Handbook of
Occupational
Health Psychology
SECOND EDITION

Handbook of

Occupational Health Psychology

SECOND EDITION

Psychology

Edited by

James Campbell Quick
and Lois E. Tetrick

American Psychological Association • Washington, DC

Published by
American Psychological Association
750 First Street, NE
Washington, DC 20002
www.apa.org

To order
APA Order Department
P.O. Box 92984
Washington, DC 20090-2984
Tel: (800) 374-2721;
Direct: (202) 336-5510
Fax: (202) 336-5502;
TDD/TTY: (202) 336-6123
Online: www.apa.org/books/
E-mail: order@apa.org

In the U.K., Europe, Africa, and the Middle East, copies may be ordered from
American Psychological Association
3 Henrietta Street
Covent Garden, London
WC2E 8LU England

Typeset in New Century Schoolbook by Circle Graphics, Inc., Columbia, MD

Printer: Maple-Vail Book Manufacturing, York, PA
Cover Designer: Naylor Design, Washington, DC

The opinions and statements published are the responsibility of the authors, and such opinions and statements do not necessarily represent the policies of the American Psychological Association.

Library of Congress Cataloging-in-Publication Data

Handbook of occupational health psychology / [edited by] James Campbell Quick and Lois E. Tetrick. — 2nd ed.
      p. ; cm.
   Includes bibliographical references and index.
   ISBN-13: 978-1-4338-0776-3
   ISBN-10: 1-4338-0776-9
   1. Industrial psychiatry—Handbooks, manuals, etc. 2. Clinical health psychology—Handbooks, manuals, etc. 3. Psychology, Industrial—Handbooks, manuals, etc. I. Quick, James C. II. Tetrick, Lois E. III. American Psychological Association.
   [DNLM: 1. Psychology, Industrial—methods. 2. Occupational Health Services.
3. Occupational Health. WA 495 H236 2011]

   RC967.5.H358 2011
   616.89—dc22

                                                                                    2009052602

British Library Cataloguing-in-Publication Data
A CIP record is available from the British Library.

Printed in the United States of America
Second Edition

Contents

Contributors

Joyce A. Adkins, United States Air Force, Langley AFB, VA

Tammy D. Allen, University of South Florida, Tampa

Dean Baker, University of California, Irvine

Julian Barling, Queen's University, Kingston, Ontario, Canada

Karen L. Belkic, University of Southern California School of Medicine, Alhambra

Joel B. Bennett, Organizational Wellness and Living Systems, Fort Worth, TX

Leonard Bickman, Vanderbilt University, Nashville, TN

Pascale Carayon, University of Wisconsin–Madison

Chu-Hsiang Chang, University of South Florida, Tampa

Royer F. Cook, The ISA Group, Alexandria, VA

Cary L. Cooper, University of Lancaster, Lancaster, United Kingdom

Michael D. Coovert, University of South Florida, Tampa

Russell Cropanzano, The University of Arizona, Tucson

Philip D. Dewe, Birkbeck College, University of London, London, United Kingdom

Michael S. Evans, Swansea University, Swansea, Wales, United Kingdom

Simon Folkard, Swansea University, Swansea, Wales, United Kingdom

Michael R. Frone, State University of New York at Buffalo

Daniel C. Ganster, Colorado State University, Fort Collins

Robert J. Gatchel, The University of Texas at Arlington

Jeffrey H. Greenhaus, Drexel University, Philadelphia, PA

Amanda Griffiths, University of Nottingham, Nottingham, United Kingdom

Catherine A. Heaney, Stanford University, Palo Alto, CA

Beth A. Jones, Yale University School of Medicine, New Haven, CT

Stanislav V. Kasl, Yale University School of Medicine, New Haven, CT

Susan Douglas Kelley, Vanderbilt University, Nashville, TN

E. Kevin Kelloway, Saint Mary's University, Halifax, Nova Scotia, Canada

Nancy Kishino, Southwestern Medical School, Dallas, TX

Paul A. Landsbergis, Mount Sinai School of Medicine, New York, NY

Lennart Levi, Karolinska Institute, Sollentuna, Sweden

Jane Mullen, Mount Allison University, Sackville, New Brunswick, Canada

Debra L. Nelson, Oklahoma State University, Stillwater

Michael P. O'Driscoll, University of Waikato, Hamilton, New Zealand

Kenneth R. Pelletier, University of Maryland School of Medicine, Baltimore

Pamela L. Perrewé, Florida State University, Tallahassee

Thomas G. Pickering (deceased), Mount Sinai School of Medicine, New York, NY

James Campbell Quick, The University of Texas at Arlington

Peter L. Schnall, University of California, Irvine

Joseph E. Schwartz, State University of New York, Stony Brook
Norbert K. Semmer, University of Berne, Berne, Switzerland
Arie Shirom, Tel Aviv University, Tel Aviv, Israel
Bret L. Simmons, University of Nevada, Reno
Carlla S. Smith (deceased), Bowling Green State University,
    Bowling Green, OH
Michael J. Smith, University of Wisconsin–Madison
Paul E. Spector, University of South Florida, Tampa
Lois E. Tetrick, George Mason University, Fairfax, VA
Philip Tucker, Swansea University, Swansea, Wales, United Kingdom
Howard M. Weiss, Purdue University, West Lafayette, IN
Thomas A. Wright, Kansas State University, Lawrence
Dov Zohar, Technion-Israel Institute of Technology, Haifa, Israel

Foreword: Narrowing the Science–Policy Gap

Lennart Levi

It is widely accepted that a broad range of physical, biological, and chemical exposures can damage health and well-being, for example, bacteria, viruses, ionizing radiation, short asbestos fibers, lead, mercury, and organic solvents. It is harder to demonstrate, and to find acceptance for, the notion that psychosocial influences brought about by social and economic conditions and conveyed by processes within the central nervous system or human behavior can have corresponding effects (Black, 2008; British Government's Office for Science, 2008; Karasek & Theorell, 1990; Kompier & Levi, 1994; Levi, 1971, 1972, 1979, 1981, 2000a, 2000b; Levi & Andersson, 1974; Shimomitsu, 2000).

Nearly two and a half millennia ago, Socrates came back from army service to report to his Greek countrymen that in one respect the Thracians were ahead of Greek civilization: They knew that the body could not be cured without the mind. "This," he continued, "is the reason why the cure of many diseases is unknown to the physicians of Hellas, because they are ignorant of the whole" (quoted in Dunbar, 1954, p. 3). About two millennia later, Paracelsus emphasized that "true medicine only arises from the creative knowledge of the last and deepest powers of the whole universe" (Dunbar, 1954, p. 3). Perhaps these assertions represent an early, intuitive understanding of what we today refer to as *ecological, cybernetic,* and *systems* approaches.

During the past century and the present one, we as psychologists have relinquished as an ideal the mastery of the whole realm of human knowledge by one person, and our training as specialists has made it difficult for us to accept the ideal of intelligent cooperation (Dunbar, 1954). This training has tended to keep each of us so closely limited by our own field that we have remained ignorant even of the fundamental principles in the fields outside our own.

The superspecialization and fragmentation of psychology are becoming increasingly problematic against the background of ongoing rapid changes in public health conditions in the Western world. Most of the major killers are now chronic, degenerative diseases. They are highly complex in their etiology, pathogenesis, manifestations, and effects. And they are not easily accessible to purely medical interventions.

At the same time, it seems likely that much of the morbidity and premature mortality is preventable. This, however, requires action beyond the health and health care sector and may involve the empowerment of the grassroots sectors. Sectors outside the traditional health and health care field, but still of major importance for our health and well-being, include education, employment, work environment, economic resources, housing, transportation and communication, leisure and recreation, social relations, political resources, safety and security, and equality.

Taking occupational factors as an example, we find that work-related stress, its causes, and its consequences are all very common in the 27 European Union (EU) member states. More than half of the 225 million workers report working at a very high speed (males 62%, females 56%) and under tight deadlines (males 68%, females 54%). More than one third have no influence on task order, and 40% report having monotonous tasks. Such work-related stressors are likely to have contributed to the present spectrum of ill health: 16% of the workforce complain of headaches, 23% of muscular pains, 23% of fatigue, 22% of "stress," and 25% of backache, and many complain of other diseases, even life-threatening ones (European Foundation, 2007).

Such a "causality" may imply a range of relationships. It can mean that a certain exposure is necessary—enough for a certain disease to develop (e.g., exposure to lead causing lead poisoning). An exposure may also be sufficient—no additional influences or vulnerabilities are necessary. Or exposure may be contributory and neither necessary nor sufficient. The question also remains about whether an exposure really causes a specific disease or if it "just" aggravates it, accelerates its course, or triggers its symptoms. If we keep all these options in mind, it becomes clear that work-related exposures may, but need not, be a prerequisite for the development of specific occupational diseases, a sine qua non. On the other hand, it becomes equally clear that they may contribute to a wide variety of morbidity and mortality, a much wider spectrum than is usually realized.

How, then, can disease be prevented and health and well-being promoted at work and elsewhere? In theory, these objectives can be achieved in accordance with principles spelled out in the EU Framework Directive (89/391/EEC), according to which employers have a "duty to ensure the safety and health of workers in every aspect related to the work," on the basis of the following general principles of prevention:

- avoiding risks; evaluating the risks that cannot be avoided;
- combating the risks at source;
- adapting the work to the individual, especially as regards the design of workplaces, the choices of work equipment and the choice of working and production methods, with a view, in particular to alleviating monotonous work and work at a predetermined work rate and to reducing their effects on health;
- *developing a coherent overall prevention policy* [italics added] which covers technology, organisation of work, working conditions, social relationships and the influence of factors related to the working environment.

To implement this set of principles, strategies need to address the root causes (primary prevention), to reduce their effects on health (secondary prevention), and also to treat the resulting ill health (tertiary prevention; e.g., Quick, Quick, Nelson, & Hurrell, 1997).

Article 152 of the European Treaty of Amsterdam states that "a high level of human health protection shall be ensured in the definition and implementation of *all* Community policies and activities" [italics added]. As pointed out in the European Commission's Guidance (Levi, 2000a), work-related disease prevention programs can aim at a variety of targets and be based on various philosophies. If the condition at work—the "shoe"—does not fit the worker—the "foot,"—one political approach is to urge the "shoe factories" to manufacture a wide variety of shoes in different sizes and configurations to fit every, or almost every, conceivable foot. Whenever possible, the instructions to the shoe factories should be evidence-based; in other words, based on measurements of a representative, random sample of all feet, of all shoes, and of the existing fit. This is a first—diagnostic—step in a primary prevention approach on a population level. Another approach, again based on primary prevention, aims at finding the right shoe for each individual foot—promoting "the right person in the right place." A third, complementary approach is that the owner of each foot should have access to and be encouraged to use a "lasting device" to adjust available shoes to fit his or her feet. The emphasis here is on empowerment, on active, responsible workers, able, willing, and encouraged to make adjustments of their working conditions, to improve the work–worker fit. All three approaches can aim at an improved fit in general terms or can address the inequity of various feet in various shoes.

So far, in the EU and elsewhere, most work-stress prevention approaches are oriented toward secondary or tertiary prevention only (Malzon & Lindsay, 1992). Most of these approaches involve, for example, the provision of on-site fitness facilities, smoking cessation programs, dietary control, relaxation and exercise classes, health screening, psychological counseling, or sometimes some combination of these packaged as a multimodular program available to employees (Cartwright, Cooper, & Murphy, 1995; Kompier & Cooper, 1999). This band-aid approach would correspond to offering corn plasters only to the owners of sore feet—or pain killers, tranquilizers, or psychotherapy to deal with the outcomes of the lack of fit between the worker and his or her conditions of work. This in no way implies a criticism against secondary and tertiary prevention approaches, particularly not as long as the latter constitute a part of a larger package that includes primary prevention also.

An obvious difficulty with primary prevention lies in the fact that one size does not fit all. It follows that what is needed is a multifaceted approach to stressor prevention and to promotion of healthy workers in healthy companies. An attempt to design such an approach has been made by the U.S. National Institute for Occupational Safety and Health (NIOSH) in its National Strategy for the Prevention of Work-Related Psychological Disorders (Sauter, Murphy, & Hurrell, 1990), which addresses

- *workload and work pace:* avoiding both under- and overload, allowing recovery from demanding tasks and increasing control by workers over various work characteristics;
- *work schedule:* designing schedules to be compatible with demands and responsibilities outside the job and addressing flex time, job sharing, and rotating shifts;
- *job future:* avoiding ambiguity in opportunities for promotion and career or skill development and in matters pertaining to job security;

- *social environment:* providing opportunities for employee interaction and support; and
- *job content:* designing job tasks to have meaning, to provide stimulation, and to provide an opportunity to use existing skills and develop new ones.

A key question, of course, concerns what is, indeed, preventable in terms of exposures and inequities in exposures to occupational stressors. Many tasks are intrinsically stressful but still need to be performed for the public good, for example, night work in an emergency ward. It can also be debated how much of the reactions to these stressors depend on excessive occupational demands and how much on individual vulnerabilities of the worker. In practice, however, there is an abundance of occupational exposures that the great majority of the labor force would experience as noxious and pathogenic. It is in the interest of all parties on the labor market to prevent, as far as possible, workers from being exposed to them. If, for one reason or another, this turns out to be unfeasible, a complementary approach is to try to reduce exposure time or to buffer or otherwise decrease the noxious effects.

Secondary or tertiary prevention can also involve improving the workers' coping repertoire. If "deep and troubled waters" cannot be eliminated, the attempt is to teach people to "swim"—that is, to cope. Coping is a cognitive and behavioral process of mastering, tolerating, or reducing internal and external demands (Lazarus & Folkman, 1984). It can be problem focused (trying to change the actual exposures), emotion focused (trying to modify the resulting emotions), or both.

In 1993, the Belgian EU Presidency, the European Commission, and the European Foundation jointly organized a major conference on "Stress at Work: A Call for Action." The conference highlighted the increasing impact of stress on the quality of working life, employees' health, and company performance. Special attention was devoted to stress monitoring and prevention at the company, national, and European levels. Instruments and policies for better stress prevention were presented and discussed (European Foundation, 1994). Finally, a roundtable on the future perspectives on stress at work in the European community brought together representatives from national governments, the European Commission, Union of Industrial and Employers' Confederations of Europe, the European Centre of Public Enterprises, European Trade Union Confederation, and the European Foundation. Based on these deliberations, the European Commission created an ad hoc group to the Advisory Committee on Health and Safety on Stress at Work. The ad hoc group proposed and the Advisory Committee (1997) endorsed the preparation by the European Commission of a "Guidance" in this field. This Guidance (Levi, 2000a) emphasizes that, according to the EU Framework Directive, employers have a "duty to ensure the safety and health of workers in every aspect related to the work." The directive's principles of prevention include "avoiding risks," "combating the risks at source," and "adapting the work to the individual." In addition, the directive indicates the employers' duty to develop "a coherent overall prevention policy." The Commission's Guidance provides a solid basis for such endeavors. Based on surveillance at individual workplaces and monitoring at national and regional levels, work-related stress should be prevented or counteracted by job redesign (e.g., by empowering the employees and avoiding both over- and underload), by improving social support, and by providing reasonable reward for the effort invested by workers, as integral parts of the overall management system, also for small- and medium-sized enterprises. And, of course, by adjusting occupational physical settings to the workers' abilities, needs, and reasonable expectations, all in line with the requirements of the EU Framework Directive and Article 152 of the Treaty of Amsterdam. Supporting actions should include not only research but also adjustments of curricula in business schools; in schools of technology, medicine, and behavioral and social sciences; and in the training and retraining of labor inspectors, occupational health officers, managers, and supervisors, in line with such goals. This overall approach was further endorsed in the Swedish EU Presidency conclusions (European Council of Ministers, 2001), according to which employment involves focusing not only on more jobs but also on better jobs. Increased efforts should be made to promote a good working environment for all, including equal opportunities for the disabled, gender equality, good and flexible work organization permitting better reconciliation of working and personal life, lifelong learning, health and safety at work, employee involvement, and diversity in working life.

In 2004, a Framework Agreement on Work-Related Stress was signed by the four central partners on the EU labor market, with the aim of preventing, eliminating, or reducing problems of work-related stress in the 160 million European workers covered by this agreement (ETUC et al., 2004). Other countries may wish to learn from European experiences in this and related fields.

All this is presented and discussed in considerable depth by the eminent scientists in the chapters of this important volume. This handbook is an essential resource for scholars, researchers, and practitioners in occupational health psychology who aim to make workplaces healthier for all concerned. It is also an essential resource for managers and labor unionists and for those in public health and medicine who are concerned with health and productivity issues in working environments.

References

Advisory Committee for Safety, Hygiene and Health Protection at Work. (1997). *Report to the Commission*. Luxembourg: European Commission.

Black, C. (2007). *Working for a healthier tomorrow*. London, England: Department for Health.

British Government's Office for Science. (2008). Mental capital and wellbeing. *Foresight*. Retrieved from http://www.foresight.gov.uk/Mental%20Capital/SR-E24_MCW.pdf

Cartwright, S., Cooper, C. L., & Murphy, L. R. (1995). Diagnosing a healthy organization: A proactive approach to stress in the workplace. In L. R. Murphy, J. J. Hurrell Jr., S. L. Sauter, & G. P. Keita (Eds.), *Job stress interventions* (pp. 217–233). Washington, DC: American Psychological Association.

Dunbar, F. (1954). *Emotions and bodily changes*. New York, NY: Columbia University Press.

European Council of Ministers. (2001). *Combating stress and depression related problems: Council conclusions*. Brussels, Belgium: Author.

ETUC, UNICE, UEAPME, and CEEP. (2004). *Framework agreement on work-related stress: EU social dialogue*. Brussels, Belgium: Author.

European Foundation. (1994). *European conference on stress at work: A call for action—Proceedings*. Luxembourg: Office for Official Publications of the European Communities.

European Foundation. (2007). *Fourth European survey on working conditions.* Dublin, Ireland: European Foundation for the Improvement of Living and Working Conditions.

Karasek, R., & Theorell, T. (1990). *Healthy work: Stress, productivity, and the reconstruction of working life.* New York, NY: Basic Books.

Kompier, M., & Cooper, C. (1999). *Preventing stress, improving productivity: European case studies in the workplace.* London, England: Routledge.

Kompier, M., & Levi, L. (1994). *Stress at work: Causes, effects, and prevention—A guide for small and medium sized enterprises.* Dublin, Ireland: European Foundation.

Lazarus, R. S., & Folkman, S. (1984). *Stress, appraisal, and coping.* New York, NY: Springer.

Levi, L. (1971). *Society, stress and disease: Vol. I. The psychosocial environment and psychosomatic diseases.* London, England: Oxford University Press.

Levi, L. (1972). Stress and distress in response to psychosocial stimuli: Laboratory and real life studies on sympathoadrenomedullary and related reactions. *Acta Medica Scandinauica, 191,* 528.

Levi, L. (1979). Psychosocial factors in preventive medicine. In D. A. Hamburg, E. O. Nightingale, & V. Kalmar (Eds.), *Healthy people: The Surgeon General's report on health promotion and disease prevention—Background papers* (pp. 207–252). Washington, DC: U.S. Government Printing Office.

Levi, L. (1981). *Society, stress and disease: Vol. IV. Working life.* London, England: Oxford University Press.

Levi, L. (2000a). *Guidance on work-related stress: Spice of life or kiss of death?* Luxembourg: European Commission.

Levi, L. (2000b). Stress in the global environment. In J. Dunham (Ed.), *Stress in the workplace: Past, present and future* (pp. 1–18). London, England: Whurr.

Levi, L., & Andersson, L. (1974). *Population, environment and quality of life: A contribution to the United Nation's World Population Conference.* Stockholm, Sweden: Royal Ministry of Foreign Affairs.

Malzon, R., & Lindsay, G. (1992). *Health promotion at the worksite: A brief survey of large organizations in Europe* (European Occupational Health Series No. 4). Copenhagen, Denmark: WHO Regional Office for Europe.

Quick, J. C., Quick, J. D., Nelson, D. L., & Hurrell, J. J., Jr. (1997). *Preventive stress management in organizations.* Washington, DC: American Psychological Association.

Sauter, S. L., Murphy, L. R., & Hurrell, J. J., Jr. (1990). Prevention of work-related psychological distress: A national strategy proposed by the National Institute of Occupational Safety and Health. *American Psychologist, 45,* 1146–1158.

Shimomitsu, T. (2000). Work-related stress and health in three post-industrial settings: EU, Japan, and USA. *Journal of Tokyo Medical University, 58,* 327–469.

Preface

The American Psychological Association–National Institute for Occupational Safety and Health (APA-NIOSH) cooperative agenda in the domain of occupational health psychology is now well established in its 3rd decade. Through a series of international conferences, the leading scientific *Journal of Occupational Health Psychology,* the first edition of the *Handbook of Occupational Health Psychology,* and the Society of Occupational Health Psychology, occupational health psychology is becoming a well-grounded specialty in the science and practice of psychology. As editors, we each have had long-standing professional and personal concerns for safe and healthy work. We are delighted that the APA has chosen to provide our field with a second edition of the *Handbook of Occupational Health Psychology* that builds on a solid foundation and then extends from there with new and important contributions. We continue to see the volume as a good fit with the International Labour Office (ILO) *Encyclopaedia of Occupational Health and Safety* (Stellman, 1997) and *Maxcy-Rosenau-Last: Public Health and Preventive Medicine* (Wallace & Doebbeling, 1998), each of which addresses much broader concerns with industrial work environments and with human health.

At the outset of the cooperative agenda, NIOSH identified job-related psychological disorders as among the top 10 occupational health concerns in the early 1980s. However, even before the identification of that concrete problem, Lennart Levi's chapter on work stress and psychologically healthy work in *Healthy People: The Surgeon General's Report on Health Promotion and Disease Prevention* (1979) signaled an emergent concern for human well-being in occupational settings. Therefore, we were delighted that Dr. Levi wrote the foreword to the first edition and has again provided a foreword for the second edition of this international handbook.

We thank our international advisory board, who were instrumental in launching the first edition of the handbook. Cary L. Cooper, Lennart Levi, Teruichi Shimomitusu, Arie Shirom, the late Carlla S. Smith, Charles D. Spielberger, and Craig Stenberg each helped us in a variety of ways as we framed, then developed, the first edition. The launch was very successful, and now here we are in the second edition. We thank Donna Ross for her invaluable administrative support throughout the entire project, beginning with her role as editorial office manager during the founding years of the *Journal of Occupational Health Psychology.* She has been a wonderful support. We would like to thank Gary VandenBos, Julia Frank-McNeil, Susan Reynolds, and other APA staff members who so ably encouraged, nurtured, and supported our editorial efforts.

Since the first edition, we lost two wonderful colleagues and collaborators. We mourn the loss of our friend, colleague, and mentor, Thomas G. Pickering, an international leader in research and patient care in hypertension and the behavioral aspects of hypertension and heart disease. Dr. Pickering, professor of medicine and director of the Center for Behavioral Cardiovascular Health at the Columbia University College of Physicians and Surgeons, died May 14, 2009, after a valiant battle against cancer. He published widely in the field and held leadership positions, including serving as president of the Society of Behavioral Medicine, the Academy of Behavioral Medicine Research, and the American Society of Hypertension's eastern regional chapter. He coined the term *white-coat hypertension* to describe patients whose blood pressure is elevated in the doctor's office but normal otherwise, and he published the first editorial describing *masked hypertension,* a condition in which an individual's blood pressure is normal in the doctor's office but elevated over the course of a day. His work in behavioral medicine stemmed from his belief that much of cardiovascular disease arises from psychosocial factors and is potentially preventable or treatable by modifying these factors.

We mourn as well the loss of our friend Carlla Smith. Her primary specialization was occupational health psychology, with particular interests in organizational stress and stress management, the effects of shiftwork on health and work effectiveness, individual differences in worker well-being and attitudes, and measurement issues in field research. At the time of her death, she was on the editorial board of the *Journal of Occupational Health Psychology.* In 1998, she received one of the first grants from NIOSH to support joint industrial–organizational (I/O) and occupational health programs. She was a founder of the Occupational Health Program at Bowling Green and served as codirector. Despite her health problems over the past decade, Carlla was hard at work right down to the last few weeks and never gave up on life. Carlla was a tough Texan who was not about to allow her condition to get in the way of the things she loved doing: socializing with her friends, caring for her cat, traveling, practicing Riznica meditation, and of course, her profession. Despite her illness, she was looking forward to spending a sabbatical year at Rice University in her native Texas. Carlla was a fellow of the American Psychological Association.

Jim thanks former University of Texas at Arlington (UT Arlington) president Robert Witt, former UT Arlington executive vice president and provost George C. Wright, dean of business Daniel D. Himarios, and many colleagues at UT Arlington for their active support and commitment to his work over the years in occupational health psychology. He is especially appreciative to UT Arlington for the 2000–2001 Faculty Development Leave, which supported the first edition of this handbook and his new research on executive health, and to Michael Moore for faithful friendship.

Lois thanks the Department of Psychology at George Mason University and the I/O Psychology Program for their support of this project. In addition, she thanks Jim and all of the authors of the handbook for their valuable contributions, support, and responsiveness throughout the publication process.

References

Healthy people: The Surgeon General's report on health promotion and disease prevention. (1979). Washington, DC: Government Printing Office.

Stellman, J. M. (Ed.). (1997). *ILO encyclopaedia of occupational health and safety.* Geneva, Switzerland: International Labour Office.

Wallace, R. B., & Doebbeling, B. N. (Eds.). (1998). *Maxcy-Rosenau-Last: Public health and preventive medicine* (14th ed.). Stamford, CT: Appleton & Lange.

Part I

Mission and History

1

Overview of Occupational Health Psychology: Public Health in Occupational Settings

Lois E. Tetrick and James Campbell Quick

People spend a significant proportion of their lives at work, and often their jobs bring meaning and structure to their lives (Jahoda, 1982; Warr, 2007). Because work is a central aspect of many people's lives, it generally is recognized that individuals should have a safe and healthy work environment. Employees should not have to worry about injury or illness, and legislation has been introduced in many industrialized countries, including the United States, the Netherlands, Sweden, and European Union, to help ensure this (Kompier, 1996; Tetrick, 2008). The focus of much of the early work on occupational safety and health was on workers' exposures to physical hazards in the work environment. Increasingly, however, the workplace is viewed as the logical, appropriate context for health promotion, not just the prevention of injuries and illness (Cooper & Cartwright, 1994; Cox, 1997). This broader perspective is concerned with healthy people and healthy organizations, especially considering the dynamic context in which organizations and individuals exist (Nelson & Quick, 2011).

The purpose of this volume is to convey an advanced understanding of what we mean by *health*—both of individuals and of organizations—and the role of occupational health psychology in promoting individual and organizational health. In the 5 years since the first edition of this book was published, the field has expanded considerably in terms of scope of content, theory, and empirical support for factors that both protect and promote the health of employees and the organizations in which they work.

In this chapter, we first describe the current conceptualization of health and the purpose and origins of occupational health psychology, a catalyst in bringing together research from multiple disciplines to promote healthy employees and healthy organizations. Next, we review current factors about the context in which work is performed, because this context plays a role in the optimal functioning of individuals and organizations. We then offer a model for integrating a public health perspective with a more psychological perspective, followed by a discussion of future directions for the field. Finally, we describe how the rest of the book is organized.

Healthy Organizations and Healthy People

In considering healthy organizations, one must consider the question of healthy for whom? Many definitions of organizational health have focused on the organization itself. For example, Miles (1965) defined a healthy organization as one that not only survives but also continues to cope adequately over the long haul, continuously developing and expanding its coping abilities. Cooper and Cartwright (1994) extended this by including the health of employees when they described a healthy organization as one that is financially successful and has a healthy workforce. A healthy organization is able to maintain a healthy and satisfying work environment over time, even in times of market turbulence and change. Similarly, Quick (1999) indicated that high productivity, high employee satisfaction, good safety records, few disability claims and union grievances, low absenteeism, low turnover, and the absence of violence characterize a healthy work environment. One could further extend the consideration of organizational health to the community in which the organization is located. Such an extension makes clear the public health perspective of occupational health psychology and its focus on prevention. Prevention programs aimed at improving the health of organizations benefit both the organization and the people in them because they reflect a value placed on people, human activities, and human relationships (Rosen, 1986; Schein, 1990). Hofmann and Tetrick (2003) suggested that organizational health should incorporate all of these aspects of organizational functioning that ensure optimal performance and sustainability.

In 1946, the World Health Organization defined health as not just the absence of disease but also as a state of complete physical, mental, and social well-being. The Ottawa Charter of the World Health Organization in 1986 defined health as a resource for everyday life, not the object of living. Health is a positive concept that includes social and personal resources as well as physical capabilities (Nutbeam, 1998). It also has been conceptualized as the ability to have and to reach goals, meet personal needs, and cope with everyday life (Raphael et al., 1999). The United States is among the countries that set national health objectives for its people with regard to health-related behavior, disease prevention, and health and safety in the workplace (U.S. Department of Health and Human Services, 1990). These developments have prompted scholars to expand the definition of individual health to include not only the absence of illness or injury and restoration of health but also the positive aspect of health to include optimal functioning and flourishing (Hofmann & Tetrick, 2003; Macik-Frey, Quick, & Nelson, 2007; Schaufeli, 2004).

Purpose and Origins of Occupational Health Psychology

The purpose of occupational health psychology is to develop, maintain, and promote the health of employees directly and the health of their families. Occupational health is important because of the associated burden of suffering from morbidity and mortality, both from an economic perspective and from a humanitarian perspective. The primary focus of occupational health psychology is the prevention of illness or injury by creating safe and healthy working environments (Quick, Quick, Nelson, & Hurrell, 1997; Sauter, Hurrell, Fox, Tetrick, & Barling, 1999). Key areas of concern are work organization factors that place individuals at risk of injury, disease, and distress. This requires an interdisciplinary, if not transdisciplinary, approach (Maclean, Plotnikoff, & Moyer, 2000) across multiple disciplines within and beyond psychology. For example, such psychology specialties as human factors, industrial and organizational psychology, social psychology, health psychology, and clinical psychology inform occupational health psychology, as do other disciplines such as public health, preventive medicine, and industrial engineering (Schneider, Camara, Tetrick, & Stenberg, 1999). Integration of these disciplines with a primary focus on prevention is the goal of occupational health psychology. Therefore, the focus is on organizational interventions rather than individual interventions such as counseling (Quick, 1999).

Figure 1.1 shows occupational health in its historical context, emerging from psychology, engineering, and the practice of preventive medicine to be uniquely recognized as occupational health psychology in the 1990s. These scientific origins are also the foundations for occupational medicine and occupational safety (Macik-Frey et al., 2007; Macik-Frey, Quick, Quick, & Nelson, 2009). Positive advances from occupational health psychology include a focus on positive health, the emergence of healthy leadership practices, an attention to the importance of mood and emotion in the workplace, and a renewed concern for workplace interventions. These positive advances carry some of the promise that occupational health psychology holds for the future.

The challenge to occupational health psychology in promoting healthy organizations and healthy people can be more fully appreciated by examining changes that are occurring in workplaces and in the workforce. These changes shape the nature of occupational risks to which people are exposed and the context within which they work. Key changes that relate to occupational health psychology are described in the following sections.

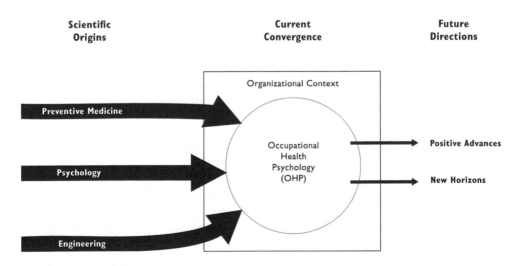

Figure 1.1.   Occupational health psychology.

The Evolving Context of Work

One of the more notable and sweeping changes in the nature of work over the past two decades concerns the process of globalization, which has increased the international competition to which organizations are subject, increased the stress for companies and individuals alike, and decreased people's job security. Globalization has been accompanied by greater global interdependencies. For example, advances in the high-technology sectors helped fuel job creation in Europe during the late 1990s. However, because of subsequent downturns in the global economy, national economic swings, and organizational restructuring, these interdependencies have created uncertainty for organizations and employees. Organizational structures, organizational practices, and work arrangements, collectively referred to as the *organization of work,* have become much more dynamic. Additionally, the workforce has become increasingly diverse in relation to many characteristics of employees.

Changes in Employment Context

Within the U.S. economy, there has been a substantial shift in the number of jobs in various sectors, with fewer jobs in manufacturing and more jobs in service industries. According to the Bureau of Labor Statistics (2007), from 1988 to 2006, the occupational groups with the slowest growth and thus the sharpest decline in percentage of overall employment were agriculture, forestry, and fishing occupations and the precision production, craft, and repair occupational groups. Operators, fabricators, and laborers as well as clerical workers experienced slower-than-average growth, while very rapid growth was seen among the professional specialty occupations and the executive, administrative, and managerial occupational groups. The Bureau of Labor Statistics (2009) predicted that from 2006 to 2016, service occupations and professional and related occupations will experience the most growth. The four occupations with the largest projected growth are personal and home care aides (50.6% growth), home health aides (48.7% growth), computer software engineers (44.6% growth), and network systems and data communications (53.4% growth). It is interesting to note that the first two of these occupations are in the lowest quartile of earnings and latter two are in the highest quartile of earnings. These predicted shifts indicate that occupational hazards reflecting both physical and psychosocial stressors in the work environment will take on more importance for the majority of employees in the United States.

The increase in service occupations and professional (executive, managerial, and administrative) occupations has also increased the number of self-employed people (Aronsson, 1999; Bureau of Labor Statistics, 2006) and the number of other forms of flexible employment, such as home-based work, temporary work, and contract work (Benach, Fernando, Platt, Diez-Roux, & Muntaner, 2000). These alternative work arrangements provide flexibility, which may enhance employees' well-being (Broschak, Davis-Blake, & Block, 2008). However, these arrangements also may lead to underemployment, in which individuals are not able to work the number of hours needed for personal growth and satisfaction or for earning potential. Because these new forms of flexible employment are likely to share some of the same unfavorable characteristics of unemployment, and because it is well established that unemployment is related to ill health (Feldman, Leana, & Bolino, 2002; Paul & Moser, 2009), there is potential for health-damaging effects (Benach et al., 2000). Therefore, it is not clear what effects these alternative employment relations may have on individuals' health.

Recent data from the Bureau of Labor Statistics (2003, 2006, 2008) reflect the effects of the current economic downturn. For example, the number of self-employed individuals working in agriculture declined 5% between 2003 and 2006 and 11% between 2003 and 2008. For self-employed individuals working in nonagricultural fields, there was a 4% increase between 2003 and 2006 but a 5% decline between 2006 and 2008. These declines for the self-employed are roughly paralleled by declines in all classes of employed individuals in the United States.

Data suggest that people have a number of different jobs in their lifetimes. The percentage of people who hold multiple jobs at the same time has increased somewhat, gradually declining for men and rapidly rising for women (Safe Work in the 21st Century, 2000), resulting in 4.9% of men and 5.2% of women holding multiple jobs in 2008 (Bureau of Labor Statistics, 2008). This pattern of employment relations suggests that people's exposure to work environments may be very dynamic, making it difficult from an epidemiological perspective to identify the sources of ill health (Berkman & Kawachi, 2000; see also Chapter 18, this volume).

Changes in the Organization of Work

In addition to the changes in work context, the organization of work has undergone significant changes. *Organization of work* refers to the management systems, supervisory practices, production processes, and their influence on the way work is performed (Sauter et al., 1999). Among these changes are globalization, increased competition and economic pressures, technological innovations, and increased complexity of organizational structures and task interdependence.

- Globalization has created several issues in relation to the health and well-being of individuals (Langan-Fox, 2005). Globalization may result in relocation, displacement, unemployment, and fear of unemployment, and these, in turn, can result in stress and negative health effects among workers and their families. The increased diversity resulting from globalization may also be stressful, perhaps as a result of difficulty in communication or conflict among cultural values or norms, thus negatively affecting employees' health (Brislin, 2008).
- Increased competition and economic pressures have resulted in new practices, such as lean production, total quality management, and advanced manufacturing techniques. These practices were developed to provide organizations with a means of responding more quickly and efficiently to production demands with better quality but may have resulted in the intensification of work to the detriment of employees' health. Typically, these practices increase the cognitive demands on

employees, their responsibilities, and the interdependence among employees, which can result in stress and negative health effects (Polanyi & Tompa, 2004).

- Technological innovations may also intensify work and/or increase employees' responsibilities to the detriment of employees' health.
- Increased complexity of organizational structures and task inter- dependence have resulted in increased downsizing and restructuring of organizations (Burke & Nelson, 1998; Tetrick, 2000). The health and safety effects of downsizing and restructuring have been found to be negative for the victims, the survivors, and the managers who imple- mented the downsizing efforts. The most common effect is depression (de Vries & Balasz, 1997; Tetrick, 2000). These findings are consis- tent with a 1996 American Management Association survey, which found that job elimination was related to increased disability claims, with the largest increase in claims being stress related (e.g., mental or psychiatric problems, substance abuse, hypertension, cardiovascu- lar disease).

Changes in Workforce Characteristics

The workforce has become more diverse with respect to age, gender, race and ethnicity, and the presence of individuals with disabilities. Today's workforce is substantially different from that of prior generations, with the changes in partic- ipation in the workforce changing dramatically over the past 3 or 4 decades (Bell, 2007). We discuss each of these factors next.

Age

The Institute of Medicine's Committee to Assess Training Needs for Occupational Safety and Health Personnel in the United States (Safe Work in the 21st Century, 2000) reported an absolute decline in the number of workers under age 25 and a growth of workers ages 25 to 54 during the 1990s. The Bureau of Labor Statistics (2009) projects for the period 2006 to 2016 that the number of individ- uals 16 to 24 years of age will continue to decline to approximately 13% of the labor force, and although the number of individuals ages 25 to 34 will increase slightly, the percentage of this age group relative to the total labor force will decline to about 65%. Individual older than age 55 will experience a substantial increase in the total workforce from 8.5% to almost 47%. This shift at least par- tially reflected the baby boom generation and the shift to an older population characteristic of Western industrialized society (Robertson & Tracy, 1998). Despite this, there have been relatively few studies of age, work productivity, and health (Robertson & Tracy, 1998). One study by Ilmarinen (cited in Robertson & Tracy, 1998) found three domains of risk factors that either singly or in combination increased the likelihood of a decline in work capacity for older workers. The first domain was work content; the common element among these risk factors was physical demands. The second domain was the nature of the work environment, which included accident hazards, extreme temperatures or changes in temperature, and general physical working conditions. The third domain was psychosocial factors, including role conflict, poor supervision, fear of failure, time pressure, lack of control, lack of development, and lack of recognition. There was an additive effect of multiple risk factors, but it appeared that changes to working conditions could be adjusted to maintain work capacity. There is also evidence suggesting that working conditions and job characteristics such as job complexity can actually serve to reduce declines in cognitive functioning (Stachowski, Fisher, Grosch, Hesson, & Tetrick, 2007). As the Institute of Medicine (Safe Work in the 21st Century, 2000) pointed out, workers over age 55 are one third less likely to be injured on the job. If they are injured, though, they take on average 2 weeks longer to recover than younger workers. Our understanding of the relations of age on workplace health and safety is just beginning to accrue.

Gender

In 1960, approximately 3% of the labor force were women, according to the Bureau of Labor Statistics; by 1990 this had increased to 45.2%, and by 2007 the percentage of women in the labor force was 46.4%, reflecting a slowing in the growth rate. There may be some unique work environment factors that put women at increased risk of ill health, such as exposure to radiation. As of 2007, 71% of women participating in the labor force had children, with 60% of women participating in the labor force having children under 3 years of age (Bureau of Labor Statistics, 1998), and the increase in working mothers may have resulted in a focus of research on work–family issues over the past decade. Flexible working arrangements (e.g., flexiplace, flexitime) have been implemented to reduce the work–family conflict; however, these may have generated other stressful working conditions, such as disappearing boundaries between work and family (Lewis & Cooper, 1999) or less safe work environments (Fairweather, 1999). These work–family issues have been demonstrated to create stress and thus result in decreased health. Although in its early phases, research has recognized that the relation between work and family can have a positive effect on employees' health as well as potential negative effects (Wayne, Grzywacz, Carlson, & Kacmar, 2007).

Race and Ethnicity

Paralleling globalization, the U.S. labor force has experienced a change in the racial and ethnic composition of the workforce mirroring changes in the population. Based on the 2000 census, the United States is more diverse than ever both racially and ethnically (Schmitt, 2001), and in some areas White non-Hispanic individuals have become the minority (Purdum, 2001). Therefore, it would be expected that the proportion of White non-Hispanics in the workforce will continue to decline as it has for the past decade (Bureau of Labor Statistics, 1998). This increased diversity in the workforce is being reflected within the workplace, with implications for health and human resources. There is a body of research that indicates differential disease rates for different racial and ethnic groups, and although this difference can be explained to a large degree by socio-economic status (SES), some non-SES-mediated differences remain (Williams, 1999). As an organization's workforce becomes more racially and ethnically diverse, there is an increased need for considering alternatives for maintaining health care costs for organizations and potential accommodations for employees with disabilities.

Disabilities

During the past decade since the implementation of the Americans With Disabilities Act of 1990, there has been a significant increase in the number of individuals with disabilities in the workplace. According to the Bureau of Labor Statistics (2009), 22% of the people in the U.S. labor force have one or more disabilities. There have been some reports that the number of severe work disabilities may be increasing (Andresen et al., 1999). However, Andresen et al. (1999) noted that people who reported fair to poor health appeared to be decreasing. Further analyses of the reasons for limited ability to work were common chronic conditions, such as arthritis, back or neck problems, heart problems, and fractures or joint injuries. It is not clear whether any of these conditions were the result of work environment factors, although there is evidence for a link between work stress and musculoskeletal problems, including back and neck problems (Griffiths, 1998; Warren, Dillon, Morse, Hall, & Warren, 2000) and heart problems (Landsbergis et al., 2003).

Disability also is related to depressive disorders, resulting in diminished quality of life, economic losses, and increased use of health services (Kouzis & Eaton, 1997). It also has been demonstrated that work impairment from psychiatric disorders indicated by lost workdays is similar across occupations, although effects on reductions in workdays or work cutback days are greater among professional workers (Kessler & Frank, 1997).

Kessler and Frank's (1997) study, based on the U.S. National Comorbidity Survey, found that pure affective disorders, including depression, were associated with the largest average number of lost workdays and work cutback days. They projected this loss of work to be 4 million lost workdays in the United States per year and 20 million work cutback days. Because there is an established link between workplace stressors and depression, it is reasonable to assume that at least some of the lost workdays were a result of the work environment. A study of work-related illness conducted in Great Britain in 1995 estimated 19.5 million lost workdays (Griffiths, 1998). Griffiths (1998) also reported 14% of the people in the United Kingdom who retired early did so because of ill health, and part of these ill-health conditions were believed to be the result of working conditions or at least made worse by working conditions. In fact, she reported that an estimated 2 million people in Great Britain were suffering from a work-related illness in 1990. With continued medical advances, it can be expected that individuals with work disability, whether work related or not, may be more likely to return to work especially with reasonable accommodations being made by employers (Krause, Dasinger, & Neuhauser, 1998).

The PATH Model

Considering the above changes in workers and the workplace and the resulting risks for physical, emotional, and mental health, it is no surprise that psychologists are giving increased attention to creating and maintaining healthy workplaces. Grawitch, Gottschalk, and Munz (2006) reviewed the literature that had been discussed and/or demonstrated to be responsible for psychologically healthy workplaces. The resulting model is the Practices for Achieving Total Health (PATH) model.

The PATH model has five categories of healthy workplace practices: work–life balance, employee growth and development, health and safety, recognition, and employee involvement. These categories are designed to result in employee well-being and organizational improvement. Employee well-being includes the physical, mental, and emotional facets of employee health, as indicated by physical health, mental health, stress, motivation, commitment, job satisfaction, and morale. Organizational improvement includes competitive advantage, performance and productivity, reduced absenteeism and turnover, reduced accident and injury rates, increased cost savings, hiring selectivity, improved service and product quality, and better customer service and satisfaction. The model promises to be a useful framework for organizing approaches to individual and organizational health.

Macik-Frey et al. (2009) cited the use of the PATH model as an underpinning of the American Psychological Association's psychologically healthy workplace agenda and awards. For example, in 2006, organizations in telecommunication, health care, and research were recognized for different strengths and excellence that made for healthy workplace practices. A very different range of healthy organizations was recognized in 2007, from a newspaper and medical center to a social service organization and National Football League franchise. The model is useful for both challenging organizations to achieve healthy workplace practices and recognizing and rewarding those who achieve success and meet the challenge.

Prevention and the Public Health Model

There are two major approaches to prevention: population-based interventions and interventions for individuals at high risk (Weich, 1997). A "prevention paradox" has been noted (Rose, 1992) in that each approach may be flawed. Some people view population-based interventions as wasteful of scarce resources. However, high-risk interventions require knowledge of the causes or etiology of particular illnesses and may be too focused to address the problem. Maclean et al. (2000) indicated that more illness may be prevented by making minor preventive changes for many people than by making major changes for those few who are at high risk. Weich (1997) suggested that "a high risk approach to prevention on its own is incapable of reducing the prevalence of the common mental disorders to any significant extent" (p. 760). However, there is some support that individual-level intervention (counseling) had clear benefits for employees' well-being, and an organizational-level intervention (increased participation and control) did not (Reynolds, 1997). The public health model actually incorporates both the population-based and at-risk individual-based models of interventions.

The public health model classifies interventions into three categories: primary interventions, secondary interventions, and tertiary interventions (Schmidt, 1994). Figure 1.2 presents a prevention and public health model showing health risk factors, asymptomatic disorders and diseases, and symptomatic disorders and diseases with the accompanying points of intervention (Wallace & Doebbeling, 1998). Primary interventions focus on prevention among people who are not at risk. This is essentially a population-based model in which the intervention is applied to entire populations or groups, although Schmidt (1994) argued that all interventions must have an individual component and therefore need to incorporate psychological theoretical approaches. Primary interventions are frequently used in health promotion and health education campaigns in which the message is sent out to everyone whether they are at risk or not, such as infomercials broadcast on television and radio about the negative health effects of smoking.

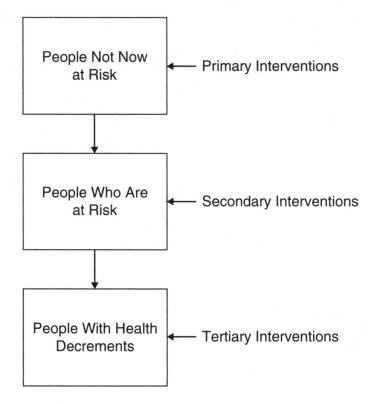

Figure 1.2.   A prevention and public health model. From "Prevention at Work: Public Health in Occupational Settings," by L. E. Tetrick and J. C. Quick. In J. C. Quick & L. E. Tetrick (Eds.), *Handbook of Occupational Health Psychology* (p. 10), 2003, Washington, DC: American Psychological Association. Copyright 2003 by the American Psychological Association.

Secondary interventions focus on people who are suspected to be at risk of illness or injury. Such interventions may be administered to groups or individuals. Staying with the health promotion and health education campaigns example, a secondary intervention would be to target the message to a particular group of people who are at risk, such as smokers. This would be akin to warning messages on packs of cigarettes.

Tertiary interventions focus on those who have experienced a loss in their health and attempt to restore them to health. Tertiary interventions are largely therapeutic and curative in nature. These interventions typically are individual based, although they can be group based, such as the difference between individual therapy and group therapy. A natural progression from our previous example would be the provision of smoking cessation programs to smokers who had experienced loss of lung capacity.

As stated earlier, occupational health psychology focuses on primary interventions, and from a public health and preventive medicine perspective primary prevention is always the preferred point of intervention (Wallace & Doebbeling, 1998). A prevention model is highly appropriate in occupational health psychology because it is systemic in nature and recognizes the life history and multifaceted complexity of many health problems (Ilgen, 1990; Quick et al., 1997). Chronic health problems stand in contrast to the infectious and contagious illnesses for which the traditional public health model was developed, originally to prevent disease epidemics.

Occupational health psychology interventions extend the public health model of prevention by addressing changes to organizations or systems, groups, and individuals. For example, changing the organizational culture to value learning would reduce stress from fear of making mistakes. Because the organizational culture affects everyone in the population, or organization in this case, it could change groups and individuals. The resultant decrease in stress at the individual level would improve the health of employees. Also, encouraging learning and development, which would be consistent with an organizational value for learning, would directly improve health (Mikkelsen, Saksvik, & Ursin, 1998). Learning organizations appear to place a premium on human resources and human development rather than treating people as simple labor costs (Forward, Beach, Gray, & Quick, 1991; Leonard-Barton, 1992), and it is proposed that this creates healthy people and healthy organizations. Cooper and Cartwright (1994) concluded that healthy organizations will tend not to need secondary and tertiary interventions. However, as Quick (1999) pointed out, there may be times when secondary or tertiary interventions may be needed because primary prevention was not feasible or individual factors create health concerns for only some people.

Integrating the PATH Model With the Public Health Model

The occupational health psychology literature has not integrated the PATH model with the public health model, perhaps because there have been relatively few empirical interventions and because the most frequent interventions focus on the individual level (see Bellarosa & Chen, 1997; Parks & Steelman, 2008;

Table 1.1   Example Interventions Integrating the PATH Model With the Public
Health Model

	Intervention		
Area of intervention	Primary	Secondary	Tertiary
Work–life balance	Benefits such as flextime, personal days off that are applicable to all employees	Work–family benefits that are applicable to those with family responsibilities	Employee assistance programs for individuals who are experiencing difficulties with nonwork responsibilities
Employee growth and development	Training both job-related (skills) and interpersonal for all employees	Training aimed at employees' needs for development of skills	Remedial training for those who have experienced illness and/or injury
Health and safety	General education campaigns relative to risk factors	Safety tips for individuals working in hazardous situations	Smoking cessation Weight loss programs for those who are experiencing health declines
Recognition	Rewards for safe behavior	Rewards for lack of accidents (which have been shown to be susceptible to negative consequences)	Incentives/ disincentives for weight loss/gain
Employee involvement	Quality of life circles	Health and safety committees for employees in hazardous environments	Peer counseling relative to substance use

Note.   PATH = Practices for Achieving Total Health.

Richardson & Rothstein, 2008). However, to illustrate how these two models could be integrated, we have included in Table 1.1 examples of the types of interventions that might fit within a matrix crossing the dimensions of the PATH model (rows) with the types of interventions of the public health model (columns).

Future Directions

Occupational health psychology is still emerging as a relatively new specialty within the science and profession of psychology. Concurrently, many business scholars are recognizing the importance of healthy organizations and healthy people (Cameron, Dutton, & Quinn, 2003). Frost and Robinson (1999) argued that emotional suffering, conflict, and pain are often endemic to organizational life for a variety of reasons. They suggested that some individuals serve the role of "organizational heroes" who effectively metabolize the emotional toxins that may build up within the system often at a price to their own health. For example, the executive who patiently listens to and absorbs the complaints of employees may be at risk, especially if these conflicts and concerns are internalized. Schein (as interviewed by Quick & Gavin, 2000) conceptualized these processes within organizations as potentially homeopathic ones in which disorder and dysfunction are metabolized before they create disability on the part of the individual, the work group, or the organization. Occupational health psychology can help organizations develop immune systems to metabolize the psychosocial and emotional toxins that may build up in work environments. Crafting organizational roles or functions for psychologists and other mental health professionals to function as immune system agents at work can contribute to the overall health and vitality of the organization and the people within it. Although there are many ways this might be achieved, two seem especially important. These growth areas concern (a) work and organizational design and (b) organizational health centers.

Luczak (1992) made the case for "good work" design from an industrial engineering perspective. From an occupational health psychology perspective, the implications of his argument are that health and safety issues must be considered on the front end of work, job, and organizational design efforts. Luczak suggested that the traditional approach to the design of work, jobs, and organizations is technocentric in nature; that is, it places technology at the center of the design process with careful deliberation over economic considerations. The implication of this approach is that people are expected to accommodate and adjust themselves to the characteristics of the work environment. In contrast, Luczak's "good work" design approach is anthropocentric in nature, placing the individual at the center of the design process. This alternative view of work, job, and organizational design is highly consistent with the emphasis we have placed on primary prevention interventions. The design of work, jobs, and organizations should be healthy and adaptive for the people who enliven them with their work efforts. This direction for occupational health psychology requires collaboration with engineers and managers for it to be effective.

A second direction for occupational health psychology is the pioneering concept of an organizational health center. This concept places a psychologist on the staff of a senior organizational leader to oversee the mental health and behavioral well-being of people throughout the organization. This elevates health and safety to the top levels in the organization. Adkins (1999) conceptualized the organizational health center as a mechanism for promoting organizational health, with its positive consequences for individual health and well-being. She pioneered the concept at the Sacramento Air Logistics Center, McClellan Air Force Base, California, during the 1990s, with the functions being prevention and intervention; training and development; and research, surveillance, and evaluation. The concept was adapted for the San Antonio Air Logistics Center, Kelly Air Force Base, Texas, to help with the largest federal industrial closure effort in U.S. national history. Preliminary indications have shown benefits in lives saved (i.e., only one suicide in a transferred workforce of 12,000 compared with 20 suicides in a comparable transferred industrial workforce of 8,000; a 0.08/1,000 rate compared with a 2.5/1,000 rate), workplace violence prevented (i.e., no incidents), and costs avoided (i.e., more than $30 million in cost avoidance; Quick & Klunder, 2000). The cost-avoidance estimate is based on a total cost of $80,000 for each employee complaint processed by the U.S. Air Force. Using this case estimator to project the number of cases expected during this closure period, civilian personnel found the number of actual cases to be 25% below what they estimated. The concept has resulted in the vice-commander of the Air Force Materiel Command placing a senior, active duty psychologist on his staff to oversee organizational health center activities.

Both the "good work" design efforts of Luczak (1992) and the organizational health center are potential mechanisms to metabolize the psychosocial and emotional toxins that may build up in work environments. In addition, both of these approaches can go beyond the prevention of illness and injury to the promotion of health within the organization. Also, these approaches exemplify the importance of occupational health psychology's multidisciplinary approach to developing and maintaining healthy people and healthy organizations. It may be that these two directions are not mutually exclusive and the practice of occupational health psychology will evolve to incorporate both approaches.

Although there is a considerable empirical base for crafting interventions that enhance organizational and employee health, more research and better methodologies are needed. Several of the teams formed around the priority areas of the U.S. National Occupational Research Agenda ("The Team Document," 2006) focus on the need for improved measurement and intervention methodologies as well as the need for surveillance and monitoring systems to identify potential risk factors associated with the organization of work.

In addition to more research evaluating the effectiveness of interventions, new phenomena are coming to the attention of occupational health psychologists (Pandey, Quick, Rossi, Nelson, & Martin, in press). These may reflect actual changes in the work environment or simply the recognition of the phenomena. One of these is bullying and incivility in the workplace, whether by supervisors, by coworkers, or by other employees. This has emerged in particular in Western industrial nations. Another such phenomenon is presenteeism, which might euphemistically be characterized as the physical presence and the psychological absence of workers and managers. This concerns the issue of engagement in the work itself and the inability to engage, perhaps due to ill health. A third such phenomenon is the seeming escalation of unfair treatment and injustice (Greenberg & Colquitt, 2005). Each of these phenomena reflects factors that may be emerging in the dynamic workplace and perhaps the larger economic situation impacting today's organizations.

Organization of This Book

In revising the *Handbook of Occupational Health Psychology,* we have reorganized the sections to better fit a risk–problem–prevention–intervention model and have added some new chapters that reflect the expanding of the field. Part I provides an overview of occupational health and its brief history. Part II provides several models and frameworks employed in occupational health psychology and in the study of stress. Part III contains information on causes of and risk factors for ill health and injury, including safety, work–family balance, shiftwork, and organizational justice. Part IV focuses on symptoms and disorders, including burnout, cardiovascular disease, musculoskeletal injuries, and substance use and abuse. Part V discusses interventions and treatment, with an emphasis on jobs, worksites, organizations, leadership, and employee assistance. The concluding section, Part VI, addresses methodology and evaluation.

Conclusion

Theory and research have not fully integrated job and work design with studies of and interventions to improve employee health, nor have studies directly addressed the linkages between employee health and organizational health. The practice of occupational health psychology requires a sound scientific basis for developing healthy organizations and healthy people. To this end, more theoretical development and supporting research are needed to define health not just as the absence of illness but as something more. Perhaps the efforts of positive psychology to understand optimum human functioning and happiness (Seligman & Csikszentmihalyi, 2000) have implications for occupational safety and health and the design of primary interventions to promote health in the workplace. Seligman (1998) chided psychology for focusing on disease to the exclusion of working toward building strength and resilience in people. It appears that occupational health psychology has heard this call, and as indicated in several of the chapters in this handbook, there is growing recognition that occupational health psychology is concerned with creating healthy people and healthy organizations, not just the prevention of injury and illness.

References

Adkins, J. A. (1999). Promoting organizational health: The evolving practice of occupational health psychology. *Professional Psychology: Research and Practice, 30,* 129–137. doi:10.1037/0735-7028.30.2.129

Americans With Disabilities Act of 1990, Pub. L. No. 101-336.

Andresen, E. M., Prince-Caldwell, A., Akinci, F., Brownson, C. A., Hagglund, K., Jackson-Thompson, J., & Crocker, R. (1999). The Missouri disability epidemiology and health project. *American Journal of Preventive Medicine, 16,* 63–71. doi:10.1016/S0749-3797(98)00151-2

Aronsson, G. (1999). Influence of worklife on public health. *Scandinavian Journal of Work, Environment and Health, 25,* 597–604.

Bell, M. P. (2007). *Diversity in organizations.* Macon, OH: South-Western/Cengage.

Bellarosa, C., & Chen, P. Y. (1997). The effectiveness and practicality of occupational stress management interventions: A survey of subject matter expert opinions. *Journal of Occupational Health Psychology, 2,* 247–262. doi:10.1037/1076-8998.2.3.247

Benach, J., Fernando, G. B., Platt, S., Diez-Row, A., & Muntaner, C. (2000). The health-damaging potential of new types of flexible employment: A challenge for public health researchers. *American Journal of Public Health, 90,* 1316–1317. doi:10.2105/AJPH.90.8.1316

Berkman, L. F., & Kawachi, I. (Eds.). (2000). *Social epidemiology.* New York, NY: Oxford University Press.

Broschak, J. P., Davis-Blake, A., & Block, E. S. (2008). Nonstandard, not substandard: The relationship among work arrangements, work attitudes, and job performance. *Work and Occupations, 35,* 3–43. doi:10.1177/0730888407309604

Brislin, R. (2008). *Working with cultural differences: Dealing effectively with diversity in the workplace.* Westport, CT: Praeger/Greenwood.

Bureau of Labor Statistics. (1998). *Current population survey: March supplements, 1998.* Washington, DC: U.S. Department of Labor. Retrieved from http://www.bls.gov/cps/cpsaat36.pdf

Bureau of Labor Statistics. (2003). *Current population survey, 2003.* Washington, DC: U.S. Department of Labor. Retrieved from http://www.bls.gov/cps/cps_aa2003.htm

Bureau of Labor Statistics. (2006). *Current population survey, 2006.* Washington, DC: U.S. Department of Labor. Retrieved from http://www.bls.gov/cps/cps_aa2006.htm

Bureau of Labor Statistics. (2007). *Occupational employment statistics, 2007.* Washington, DC: U.S. Department of Labor. Retrieved from http://www.bls.gov/oes/oes_arch.htm

Bureau of Labor Statistics. (2008). *Current population survey, 2008.* Washington, DC: U.S. Department of Labor. Retrieved from http://www.bls.gov/cps/cpsaat36.pdf

Bureau of Labor Statistics. (2009). *Occupational projects and training data, 2008–09 edition.* Washington, DC: U.S. Department of Labor. Retrieved from http://www.bls.gov/emp/optd/

Burke, R. J., & Nelson, D. (1998). Mergers and acquisitions, downsizing, and privatization: A North American perspective. In M. K. Gowing, J. D. Kraft, & J. C. Quick (Eds.), *The new organizational reality: Downsizing, restructuring, and revitalization* (pp. 21–54). Washington, DC: American Psychological Association. doi:10.1037/10252-001

Cameron, K. S., Dutton, J. E., & Quinn, R. E. (2003). *Positive organizational scholarship: Foundations of a new discipline.* San Francisco, CA: Berrett-Koehler.

Cooper, C. L., & Cartwright, S. (1994). Healthy mind, healthy organization: A proactive approach to occupational stress. *Human Relations, 47,* 455–471. doi:10.1177/001872679404700405

Cox, T. (1997). Workplace health promotion. *Work and Stress, 11,* 1–5.

de Vries, M. F. R. K., & Balasz, K. (1997). The downside of downsizing. *Human Relations, 50,* 11–50. doi:10.1177/001872679705000102

Fairweather, N. B. (1999). Surveillance in employment: The case of teleworking. *Journal of Business Ethics, 22,* 39–49. doi:10.1023/A:1006104017646

Feldman, D. C., Leana, C. R., & Bolino, M. C. (2002). Underemployment and relative deprivation among re-employed executives. *Journal of Occupational and Organizational Psychology, 75,* 453–471. doi:10.1348/096317902321119682

Forward, G. E., Beach, D. E., Gray, D. A., & Quick, J. C. (1991). Mentofacturing: A vision for American industrial excellence. *Academy of Management Executive, 5,* 32–44.

Frost, P., & Robinson, S. (1999). The toxic handler. *Harvard Business Review, 77,* 97–106.

Grawitch, M. J., Gottschalk, M., & Munz, D. C. (2006). The path to a healthy workplace: A critical review linking healthy workplace practices, employee well-being, and organizational improvements. *Consulting Psychology Journal: Practice and Research, 58,* 129–147. doi:10.1037/10659293.58.3.129

Greenberg, J., & Colquitt, J. A. (2005). *Handbook of organizational justice.* London, England: Taylor & Francis.

Griffiths, A. (1998). Work-related illness in Great Britain. *Work and Stress, 12,* 1–5.

Hofmann, D. A., & Tetrick, L. E. (2003). The etiology of the concept of health: Implications for "organizing" individual and organizational health. In D. A. Hofmann & L. E. Tetrick (Eds.), *Health and safety in organizations* (pp. 1–28). San Francisco, CA: Jossey-Bass.

Ilgen, D. R. (1990). Health issues at work: Opportunities for industrial organizational psychology. *American Psychologist, 45,* 273–283. doi:10.1037/0003-066X.45.2.273

Jahoda, M. (1982). *Employment and unemployment: A social psychological analysis.* Cambridge, England: Cambridge University Press.

Kessler, R. C., & Frank, R. G. (1997). The impact of psychiatric disorders on work loss days. *Psychological Medicine, 27,* 861–873. doi:10.1017/S0033291797004807

Kompier, M. A. J. (1996). Job design and well-being. In M. J. Schabracq, J. A. M. Winnubst, & C. L. Cooper (Eds.), *Handbook of work and health psychology* (pp. 349–368). New York, NY: Wiley.

Kouzis, A. C., & Eaton, W. W. (1997). Psychopathology and the development of disability. *Social Psychiatry and Psychiatric Epidemiology, 32,* 379–386.

Krause, N., Dasinger, L. K., & Neuhauser, F. (1998). Modified work and return to work: A review of the literature. *Journal of Occupational Rehabilitation, 8,* 113–139. doi:10.1023/A:1023015622987

Landsbergis, P. A., Schnall, P. L., Belkic, K. L., Baker, D., Schwartz, J. E., & Pickering, T. G. (2003). The workplace and cardiovascular disease: Relevance and potential role for occupational health psychology. In J. C. Quick & L. E. Tetrick (Eds.), *Handbook of occupational health psychology* (pp. 265–287). Washington, DC: American Psychological Association. doi:10.1037/10474-013

Langan-Fox, J. (2005). New technology, the global economy and organizational environments: Effects on employee stress, health and well-being. In A.-S. G. Antoniou & C. L. Cooper (Eds.), *Research companion to organizational health psychology* (pp. 413–429). Northampton, MA: Edward Elgar.

Leonard-Barton, D. (1992). The factory as a learning laboratory. *Sloan Management Review, 34,* 23–39.

Lewis, S., & Cooper, C. L. (1999). The work–family research agenda in changing contexts. *Journal of Occupational Health Psychology, 4,* 382–393. doi:10.1037/1076-8998.4.4.382

Luczak, H. (1992). "Good work" design: An ergonomic, industrial engineering perspective. In J. C. Quick, L. R. Murphy, & J. J. Hurrell Jr. (Eds.), *Stress and well-being at work: Assessments and interventions for occupational mental health* (pp. 96–112). Washington, DC: American Psychological Association.

Macik-Frey, M., Quick, J. C., & Nelson, D. L. (2007). Advances in occupational health: From a stressful beginning to a positive future. *Journal of Management, 33,* 809–840. doi:10.1177/0149206307307634

Macik-Frey, M., Quick, J. D., Quick, J. C., & Nelson, D. L. (2009). Occupational health psychology: From preventive medicine to psychologically healthy workplaces. In A.-S. G. Antoniou, C. L. Cooper, G. P. Chrousos, C. D. Spielberger, & M. W. Eysenck (Eds.), *Handbook of managerial behavior and occupational health* (pp. 3–19). Northampton, MA: Edward Elgar.

Maclean, L. M., Plotnikoff, R. C., & Moyer, A. (2000). Transdisciplinary work with psychology from a population health perspective: An illustration. *Journal of Health Psychology, 5,* 173–181. doi:10.1177/135910530000500208

Mikkelsen, A., Saksvik, P. O., & Ursin, H. (1998). Job stress and organizational learning climate. *International Journal of Stress Management, 5,* 197–209. doi:10.1023/A:1022965727976

Miles, M. B. (1965). Planned change and organizational health: Figure and ground. In F. D. Carver & T. J. Sergiovanni (Eds.), *Organizations and human behavior: Focus on schools* (pp. 375–391). New York, NY: McGraw-Hill.

Nelson, D. L., & Quick, J. C. (2011). *Organizational behavior: Science, the real world, and you* (7th ed.). Mason, OH: Cengage/South-Western.

Nutbeam, D. (1998). Health promotion glossary. *Health Promotion International, 13,* 349–364. doi:10.1093/heapro/13.4.349

Pandey, A., Quick, J. C., Rossi, A. M., Nelson, D. L., & Martin, W. (in press). Stress and the workplace: Ten years of science, 1997–2007. In R. Contrada & A. Baum (Eds.), *The handbook of stress science: Biology, psychology, and health.* New York, NY: Springer.

Parks, K. M., & Steelman, L. A. (2008). Organizational wellness programs: A meta-analysis. *Journal of Occupational Health Psychology, 13,* 58–68. doi:10.1037/1076-8998.13.1.58

Paul, K. I., & Moser, K. (2009). Unemployment impairs mental health: Meta-analyses. *Journal of Vocational Behavior, 74,* 264–282. doi:10.1016/j.jvb.2009.01.001

Polanyi, M., & Tompa, E. (2004). Re-thinking work-health models for the new global economy: A qualitative analysis of emerging dimensions of work. *Work: Journal of Prevention, Assessment and Rehabilitation, 23,* 3–18.

Purdum, T. S. (2001, March 3). Non-Hispanic Whites a minority, California census figures show. *New York Times,* pp. A1, A16.

Quick, J. C. (1999). Occupational health psychology: The convergence of health and clinical psychology with public health and preventive medicine in an organizational context. *Professional Psychology: Research and Practice, 30,* 123–128. doi:10.1037/0735-7028.30.2.123

Quick, J. C., & Gavin, J. H. (2000). The new frontier: Edgar Schein on organizational therapy. *Academy of Management Executive, 14,* 31–44.

Quick, J. C., & Klunder, C. (2000). Preventive stress management at work: The case of San Antonio Air Logistics Center (AFMC). In *Proceedings of the Eleventh International Congress on Stress.* Yonkers, NY: American Institute of Stress.

Quick, J. C., Quick, J. D., Nelson, D. L., & Hurrell, J. J., Jr. (1997). *Preventive stress management in organizations.* Washington, DC: American Psychological Association. doi:10.1037/10238-000

Raphael, D., Steinmetz, B., Renwick, R., Rootman, I., Brown, I., Sehdev, H., . . . Smith, T. (1999). The community quality of life project: A health promotion approach to understanding communities. *Health Promotion International, 14,* 197–209. doi:10.1093/heapro/14.3.197

Reynolds, S. (1997). Psychological well-being at work: Is prevention better than cure? *Journal of Psychosomatic Research, 43,* 93–102. doi:10.1016/S0022-3999(97)00023-8

Richardson, K. M., & Rothstein, H. (2008). Effects of occupational stress management intervention programs: A meta-analysis. *Journal of Occupational Health Psychology, 13,* 69–93.

Robertson, A., & Tracy, C. S. (1998). Health and productivity of older workers. *Scandinavian Journal of Work, Environment and Health, 24,* 85–97.

Rose, G. (1992). *The strategy of preventive medicine.* Oxford, England: Oxford University Press.

Rosen, R. H. (1986). *Healthy companies.* New York, NY: American Management Association.

Safe Work in the 21st Century: Education and Training Needs for the Next Decade's Occupational Safety and Health Personnel. (2000). Washington, DC: Institute of Medicine, National Academy Press.

Sauter, S. L., Hurrell, J. J., Fox, H. R., Tetrick, L. E., & Barling, J. (1999). Occupational health psychology: An emerging discipline. *Industrial Health, 37,* 199–211. doi:10.2486/indhealth.37.199

Schaufeli, W. B. (2004). The future of occupational health psychology. *Applied Psychology: An International Review, 53,* 502–517.

Schein, E. H. (1990). Organizational culture. *American Psychologist, 45,* 109–119. doi:10.1037/0003-066X.45.2.109

Schmidt, L. R. (1994). A psychological look at public health: Contents and methodology. In S. Maes, H. Leventhal, & M. Johnston (Eds.), *International review of health psychology* (Vol. 3, pp. 3–36). Chichester, England: Wiley.

Schmitt, E. (2001, April 1). U.S. now more diverse, ethnically and racially. *New York Times,* p. A20.

Schneider, D. L., Camara, W. J., Tetrick, L. E., & Stenberg, C. R. (1999). Training in occupational health psychology: Initial efforts and alternative models. *Professional Psychology: Research and Practice, 30,* 138–142. doi:10.1037/0735-7028.30.2.138

Seligman, M. E. P. (1998, January). Building human strength: Psychology's forgotten mission. *APA Monitor, President's Column.* Retrieved from http://www.apa.org/monitor/jan98/pres.html

Seligman, M. E. P., & Csikszentmihalyi, M. (2000). Positive psychology: An introduction. *American Psychologist, 55,* 5–14. doi:10.1037/0003-066X.55.1.5

Stachowski, A., Fisher, G. G., Grosch, J. W., Hesson, J., & Tetrick, L. E. (2007, April). *Job complexity: Prevention of cognitive functioning decline?* Paper presented at the annual meeting of the Society for Industrial and Organizational Psychology, New York, NY.

The Team Document: Ten Years of Leadership Advancing the National Occupational Research Agenda. (2006). Retrieved from http://www.cdc.gov/niosh/nora/pastnora.html

Tetrick, L. E. (2000). Linkages between organizational restructuring and employees' wellbeing. *Journal of Tokyo Medical University, 58,* 357–363.

Tetrick, L. E. (2008). Prevention: Integrating health protection and health promotion perspectives. In M. Sverke, K. Näswall, & J. Hellgren (Eds.), *The individual in the changing work life* (pp. 403–418). Cambridge, England: Cambridge University Press.

U.S. Department of Health and Human Services. (1990). *Healthy People 2000: National health promotion and disease prevention objectives.* Washington, DC: National Academy of Sciences.

Wallace, R. B., & Doebbeling, B. N. (1998). *Maxcy-Rosenau-Last public health and preventive medicine* (14th ed.). Stamford, CT: Appleton & Lange.

Warr, P. (2007). *Work, happiness and unhappiness.* Mahwah, NJ: Erlbaum.

Warren, N., Dillon, C., Morse, T., Hall, C., & Warren, A. (2000). Biomechanical, psychosocial, and organizational risk factors for WRMSD population-based estimates from the Connecticut Upper-extremity Surveillance Project (CUSP). *Journal of Occupational Health Psychology, 5,* 164–181. doi:10.1037/1076-8998.5.1.164

Wayne, J. H., Grzywacz, J. G., Carlson, D. S., & Kacmar, K. M. (2007). Work–family facilitation: A theoretical explanation and model of primary antecedents and consequences. *Human Resource Management Review, 17,* 63–76. doi:10.1016/j.hrmr.2007.01.002

Weich, S. (1997). Prevention of the common mental disorders: A public health perspective. *Psychological Medicine, 27,* 757–764. doi:10.1017/S0033291797005394

Williams, D. R. (1999). Race, socioeconomic status, and health: The added effects of racism and discrimination. In N. E. Adler, M. Marmot, B. S. McEwen, & J. Stewart (Eds.), *Annals of the New York Academy of Sciences: Socioeconomic status and health in industrial nations: Social, psychological, and biological pathways* (Vol. 896, pp. 173–188). New York, NY: New York Academy of Science.

2

A History of Occupational Health Psychology

Julian Barling and Amanda Griffiths

Interest in questions about occupational health psychology is by no means a recent phenomenon. The question of how workplace practices and policies, supervision, and leadership affect employees' physical and psychological well-being has attracted a considerable amount of interest for much of the 20th century. The importance of the more intangible aspects of work and their effects on individual health, both psychological and physical, began to be recognized in the 19th century, particularly after the Industrial Revolution. At that time, psychology was only a fledgling discipline; it was largely confined to purely experimental matters, making little contribution to applied issues. However, individuals from disciplines with a more substantial history—such as philosophy, politics, sociology, art, and literature—had begun to air concerns about the impact of the changing world of work on employees' physical and psychological health. The strange and dehumanizing world of factories and offices began to appear not only in the sociological and political commentaries of that time but also in novels throughout much of Europe in the late 19th and early 20th centuries, for example, in the writings of authors such as Franz Kafka.

In this chapter, we trace the development of occupational health psychology in the 20th century. In doing so, we take the position that the interactions among people, ideas, events, and institutions are critical. We trace various events throughout the 20th century and note how they influenced what today we refer to as *occupational health psychology*. We also examine some of the institutions that have had a critical impact on the development of occupational health psychology. Throughout, we introduce some of the people whose research, ideas, and personal efforts helped to create occupational health psychology as a recognizable discipline and who may have begun to make a difference to the lives of working people.

Writing a history of any newly emerging field presents particular challenges, notably in attempting to document the contribution of specific individuals or events. With the benefit of more hindsight—perhaps a century or two rather than a few decades—one might make a more informed judgment. But even

Financial support from the Social Sciences and Humanities Research Council of Canada to Julian Barling is gratefully acknowledged. Amanda Griffiths acknowledges helpful correspondence from many colleagues in Europe, particularly from members of the European Academy of Occupational Health Psychology.

200 years may not be enough. Chou En-Lai, the former Chinese leader, when asked in the late 1970s for his opinion on the impact of the French Revolution of 1789, is reputed to have responded, "I don't know. It's too soon to tell." It is clear that tracing influential early developments in an area as new as occupational health psychology presents an intriguing challenge, but one with which we nonetheless readily engage.

There are two further notes of caution. First, a significant proportion of the subject matter included in this analysis is largely restricted to that published in, or translated into, English. Second, perceptions of important conceptual frameworks in the discipline vary between North America and Europe and among the various countries of Europe. This chapter may be ambitious in trying to reconcile many different viewpoints and distill them in so few pages. In many ways, therefore, what is offered is *a* history rather than *the* history of occupational health psychology.

Early Philosophical Developments

One of the first to voice concern, in the mid-19th century, was Friedrich Engels in *The Condition of the Working Class in England* (1845/1987), first published in German. He described in detail the physical and psychological health problems suffered by workers from many different trades. He believed the origins of these problems to be in the organization of work and its associated social and physical environments. Karl Marx subsequently wrote about the horrific ways in which industrial capitalism exploited employees in *Das Kapital* (1867/1999), the first volume of which he published himself. He famously described the "alienation" of workers when treated as commodities within a capitalist economic system in which workplaces were increasingly characterized by specialization and division of labor. Many in Europe who subsequently became interested with the health effects of work organization have acknowledged an intellectual debt to both Marx and Engels: Both of the works referred to previously are still in print and widely read today.

However, despite these concerns, a considerable period of time elapsed before the effects of the organization of work (as opposed to the physical working environment) on health were subject to serious scientific attention. A more substantial investigation of the nature of the relationship between health and work from a psychological perspective began to emerge in publications from Northern Europe and the United States in the mid-20th century. This occurred partly as a result of the cross-fertilization of ideas between the disciplines of medicine, psychology, sociology, and management. It could be argued that it was from these developments that the discipline of occupational health psychology, as we now know it, emerged.

Early Developments in the United States

Although many developments relating to occupational health psychology throughout the 20th century were positive from the perspective of employees, one of the earliest events in the United States was certainly not. We refer to the seminal work of Frederick Taylor, whose book, *The Principles of Scientific Management* (1911), was to attract considerable attention for the remainder of the century. Taylor, initially a machine-shop foreman, proposed that low productivity was partly the result of management's ignorance of working processes. This ignorance allowed workers to deceive managers, to control those processes, and thus to determine the speed of work. He advocated, in the interests of financial economy, that tasks should be carefully analyzed, simplified, compartmentalized, and standardized and that worker influence should be removed. In effect, this reduced the amount of skill required to complete tasks and removed all worker control and discretion. These principles appeared to make economic sense to many managers at the time and had a significant impact on management practice both inside and outside the United States. *Scientific management* was a critical development in the emergence of occupational health psychology because of its two inherent assumptions. First, as a forerunner of the industrial engineering approach, it separated "thinking" about work from "doing" work. Specifically, one class of employees, industrial engineers, would have the specialized skills (and as it later transpired, the organizational power) that would allow them to design the work of other people, whose only role was to perform whatever tasks were assigned to them. In this sense, scientific management may represent the first concerted effort to "de-skill" work. Second, scientific management demanded that consideration of employee emotions at work be eliminated, on the assumption that they interfered with productive work. As readers shall see, at the end of the 20th century, occupational health psychology would be embracing the very opposite of these two concepts.

Additional research in the United States that had a widespread influence in many countries included the experiments carried out in the 1920s at the Western Electric Company at Hawthorne Plant (Mayo, 1933; Roethlisberger & Dickson, 1939). Using a Tayloristic framework, these studies explored the relationships between various working conditions (e.g., lighting, wages, rest breaks) and productivity. But whatever changes were made, productivity usually rose. It was eventually concluded that receiving special attention, being aware that they were the focus of research, and guessing what the researchers were investigating affected the way workers behaved. It became apparent that workers' perceptions of, and feelings about, what was happening to them were important (the antithesis of the Tayloristic emphasis on removing emotions from the workplace). This effect was henceforth named the *Hawthorne effect*. The significance of this development lay in the recognition of the importance of human relations—the social, psychological, and cultural aspects of work. It gradually became apparent that although Taylor's principles may have appeared to managers to make economic sense, scientific management was not necessarily followed by increases in productivity and was in fact often associated with negative attitudes and poor health outcomes. Two subsequent investigations into the physical and mental health problems experienced by automobile workers in the United States substantiated this view (Chinoy, 1955; Kornhauser, 1965). Such findings were also being documented in Europe. Before we note these, however, it is worth mentioning two other significant theoretical developments for occupational health psychology that arose from quite different streams of research in the United States. First, from a perspective of personality and clinical psychology, Abraham Maslow published his theory of self-actualization (Maslow, 1943) and some 20 years later applied it specifically to work organizations (Maslow, 1965). Although it has been generally underappreciated from the perspective of occupational health psychology, Maslow stated explicitly that only individuals who are psychologically healthy could be motivated to work, arguing that repressive environments, including work environments, would inhibit individuals from reaching their fullest potential.

Perhaps one of the other most salient developments in the 20th century was the advent of job design theories. Credit for much of the initial thinking about those working conditions that influence job performance and mental health can be given to Frederick Herzberg (1966). He suggested that motivation and job satisfaction could be improved by improving people's work—for example, by enriching their jobs through increased skill use, challenge, or recognition. Although some of his research has been subsequently criticized, these basic suggestions about job enrichment remain useful, and his ideas stimulated a considerable amount of research on this topic. Some years later, Hackman and Oldham (1976, 1980) provided a more specific "job characteristics" model, rejuvenating research and thinking on the topic of job design.

Many other important theoretical contributions in the early development of occupational health psychology and social psychology are acknowledged to have originated at the University of Michigan. In 1948, Rensis Likert established the Institute for Social Research at the University of Michigan, and the institute's influence was to be felt for the rest of the century. It is the oldest institute for interdisciplinary research in the social sciences in the United States, currently employing about 350 individuals. Its earlier substantive contributions included Quinn and Staines's (1977) Quality of Employment Survey and House's (1981) research on work stress and social support. The early theoretical contributions (e.g., person–environment fit) of what was known as the "Michigan School" (e.g., Caplan, Cobb, French, van Harrison, & Pinneau, 1975; Kahn, Wolfe, Quinn, Snoek, & Rosenthal, 1964; Katz & Kahn, 1966) were widely acknowledged in Europe. More recently, the influence of the Institute for Social Research is maintained through, for example, its research program on the effects of unemployment as well as on the factors that influence reemployment (e.g., Caplan, Vinokur, Price, & van Ryn, 1989; Kessler, Turner, & House, 1987; Vinokur, Schul, Vuori, & Price, 2000).

Early Influences From Europe

Research in Europe was demonstrating the dangers of scientific management. In Britain, for example, the negative effects of the disregard for workers' psychological well-being in job design in coal mines were explored in some detail by researchers from the Tavistock Institute of Human Relations in London (Trist & Bamforth, 1951). Trist (a psychiatrist) and Bamforth (a former miner with 18 years experience at the coal-face) described in considerable detail the psychological and social consequences of a particular change in coal mining methods. They explored the relationship between the health and productivity of miners as a function of the social structure of the work system. Miners' work had changed from a whole-task, skilled, autonomous system to a mechanized, fractured system with isolated but heavily interdependent groups of workers. In this new system, miners were observed to experience high levels of anxiety, anger, and depression, problems that had previously been largely absent. Major disruptions in social support also were observed. Trist and Bamforth (1951) concluded that it was

> difficult to see how these problems can be solved effectively without restoring responsible autonomy to primary groups within the system and ensuring that each of these groups has a satisfying sub-whole as its work task, and some scope for flexibility in workplace. (p. 41)

They concluded that the nature of demand and employee participation in decision making were important for employee health.

At this time, although it is hard to trace, there was much cross-fertilization of ideas about work organization in the Nordic countries (e.g., Scandinavia, Finland). Many Nordic academics read fluently in several languages, including English. Trist and his colleagues from London, notably Fred Emery, collaborated closely with a Norwegian, Einar Thorsrud, who is often regarded as the founding figure of what would now be recognized as occupational health psychology in Norway. Thorsrud and Emery's empirical research on the empowering of work groups (essentially, an anti-Tayloristic approach) and their theory of psychological job demands were widely read and inspired many researchers in Denmark and Sweden (Thorsrud & Emery, 1970). Similarly, the sociologist Sverre Lysgaard's (1961) writings on workers' collectives were influential. Also in Norway, a separate research group led by Holger Ursin began publishing work on stress-related psychophysiological mechanisms (Ursin, 1980; Ursin, Baade, & Levine, 1978). In Finland, there had been a long-term interest in the mental health outcomes of work design. The Finnish Institute of Occupational Health, for example, acknowledged major influences from the United States, Germany, and the United Kingdom, with some of their psychologists visiting Trist and colleagues in London in the 1950s. In 1974, Finland employed its first practicing occupational health psychologist in the UPM Kymmene paper mill. In Denmark, an interest was also flourishing in the importance of working conditions and related interventions: Indeed, the translation of occupational health psychology in Danish is "work environment psychology." Much of the Danish interest was inspired by work in Sweden, where major direct challenges to Taylor's ideas are widely acknowledged to have emerged in the 1970s and 1980s—much of it published in English. We return to this work in more detail below.

Moving ahead for a moment, the publications that have probably had the most impact in occupational health psychology, and that demonstrated to a wide audience the inadvisability of adopting a Tayloristic approach to job design, were Robert Karasek's (1979) article on job demands, job decision latitude, and mental health, and his subsequent article on the importance of such factors for cardiovascular health in a prospective study of Swedish men (Karasek, Baker, Marxer, Ahlbom, & Theorell, 1981). A third publication, the influential book that Karasek coauthored with Tores Theorell titled *Healthy Work* (Karasek & Theorell, 1990) brought the subject matter to an even wider audience. The historical importance of the job demands–job control theory lies not so much in the subsequent attempts at its validation by other workers but in the enormous amount of research that later focused on those psychosocial aspects of work that might be critical for psychological and physical health. Within a decade of the appearance of *Healthy Work,* research findings were suggesting that the factors responsible for psychological and physical health were the same as those associated with higher levels of job performance (e.g., Parker & Wall, 1998; Wall, Corbett, Martin, Clegg, & Jackson, 1990).

The work of Karasek and Theorell did not emerge in a vacuum. It followed directly from the strong tradition of research on, and thought about, work design and health in the Nordic countries. In those countries, activities typical of traditional industrial–organizational psychology, such as personnel selection and performance assessment, had been criticized (largely by the labor movement) and had not prospered, but research and practice concerned with work reform and worker well-being flourished.

It is widely acknowledged in Europe that many of the major intellectual developments that heralded interest in the relationship between work and health from a psychological and psychophysiological perspective, and that provided an empirical base for such concerns, emerged in Sweden and in Norway. Karasek and Theorell had worked, separately, in two key institutions in Sweden that had a major impact on the early development of occupational health psychology and under the guidance of two influential figures: Bertil Gardell (a psychologist) at the University of Stockholm and Lennart Levi (a physician) at the Karolinska Institute in Stockholm.

Gardell is widely recognized in Europe as one of the founding figures of work and organizational psychology. He worked at the University of Stockholm from the 1960s, becoming professor of psychology, studying work reform. He described in detail how work (e.g., as advocated by Taylor) could lead to alienation and withdrawal, and he published widely on the relationship between technology, autonomy, participation, and mental health (e.g., Gardell, 1971, 1977) and on the relationship between work reform research and social change (Gardell & Gustavsen, 1980). In a series of empirical studies, he and others in Sweden (e.g., Gunnar Aronsson and Gunn Johansson) established credibly throughout the 1970s and 1980s that, among other matters, machine-paced work, lack of control at work, monotonous work, and fragmented and isolated work all had adverse effects (e.g., Johansson, Aronsson, & Lindstrom, 1978). The importance of worker participation and control was particularly central to many of these investigations: Aronsson (1987) later published a book on the concept of control in work psychology.

Many of Gardell's ideas, before and after his unfortunate early death, were developed further by his colleagues and researchers in Sweden. Marianne Frankenhaeuser was one such collaborator, among the first to explore the psychophysiological mechanisms involved in the relationship between working conditions and ill health as a means of broadening the "scientific" case for job redesign. She and her colleagues investigated the neuroendocrinological changes associated with various environmental conditions such as understimulation, low control, monotonous activity, or fast-paced work (Frankenhaeuser & Gardell, 1976; Frankenhaeuser & Johansson, 1986; Frankenhaeuser, Lundberg, & Forsman, 1980).

Also in Stockholm in the 1950s, Lennart Levi, a physician, had created his stress laboratory as part of the Karolinska Institute. He had previously spent some time working with Hans Selye in Montreal, Quebec, Canada, and his initial focus, largely experimental, was on the physiological aspects of stress. However, he gradually adopted a multidisciplinary focus and began working with psychologists and sociologists in the 1960s on large-scale studies, some with Aubrey Kagan, of working conditions and their associations with various health indicators. Levi also explored the psychophysiological mechanisms associated with stressful conditions. He was influential in international circles, advancing the importance of the psychosocial work environment and systems-level thinking for worker health at a time when such notions, and social medicine in general, were not widely accepted by the medical establishment (Levi, 1971). Researchers at the Karolinska Institute conduct many studies on work stress as well as on stress in general. In 1981, Levi founded the Institute for Psychosocial Factors and Health, an independent government institute associated with the Karolinska Institute, and became its first director.

Tores Theorell, one of Levi's younger colleagues, was a specialist in clinical cardiology with an initial interest in the role of life events. He went on to make a significant impact on the field, both with Karasek and with colleagues at the Karolinska Institute. On Levi's retirement in 1996, Theorell took over as director of the institute. The results of his work partly inspired the Whitehall Study, a longitudinal study on the relationship between working conditions and cardiovascular disease, carried out by Michael Marmot and colleagues in the United Kingdom. Marmot and Theorell (1988) pioneered the notion that differences in the psychosocial work environment may be partly responsible for the association between social class and the incidence of coronary heart disease.

Unemployment and Nonwork

So far, we have examined the issue of the organization of work and its effects on mental or physical health. A comprehensive study of the field of occupational health psychology today, however, would include not just a focus on psychosocial factors at work but also an understanding of the effects of nonwork and unemployment. Although research on the interdependence of work and nonwork has been conducted since the early 1980s, there is substantially more research on this topic than on unemployment. The primary focus of this research endeavor has been on the mutual effects of work on family and of family on work (Barling, 1990). In contrast, the effects of unemployment have been the focus of research for at least 7 decades, with interest peaking after bouts of high unemployment.

The contribution of Marie Jahoda was substantial throughout most of this period. Jahoda's earliest research focused on the effects of unemployment on a particular group in Europe, the Marienthal community, which had previously experienced sustained industrial development (Jahoda, Lazarsfeld, & Zeisel, 1933). Much later, she provided a theory of the psychological meaning of both employment and unemployment, reasoning that neither exerts uniform effects; instead, it is the quality of the employment and unemployment experience that is critical (Jahoda, 1982). Remarkably, her contribution did not end there, as was evident from her review of the effects of economic recession on psychological well-being in 1988, some 55 years after her initial research findings were first published (Jahoda, 1988). Indeed, on her death on April 28, 2001, at the age of 94, the byline of one obituary noted, "Psychologist who examined the corrosive effects of unemployment" (Professor Marie Jahoda, 2001).

Separately, research was being conducted within Australia and the United States. Although no individual researcher matched the length of Jahoda's career, the findings of Stan Kasl and Sidney Cobb (Kasl & Cobb, 1970; Kasl, Gore, & Cobb, 1975) helped to legitimize the study of unemployment in the United States, as did those of Peter Warr (1987) in the United Kingdom. Similarly, like Jahoda's (1982) theory, the archival analyses of the Great Depression by Glen Elder (1974) helped to dispel the notion that unemployment exerted uniform negative effects. Research by Boris Kabanoff, Norman Feather, and Gordon O'Brien (e.g., Feather, 1990; O'Brien & Feather, 1990) advanced the breadth of occupational health psychology by providing a comprehensive understanding of the nature and effects of both employment and unemployment. At the time of going to press, there is a growing recognition that long-term worklessness is bad for physical and mental health, that work confers a wide range of benefits, and that wherever possible people with long-term health conditions and disabilities should be encouraged to remain in or return to work as soon as possible (Waddell & Burton, 2006). These latter authors, having undertaken a systematic review of the literature, conclude that overall the beneficial effects of work outweigh the risks of work.

Other Significant Institutions

The U.S. National Institute for Occupational Safety and Health (NIOSH) is widely acknowledged as having played an important role in furthering the cause of occupational health psychology since the early 1990s. NIOSH is mandated by federal law in the United States to conduct research on working conditions that could be hazardous to employee mental or physical well-being. An additional mandate is to make recommendations and disseminate knowledge that could be used to prevent workplace injuries. NIOSH has made three substantial contributions to the field. First, Sauter, Murphy, and Hurrell (1990) published a seminal article, based on extensive consultations with researchers, practitioners, and policymakers, that presented a comprehensive national strategy both to promote and to protect the psychological well-being of workers. Second, NIOSH entered into a cooperative agreement with the American Psychological Association (APA) to fund the initial development of graduate training in occupational health psychology in the United States. Several universities in the United States (e.g., Bowling Green State University, Clemson University, Kansas State University, Tulane University, the Universities of Houston and Minnesota) received funding toward the design and delivery of modules on this subject. Third, NIOSH and the APA joined forces in the 1990s to host major international conferences on the broad topic of work and well-being. These took place in 1990, 1992, 1995, 1999, 2003, 2006, and 2008. The most recent conference took place in Puerto Rico in November 2009.

In many countries, distinct institutions can be identified that have been influential in the development of occupational health psychology. We have already mentioned some from the United States and Sweden. But there are others. In the United Kingdom, for example, at least three separate research groups made an important contribution in early developments. The Institute of Work, Health and Organisations (I-WHO; formerly the Stress Research Group, and then the Centre for Organisational Health and Development) at the University of Nottingham has had a commitment to occupational health psychology as a distinct discipline since its beginnings in the early 1970s. Under the direction of Tom Cox, it made a notable contribution to the development of research, particularly in the fields of work stress (e.g., Cox, 1978). Cox's approach was driven by transactional theories such as that of Richard Lazarus (e.g., Lazarus, 1966; Lazarus & Folkman, 1984) highlighting the importance of cognitive and perceptual processes in people's reactions to their environments. However, the focus of Cox's early work was more on the psychophysiological processes that might mediate between various aspects of the environment and health. Cox and his colleagues moved on to apply theory in the workplace via interventions using a risk management paradigm (Cox, Griffiths, & Rial-Gonzalez, 2000). They acknowledged the significant influence of the Nordic emphasis on design, prevention, and systems-level rather than individual-level analysis. I-WHO has also been a leader in the field of postgraduate education in occupational health psychology since the late 1990s when Amanda Griffiths established the first master's-level degree in the world devoted entirely to occupational health psychology.

The Institute for Work Psychology at Sheffield (formerly the Social and Applied Psychology Unit) has been one of the longest standing and most highly respected research institutions in the United Kingdom for research and education in work and organizational psychology. It has also made major contributions that are relevant to occupational health psychology, notably in terms of the relationship between work, well-being, and effectiveness. Peter Warr's "vitamin model" and his work on the relationship between work, well-being, and unemployment (Warr, 1987, 1999) were notable early examples, as was Toby Wall's research on the nature and consequences of job redesign (Wall, 1982). At the University of Manchester Institute for Science and Technology, and more recently at the University of Lancaster, Cary Cooper has promoted the general field of occupational health psychology through the development of a number of broadly based journals, including the *Journal of Organizational Behavior,* by bringing together numerous collections of the works of authors in various areas of occupational psychology as informative and influential edited collections, and by being a prolific and effective publicist for the subject. There was clearly much activity in various institutions elsewhere in Europe in the 1970s and 1980s that was relevant to occupational health psychology's concerns, but much of what happened then is not as widely known as is deserved, simply because the significant authors operated and published in their native languages. But there is no doubt that some of these individuals have been influential. Winfried Hacker and his colleagues from Dresden (in the former East Germany), for example, undertook much admired early research on working conditions and the psychophysiology of stress (Hacker, 1978; Hacker & Richter, 1980). There are other major contributors, such as Johannes Siegrist (1996), also working in

Germany. His research, from a social equity perspective, has given rise to the effort–reward imbalance model and substantial recent interest in its contribution as an alternative or complement to other models of the relationship between work and health.

We would be remiss in discussing the influence of exogeneous organizations if we did not highlight the significant role that labor unions have historically exerted on employee well-being, both physical and psychological. Specifically, this influence has come about in several different ways. In the first instance, labor unions have generally influenced governments to introduce legislation that protects employees' physical well-being. Labor unions have also had an impact on employee well-being through the collective bargaining process. Within organizations, labor unions have also had a direct effect on management and worker awareness of occupational health and safety issues and risks (Barling, Fullagar & Kelloway, 1992; Kochan, 1980). Last, where it has not been possible to reduce the hazardous nature of work, labor unions have generally been successful in obtaining wage premiums for engagement in hazardous work (e.g., Freeman & Medoff, 1981; Olson, 1981).

One final observation concerning the role of labor unions in employee well-being: If we do accept the beneficial effects that unions have had for close to a century, then the decrease in union density in most Western countries over the past 2 decades is disquieting at best, especially in the face of potential stressors such as the ever-increasing work intensification and external economic crises.

Professional Organizations and Their Activities

Several other recent developments warrant attention, because they point to the emergence of occupational health psychology as an institutionalized, mature discipline. One of these is the publication of two journals that are devoted specifically to occupational health psychology. *Work and Stress* has been edited by Cox at the University of Nottingham since its inception in 1987. The *Journal of Occupational Health Psychology* has been published by the APA since 1996, first edited by James Campbell Quick, from 2000 by Julian Barling, and from 2006 by Lois Tetrick. Like other journals, *Work and Stress* and the *Journal of Occupational Health Psychology* provide a forum for researchers and practitioners and for the dissemination of knowledge. The presence of two such international quarterlies lends further support to the notion that occupational health psychology has emerged as a distinct discipline.

The emergence of organizations for scientists and practitioners could be taken as further evidence of maturity of a field. The European Academy of Occupational Health Psychology was established in 1998 by Cox and coworkers in the United Kingdom, together with colleagues from Sweden and Denmark. Its purpose is to promote research, practice, and education in the discipline. It hosted its first conference in Lund, Sweden (1999), its second in Nottingham, England (2000), and subsequent conferences in Barcelona (2001), Vienna (2002), Berlin (2003), Porto (2004), Dublin (2006), Valencia (2008), and at the time of going to press is planning for Rome in 2010.

The International Commission on Occupational Health ratified a new Scientific Committee in 1999 on Work Organization and Psychosocial Factors (ICOH-WOPS), with Raija Kalimo from the Finnish Institute of Occupational Health as its first chair and Michiel Kompier from the University of Nijmegen in the Netherlands as its second. Its focus is largely occupational health psychology. ICOH-WOPS hosted its first special conference on Psychosocial Factors at Work in Copenhagen in 1998, its second in Japan in 2005, and a third in Quebec in 2008.

In 2000, an informal International Coordinating Group for Occupational Health Psychology (ICGOHP) was formed, its purpose being to promote and facilitate the development of the discipline and to coordinate conference scheduling within an international framework. The initial members of the ICGOHP constituted representatives from the two major journals, NIOSH, the APA, and the European Academy of Occupational Health Psychology (EAOHP). In 2006, the body was reviewed, and representatives from the Society for Occupational Health Psychology (SOHP) were added to the membership. The SOHP, founded in 2005, with Leslie Hammer as first president, is the first organization in the United States to be devoted to occupational health psychology. Its now plays a role, with APA and NIOSH, in organizing Work, Stress, and Health conferences and coordinates activities with its European counterpart, the EAOHP.

Recent Developments

One of the ultimate criteria for the contribution and maturity of occupational health psychology is that some of its central tenets (e.g., the importance of employee control and participation) have become enshrined in government legislation and advice for employers in many countries. The following examples demonstrate the developing situation.

One of the first countries to establish such legislation was Sweden. The Swedish Work Environment Act of 1978 specified, among other things, that working methods, equipment, and materials should be adapted to fit people—both from a physiological and from a psychological point of view. Sweden's Act of Co-determination of 1977 had already given workers influence over job design, production methods, and the work environment, as well as the right to influence major decisions and planning processes via representation at board level (Gardell & Johansson, 1981). Somewhat later, the European Commission (1989) published their framework directive, titled "Council Framework Directive on the Introduction of Measures to Encourage Improvements in the Safety and Health of Workers at Work." Every member state of the European Union was required to translate the requirements of this directive into their own national legislative frameworks by 1992. Major requirements were that employers should assess all major risks to employee health and that employees or their representatives should be consulted on all matters that might affect their health and safety. In the United Kingdom, some of these requirements were already in place, but those that were not were incorporated into the Management of Health and Safety at Work Regulations in 1992 and 1999. The 1999 Approved Code of Practice for these regulations states, for example, that "employers should increase the control individuals have over the work they are responsible for" and that they should "adapt work to the requirements of the individual (consulting those who will be affected when designing workplaces" (paragraph 30d). Similar provisions are now in place or in development in all countries of the European Union. In the United States, while legislation is not so advanced, NIOSH has been advising employers for some time; for example, that workers should be given the opportunity to participate in decisions that affect their jobs and task performance (Sauter et al., 1990).

Given that occupational health psychology is still a newly emerging field, we hope that this brief introduction to its origins—people, ideas, events, and institutions—has demonstrated how far it has come in a short time. Whereas at the beginning of the 20th century work was designed largely with managers' best interests at heart, at the beginning of the 21st century we are witnessing a desire to promote and protect the psychological and physical health of workers themselves, through prevention and job design. If this level of progress continues, we can be cautiously optimistic that occupational health psychology will make a worthwhile and lasting contribution.

References

Aronsson, G. (1987). *Arbetspsykologi: Stress och kvalifikationsperspektiv* [The concept of control in work psychology]. Lund, Sweden: Studentlitteratur.

Barling, J. U. (1990). *Employment, stress and family functioning.* New York, NY: Wiley.

Barling, J., Fullagar, C., & Kelloway, E. K. (1992). *The union and its employees: A psychological approach.* , New York, NY: Oxford University Press.

Caplan, R., Cobb, S., French, J., van Harrison, R., & Pinneau, S. (1975). *Job demands and worker health.* Washington, DC: National Institute for Occupational Safety and Health.

Caplan, R. D., Vinokur, A. D., Price, R. H., & van Ryn, M. (1989). Job seeking, reemployment and mental health: A randomized field experiment in coping with job loss. *Journal of Applied Psychology, 74,* 759–769. doi:10.1037/0021-9010.74.5.759

Chinoy, E. (1955). *Automobile workers and the American dream.* Garden City, NJ: Doubleday.

Cox, T. (1978). *Stress.* London, England: Macmillan.

Cox, T., Griffiths, A., & Rial-Gonzalez, E. (2000). *Research on work-related stress.* Luxembourg: Office for Official Publications of the European Communities, European Agency for Safety & Health at Work.

Elder, G. H. (1974). *Children of the Great Depression.* Chicago, IL: University of Chicago Press.

Engels, F. (1987). *The condition of the working class in England.* London, England: Penguin Books. (Original work published 1845)

European Commission. (1989). Council framework directive on the introduction of measures to encourage improvements in the safety and health of workers at work (89/391/EEC). *Official Journal of the European Communities, 32* (No. L183), 1–8.

Feather, N. T. (1990). *The psychological impact of unemployment.* New York, NY: Springer.

Frankenhaeuser, M., & Gardell, B. (1976). Underload and overload in working life: Outline of a multidisciplinary approach. *Journal of Human Stress, 2,* 35–46.

Frankenhaeuser, M., & Johansson, G. (1986). Stress at work: Psychobiological and psychosocial aspects. *International Review of Applied Psychology, 35,* 287–299. doi:10.1111/j.1464-0597.1986.tb00928.x

Frankenhaeuser, M., Lundberg, U., & Forsman, L. (1980). Dissociation between sympathetic-adrenal and pituitary-adrenal responses to an achievement situation characterized by high controllability: Comparison between Type A and Type B males and females. *Biological Psychology, 10,* 79–91. doi:10.1016/0301-0511(80)90029-0

Freeman, R. B., & Medoff, J. L. (1981). The impact of the percent organized on union and nonunion wages. *Review of Economics and Statistics, 63,* 561–572. doi:10.2307/1935852

Gardell, B. (1971). Alienation and mental health in the modern industrial environment. In L. Levi (Ed.), *Society, stress and disease* (Vol. 1, pp. 148–180). Oxford, England: Oxford University Press.

Gardell, B. (1977). Autonomy and participation at work. *Human Relations, 30,* 515–533. doi:10.1177/001872677703000603

Gardell, B., & Gustavsen, B. (1980). Work environment research and social change: Current developments in Scandinavia. *Journal of Occupational Behaviour, 1,* 3–17.

Gardell, B., & Johansson, G. (1981). *Working life: A social science contribution to work reform.* Chichester, England: Wiley.

Hacker, W. (1978). *Allgemeine arbeits-und ingenieurpsychologie* [General work and engineering psychology]. Bern, Switzerland: Huber.

Hacker, W., & Richter, P. (1980). *Psychische fehlbeanspruchung, psychische ermiidung, monotonie, sdttigung und strep* [Psychological mis-strain, psychological fatigue, monotony, satiation, and stress]. Berlin, Germany: Deutscher Verlag der Wissenschaften.

Hackman, J. R., & Oldham, G. R. (1976). Motivation through the design of work test of a theory. *Organizational Behavior and Human Performance, 16,* 250–279. doi:10.1016/0030-5073(76)90016-7

Hackman, J. R., & Oldham, G. R. (1980). *Work redesign.* Reading, MA: Addison-Wesley.

Herzberg, F. (1966). *Work and the nature of man.* Cleveland, OH: World.

House, J. S. (1981). *Work stress and social support.* Reading, MA: Addison-Wesley.

Jahoda, M. (1982). *Employment and unemployment: A social psychological analysis.* Cambridge, England: Cambridge University Press.

Jahoda, M. (1988). Economic recession and mental health: Some conceptual issues. *Journal of Social Issues, 44,* 13–23.

Jahoda, M., Lazarsfeld, P. F., & Zeisel, H. (1933). *Marienthal: The sociography of an unemployed community.* London, England: Tavistock.

Johansson, G., Aronsson, G., & Lindstrom, B. O. (1978). Social psychological and neuro-endocrine stress reactions in highly mechanized work. *Ergonomics, 21,* 583–599. doi:10.1080/00140137808931761

Kahn, R., Wolfe, D. M., Quinn, K. P., Snoek, J. D., & Rosenthal, R. A. (1964). *Organizational stress: Studies in role conflict and ambiguity.* New York, NY: Wiley.

Karasek, R. A. (1979). Job demands, job decision latitude, and mental strain: Implications for job redesign. *Administrative Science Quarterly, 24,* 285–307. doi:10.2307/2392498

Karasek, R. A., Baker, D., Marxer, F., Ahlbom, A., & Theorell, T. (1981). Job decision latitude, job demands, and cardiovascular disease: A prospective study of Swedish men. *American Journal of Public Health, 71,* 694–705. doi:10.2105/AJPH.71.7.694

Karasek, R. A., & Theorell, T. (1990). *Healthy work: Stress, productivity and the reconstruction of work life.* New York, NY: Basic Books.

Kasl, S. V., & Cobb, S. (1970). Blood pressure changes in men undergoing job loss: A preliminary report. *Psychosomatic Medicine, 32,* 19–38.

Kasl, S. V., Gore, S., & Cobb, S. (1975). The experience of losing a job: Reported changes in health, symptoms and illness behavior. *Psychosomatic Medicine, 37,* 106–122.

Katz, D., & Kahn, R. (1966). *Social psychology of organizations.* New York, NY: Wiley.

Kessler, R. C., Turner, J. B., & House, J. S. (1987). Intervening processes in the relationship between unemployment and health. *Psychological Medicine, 17,* 949–961. doi:10.1017/S0033291700000763

Kochan, T. A. (1980). *Collective bargaining and industrial relations: From theory to policy and practice.* Homewood, IL: Richard D. Irwin.

Kornhauser, A. (1965). *Mental health and the industrial worker.* New York, NY: Wiley.

Lazarus, R. S. (1966). *Psychological stress and the coping process.* New York, NY: McGraw-Hill.

Lazarus, R. S., & Folkman, S. (1984). *Stress, appraisal and coping.* New York, NY: Springer.

Levi, L. (1971). *Society, stress and disease* (4 vols.). Oxford, England: Oxford University Press.

Lysgaard, S. (1961). *Arbeiderkollektivet: En studie i de underordnedes sosiologi* [Workers' collective: A study of the sociology of the subordinated]. Oslo, Norway: Universitetsforlaget.

Marmot, M. G., & Theorell, T. (1988). Social class and cardiovascular disease: The contribution of work. *International Journal of Health Services, 18,* 659–674.

Marx, K. (1999). *Das Kapital.* Oxford, England: Oxford University Press. (Original work published 1867)

Maslow, A. H. (1943). A theory of human motivation. *Psychological Review, 50,* 370–396. doi:10.1037/h0054346

Maslow, A. H. (1965). *Eupsychian management: A journal.* Homewood, IL: Irwin-Dorsey.

Mayo, E. (1933). *The human problems of an industrial civilization.* New York, NY: MacMillan.

O'Brien, G. E., & Feather, N. T. (1990). The relative effects of unemployment and quality of employment on the affect, work values and personal control of adolescents. *Journal of Occupational Psychology, 63,* 151–165.

Olson, C. A. (1981). An analysis of wage differentials received by workers on dangerous jobs. *Journal of Human Resources, 16,* 167–185. doi:10.2307/145507

Parker, S. K., & Wall, T. (1998). *Job and work design.* Thousand Oaks, CA: Sage.

Professor Marie Jahoda. (2001, May 17). Obituary. Retrieved from http://www.thetimes.co.uk/article/0,60-203019,00.html

Quinn, R. P., & Staines, G. L. (1977). *The 1977 quality of employment survey.* Ann Arbor: University of Michigan, Institute for Social Research.

Roethlisberger, F., & Dickson, W. J. (1939). *Management and the worker.* Cambridge, MA: Harvard University Press.

Sauter, S. L., Murphy, L. R., & Hurrell, J. J. (1990). Prevention of work-related psychological disorders: A national strategy proposed by the National Institute for Occupational Safety and Health (NIOSH). *American Psychologist, 45,* 1146–1158. doi:10.1037/0003-066X.45.10.1146

Siegrist, J. (1996). Adverse health effects of high-effort–low-reward conditions. *Journal of Occupational Health Psychology, 1,* 27–41. doi:10.1037/1076-8998.1.1.27

Taylor, F. W. (1911). *The principles of scientific management.* New York, NY: Harper.

Thorsrud, E., & Emery, F. E. (1970). *Mot en ny bedrifsorganisasjon* [Toward a new organization of enterprises]. Oslo, Norway: Tanum.

Trist, E. L., & Bamforth, K. W. (1951). Some social and psychological consequences of the longwall method of coal-getting. *Human Relations, 4,* 3–38. doi:10.1177/001872675100400101

Ursin, H. (1980). Personality, activation and somatic health: A new psychosomatic theory. In S. Levine & H. Ursin (Eds.), *Coping and health* (pp. 259–279). New York, NY: Plenum Press.

Ursin, H., Baade, E., & Levine, S. (1978). *Psychobiology of stress: A study of coping men.* New York, NY: Academic Press.

Vinokur, A. D., Schul, Y., Vuori, J., & Price, R. H. (2000). Two years after a job loss: Long-term impact of the JOBS program on reemployment and mental health. *Journal of Occupational Health Psychology, 5,* 32–47. doi:10.1037/1076-8998.5.1.32

Waddell, G., & Burton, A. K. (2006). *Is work good for your health and well-being?* London, England: The Stationery Office.

Wall, T. D. (1982). Perspectives on job redesign. In J. E. Kelly & C. W. Clegg (Eds.), *Autonomy and control in the workplace* (pp. 1–20). London, England: Croom Helm.

Wall, T. D., Corbett, M. J., Martin, R., Clegg, C. W., & Jackson, P. R. (1990). Advanced manufacturing technology, work design, and performance: A change study. *Journal of Applied Psychology, 75,* 691–697. doi:10.1037/0021-9010.75.6.691

Warr, P. B. (1987). *Work, unemployment, and mental health.* Oxford, England: Oxford University Press.

Warr, P. B. (1999). *Work, well-being and effectiveness: A history of the MRCIESRC Social and Applied Psychology Unit, Sheffield, UK.* Sheffield, England: Academic Press.

Part II ——————————————

Models and Frameworks

3

Theories of Occupational Stress

Daniel C. Ganster and Pamela L. Perrewé

In this chapter, we review the work stress theories that have had the most prominent impact on the field of work and occupational health psychology. We begin
with a review of basic stress theory from the physiology literature as this work
provides the conceptual substrate for most of the work-based theory and research
in occupational health psychology. In this realm of basic research, the allostatic
load model (McEwen, 1998) has taken center stage and represents the latest
in an evolution of models proposed by Cannon (1932) and Selye (1955). Our
review provides a brief overview of this model and its related research as a back-
drop to occupationally based research. We then discuss some of the more influential job stress theories, including the demands–control model (Karasek, 1979),
the person–environment fit approach, conservation of resources theory (Hobfoll,
1989), and the effort–reward imbalance model (Siegrist, 1996, 2001).

Basic Conceptualizations of Stress and Physiology

The concept of *homeostasis*—that is, the body maintaining steady states in various physiological systems—has been at the core of explanations for how individuals react to environmental demands. According to Cannon (1932), experienced
stress was the result of an external environmental demand that was disturbing
to an individual's natural homeostatic balance. Cannon's early writings provided
the groundwork for the fight-or-flight response. Cannon described experienced
stress as a survival response to environmental threats. The fundamental process
that occurs when one is confronted with an environmental demand or threat is
one of defending oneself (i.e., fight) or fleeing (i.e., flight). Cannon placed stress
within a reactive stimulus–response framework and emphasized the importance
of outside demands external to the person.

Cannon (1932) argued that experienced stress triggered the body's response
to threats (i.e., fight or flight), characterized by responses of the sympathetic
nervous system. These responses give the human body a burst of energy enabling
individuals to physically fight or run away from the danger or threat. When the
perceived threat is gone, the autonomic system should return to normal.
However, when individuals experience chronic, sustained stress, the recovery
process may not occur, leading to ill health.

Selye (1955) conceptualized the stress experience as a process of adaptation
that he termed the *general adaptation syndrome* (GAS). His initial inspiration for

the GAS came from an endocrinology experiment in which he injected mice with extracts of various organs. He initially believed he had discovered a new hormone but was proven wrong when every irritating substance he injected produced the same physiological symptoms. This discovery, paired with his observation that people with different diseases exhibited similar symptoms, led to his description of the effects of "noxious agents," as he first described them. He later coined the term *stress,* which has been accepted into the lexicon of languages around the world.

Selye (1955) argued that the human body goes through three stages (i.e., GAS) when confronted with an intense demand. First is the alarm reaction, characterized by hormonal changes in the body, analogous to Cannon's (1932) fight-or-flight response. The second stage is the adaptation that is character-ized by diminishing symptoms as the body achieves optimal adaptation. If the exposure to the stressor is prolonged, acquired adaptation is lost and the third stage, exhaustion, sets in. Selye argued that this last stage would lead to death unless there was some aid from an outside source. According to Selye, the adaptability of an organism is finite. In general, he argued that stress is the nonspecific response of the body to a demand, regardless of whether the demand resulted in pleasant or unpleasant conditions. When demands result in unpleasant conditions, this is called *distress;* when demands result in pleas-ant conditions, this is called *eustress.* However, it is important to note that most of the damage occurs when individuals are under distress rather than eustress (Selye, 1974). Selye's nonspecific, or stereotyped, model of responses to stress has been challenged by subsequent research that demonstrated a great variety in physiological responses depending on the different cues and situations fac-ing the individual (Goldstein & Eisenhofer, 2000).

Allostatic Load Model

More recently, physiologists have noted limitations of the homeostasis concept. Homeostasis refers to the body's attempt to maintain a stable internal environ-ment through a complex system of feedback mechanisms. Thus, for example, when encountering low ambient temperatures, the body will take steps to reduce heat loss by directing blood flows away from the periphery and/or increase the use of energy through the metabolism of stored fats and carbohydrates to keep the internal temperature within a narrow range. Similarly, perspiration is a mechanism to lower body temperatures that are above the acceptable range. Research following Cannon's and Selye's work increasingly found, however, that organisms exhibited a broad range of behavioral responses to environmental demands and that the homeostasis model provided an inadequate accounting for their effects. According to McEwen (1998), there are several true homeostatic systems, such as temperature and oxygen levels. But many other systems are very responsive to the external environment and operate within a wider range. The concept of *allostasis* was first proposed by Sterling and Eyer (1988). Frequently referred to as *stability through change,* allostasis refers to physiolog-ical response systems that supplement the basic homeostatic systems and respond to environmental demands and anticipated demands. Whereas such sys-tems, such as the hypothalamic–pituitary–adrenal (HPA) axis, operate around certain set points, some of which are subject to diurnal or even seasonal rhythms, these set points can also be reset after exposure to chronic demands that continually push them beyond their normal ranges. Another important distinction of the allostasis model is the critical role played by the central nervous system, which controls physiological reactions, often directly, by using prior knowledge and experience in conjunction with environmental events, to anticipate the need for adaptation. The transactional model, discussed below, is entirely consistent with this allostatic perspective.

Allostasis, then, refers to the process of adjustment of various effector systems (cardiovascular, neuroendocrine, and others) to cope with real or imagined challenges to homeostatic systems. *Allostatic state* refers to a chronic overactivation of allostatic regulatory systems and the alteration of set points. Finally, *allostatic load* refers to various symptoms of pathology caused by a chronic allostatic state. This perspective highlights two points that are especially salient to the topic of work stress and health. First, unlike in Selye's model, which defines stress as a nonspecific response of the body (primarily the HPA axis) to challenge or threat, the allostasis model allows for a great diversity of physiological responses. Often, multiple effectors are used to control values for a given homeostatic variable. For example, blood glucose levels can be affected by insulin, adrenaline, cortisol, glucagon, and growth hormone. This is an example of the diversity of responses that the body can make to perturbations in internal homeostatic systems. Similarly, there can be a variety of different physiological responses to different environmental demands. This variety of allostatic mechanisms makes stress research more complicated because it argues against a simple reliance on single indicators. Likewise, the operationalization of allostatic load, which is a pathological state caused by chronic stress, also requires a consideration of different indicators. Singer, Ryff, and Seeman (2004) provided a detailed review of allostatic load measurement models. The criteria for assessing operationalizations of allostatic load ultimately depend on their value as risk factors that presage morbidity and mortality.

A second implication of the allostatic load model comes from the key role that the central nervous system plays in orchestrating the array of allostatic responses and in triggering these responses in the first place. Compared with Selye's perspective, the allostasis model emphasizes the mind–body connection in the stress process. For stress researchers, this means, of course, that many of the stressors of interest in the workplace, and probably all of the psychosocial ones, exert their effects on the body through cognitive processing. Compared with earlier homeostasis conceptualizations, the allostasis perspective views the individual (human or otherwise) not solely as a reactive organism but as one who perceives aspects of the environment and initiates allostatic responses in anticipation of predicted needs. This perspective is very much in accord with the transactional model of stress as developed by Lazarus (1966).

Transactional Model

One of the most popular frameworks for understanding psychosocial stress remains the transactional model (Folkman & Lazarus, 1990; Lazarus, 1966), which suggests that stress cannot be found in the person or the environment alone but in the interaction between the two. The model views stressors subjectively, meaning that what is stressful to one individual may not be stressful to another individual. Stress, therefore, is cognitively determined. Lazarus was more concerned about the appraisal and cognitive components of stress as opposed to the medical and physiological approaches of Cannon and Selye. Similar to Cannon and Selye, Lazarus saw experienced stress as a response to an environmental demand; however, Lazarus emphasized the person's cognitive appraisal of events. The primary role of cognition (i.e., the central nervous system) in the stress process bridges the allostasis and transactional models. Curiously, the allostasis model, developed in the biological literature, seems to have evolved more or less independently of the transactional model in psychology. Lazarus's work is rarely cited in the former.

Based on Lazarus's (1991) belief in the primacy of cognition, the transactional model posits that two processes (i.e., cognitive appraisal and coping) mediate between environmental stressors and resulting responses. According to the model, an event in the work environment engages the cognitive appraisal process: the primary appraisal. This consists of an evaluation of whether the event is a threat to the individual's well-being or whether it can be dismissed as benign or perhaps challenging. If the individual perceives a threat to well-being, the secondary appraisal process is engaged to determine if anything can be done to handle the situation. In this secondary appraisal stage, individuals are said to evaluate their available options for coping with the stressor. An individual may use either problem-focused or emotion-focused coping. The perception that the stressful situation cannot be changed is argued to lead to emotion-focused coping, whereby the individual engages in strategies (e.g., meditation) to help alleviate the negative effects of the situation on well-being. If the stressful situation is deemed controllable, the individual is predicted to use problem-focused coping, whereby the individual attempts to alter the stressful situation in some way.

Sterling (2004), of the biological allostasis position, might refer to emotion-focused coping as analogous to allostatic responding to lower level physiological targets, which is to say attempting to intervene at the level of physiological perturbation of homeostatic systems. An analogy from the medical perspective would be the different ways to intervene to control hypertension or chronically elevated blood pressure. Treating hypertension at the low level of homeostasis involves the use of drugs such as diuretics to reduce blood volume or heart rate antagonists to reduce cardiac output. Alternatively, intervening at a higher level involves modifying the environmental demands that triggered the allostatic load (expressed as hypertension) in the first place. In the work stress domain, this distinction is analogous to the difference between intervention approaches that aim at helping stressed individuals deal with their stress symptoms (e.g., through meditation, cognitive–behavioral modification, or relaxation) and those that aim to change the characteristics of the work environment that are driving the allostatic state (e.g., through job redesign).

The transactional model is not without its critics. In a published academic debate, Zajonc (1984) refuted Lazarus's belief that cognitive processes were necessary for affective processes to occur, arguing instead that affect often occurs without any temporally antecedent cognitive processing. This might also occur for gradual threats to health as well. For example, some stressors in the workplace, such as rotating shift schedules, might affect stress responses without any significant cognitive mediation. Although the transactional approach is still a prominent theoretical approach to psychosocial stress, it does not enumerate specific workplace events or characteristics that are apt to be interpreted as stressors. Explaining the conditions of work that produce stress responses is the province of occupational stress theories.

Occupational Stress Theories

In the following sections, we review the prominent theoretical approaches to job stress. Although this is not a comprehensive listing of all work stress theories, we chose those that have had a historical and continuing impact on the development of the field.

Person–Environment Fit Approach

The idea that the psychological outcomes that workers experience stem from the degree of correspondence between their personal characteristics and the outcomes and demands of their jobs has been central in the work psychology literature for at least 40 years (Lofquist & Dawis, 1969). Caplan and his colleagues elaborated and operationalized the person–environment (P-E) fit model in the field of job stress and conducted much of the early research testing it (Caplan, Cobb, French, Harrison, & Pinneau, 1975). The stressfulness (or strain) experienced at work is theorized to be caused by a lack of fit between (a) outcomes provided by the job and the needs, motives, and preferences of the worker and (b) the requirements of the job and the skills and abilities of the worker. Some large-scale tests of the P-E fit model have been conducted, including the study of 23 occupations by Caplan et al. (1975). In his review of this literature, Harrison (1985) concluded that fit scores, generally operationalized as the differences between self-reported environment and person components, often, but not always, predicted strain outcomes better than did the components themselves.

The evidence supporting P-E fit theory has been subjected to some significant criticism. Edwards and Cooper (1990), for example, articulated four major shortcomings of this research. First, researchers generally did not specify their models in terms of how the two types of fit related to different kinds of outcomes. Second, there are theoretically distinct mathematical forms of fit, including discrepancy, interactive, and proportional models, but investigators failed to statistically model these different forms. Third, researchers often used inappropriate measures of the P-E components and relied exclusively on self-report approaches. Finally, statistical models of fit most often relied on simple difference score measures that yielded mostly uninterpretable results. Later work by Edwards (1995) addressed the statistical problems arising from the use of difference scores to assess fit and proposed polynomial regression and response surface analysis strategies for testing theoretically specified fit models. Edwards's critique of the use of difference scores generally calls into question most of the P-E fit findings reported in the work stress literature.

Although P-E fit theory addressed the phenomenon of stress in the workplace, the theory itself does not necessarily specify the components of the person and the work environment that should be most salient. In this sense, it is a process theory, much as Lazarus and Folkman's (1984) more general transactional model, and does not enumerate those features of the work environment that should be the key constructs generating a stress response. Most investigators of P-E fit have used the same small set of eight components used in Caplan et al.'s (1975) study. The P-E fit model has played a much less prominent role in the work stress and health literature in recent years, although the basic notion of fit undergirds, at least implicitly, many conceptualizations of stress in the workplace.

Job Demands–Control Model

The demands–control model of job stress was introduced by Karasek (1979) about 30 years ago and has had a dominant role in shaping the research agenda in the field of work stress and health. Unlike earlier models, the demands–control model can be classified as a content model because it specifies the particular job characteristics that are thought to be the primary stressors in the workplace. Job demands are conceptualized as the task requirements at work and involve issues such as role conflict or time pressure (Karasek & Theorell, 1990). Control (i.e., decision latitude) includes both the worker's authority to make decisions and the breadth of skills that are employed (Verhoeven, Maes, Kraaij, & Joekes, 2003). Karasek (1979) argued that in jobs with high control, workers experience low strain if they have low demands, whereas they play an active or learning role if they have a job with high demands. On the other hand, workers with low job demands have passive jobs if they have low control but experience high strain if high demands are made of them.

Karasek (1979) thus argued that experienced stress and job dissatisfaction result from the interactive effects of job demands and the range of decision latitude or job control. Karasek's model makes two predictions. First, experienced stress will occur when job demands are high and decision latitude is low. Second, optimal competency is argued to occur when the challenge of the situation is matched with the individual's decision latitude (i.e., control) in dealing with the challenge. The implication is that although job demands remain high, experienced stress and dissatisfaction can be reduced by providing workers with more control over their work.

The many studies examining the joint effects of job demands and situational control have not been overwhelmingly supportive of Karasek's model (e.g., Ganster & Fusilier, 1989; Taris, 2006). Some studies have supported the proposed interaction between demands and control (e.g., Fox, Dwyer, & Ganster, 1993; Ganster, Fox, & Dwyer, 2001). However, many studies across organizations (e.g., Daniels & Guppy, 1994), within homogenous occupational groups (Morrison, Dunne, Fitzgerald, & Cloghan, 1992), and longitudinally (e.g., Parkes, Mendham, & von Rabenau, 1994) have found little or incomplete support for the demands–control model. Therefore, some (e.g., Parkes et al., 1994) have argued that moderators of the demand–control interaction, or variables that directly affect the outcomes, deserve further consideration. The results of one study demonstrated that by distinguishing between job control (measured via task autonomy) and skill discretion (measured via skill utilization), skill discretion was found to be a more important construct than control (van Veldhoven, Taris, de Jonge, & Broersen, 2005). However, the majority of researchers have investigated moderators of the demands–control model utilizing variables that were not explicitly stated within Karasek's (1979) conceptualization of workplace stress.

In an update to the original model, Karasek and Theorell (1990) proposed the demands–control–support model, adding the component of social support as another critical factor in determining responses to job demands. A number of researchers tested the moderating effects of social support in the demand–control model (e.g., Karasek & Theorell, 1990). However, although the demands–control–social support conceptualization has demonstrated relationships with strain outcomes, only modest support has been found for the buffering effect of control, at most demonstrating that in order for control to have a buffering effect, it needs to correspond to the types of demands placed on the individual (Van der Doef & Maes, 1998, 1999). Concerning the strain hypothesis of the demands–control model, some (e.g., De Lange, Taris, Kompier, Houtman, & Bongers, 2003) have suggested that the effects of demands and control could be either additive or interactive and that more research to date supports an additive rather than interactive model (Turner, Chmiel, & Walls, 2005). Relatively little research has been conducted regarding the activity level hypothesis; however, some evidence suggests that high control promotes learning, and high demands are harmful to these same outcomes (Taris, Kompier, De Lange, Schaufeli, & Schreurs, 2003). Furthermore, the demands–control–support model has been criticized by some as being too simplistic for explanations of individual health and well-being, at least for certain populations (e.g., Verhoeven et al., 2003).

Some research suggests that the mixed results found by the job demands–control model indicate the importance of individual difference variables. Schaubroeck and Merritt (1997) found that individuals with high self-efficacy benefited from increased control, whereas those with low self-efficacy did not. Similarly, the results of another study (de Rijk, Le Blanc, Schaufeli, & de Jonge, 1998) indicated that individuals high in active coping benefited from greater control, but those low in active coping were more likely to suffer burnout from increased control. In addition, Parker and Sprigg (1999) found general support for both the strain and learning (active) aspects of the demands–control model for those high in proactive personality.

Like any theory, the demands–control model also has critics. For example, Taris (2006) discussed the limited research support for the interaction of job demands and decision latitude. Although researchers generally find that high job demands and low decision latitude independently predict strain, studies on the interaction of the two are not always supportive. Specifically, Taris argued that although the variables of demands and control work well as predictors of work stress and ill health, this does not mean that the statistical interaction between demands and control affects stress and health. Further, Taris argued that the assumptions about the curvilinear relations among job demands, control, and social support to employee health have not been well documented.

Many researchers still assume that too little or too many of these characteristics at work (i.e., demands, control, social support) may lead to experienced stress. Although a few researchers have found modest curvilinear relations between work characteristics and employee well-being (e.g., de Jonge & Schaufeli, 1998), some large-scale studies have failed to find these nonlinear relationships. For example, based on several thousand participants in the Whitehall II studies of British civil servants, there was very little support for curvilinear relationships among work characteristics and well-being (Rydstedt, Ferrie, & Head, 2006). Taris (2006) argued that based on these latter results from such a large-scale sample, redesigning the workplace to reduce stress should target all employees, not only those who have too much or too little of a certain work characteristic. Additional stress research is still needed before organizational scientists can be confident in the linear or nonlinear effects of work characteristics on employee stress and well-being.

Perhaps the greatest contribution of the demands–control model has been its heuristic value for the field of stress research. It clearly has stimulated a large body of research, and importantly, has had a significant influence on the thinking and research of those in epidemiology and medicine. As a content theory of job stress, it brought to the forefront of researchers' attention the two constructs of demands and control. But both of these constructs were defined in ways that have lessened the falsifiability of the model. *Demands,* for example, refer to requirements for working hard, having too much to do, and having conflicting demands. On the one hand, this is a broad conceptualization reflecting both amount of work requirements and their nature; on the other, it rather narrowly focuses on workload demands to the exclusion of other types of stressors such as negative social interactions like undermining (Duffy, Ganster, & Pagon, 2002) or even threats to economic security (Brief & Atieh, 1987). Because of this imprecise definition of job demands, it is difficult to discern the extent to which conflicting findings might be caused by differing demand operationalizations.

The demands–control model should also be credited with bringing the construct of control, which has been so fundamental to psychology, to the forefront in work stress research. But the job decision latitude construal of the model, as defined by Karasek (1979), can be seen as overly broad and as mixing conceptually different constructs. In Karasek's original 1979 study, as in many epidemiological studies that followed, job decision latitude was operationalized in different ways in different samples. For example, in Karasek's 1979 U.S. sample, the measure of job decision latitude included indicators that most would classify as behavioral control or autonomy, such as *freedom of how to do work, allows a lot of decisions,* and *have a say over what happens.* But it also included indicators like *high skill level required, required to learn new things, nonrepetitious work,* and *creativity required.* In the sample from Sweden, job decision latitude consisted entirely of skill level ratings and repetition and monotony of the work, and no specific referents to behavioral control at all. Most researchers in the work stress domain have subsequently narrowed the operationalization to behavioral control indicators (Terry & Jimmieson, 1999), but in field research it is generally not possible to isolate the effects of control itself from other characteristics of work, such as complexity and skill level, that are confounded with it.

Conservation of Resources Theory

Another stress theory related to employees' feelings of control is Hobfoll's (1989) conservation of resources (COR) theory. According to COR theory, *resources* are the objects, energies, personal characteristics, and conditions that are valued by the individual or that assist the individual in obtaining these things. Stress is said to result from an actual or threatened net loss of resources or from a lack of resource gain following the investment of resources. The theory posits that the effects of stressful situations may be buffered or attenuated if the individual perceives he or she has the resources to cope with the stressor. Similar to the transactional model, the COR model views control, or the ability to cope, in subjective terms. COR theory proposes that experienced stress is most likely to occur when there is an actual resource loss, a perceived threat of resource loss, a situation in which one's resources are perceived to be inadequate to meet work demands, or the anticipated returns are not obtained on an investment of resources (Hobfoll, 1989, 2001).

COR theory posits four principal resource categories: (a) object resources (e.g., home, vehicles), (b) condition resources (e.g., socioeconomic status, valued work role), (c) personal resources (e.g., self-esteem, mastery), and (d) energy resources (e.g., money, time, credit) that are valued by the individual and that serve as a means for the attainment of goals. Thus, events are stressful to the extent that they threaten or result in loss of critical individual resources.

More directly, COR theory states that stress occurs with resource loss, that events are stressful to the extent they make demands that outstrip resources, and that resources are those things that are used to meet demands. Environmental conditions in the workplace (e.g., perceptions of organizational politics) may threaten or cause a depletion of employees' resources such as status, position, or self-esteem. During a stressful situation, an individual has to offset one resource loss with other resources (Hobfoll, 1989). It is commonly held that the loss of resources can be cumulative as stressors pile up. After initial losses, fewer resources are available for stress resistance; hence, the individual is less resilient and more vulnerable to stressors.

Hobfoll and Shirom (2000) offered four corollaries of the COR theory: (a) Individuals must bring in resources to prevent the loss of resources, (b) individuals with a greater pool of resources are less susceptible to resource loss and are more capable of resource gain, (c) those individuals who do not have access to strong resource pools are more likely to experience increased resource loss (i.e., initial losses lead to further losses), and (d) strong resource pools lead to a greater likelihood that individuals will seek opportunities to risk resources for increased resource gains. Hobfoll (2001) related these corollaries to workplace stress research and noted factors such as optimism–pessimism, self-efficacy (mastery), and self-esteem as resources in reducing stress. For example, Hobfoll and Shirom (2000) argued that personality traits that made individuals more inclined toward a sense of resiliency and control over their environment appeared to partially protect individuals from experienced stress.

Previous research has used the COR framework as an explanation for a stressor–job performance link. For example, Wright and Cropanzano (1998) argued that emotional exhaustion represented a condition in which an employee was drained of resources. As such, they argued that these individuals would be unable to rally the resources necessary to overcome the organizational stressors and maintain adequate levels of performance.

COR theory has influenced work stress research primarily in the areas of burnout, work–family conflict, and respites from work (e.g., vacations). A review by Westman, Hobfoll, Chen, Davidson, and Laski (2005) concluded that studies in these areas demonstrate the utility of the COR conceptualization of stress in terms of resource losses and gains. It is unclear, however, whether COR propositions provide a superior explanation for the results in many of these studies. Much of the research stimulated by COR theory principles demonstrates relationships between strain outcomes and various demands but does not effectively demonstrate that COR theory makes predictions that are really different from those made by other models or that it can account for empirical results that other conceptualizations cannot. What really distinguishes COR theory from other approaches to work stress are propositions such as "resource loss is disproportionately more salient than resource gain" (Westman et al., 2005, p. 169) and resource losses will trigger loss spirals. Elaborating on the loss spiral prediction, Westman et al. (2005) described it as "a critical aspect of the theory, because it predicts that loss cycles will occur quickly and powerfully. Further, at each iteration of loss in the sequence, the cycle will gain in strength and momentum" (p. 169). The theoretical strength of these propositions is that their specificity enhances the falsifiability of the model. But the model can also be criticized for its lack of specificity in enumerating exactly what will be a resource, because although it lays out broad categories such as objects, conditions, personal characteristics, and energies, it is conceivable that almost any construct in the context of the work environment could be labeled as a resource. This lack of specificity renders the model less falsifiable. The critical research needed to test the COR model in the work setting must overcome the challenge of defining resources in an a priori way such that the theoretical propositions can be falsified. Such specificity will allow researchers to critically test the central propositions of loss versus gain salience and loss spirals. To adequately test these propositions, moreover, investigators need longitudinal designs in which they can capture both gains and losses of resources over multiple measurement occasions.

Effort–Reward Imbalance Theory

The model of effort–reward imbalance (ERI) at work is derived from a more general approach toward analyzing the psychosocial dimension of human health and well-being. Siegrist (2001) proposed that personal self-regulation is important for health and well-being in adult life and that this is largely contingent on the successful social exchange through individual roles. The ERI approach focuses on social reciprocity and social exchange, characterized by mutual cooperative investments based on the norm of return expectancy in which efforts are balanced by respective rewards. Failed reciprocity violates this norm and leads to strong negative emotions and sustained strain responses because it threatens the fundamental reciprocity/exchange principle. Further, the ERI model suggests that failed reciprocity (i.e., high efforts spent and low rewards received in turn) is likely to elicit recurrent negative emotions and sustained stress responses in exposed individuals. Conversely, positive emotions evoked by appropriate social rewards and exchanges promote well-being, health, and survival.

The ERI model maintains that availability of a work role is associated with recurrent options of contributing and performing, of being rewarded, and of belonging to some meaningful group (e.g., work colleagues). Yet these potentially beneficial effects are contingent on a basic prerequisite of exchange (i.e., reciprocity). Effort at work is part of a socially organized exchange process to which society contributes in terms of rewards. Rewards are distributed by three systems: money, esteem, and career opportunities. The ERI model claims that lack of reciprocity between the costs and gains (i.e., high cost/low gain conditions) elicits negative emotions with a propensity to sustained autonomic and neuroendocrine activation (Siegrist, 1996).

The following three hypotheses are derived from the ERI model:

1. An imbalance between high effort and low reward (i.e., nonreciprocity) increases the risk of reduced health over and above the risk associated with each one of the components.
2. Overcommitted people are at increased risk of reduced health, whether or not this pattern of coping is reinforced by work characteristics.
3. Relatively highest risks of reduced health are expected in people who are characterized by Conditions 1 and 2.

The imbalance often results from the fact that the social exchange between employee and employer is based on an incomplete contract. In incomplete contracts, assumptions of trust in mutual commitment are made. However, under certain conditions it is likely that incomplete contracts result in high cost/low gain conditions for employees. The risk of nonreciprocity in exchange is particularly high if employees have no other reasonable choices in the labor market. Further, if employees' skills are poor or if they subscribe to short-term contracts, nonreciprocity may occur.

Employees themselves may also contribute to high cost/low gain conditions at work, either intentionally or unintentionally. For example, they may accept job assignments that are considered unfair for a short period of time for strategic reasons as they tend to improve their opportunities for career promotion or other rewards at a later date.

Finally, there are psychological reasons of a continued mismatch between efforts and rewards at work. People characterized by a motivational pattern of excessive overcommitment to work and a high need for approval may suffer from inappropriate perceptions of demands and their own coping resources more often than their less involved colleagues (Siegrist, 1996, 2002). Perceptual distortion prevents them from accurately assessing cost–gain relations. As a consequence, they underestimate the demands and overestimate their own coping resources while not being aware of their own contribution to nonreciprocal exchange.

In summary, the ERI model is based on the sociological hypothesis that structured social exchange, as mediated through core work roles, is rooted in contracts of reciprocity. In addition to its importance to basic social functioning, this reciprocal contractual exchange is argued to produce beneficial effects on individual health and well-being.

The key hypothesis of the ERI model is that it is the imbalance between efforts and rewards that produces strain and ill health. Siegrist and others (Bosma, Peter, Siegrist, & Marmot, 1998; Siegrist, 1996) have mostly operationalized this imbalance using a similar set of self-report scales. The use of self-report scales is common, of course, in the work stress literature, but often they are used as substitutes for more direct measurement of work stressors. For example, scales used in testing the demands–control model ask workers to report the levels of work demands and job decision latitude, and the effects of these constructs on strain are inferred from their statistical associations with psychological and physiological indicators of strain, as well as with more distal medical outcomes such as heart disease. In contrast, the self-report of effort and reward combines not only a report of the stressor but also the effect that the stressor has on the respondent. For example, one item is "I have constant time pressure due to a heavy workload." The response options are 1 = *Disagree;* 2 = *Agree, but I am not at all distressed;* 3 = *Agree, and I am somewhat distressed;* 4 = *Agree, and I am distressed;* and 5 = *Agree, and I am very distressed* (http://www.uni-duessel dorf.de/medicalsociology/Psychometric_information_and_d.145.0.html; accessed September 28, 2008). Similarly, items soliciting reward perceptions combine a reporting of a condition (e.g., "I receive the respect I deserve from my superiors") with the subjective distress level that it elicits. This procedure makes the interpretation of the measures ambiguous and raises the question as to what the causal constructs in the model really are. Are the causal constructs referring to workplace conditions, albeit through the perceptions of the respondent, or are they types of psychological distress itself? This mixing of the perceptions of conditions (effort and reward) with their effects is further complicated by the computation of ERI as the ratio of the two scales. This ratio score seems to be a complicated construct. The numerator describes working conditions in terms of the amount of distress that they produce, and the denominator describes other sources of distress. Moreover, the reward items appear to incorporate equity judgments as well. In other words, the reward scale might itself be interpreted as strain resulting from inequitable rewards. At this point, empirical relationships between this measure of ERI and health outcomes may mostly reflect the relationship of psychological strain (or distress) on health.

Summary and Suggestions for Future Research

Each of the work stress models discussed heretofore contributes unique perspectives to the understanding of the role of work experiences on health and general well-being. In reality, however, they are not competing theories, and efforts to pit them against one another in critical experiments are unlikely to be successful. The demands–control model is the one that is most clearly rooted in the objective conditions facing the worker. Although tests of the model often use self-reports as measures of the model components, these are viewed as substitutes for more objective assessments. In contrast, the ERI model begins with the subjective appraisals of working conditions and outcomes and their emotional effects on the respondent, and objective assessments of the model components are not even considered. Thus, whereas the demands–control model is a stressor–strain–health conceptualization, the ERI model, at least in terms of how it is operationalized, appears to be a strain–health conceptualization. Results from studies in which the predictive powers of each model have been directly compared (e.g., Bosma et al., 1998; Peter et al., 1998) indicate that measures representing each of them significantly and independently account for variance in health outcomes. We suspect that if the COR model were similarly compared, it too would add significant, independent explained variance in health outcomes, given the wide array of resource measures (including even socioeconomic status) that it would bring to the study. Finally, although the P-E fit model is rarely directly tested anymore, the idea of fit still imbues much of our thinking. For example, Schaubroeck and Merritt (1997) found that individual differences in self-efficacy moderated the impact of demands and control on health outcomes, suggesting that amount of control that one experienced at work needed to fit with one's perceived capability of using it effectively. Similarly, Schaubroeck, Ganster, and Kemmerer (1994) found that cardiovascular disorder was predicted not solely by job demands or the Type A behavior pattern but by their interaction, again suggesting a fit model.

Each of the stress theories discussed has played an important heuristic function in the field of work stress. Even though they represent complementary approaches more than competing ones, each has stimulated a line of investigation into factors that predict health outcomes that might have otherwise been neglected. We would encourage investigators to continue to combine elements of the different models in prospective studies of work stress and well-being while expanding their research strategy to better incorporate both measures of the objective environment and measures of allostatic state.

We recommend more emphasis on the objective work environment for at least two reasons. First, even if we believe that environmental demands exert their effects mostly through a cognitive appraisal process, we know relatively little about how and why individuals differ in this process. Why is it that some people interpret a given workload as onerous and a possible threat, whereas others interpret it as manageable and a challenge? Each of the major theoretical perspectives suggests alternative explanations. For example, the COR model might suggest that personal resources such as mastery or self-esteem would play a critical role in how the individual interpreted a given level of workload demands. Alternatively, the ERI model might inspire us to examine aspects of the exchange process regarding the rewards that are attached to a given workload, or even to aspects that individuals bring with them to the job, such as personal commitment (or overcommitment). The P-E fit model, of course, suggests that we examine the skills and abilities of the worker in relation to the demands of the job. Which of these perspectives is most useful in explaining how different individuals cognitively appraise their workload and see it as overload? These questions can never be explored if we do not attempt to independently capture characteristics of the workplace that, in conjunction with individual differences, trigger cognitive appraisals. Specific methods for measuring work characteristics in independent ways have been discussed by others, and we refer the reader to them (e.g., Ganster, in press; Semmer, Grebner, & Elfering, 2004).

A second reason to direct more attention to the objective work environment is to help us understand how best to intervene in the workplace to improve health outcomes. For example, if control is indeed a critical factor in how the work environment affects well-being, how would one change control appraisals in a meaningful way that would have a measurable impact on most, if not all, workers? How do characteristics of reward systems such as performance-based pay or promotion procedures affect responses to the ERI measure of rewards and, consequently, the effort–reward imbalance? These are critical questions for testing both the validity and the applicability of our theories in the real world of work. Some evidence suggests that how changes in specific aspects of the work environment affect cognitive appraisals of those aspects is not a simple process. For example, Logan and Ganster (2005) found in an experimental intervention targeting employee control that subsequent control perceptions were determined jointly by the intervention and the level of social support that the participants received from their supervisors. Thus, a productive, though still rare, approach to studying objective work stressors is to actively change them and evaluate change interventions using not only measures of strain and well-being but also measures of the various cognitive appraisals that are theorized to intervene.

We also need to further develop ways of measuring the allostasis process in the context of work stress, for this is the process that is generally theorized to intervene between the workplace conditions described by work stress theories and the health outcomes that they are hypothesized to cause. To some extent, researchers have rather extensively examined indicators of allostatic load, the condition resulting from a sustained allostatic state. Markers of allostatic load include resting blood pressure, cholesterol levels, and waist/hip ratio. Singer et al. (2004) reviewed the predictability of such indicators for morbidity and mortality. But what are the allostasis markers whose persistence over time is expected to produce changes in the allostatic load markers? Do repeated increases in blood pressure during stressful work lead to stable elevated resting levels (hypertension)? Do regular increases in cortisol during the workday presage more stable dysregulation of cortisol, or do we need to focus on after-work cortisol levels as indicators of failure to unwind (Ganster et al., 2001)? McEwen (2004) considered markers of allostasis as primary mediators and indicators of allostatic load as secondary outcomes. It is unlikely that investigators studying work stress and health can make strong causal inferences, based on experimental interventions, regarding the effects of work stressors on health, or even on the allostatic load markers that are predictive of health outcomes. Disease endpoints, at least those believed to be related to psychosocial stress, generally develop slowly, reflecting chronic exposures to allostatic states that may span years. It is difficult to relate work stressors to such endpoints in prospective designs that have high internal validity because exposure to stressors can vary significantly over the years of the study. Linking stressors to health outcomes in experimental intervention studies is virtually impossible for much the same reason: The integrity of the experimental design would need to be maintained for perhaps years. Thus, a focus on the relatively short-term markers of allostatic state holds much promise for bridging this gap. Which of these is the most useful remains to be seen, but McEwen (2004) suggested several candidates, including elevated levels of inflammatory cytokines, elevated and flattened diurnal cortisol rhythms, and elevated overnight levels of urinary catecholamines.

In conclusion, the theories we reviewed here have all had a significant impact on the course of work stress research. Rather than offering competing perspectives, we view them more as complementary approaches. It is unlikely that one of the theories will "win out" over the others from head-to-head empirical competition. But we believe that our understanding of how work experiences affect health and well-being will be advanced by combining the elements of these theories in more comprehensive examinations of working conditions and health. We also believe that such comprehensive investigations will make considerably more progress if they directly address the phenomenology of stress by examining how objective environments get translated into subjective appraisals. And finally, we will better understand how job experiences lead to health outcomes by examining how they are related to relatively short-term indicators of allostatic state, and how such chronic states produce allostatic load and disease.

References

Bosma, H., Peter, R., Siegrist, J., & Marmot, M. (1998). Two alternative job stress models and the risk of coronary heart disease. *American Journal of Public Health, 88,* 68–74. doi:10.2105/AJPH.88.1.68

Brief, A., & Atieh, J. (1987). Studying job stress: Are we making mountains out of molehills? *Journal of Occupational Behavior, 8,* 115–126. doi:10.1002/job.4030080203

Cannon, W. B. (1932). *The wisdom of the body* (2nd ed.). New York, NY: Norton.

Caplan, R. D., Cobb, S., French, J. R. P., Harrison, R. V., & Pineau, S. R. (1975). *Job demands and worker health* (Publication No. 75-168). Cincinnati, OH: National Institute for Occupational Safety and Health.

Daniels, K., & Guppy, A. (1994). Occupational stress, social support, job control, and psychological well-being. *Human Relations, 47,* 1523–1544. doi:10.1177/001872679404701205

de Jonge, J., & Schaufeli, W. B. (1998). Job characteristics and employee well-being: A test of Warr's vitamin model in health care workers using structural equation modelling. *Journal of Organizational Behavior, 19,* 387–407. doi:10.1002/(SICI)1099-1379(199807)

De Lange, A. H., Taris, T. W., Kompier, M. A. J., Houtman, I. L. D., & Bongers, P. M. (2003). "The very best of the millennium": Longitudinal research and the demand–control–(support) model. *Journal of Occupational Health Psychology, 8,* 282–305. doi:10.1037/1076-8998.8.4.282

de Rijk, A. E., Le Blanc, P. M., Schaufeli, W. B., & de Jonge, J. (1998). Active coping and need for control as moderators of the job demand–control model: Effects on burnout. *Journal of Occupational and Organizational Psychology, 71,* 1–18.

Duffy, M., Ganster, D. C., & Pagon, M. (2002). Social undermining in the workplace. *Academy of Management Journal, 45,* 331–351. doi:10.2307/3069350

Edwards, J. R. (1995). Alternatives to difference scores as dependent variables in the study of congruence in organizational research. *Organizational Behavior and Human Decision Processes, 64,* 307–324. doi:10.1006/obhd.1995.1108

Edwards, J. R., & Cooper, C. L. (1990). The person–environment fit approach to stress: Recurring problems and some suggested solutions. *Journal of Organizational Behavior, 11,* 293–307. doi:10.1002/job.4030110405

Folkman, S., & Lazarus, R. S. (1990). Coping and emotion. In N. L. Stein, B. Leventhal, & T. Trabasso (Eds.), *Psychological and biological approaches to emotion* (pp. 313–332). Hillsdale, NJ: Erlbaum.

Fox, M. L., Dwyer, D. J., & Ganster, D. C. (1993). Effects of stressful job demands and control on physiological and attitudinal outcomes in a hospital setting. *Academy of Management Journal, 36,* 289–318. doi:10.2307/256524

Ganster, D. C. (in press). Measurement challenges for studying work-related stressors and strains. *Human Resource Management Review.*

Ganster, D. C., Fox, M., & Dwyer, D. (2001). Explaining employee health care costs: A prospective examination of stressful job demands, personal control, and physiological reactivity. *Journal of Applied Psychology, 86,* 954–964. doi:10.1037/0021-9010.86.5.954

Ganster, D. C., & Fusilier, M. R. (1989). Control in the workplace. In C. L. Cooper & I. T. Robertson (Eds.), *International review of industrial and organizational psychology* (pp. 235–280). London, England: Wiley.

Goldstein, D. S., & Eisenhofer, G. (2000). Sympathetic nervous system physiology and pathophysiology in coping with the environment. In B. S. McEwen (Ed.), *Handbook of physiology: Coping with the environment* (pp. 21–43). New York, NY: Oxford University Press.

Harrison, R. V. (1985). The person–environment fit model and the study of job stress. In T. A. Beehr & R. S. Bhagat (Eds.), *Human stress and cognition in organizations* (pp. 23–55). New York, NY: Wiley.

Hobfoll, S. E. (1989). Conservation of resources: A new attempt at conceptualizing stress. *American Psychologist, 44,* 513–524. doi:10.1037/0003-066X.44.3.513

Hobfoll, S. E. (2001). The influence of culture, community, and the nested-self in the stress process: Advancing conservation of resources theory. *Applied Psychology: An International Review, 50,* 337–421. doi:10.1111/1464-0597.00062

Hobfoll, S. E., & Shirom, A. (2000). Conservation of resources theory: Application to stress and management in the workplace. In R. T. Golembiewski (Ed.), *Handbook of organization behavior* (pp. 57–81). New York, NY: Dekker.

Karasek, R. (1979). Job demands, job decision latitude, and mental strain: Implications for job redesign. *Administrative Science Quarterly, 24,* 285–307. doi:10.2307/2392498

Karasek, R. A., & Theorell, T. (1990). *Healthy work, stress, productivity and the reconstruction of working life.* New York, NY: Basic Books.

Lazarus, R. S. (1966). *Psychological stress and the coping process.* New York, NY: McGraw-Hill.

Lazarus, R. S. (1991). Psychological stress in the workplace. *Journal of Social Behavior and Personality, 6,* 1–13.

Lazarus, R. S., & Folkman, S. (1984). *Stress, appraisal, and coping.* New York, NY: Springer.

Lofquist, L. H., & Dawis, R. B. (1969). *Adjustment to work.* New York, NY: Appleton-Century-Crofts.

Logan, M., & Ganster, D. C. (2005). An experimental evaluation of a control intervention to alleviate job stress. *Journal of Management, 31,* 90–107. doi:10.1177/0149206304271383

McEwen, B. S. (1998). Stress, adaptation, and disease: Allostatis and allostatic load. *Annals of the New York Academy of Sciences, 840,* 33–44. doi:10.1111/j.1749-6632.1998.tb09546.x

McEwen, B. S. (2004). Protective and damaging effects of the mediators of stress and adaptation: Allostasis and allostatic load. In J. Schulkin (Ed.), *Allostasis, homeostasis, and the costs of physiological adaptation* (pp. 65–98). Cambridge, England: Cambridge University Press.

Morrison, D. L., Dunne, M. P., Fitzgerald, R., & Cloghan, D. (1992). Job design and levels of physical and mental strain among Australian prison officers. *Work and Stress, 6,* 13–31. doi:10.1080/02678379208257036

Parker, S. K., & Sprigg, C. A. (1999). Minimizing strain and maximizing learning: The role of job demands, job control, and proactive personality. *Journal of Applied Psychology, 84,* 925–939. doi:10.1037/0021-9010.84.6.925

Parkes, K. R., Mendham, C. A., & von Rabenau, C. (1994). Social support and the demand-discretion model of job stress: Tests of additive and interactive effects in two samples. *Journal of Vocational Behavior, 44,* 91–113. doi:10.1006/jvbe.1994.1006

Peter, R., Alfredsson, L., Hammar, N., Siegrist, J., Theorell, T., & Westerholm, P. (1998). High effort, low reward, and cardiovascular risk factors in employed Swedish men and women: Baseline results from the WOLF study. *Journal of Epidemiology and Community Health, 52,* 540–547. doi:10.1136/jech.52.9.540

Rydstedt, L. W., Ferrie, J., & Head, J. (2006). Is there support for curvilinear relationships between psychosocial work characteristics and mental wellbeing? Cross-sectional and long-term data from the Whitehall II study. *Work and Stress, 20,* 6–20. doi:10.1080/02678370600668119

Schaubroeck, J., Ganster, D. C., & Kemmerer, B. E. (1994). Job complexity, Type A behavior, and cardiovascular disorder: A prospective study. *Academy of Management Journal, 37,* 426–439. doi:10.2307/256837

Schaubroeck, J., & Merritt, D. E. (1997). Divergent effects of job control on coping with work stressors: The key role of self-efficacy. *Academy of Management Journal, 40,* 738–754. doi:10.2307/257061

Selye, H. (1955, October 7). Stress and disease. *Science, 122,* 625–631. doi:10.1126/science.122. 3171.625

Selye, H. (1974). *Stress without distress.* Philadelphia, PA: Lippincott.

Semmer, N. K., Grebner, S., & Elfering, A. (2004). Beyond self-report: Using observational, physiological, and situation-based measures in occupational stress research. In P. L. Perrewé & D. C. Ganster (Eds.), *Research in occupational stress and well being: Vol. 3. Emotional and physiological processes and positive intervention strategies* (pp. 205–263). Amsterdam, the Netherlands: Elsevier/JAI.

Siegrist, J. (1996). Adverse health effects of high-effort/low reward conditions. *Journal of Occupational Health Psychology, 1,* 27–41. doi:10.1037/1076-8998.1.1.27

Siegrist, J. (2001). A theory of occupational stress. In J. Dunham (Ed.), *Stress in the workplace: Past, present, and future* (pp. 52–66). Philadelphia, PA: Whurr.

Siegrist, J. (2002). Effort-reward imbalance at work and health. In P. L. Perrewé & D. C. Ganster (Eds.), *Research in occupational stress and well being: Vol. 2. Historical and current perspectives on stress and health* (pp. 261–291). Amsterdam, the Netherlands: Elsevier/JAI.

Singer, B., Ryff, C. D., & Seeman, T. (2004). Operationalizing allostatic load. In J. Schulkin (Ed.), *Allostasis, homeostasis, and the costs of physiological adaptation* (pp. 113–149). Cambridge, England: Cambridge University Press.

Sterling, P. (2004). Principles of allostasis: Optimal design, predictive regulation, pathophysiology, and rational therapeutics. In J. Schulkin (Ed.), *Allostasis, homeostasis, and the costs of physiological adaptation* (pp. 17–64). Cambridge, England: Cambridge University Press.

Sterling, P., & Eyer, J. (1988). Allostasis: A new paradigm to explain arousal pathology. In S. Fisher & J. Reason (Eds.), *Handbook of life stress, cognition, and health* (pp. 629–649). New York, NY: Wiley.

Taris, T. W. (2006). Bricks without clay: On urban myths in occupational health psychology. *Work and Stress, 20,* 99–104. doi:10.1080/02678370600893410

Taris, T. W., Kompier, M. A. J., De Lange, A. H., Schaufeli, W. B., & Schreurs, P. J. G. (2003). Learning new behaviour patterns: A longitudinal test of Karasek's active learning hypothesis among Dutch teachers. *Work and Stress, 17,* 1–20. doi:10.1080/0267837031000108149

Terry, D. J., & Jimmieson, N. L. (1999). Work control and well-being. In C. L. Cooper & I. T. Robertson (Eds.), *International review of industrial and organizational psychology* (pp. 95–148). London, England: Wiley.

Turner, N., Chmiel, N., & Walls, M. (2005). Railing for safety: Job demands, job control, and safety citizenship role definition. *Journal of Occupational Health Psychology, 10,* 504–512. doi:10.1037/1076-8998.10.4.504

Van der Doef, M., & Maes, S. (1998). The job demand–control(–support) model and physical health outcomes: A review of the strain and buffer hypotheses. *Psychology and Health, 13,* 909–936. doi:10.1080/08870449808407440

Van der Doef, M., & Maes, S. (1999). The job demand–control(–support) model and psychological well-being: A review of 20 years of empirical research. *Work and Stress, 13,* 87–114. doi:10.1080/026783799296084

van Veldhoven, M., Taris, T. W., de Jonge, J., & Broersen, S. (2005). The relationship between work characteristics and employee health and well-being: How much complexity do we *really* need? *International Journal of Stress Management, 12,* 3–28. doi:10.1037/1072-5245.12.1.3

Verhoeven, C., Maes, S., Kraaij, V., & Joekes, K. (2003). The job-demand–control–social support model and wellness/health outcomes: A European study. *Psychology and Health, 18,* 421–440. doi:10.1080/0887044031000147175

Westman, M., Hobfoll, S., Chen, S., Davidson, O., & Laski, S. (2005). Organizational stress through the lens of conservation of resources (COR) theory. In P. L. Perrewé & D. C. Ganster (Eds.), *Research in occupational stress and well being: Vol. 4. Exploring interpersonal dynamics* (pp. 167–220). Amsterdam, the Netherlands: Elsevier/JAI.

Wright, T. A., & Cropanzano, R. (1998). Emotional exhaustion as a predictor of job performance and voluntary turnover. *Journal of Applied Psychology, 83,* 486–493. doi:10.1037/0021-9010.83.3.486

Zajonc, R. B. (1984). On the primacy of affect. *American Psychologist, 39,* 117–123.

4

Savoring Eustress While Coping With Distress: The Holistic Model of Stress

Debra L. Nelson and Bret L. Simmons

The extension of the positive psychology movement into the realm of occupational health psychology, and specifically into the study of work stress, allows us to study the positive aspects of the stress experience—eustress. Winning a marathon, giving that all-important speech, becoming resonant as a performing artist or with the audience, or simply engaging in pleasurable work can trigger the positive response to stress. Time may suspend, distractions are screened out, and work is completed in a pleasurable manner. Although quite a lot is known about distress, the negative response to stressors, and its dysfunctional outcomes, shouldn't the positive outcomes that arise at work from eustress, the positive response to stress, be equally known? Is it possible that individuals savor with delight the experience of eustress, wanting to prolong this fleeting but engaging experience? These are the questions our chapter addresses.

We assert that the proper way to advance the study of eustress is to avoid an exclusive focus on the positive and develop inclusive theoretical models that incorporate and extend our vast knowledge of negative causes, consequences, and outcomes (Simmons, 2000). To focus exclusively on the positive would send us down the same path that we now take such strong exception to with respect to the psychology of disease and dysfunction. In this chapter, we focus on eustress as captured within the holistic stress model (Nelson & Simmons, 2003). We present an updated and refined version of the model, elaborating on the indicators of eustress. In addition, we propose a more holistic framework for managing work stress, one with an emphasis on eustress generation as a complement to distress prevention.

The Concept of Eustress

We believe that eustress can best be conceptualized by identifying it as positive aspects of the stress response itself. We propose a more holistic model of stress, shown in Figure 4.1, that incorporates both positive and negative psychological responses to demands. The model also incorporates a broad range of demands—select individual difference variables that may be especially salient for cognitive appraisal, coping, and outcome variables representing things important to the individual both at work and away from work. We also propose a new concept,

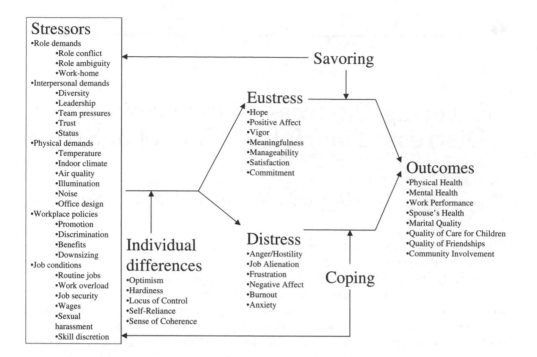

Figure 4.1. A holistic model of stress. From "Health Psychology and Work Stress: A More Positive Approach," by D. L. Nelson & B. L. Simmons, 2003. In J. C. Quick & L. E. Tetrick (Eds.), *Handbook of Occupational Health Psychology* (p. 102), Washington, DC: American Psychological Association. Copyright 2003 by the American Psychological Association.

savoring, that is the parallel for the positive response of coping for the negative response. The demands, distress response, coping, and outcomes portion of the model are well-known in the occupational stress literature, so they are discussed only briefly. The unique aspects of this model, the indicators of eustress, the individual differences that may promote eustress, and savoring eustress are discussed in greater detail. The central tenets of our model (Simmons & Nelson, 2007) are as follows:

- Demands or stressors are inherently neutral.
- The cognitive appraisal of any given demand or stressor produces a simultaneous positive and negative response. It is the response to demands that has positive and/or negative valence based on the degree of attraction and/or aversion the individual experiences toward the event or object.
- Individual differences/traits affect the way in which demands are appraised; therefore, they moderate the relationship between demands and responses.
- Positive and negative responses are complex and mixed; therefore, they manifest themselves in a variety of distinct physiological, psychological, and behavioral indicators. Degrees of both positive and negative

indicators of response will be present for any given demand. (Our model does not focus on physiological indicators because they are less observable by managers interacting with employees, and therefore are less subject to managerial intervention.)

- Individuals select strategies either to eliminate or alleviate their negative responses to demands or to accentuate or potentially dampen their positive responses. These strategies can be focused either on the perceived demand or on the perceived response.
- Positive and negative responses differentially affect valued outcomes at work.
- The relationship between responses and outcomes is moderated by both explicit and implicit contracts that govern what is expected of and accepted from employees at work.

The physical or psychological stimuli to which the individual responds are commonly referred to as either *stressors* or *demands*. Stressors at work take the form of role demands, interpersonal demands, physical demands, workplace policies, and job conditions (Quick, Quick, Nelson, & Hurrell, 1997). Some of these demands will be less salient for some individuals, yet may produce significant responses in others. Because our knowledge of these demands is embedded in the pathological perspective of stress and health, these demands are commonly interpreted as *distressors*. We suggest that to be consistent with the cognitive appraisal approach to stress that provides the theoretical foundation of this model, the assignment of valence should be reserved for the individual stress response.

Because the stress response is complex, we contend that most, if not all, of these stressors will elicit both a degree of negative and a degree of positive response for any individual. For example, one of the most significant sources of stress for hospital nurses is the death of a patient (Gray-Toft & Anderson, 1981). It is easy to understand how the loss of a patient could result in distress for a nurse. Yet along with the loss, the death of a patient may at the same time be appraised as positive. One study found that contrary to expectations, the variable death–dying had a significant, positive relationship with eustress and a nonsignificant, negative relationship with distress. The interpretation was that when the nurses in the study were faced with the demand of dealing with death–dying in their patients, they apparently became significantly more engaged in their work (Simmons, 2000).

Although there is substantial evidence of the links between distress and ill health (Quick et al, 1997), there is less evidence concerning the relationship between eustress and health. Edwards and Cooper (1988) speculated that eustress may improve health directly through physiological changes or indirectly by reducing existing distress. They reviewed findings from a variety of sources and found that the bulk of the evidence suggests a direct effect of eustress on health. They noted that this evidence is merely suggestive rather than conclusive, and that only one study was able to demonstrate that eustress is associated with an improvement in physiological functioning rather than just a reduction in damage. There was no evidence to suggest that eustress was associated with a deterioration in health.

One review of the literature stated that "positive emotional states *may* promote healthy perceptions, beliefs, and physical well-being itself" (Salovey, Rothman, Detweiler, & Steward, 2000, p. 110, italics added). Yet several empirical studies of hospital nurses operationalized eustress and distress as separate responses indicated by the presence of multivariate positive and negative psychological states (Simmons & Nelson, 2001). These cross-sectional studies hypothesized that in response to the demands of the job, hospital nurses would experience significant levels of both eustress and distress, and each stress response would have a separate effect on the nurses' perceptions of their health. They found that even in the presence of a demanding work environment, the hospital nurses were actively engaged in their work and reported significant levels of eustress, and eustress in turn had a significant positive relationship with their perception of their own health. Hope was the indicator of eustress with the strongest positive relationship with the nurses' perception of health. In addition to being healthy and productive themselves, eustressed nurses may have a concrete impact on the health of patients by inspiring positive expectations and raising the patients' levels of hope (Salovey et al., 2000).

Eustressed workers are engaged, meaning that they are enthusiastically involved in and pleasurably occupied by the demands of the work at hand. Workers can be engaged and perceive positive benefits even when confronted with extremely demanding stressors. A study of female and male soldiers participating in the U.S. peacekeeping mission in Bosnia found that soldiers who were engaged in meaningful work during the deployment found it to be a positive experience (Britt, Adler, & Bartone, 2001). It is interesting to note that a factor such as witnessing the destruction caused by warring factions was associated with reporting greater positive benefits. In the context of the mission, the destruction was likely seen as justification for the mission, which added meaning to the soldiers' work. Female soldiers in this study self-reported more positive benefits as a result of the deployment than men, although the effect size for gender was small.

Research shows that positive aspects of work for women are also positive influences in the home environment (Barnett, Marshall, & Sayer, 1992). In a study of licensed practical nurses and social workers, there were no negative spillover effects from job to parenting or from parenting to job, but there were positive spillover effects from job to parenting (Barnett et al., 1992). Women who perceived their jobs as rewarding experienced less of the mental health effects of troubled relationships with their children. Challenge was the specific aspect of a rewarding job that provided the positive spillover effect (Barnett et al., 1992). When employed mothers enjoyed high rewards from challenge at work, they reported low distress, regardless of their level of disaffection they experienced in their relationship with their children.

Indicators of Eustress

Each stress response, both positive and negative, will have its associated effect indicators and can be expected to produce differential effects on the outcome variables (e.g., health). Indicators of the stress response could be physiological, behavioral, and psychological. The model presented focuses only on the psychological response. As suggested by Edwards and Cooper (1988), the indicators of the positive response will be positive psychological states (e.g., positive affect, meaningfulness, hope), and the indicators of the negative response will be negative psychological states (e.g., negative affect). Consistent with this holistic representation of stress, *eustress* can be operationally defined as a positive psychological response to a stressor, as indicated by the presence of positive psychological states, and *distress* can be operationally defined as a negative psychological response to a stressor, as indicated by the presence of negative psychological states (Simmons, 2000).

Eustress reflects the extent to which cognitive appraisal of a situation or event is seen to either benefit an individual or enhance his or her well-being. Our approach is squarely rooted in the transactional model of stress articulated by Lazarus and Folkman (1984). The transactional model suggests that stress can be conceived of as an imbalance between demands and resources. The part of the transactional model most germane to our holistic model of stress is that stressors can be perceived not only as threats but also as challenging or positive. We expect that most work situations elicit a mixed bag of both positive and negative responses in individuals. For example, a recently promoted individual should be expected to experience joy and satisfaction associated with the recognition of achievement and excitement about the opportunity to pursue new goals and challenges at work. At the same time, and as a result of the same situation, the individual may also experience a degree of disappointment if the additional compensation associated with the promotion is perceived as inadequate, or may experience the beginnings of the anxiety the individual anticipates about having to tell friends, family, and colleagues that the new promotion involves relocation to another city. On the other hand, an individual recently downsized out of a job can be expected to experience hostility associated with the loss and anxiety as a result of the uncertainty of having to find a new job. Yet at the same time he or she may feel relief to be leaving an overworked job in a sinking ship or may see it as an opportunity to spend more coveted time with family.

Positive and negative responses are separate, distinct, multidimensional, and potentially interactive in nature. To assume the presence of the positive by simply observing the absence of the negative, or vice versa, is an unacceptably simplistic approach to understanding the sources, responses, and consequences of stress. The full range of the stress response cannot be appreciated without a strategy to assess eustress and distress concurrently.

When eustress is assessed as we have defined it, the indicators of eustress should be positive psychological states, such as attitudes or emotions. Stable dispositional variables are not acceptable indicators of eustress, which must be subject to change according to cognitive appraisals of stressors. Work attitudes are preferable indicators. The work attitudes positive affect, meaningfulness and manageability, hope, and vigor may be good indicators of eustress (Simmons, 2000; Simmons & Nelson, 2001; Simmons, Nelson, & Neal, 2001). Although conceptually distinct, these constructs all represent an aspect of engagement, one of the primary indicators of the eustress response.

Positive Affect

Positive affect is a state of pleasurable engagement and reflects the extent to which a person feels enthusiastic, active, and alert (Watson, Clark, & Tellegen, 1988). Positive affect can be measured as a state or trait, with state positive affect capturing how one feels at given points in time and the trait positive affect representing stable individual differences in the level of affect generally experienced. State and trait positive affect are both conceptually and empirically distinct, and state positive affect is a separate factor from negative affect (George & Brief, 1992).

People in a positive state process information more heuristically or strategically, and people in a negative state process information more systematically. Positive affect is associated with seeing the opportunity in an issue as well as lower levels of risk taking (Mittal & Ross, 1998). Others have described those in a positive mood as "smarter" at processing information than those in a negative mood (Staw & Barsade, 1993). Positive affect has been shown to be effective in medical contexts, improving decision making among medical students and creative problem solving and diagnostic reasoning processes among practicing physicians (Estrada, Isen, & Young, 1994, 1997; Isen, Rosenzweig, & Young, 1991).

Meaningfulness and Manageability

Meaningfulness and manageability are part of a new scale developed by a nurse to measure situational sense of coherence. Sense of coherence was a term developed to denote factors that promote a healthy response to stressful situations (Antonovsky, 1993). It has traditionally been measured as a trait variable but was adapted by Artinian (1997) as a situational or state measure. Two of three subscales are appropriate as indicators of eustress.

Meaningfulness is the extent to which one feels that work makes sense emotionally and that problems and demands are worth investing energy in, are worthy of commitment and engagement, and are challenges that are welcome. The literature on psychological empowerment has described meaningfulness as a sense of purpose or personal connection about work (Spreitzer, 1995). A representative item of the meaningfulness subscale of Artinian's (1997) Sense of Coherence Scale is, "At work, do you have the feeling that you don't really care about what goes on around you (very seldom/very often)?" (Simmons, 2000, p. 127).

In their study of peacekeepers in Bosnia, Britt et al. (2001) operationalized meaningful work with indicators of job importance, soldier engagement, and the relevance of peacekeeping to the soldier's identity. The meaningfulness of work was a significant predictor of deriving benefit from the mission. The strongest zero-order correlation in the study was the significant positive relationship between soldier engagement and job importance.

Manageability is the extent to which one perceives that resources at one's disposal are adequate to meet the demands posed by the work situation. This is not a common construct in the work stress literature, but it functions somewhat similarly to the concept of control. For example, even in a demanding work situation (e.g., a hospital critical care unit), the attitude of manageability will develop as a positive response to the extent that adequate resources (e.g., proper equipment, adequate staffing and training) are available. Items from the manageability subscale of the Sense of Coherence scale are, "When you think of the challenges you are facing at work, do you feel that (there is no solution or you can find a solution)?" and "People you count on at work often disappoint you (always happens/never happens)" (Simmons, 2000, p. 127).

Hope

Hope has been identified as a positive emotion reflecting a degree of expected benefit resulting from an evaluation of a particular situation (Lazarus, 1993). Hope was defined as a cognitive set that is based on a sense of successful goal-directed determination and planning to meet goals (Snyder et al., 1996). As a belief that one has both the will and the way to accomplish one's goals, hope has also been suggested as an attribute of emotional intelligence (Huy, 1999). The State Hope Scale (Snyder et al., 1996) thus provides a snapshot of a person's goal-directed thinking and engagement.

Gender differences in state hope did not emerge in any of the studies conducted to develop and validate the State Hope Scale. The lack of gender differences for hope is consistent with findings of the Scale for Dispositional Hope (Snyder et al., 1991), which has been administered to thousands of men and women of different backgrounds, education, and occupations (Snyder, 1994). The positive spin on this finding is that men and women are equally hopeful.

Conversely, it may be that the goals toward which hope is applied are different for women and men (Snyder, 1994). Like a glass ceiling effect, some women may have been socially conditioned to expect to have fewer of life's goals, especially those associated with work, open to them. If women perceive that many goals at work are not available to them, they may not even think of certain goals as being attainable. In effect, women may limit their goals to those left open to them. Thus women may report high hope for the goals they perceive they are "allowed" to have.

Vigor

Vigor is a positive psychological state experienced at work that encompasses both an emotion and a mood state (Shirom, 2007). The three dimensions of vigor are physical strength, emotional energy, and cognitive liveliness, each of which arises from an appraisal of the individual's energy resources (Shirom, 2003). Because vigor at work is an energy resource, it is related to motivational processes that initiate and sustain behavior at work. Vigor is positively related to individual health and well-being and is proposed to have a reciprocal relationship with job performance.

As an indicator of eustress, vigor is important because it represents the energy resources necessary to experience a positive response to a demand. Individuals who feel invigorated can approach a stressor with the convictions that they possess the physical, emotional, and cognitive powers to cope successfully.

A recent study by Shraga and Shirom (2009) indicated that the most frequent work-related antecedents of vigor were meaningful interactions with others, coping with challenging situations, and achieving success on a project.

The positive psychological states meaningfulness, manageability, hope, positive affect, and vigor are examples of constructs that may be good indicators of eustress. A study of eustress in hospital nurses found that all of these indicators loaded positively and significantly on a second-order factor analysis of eustress (Simmons, 2000). The indicator with the strongest factor loading on eustress was meaningfulness. In this study, eustress was differentiated from a second-order factor distress. Eustress was significantly and positively related to the nurses' perceptions of their health, and the relationship between distress and health was negative but nonsignificant.

Although we have briefly discussed these indicators of eustress, they should not be considered the only or even the best indicators of eustress. In theory, any positive psychological state could be a potential indicator of eustress, and much more research is needed on positive psychological states at work. For example, in a meta-analysis the familiar constructs of job satisfaction and affective organizational commitment were referred to as *overall positive job attitude* (Harrison, Newman, & Roth, 2006). The meta-analysis found job satisfaction and affective commitment to be strong predictors of individual effectiveness, which Harrison and colleagues called *work engagement*. They concluded that "a general, positive job attitude leads individuals to contribute rather than withhold desirable inputs from their work roles" (p. 320). We believe that satisfaction and commitment are additional valid indicators of eustress at work.

Individual Differences That Promote Eustress

Because individual differences have been studied in conjunction with the stress process, the focus has been largely on identifying individual factors that predispose individuals to cope less well with stress. Type A behavior, for example, has been implicated as a risk factor for cardiovascular disease, with studies indicating that the hostility–anger component of Type A appears to be the most noxious one (L. Wright, 1988). Negative affect's role in the stressor–strain connection has also been extensively examined, with the conclusion that individuals with negative affect possess more negative appraisals and perceptions (Watson, Pennebaker, & Folger, 1987). Thus, those individuals with negative affect experience a stronger connection between stressors and strains, either because they are more sensitive to stressors or because they create more stressors because of their negative view of the world (McCrae & Costa, 1994).

In accordance with a more positive emphasis, we believe there is benefit in identifying those individual differences that would promote eustress through their role in generating more positive appraisals (challenge, as opposed to threat) of demands. Alternatively, these characteristics could work to arm individuals with the belief that they are equipped to handle a demand (secondary appraisal) or even encourage the savoring process. Five possible candidates for inclusion in studies of eustress are optimism, locus of control, hardiness, secure attachment, and sense of coherence.

Optimism

As an individual difference variable, optimism has been associated with good mood, perseverance, achievement, health, and longevity. Peterson (2000) recommended distinguishing between *little* and *big* optimism to gain a greater understanding of optimism's benefits. Little optimism encompasses specific expectations about positive outcomes. An example of little optimism would be, "I expect to perform well in my presentation today." This form of optimism is typified by Seligman's (1991) learned optimism construct, which is related to an optimistic explanatory style. Links have been established between attributions for positive events and well-being (Peterson & Seligman, 1987).

In contrast, big optimism involves a larger and more global expectation, for example, "Mankind is on the verge of a great discovery." This type of optimism is more in line with Scheier and Carver's (1992) description of dispositional optimism. Scheier and Carver defined *dispositional optimism* as the global expectation that good things will be plentiful in the future and that bad things will be scarce. Dispositional optimism's relationship with health has mainly been explored in terms of coping. Optimists engage in more active problem-solving types of coping as opposed to avoidant coping. Other mechanisms linking optimism and health include enhanced immune function (Segerstrom, Taylor, Kemeny, & Fahey, 1998) and better health habits (Morrill, Ickovics, Golubchikov, Beren, & Rodin, 1996). Peterson (2000) suggested that big optimism could be a biological tendency and that it is socially encouraged and modeled.

Peterson's (2000) argument is that optimism can exist at very different levels of abstraction. Big optimism, according to Peterson, produces a general state of vigor and resilience. Little optimism may be the product of an individual's learning. It is associated with positive outcomes because it produces behaviors that help individuals adapt to specific situations.

Optimism may relate to the eustress process in any of several ways. It may lead individuals to initiate more positive primary appraisals. It could equip individuals with the belief that they can handle a certain situation (as in little optimism). Certainly, because the eustress process is heavily dependent on appraisal, optimism is a reasonable individual difference to examine in future studies of eustress. The big versus little distinction is an intriguing one and may be useful in helping to explain optimism's role in promoting eustress.

Locus of Control

Locus of control is a generalized expectancy that is dichotomized into internal and external categories. An individual with an internal locus of control believes that outcomes occur as a result of his or her own actions. In contrast, an individual with an external locus of control believes that outcomes occur as a result of other people's actions or uncontrollable factors such as fate, chance, or luck (Rotter, 1966). Cohen and Edwards (1988) conducted an extensive review of personality as a moderator in the stress–strain relationship and concluded that generalized expectancy of control (i.e., locus of control) was a construct with a powerful moderating effect. Thus, locus of control can buffer the sequence of events that links stress with health problems.

Lefcourt and Davidson-Katz (1991) explained that this buffering could occur as part of the primary appraisal process. People with an external locus of control, with their belief that their actions have little effect over outcomes, are more likely to perceive demands as threats. Locus of control can also come into play in the secondary appraisal phase. During secondary appraisal (the self-assessment appraisal), individuals evaluate their resources for dealing with the demand, and those with an externals locus of control are more likely to feel that they do not have sufficient resources for coping with the demand they are facing.

Stating this within the positive framework, we can conclude that people with an internal locus of control are more likely to enjoy the stress-buffering properties of locus of control. They are more likely to appraise demands as opportunities rather than threats (primary appraisal) and to believe that they possess the necessary resources for coping with the demand (secondary appraisal). In addition, they are more likely to select problem-solving forms of coping as a first choice and resort to emotion-focused coping only when they see that their own efforts will not solve the problem. People with an internal local of control are more flexible in their choice of coping methods than people with an external locus of control. As a result of this process, their efforts are associated with vigor, humor, and life satisfaction rather than dysphoria, immune-system dysfunctions, and related illnesses experienced by those with an external locus of control.

Hardiness

Hardiness, as originally conceived by Kobasa and Maddi (Kobasa, 1979; Kobasa, Maddi, & Kahn 1982), is people's view of their place in the environment that is simultaneously expressed through commitment, challenge, and control in their actions, thoughts, and feelings. Commitment involves finding persons and situations interesting and meaningful; it refers to engagement in life. People who are committed view their activities as purposeful. Challenge, as a dimension of hardiness, is the view that changes are opportunities for growth rather than threats, and it also reflects the ability to tolerate ambiguity. Control is reflected in the belief that one has influence over one's life. The combination of commitment, challenge, and control is proposed to facilitate psychological and physical health.

Hardiness also relates to transformational coping, or reframing a stressor such that it is less threatening or is perceived as an opportunity rather than a threat. In addition, it is associated with seeking social support and with engaging in health-promoting behaviors (Maddi, 1998). The early research on hardiness was conducted at a large telephone company in which executives were studied for 5 years using questionnaires. Hardy executives were less likely to report physical illness than those executives who were low on hardiness (Maddi, 1998). Several additional studies have supported the relationship between hardiness and health (Wiebe & Williams 1992) and between hardiness and performance (e.g., Westman, 1990).

Research on the potential mechanisms whereby hardiness is related to health is helpful in speculating about the potential role of hardiness in the eustress process. For example, hardy individuals are less likely to appraise events pessimistically (Wiebe, 1991); perhaps this would enable them to appraise stressors as challenges or to engage in transformational coping and therefore to respond eustressfully. It may be of benefit to assess the three dimensions of hardiness separately in their relation to eustress. Florian, Mikulincer, and Taubman (1995) found that the three facets of hardiness showed different relationships with cognitive appraisal processes and coping mechanisms. Control was related to reduced threat appraisals and to the increased use of problem-focused coping and support-seeking behaviors. Commitment also was associated with lower threat appraisals but was associated with the emotion-focused form of coping.

Many questions can arise when considering the relationship between hardiness and eustress. Presumably, a greater sense of control would result in more opportunity appraisals, and the support-seeking behavior associated with hardiness would permit individuals to engage in positive secondary appraisals (i.e., to believe that they could cope with the demand). Commitment, as a sense of engagement, might facilitate the savoring process. Hardy individuals might be committed to enacting and prolonging that sense of flow associated with savoring.

Secure Attachment

As an individual difference, secure attachment is a healthy characteristic pattern of forming relationships with others. Ainsworth and Bowlby (1991) studied infants' attachments with their primary caregivers and concluded that the attachment process is a biological imperative that is related to survival of the human species. In observing the interactions between infants and their mothers, they identified three distinct patterns of attachment: secure, avoidant, and anxious–ambivalent, with the latter two being unhealthy, insecure attachment patterns. Secure infants believe their caregiver will be available and helpful in times of distress, whereas insecure infants believe no one will be available in their times of need. This early history with caregivers forms the basis for individuals' beliefs about the responsiveness of others and for the formation of attachments to others in later life. These beliefs crystallize into internal working models of how one should relate to other people.

Attachment orientations extend into adulthood, and they are related to effectiveness and satisfaction at work (Hazan & Shaver, 1990). The attachment orientations have been labeled in the management literature as self-reliant or secure, counterdependent (avoidant), and overdependent (anxious–ambivalent; Nelson, Quick, & Joplin, 1991; Simmons, Gooty, Nelson, & Little, 2009). Secure individuals, possessing a sense of security, form interdependent, flexible relationships with others. Adults who are secure form close and supportive relationships with others both inside and outside the organization. They are comfortable working alone or asking for assistance from others as each situation demands. They report fewer symptoms of distress and are better able to develop the social support necessary for effective performance at work (Nelson, Quick, & Simmons, 2001).

In a study of assisted living center employees, secure attachment was shown to positively affect hope and trust and negatively affect burnout. Individuals with secure attachment formed more trusting relationships with their supervisors, which ultimately had a positive affect on their work performance (Simmons et al., 2009). This study also serves as an example of our call for more holistic research models by including both positive (e.g., hope, trust) and negative (e.g., burnout) variables as antecedents of employee performance.

Counterdependent individuals often overinvest in work and prefer to work alone rather than seek out support and assistance. As a result, they find themselves isolated and may even refuse support when it is offered. Counterdependence is rooted in the belief that others will not be there when one needs them and that it is best to depend only on oneself. Overdependent individuals search out and depend on more support than is appropriate, and they often appear clingy and unable to reciprocate by providing support to others. Like counterdependence, overdependence has its roots in the belief that others cannot be counted on for support. As a result, overdependent people may drain their social support sources by exhausting others' resources. Both counterdependent and overdependent individuals report greater distress symptoms and diminished well-being.

Secure attachment holds promise as an individual difference that may affect the eustress process. Secure individuals, with their inherent belief that others are dependable and can be trusted to provide support, may be bolstered to either appraise demands as challenges or believe that they have access to the resources (social support systems) that will allow them to manage these demands. In addition, their comfort in both working alone or interdependently gives these individuals security and flexibility in meeting demands that may be related to the confidence of viewing demands as challenging rather than threatening. Through its relationship with hope and trust, secure attachment is a positive psychological strength that can enhance eustress and ultimately performance at work (Simmons et al., 2009).

Sense of Coherence

Another appealing individual difference that can be studied within the context of eustress is sense of coherence, a view of life as comprehensible, manageable, and meaningful (Antonovsky, 1987, 1993). Having a sense of purpose in life is central to sense of coherence. Ryff and Singer (1998) noted that this is a core feature of positive human health. Part of the appeal of sense of coherence lies in its connection with salutogenesis, the process of successfully resolving stressors and maintaining health, rather than pathogenesis, failures in coping that lead to disease. Sense of coherence is thus a salutogenic strength for adaptively coping with stress.

Central to Antonovsky's theory is the notion that under stress, people with a strong sense of coherence cope more effectively, are better able to use their own resources and those of others, and therefore experience better health and well-being. In reviewing the research on sense of coherence, Ouellette and DiPlacido (2001) noted that the evidence for the salutogenic effects is stronger with regard to psychological health than physical health. They also noted that sense of coherence facilitated health and well-being among patients recovering from joint replacement surgery and those living with rheumatoid arthritis.

The mechanisms through which sense of coherence operates to have a salu-togenic effect are informative in terms of its potential relationship with eustress. It has been positively related to health-promoting behaviors, social support use, and problem-focused coping (Antonovsky, 1993). We propose that individuals with a strong sense of coherence are more likely to appraise demands as challenges, to believe that they have (or can get from others) the resources they require to manage a demand, and to engage in effective coping methods for dealing with demands. Also, they may be more likely to enact eustressful, rather than distressful, responses to demands.

A Holistic Approach to Managing Health at Work

The research literature on work stress has focused strongly on pathology and on healing the wounded. The importance of this venture cannot be denied. We have learned much about stressors (causes of stress), coping, and symptoms of distress. Great strides have been made in assisting both individuals and organizations in managing distress. This, however, is only half the battle. As a complement to healing the wounded, we must also find ways of building and capitalizing on strengths. Distress prevention and eustress generation together provide a more holistic framework for managing occupational health issues.

Distress Prevention

As mentioned earlier in this chapter, one framework that allows for a comprehensive gathering of distress-focused interventions is that of preventive stress management, as originally proposed by Quick and Quick (1984) and as elaborated on by Quick et al. (1997). Central to the preventive stress management philosophy is the idea that stress is inevitable, but distress is not. Rooted in a public health framework, the three levels of preventive stress management are primary prevention, which is intended to reduce, change, or eliminate stressors; secondary prevention, which is focused on modifying the individual's or organization's response to stressors; and tertiary prevention, which attempts to heal individual or organizational symptoms of distress.

Primary prevention includes activities to directly change or eliminate the stressor and would encompass job redesign efforts. Karasek's (1979) job strain model, for example, indicated that it is possible to increase the demand level of a job without making it distressful so long as job discretion is also increased. Time management efforts also focus on eliminating or changing stressors. Also included in primary prevention, however, are efforts to change the individual's perception of the stressor. Cognitive restructuring and learned optimism, which alter the individual's internal self-talk, are primary prevention methods.

Secondary prevention efforts target the individual or organizational response to stress. Exercise, meditation, and other forms of relaxation and nutrition would all fall under the heading of secondary prevention. These techniques focus on lowering the risk of disease. Notable among the secondary prevention efforts is the work of Pennebaker and his colleagues (e.g., Smyth & Pennebaker, 2001), which demonstrates the psychological and somatic health benefits of writing about traumatic events and stressors.

Tertiary prevention is the most direct form of healing the wounds of distress. It consists of getting professional help (e.g., counseling, physical therapy, medical treatment) for symptoms of distress. Organizational efforts at tertiary prevention are often facilitated by employee assistance programs.

Our knowledge of preventing distress has grown. We can tell individuals a lot about how to prevent or resolve distress. Our next task, and a formidable one, is to learn how to help individuals and organizations generate eustress, savor it, and reap the benefits in terms of increased health, well-being, and performance.

Eustress Generation

As a complement to preventing distress, we must learn to generate eustress at work. Accordingly, if we are truly interested in eustress generation, we must measure and assess wellness and positive functioning. A model of eustress generation must go beyond positive coping with distress and distress prevention.

The contrast between the view of positive psychology presented and the more common view is captured by Folkman and Moskowitz (2000). They accepted the fact that positive and negative affect can co-occur during a stressful period of time. They suggested that positive and negative responses are produced by different events (stressors). In their study, the effects of the positive response are viewed as a coping strategy, a way to adapt to distress and its negative effects. Several studies of the happy–productive worker hypothesis provide additional support for the need to develop a model of eustress generation. One study found that a pleasantness-based measure of dispositional affect predicted rated job performance, although the same was not true of state positive affect in this study (T. A. Wright & Staw, 1999). A second set of studies found that psychological well-being was predictive of job performance for 47 human service workers (T. A. Wright & Cropanzano, 2000). Unfortunately, psychological well-being was operationalized as the absence of the negative (e.g., "How often have you felt depressed or very unhappy?"), again supporting the prevailing primacy of distress.

A model of eustress generation recognizes that the interpretation of and response to work demands can be positive as well as negative. Managers interested in eustress generation might identify which aspects of the work employees find most engaging, and then, more importantly, identify why individuals find the work pleasurable and consider what could be done to enhance the positive aspects of the work experience. Similar to Quick et al.'s (1997) concept of primary distress prevention, this could be thought of as primary eustress generation via job redesign. Accordingly, we suggest that job redesign efforts must be assessed for their ability to generate the eustress as well as to prevent distress. It is important to note that any assignment of positive valence to work demands must be employee generated and should not be considered a one-size-fits-all solution.

If hopeful employees are healthy employees, then the generation of hope in workers as an indicator of eustress merits additional attention. The ability to generate hope among an organization's members may be particularly important during radical change efforts. When people believe that their actions will lead to positive results, they may be more willing to accept difficult and uncertain challenges. Managers can generate hope by establishing goals that are meaningful to all members, allocating the organizational resources necessary for individuals to excel at their jobs, and maintaining a frequent and inspirational dialogue with their constituents (Huy, 1999). Others have suggested that trust in management and procedural justice may result in primary appraisals that result in more hopeful employees during periods of organizational downsizing by reducing the extent to which downsizing is evaluated as a threat (Mishra & Spreitzer, 1998).

An example of an organizational resource that may be important for generating both manageability and hope is information. Role ambiguity has been shown to have a strong negative impact on hope (Simmons & Nelson, 2001). Role ambiguity is the confusion a person experiences related to not understanding what is expected, not knowing how to perform or change to meet new expectations, or not knowing the consequences of failing to meet expectations (Nelson & Quick, 2000). Relationships between employees and their supervisors that are open and supportive can reduce the role ambiguity and increase satisfaction. Managers who are easily accessible, who actively share information regarding current as well as evolving expectations with their constituents, and who encourage their management staff to do the same should establish a solid foundation for the generation of hope by lessening role ambiguity.

In parallel to the preventive stress management model, secondary eustress generation would target the individual response to work demands. Strategies for identifying and then managing negative responses, or coping, are well documented (Quick et al., 1997). Similar strategies are needed to help individuals identify and manage, or savor, positive responses.

This will first require the previously mentioned effort to identify valid eustress responses, describe them in terms that clearly differentiate them from distress responses, and link them to health benefits in the same way that distress responses have been linked to health consequences. If the health benefit has significant valence for the individual, and the expectancy that eustress could promote the health benefit is firmly established, then the individual could choose strategies to enhance their exposure to demands that they appraise to be appreciably positive.

The key to eustress generation may be helping individuals develop competencies for recognizing eustress in themselves and others to complement existing competencies for recognizing distress. The challenge for researchers will be to propose, validate, improve, and articulate ways that the presence of the positive can be recognized and understood as more than just the absence of the negative.

In situations in which jobs have a high degree of control, individuals can savor eustress by enhancing their exposure to the demands that they believe precipitated the responses recognized as positive. For example, if an individual identifies a trusting relationship with a supervisor as a source of hope for them at work, then the individual might engage in behaviors that make themselves more trustworthy in the eyes of the supervisor. Having linked trusting relationships with a positive response for themselves at work, individuals may also seek to develop more trusting relationships with others at work, especially with those whom they may have a stressful relationship. In this example of dealing with a stressful relationship, the eustress-generation approach of promoting the positive stands in contrast to the distress prevention approach of avoiding the stressor by avoiding the person (Quick et al., 1997).

In jobs that do not have a high degree of control, organizations can facilitate individuals savoring the positive. This may be challenging because as a result of cognitive appraisal, eustress recognition and interest in eustress generation will always be highly individualistic. Yet even in jobs with high demands and low decision latitude, the potential for positive appraisals remains. For example, the previously cited study of soldiers participating in a U.S. peacekeeping mission in Bosnia showed that the soldiers found meaningfulness in the challenge of their mission (Britt et al., 2001). Recall that a factor such as witnessing the destruction caused by warring factions was associated with reporting greater positive benefits, because in the context of the mission the destruction was likely seen as justification for the mission, which added meaning to the soldier's work. The degree of eustress experienced by the soldiers did not result from witnessing the destruction; rather it resulted from the organization providing the opportunity for purposeful engagement by defining a clear mission that was perceived beneficial, and then providing the resources necessary to accomplish the mission (i.e., manageability).

We have also suggested the concept of savoring eustress (Simmons & Nelson, 2007). Savoring the positive would literally mean enjoying the positive response, with anticipation or dwelling on it with satisfaction or delight (Nelson & Simmons, 2004). Savoring the positive is a deliberate attempt to make it last (Peterson, 2006). An instrument for assessing the savoring process, the Savoring Beliefs Inventory, has also been developed (Brant & Veroff, 2007).

We see savoring eustress as a contrast to coping with distress and as a related but separate and distinct mechanism. Coping, as reactions to feelings of distress, consists of voluntary activities involving cognition, emotion, and behavior in a process of self-regulation (Ashkanasy, Ashton-James, & Jordan, 2004). The strategies an individual formulates to reduce or eliminate distress can be problem focused, intended to address the perceived source of distress, or emotion focused, intended to deal with the perceived experience and ramifications of distress (Lazarus & Folkman, 1984).

Some use the concept of positive coping in an attempt to focus on the positive (Folkman & Moskowitz, 2000). Consistent with our model, positive coping accepts the fact that both positive and negative response (e.g., affect) can co-occur during a stressful period of time. In contrast to the approach presented here, positive coping suggests that positive and negative responses are produced by different events (stressors); furthermore, the effects of the positive response are viewed as a coping strategy, a way to adapt to distress and its negative effects. As such, we believe that positive coping is still embedded in the disease model of stress.

Fredrickson's (2002) broaden-and-build theory of positive emotions posits that positive emotions broaden people's habitual models of thinking and acting and build enduring personal resources. The experience of positive emotions can help individuals transform themselves to become more creative, connected, resilient, and ultimately healthy individuals. The concept of broad-minded coping is part of the broaden-and-build approach, and although it is very appealing, we believe that it is still ultimately conceptualized and operationalized as a distress/disease model, as a method to help individuals cope with adversity.

Although research on coping with distress is plentiful, research involving positive affect regulation is relatively rare. There is, however, research to suggest that processes of positive affect regulation are separate and distinct from processes of negative affect regulation (Larsen, 2000). People who are experiencing positive emotions typically strive to maintain the emotions by approaching things they believe caused the experience and avoiding things that threaten to cut short their good feelings. Yet there may be times when people attempt to dampen positive feelings by calming down and refocusing themselves. They may do this, for example, when they anticipate engaging in a demanding task or interacting with someone of importance (Wood, Heimpel, & Michela, 2003).

A comprehensive review of the past 15 years of occupational health psychology research called for a greater emphasis on positive health (Macik-Frey, Quick, & Nelson, 2007). This chapter has proposed a more positive, holistic approach for understanding work stress by incorporating eustress, the positive response to stress. This approach is embedded in a view of health that emphasizes the presence of the positive mental, spiritual, and physical well-being in addition to the absence of disease and dysfunction. A tremendous opportunity exists for researchers to clarify and validate this more holistic approach to stress and health. This is a worthy endeavor, the goal of which is to influence a change in the refrain of many workers from "I'm stressed out" to "I'm engaged."

References

Ainsworth, M. D. S., & Bowlby, J. (1991). An ethological approach to personality. *American Psychologist, 46,* 333–341. doi:10.1037/0003-066X.46.4.333

Antonovsky, A. (1987). *Unraveling the mysteries of health.* San Francisco, CA: Jossey-Bass.

Antonovsky, A. (1993). The structure and properties of the sense of coherence scale. *Social Science and Medicine, 36,* 725–733. doi:10.1016/0277-9536(93)90033-Z

Artinian, B. M. (1997). Situational sense of coherence: Development and measurement of the construct. In B. M. Artinian & M. M. Conger (Eds.), *The intersystem model: Integrating theory and practice* (pp. 18–30). Thousand Oaks, CA: Sage.

Ashkanasy, N. M., Ashton-James, C. E., & Jordan, P. J. (2004). Performance impacts of appraisal and coping with stress in workplace settings. In P. L. Perrewe & D. C. Ganster (Eds.), *Research in occupational stress and well being: Vol. 3. Emotional and physiological processes and positive intervention strategies* (pp. 1–43). Oxford, England: Elsevier.

Barnett, R. C., Marshall, N. L., & Sayer, A. (1992). Positive-spillover effects from job to home: A closer look. *Women and Health, 19,* 13–41. doi:10.1300/J013v19n02_02

Brant, F. B., & Veroff, J. (2007). *Savoring: A new model of positive experience.* Mahwah, NJ: Erlbaum.

Britt, T. W., Adler, A. B., & Bartone, P. T. (2001). Deriving benefits from stressful events: The role of engagement in meaningful work and hardiness. *Journal of Occupational Health Psychology, 6,* 53–63. doi:10.1037/1076-8998.6.1.53

Cohen, S., & Edwards, J. R. (1988). Personality characteristics as moderators of the relationship between stress and disorder. In W. J. Neufeld (Ed.), *Advances in the investigation of psychological stress* (pp. 235–283). New York, NY: Wiley.

Edwards, J. R., & Cooper, C. L. (1988). The impacts of positive psychological states on physical health: A review and theoretical framework. *Social Science and Medicine, 27,* 1447–1459. doi:10.1016/0277-9536(88)90212-2

Estrada, C. A., Isen, A. M., & Young, M. J. (1994). Positive affect improves creative problem solving and influences reported sources of practice satisfaction in physicians. *Motivation and Emotion, 18,* 285–299. doi:10.1007/BF02856470

Estrada, C. A., Isen, A. M., & Young, M. J. (1997). Positive affect facilitates integration of information and decreases anchoring in reasoning among physicians. *Organizational Behavior and Human Decision Processes, 72,* 117–135. doi:10.1006/obhd.1997.2734

Florian, V., Mikulincer, M., & Taubman, O. (1995). Does hardiness contribute to mental health during a stressful real-life situation? The roles of appraisal and coping. *Journal of Personality and Social Psychology, 68,* 687–695. doi:10.1037/0022-3514.68.4.687

Folkman, S., & Moskowitz, J. T. (2000). Positive affect and the other side of coping. *American Psychologist, 55,* 647–654. doi:10.1037/0003-066X.55.6.647

Fredrickson, B. L. (2002). Positive emotions. In R. Snyder & S. J. Lopez (Eds.), *Handbook of positive psychology* (pp. 120–134). New York, NY: Oxford University Press.

George, J. M., & Brief, A. P. (1992). Feeling good–doing good: A conceptual analysis of mood at work–organizational spontaneity relationship. *Psychological Bulletin, 112,* 310–329. doi:10.1037/0033-2909.112.2.310

Gray-Toft, P., & Anderson, J. G. (1981). Stress among hospital nursing staff: Its causes and effects. *Social Science and Medicine, 15,* 639–647.

Harrison, D. A., Newman, D. A., & Roth, P. L. (2006). How important are job attitudes? Meta-analytic comparisons of integrative behavioral outcomes and time sequences. *Academy of Management Journal, 49,* 305–325.

Hazan, C., & Shaver, P. R. (1990). Love and work: An attachment-theoretical perspective. *Journal of Personality and Social Psychology, 29,* 270–280. doi: 10.1037/0022–3514.59.2.270

Huy, Q. N. (1999). Emotional capability, emotional intelligence, and radical change. *Academy of Management Review, 24,* 325–345. doi:10.2307/259085

Isen, A. M., Rosenzweig, A. S., & Young, M. J. (1991). The influence of positive affect on clinical problem solving. *Medical Decision Making, 11,* 221–227. doi:10.1177/0272989X9101100313

Karasek, R. A. (1979). Job demands, job decision latitude, and mental strain: Implications for job redesign. *Administrative Science Quarterly, 24,* 285–308. doi:10.2307/2392498

Kobasa, S. C. (1979). Stressful life events, personality, and health: An inquiry into hardiness. *Journal of Personality and Social Psychology, 37,* 1–11. doi:10.1037/0022-3514.37.1.1

Kobasa, S. C., Maddi, S. R., & Kahn, S. (1982). Hardiness and health: A prospective study. *Journal of Personality and Social Psychology, 42,* 168–177. doi:10.1037/0022-3514.42.1.168

Larsen, R. J. (2000). Toward a science of mood regulation. *Psychological Inquiry, 11,* 129–141. doi:10.1207/S15327965PLI1103_01

Lazarus, R. S. (1993). From psychological stress to the emotions: A history of changing outlooks. In L. W. Porter & M. R. Rosenzweig (Eds.), *Annual review of psychology* (Vol. 44, pp. 1–21). Palo Alto, CA: Annual Reviews.

Lazarus, R. S., & Folkman, S. (1984). *Stress, appraisal and coping.* New York, NY: Springer.

Lefcourt, H. M., & Davidson-Katz, K. (1991). Locus of control and health. In C. R. Snyder & D. R. Forsyth (Eds.), *Handbook of social and clinical psychology* (pp. 246–266). New York, NY: Pergamon Press.

Macik-Frey, M., Quick, J. C., & Nelson, D. L. (2007). Advances in occupational health: From a stressful beginning to a positive future. *Journal of Management, 33,* 809–840. doi:10.1177/0149206307307634

Maddi, S. (1998). Hardiness in health and effectiveness. In H. S. Friedman (Ed.), *Encyclopedia of mental health* (Vol. 2, pp. 323–335). San Diego, CA: Academic Press.

McCrae, R. R., & Costa, P. T., Jr. (1994). The stability of personality: Observations and evaluations. *Current Directions in Psychological Science, 3,* 173–175. doi:10.1111/1467-8721.ep10770693

Mishra, A. K., & Spreitzer, G. M. (1998). Explaining how survivors respond to downsizing: The roles of trust, empowerment, justice, and work redesign. *Academy of Management Review, 23,* 567–588. doi:10.2307/259295

Mittal, V., & Ross, W. T., Jr. (1998). The impact of positive and negative affect and issue framing on issue interpretation and risk taking. *Organizational Behavior and Human Decision Processes, 76,* 298–324. doi:10.1006/obhd.1998.2808

Morrill, A. C., Ickovics, J. R., Golubchikov, V. V., Berens, S. E., & Rodin, J. (1996). Safer sex: Social and psychological predictors of behavioral maintenance and change among heterosexual women. *Journal of Consulting and Clinical Psychology, 64,* 819–828. doi:10.1037/0022-006X.64.4.819

Nelson, D. L., & Quick, J. C. (2000). *Organizational behavior: Foundations, realities, and challenges* (3rd ed.). Cincinnati, OH: South-Western.

Nelson, D. L., Quick, J. C., & Joplin, J. (1991). Psychological contracting and newcomer socialization: An attachment theory foundation. *Journal of Social Behavior and Personality, 6,* 55–72.

Nelson, D. L., Quick, J. C., & Simmons, B. L. (2001). Preventive management of work stress: Current themes and future challenges. In A. Baum, T. Revenson, & J. Singer (Eds.), *Handbook of health psychology* (pp. 349–364). Mahwah, NJ: Erlbaum.

Nelson, D. L., & Simmons, B. L. (2003). Health psychology and work stress: A more positive approach. In J. Quick & L. Tetrick (Eds.), *Handbook of occupational health psychology* (pp. 97–119). Washington, DC: American Psychological Association.

Nelson, D. L., & Simmons, B. L. (2004). Eustress: An elusive construct, an engaging pursuit. In P. L. Perrewe & D. C. Ganster (Eds.), *Research in occupational stress and well being: Vol. 3. Emotional and physiological processes and positive intervention strategies* (pp. 265–322). Oxford, England: Elsevier.

Ouellette, S. C., & DiPlacido, J. (2001). Personality's role in the protection and enhancement of health: Where the research has been, where it is stuck, how it might move. In A. Baum, T. Revenson, & J. Singer (Eds.), *Handbook of health psychology* (pp. 175–193). Mahwah, NJ: Erlbaum.

Peterson, C. (2000). The future of optimism. *American Psychologist, 55,* 44–55. doi:10.1037/0003-066X.55.1.44

Peterson, C. (2006). *A primer in positive psychology.* New York, NY: Oxford University Press.

Peterson, C., & Seligman, M. E. P. (1987). Explanatory style and illness. *Journal of Personality, 55,* 237–265. doi:10.1111/j.1467-6494.1987.tb00436.x

Quick, J. C., & Quick, J. D. (1984). *Organizational stress and preventive management.* New York, NY: McGraw-Hill.

Quick, J. C., Quick, J. D., Nelson, D. L., & Hurrell, J. J. (1997). *Preventive stress management in organizations.* Washington, DC: American Psychological Association. doi:10.1037/10238-000

Rotter, J. B. (1966). Generalized expectancies for internal versus external control of reinforcements. *Psychological Monographs, 80,* 1–28.

Ryff, C. D., & Singer, B. (1998). The contours of positive human health. *Psychological Inquiry, 9,* 1–28. doi:10.1207/s15327965pli0901_1

Salovey, P., Rothman, A. J., Detweiler, J. B., & Steward, W. T. (2000). Emotional states and physical health. *American Psychologist, 55,* 110–121. doi:10.1037/0003-066X.55.1.110

Scheier, M. F., & Carver, C. S. (1992). Effects of optimism on psychological and physical well being: Theoretical overview and empirical update. *Cognitive Therapy and Research, 16,* 201–228. doi:10.1007/BF01173489

Segerstrom, S. C., Taylor, S. E., Kemeny, M. E., & Fahey, J. L. (1998). Optimism is associated with mood, coping, and immune change in response to stress. *Journal of Personality and Social Psychology, 74,* 1646–1655. doi:10.1037/0022-3514.74.6.1646

Seligman, M. E. P. (1991). *Learned optimism.* New York, NY: Knopf.

Shirom, A. (2003). Feeling vigorous at work? The construct of vigor and the study of positive affect in organizations. In D. Ganster & P. L. Perrewe (Eds.), *Research in organizational stress and well-being* (Vol. 3, pp. 135–165). Greenwich, CT: JAI Press.

Shirom, A. (2007). Explaining vigor: On the antecedents and consequences of vigor as a positive affect at work. In C. L. Cooper & D. Nelson (Eds.), *Organizational behavior: Accentuating the positive at work* (pp. 86–100). Thousand Oaks, CA: Sage.

Shraga, O., & Shirom, A. (2009). The construct validity of vigor and its antecedents. *Human Relations, 62,* 271–291. doi:10.1177/0018726708100360

Simmons, B. L. (2000). *Eustress at work: Accentuating the positive.* Unpublished doctoral dissertation, Oklahoma State University.

Simmons, B. L., Gooty, J., Nelson, D. L., & Little, L. M. (2009). Secure attachments: Implications for trust, hope, burnout, and performance. *Journal of Organizational Behavior, 30,* 233–247. doi:10.1002/job.585

Simmons, B. L., & Nelson, D. L. (2001). Eustress at work: The relationship between hope and health in hospital nurses. *Health Care Management Review, 26,* 7–18.

Simmons, B. L., & Nelson, D. L. (2007). Eustress at work: Extending the holistic stress model. In D. L. Nelson & C. L. Cooper (Eds.), *Positive organizational behavior* (pp. 40–53). Thousand Oaks, CA: Sage.

Simmons, B. L., Nelson, D. L., & Neal, L. J. (2001). A comparison of the positive and negative work attitudes of home healthcare and hospital nurses. *Health Care Management Review, 26,* 63–74.

Smyth, J. M., & Pennebaker, J. W. (2001). What are the health effects of disclosure? In A. Baum, T. A. Revenson, & J. E. Singer (Eds.), *Handbook of health psychology* (pp. 339–348). Mahwah, NJ: Erlbaum.

Snyder, C. R. (1994). *The psychology of hope: You can get there from here.* New York, NY: Free Press.

Snyder, C. R., Harris, C., Anderson, J. R., Holleran, S. A., Irving, L. M., & Sigman, S. T., . . . Harney, P. (1991). The will and the ways: Development and validation of an individual differences measure of hope. *Journal of Personality and Social Psychology, 60,* 570–585.

Snyder, C. R., Sympson, S. C., Ybasco, F. C., Borders, T. F., Babyak, M. A., & Higgins, R. L. (1996). Development and validation of the state hope scale. *Journal of Personality and Social Psychology, 70,* 321–335. doi:10.1037/0022-3514.70.2.321

Spreitzer, G. M. (1995). Psychological empowerment in the workplace: Dimensions, measurement, and validation. *Academy of Management Journal, 38,* 1442–1465. doi:10.2307/256865

Staw, B. M., & Barsade, S. G. (1993). Affect and managerial performance: A test of the sadder-but-wiser vs. happier-and-smarter hypothesis. *Administrative Science Quarterly, 38,* 304–331. doi:10.2307/2393415

Watson, D., Clark, L. A., & Tellegen, A. (1988). Development and validation of brief measures of positive and negative affect: The PANAS scale. *Journal of Personality and Social Psychology, 54,* 1063–1070. doi:10.1037/0022-3514.54.6.1063

Watson, D., Pennebaker, J. W., & Folger, R. (1987). Beyond negative affectivity: Measuring stress and satisfaction in the workplace. *Journal of Organizational Behavior Management, 8,* 141–157. doi:10.1300/J075v08n02_09

Westman, M. (1990). The relationship between stress and performance: The moderating effect of hardiness. *Human Performance, 3,* 141–155. doi:10.1207/s15327043hup0303_1

Wiebe, D. J. (1991). Hardiness and stress moderation: A test of proposed mechanisms. *Journal of Personality and Social Psychology, 60,* 89–99. doi:10.1037/0022-3514.60.1.89

Wiebe, D. J., & Williams, P. G. (1992). Hardiness and health: A social psychophysiological perspective on stress and adaptation. *Journal of Social and Clinical Psychology, 11,* 238–262.

Wood, J. V., Heimpel, S. A., & Michela, J. L. (2003). Savoring versus dampening: Self-esteem differences in regulating positive affect. *Journal of Personality and Social Psychology, 85,* 566–580. doi:10.1037/0022-3514.85.3.566

Wright, L. (1988). The Type A behavior pattern and coronary artery disease. *American Psychologist, 43,* 2–14. doi:10.1037/0003-066X.43.1.2

Wright, T. A., & Cropanzano, R. (2000). Psychological well-being and job satisfaction as predictors of job performance. *Journal of Occupational Psychology, 5,* 84–94. doi:10.1037/1076-8998.5.1.84

Wright, T. A., & Staw, B. M. (1999). Affect and favorable work outcomes: Two longitudinal tests of the happy–productive worker thesis. *Journal of Organizational Behavior, 20,* 1–23.

5

Controlling Occupational Safety
and Health Hazards

Michael J. Smith and Pascale Carayon

Employees are injured or killed at work every day in the United States. In 2005, it was estimated that the annual toll was 55,000 U.S. employees killed by injuries or illnesses and 3.8 million incurring disabling injuries that required time off from work (Schulte, 2005). The U.S. Bureau of Labor Statistics reported 5,657 deaths from injury for 2007 and about 4 million recordable injuries, both a reduction from previous years. Although the trend in U.S. workplace deaths by injury and disabling injuries has steadily declined since the Bureau of Labor Statistics first started collecting data in 1972, the current numbers indicate a serious need to continue to make improvements in occupational safety and health efforts.

In this chapter, we examine the major causes of occupational injuries and illnesses and ways to reduce employee risk of injury, illness, or death, as well as directions for establishing effective detection and control methods. We first present a model for examining safety risks. Then we define different types of workplace hazards that have been shown to cause injuries and illnesses. Next, we examine ways to measure hazards and injuries. The remainder of the chapter describes methods (both engineering and human factors) for controlling hazards.

The Balance Model: Factors That Can Lead
to Exposures and Accidents

An important consideration in conceptualizing an approach to occupational health and safety is an understanding of the various personal and workplace factors that lead to exposures and accidents. Any strategy to control these exposures and accidents should consider a range of factors and their influences on each other. A concept of human workplace interaction was proposed by M. J. Smith and Sainfort (1989). This *balance* model has five components: (a) person; (b) machinery, technology, and materials; (c) task activities; (d) the environment; and (e) organization and supervision. For each element of this concept there can be hazardous exposures, for instance, a machine with an unguarded drive shaft or a person using unsafe work methods. The elements of the concept can also interact together to produce hazardous exposures, for example, a high workload task that is performed in an environment with chemical exposures by an untrained worker is a combination of hazards. Or when the person uses machinery and tools that have hazardous characteristics and there is high work pressure to complete a task quickly.

The balance model uses a system-level approach for analyzing tasks and hazards. Each separate element of the balance model has specific characteristics that can influence (create, enhance, modify) exposures to hazards and accident potential or disease risk. At the same time, each element interacts with the others to increase or mitigate risks. The use of system-level approaches to examine occupational health and safety issues has been promoted for many years (Carayon & Smith, 2000; Hendrick & Kleiner, 2002; O'Neill, 1998; M. J. Smith & Carayon, 1995).

The Person

A wide range of individual attributes can affect exposure and accident potential. These include a person's intellectual capabilities and aptitudes, perceptual–motor abilities, physical capabilities such as strength and endurance, current health status, susceptibilities to disease, and personality. Intelligence affects the ability for hazard recognition and aptitude for training in hazard recognition and elimination. An important aspect of injury prevention is to have knowledgeable employees who can determine the potential danger of an exposure and respond appropriately. This requires some previous experience with a hazard and/or training about the nature of the hazard, its injury potential, and ways to control it.

Employees must have the intellectual capability to learn and retain the information that they are given in training classes. There is a fundamental need for employees to have an adequate background and education to be able to acquire new knowledge through training. Of specific importance are observational, reading, listening, and language skills so employees can be trained and instructed properly.

Physiological considerations such as strength, endurance, and susceptibilities to fatigue, stress, or disease are also important aspects of injury potential. Some jobs demand high energy expenditure and strength requirements. For these, employees must have adequate physical resources to do the work safely. Another attribute related to physical capacity is perceptual–motor skills and abilities such as eye–hand coordination. These skills come into play in the moment-by-moment conduct of work tasks and interactions with hazards. Although strength may influence the ability to do a specific component of a task, perceptual–motor skills are involved in all aspects of manual tasks and the accuracy of performance. Thus, perceptual–motor skills affect the quality with which a task is carried out as well as the probability of a mistake that could cause an exposure or accident.

It is critical that a proper "fit" is achieved between an employee's capabilities and other elements of the balance model. This can occur with proper selection, training, skill enhancement, hazard orientation, ergonomic improvements, and proper engineering of the tasks, technology, and environment.

Machinery, Technology, and Materials

Characteristics of the machinery, tools, technology, and materials used by the worker can influence the potential for an exposure or accident. One consideration is the extent to which machinery and tools influence the worker's use of the most appropriate and effective perceptual–motor skills and energy resources. The relationship between the controls of a machine and the action of that machine dictates the level of perceptual–motor skill necessary to perform a task. The action of the controls and the subsequent reaction of the machinery must be compliant and compatible with basic human perceptual–motor patterns and cognitive models. If not, significant interference with performance can occur that may lead to improper responses that can cause accidents.

In addition, the adequacy of feedback about the action of the machine affects the performance efficiency that can be achieved and the potential for an operational error. An excellent resource for determining if a machine is compliant with human factors is the *Handbook of Human Factors and Ergonomics* (Salvendy, 2006). Additional hazard control resources are the *Accident Prevention Manual* (Vols. I and II; Hagan, Montgomery, & O'Reilly, 2001) and *The Safety Professional's Handbook* (Vols. I and II; Haight, 2008).

The inherent characteristics of materials, such as flammability or toxicity, affect exposures and risk. Those materials that are more hazardous clearly have a greater probability of adverse safety or health outcomes if there is an exposure. Sometimes employees will be more careful when using materials that they know have a high hazard potential. But this can only be possible when they have adequate knowledge of the material's hazard level. When a material is very hazardous, there are often other, less hazardous materials available that can be substituted to reduce the extent of risk. When such substitution is not possible, then closed-system production methods with extensive engineering controls should be considered.

There are similar issues of substitution for hazardous work processes. Proper substitution of better methods, materials, or machinery can decrease the risk of injury or illness. However, care must be taken to ensure that the material or process being substituted is really safer and that it mixes well with the entire product formulation or production-assembly process. This calls for an analysis of the systemic influences of changes. Resources for industrial hygiene controls include *The Occupational Environment: Its Evaluation and Control* (DiNardi, 1997), *Fundamentals of Industrial Hygiene* (5th ed.; Plog & Quinlan, 2002), *2008 TLVs and BEIs* (American Conference of Government Industrial Hygienists [ACGIH], 2008), and *Modern Industrial Hygiene* (Vols. I and II; Perkins, 2008).

Task Activities

The demands of a work activity and the way in which it is conducted can influence the probability of an exposure or accident. In addition, the influence of the work activity on employee attention, satisfaction, and motivation can affect behavior patterns that increase exposure and accident risk. Work-task considerations can be broken into the physical requirements, the mental requirements, and psychological considerations. The physical requirements influence the amount of energy expenditure necessary to carry out a task. Excessive physical requirements can lead to fatigue, both physiological and mental, which can reduce worker capabilities to recognize and respond to workplace hazards. Typically, relatively high workloads can be tolerated for only short periods of time. Longer exposure to heavy workloads or multiple exposures to shorter duration heavy workloads leads to diminished employee capacity to respond. Salvendy's (2006) *Handbook of Human Factors and Ergonomics,* the Human Factors and Ergonomic Society (HFES) website, the International Ergonomic Association (IEA) website, and the National Institute for Occupational Safety and Health (NIOSH) website all describe physiological aspects of work and fatigue. (See Appendix 5.1 at the end of the chapter for a list of helpful websites.)

Other task considerations related to the physical work requirements include the pace or rate of work, the amount of repetition in task activities, and work pressure as a result of production demands. Task activities that are highly repetitive and paced by machinery rather than by employee tend to be stressful. Such conditions diminish an employee's attention to hazards and the capability to respond to a hazard because of boredom (Cooper & Smith, 1985). These conditions may produce cumulative trauma disorders to the musculoskeletal system when the task activity cycle time is very short and constant, the repetition is frequent, and biomechanical loads are high. Tasks with relatively low workload and low energy expenditure can result in boredom that leads to employee inattention to hazards (National Academy of Sciences, 2001).

Psychological task content considerations, such as satisfaction with job tasks, the amount of control over the work process, participation in decision making, the ability to use knowledge and skills, the amount of esteem associated with the job, and the ability to identify with the end products of the task activity, can influence employee attention and motivation (M. J. Smith & Sainfort, 1989). Poor task content can cause psychosocial job stress. Job stress can affect employee ability to attend to, recognize, and respond to hazards, as well as the motivation needed to be concerned with personal health and safety considerations. Job stress can bring about emotional disturbances that limit the employee's capabilities to respond, as well as general motivation to safety issues. Task considerations are a central aspect in reducing worker fatigue and psychosocial stress and in enhancing worker motivation for positive safety behavior. Tasks must be designed to fit an employee's capabilities and needs and be compatible with the other elements of the balance model.

The Work Environment

In the work environment, employees are exposed to materials, chemicals, and physical agents that can cause harm or injury if the exposure exceeds safe limits. Such exposures vary widely from industry to industry, from job to job, and from task to task. Exposures from the work environment influence the probability for an injury or illness, and the extent of exposure often determines the seriousness of the injury. The extent of environmental exposures is an important basis for determining the rates companies pay for worker's compensation insurance. The central concept is one of relative risk. For assessment of relative risk, it is assumed that the greater the number of hazards, and the more serious their potential to inflict injury or illness, then the greater the probability of an accident. It follows that the greater the probability of accidents, then the higher the insurance premium. The hazard potential of different environmental factors can be evaluated using various federal, state, and local codes and standards, as well as consensus standards for worker protection and exposure limits that have been established by scientific and consensus groups. Details about standards and guidelines for particular chemicals, materials, technologies, processes, and industries are available from the Occupational Safety and Health Administration (OSHA), NIOSH, ACGIH, American National Standards Institute (ANSI), Environmental Protection Agency (EPA), and ASTM International (originally known as the American Society for Testing and Materials).

Environmental conditions may also hamper the ability of employees to use their senses (e.g., poor lighting, excessive noise, overpowering smells) and thus reduce employees' abilities to respond or react to hazardous situations. The environment should be compatible with worker sensory capabilities, perceptual–motor skills, energy expenditure and endurance limits, and the motivational desire to do tasks in the proper and safe way.

Organizational Design and Management

Several aspects of organizational design and management can have an influence on accident risk. These include management policies and procedures, the way in which work tasks are organized into plantwide activities, the style of employee supervision, the motivational climate in the plant, the amount of socialization and interaction between employees, the amount of social support employees receive, and management attitude toward safety. Management attitude has often been cited as a critical element in a successful safety program (Cohen, 1977; Dejoy, 2005; DeJoy, Schaffer, Wilson, Vanderberg, & Butts, 2004; Neal & Griffin, 2006; M. J. Smith, Cohen, Cohen, & Cleveland, 1978; Zohar, 1980; Zohar & Luria, 2005). If the individuals who manage an organization have a disregard for safety considerations, then employees tend not be very motivated to work safely. Conversely, if the management attitude is one in which safety considerations are paramount—even more important than production goals—then managers, supervisors, and employees will put a great effort into health and safety considerations.

Other organizational considerations that are important in safety performance are related to management atmosphere and attitudes. For instance, a management structure that provides for frequent employee interaction with other employees, the style of the supervisor, and frequent social support will lead to an organizational climate that is conducive to cooperative efforts in hazard recognition and control. Such a structure also allows for the motivational climate necessary to encourage appropriate safety behavior.

A consistent factor in accident causation is work pressure for greater production, for faster output, to quickly correct problems to continue production, or to reduce customer waiting time. Such work pressure issues have been defined in a series of catastrophic accident disasters that have been documented by OSHA (2001, 2002, 2003a, 2003b, 2004) and that led to the development of a process safety standard. These case studies demonstrate how poor management decisions about production issues led to critical employee, supervisor, or contract worker mistakes causing disastrous results. Abkowitz (2008) and Kletz (2009) have written books describing several industrial catastrophes.

Management emphasis on reducing costs, enhancing profits, and increasing stock price often stretches the limits of the capabilities of the workforce and technology. When breakdowns occur or operations are not running normally, employees tend to take risks to keep production online or to get it back online quickly. It is during these nonnormal operations that many accidents occur. Management must provide adequate resources to meet production goals and to accommodate nonnormal operations. Management must also establish policies to ensure that employees and supervisors do not take unnecessary risks just to ensure high production. Modern concepts of "lean production" can lead to situations in which employees do not have the necessary resources to meet nonnormal operational demands. Management should recognize that nonnormal operations put additional demands on the workforce, and efforts should be made to control these increased demands.

Workplace Hazards

To list of all of the currently recognized and potential workplace hazards would take a document larger than this handbook; for example, the OSHA standards are multiple volumes (available on DVD or online). Hazard information pertinent to one's operations can be found in OSHA standards, NIOSH documents, government reports, and publications and resources from professional organizations and societies such as the National Safety Council, ACGIH, American Industrial Hygiene Association, American Society of Safety Engineers (ASSE), and HFES. The National Safety Council's *Accident Prevention Manual* (Vols. I and II; Hagan et al., 2001), ASSE's *The Safety Professionals Handbook* (Vols. I and II; Haight, 2008), ACGIH's *2008 TLVand BEIs* (ACGIH, 2008), and *Best's Loss Control Manual* (2008) are also good resources. There are also other federal, state, and local agencies that can provide information on some aspects of occupational health and safety hazard information. At the U.S. federal level, these include the Environmental Protection Agency, the National Institute for Environmental Health Sciences, and the Centers for Disease Control and Prevention. At the international level, there is the International Labour Office (ILO), World Health Organization, International Organization for Standardization, and European Agency for Safety and Health at Work.

It is important to comprehend the breadth and nature of occupational hazard exposures. Workplace hazard sources are classified into broad categories that help explain their nature and potential controls. These are (a) physical agents such as noise and heat; (b) powered mechanical agents such as machinery and tools; (c) nonpowered mechanical agents such as hammers, axes, and knives; (d) liquid chemical agents such as benzene and toluene; (e) powdered materials such as pesticides, asbestos, sand, and coal dust; (f) gaseous or vaporous chemical agents such as nitrous oxide, carbon monoxide, and anhydrous ammonia; (g) heavy metals such as lead, mercury, and chromium; (h) biological agents such as bacteria and viruses; (i) genetically engineered agents; (j) nanotechnology; and (k) other hazards such as wet working surfaces, unguarded floor openings, job stress, and the unsafe behavior of others. These hazards enter the body through various routes, including inhalation into the lungs and nose, absorption through the skin and other membranes, ingestion into the throat and stomach, traumatic contact with various body surfaces and organs, and in the case of job stress through the cognitive mental processes.

Traditional hazards such as unexpected energy release and chemicals are still major concerns in the workplace. Lasers, robots, microwaves, x-rays, and imaging devices have become more common. Their use makes many of the traditional problems of controlling energy release and limiting worker access to hazardous machine components even more challenging. These technologies will become even more problematic because of the complex nature of the mechanisms of energy release and because of the increased power of the forces involved. For instance, using x-rays for lithographic etching of computer chips could produce exposures that are substantially higher than conventional diagnostic x-rays. The safety precautions for this type of instrument have to be much better than current standards for diagnostic equipment. In addition, emerging hazards are appearing. Some will be the exotic products of genetic engineering and biotechnology, and others will be the products of scientists' ability to harness the laws of physics and chemistry with advanced engineering designs (e.g., nanotechnology). These will become everyday tools used by thousands of workers, many whom will not be well educated or knowledgeable of the tremendous power of the technology with which they will be working.

Although these physical and biological hazards will become more prevalent and dangerous than they are today, there will also be more physical and psychological work demands that can lead to psychological stress problems. Two of the fastest rising worker's compensation claims areas in the United States are cumulative musculoskeletal trauma and psychological distress. The rise in these problems can generally be related to two factors. First, there is greater media, worker, and employer awareness and knowledge of how the workplace can contribute to such problems. Second, there has been a substantial increase in workplace automation over the past decade that has produced working conditions that can influence the development of these disorders. It is possible that dealing with the stress-induced problems may be even more difficult than dealing with the biological, chemical, and physical hazards.

Measuring Hazard Potential and Safety Performance

To successfully control occupational hazards and related illness and injuries, one needs to define their nature and predict when and where they will occur. This requires that some system of hazard detection be developed that can define the frequency of the hazard, its seriousness, and its amenability to control. Traditionally, two parallel systems of information have been used to attain this purpose. One system is hazard identification, such as plant inspections, fault-free analysis, failure mode analysis, and employee hazard reporting programs. These methods have been used to define the nature and frequency of potential and/or actual company hazards. The definition of serious hazards permits an employer to abate the risks before injury or illness occurs. The second system is after the fact in that it uses employee injury and company loss control information to define problem spots on the bases of the extent of injuries and costs to the organization. In hazardous and complex work systems, incident reporting is often used before injuries or property damage occurs. When pre- and postinjury systems can be integrated, an organization can have greater success in predicting high-risk plant areas or working conditions in which programs can be established for hazard control. The next two sections illustrate ways to measure hazards and injuries.

Hazard Inspection Programs

Hazard identification before the occurrence of an occupational injury is a major goal of a hazard inspection program. In the United States, such programs have been formalized in terms of federal and state regulations that require employers to monitor and abate recognized occupational health and safety hazards. These recognized hazards are defined in the federal and state regulations that provide explicit standards of unsafe exposures. The standards can be the basis for establishing an in-plant inspection program, as they specify the explicit subject matter to be investigated and corrected.

Inspections are more effective in identifying permanent fixed physical and environmental hazards that do not vary over time than in identifying transient physical and environmental hazards or improper workplace behaviors, as these hazards may not be present when the inspection is taking place (Boiano & Hull, 2001; Sieber, Sundin, Frazier, & Robinson, 1991; K. U. Smith, 1990). A major benefit from inspections, beyond hazard recognition, is the positive motivational influence on employees. Inspections demonstrate management's interest in the health and safety of employees and a commitment to a safe working environment. To capitalize on this positive motivational influence, an inspection should not be a punitive process of placing blame, confrontation, or punishment. Indicating the good aspects of a work area and not just focusing on the hazards is important in this respect because it recognizes the positive aspects of employer and employee safety efforts. It is also important to have employees participate in hazard inspections because such participation can increase their hazard recognition skills and their motivation for safe behavior.

The first step in an inspection program is to develop a checklist that identifies all potential hazards. A good starting point is the state and federal standards. Many insurance companies have developed general checklists of OSHA standards that can be tailored to a particular plant.

A systematic inspection procedure is preferred. This requires that the inspector knows what to look for, knows where to look for it, and has the proper tools to conduct an effective assessment. It is important that the checklist be tailored to each work area after an analysis of that work area's needs has been undertaken. This analysis should determine the factors to be inspected, including (a) the technology, machinery, tools, and materials; (b) chemicals, gases, vapors, and biological agents; and (c) environmental conditions. The analysis will also determine the frequency of inspection necessary to detect and control hazards, the individuals who should conduct or participate in the inspection, and the instrumentation needed to make measurements of the hazards.

The hazards that require inspection can be determined by (a) their potential to cause an injury or illness; (b) the seriousness of a resulting injury or illness; (c) the number of injuries and illnesses a specific workplace factor has been identified with; and (d) conditions that have been defined by federal, state, and local regulations. The frequency of inspections should be based on the nature of the hazards being evaluated. For instance, once a serious fixed physical hazard has been identified and controlled, it is no longer a hazard. It will only have to be reinspected periodically to be sure the fixed hazard is still being controlled. Random spot-checking is another method that can indicate whether the hazard control remains effective.

Other types of hazards that are intermittent will require more frequent inspection to ensure proper hazard abatement. In many cases, weekly or monthly inspections are warranted, and in some cases daily inspections are reasonable. Inspections should take place when and where the highest probability of a hazard exists, and reinspection can occur on an incidental basis to ensure that hazard control is effectively maintained. The timing of inspections should be when work processes are operating and should be conducted on a recurring basis at regular intervals.

Annual inspections should be considered a maximum time period for evaluation of hazards because many hazards are intermittent, temporary, recurring, or due to procedural failures and not just fixed hazards. Because housekeeping is an important aspect of hazard control, inspection of all work areas should occur at least monthly for cleanliness, clutter, and traffic flow.

A checklist can be used to identify each hazard, its nature, exact location, potential to cause serious damage, and possible control measures. During the walk-through, employee input should be solicited. Photographs and videotapes of hazards are effective in documenting the nature and potential seriousness of hazards. Once the inspection is completed, a report is prepared that specifies pertinent information about the nature of the hazards, illness, and injury potential and abatement recommendations. This report needs to be detailed and provide step-by-step instructions for instituting hazard control procedures in a timely manner. It is not sufficient to simply write up the results; they should be shared with all concerned parties, preferably in a face-to-face meeting. This meeting will give the results greater significance and serve as the basis for further interaction and possible modification of recommendations. Such meetings will enhance employee understanding and allow for in-depth discussion of the findings and recommendations. This makes the entire inspection process more relevant to supervision and employees and facilitates the favorable acceptance of the results and any subsequent recommendations.

Illness and Injury Statistics

Injury statistics have four main uses: (a) to identify high-risk jobs or work areas, (b) to evaluate company health and safety performance, (c) to evaluate the effectiveness of hazard abatement approaches, and (d) to identify factors related to illness and injury causation. An illness and injury reporting and analysis system requires that detailed information be collected about the characteristics of illness and injuries and their frequency and severity. The Occupational Safety and Health Act of 1970 (OSH Act) establishes illness and injury reporting and recording requirements that are mandatory for all employers, with certain exclusions such as small establishments and local government agencies. Regulations have been developed to define how employers are to adhere to these requirements.

The OSH Act requirements specify that any illness or injury to an employee that causes time lost from the job, treatment beyond first-aid, transfer to another job, loss of consciousness, or any occupational illness must be recorded on a daily log of injuries (OSHA 300 form). This log identifies the injured person, the date and time of the injury, the department or plant location where the injury occurred, and a brief description about the occurrence of the injury, highlighting salient facts such as the chemical, physical agent, or machinery involved and the nature of the injury. An injury should be recorded on the day that it occurs, but this is not always possible with cumulative musculoskeletal disorders and other cumulative trauma injuries. The number of days that the person is absent from the job is also recorded on the employee's return to work.

In addition to the daily log, a more detailed form is filled out for each injury that occurs (OSHA 301 form). This form provides a description of the nature of the injury, the extent of damage to the employee, the factors that could be related to the cause of the injury (e.g., the source or agent that produced the injury), and events surrounding its occurrence. A worker's compensation form can be substituted for the OSHA 301 form because equivalent information is gathered on these forms.

The OSH Act injury and illness system specifies a procedure for calculating the frequency of occurrence of occupational injuries and illnesses and an index of their severity. Companies can use these to monitor their health and safety performance. National data by major industrial categories are compiled by the U.S. Bureau of Labor Statistics annually and can serve as a basis of comparison of individual company performance within an industry in the United States. Thus, a company can determine whether its injury rate is better or worse than those of other companies in its industry.

The OSHA system uses the following formula in determining company annual injury and illness incidence. The total number of recordable injuries is multiplied by 200,000 and then divided by the number of hours worked by the company employees. This gives an injury frequency per 100 person-years of work (injury incidence). These measures can be compared with an industry average.

$$\text{Incidence} = \text{Number of recordable injuries and illnesses} \times 200,000 /$$
$$\text{Number of hours worked by company employees in a year,}$$

where (a) the number of recordable injuries and illnesses is taken from the OSHA 300 daily log of injuries; (b) 200,000 is equal to the annual hours worked by 100 full-time employees; and (c) the number of hours worked by employees is taken from payroll records and reports prepared for the Department of Labor or the Social Security Administration for the reporting year.

It is also possible to determine the severity of company injuries. Two methods are typically used. In the first, the total number of days employees were away from work because of injuries is compiled from the OSHA 300 daily log and divided by the total number of injuries recorded on the OSHA 300 daily log. This gives an average number of days away from work per injury. In the second method, the total number of days away from work for the year are multiplied by 200,000 and then divided by the number of annual hours worked by the company employees. This gives a severity index per 100 person-years of work. These measures can also be compared with an industry average.

Injury incidence and severity information can be used by a company to monitor its injury and illness performance over the years to examine improvement and the effectiveness of health and safety interventions. Such information provides the basis for making corrections in the company's approach to health and safety and can serve as the basis of rewarding managers and workers for good performance. However, it must be understood that injury statistics give only a crude indicator of safety performance. Because injuries are rare events, they do not reflect the sum total of daily performance of company employees and managers.

Methods for Controlling Workplace Hazards

The next logical step after identifying and defining workplace hazards is to eliminate or control them. There are four types of interventions for achieving this, and these are not always mutually exclusive: eliminating the hazard or blocking employee access to the hazard, warning the employee of the hazard, training the employee to avoid the hazard, and improving work practices. The first type of intervention involves engineering, whereas the remaining types involve human factors. Each type is described below.

Eliminating the Hazard or Blocking Employee Access to the Hazard

The most effective way to deal with a hazard is to get rid of it. This can be accomplished by redesigning a product, tool, machine, process, or environment or through substitution of a nonhazardous or less hazardous method, material, or technology. For example, the loading of a mechanical punch press can be accomplished by placing a part directly onto the die by the employee's hand, which puts the hand directly into the point of operation. If the press should inadvertently cycle, the employee's hand could be injured. To eliminate this hazard, a fixture can be designed that the employee places the part on, and then the fixture with the part can be slid into the point of operation. With this system the employee's hand is not put into the point of operation. This redesign removes the hand from the hazardous area of the machine. Another example is substituting a less hazardous chemical to replace a more hazardous chemical and thereby reducing the extent of risk or the level of exposure. An example is replacing benzene with toluene as a solvent.

The second class of engineering controls is blocking employee access to the hazard. This can be achieved by putting up a barrier that keeps the employee from entering a hazardous area. The best example of this is fencing off an area such as a high voltage transformer. With this type of intervention, the hazard remains but is controlled by keeping employees blocked from the hazardous area. However, it is often the case that the hazardous area must be accessed for maintenance or other reasons. In such a case, there are often secondary hazard controls to protect those who cross the barrier. For example, robots usually have a barrier around them to keep employees outside of their arc of swing so that they do not inadvertently come into contact with the robot's arm. But when the robot has to be programmed or maintained, then an employee has to cross the barrier to access the robot. A secondary control is to have the robot automatically shut down when the barrier is breached. This is a form of "interlock" that keeps the hazard inactive while employees are present in the danger zone.

Containment is a form of a barrier guard that is used primarily with very dangerous chemical and physical hazards. An example is the ionizing radiation from a nuclear reactor. The radiation at the core of the reactor is restrained from leaving the reactor by lead-lined walls, but if leakage should occur through the walls, then a back-up barrier contains the leakage. In the case of a closed system, the employee never comes in contact with the hazard source (e.g., the reactor core). The system is designed to protect the employee from the hazard source without requiring any special action by the employee. Many chemical plants use the concept of a closed system of containment. The only time an employee would come into contact with these specific deadly hazards would be in the case of a disaster in which the containment devices failed.

Another form of barrier control is a guard. A guard is used when there is a hazard only during certain aspects of an operation or when the hazardous area can be covered during normal operations. For example, when a power press is inactive, there is no hazard at the point of operation. But when it is activated, the punch bit is set in motion and this becomes a hazard. In such a case, a guard is engaged that blocks the employee from contact with the bit whenever this hazard is present. In this situation of using guards, there is a barrier to keep the employee from the area of the hazard only when the hazard is present. The guard allows access to the operational area of the machine for loading, unloading, and other job operations before the activation of the machine and when the machine cycle is completed. But when the energy is activated, then the guard moves into place to block the employee from access to the site of the action (the hazard).

Many machines use permanent guards to cover moving parts that do not have to be accessed during operations, such as drive shafts, belts, and gears. These permanent guards make the hazard inaccessible when the guard is in place. The guard is only removed for machine maintenance or when a malfunction occurs. These fixed guards often have an interlock similar to the robot example. When the fixed guard is removed, then the interlock ensures that the machine cannot operate by shutting off the power.

Yet another engineering control is the active removal of the hazard before it contacts the employee during the work process. An example of this would be a local scavenger ventilation system that sucks the fumes produced by an operation such as welding or laser surgery away from the employees during operations. This transfers the fumes into a filtering system that removes the contaminants and then exhausts the air outside of the plant (surgery room) away from the employees and the public. The ventilation systems must comply with federal, state, and local regulations in design and in the level of emissions into the environment. Thus, the fumes may need to be "scrubbed" clean before being released into the open environment.

A related ventilation approach is to dilute the employee exposure to airborne contaminants by bringing in more fresh air from outside of the plant (or room) on a regular basis, which will reduce the concentration of the contaminant. Because the fresh air dilutes the concentration of the contaminant, the employees' extent of exposure to the contaminant is lowered to a safe level. The effectiveness of this approach can be verified by measuring the ambient air level of contamination in the plant (room) and also measuring the specific exposure level for a particular employee(s) on a regular basis. When new materials or chemicals are introduced into the work process, or when other new airborne exposures are introduced into the plant, the adequacy of the ventilation dilution approach to provide safe levels of exposure(s) must be verified.

When regular engineering controls cannot provide adequate employee protection, then personal protective equipment must be worn by the employees. This is not a preferred method of control because there is a possibility that an employee may still come in contact with the hazard due to equipment failure, inadequacy of the equipment, poor fit, poor maintenance, or lack of use.

It is a cardinal rule of safety and health engineering that the primary method of controlling hazards is through engineering controls. Human factors controls are to be used primarily when engineering controls are not practical, feasible, solely effective in hazard control, or cost-effective. It is recognized that human factors controls are often necessary as adjuncts (supplements) to engineering controls, but there are some instances in which human factors controls are the only feasible and effective controls.

Warning the Employee of the Hazard

When informing employees about workplace hazards, employers must convey three things: (a) what the hazard exposures are, (b) what the dangerous conditions and materials are, and (c) how to be protected from the hazards. Federal safety and health regulations and many state and local regulations specify that an employer has the obligation to inform employees of hazardous workplace exposures to chemicals, materials, physical agents, and/or biological agents that are known to cause harm. The requirements of informing vary from locale to locale, and employers must be aware of the informing and reporting requirements in their area.

In general, an employer must provide information on the name of the material (hazard), its potential health effects, exposure levels that produce adverse health (safety), and the typical kinds of exposures encountered in the facility. For each chemical or material or agent classified as hazardous by OSHA (and EPA), employers are required to maintain a standard data safety sheet called a *material safety data sheet* that provides detailed information about the toxicity, control measures, and standard operating procedures for using the product. A list of hazardous chemicals, materials, and physical agents can be obtained from OSHA or the EPA.

These standard data sheets must be supplied by the manufacturer of the product. These data sheets must be shared with employees who are exposed to specific hazardous products and must be available at a plant location where the data sheet(s) can be accessed by employees using the material. The sheet is an information resource that provides instructions and information in case of an exposure or emergency. The motivation behind the right-to-know concept is that employees have a basic human right to knowledge about their workplace exposures and that employees will make better choices and use better judgment when working with hazardous materials if they are informed.

Warnings are used to convey the message of extreme danger. They are designed to catch the attention of the employee, to inform the employee about a hazard, and to instruct the employee about how to avoid the hazard. The American National Standards Institute (ANSI; 1991, 1998) developed a series of standards for the design of visual warnings that provide guidelines as a starting point for designing warnings (e.g., ANSI Z535.1: safety color code; ANSI Z535.2: environmental and facility safety signs; ANSI Z535.3: criteria for safety symbols; ANZI Z535.4: product safety signs and labels). Warnings are primarily visual but can also be auditory, as in the case of a fire alarm. Warnings use sensory techniques that capture the attention of the employee; for instance, the use of the color red has been identified with danger, as has the use of a loud, discontinuous noise in emergency situations. After catching employees' attention, the warning provides information about the nature of the hazard and its potential effects on health and safety. This provides the employee with an opportunity to assess the risk of ignoring the warning. Finally, the warning provides some information about specific actions to take to avoid the hazard, such as "stay clear of the boom," or "stand back 50 feet from the crane," or "stay away from this area."

Developing good warnings starts with reviewing the ANSI standards, using the results of current scientific studies, and using good judgment. *The Handbook of Warnings* (Wogalter, 2006) is a good resource regarding the use and design of warnings. Considerations such as the educational level of employees and word comprehension, the placement of the warning, potential environmental distortions, wording of instructions, and employee sensory overload, just to name a few, must be taken into account. Even when good warnings are designed, their ability to influence employee behavior varies greatly. Even so, they provide the employee with an opportunity to make a reasoned choice regarding exposure. Warnings should never be used in place of engineering controls and should always serve as an adjunct to other means of hazard control unless other controls are not feasible.

Instructions provide direction to employees that will help them to avoid hazards or to more effectively deal with hazards. They are the behavioral model that can be followed to increase the probability of safe behavior to reduce risk of exposure. The basis of good instructions is a job analysis that provides detailed information on the job tasks, the environment, the tools, and materials used by employees. The job analysis will identify high-risk materials and situations. Based on verification of the information in the job analysis, a set of instructions on how to avoid hazardous situations can be developed. The implementation of such instructions to influence proper employee behavior is covered in the next section under training and safe behavior improvement.

Training the Employee to Avoid the Hazard

Training workers to improve their skills and to recognize hazardous conditions is a primary means for reducing exposures and accidents. Studies have found that safety and health training was effective in reducing employee risk (Burke et al., 2006; Cohen & Colligan, 1998; Lippin, Eckman, Calkin, & McQuiston, 2000; Luskin, Somers, Wooding, & Levenstein, 1992). *Training* can be defined as a systematic acquisition of knowledge, concepts, or skills that can lead to improved performance or behavior. Eckstrand (1964) detailed seven basic steps in training that are still useful today: (a) defining the training objectives, (b) developing criterion measures for evaluating the training process and outcomes, (c) developing or deriving the content and materials to be learned, (d) designing the techniques to be used to teach the content, (e) integrating the learners and the training program to achieve effective earning, (f) evaluating the extent of learning, and (g) modifying the training process to improve learner comprehension and retention of the content. These steps provide the foundation for the application of basic guidelines that can be used for designing the training content and integrating the content and the learner. Revelle (1980) examined a number of safety training methods that provide different approaches to achieve better safety performance in a variety of situations.

Two levels of objectives, global and specific, can be established in defining training objectives. The global objectives are the end goals that are to be met by the training program. For instance, a global objective might be the reduction of eye injuries by 50%. The specific objectives are those that are particular to each segment of the training program, including the achievements to be reached by the completion of each segment of training. A specific objective might be the ability to recognize eye injury hazards by the end of the hazard education segment. A basis for defining training objectives is the assessment of company safety problem areas. This can be done using hazard identification methods described earlier, such as injury statistics, inspections, and hazard surveys. Problems should be identified, ranked in importance, and then used to define training objectives.

To determine the success of the training process, criteria for evaluation need to be established. Hazard identification measures can be used to determine overall effectiveness. Thus, global objectives can be verified by determining a reduction in injuries (such as eye injuries) or the elimination of a substantial number of eye hazards.

The content of the training program should be developed on the basis of the learners' knowledge level, current skills, and aptitudes. The training content should be flexible enough to allow for individual differences in aptitudes, skills, and knowledge, as well as for individualized rates of learning. The training content should allow all learners to achieve a minimally acceptable level of health and safety knowledge and competence by the end of training. The specifics of the content deal with the desired skills to be learned and the hazards to be recognized and controlled.

Various techniques can be used to train workers. On-the-job training (OJT) has been used often to teach workers job skills and health and safety considerations. The effectiveness of such training can be influenced by the skill and effort of the supervisor and/or experienced workers doing the training. OJT emphasizes enhancing skills through observation and practice. In addition to OJT, classroom training can be used to teach concepts and to improve knowledge. Classroom training is best carried out in small groups in an area free of distractions to allow learners to concentrate on the subject matter. Training sessions should not be too long; we suggest not exceeding 30 min per session.

Once the success of the training program has been determined, the final stage is to make modifications as determined by the results of the evaluation. Such modifications can be done on a continuous basis as feedback on learners' performance and training deficiencies are acquired.

Improving Work Practices

Many workplace hazards are produced by the interaction between employees and their tools and environment, and some of these hazards cannot be eliminated through engineering controls. These hazards can be controlled when employees recognize the risks of the hazards and use safe behavior when they encounter the hazards. Such safe behavior may include following proper work procedures to ensure that hazards will not occur or taking special care to avoid a hazard when the hazard occurs. There are very few hazard control efforts that are not in some way dependent on the safe behavior of employees.

Conard (1983) listed a series of steps that can be used in developing and implementing work practices for eliminating occupational hazards: (a) define the hazardous work practices, (b) define the new work practices to reduce the hazards, (c) train employees when and how to do the desired work practices, (d) test the new work practices in the job setting, (e) install the new work practices using motivators, (f) monitor the effectiveness of the new work practices, (g) redefine the new work practices as needed, and (h) maintain proper employee habits regarding work practices using applied behavioral methods.

Hopkins, Conard, and Smith (1986) demonstrated the effectiveness of modifying employee work practices in reducing employee chemical exposures using the steps identified by Conard (1983). Hopkins (1999) discussed the principles of behavior modification as a means to control workplace exposures, and DeJoy (2005) discussed how behavior change programs could be complementary to organizational efforts to improve organizational safety climate and safety performance.

Hopkins (1999) recommended the use of incentives to sustain the improved work practices. There are many types of incentives, including money, tokens, privileges, social rewards, recognition, feedback, and participation. Positive incentives can be used to develop consistent work practice patterns, whereas negative incentives, such as punishment, often lead to employee resentment and long-term motivational problems. Research has demonstrated that the use of financial rewards in the form of increased hourly wage can have a beneficial effect on employee safety behaviors and reduced hazard exposure (Hopkins, 1999; Hopkins et al., 1986; M. J. Smith, Anger, Hopkins, & Conrad, 1983).

Conclusion

Reducing occupational injuries and illnesses requires a multifaceted approach that can define hazards, evaluate risks, establish means to control risks, and incorporate management, supervision, and employees actively in the process. This chapter has defined various workplace hazards and described methods to involve employees and managers in defining and controlling the identified risks. These specific methods for defining hazards, assessing the level of risk, engaging employees in hazard recognition and control, and implementing organizational structures for safety programs are the major elements of an occupational hazard control program that can lead to improved organizational safety.

Appendix 5.1

Useful Web Information Sources
American Association of Occupational Health Nurses. http://www.aaohn.org
American Board of Industrial Hygiene. http://www.abih.org
American College of Occupational and Environmental Medicine.
  http://www.acoem.org
American Council of Government Industrial Hygicnists. http://www.acgih.org
American Industrial Hygiene Association. http://www.aiha.org
American National Standards Institute. http://www.ansi.org
American Psychological Association. http://www.apa.org
American Society of Safety Engineers. http://www.asse.org
ASTM International. http://www.astm.org
Bureau of Labor Statistics. http://www.bls.gov
Centers for Disease Control and Prevention. http://www.cdc.gov
Human Factors and Ergonomics Society. http://www.hfes.org
International Ergonomics Association. http://www.iea.cc
International Labour Office. http://www.ilo.org
International Organization for Standardization. http://www.iso.org
National Institute for Environmental Health Sciences. http://www.niehs.nih.gov
National Institute for Occupational Safety and Health. http://www.cdc.gov/niosh
National Safety Council. http://www.nsc.org
Occupational Safety and Health Administration. http://www.osha.gov
U.S. Department of Justice. http://www.justice.gov
U.S. Department of Labor. http://www.dol.gov
U.S. Environmental Protection Agency. http://www.epa.gov
World Health Organization. http://www.who.int/en

References

Abkowitz, M. D. (2008). Study approach to effective planning and response. New York, NY: Wiley.

American Conference of Government Industrial Hygienists. (2008). *2008 TLVs and BEIs* [CD ROM]. Cincinnati, OH: Author.

American National Standards Institute. (1991). *ANSI Z535.1: Safety color code; ANSI Z535.2: environmental and facility safety signs; ANSI Z535.3: criteria for safety symbols; ANSI Z535.4: Product safety signs and labels.* Washington, DC: National Electrical Manufacturers Association.

American National Standards Institute. (1998). *ANSI Z535.1–ANSI Z535.4: Revised.* Washington, DC: National Electrical Manufacturers Association.

Best, A. M. (2008). *Best's loss control manual.* Oldwick, NJ: A. M. Best Company.

Boiano, J. M., & Hull, R. D. (2001). Development of a national occupational exposure survey and database associated with NIOSH hazard surveillance initiatives. *Applied Occupational and Environmental Hygiene, 16,* 128–134. doi:10.1080/104732201460217

Burke, M. J., Sarpy, S. A., Smith-Crowe, K., Chan-Serafin, S., Salvador, R. O., & Islam, G. (2006). Relative effectiveness of worker safety and health training methods. *American Journal of Public Health, 96,* 315–324. doi:10.2105/AJPH.2004.059840

Carayon, P., & Smith, M. J. (2000). Work organization and ergonomics. *Applied Ergonomics, 31,* 649–662. doi:10.1016/S0003-6870(00)00040-5

Cohen, A. (1977). Factors in successful occupational safety programs. *Journal of Safety Research, 9,* 168–178.

Cohen, A., & Colligan, M. J. (1998). *Assessing occupational safety and health training: A literature review.* Cincinnati, OH: U.S. Department of Health and Human Services, National Institute for Occupational Safety and Health.

Conard, R. (1983). *Employee work practices.* Cincinnati, OH: U.S. Department of Health and Human Services, National Institute for Occupational Safety and Health.

Cooper, C., & Smith, M. J. (1985). *Job stress in blue collar work.* London, England: Wiley.

DeJoy, D. M. (2005). Behavior changes versus culture change: Divergent approaches to managing workplace safety. *Safety Science, 43,* 105–129. doi:10.1016/j.ssci.2005.02.001

DeJoy, D. M., Schaffer, B. S., Wilson, M. G., Vandenberg, R. J., & Butts, M. M. (2004). Creating safer workplaces: Assessing the determinants and role of safety climate. *Journal of Safety Research, 35,* 81–90. doi:10.1016/j.jsr.2003.09.018

DiNardi, S. R. (1997). *The occupational environment: Its evaluation and control.* Washington, DC: American Industrial Hygiene Association Press.

Eckstrand, G. (1964). *Current status of the technology of training* (AMRL Document Technical Report). Fairfax, VA: U.S. Department of Defense.

Hagan, P. E., Montgomery, J. F., & O'Reilly, J. T. (2001). *Accident prevention manual: Vols. I and II* (12th ed.). Itasca, IL: National Safety Council.

Haight, J. M. (2008). *The safety professional's handbook: Vols. I and II.* Des Plains, IL: American Society of Safety Engineers.

Hendrick, H., & Kleiner, B. (2002). *Macroergonomics: Theory, methods, and applications.* Mahwah, NJ: Erlbaum.

Hopkins, B. L. (1999). The principles of behavior as an empirical theory and the usefulness of that theory in addressing practical problems. *Journal of Organizational Behavior Management, 19*(3), 67–74. doi:10.1300/J075v19n03_07

Hopkins, B. L., Conard, R. J., & Smith, M. J. (1986). Effective and reliable behavioral control technology. *American Industrial Hygiene Association Journal, 47,* 785–791. doi:10.1080/15298668691390665

Kletz, T. (2009). *What went wrong? Process plant disasters and how they could have been avoided* (5th ed.). Oxford, England: Elsevier (Butterworth Heinemann/ChemE).

Lippin, T. M., Eckman, A., Calkin, K. R., & McQuiston, T. H. (2000). Empowerment-based health and safety training: Evidence of workplace change from four industrial sectors. *American Journal of Industrial Medicine, 38,* 697–706. doi:10.1002/1097-0274(200012)38:6<697::AID-AJIM9>3.0.CO;2-T

Luskin, J., Somers, C., Wooding, J., & Levenstein, C. (1992). Teaching health and safety: Problems and possibilities for learner-centered training. *American Journal of Industrial Medicine, 22,* 665–676. doi:10.1002/ajim.4700220505

National Academy of Sciences. (2001). *Musculoskeletal disorders and the workplace.* Washington, DC: National Academy Press.

Neal, A., & Griffin, M. (2006). A study of the lagged relationships among safety climate, safety motivation, safety behavior, and accidents at the individual and group levels. *Journal of Applied Psychology, 91,* 946–953. doi:10.1037/0021-9010.91.4.946

Occupational Safety and Health Administration. (2001). *Motiva Enterprises LLC.* Retrieved from http://www.osha.gov/pls/imis/accidentsearch.accident_detail?id=200410611

Occupational Safety and Health Administration. (2002). *Hi-Temp Specialty Metals, Inc.* Retrieved from http://www.osha.gov/pls/imis/accidentsearch.accident_detail?id=201771698

Occupational Safety and Health Administration. (2003a). *CTa Acoustics Inc.* Retrieved from http://www.osha.gov/pls/imis/accidentsearch.accident_detail?id=201857570

Occupational Safety and Health Administration. (2003b). *West Pharmaceutical Services.* Retrieved from http://www.osha.gov/pls/imis/accidentsearch.accident_detail?id=200352961

Occupational Safety and Health Administration. (2004). *Formosa Plastics Corporation.* Retrieved from http://www.osha.gov/pls/imis/accidentsearch.accident_detail?id=2002712914

O'Neill, M. (1998). *Ergonomic design for organizational effectiveness.* New York, NY: CRC Press, Taylor & Francis Group.

Perkins, J. L. (2008). *Modern industrial hygiene: Vols. I and II.* Cincinnati, OH: American Conference of Government Industrial Hygienists.

Plog, B. A., & Quinlan, P. J. (2002). *Fundamentals of industrial hygiene.* Itasca, IL: National Safety Council.

Revelle, J. B. (1980). *Safety training methods.* New York, NY: Wiley-Interscience.

Salvendy, G. (2006). *Handbook of human factors and ergonomics.* New York, NY: Wiley. doi:10.1002/0470048204

Schulte, P. A. (2005). Characterizing the burden of occupational injury and disease. *Journal of Occupational and Environmental Medicine, 47,* 607–622. doi:10.1097/01.jom.0000165086.25595.9d

Sieber, W. K., Sundin, D. S., Frazier, T. M., & Robinson, C. F. (1991). Development, use and availability of a job exposure matrix based on national occupational hazard survey data. *American Journal of Industrial Medicine, 20,* 163–174. doi:10.1002/ajim.4700200204

Smith, K. U. (1990). Hazard management. In *Proceedings of the Human Factors and Ergonomics Society annual meeting* (pp. 1020–1024). Santa Monica, CA: Human Factors and Ergonomics Society.

Smith, M. J., Anger, K., Hopkins, B., & Conrad, R. (1983). Behavioral–psychological approaches for controlling employee chemical exposures. In *Proceedings of the tenth world congress on the prevention of occupational accidents and diseases.* Geneva, Switzerland: International Social Security Association.

Smith, M. J., & Carayon, P. (1995). New technology, automation and work organization: Stress problems and improved technology implementations strategies. *International Journal of Human Factors in Manufacturing, 5,* 99–116. doi:10.1002/hfm.4530050107

Smith, M. J., Cohen, H. H., Cohen, A., & Cleveland, R. (1978). Characteristics of successful safety programs. *Journal of Safety Research, 10,* 5–15.

Smith, M. J., & Sainfort, P. C. (1989). A balance theory of job design and for stress reduction. *International Journal of Industrial Ergonomics, 4,* 67–79. doi:10.1016/0169-8141(89)90051-6

Wogalter, M. S. (2006). *Handbook of warnings.* Mahwah, NJ: Erlbaum.

Zohar, D. (1980). Safety climate in industrial organizations: Theoretical and applied implications. *Journal of Applied Psychology, 65,* 96–102. doi:10.1037/0021-9010.65.1.96

Zohar, D., & Luria, G. (2005). A multilevel model of safety climate: Cross-level relationship between organization and group-level climates. *Journal of Applied Psychology, 90,* 616–628. doi:10.1037/0021-9010.90.4.616

6

An Integral Framework for Organizational Wellness: Core Technology, Practice Models, and Case Studies

Joel B. Bennett, Royer F. Cook,
and Kenneth R. Pelletier

Cross-disciplinary, scientific training of occupational health psychologists prepares them to play an important, strategic role in helping employers. With increases in work stress and health costs, employers use cost-cutting tactics such as reductions in health benefits and service integration (e.g., Finch & Phillips, 2005; Society for Human Resource Management, 2009). But employers can also achieve cost savings by integrating working conditions, behavior, and individual risk factors. They also can apply evidence-based knowledge to build efficient and effective interventions and work across different service areas (Guidotti, 2008).

This chapter seeks to help psychologists create healthy companies. We use an *integral* model of organizational wellness (Bennett, Cook, & Pelletier, 2003) to propose core practitioner competencies and review case studies showing how we have practiced these competencies in attempts to apply evidence-based knowledge.

Because of the cross-disciplinary nature of their work (Smith & Carayon, 2003; see also Chapter 5, this volume), occupational health psychologists benefit from collaboration with neighboring fields: risk managers, medical directors, employee assistance program (EAP) professionals, human resource professionals, and directors of prevention and wellness. Although the past decade has seen much growth in evidence-based programs (Harper, Mulvey, & Robinson, 2003; Levant, 2005; Walker & London, 2007), there is a great need to integrate these programs into work settings. We face a challenge of *scalability*—that is, the capacity to take programs from research and make them work in larger, business, or commercial settings.

We call this framework *integral* for several reasons. First, most wellness programs focus on physical health. It is time to integrate curricula that prevent depression, substance abuse, and other mental health concerns and to collaborate with EAPs (see Cooper, Dewe, & O'Driscoll, 2003; see also Chapter 18, this

Some of the research described in this chapter was supported in part by Grants DA015283 (National Institute of Drug Abuse) and UD1 SP11129 (Center for Substance Abuse Prevention, Substance Abuse and Mental Health Administration).

volume). Second, there is a growing trend to integrate health promotion with cousin disciplines (e.g., health and safety, health and productivity). Third, research utilization will be optimal when research participants or clients are partners and empowered as prevention advocates. A sincere science-to-practice approach should encourage lay practitioners to use evidence-based knowledge at the local level (Shain & Suurvali, 2003). Finally, effective health promotion requires a systemic approach with equal support for positive work conditions and healthy lifestyle (e.g., LaMontagne, Keegel, Louie, Ostry, & Landsbergis, 2007).

In the previous edition of this handbook, we identified seven themes in definitions of organizational health (Bennett et al., 2003) that can shape a core technology for occupational health psychology (see Table 6.1). By *core technology,* we mean a set of agreed-upon competencies that define the profession. Such competencies include the ability to design efforts that (a) treat multiple aspects of worker well-being; (b) align group, departmental, and leadership levels and not solely focus on individual health (see Heaney, 2003; see also Chapter 17, this volume); (c) utilize psychometric tools for assessment; (d) are evidence based (i.e., the practitioner pays attention to outcomes and standards of quality, efficacy, fidelity, and replicability); (e) attend to environmental, economic, and other extraorganizational factors that can enhance program success; (f) maintain awareness of climactic stresses in worksites and design programs to address risks; and (g) remain sensitive to an organization's readiness for programs.

The first part of this chapter reviews various practitioner models for promoting organizational wellness, updates the evidence base on health promotion (e.g., LaMontagne et al., 2007; Pelletier, 2005, 2009), and discusses the Internet as a method for promoting workplace health. The second part reviews case studies to demonstrate applications of an integral approach.

The Healthy Company: Practice Models

Most companies will not commit to healthy organizational practices unless they cut costs and improve productivity. Practitioners can align healthy practices, cost containment, and productivity goals through health promotion approaches (Heaney & Goetzel, 1997), cultural interventions (J. Allen, 2008a), and their combination. Before we review these approaches, it helps to know the relationship between behavioral risks and health care costs.

Introduction to Modifiable Health Risks and Cost Expenditures

A number of studies have documented clear relationships between health risks and financial and productivity loss. Perhaps the most influential study (Anderson et al., 2000; Goetzel et al., 1998; $N = 46,026$) found that medical expenditures were significantly higher for employees high versus low risk in seven of 10 risk categories (depression, stress level, blood glucose, body weight, tobacco, blood pressure, and exercise habits). The difference between those with and without a risk was highest for those reporting depression (70.2% higher) and stress

Table 6.1. Postulates of Integral Organizational Wellness and Core Technology

Theme	Postulate of organizational health (and key references)	Core technology for practice of integral wellness
1. Multiple dimensions of health	A healthy organization considers multiple dimensions of well-being (social, emotional, physical, spiritual; Adams et al., 2000; Fleisher et al., 1996).	Provide health promotion programs that simultaneously focus on multiple dimensions of well-being.
2. Multiple levels of health	A healthy organization considers multiple levels of health (individual, groups, departments, as well as the entire organization) and is aware of cross-level relationships across areas (Kidwell, Mossholder, & Bennett, 1997; Söderfeldt et al., 1997).	Provide (systemic or comprehensive) programs that address individual, group, leadership, and environmental aspects of the organizations.
3. Include self-assessments for adaptability	Using information from above, a healthy organization continually monitors its state of health and adapts to maintain optimal well-being across levels and dimensions (Bennis, 1993; Schein, 1965).	Utilize reliable and valid (psychometrically sound) instruments to proactively assess well-being across levels and to drive programs that meet identified risks and needs.
4. Make effort in health promotion	A healthy organization makes an ongoing effort to provide programs and policies that increase the well-being of employees (O'Donnell, 2001, and *American Journal of Health Promotion*).	Provide evidence-based programs or programs with grounding in scientific principles.
5. Maintain awareness of fitness and congruence	A healthy organization maintains levels of relative fitness or congruence at two levels: (a) between the organization and the external environment (market, economy, and community), and (b) between components within the organization (i.e., communication between individuals, groups, and executive levels) (Brown & Eisenhardt, 1998; Kelly & Allison, 1999; Kozlowski & Salas, 1997).	Maintain awareness of how "fit" the organization is both within the market (economy) and internally. Caveat: Do not provide programs and assessments (1–4 above) in a vacuum.

(continued)

Table 6.1. Postulates of Integral Organizational Wellness and Core Technology *(Continued)*

Theme	Postulate of organizational health (and key references)	Core technology for practice of integral wellness
6. Maintain awareness of core tension	A healthy organization is aware of and addresses the various tensions involved in maintaining levels of optimal health (e.g., serving internal and external customers) (Mayrhofer, 1997).	Assess the work climate to determine areas of relative risk and strength.
7. Maintain awareness of regression and development	A healthy organization maintains an awareness of cycles of growth, regression, and deterioration in overall organizational vitality. This awareness is used to make adjustments in health efforts (see theme 4) and respond to different levels of incongruence (theme 5) and tension (theme 6) (Kilburg, Stokes, & Kuruvilla, 1998).	Remain sensitive to organizational stages of changes and the level of organizational readiness for different types of programs.

Adapted from "Toward an Integrated Framework for Comprehensive Organizational Wellness: Concepts, Practices, and Research in Workplace Health Promotion," by J. B. Bennett, R. F. Cook, & K. R. Pelletier, 2003. In J. C. Quick & L. E. Tetrick (Eds.), *Handbook of Occupational Health Psychology* (pp. 71–78). Washington, DC: American Psychological Association.

(46.3% higher). Moreover, employees at high risk of stress accounted for the largest incremental expenditures of any high-risk category. Findings suggest mental health risks may be more important than other (e.g., cardiovascular) risks.

Subsequent studies from the University of Michigan highlight the impact of health on employer costs. Wang et al. (2003) found a significant relationship between gradations of body mass index (BMI) and medical costs ($N = 177,971$). Except for the underweight group, medical costs increased with BMI. In studies with different samples, Edington and colleagues (Edington, 2001; Musich, Hook, Barnett, & Edington, 2003) have shown that increased health risks are associated with greater incurred medical expenses. Burton et al. (2005) found that 10 health risk factors were significantly associated with work limitations (from greatest to least, these were use of relaxation medication, life dissatisfaction, high stress, safety belt usage, job dissatisfaction, current smokers, physical inactivity, poor physical health, BMI $\geq$ 30, and high blood pressure; $N = 28,375$).

A review of 113 studies demonstrated a clear relationship between health conditions and presenteeism (Schultz & Edington, 2007). *Presenteeism* is defined as lost productivity that occurs when employees come to work but perform below par because of any kind of illness. Musich, Hook, Baaner, and Edington (2006) found that increased presenteeism was significantly associated with poor working conditions, ineffective management/leadership, and work–life imbalance (adjusting for age, gender, health risks, and medical conditions). Many other studies, some reviewed in this volume, document that working conditions contribute to presenteeism (Allen, 2009) and employee health and productivity status (Benavides, Benach, Diez-Roux, & Roman, 2000; Lowe, Schellenberg, & Shannon, 2003; Mausner-Dorsch & Eaton, 2000).

Although health risks predict medical and productivity costs, such risks can be modified through employer efforts. The following sections review four practitioner models that can assist in these efforts. Common elements across these models include linking health with productivity, managing risk, building healthy cultures (R. F. Allen & Allen, 1987), and promoting leadership health (e.g., Quick, Cooper, Gavin, & Quick, 2002). We also review various awards that recognize healthy companies as these may shape or impact practices efforts.

Health and Productivity Management

Broadly defined, health and productivity management (HPM) has three goals: (a) to integrate and coordinate different types of services that promote health when workers are sick, injured, or balancing work–life issues; (b) to increase productivity; and (c) to link the first and second goals—that is, to manage services (medical benefits, workers' compensation, risk management, EAPs, occupational safety) in ways that promote health and productivity. Overviews of HPM can be found in Goetzel and Ozminkowski (2000) and Goetzel, Guindon, Turshen, and Ozminkowski (2001). The Institute for Health and Productivity Management (http://www.ihpm.org) publishes a quarterly magazine, *Health and Productivity Management,* with articles on specific tools and practices. For example, Hagen (2004) described organizational solutions to obesity. Brennan (2005) explained Boeing's approach to risk reduction through health risk appraisals and web-based and telephonic interventions. Baase (2005) reported a study at Dow Corporation showing that emotional disorders have the highest cost to the company.

In a benchmarking study of 43 organizations, Goetzel et al. (2001) identified 10 best-practice HPM themes: (a) alignment between HPM and business strategy; (b) an interdisciplinary team focus in which diverse areas work together (e.g., human resources, employee benefits, safety, legal, and health promotion); (c) a champion or a team of champions with a sense of purpose; (d) senior management and business operations as key members of the team; (e) prevention, health promotion, and wellness staff; (f) emphasis on quality-of-life improvement, not just cost cutting; (g) data, measurement, reporting, and evaluation becoming increasingly important over time; (h) constant communication directed throughout the organization; (i) constant need to improve by learning from others; and (j) having fun.

Behavioral Risk Management

Behavioral risk management (BRM), often associated with the EAP field, was described by Yandrick (1996) as addressing nine different risks: (a) problems resulting from high stress, (b) work–life imbalances, (c) employee negligence or indifference, (d) job-related violence, (e) disgruntlement/litigiousness, (f) sabotage and theft, (g) conflicts due to racial or gender disharmony, (h) alcohol and drug abuse, and (i) malingering on disability health insurance or workers' compensation. Effective BRM requires that organizations maintain a close relationship with the service organization that provides behavioral health care and collaborate with those providers or EAPs in managing risk through prevention and health care promotion.

BRM combines needs assessment with customized programming for reducing behavioral risks in five core steps: (a) conduct a behavioral risk audit (using survey, interviews, and organizational records) to determine the level of risks in the nine categories; (b) aggregate these data to derive an overall picture of risk; (c) assess both individual and organizational risk, as well as effectiveness of current risk management practices; (d) integrate this information through a management information system to help determine which activities are having an impact on individual/organizational risk and which programs are needed; and (e) use information from Steps a through d to develop a prevention, early intervention, or health promotion strategy. Returning to Step a, examine changes to assess program effectiveness. Thus, BRM is an ongoing integrated process. Yandrick (1996) provided several case examples of organizations that are attempting to control costs through BRM processes, including DuPont, the University of California, U.S. Oil, and the World Bank. Readers interested in BRM may also consult Wolfe and Parker (1994) and Steinbach (2000).

Healthy Culture Planning

Judd Allen and colleagues developed the healthy culture model in organizational health (J. Allen & Bellingham, 1994; R. F. Allen & Allen, 1987). Core premises are that workplace social norms promote either healthy or unhealthy lifestyles, and the organization-level interventions can effectively develop norms that promote health. This culture change model has evolved over 30 years and has recently produced two trade texts (J. Allen 2008a, 2008b). The emphasis on healthy work culture is also seen in Canada's National Quality Institute (http://www.nqi.org) healthy workplace initiative (see McKeown, 2001).

There are four phases for building supportive cultures. Phase 1 analyzes the current culture and seeks leadership commitment. Phase 2 creates high involvement of all those in the change effort, often through a workshop that enables participants to visualize the desired culture. Phase 3 integrates systems through programs for individual self-help, peer support, organizational support, and leadership development. Phase 4 repeats evaluation of performance, programs, and culture to determine progress and set new objectives. Healthy culture planning is akin to other large-scale interventions in organizational development but with a special focus on health. *The Change Handbook* (Holman, Devane, & Cady, 2007) also provides a compendium of over 60 approaches to creating positive cultural change.

Healthy Leadership (The Ripple Effect)

Leadership is a key feature in each of the above approaches. Research suggests that managers have a ripple effect: Leader behavior affects employee well-being (Arnold, Turner, Barling, Kelloway, & McKee, 2007; Gavin & Kelley, 1978; Gilbreath & Benson, 2004). In one study, workers who felt that they were treated fairly by their bosses had lower cardiovascular risk up to 8 years later (Kivimäki et al., 2005). Many studies found an inverse relationship between supportive behavior in immediate supervisors and employee ratings of burnout (Burke, Shearer, & Deszca, 1984; Constable & Russell, 1986; Russell, Altmaier, & Van Velzen, 1987; Seltzer & Numerof, 1988). When leaders were perceived as being concerned, honest, and consistent, subordinates experienced reduced stress (Alimo-Metcalfe & Alban-Metcalfe, 2003). Conversely, workers with supervisors who ridiculed or mistreated subordinates reported higher levels of depression, anxiety, and emotional exhaustion 6 months later (Tepper, 2000).

A longitudinal study of female hospital workers across 10 different locations showed that managerial practices predicted sickness absence, minor psychiatric morbidity, and self-rated health status 2 years later (Kivimäki, Elovainio, Vahtera, & Ferrie, 2003). In a meta-analysis of 73 independent studies of perceived organizational support (POS), Rhoades and Eisenberger (2002) found supervisor support had the greatest relationship with POS and that POS itself correlated with reduced strain such as reduced fatigue, burnout, anxiety, and headaches. Finally, a meta-analysis showed that worker perceptions of leadership had a significant relationship with their psychological well-being (Parker et al., 2003).

There are a number of efforts to improve leadership health or guidance to integrate health promotion with manager development. These include the "Corporate Athlete" program (http://hpinstitute.com; Loehr & Schwartz, 2003) and two new initiatives, "Leading by Example: CEOs on the Business Case for

Worksite Health Promotion" (Partnership for Prevention, 2009) and "CEO Cancer Gold Standard" (http://www.cancergoldstandard.com). These initiatives foster CEOs as role models for corporate health promotion. The model by Quick, Macik-Frey, and Cooper (2007) identifies unique risk and strength factors associated with executive health. Risks include loneliness of command, work demands, and failures. Strengths include physical fitness and maintaining an executive support network. Management interventions have shown to improve leadership practices (Cunningham & Kitson, 2000; Kelloway & Barling, 2000; Zohar, 2002) as well as health outcomes (Theorell, Emdad, Arnetz, & Weingarten, 2001). The executive coaching literature also suggests promising results (Kampa-Kokesch, 2001; Smither, London, Flautt, Vargas, & Kucine, 2003; Wasylyshyn, 2003).

Awarding Healthy Company Practices

A company may adopt any of these practice models to be recognized as being a good and healthy place to work. A growing number of awards provide such recognition. The list has more than doubled in the past 10 years. These awards may contribute to the crystallization of a cross-industry social norm and an increase in the overall level of organizational health in the economy:

- *Psychologically Healthy Workplace Awards* (http://www.phwa.org) include an annual national award as well as awards made by state, provincial, and territorial psychological associations. Since 1999, 48 associations across the United States and Canada have recognized more than 300 organizations.
- *The Corporate Health Achievement Award* (http://www.chaa.org) was established in 1996 by the American College of Occupational and Environmental Medicine.
- *Behavioral Health Awards,* established in 2007 by the National Business Group on Health, recognize employers that design innovative benefits or programs in behavioral health (see Slavit & Flood, 2007).
- *The C. Everett Koop National Health Award* acknowledges companies for comprehensive wellness efforts (Ziegler, 1998; see http://healthproject. stanford.edu/koop/work.html for a list of winners since 1994, along with evaluation summaries).
- *Corporate Health and Productivity Management Awards* are provided by the Institute of Health and Productivity Management (http://www.ihpm. org). Since 2001, IHPM have given awards to about 30 large-sized employers.
- *Wellness Councils of America* has developed seven benchmarks for exemplary wellness initiatives and presents bronze, silver, and gold "well workplace" awards (Hunnicutt, 2006; see http://www.welcoa.org for a list of winners since 1993, also organized by U.S. state).
- *The Canadian Healthy Workplace Award* (see http://www.nqi.ca) provides significant guidance on how to work toward receiving an award.
- *Workforce Magazines "Optimas Award"* for promoting employee quality of life (http://www.workforce.com)

- *Fortune Magazine's "Top 100 Companies to Work For"* (http://www. fortune.com). This entails surveying employees with a "Great Place to Work Trust Index" (a climate measure), a culture audit, and analysis of supporting materials (e.g., employee handbooks, newsletters, and videos; see Fawcett, Rhoads, & Burnah, 2004; Levering & Moskowitz, 1994; http://www.greatplacetowork.com).

Research is needed to identify common elements of award criteria and also determine the after-effects of these awards.

Summary and Application of Practitioner Approaches: Redundancy and Integration

Healthy companies use strategies that integrate elements across the five practices: link health with productivity, manage risk, build healthy cultures, develop leaders, and seek recognition for health efforts. These practices appear to serve interdependent functions. Each may entail routines that help other practices such that mastery in one practice may eventually compensate for deficiencies in others. For example, if a company ineffectively manages risk, it is possible that efforts in leadership development (i.e., around safety) may mitigate risk.

Health Promotion and Stress and Disease Management: Building the Evidence Base

In this section, we review two streams of intervention research relevant to an integral approach: comprehensive health promotion and systemic-level stress management. We also point out areas for improvement and list insights abstracted from these previous reviews. There is substantial evidence that the workplace can be an effective vehicle for educating workers on the powerful role of behavior on health and for promoting both health behavior and healthy workplaces to prevent disease. Collectively, almost 150 studies were conducted between 1980 and 2008 that demonstrate the clinical and cost effectiveness of comprehensive health promotion and disease management programs delivered at worksites (Pelletier, 2005, 2009). A review (1990–2005) of the job stress intervention literature also reveals 90 studies (LaMontagne et al., 2007) that demonstrate positive outcomes with a wide variety of populations, sizes of worksites, and varying degrees of methodological quality.

Results from health promotion research suggest that providing individualized risk reduction for all employees, including high-risk employees in the context of comprehensive programming, is the critical element of worksite interventions. Results from the stress management literature also suggest that systems-level interventions may be most effective. Systemic interventions simultaneously target the physical work environment (e.g., noise level), the organization (e.g., job design), and the individual employee (e.g., employee participation). One caveat is that studies lacking statistically significant results tend not to be published and may result in a publication bias of positive outcomes.

There have been several reviews of health promotion studies (Goetzel, 2001; Pelletier, 1991, 1993, 1996) and updates on 28 studies conducted between 2000 and 2008 (Pelletier, 2005, 2009). Comprehensive health promotion and disease management programs are

> programs that provide an ongoing, integrated, program of health promotion and disease prevention that integrates the particular components (i.e. smoking cessation, stress management, lipid reduction, etc.) into a coherent, ongoing program that is consistent with corporate objectives and includes program evaluation. (Pelletier, 2005, p. 1053)

The most significant clinical and cost outcomes are likely to be evidenced when an intervention is selective or focused on identified individualized risks. Such a disease management intervention needs to provide focused, consistent, sustained behavioral change, plus appropriate medical oversight. A multiple risk factor intervention model is also applicable to single risk factors, such as smoking and hypertension, as well as to other chronic conditions, such as stress, arthritis, musculoskeletal disorders, video display terminal disabilities, back injuries or pain, and cancer, which constitute major clinical and cost liabilities to employers.

One of the most rigorous worksite studies assessed multiple risk interventions for cardiovascular disease at General Motors. The initial study addressed weight loss and smoking cessation among 7,804 employees in four different GM worksites over a 3-year intervention period (e.g., Erfurt, Foote, & Heirich, 1991; Erfurt & Holtyn, 1991) and found that more frequent follow-up counseling was associated with greater participation in smoking cessation, weight loss, and greater reduction in blood pressure among employees with hypertension.

Pelletier (2005, 2009) described methodological trends in clinical trials research on health promotion: (a) a decrease in formal randomized clinical trials (RCTs) in worksites, (b) an increase in companies conducting focused disease management programs with pre/post designs but not formal RCTs, and (c) an increase in companies conducting observational studies to track outcomes of participants versus nonparticipants in programs. Studies suggest that comprehensive and high-risk intervention programming is critical to successful interventions.

In addition to Pelletier's reviews, Aldana (1998) identified 24 studies that assessed the effect of health promotion on medical expenses. Reductions in medical care cost and absenteeism were significant in most cases, and the average cost–benefit ratio for studied health care costs and calculated cost–benefit ratios was $3.35 for every $1.00 spent. Aldana and Pronk (2001) concluded that even the most effective health promotion programs can affect only a portion, perhaps up to 20%, of all absenteeism.

Unfortunately, although many of the studies reviewed have exhibited adequate-to-strong methodologies, some have been characterized by methodological weaknesses, including weak designs, brief follow-up periods, low participation rates and selection bias, and sample attrition. Randomized designs are seldom used, and too often the worksite has not been appropriately used as the unit of analysis. Because virtually all worksite programs are voluntary, low participation rates (sometimes only 10%) and self-selection plague such studies.

On the basis of the accumulated evidence, we extract a few insights on the effectiveness of worksite wellness. First, programs integrated with human resource strategy and accepted as the norm are likely to be well implemented and effective. Second, feeling valued as an employee, having job control to reduce job strain, and being satisfied with work predict employee health behaviors. However, cultural factors cannot fully address employees at high risk for disease; they also need programs that target specific risks. Finally, it is important to consider the type of outcome and the temporal dimension when assessing effectiveness (see Bennett et al., 2003).

Workplace Health Promotion and the Internet

An increasing number of working adults search the Internet for personal health information. In recent years, an area of "eHealth" has developed, representing the use of emerging information and communication technology, especially the Internet, to improve or enable health and health care (Eng, 2001; Norman et al., 2007). Many web-based health programs have been successful in reaching workers and promoting positive outcomes (see reviews by Griffiths, Lindenmeyer, Powell, Lowe, & Thorogood, 2006; Wantland, Portillo, Holzemer, Slaughter, & McGhee, 2004). The most effective have been characterized by a short duration, interactivity, some tailoring to fit users' individual needs, a cognitive or behavioral approach, and being evidence based (Lustria, Brown, & Davis, 2007). In addition, participants who used programs more tended to have the best outcomes (Norman et al., 2007). Studies also support eHealth programs for stress, mood, and substance use concerns (Billings, Cook, Hendrickson, & Dove, 2008; Cook, Billings, Hersch, Back, & Hendrickson, 2007; McPherson, Cook, Back, Hersch, & Hendrickson, 2006).

Several features of the Internet make it attractive for eHealth at work. In their review of 83 studies, Lustria et al. (2007) identified several of these features, such as relatively low development costs and ease of personalization. Although younger users are the most numerous, Internet use among older users increased dramatically from 2005 to 2008, reaching rates above 80% for adults between the ages of 40 and 64 (Jones & Fox, 2009).

Case Studies in Integral Organizational Wellness

The following case studies may bring pragmatic grounding to the above reviews. The first half of this chapter focused more on content issues, trends, and findings in the research literature. This section describes intervention and process issues gleaned from practical experience. We hope these case studies convey practice-based knowledge and help students think about how they might apply insights from science. Both cases pertain to the dissemination of evidence-based programs in workplace substance abuse prevention (Bennett & Lehman, 2003; see also the National Registry of Evidence-Based Programs and Practices website: http://www.nrepp.samhsa.gov).

Integral Case Study 1: Understanding Neighbor Disciplines

The first case highlights perspectives associated with different practitioner roles. We assessed perceptions of three professional groups: wellness practitioners (i.e., those who deliver health promotion programs to workers), EAP providers, and human resource professionals. Groups used an Internet (e-learning) program that educated in evidence-based wellness.

BACKGROUND. National surveys of professions suggest a drive toward greater integration of health services and a need for evidence-based wellness. Herlihy and Attridge (2005) reported results from several surveys of professional groups, including human resources, EAPs, and both wellness and work-life service providers. Findings showed greater market demand for service integration and increasingly complex vendor arrangements. Another survey of wellness practitioners ($N \approx 1,000$) found many partnering with EAPs, health, and insurance providers (Hunnicutt, 2006). Practitioners wanted further assistance to strengthen their wellness program, especially for collecting data to drive their health efforts.

The lack of integration appears to have negative consequences for human resources (HR) professionals. Finch and Phillips (2005) reported a lack of integration among health care vendors, including managed behavioral health, and pharmacy benefits. They claimed significant quality and accountability problems have resulted, making it difficult for HR consumers to monitor success of behavioral health programs. Poor integration is partly due to the greater proliferation of wellness benefits over the past 5 years. Surveys on health benefits conducted by the Society for Human Resource Management (2007, 2008, 2009) show general year-to-year increases in wellness, health screening, smoking cessation, chiropractic, and EAP programs. Of interest is a steady decrease in worksites offering stress reduction programs, from 19% in 2006 to 11% in 2009.

APPLICATION. In response to these trends, we developed an Internet-based expert system that trains professionals in assessing, designing, delivering, and evaluating prevention programs (Bennett, 2007). The program is an "expert" system in that it trains individuals to develop knowledge that would otherwise require the use of expert consultants. The goal of the program is to provide professionals knowledge and tools for using more evidence-based approaches in their work. Program features include a return-on-investment estimation tool, program planning tools, access to a library of evidence-based programs, a list of strategies for program delivery, and a deployable survey of healthy work climate with a database for compiling results. Professionals ($N = 200$) from businesses of varying size ($M = 3,200$; $Mdn = 600$) representing 42 states and 15 industries around the United States were recruited to receive the program. Their job was in health promotion/occupational health, employee assistance/behavioral health, or human resources.

Practitioners were surveyed about their roles and efforts in health promotion and their response to the expert program. We hypothesized that the program would affect occupations in different ways. While we expected that wellness practitioners would be at the forefront in implementing physical health programs, HR professionals may have more decision-making power regarding implementation, and EAP practitioners would have the greatest understanding of mental health concerns among working adults. Study participants indicated the degree to which their worksite ("target worksite") used various health programs (see Table 6.2). Findings indicated a greater emphasis on programs that target physical health, an equal emphasis on mental health for both wellness and EAP practitioners, and less implementation by HR professionals.

HR professionals may be the least likely to implement programs as they generally decide to outsource that function. Figure 6.1 shows the percentage of participants responding to items about role implementation, decision-making power, actual program delivery, and understanding that programs can address substance abuse. These data were collected in a posttraining survey, and the figure combines participants across experimental and control conditions. As expected, HR professionals have the greatest decision-making power, EAP professionals have the most knowledge to address substance abuse, and wellness professionals are most likely to provide programs but have less knowledge to address substance abuse.

Table 6.2. Mean Frequency That Target Worksite Offers Programs (According to Three Primary Job Types)

| | Primary job in organization | | | |
Target worksite	Health promotion (n = 44)	EAP (n = 60)	Human resources (n = 45)	$F(2, 146)$ (combined effects)
Wellness programs targeting physical health	3.55	2.20	2.22	18.68***
Wellness programs targeting mental health	2.39	2.38	1.73	6.98***
Wellness programs targeting energy	2.00	1.92	1.53	2.84
Wellness programs targeting alcohol/drug misuse	1.56	2.18	1.58	7.99***
Stress management programs	2.16	2.30	1.60	6.60**
Work–life balance programs	2.07	1.87	1.58	2.99
Safety programs	1.91	1.64	2.09	2.39
Communication or team work programs	1.84	1.84	1.71	<1
EAP awareness programs	2.16	2.78	2.07	6.50**
Tobacco programs	1.77	1.54	1.24	3.95*
Alcohol awareness	1.40	1.69	1.27	<1
Programs on use/misuse of prescription drugs	1.30	1.31	1.22	<1

Note. Participants were asked, "Over the past few months, indicate the frequency with which each of the following was provided." Response categories were 1 = *never,* 2 = *once or twice,* 3 = *almost weekly,* 4 = *weekly,* 5 = *weekly or daily.* EAP = employee assistance program.
*$p < .05$. **$p < .01$. ***$p < .001$.

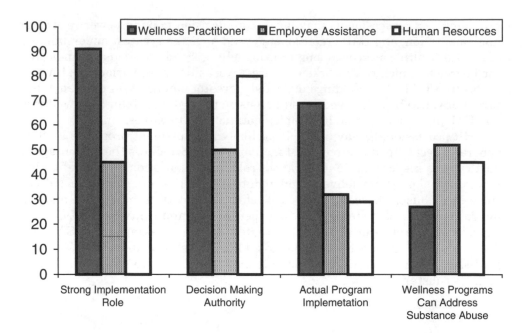

Figure 6.1. Cross-occupational comparisons in health promotion program implementation and knowledge. For all four items, there were significant differences across the practitioner groups ($phi > .37$, ps < .05): wellness practitioner ($n = 46$), employee assistance program (EAP) practitioner ($n = 60$), and human resources ($n = 45$). Strong Implementation Role shows the percentage of respondents indicating "play a strong, very important, or most significant role" in implementing any of the programs listed in Table 6.1. Decision Making Authority shows the percentage indicating "much, very much, or great" decision-making authority in implementing programs. Actual Program Implementation depicts the percentage indicating "we have delivered programs, delivered them for a while, or continually deliver programs." Wellness Programs Can Address Substance Abuse shows the percentage agreeing with the statement, "It is possible to implement a wellness program that addresses alcohol or drug abuse at the same time."

We randomly assigned practitioners to receive the expert system or to a no-training control group. Posttraining surveys revealed significant differences on several outcomes; for example, compared with controls, program recipients reported greater knowledge of and intentions to use evidence-based programs, greater ability to assess workplace needs, and greater expectations about their role as wellness advocates. Findings generally applied across professional groups, but EAPs were most likely to report that wellness programs can also address substance abuse. This study is important for several reasons. First, it is possible to educate professionals from neighboring disciplines about evidence-based wellness using a common e-learning platform. Second, the platform enhanced intentions to use such programs. The study also allowed us to use the core occupational health competencies described in Table 6.1. Most important, we helped professionals use a climate measure to assess multiple levels of health as part of a wellness effort, improving their own self-efficacy (also see Schwab & Bennett, 2007, 2008).

Integral Case Study 2: Integral Prevention and Bringing Programs to Scale

The second case highlights a model we used to address forces that come into play when adapting evidence-based programs.

BACKGROUND. Employee perception of social support at work predicts well-being and reduced health risks (Humphrey, Nahrgang, & Morgeson, 2007; Parker et al., 2003; Rhoades & Eisenberger, 2002). In one study, perceived group cohesion was associated with reduced risk of worker substance abuse (Bennett & Lehman, 1996, 1998). Such findings dictated the development of a new program, titled Team Awareness, that was recently entered into the National Registry of Evidence Based Programs (Brounstein, Gardner, & Backer, 2006), along with positive ratings for effectiveness and capacity for dissemination. Team Awareness (TA)—combining peer referral, team building, and drug-free workplace programming—has been shown to reduce health risks in research trials (Bennett & Lehman, 2001, 2002; Bennett, Patterson, Reynolds, Wiitala, & Lehman, 2004; Lehman, Reynolds, & Bennett, 2003; Patterson, Bennett, & Wiitala, 2005; Reynolds & Lehman, 2008). The classroom-based program includes interactive modules on stress management, communication, policy awareness, and peer-to-peer encouragement for health problems. Since 2002, more than 7,000 workers have been reached in various settings, including health care, small businesses, and the military. To adapt TA to these settings, we have used focus groups, adaptation retreats, culture assessments, and policy analyses.

APPLICATION. These experiences led us to develop an integral model of prevention to assist workplaces in bringing experimental programs to scale. This model was informed from previous work on collaboration, local adaptation, and capacity building (Backer, 2000; Chinman, Imm, & Wandersman, 2004; MacLean et al., 2003; Shain & Suurvali, 2003; Stevenson & Mitchell, 2003; Wandersman, 2003).

The model views efforts to take evidence-based programs to scale as a coordination of four distinct processes (see Figure 6.2). We propose that each process is necessary to make a program developed in a research setting work effectively in a business context for worker health. Each process comes to the foreground at different points during the adaptation to delivery to dissemination process. The four processes exist in two pairs, with each pair viewed on a continuum rather than as polar opposites. The first pair is Adaptation (modification of program elements for enculturation and success at local levels), which compares with Fidelity (ensuring that core principles and program elements are preserved). The second pair is Capacity Building (marketing, efforts at collaboration, sensitivity to readiness, relationship building, and stakeholder involvement), which compares with Prevention Intervention (final program design, delivery, and evaluation).

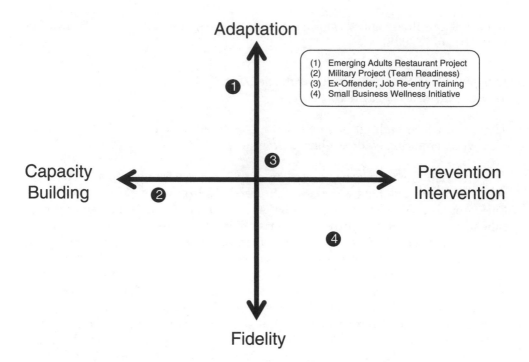

Figure 6.2. Graphic display of integral model of prevention. The figure places each of the four projects according to their emphasis along the two dimensions: Capacity Building–Prevention Intervention and Adaptation–Fidelity. For example, the small business wellness initiative (4) emphasized delivering the intervention with fidelity, whereas the military project (2) focused almost entirely on capacity building.

The integral model emphasizes features of organizational change (adaptation) as they relate to implementing an evidence-based program rather than focusing on the specific content of the program itself. During adaptation, a significant amount of capacity building and attention to fidelity is often required. The core assumptions of the integral model are that (a) the four processes are part of (integral to) the entire prevention effort and (b) success is improved when both client readiness and program impact are high.

Table 6.3 gives capsule descriptions of how TA was adapted in four different settings. In some cases (restaurant project), the curriculum was adapted through intensive meetings (capacity building) over an extended period of time prior to program delivery. The final program represents a single adaptation implemented with high fidelity. In other cases (military setting), capacity building was emphasized to gain management-level support. There was less immediate concern on whether the program is implemented with consistency and fidelity.

The first setting involved a Substance Abuse and Mental Health Administration (SAMHSA) grant-funded project to adapt TA for a national restaurant chain with a sample of at-risk young adults (ages 16 to 25 years). Many factors (e.g., hectic work climate, high turnover) led to a total revision of the original TA curriculum with a new focus on resilience in emerging adulthood (Arnett, 2001). The second setting involved a national military organization that sought to adapt

Table 6.3. Four Projects Using the Integral Model of Prevention
with Emphasis in Quadrant

Project/organization	Capacity building ←→ Prevention intervention	Adaptation ←→ Fidelity
1. Emerging adults restaurant project (Team Resilience)	Over a 12-month period, we developed multiple focus groups, a management steering committee, and an employee advisory group. Input from these groups shaped an entirely new program. The new program was delivered in 14 different restaurants.	The new program, Team Resilience, focused more on special risks of emerging adulthood and restaurant work. Employee turnover also dictated the addition of a new peer-nominated "ambassador" program.
	Capacity building ← → Prevention intervention [grid with X at 6th cell]	**Adaptation ← → Fidelity** [grid with X at 1st cell]
2. Military project (Team Readiness)	Over an 8-month period, we trained and coached prevention specialists to adapt the Team Awareness program, each in their own respective localities. A key factor is the need for commander-level support. The process of obtaining such support became a more critical focus than adaptation.	The new program, Team Readiness, is currently being continually developed and refined. It is possible that the program may be delivered in different ways in each setting. At the same time, there is some emphasis on adherence to core principles (if not content) of the original program.
	Capacity building ← → Prevention intervention [grid with X at 1st cell]	**Adaptation ← → Fidelity** [grid with X at middle cell]
3. Ex-offenders working in nonprofit reentry job training program (see http://www.boazadnruth.com)	Focus groups were conducted with the target population, staff, and owners of the job program. A staff member attended a pretraining session to help adaptation. These meetings helped build rapport between the developer and jobsite.	A key adaptation was the addition of a new module on relapse prevention. All staff were trained on fidelity in the original model, with the target population attending the program.
	Capacity building ← → Prevention intervention [grid with X at 6th cell]	**Adaptation ← → Fidelity** [grid with X at 3rd cell]

(continued)

Table 6.3.   Four Projects Using the Integral Model of Prevention
with Emphasis in Quadrant (*Continued*)

Project/ organization	Capacity building ←→ Prevention intervention	Adaptation ←→ Fidelity
4. Small business wellness initiative (see http://www. sbwi.org)	Prior to program delivery, a needs assessment was conducted with the small business owner. The needs assessment helped to gain management support, and a program was customized to meet needs identified. The intervention was delivered in 20 different businesses but also adhered to fidelity guidelines.	Due to limited resources in small businesses, sessions were reduced to 4 hr. Also, a new program was created that included eight modules. Any given session include two or three modules. Each module was delivered with fidelity guidelines but modules varied across businesses.

Capacity building ← → Prevention intervention	Adaptation ← → Fidelity
						X									X		

Note. The placement of each project on the two continua represents a snapshot of the project at a particular point in time based on the overall effort for that project. Emphasis of effort may vary as projects develop.

TA as part of a prevention effort. The chain-of-command and strong hierarchical structure required significant emphasis on capacity building long before any intervention could be administered. The third setting involved ex-offenders in a job reentry training program. We preserved original content, but owing to the addiction history of this population, we added a new module on relapse prevention. The program has been incorporated as part of a prisoner reentry program. Finally, we adapted both TA and another "model" program, "The Healthy Workplace" (Cook et al., 2007), to at-risk small businesses. TA was shortened in length because small businesses have less time to offer programs.

When adapting programs, different workplaces require different emphases in the four quadrants and benefit from capacity building and adaptation as much as from direct program delivery with high standards of fidelity. To be clear, the quadrants do not represent four kinds of organizational contexts for interventions but four processes to emphasize when adapting programs. Figure 6.2 displays such emphases. However, in each project, program implementation required working in each quadrant at some point. We believe that the integral model is useful for several reasons. First, it broadens practitioners' perspective of the processes involved in moving occupational health psychology "out of the laboratory." Second, it can be useful as a guide for bringing a program into diverse settings. Moreover, working with organizations required us to draw on competencies that pertain to understanding their stressors (e.g., Themes 5, 6, and 7 in Table 6.1). As consultants, we needed to remain sensitive to organizational changes that co-occurred with the intervention.

Summary and Implications

Any profession in occupational health will prosper to the degree it can provide competencies that do not exist in other fields and, at the same time, help neighboring professions in a common quest to enhance workplace health. These competencies are not based merely in research or academic knowledge but in insights gained from practices, consultation, and face-to-face applications with businesses, managers, and workers. As occupational health psychology grows, so will its practical knowledge.

This chapter provides a broad or integral map through which to navigate this growth. We believe such a map is needed because of increased health care costs, the growing complexity of health care, health care reform, work stress, and the expansion of a diverse service workforce that seeks to reduce these problems. We hope students will find some path on this map through which they can contribute their talents. They may draw from knowledge of other practice models (e.g., health and productivity management, behavioral risk management, healthy culture planning, healthy leadership) as well as growing trends in healthy company award practices and eHealth programming. They may also directly apply evidence-based knowledge from clinical research trials. Whatever path they pursue, occupational health psychologists can bring a unique, science-based, and needed set of competencies to their consultations and interventions. We suggest that mastery of the core competencies proposed here will help them in this pursuit.

References

Adams, T., Bezner, J., Drabbs, M., Zambarano, R., & Steinhardt, M. (2000). The relationship of spiritual and psychological dimensions of wellness to perceived wellness. *Journal of American College Health, 48,* 165–173.

Aldana, S. (1998). Financial impact of worksite health promotion and methodological quality of evidence. *The Art of Health Promotion, 2*(1), 1–8.

Aldana, S., & Pronk, N. (2001). Health promotion programs, modifiable health risk, and employee absenteeism. *Journal of Occupational and Environmental Medicine, 43,* 36–46. doi:10.1097/00043764-200101000-00009

Alimo-Metcalfe, B., & Alban-Metcalfe, J. (2003, March 6). Under the influence. *People Management,* 32–35.

Allen, H. (2009). Measuring productivity loss to reduce it. *Journal of Health and Productivity, 4*(1), 21–28.

Allen, J. (2008a). *Wellness leadership.* Burlington, VT: Human Resources Institute.

Allen, J. (2008b). *Health habits, healthy friends.* Burlington, VT: Human Resources Institute.

Allen, J., & Bellingham, R. (1994). Building supportive cultural environments. In M. O'Donnell & J. Harris (Eds.), *Health promotion in the workplace* (pp. 204–216). Albany, NY: Delmar.

Allen, R. F., & Allen, J. (1987). A sense of community and positive culture: Core enabling factors in successful cultural base health promotion programs. *American Journal of Health Promotion, 1*(3), 40–47.

Anderson, D. R., Whitmer, W., Goetzel, R., Ozminkowski, R., Wasserman, J., & Serxner, S. (2000). The relationship between modifiable health risks and group-level health care expenditures. *American Journal of Health Promotion, 15*(1), 45–52.

Arnett, J. J. (2001). Conceptions of the transition to adulthood: Perspectives from adolescence to midlife. *Journal of Adult Development, 8,* 133–143. doi:10.1023/A:1026450103225

Arnold, K., Turner, N., Barling, J., Kelloway, E., & McKee, M. (2007). Transformational leadership and psychological well-being: The mediating role of meaningful work. *Journal of Occupational Health Psychology, 12,* 193–203. doi:10.1037/1076-8998.12.3.193

Baase, C. (2005). Effect of chronic health conditions on work performance and absence, and total economic impact for employers. *Health and Productivity Management, 4*(3), 14–16.

Backer, T. E. (2000). *Balancing program fidelity and adaptation in substance abuse prevention: A state-of-the-art review.* Rockville, MD: Center for Substance Abuse Prevention.

Benavides, F., Benach, J., Diez-Roux, A., & Roman, C. (2000). How do types of employment relate to health indicators? Findings from the second European survey on working conditions. *Journal of Epidemiology and Community Health, 54,* 494–501. doi:10.1136/jech.54.7.494

Bennett, J. B. (2007). *Internet facilitation for adapting workplace substance abuse prevention: An expert-system for human resource professionals* (Final Research Report to National Institutes of Drug Abuse). Fort Worth, TX: Organizational Wellness and Learning Systems.

Bennett, J. B., Cook, R. F., & Pelletier, K. R. (2003). Toward an integrated framework for comprehensive organizational wellness: Concepts, practices, and research in workplace health promotion. In J. C. Quick & L. E. Tetrick (Eds.), *Handbook of occupational health psychology* (pp. 69–95). Washington, DC: American Psychological Association. doi:10.1037/10474-004

Bennett, J. B., & Lehman, W. E. K. (1996). Alcohol, antagonism, and witnessing violence in the workplace: Drinking climates and social alienation–integration. In G. R. VandenBos & E. Q. Bulatao (Eds.), *Violence on the job: Identifying risks and developing solutions* (pp. 105–152). Washington, DC: American Psychological Association. doi:10.1037/10215-004

Bennett, J. B., & Lehman, W. E. K. (1998). Workplace drinking climate, stress, and problem indicators: Assessing the influence of team work (group cohesion). *Journal of Studies on Alcohol, 59,* 608–618.

Bennett, J. B., & Lehman, W. E. K. (2001). Workplace substance abuse prevention and help seeking: Comparing team oriented and informational training. *Journal of Occupational Health Psychology, 6,* 243–254. doi:10.1037/1076-8998.6.3.243

Bennett, J. B., & Lehman, W. E. K. (2002). Supervisor tolerance-responsiveness to substance abuse and workplace prevention training: Use of a cognitive mapping tool. *Health Education Research, 17,* 27–42. doi:10.1093/her/17.1.27

Bennett, J. B., & Lehman, W. E. K. (2003). *Workplace substance abuse prevention: Beyond drug testing to wellness.* Washington, DC: American Psychological Association. doi:10.1037/10476-000

Bennett, J. B., Patterson, C. R., Reynolds, G. S., Wiitala, W. L., & Lehman, W. E. K. (2004). Team awareness, problem drinking, and drinking climate: Workplace social health promotion in a policy context. *American Journal of Health Promotion, 19,* 103–113.

Bennis, W. (1993). Toward a "truly" scientific management. The concept of organizational health. In W. Bennis (Ed.), *Beyond bureaucracy: Essays on development and evolution of human organization* (pp. 39–74). San Francisco, CA: Jossey-Bass.

Billings, D. W., Cook, R.F., Hendrickson, A., & Dove, D. C. (2008). A web-based approach to managing stress and mood disorders in the workforce. *Journal of Occupational and Environmental Medicine, 50,* 960–968. doi:10.1097/JOM.0b013e31816c435b

Brennan, M. (2005). Managing health at Boeing: It's all about risk. *Health and Productivity Management, 2*(1), 19–23.

Brounstein, P., Gardner, S., & Backer, T. (2006). Research to practice: Bringing effective prevention to every community. *Journal of Primary Prevention, 27,* 91–109. doi:10.1007/s10935-005-0024-6

Brown, S., & Eisenhardt, K. (1998). *Competing on the edge: Strategy as a structured chaos.* Boston, MA: Harvard Business School.

Burke, R. J., Shearer, J., & Deszca, G. (1984). Burnout among men and women in police work: An examination of the Cherniss model. *Journal of Health and Human Resources Administration, 7,* 249–263.

Burton, W. N., Chen, C., Conti, D., Schultz, A. B., Pransky, G., & Edington, D. (2005). The association of health risks with on-the-job productivity. *Journal of Occupational and Environmental Medicine, 47,* 769–777.

Chinman, M., Imm, P., & Wandersman, A. (2004). *Getting to outcomes: Promoting accountability through methods and tools for planning, implementation, and evaluation.* Retrieved from http://wwwcgi.rand.org/pubs/technical_reports/TR101/

Constable, J., & Russell, D. (1986). The effect of social support and the work environment upon burnout among nurses. *Journal of Human Stress, 12,* 20–26.

Cook, R. F., Billings, D. W., Hersch, R. K., Back, A. S., & Hendrickson, A. (2007). A field test of a web-based workplace health promotion program to improve dietary practices, reduce stress, and increase physical activity: Randomized controlled trial. *Journal of Medical Internet Research, 9*(2), e17. doi:10.2196/jmir.9.2.e17

Cooper, C. L., Dewe, P., & O'Driscoll, M. (2003). Employee assistance programs. In J. C. Quick & L. E. Tetrick (Eds.), *Handbook of occupational health psychology* (pp. 289–304). Washington, DC: American Psychological Association. doi:10.1037/10474-014

Cunningham, G., & Kitson, A. (2000). An evaluation of the RCN clinical leadership development programme. *Nursing Standard, 15*(12), 34–37.

Edington, D.W. (2001). Emerging research: A view from one research center. *American Journal of Health Promotion, 15,* 341–349.

Eng, T. R. (2001). *The eHealth landscape: A terrain map of emerging information and communication technologies in health and health care.* Princeton, NJ: The Robert Wood Johnson Foundation.

Erfurt, J. C., & Holtyn, K. (1991). Health promotion in small business: What works and what doesn't work. *Journal of Occupational Medicine., 33,* 66–73. doi:10.1097/00043764-199101000-00017

Erfurt, J. C., Foote, A., & Heirich, M. (1991). Worksite wellness programs: Incremental comparisons of screening and referral alone, health education, follow-up counseling, and plant organization. *American Journal of Health Promotion, 5,* 438–448.

Fawcett, S. E., Rhoads, G. K., & Burnah, P. (2004). People as the bridge to competitiveness: Benchmarking the "ABCs" of an empowered workforce. *Benchmarking: An International Journal, 11,* 346–360. doi:10.1108/14635770410546755

Finch, R., & Phillips, K. (2005). *An employer's guide to behavioral health services.* Retrieved from http://www.businessgrouphealth.org/pdfs/fullreport_behavioralhealthservices.pdf

Fleisher, C., Brown, W., & Fleisher, A. (1996). Comprehensive organizational wellness. In M. Rahim, G. Golembiewski, & C. Lundberg (Eds.), *Current topics in management* (pp. 167–185). Greenwich, CT: JAI Press.

Gavin, J., & Kelley, R. (1978). The psychological climate and reported well-being of underground miners: An exploratory study. *Human Relations, 31,* 567–581. doi:10.1177/001872677803100701

Gilbreath, B., & Benson, P. G. (2004). The contribution of supervisor behaviour to employee psychological well-being. *Work and Stress, 18,* 255–266. doi:10.1080/02678370412331317499

Goetzel, R. Z. (2001). The financial impact of health promotion and disease prevention programs. *American Journal of Health Promotion, 15,* 277–280.

Goetzel, R. Z., Guindon, A., Turshen, I., & Ozminkowski, R. (2001). Health and productivity management: Establishing key performance measures, benchmarks, and best practices. *Journal of Environmental and Occupational Medicine, 43,* 10–17. doi:10.1097/00043764-200101000-00003

Goetzel, R. Z., Anderson, D. R., Whitmer, R. W., Ozminkowski, R. J., Dunn, R. L., Wasserman, J. , & the HERO Research Committee. (1998). The relationship between modifiable health risks and health care expenditures: An analysis of the multi-employer HERO health risk and cost database. *Journal of Occupational and Environmental Medicine, 40,* 843–854.

Goetzel, R. Z., & Ozminkowski, R. (2000). Health and productivity management: Emerging opportunities for health promotion professionals for the 21st century. *American Journal of Health Promotion, 14,* 211–214.

Griffiths, F., Lindenmeyer, A., Powell, J., Lowe, P., & Thorogood, M. (2006). Why are health care interventions delivered over the Internet? A systematic review of the published literature. *Journal of Medical Internet Research, 8*(2), e10.

Guidotti, T. L. (2008). Comparative models for workplace wellness. *Journal of Health and Productivity, 3*(1), 15–21.

Hagen, P. (2004). Organizational solutions to obesity. *Health and Productivity Management, 1*(2), 25–28.

Harper, D., Mulvey, R. M., & Robinson, M. (2003). Beyond evidence-based practice: Rethinking the relationship between research, theory and practice. In R. Bayne & I. Horton (Eds.), *Applied psychology: Current issues and new directions* (pp. 158–171). London, England: Sage.

Heaney, C. (2003). Worksite health interventions: Targets for change and strategies for attaining them. In J. C. Quick & L. E. Tetrick (Eds.), *Handbook of occupational health psychology* (pp. 305–323). Washington, DC: American Psychological Association. doi:10.1037/10474-015

Heaney, C. A., & Goetzel, R. Z. (1997). A review of health-related outcomes of multi-components worksite health promotion programs. *American Journal of Health Promotion, 11,* 290–307.

Herlihy, P. A., & Attridge, M. (2005). Research on the integration of employee assistance, work-life and wellness services: Past, present and future. In M. Attridge, P. A. Herlihy, & R. P. Maiden (Eds.), *The integration of employee assistance, work/life, and wellness services* (pp. 67–93). London, England: Haworth Press.

Holman, P., Devane, T., & Cady, S. (2007). *The change handbook: The definitive resource on today's best methods for engaging whole systems.* San Francisco, CA: Berrett-Koehler.

Humphrey, S., Nahrgang, J., & Morgeson, F. (2007). Integrating motivational, social, and contextual work design features: A meta-analytic summary and theoretical extension of the work design literature. *Journal of Applied Psychology, 92,* 1332–1356. doi:10.1037/0021-9010.92.5.1332

Hunnicutt, D. (2006). WELCOA's annual membership survey. *Absolute Advantage, 5*(9), 1–32.

Jones, S., & Fox, S. (2009). *Generations online in 2009.* Retrieved from http://www.pewinternet.org/~/media//Files/Reports/2009/PIP_Generations_2009.pdf

Kampa-Kokesch, S. (2001). Executive coaching as an individually tailored consultation intervention: Does it increase leadership? *Dissertation Abstracts International Section B: Sciences and Engineering, 62*(7-B), 3408.

Kelloway, E., & Barling, J. (2000). What we have learned about developing transformational leaders. *Leadership and Organization Development Journal, 21,* 355–362. doi:10.1108/01437730010377908

Kelly, S., & Allison, M. (1999). *The complexity advantage: How the science of complexity can help your business achieve peak performance.* New York, NY: McGraw Hill.

Kidwell, R. J., Mossholder, K., & Bennett, N. (1997). Cohesiveness and organizational citizenship behavior: A multilevel analysis using work groups and individuals. *Journal of Management, 23,* 775–793. doi:10.1177/014920639702300605

Kilburg, R., Stokes, E., & Kuruvilla, C. (1998). Toward a conceptual model of organizational regression. *Consulting Psychology Journal: Practice and Research, 50,* 101–119. doi:10.1037/1061-4087.50.2.101

Kivimäki, M., Elovainio, M., Vahtera, J., & Ferrie, J. (2003). Organisational justice and health of employees: Prospective cohort study. *Journal of Occupational and Environmental Medicine, 60,* 27–34. doi:10.1136/oem.60.1.27

Kivimäki, M., Head, J., Ferrie, J., Hemingway, H., Shipley, M., Vahtera, J., & Marmot, M. (2005). Working while ill as a risk factor for serious coronary events: The Whitehall II study. *American Journal of Public Health, 95,* 98–102. doi:10.2105/AJPH.2003.035873

Kozlowski, S., & Salas, E. (1997). A multilevel organizational systems approach for the implementation and transfer of training. In J. Ford (Ed.), *Improving training effectiveness in work organizations* (pp. 247–287). Mahwah, NJ: Erlbaum.

LaMontagne, A. D., Keegel, T., Louie, A. M., Ostry, A., & Landsbergis, P. A. (2007). A systematic review of the job-stress intervention evaluation literature, 1990–2005. *International Journal of Occupational and Environmental Health, 13,* 268–280.

Lehman, W. E. K., Reynolds, G. S., & Bennett, J. B. (2003). Team and informational training for workplace substance abuse prevention. In J. Bennett & W. Lehman (Eds.), *Preventing workplace substance abuse: Beyond drug testing to wellness* (pp. 165–201). Washington, DC: American Psychological Association.

Levant, R. (2005). *Report of the 2005 presidential task force on evidence-based practice.* Washington, DC: American Psychological Association.

Levering, R., & Moskowitz, M. (1994). *The best 100 companies to work for in America.* New York, NY: Plume Books.

Loehr, J., & Schwartz, T. (2003). *The power of full engagement.* New York, NY: Free Press.

Lowe, G., Schellenberg, G., & Shannon, H. (2003). Correlates of employees' perceptions of a healthy work environment. *American Journal of Health Promotion, 17,* 390–399.

Lustria, M., Brown, L. L., & Davis, R. (2007, November). *10 years of consumer health informatics: What have we learned about how to design successful web-based interventions?* Paper presented at the annual meeting of the National Communication Association, Chicago, IL.

MacLean, D. R., Farquarhson, J., Heath, S., Barkhouse, K., Latter, C., & Joffres, C. (2003). Building capacity for heart health promotion: Results of a 5-year experience in Nova Scotia, Canada. *American Journal of Health Promotion, 17,* 202–212.

Mausner-Dorsch, H., & Eaton, W. (2000). Psychosocial work environment and depression: Epidemiologic assessment of the demand–control model. *American Journal of Public Health, 90,* 1765–1770. doi:10.2105/AJPH.90.11.1765

Mayrhofer, W. (1997). Warning: Flexibility can damage your organizational health! *Employee Relations, 19,* 519–534. doi:10.1108/01425459710193081

McKeown, G. (2001, March 4). *Workplace wellness: Something's happening here.* Retrieved from http://www.nqi.ca/articles/article.aspx?ID=80

McPherson, T. L., Cook, R. F., Back, A. S., Hersch, R. K., & Hendrickson, A. (2006). A field test of a web-based substance abuse prevention training program for health promotion professionals. *American Journal of Health Promotion, 20,* 396–400.

Musich, S., Hook, D., Baaner, S., & Edington, D. (2006). The association of two productivity measures with health risks and medical conditions in an Australian employee population. *American Journal of Health Promotion, 20,* 353–363.

Musich, S., Hook, D., Barnett, T., & Edington, D. W. (2003). The association between health risk status and health care costs among the membership of an Australian health plan. *Health Promotion International, 18,* 57–65. doi:10.1093/heapro/18.1.57

Norman, G. J., Zabinski, M. F., Adams, M. A., Rosenberg, D. E., Yaroch, A. L., & Atienza, A. A. (2007). A review of eHealth interventions for physical activity and dietary behavior change. *American Journal of Preventative Medicine, 33,* 336–345, e16.

O'Donnell, M. (2001). *Health promotion in the workplace* (3rd ed.). Albany, NY: Delmar.

Parker, C., Baltes, B., Young, S., Huff, J., Atlmann, R., LaCost, H., & Roberts, J. (2003). Relationships between psychological climate perceptions and work outcomes: A meta-analytic review. *Journal of Organizational Behavior, 24,* 389–416. doi:10.1002/job.198

Partnership for Prevention. (2009). *Leading by example.* Retrieved from http://prevent.org/content/view/30/57/

Patterson, C. R., Bennett, J. B., & Wiitala, W. L. (2005). Healthy and unhealthy stress unwinding: Promoting health in small businesses. *Journal of Business and Psychology, 20,* 221–247. doi:10.1007/s10869-005-8261-5

Pelletier, K. (1991). A review and analysis of the health and cost-effective outcomes studies of comprehensive health promotion and disease prevention programs. *American Journal of Health Promotion, 5,* 311–313.

Pelletier, K. (1993). A review and analysis of the health and cost-effective outcomes studies of comprehensive health promotion and disease prevention programs at the worksite: 1991–1993 update. *American Journal of Health Promotion, 8,* 43–49.

Pelletier, K. (1996). A review and analysis of the health and cost-effective outcomes studies of comprehensive health promotion and disease prevention programs at the worksite: 1993–1995 update. *American Journal of Health Promotion, 10,* 380–388.

Pelletier, K. (2005). A review and analysis of the clinical and cost-effectiveness studies of comprehensive health promotion and disease management programs at the worksite: Update VI 2000–2004. *Journal of Occupational and Environmental Medicine, 47,* 1051–1058. doi:10.1097/01.jom.0000174303.85442.bf

Pelletier, K. (2009). A review and analysis of the clinical and cost-effectiveness studies of comprehensive health promotion and disease management programs at the worksite: Update VII 2004–2008. *Journal of Occupational and Environmental Medicine, 51,* 822–837. doi:10.1097/JOM.0b013e3181a7de5a

Quick, J., Cooper, C., Gavin, J., & Quick, J. (2002). Executive health: Building self-reliance for challenging times. In I. Roberston & C. Cooper (Eds.), *International review of industrial and organizational psychology* (pp. 187–216). New York, NY: Wiley.

Quick, J., Macik-Frey, M., & Cooper, C. (2007). Managerial dimensions of employee health. *Journal of Management Studies, 44,* 189–205. doi:10.1111/j.1467-6486.2007.00684.x

Reynolds, G., & Lehman, W. (2008). Workgroup temperance of alcohol and safety climate moderate the cognitive effects of workplace substance-abuse prevention. *Journal of Applied Social Psychology, 38,* 1827–1866. doi:10.1111/j.1559-1816.2008.00371.x

Rhoades, L., & Eisenberger, R. (2002). Perceived organizational support: A review of the literature. *Journal of Applied Psychology, 87,* 698–714. doi:10.1037/0021-9010.87.4.698

Russell, D., Altmaier, E., & Van Velzen, D. (1987). Job-related stress, social support, and burnout among classroom teachers. *Journal of Applied Psychology, 72,* 269–274. doi:10.1037/0021-9010.72.2.269

Schein, E. (1965). *Organizational psychology.* Englewood Cliffs, NJ: Prentice Hall.

Schwab, A., & Bennett, J. B. (2007, October). *E-coaching for promoting organizational wellness: Applications from research on EAPs.* Paper presented at the annual conference of the Employee Assistance Society of North America, San Diego, CA.

Schwab, A., & Bennett, J. B. (2008). *Process evaluation of user-system interface: Predicting e-learning program effectiveness.* Paper presented at American Psychological Association–National Institute of Occupational Safety and Health Interdisciplinary Conference on Work, Stress, and Health, Washington, DC.

Schultz, A. B., & Edington, D. (2007). Employee health and presenteeism: A systematic review. *Journal of Occupational Rehabilitation, 17,* 547–579. doi:10.1007/s10926-007-9096-x

Seltzer, J., & Numerof, R. (1988). Supervisory leadership and subordinate burnout. *Academy of Management Journal, 31,* 439–446. doi:10.2307/256559

Shain, M., & Suurvali, H. (2003). Lay and scientific perspectives on harm prevention: Enabling theory and program innovation. In J. Bennett & E. Lehman (Eds.), *Preventing workplace substance abuse* (pp. 203–226). Washington, DC: American Psychological Association. doi:10.1037/10476-006

Slavit, W., & Flood, G. (2007). *Center for Prevention and Health Services behavioral health awards: Employer implementation and best practices.* Washington, DC: National Business Group on Health. Retrieved from http://www.businessgrouphealth.org/pdfs/issuebrief_awardsoct2007.pdf

Smith, M. J., Karsh, B. T., Carayon, P., & Conway, F. T. (2003). Controlling occupational safety and health hazards. In J. C. Quick & L. E. Tetrick (Eds.), *Handbook of occupational health psychology* (pp. 35–68). Washington, DC: American Psychological Association. doi:10.1037/10474-003

Smither, J. W., London, M., Flautt, R., Vargas, Y., & Kucine, I. (2003). Can working with an executive coach improve multisource feedback ratings over time? A quasi-experimental field study experimental field study. *Personnel Psychology, 56,* 23–44. doi:10.1111/j.1744-6570.2003.tb00142.x

Society for Human Resource Management. (2007). *2007 employee benefits: A survey report.* Retrieved from http://www.shrm.org/research

Society for Human Resource Management. (2008). *2008 employee benefits: A survey report.* Retrieved from http://www.shrm.org/research

Society for Human Resource Management. (2009). *2009 employee benefits: A survey report-examining employee benefits in a fiscally challenged economy.* Retrieved from http://www.shrm.org/research

Söderfeldt, B., Söderfeldt, M., Jones, K., O'Campo, P., Muntaner, C., Ohlson, C., & Warg, L. (1997). Does organization matter? A multilevel analysis of the demand–control model applied to human services. *Social Science and Medicine, 44,* 527–534. doi:10.1016/S0277-9536(96)00179-7

Steinbach, T. (2000). Workplace strategies for removing obstacles to employee health. *Employee Benefits Journal, 25,* 9–10.

Stevenson, J., & Mitchell, R. (2003). Community-level collaboration for substance abuse prevention. *Journal of Primary Prevention, 23,* 371–404. doi:10.1023/A:1021397825740

Tepper, B. (2000). Consequences of abusive supervision. *Academy of Management Journal, 44,* 178–190. doi:10.2307/1556375

Theorell, T., Emdad, R., Arnetz, B., & Weingarten, A. (2001). Employee effects of an educational program for managers at an insurance company. *Psychosomatic Medicine, 63,* 724–733.

Walker, B. B., & London, S. (2007). Novel tools and resources for evidence-based practice in psychology. *Journal of Clinical Psychology, 63,* 633–642. doi:10.1002/jclp.20377

Wandersman, A. (2003). Community science: Bridging the gap between science and practice with community-centered models. *American Journal of Community Psychology, 31,* 227–242. doi:10.1023/A:1023954503247

Wang, F., Schultz, A., Musich, S., McDonald, T., Hirschland, D., & Edington, D. (2003). The relationship between National Heart, Lung, and Blood Institute weight guidelines and concurrent medical costs in a manufacturing population. *American Journal of Health Promotion, 17,* 183–189.

Wantland, D. J., Portillo, C. J., Holzemer, W. L., Slaughter, R., & McGhee, E. M. (2004). The effectiveness of web-based vs. non-web-based interventions: A meta-analysis of behavioral change outcomes. *Journal of Medical Internet Research, 6*(4), e40. doi:10.2196/jmir.6.4.e40

Wasylyshyn, K. (2003). Executive coaching: An outcome study. *Consulting Psychology Journal: Practice and Research, 55,* 94–106. doi:10.1037/1061-4087.55.2.94

Wolfe, R., & Parker, D. (1994). Employee health management: Challenges and opportunities. *Academy of Management Executive, 8*(2), 22–31.

Yandrick, R. (1996). *Behavioral risk management: How to avoid preventable losses from mental health problems in the workplace.* San Francisco, CA: Jossey-Bass.

Ziegler, J. (1998). America's healthiest companies. *Business and Health, 16*(12), 29–31.

Zohar, D. (2002). The effects of leadership dimensions, safety climate, and assigned priorities on minor injuries in work groups. *Journal of Organizational Behavior, 23,* 75–92. doi:10.1002/job.130

7

Cross-Cultural Occupational Health Psychology

Chu-Hsiang Chang and Paul E. Spector

Occupational health psychology (OHP) is a new field dedicated to understanding how workplace psychological and social aspects affect workers' physical and psychological health. The emergence of OHP has been attributed to early work by European scholars (Barling & Griffiths, 2002). In Sweden, Karasek (1979) first recognized the joint effects of job demands and decision latitude on employees' mental health and cardiovascular disease in Swedish men (Karasek, Baker, Marxer, Ahlbom, & Theorell, 1981). Since then, interest in building a healthy work organization—one that emphasizes the health of the workplace and the well-being of employees equally—through a better understanding of OHP-related issues has gained prominence among researchers, employers, and policymakers around the world (Cooper, 2000).

Culture can have a substantial influence on employee psychological processes underlying health-related outcomes, thereby affecting how a healthy workplace can be created. At the macrolevel, culture influences the sociopolitical as well as the organizational context in which employees work (Beehr & Glazer, 2001; Janssens, Brett, & Smith, 1995). Additionally, culture shapes employees' value systems and how they perceive and respond to environmental features. Indeed, as the economy becomes more diverse and as more organizations operate in a global environment, the challenge for the OHP field is not only to better understand the psychological mechanisms contributing to employee health but also to do so in a multicultural context.

This chapter provides a global, cross-cultural perspective on OHP. We first present cultural dimensions that are particularly informative for considering OHP-related issues. We then review the cross-cultural works in the major OHP areas. Finally, we discuss methodological issues and future directions for cross-cultural OHP.

The Cultural Context

Much cross-cultural research has focused on national differences in values, which are general, motivational concerns that describe desirable end states and help guide the selection and evaluation of behaviors and events across different contexts (Schwartz, 1994). Hofstede (1980) provided the most used values scheme, which includes five dimensions (power distance, uncertainty avoidance, individualism–collectivism, masculinity, and long-term orientation). Schwartz (1994) expanded on Hofstede's value scheme with a system of 10 basic values (universalism, benevolence, conformity, tradition, security, power, achievement, hedonism, stimulation, and self-direction) and two orthogonal axes: self-enhancement–self-transcendence and openness to change–conservation. Next, we introduce these two dimensions and discuss how they relate to Hofstede's original cultural value dimensions, as they offer a theoretical framework to organize cross-cultural studies in OHP topics. We also discuss one important cultural norm—display rules—and its implications for employee emotional regulation and well-being.

Self-Enhancement–Self-Transcendence

The dimension of self-enhancement–self-transcendence is akin to Hofstede's (1980) cultural dimension of individualism–collectivism. Self-enhancement emphasizes personal achievement and power, and people from individualistic societies tend to act on the basis of their personal beliefs and attitudes, have loose ties with their social groups, and be motivated to maximize their own benefits (Hofstede, 1980; Triandis, 2001). In contrast, self-transcendence values feature universalism and benevolence, and people from collectivist cultures are concerned with pursuing the welfare of the social groups to which they belong, as well as successfully performing their assigned group roles (Hofstede, 1980; Schwartz, 1994).

Implications of this cultural dimension have been noted for a number of OHP topics. For example, employees from collectivist cultures show a preference for a group-based over an individual-based decision-making style, which can influence how managers anticipate and respond to workplace accidents (Li, Harris, & Chen, 2007). Additionally, employees from individualistic versus collectivist cultures tend to face different occupational stressors (e.g., Liu, Spector, & Shi, 2007) and respond to the same stressors differently (e.g., Schaubroeck, Lam, & Xie, 2000). More evidence regarding the implications of this dimension is presented in the later sections.

Openness to Change–Conservation

The dimension of openness to change–conservation captures whether individuals prefer novel experiences versus known, structured events (Rohan, 2000; Schwartz, 1994). Values associated with openness to change emphasize the importance of embracing new challenges in one's life, expressing innovation and creativity, and seizing opportunities that may lead to gains. In contrast, conservation values underscore the respect and acceptance of traditions and customs, fulfillment of assigned duties and responsibilities, and avoidance of impulsive actions and rule-breaking behaviors (Bardi & Schwartz, 2003). As such, Hofstede's (1980) uncertainty avoidance variable can be seen as part of this dimension, with openness to change corresponding to high uncertainty tolerance and conservation corresponding to high uncertainty avoidance.

Although less work has been done to explore the implications of this dimension for various OHP topics, research does point to its importance. For example, in a meta-analysis across 14 countries, the cultural value of uncertainty avoidance was associated with workplace accidents and injuries through its impact on the effectiveness of safety training. In particular, the effectiveness of training was negatively affected in countries with a higher level of uncertainty avoidance (Burke, Chan-Serafin, Salvador, Smith, & Sarpy, 2008). Similarly, another meta-analysis found that employees from countries that are exposed to constant political turmoil and challenges responded less negatively to job stressors, such as perceptions of organizational politics (Chang, Rosen, & Levy, 2009).

Display Rules

In addition to values, display rules represent another important cross-cultural difference that may influence employees' well-being at work, particularly for those engaging in emotional labor. *Display rules* refer to cultural differences in facial and other nonverbal, nonvocal (e.g., eye contact) expressions of emotion (Ekman & Friesen, 1975). These rules are learned early in childhood and help individuals regulate their emotional expressions based on different social circumstances. Studies have identified differences in display rules between individualistic and collectivist cultures. Particularly, people from individualistic cultures tend to be more expressive of their emotions than those from collectivist cultures, especially when it comes to showing negative emotions to in-group members. Conversely, collectivist cultures are linked with more expressions of positive emotions toward ingroup members and more negative emotions toward outgroup members (Matsumoto, Yoo, Hirayama, & Petrova, 2005).

Because display rules are well learned and operate outside of the conscious awareness, they can create communication barriers between individuals following different rules. For example, maintaining eye contact during conversation indicates interest and respect in North American and European cultures. However, such behavior is considered rude in Japanese and Arab cultures, in which looking down during social interaction is a sign of respect (Argyle & Cook, 1976; Collett, 1971). As such, differences in display rules represent a potential source of implicit interpersonal conflicts among workers with different cultural backgrounds and may contribute to employee job stress in cross-cultural interactions.

In addition to the inherent cross-cultural differences in display rules, there may be unique, job-based display rules. For example, employees in service and retail industries are required to display cheer and other positive emotions (Pugh, 2001), whereas bill collectors are trained to show irritation and urgency toward debtors (Sutton, 1991). These display expectations create additional demands for employees to regulate their emotions at work (Grandey & Brauberger, 2002) and can have detrimental effects on employee physical and psychological health (Bono & Vey, 2005). The job-specific display rules may be particularly challenging if they contradict employees' own cultural display rules (Grandey, Fisk, & Steiner, 2005), and as such, may demand extra attentional resources from employees to show the "proper" emotions. Moreover, there are cross-cultural differences in *how* employees regulate their emotions (Matsumoto, Yoo, &

Nakagawa, 2008), and these different regulatory strategies can have health implications (Goldberg & Grandey, 2007).

In the following sections, we review empirical studies that examined five major topics of OHP in the cross-cultural or international settings: job stress, work–family issues, accidents and injuries, musculoskeletal disorders, and workplace violence.

Job Stress

Job stress is the process by which individuals respond to potentially adverse or challenging job conditions that may have both psychological and physical effects on them. Perhaps no topic in OHP is more central to occupational health, safety, and well-being than job stress, which relates significantly to each of the other topics. In addition, more cross-cultural and cross-national (CC/CN) research has been done in the job stress area than any other OHP topics.

Most theories of job stress adopt either explicitly or implicitly the environment–response framework (Spector, 1992), best reflected in the transactional approach (Lazarus, 1991; Perrewé & Zellars, 1999) in which the work environment (stressor) is assumed to cause responses by or in the person (strains). *Stressors* are conditions in the environment that require adaptive responses (Jex, 1998). There are a variety of stressor types, some of which are inherent in the nature of the job (e.g., uncertainty over required job tasks), whereas others are more social by nature (e.g., being bullied). *Strains* are reactions to stressors that can be classified as physical (e.g., increased blood pressure), psychological (anger), or behavioral (alcohol consumption; Jex, 1998). Prolonged exposure to stressors over time can contribute to more serious illness, such as heart disease (Frankenhaeuser & Johansson, 1986). Chapter 3 of this volume discusses the transactional model in greater detail.

Models of job stress have suggested a variety of potential moderator variables that make the process more complex. The most influential has been the demand–control model, which suggests that control buffers the adverse impact of stressors on strains (Karasek, 1979). An extension of this model is the demand–control–support model that suggests that the impact of demands is reduced by the combination of high control and social support (Karasek & Theorell, 1990).

International Replications

By far the most common international studies are international replications in a single country. Such studies generally make no explicit attempt to compare results quantitatively to another country, and most make no claim at being cross-cultural. For example, Bishop et al. (2003) found support for the demand–control model in a sample of Singaporean police officers. C.-Q. Lu, Siu, and Cooper (2005) noted that extending Western findings to China was the purpose of their study of the role of self-efficacy in the job stress process. Similarly, Chen, Wong, Yu, Lin, and Cooper (2003) were interested in exploring sources of stress specifically among the Chinese and how they might vary as a function of personality. From the perspective of a CC/CN researcher, this literature is fragmented and provides limited insights concerning generalizability because there are too few studies in too few countries using too many diverse measures and samples from which to draw definitive conclusions.

Comparative Studies

There is a growing body of comparative studies that include two or more countries in an attempt to draw inferences about country differences and similarities. By far, the vast majority are two-country comparisons of Canada or the United States with another culturally dissimilar country, such as China or India. Some studies have compared levels of job stressors and strains among two or more countries. For example, Kim (2007) compared samples of psychotherapists between Korea and the United States, finding that Koreans tended to report higher levels of overall stress. Looking at particular stressors and strains, studies have found that Chinese tend to have lower job satisfaction and higher stressors than Americans (Chiu & Kosinski, 1999; Liu et al., 2007; Spector, Sanchez, Siu, Salgado, & Ma, 2004). Furthermore, Asians tend to report more physical symptoms than Americans and Australians (Chiu & Kosinski, 1999; Liu et al., 2007). On the other hand, Americans tend to report more strains than do Iranians, although Iranians report more stressors (Spector, Cooper, & Aguilar-Vafaie, 2002). The Nurses' Early Exit Study (NEXT; Hasselhorn, Müller, & Tackenberg, 2005) compared burnout levels in 11 European countries, finding the highest incidence in France and Slovakia and the lowest incidence in the Netherlands and Norway. In the 26-country Collaborative International Study of Managerial Stress, Spector et al. (2001) reported mean comparisons on job satisfaction, physical strain, and psychological strain. Of course, one must be cautious in interpreting results of such studies as there can be culturally determined response tendencies that make it difficult to accurately compare mean levels of stressors and strains.

An alternative approach to exploring country differences is to rely on qualitative methods in which subjects report stressful incidents they have encountered. Two such studies compared Americans with Indians (Narayanan, Menon, & Spector, 1999) and Chinese (Liu et al., 2007) and found that their reports of stressors and strains varied by country.

Perhaps a more important issue is the extent to which relationships among stressors, strains, and other variables are similar across countries. Studies found that some relationships between stressors and strains are similar in magnitude between the United States and Iran (Spector, Cooper, & Aguilar-Vafaie, 2002), Hong Kong (Schaubroeck et al., 2000), People's Republic of China (Liu et al., 2007), and South Africa (Bhagat et al., 2001). Perhaps somewhat less consistent are results from the EUROTEACH project, which surveyed 2,796 school teachers from 13 European countries on job stressors and strains (Verhoeven, Maes, Kraaij, & Joekes, 2003). Although most corresponding correlations were similar across countries, there were some differences as well. For example, control correlated .45 with job satisfaction in the Netherlands but correlated a nonsignificant .14 in the United Kingdom. An analysis of turnover intentions from six countries in the NEXT study found that unemployment rate at the country level affected whether the three-way interaction of demands by control by support was significant (Widerszal-Bazyl, Radkiewicz, Hasselhorn, Conway, & van der Heijden, 2008). Specifically, the three-way interaction was significant for countries with low unemployment but not high unemployment.

Studies have also explored relationships of stressors and/or strains with a limited number of personality variables. Perhaps the most studied personality variable in CC/CN research is work locus of control (Spector, 1988), that is, the extent to which an individual believes he or she has control over promotions, raises, and other rewards at work. Spector, Cooper, Sanchez, et al. (2002) found that correlations of work locus of control were consistent for job satisfaction but not physical strains. However, Spector, Sanchez, et al. (2004) found that an external locus of control was associated with high levels of several stressors and strains in Americans but not Chinese.

Few studies have investigated other personality variables in a very restricted number of country comparisons. Type A behavior was shown to relate similarly to burnout and turnover intentions and to moderate the stress–burnout relationship in both Canada and Pakistan (Jamal, 1999). Evans, Palsane, and Carrere (1987) found that Type A behavior related to accidents and psychological strain (irritability) in a sample of bus drivers in both India and the United States. However, Type A was associated with aggressive driving in India but not in the United States.

Country-Level Studies

Country-level studies treat country as the unit of analysis by computing country means on the variables of interest. Perhaps the best example is Peterson et al. (1995), who related mean levels of Hofstede's (1980) culture values to mean levels of role stressors for 21 nations. Countries that were individualistic were higher in role ambiguity and lower in role overload than countries that were collectivistic. Countries high in power distance were higher on role overload and lower on role ambiguity than countries low in power distance.

Similarly, Spector, Cooper, Sanchez, et al. (2002) related mean levels of individualism–collectivism, work locus of control, physical strain, and psychological strain among 26 countries. They showed that countries where people tend to be internal in their work locus of control had lower levels of strain. Although country-level individualism–collectivism was related to work locus of control (people in individualist countries tend to be internal), individualism–collectivism was unrelated to strains. Taken together, these two studies show that there can be aspects of culture that are related to both job stressors and job strains. However, these studies do not provide a great deal of insight into why those relationships might occur, as the designs were cross-sectional.

Work–Family Issues

It has become increasingly apparent that the interplay between work and family has implications for employee health and well-being. Of particular concern is *work–family conflict* (WFC), which is the incompatibility of demands between the work and family domains (Greenhaus & Beutell, 1985). Most WFC research has been conducted in the United States and other Western countries, where such relationships have been fairly consistent. For example, studies in northern Europe have found consistent relationships between WFC and other variables (e.g., Cousins & Tang, 2004; Geurts, Kompier, Roxburgh, & Houtman, 2003). Research in culturally dissimilar regions of the world, such as Asia, has found less consistent relationships, and cross-national studies have suggested some cultural reasons. Work demands have been shown to significantly relate to WFC in India (Aryee, Srinivas, & Tan, 2005) and Hong Kong (Aryee, Luk, Leung, & Lo, 1999) but not Japan (Matsui, Ohsawa, & Onglatco, 1995). A series of cross-national studies explored the possibility of cultural differences in relationships between WFC and demands and outcomes. Yang, Chen, Choi, and Zou (2000) proposed that individualism–collectivism affects the way people view the interplay between work and family. Support for the idea that the relationship between demands and WFC would be stronger in individualist countries can be found in studies showing that number of working hours relates more strongly to WFC in the United Kingdom than Taiwan (L. Lu, Gilmour, Kao, & Huang, 2006) and more strongly in Norway than in India (Pal & Saksvik, 2008). Two larger scale studies compared relationships between demands and WFC in several countries combined into regions. Spector, Cooper, et al. (2004) found that working hours related to work–family pressure in Anglo countries (Australia, Canada, New Zealand, United Kingdom, and United States) but not in collectivist regions (Greater China and Latin America). Similarly, Spector et al. (2007) compared individualist Anglo countries with collectivist regions of Asia, Eastern Europe, and Latin America and found that both working hours and perceived workload related more strongly to WFC in the individualist region.

Not all studies have been consistent in showing that WFC relates more strongly to other variables in individualistic countries. In a 48-country study, the same model relating demands to WFC and job attitudes was supported across four country clusters (Hill, Yang, Hawkins, & Ferris, 2004). Although the same model fit universally, Hill et al. (2004) did not test to see if relationships were stronger in some regions than others. Finally, Yang et al. (2000) found that the relationship between demands and WFC was stronger in China than the United States, which is opposite to the findings of other studies.

The conclusion from the cross-national literature is that work–family issues are important internationally, but some relationships appear to vary across countries and regions of the world. The reasons for discrepancies among studies are not entirely clear. However, it is reasonable to expect that cultural differences in individualism–collectivism might be partially responsible.

Accidents and Injuries

Some safety researchers have focused on the issues at the national level, such as comparing legislation related to worker safety and health, or comparing education policies and worker qualifications between countries (e.g., Barish, 2001; Spangenberg et al., 2003). Spangenberg et al. (2003) compared the accident and injury rates between Danish and Swedish construction workers and found that between 1996 and 2000, Danish workers had consistently higher rates of both minor and serious accidents and suffered more lost-time injuries. Spangenberg and colleagues attributed these findings partly to the national differences in sick leave pay, as well as differences in the lengths and structures of apprenticeship between the two countries.

Other research has focused on understanding the connection between cross-cultural value differences and workplace accident and injury prevention. For example, because of the preference for consistency and predictability in safety training delivery, organizations in countries that are high on the conservation cultural values tend to utilize less engaging safety training methods (e.g., lectures, pamphlets; Burke et al., 2008). Unfortunately, these training methods have often led to lower safety knowledge acquisition and safety performance and have had less impact on health and safety outcomes (Burke et al., 2006). Consequently, researchers have observed the paradoxical effect that safety training resulted in limited accident and injury reduction in countries with a high uncertainty avoidance tendency (Burke et al., 2008).

CC/CN studies have also identified different organizational and management practices as the factor underlying differences in accident rates in the same industry among different countries. Compared with organizations in the United States and Taiwan, organizations in developing countries such as India often had inadequate safety training for their employees, lower quality human resource management, and unclear organizational structure and chains of command. The poor organizational designs and processes were associated with higher accident rates (e.g., Li et al., 2007). Hsu, Lee, Wu, and Takano (2008) compared the organizational factors on safety between Japanese and Taiwanese oil refinery plants and found that Japanese plants featured higher empowerment and team-based structure, as well as a better reward system, which increased employees' awareness of and willingness to report safety-related issues and their safety behaviors. On the other hand, Taiwanese management had a stronger commitment to safety, which led to supervisors' greater efforts in monitoring and instructing safety-related issues.

In a similar study that explored the differences in management practices between business owners in the United Kingdom and Spain, it was found that U.K. managers were more informed about the health and safety legislation and more likely to be involved in safety management than were their Spanish counterparts (Vassie, Tomàs, & Oliver, 2000). Janssens et al. (1995) compared the impact of management overall concerns for employees on employee safety perceptions across U.S., French, and Argentine plants. They found that because of the collectivist feature of Argentine culture, management concern for employees had a greater impact on employees' perceived safety priority. On the other hand, because U.S. and French cultures emphasized individualism and competition, managers from those countries placed a higher premium on meeting the production target, and as a result, employees had a lower perceived safety level.

In addition to improving organizational factors and management practices, another approach to reduce accidents and injuries focuses on creating a positive safety climate (Zohar & Luria, 2005). Safety climate is conceptualized as the shared perceptions among members of a group or an organization regarding the safety policies, procedures, and practices (Zohar & Luria, 2005), and it has been linked to important safety outcomes, including accidents, injuries, and safety performance (Zacharatos, Barling, & Iverson, 2005) in the North American context. Researchers have begun to explore the effects of safety climate in settings other than North America or Europe (Mearns, Rundmo, Flin, Gordon, & Fleming, 2004). For example, in a study with construction workers in Hong Kong, the safety climate was found to reduce accident rates and injuries via its effects on psychological strains (Siu, Phillips, & Leung, 2004). C.-S. Lu and Tsai (2008) found that a positive safety climate was linked to reduced vessel accidents and crew fatalities in a container shipping company in Taiwan. A positive safety climate improved Australian health care employees' safety motivation, and subsequent safety performance (Neal & Griffin, 2006), and reduced employee vehicular accidents in Australia (Newnam, Griffin, & Mason, 2008). Thus far, research evidence supports the general positive effects associated with a good safety climate across different countries.

Finally, a unique line of CC/CN research in workplace accidents and injuries involves comparing different attributions made after accidents. The cultural dimension of self-enhancement–self-transcendence has been associated with different attribution styles for accidents. Workers from collectivist cultures (e.g., Ghana) were likely to attribute the accidents to external, contextual causes (e.g., dangerous work), whereas workers from individualist cultures (e.g., Finland) were likely to attribute accidents to internal, individual-based causes (e.g., workers failing to follow safety procedures; Gyekye & Salminen, 2005). Zemba, Young, and Morris (2006) found that Japanese observers were more likely to blame the organization and the organizational representative (e.g., managers) for the accident. On the other hand, U.S. observers were more likely to hold the individual who caused the accident responsible and less likely to consider the organization or its representatives liable. These differences in attributions are likely to have implications for workplace accident investigation, the reporting mechanisms for near misses and other safety-related issues, and the development and modification of safety management policies. As such, cultural orientations and values of the employment context should be taken into consideration when implementing safety interventions.

Musculoskeletal Disorders

Work-related musculoskeletal disorders (WRMSDs) affect tendons, tendon sheaths, muscles, nerves, bursae, and blood vessels in the upper and lower extremities and the back. Studies exploring the risk factors underlying WRMSDs have typically focused on physical job demands, such as manual material handling and awkward positions (National Institute for Occupational Safety and Health [NIOSH], 1997). However, researchers have recognized psychosocial stressors and strain from jobs as additional risk factors for WRMSDs (e.g., Simon et al., 2008; Sobeih, Salem, Daraiseh, Genaidy, & Shell, 2006). In particular, employee job dissatisfaction, lack of autonomy and social support, and high workload have been consistently linked to increased WRMSDs among U.S. workers (NIOSH, 1997; Sobeih et al., 2006).

In terms of CC/CN work in the area of WRMSDs, some studies have compared the symptoms of workers in the same industry from different countries.

For example, Smith (2003) compared nurses in Australia, Japan, South Korea, and Taiwan and found that Japanese nurses suffered from the highest rates of WRMSDs. Additionally, Waluyo, Ekberg, and Eklund (1996) compared the assembly workers in Indonesia and Sweden and found that although Swedish workers reported significantly higher job strain and dissatisfaction, the prevalence for WRMSD symptoms was high for workers in both countries.

Other studies have focused on examining the relationships between psychosocial factors and WRMSD symptoms in cultural settings other than the United States. For example, mental stress was related to increased WRMSD symptoms in a sample of Japanese nurses (Smith, Mihashi, Adachi, Koga, & Ishitake, 2006). Similarly, mental pressure and lack of social support at work were significant risk factors for the WRMSD complaints made by Chinese physicians (Smith, Wei, Zhang, & Wang, 2006). Thus, it appears that links between psychosocial factors such as stress and lack of support and WRMSD symptoms were replicated in some non-Western settings.

Workplace Violence

Workplace violence is one of the leading causes of workplace fatalities in the United States (U.S. Department of Labor, 2008). Violence can be categorized into four types (Merchant & Lundell, 2001). Type 1 violence is committed by individuals with no connection with the organization or the victim, such as someone committing a robbery against convenience store clerks and taxi cab drivers. Clients and customers of the organization are responsible for Type 2 violence. For example, health care professionals can be assaulted by patients (Lanza, 2006). Type 3 violence is performed by the coworkers of the victim, and Type 4 is relationship violence (e.g., spouse abuse) that spills over to the workplace.

Similar to work related to WRMSDs, CC/CN studies on workplace violence have compared the prevalence of violence among workers in the same industry from different countries. For example, in a study comparing nurses' exposure to physical violence across eight European Union countries, French and German nurses had the most frequent exposure to violence, whereas nurses in the Netherlands were the least likely to be assaulted (Camerino, Estryn-Beharc, Conway, van Der Heijden, & Hasselhorn, 2008). The different exposure rates between countries corresponded to nurses' report of poor working conditions (e.g., high job uncertainty, role conflict) in those countries. Another study found that psychiatric nurses and psychiatrists in the United Kingdom were more likely to be assaulted in the past 12 months than their Swedish counterparts (Lawoko, Soares, & Nolan, 2004). These differences were attributed to both organizational characteristics (e.g., policies, working conditions) and societal differences (e.g., patient access to psychiatric services; Lawoko et al., 2004). Finally, Guterman, Jayaratne, and Bargal (1996) compared exposure to violence among social workers in the United States and Israel. They found that although Israeli social workers were more likely to be physically threatened than their U.S. counterparts, the two groups had experienced similar numbers of physical attacks. Moreover, whereas inexperienced and male American social workers were more likely to be assaulted, tenure and gender had little impact on Israeli social workers' likelihood of exposure.

In addition to physical violence, researchers have also compared the pervasiveness of nonphysical aggression at work, such as verbal assaults, sexual harassment, and uncivil treatment, across different countries. Among eight European Union countries, Camerino et al. (2008) found that nurses in Poland were most likely to be verbally abused by their supervisors and colleagues, followed by those in France and Germany. On the other hand, Dutch nurses were least likely to suffer from verbal harassment. Guterman et al. (1996) found that almost half of the social workers in the American and Israeli samples had been verbally assaulted in the past 12 months. However, the American social workers were more likely to be sexually harassed than their Israeli counterparts. It is interesting to note that while inexperienced American social workers were more likely to be verbally abused, tenure was unrelated to Israeli social workers' experiences of verbal aggression. Finally, researchers have compared the experiences between Caribbean women who immigrated to Canada versus those who lived in the Caribbean (Ali & Toner, 2005). It was found that Caribbean women reported more abuse in intimate relationships and attributed the abuse to bad relationship partners. On the other hand, Caribbean–Canadian women experienced more abuse at work and cited systematic causes (e.g., racism) for their experiences. Overall, there appeared to be significant differences in exposure to both physical and nonphysical violence among workers from different parts of the world.

Other studies focused on identifying cross-cultural differences in values and attitudes that may explain the variations in the prevalence of workplace violence. For example, in a meta-analysis, cultures that are characterized by higher levels of individualism and conservation values had higher levels of general, societal aggression (Bergeron & Schneider, 2005). Extending to the workplace, this may explain why nurses in France and Germany, two highly individualistic countries, were exposed to more violence at work (Camerino et al., 2008). Another study explored the cross-cultural differences in the attitudes of nursing staff members toward the aggression from psychiatric patients. Jansen, Middel, Dassen, and Reijneveld (2006) found that U.K. nurses were most likely to view aggression from psychiatric patients as insulting and unacceptable behavior with the intention to harm others. On the other hand, Norwegian nurses tended to view aggression from psychiatric patients as defending or shielding their physical and emotional spaces. These differences in attitudes may influence how nurses respond to a violent episode and their subsequent treatment of the patient perpetrators, such that more coercive and restrictive strategies (e.g., mechanical restraint, seclusion) are likely to be adopted in countries where patient aggression is considered as threatening rather than a cry for help.

Methodological Concerns

CC/CN research has two particular methodological challenges: measurement equivalence and sample equivalence (Sanchez, Spector, & Cooper, 2006). *Measurement equivalence* is the extent to which an instrument (usually a self-report scale) maintains its calibration across samples. In other words, do people in different countries understand the items in the scale to mean the same thing, and are their responses to items given the same level of the underlying trait the same? *Sample equivalence* means that there is no confound between country and sample characteristics.

CC/CN studies most often use existing scales, often translating them into the appropriate language. The accepted procedure is *back-translation* (van de Vijver & Leung, 1997), in which an instrument is translated into a target language by one translator, and then the translation is independently translated back to the source language by another translator, and discrepancies are fixed. Whereas back-translation is an essential tool for CC/CN survey research, statistical tools are required to determine if equivalence has been achieved (Vandenberg, 2002; Vandenberg & Lance, 2000). The two approaches most often used are confirmatory factor analysis (CFA) and item response theory (IRT). CFA allows for comparisons of factor structure of a set of items, either from a single scale or from multiple scales simultaneously. There are a number of specific comparisons that range from stringent tests that interitem relationships (correlations or covariances) are the same, to tests that allow for less perfect equivalence, for example, that the same items load on the same factors although the magnitude of loadings are not the same (Vandenberg & Lance, 2000). IRT procedures allow for determination that items behave similarly across samples. It is generally used with scales that are unidimensional, and when multiple scales are analyzed they are done one at a time. It can be quite useful in refining scales by showing which items do not perform well across samples and should be eliminated. Of course, this assumes that there exist a sufficient number of remaining items that behave equivalently across samples.

CFA procedures are the most frequently used in CC/CN research. In fact, it has become common procedure to report results of CFA equivalence tests in papers describing cross-national comparative studies. There are two likely reasons for the greater popularity of CFA methods. First, CFA allows more flexibility in that it does not require unidimensional measures. Thus one can conduct CFA on scales that are multidimensional or on multiple scales at the same time. Second, methods for conducting CFA are more accessible and better developed in terms of providing a variety of fit statistics that allow for conclusions concerning equivalence (Reise, Widaman, & Pugh, 1993). Although CFA and IRT are very different approaches to establishing measurement equivalence, and each has its advantages, comparisons of both methods on the same data suggest they both will lead to the same overall conclusion (Maurer, Raju, & Collins, 1998; Reise et al., 1993), at least with data that are appropriate for both methods.

Sample equivalence can best be achieved by sampling the same occupation or occupations across countries. Evans et al. (1987), for example, sampled bus drivers in India and the United States. Although this approach can control for many confounds between country and nature of work, it is not always sufficient. There can be many differences across countries in the same occupation, for example, in demographics and in relative economic and social status. Although the nature of the work might be very much the same, the context in which that work is done can vary so that in one country the sample consists mainly of individuals working for large private organizations whereas in the other respondents are mainly from government agencies.

There are additional strategies that can help rule out confounds. One simple approach is to include additional measures of demographics and other variables suspected of being important. A series of analyses can be conducted to rule in or out the possibility that these additional variables are either accounting for or obscuring country differences. A second approach is to choose several matched occupations across studies to see if differences among countries are consistent. If a pattern of differences with elementary school teachers, for example, cannot be replicated with samples of accountants, nurses, or physicians, one might suspect that the teacher results might not have been due to country differences.

Future Research Directions

Four main directions are recommended for future research in cross-cultural OHP. First, studies should move beyond cross-national comparisons and start exploring the specific cultural values (or other country-level variables) that can explain the observed differences in various OHP areas between countries. For example, although multiple studies have shown cross-national differences in prevalence of workplace violence against the nursing profession (e.g., Camerino et al., 2008; Lawoko et al., 2004), none have examined the reasons behind these differences. Variations at the national policy level, specific cultural values, and/or display rules may explain the differences. Thus, more research is necessary to better understand the mechanisms underlying these observed cross-national differences.

Second, it is worthwhile to acknowledge that within-country variance in cultural values exists and deserves more research attention. For example, Triandis (1995) distinguished between the culture-level classification of individualism–collectivism from the psychological-level classification of idiocentrism (individual-level individualism)–allocentrism (individual-level collectivism). Research has shown that within-country variance in cultural values can have meaningful impact on employees' attitudes (e.g., organizational commitment; Clugston, Howell, & Dorfman, 2000). Thus, future research should explore how within-country differences in various cultural values may manifest themselves in different areas of OHP.

Third, more research needs to focus on the design and delivery of interventions intended to improve employee health, safety, and well-being in a cross-cultural setting. Comparative studies are necessary to better evaluate the effectiveness of the same intervention in different cultural contexts. As evident in some studies mentioned earlier (e.g., Janssens et al., 1995), the same set of organizational policies or programs may be implemented or received very differently depending on the cultural values. As such, effective interventions must be culturally sensitive in their design and delivery methods. More studies are necessary to identify the best practice for each unique cultural setting.

Finally, researchers should pay particular attention to the worker population that is especially vulnerable in today's global economy. For example, more organizations are sending their employees on overseas assignments. These expatriate employees often feel isolated in an unfamiliar setting, experience high levels of stress, and often abandon their post prematurely if their organizations do not provide adequate support (Kraimer & Wayne, 2004). They need to learn about and adapt to the host culture, which can be a daunting task even when their native culture is similar to the host one (e.g., United States and Canada; Selmer, 2007). Moreover, international assignments often involve the relocation of the whole family, which blurs the line between work and nonwork domains and can create additional stress for expatriates if their family members experience adjustment problems (Harris, 2004). Thus, expatriates may be a group that faces unique challenges and deserves research attention.

References

Ali, A., & Toner, B. (2005). A cross-cultural investigation of emotional abuse in Caribbean women and Caribbean-Canadian women. *Journal of Emotional Abuse, 5,* 125–140. doi:10.1300/J135v05n01_05

Argyle, M., & Cook, M. (1976). *Gaze and mutual gaze.* Cambridge, England: Syndics of the Cambridge University Press.

Aryee, S., Luk, V., Leung, A., & Lo, S. (1999). Role stressors, interrole conflict, and well-being: The moderating influence of spousal support and coping behaviors among employed parents in Hong Kong. *Journal of Vocational Behavior, 54,* 259–278. doi:10.1006/jvbe.1998.1667

Aryee, S., Srinivas, E., & Tan, H. H. (2005). Rhythms of life: Antecedents and outcomes of work–family balance in employed parents. *Journal of Applied Psychology, 90,* 132–146. doi:10.1037/0021-9010.90.1.132

Bardi, A., & Schwartz, S. H. (2003). Values and behaviors: Strength and structure of relations. *Personality and Social Psychology Bulletin, 29,* 1207–1220. doi:10.1177/0146167203254602

Barish, R. C. (2001). Legislation and regulations addressing workplace violence in the United States and British Columbia. *American Journal of Preventive Medicine, 20,* 149–154. doi:10.1016/S0749-3797(00)00291-9

Barling, J., & Griffiths, A. (2002). A history of occupational health psychology. In J. C. Quick & L. E. Tetrick (Eds.), *Handbook of occupational health psychology* (pp. 19–33). Washington, DC: American Psychological Association.

Beehr, T. A., & Glazer, S. (2001). A cultural perspective of social support in relation to occupational stress. In P. L. Perrewe & D. C. Ganster (Eds.), *Exploring theoretical mechanisms and perspectives* (pp. 97–142). New York, NY: JAI Press.

Bergeron, N., & Schneider, B. H. (2005). Explaining cross-national differences in peer-directed aggression: A quantitative synthesis. *Aggressive Behavior, 31,* 116–137. doi:10.1002/ab.20049

Bhagat, R. S., Ford, D. L., Jr., O'Driscoll, M. P., Frey, L., Babakus, E., & Mahanyele, M. (2001). Do South African managers cope differently from American managers? A cross-cultural investigation. *International Journal of Intercultural Relations, 25,* 301–313. doi:10.1016/S0147-1767(01)00005-0

Bishop, G. D., Enkelmann, H. C., Tong, E. M., Why, Y. P., Diong, S. M., Ang, J., & Khader, M. (2003). Job demands, decisional control, and cardiovascular responses. *Journal of Occupational Health Psychology, 8,* 146–156. doi:10.1037/1076-8998.8.2.146

Bono, J. E., & Vey, M. A. (2005). Toward understanding emotional management at work: A quantitative review of emotional labor research. In C. E. Härtel, W. J. Zerbe, & N. M. Ashkanasy (Eds.), *Emotions in organizational behavior* (pp. 213–233). Mahwah, NJ: Erlbaum.

Burke, M. J., Chan-Serafin, S., Salvador, R., Smith, A., & Sarpy, S. A. (2008). The role of national culture and organizational climate in safety training effectiveness. *European Journal of Work and Organizational Psychology, 17,* 133–152. doi:10.1080/13594320701307503

Burke, M. J., Sarpy, S. A., Smith-Crowe, K., Chan-Serafin, S., Salvador, R. O., & Islam, G. (2006). Relative effectiveness of worker safety and health training methods. *American Journal of Public Health, 96,* 315–324. doi:10.2105/AJPH.2004.059840

Camerino, D., Estryn-Beharc, M., Conway, P. M., van Der Heijden, B. I. J. M., & Hasselhorn, H.-M. (2008). Work-related factors and violence among nursing staff in the European NEXT study: A longitudinal cohort study. *International Journal of Nursing Studies, 45,* 35–50. doi:10.1016/j.ijnurstu.2007.01.013

Chang, C.-H., Rosen, C. C., & Levy, P. E. (2009). The relationship between perceptions of organizational politics and employee attitudes, strain, and behavior: A meta-analytic examination. *Academy of Management Journal, 52,* 779–801.

Chen, W.-Q., Wong, T.-W., Yu, T.-S., Lin, Y.-Z., & Cooper, C. L. (2003). Determinants of perceived occupational stress among Chinese offshore oil workers. *Work and Stress, 17,* 287–305. doi:10.1080/02678370310001647302

Chiu, R. K., & Kosinski, F. A., Jr. (1999). The role of affective dispositions in job satisfaction and work strain: Comparing collectivist and individualist societies. *International Journal of Psychology, 34,* 19–28. doi:10.1080/002075999400078

Clugston, M., Howell, J. P., & Dorfman, P. W. (2000). Does cultural socialization predict multiple bases and foci of commitment? *Journal of Management, 26,* 5–30. doi:10.1016/S0149-2063(99)00034-3

Collett, P. (1971). On training Englishmen in the non-verbal behaviour of Arabs: An experiment in intercultural communication. *International Journal of Psychology, 6,* 209–215. doi:10.1080/00207597108246684

Cooper, C. L. (2000). Editorial: Future research in occupational stress. *Stress Medicine, 16,* 63–64. doi:10.1002/(SICI)1099-1700(200003)16:2<63::AID-SMI865>3.0.CO;2-8

Cousins, C. R., & Tang, N. (2004). Working time and work and family conflict in the Netherlands, Sweden and the UK. *Work, Employment and Society, 18,* 531–549. doi:10.1177/0950017004045549

Ekman, P., & Friesen, W. V. (1975). *Unmasking the face: A guide to recognizing emotions from facial clues.* Upper Saddle River, NJ: Prentice-Hall.

Evans, G. W., Palsane, M. N., & Carrere, S. (1987). Type A behavior and occupational stress: A cross-cultural study of blue-collar workers. *Journal of Personality and Social Psychology, 52,* 1002–1007. doi:10.1037/0022-3514.52.5.1002

Frankenhaeuser, M., & Johansson, G. (1986). Stress at work: Psychobiological and psychosocial aspects. *International Review of Applied Psychology, 35,* 287–299. doi:10.1111/j.1464-0597.1986.tb00928.x

Geurts, S. A., Kompier, M. A., Roxburgh, S., & Houtman, I. L. (2003). Does work–home interference mediate the relationship between workload and well-being? *Journal of Vocational Behavior, 63,* 532–559. doi:10.1016/S0001-8791(02)00025-8

Goldberg, L. S., & Grandey, A. A. (2007). Display rules versus display autonomy: Emotion regulation, emotional exhaustion, and task performance in a call center simulation. *Journal of Occupational Health Psychology, 12,* 301–318. doi:10.1037/1076-8998.12.3.301

Grandey, A. A., & Brauberger, A. L. (2002). The emotion regulation behind the customer service smile. In R. G. Lord, R. J. Klimoski, & R. Kanfer (Eds.), *Emotions in the workplace: Understanding the structure and role of emotions in organizational behavior* (pp. 260–294). San Francisco, CA: Jossey-Bass.

Grandey, A. A., Fisk, G. M., & Steiner, D. D. (2005). Must "service with a smile" be stressful? The moderating role of personal control for American and French employees. *Journal of Applied Psychology, 90,* 893–904. doi:10.1037/0021-9010.90.5.893

Greenhaus, J. H., & Beutell, N. J. (1985). Sources and conflict between work and family roles. *Academy of Management Review, 10,* 76–88. doi:10.2307/258214

Guterman, N. B., Jayaratne, S., & Bargal, D. (1996). Workplace violence and victimization experienced by social workers: A cross-national study of Americans and Israelis. In G. R. VandenBos & E. Q. Bulatao (Eds.), *Violence on the job: Identifying risks and developing solutions* (pp. 175–188). Washington, DC: American Psychological Association. doi:10.1037/10215-007

Gyekye, S. A., & Salminen, S. (2005). Responsibility assignment at the workplace: A Finnish and Ghanaian perspective. *Scandinavian Journal of Psychology, 46,* 43–48. doi:10.1111/j.1467-9450.2005.00433.x

Harris, H. (2004). Global careers: Work-life issues and the adjustment of women international managers. *Journal of Management Development, 23,* 818–832. doi:10.1108/02621710410558431

Hasselhorn, H. M., Müller, B. H., & Tackenberg, P. (2005). *NEXT scientific report.* Retrieved from http://www.next.uni-wuppertal.de/download/NEXTscientificreportjuly2005.pdf

Hill, E., Yang, C., Hawkins, A. J., & Ferris, M. (2004). A cross-cultural test of the work–family interface in 48 countries. *Journal of Marriage and the Family, 66,* 1300–1316. doi:10.1111/j.0022-2445.2004.00094.x

Hofstede, G. (1980). *Culture's consequences: International differences in work-related values.* Beverly Hills, CA: Sage.

Hsu, S. H., Lee, C.-C., Wu, M.-C., & Takano, K. (2008). A cross-cultural study of organizational factors on safety: Japanese vs. Taiwanese oil refinery plants. *Accident; Analysis and Prevention, 40,* 24–34. doi:10.1016/j.aap.2007.03.020

Jamal, M. (1999). Job stress, type-A behavior, and well-being: A cross-cultural examination. *International Journal of Stress Management, 6,* 57–67. doi:10.1023/A:1021962320645

Jansen, G. J., Middel, B., Dassen, T. W. N., & Reijneveld, M. S. A. (2006). Cross-cultural differences in psychiatric nurses' attitudes to inpatient aggression. *Archives of Psychiatric Nursing, 20,* 82–93. doi:10.1016/j.apnu.2005.08.012

Janssens, M., Brett, J. M., & Smith, F. J. (1995). Confirmatory cross-cultural research: Testing the viability of a corporation-wide safety policy. *Academy of Management Journal, 38,* 364–382. doi:10.2307/256684

Jex, S. M. (1998). *Stress and job performance: Theory, research, and implications for managerial practice.* Thousand Oaks, CA: Sage.

Karasek, R. A. (1979). Job demands, job decision latitude, and mental strain: Implications for job redesign. *Administrative Science Quarterly, 24,* 285–307. doi:10.2307/2392498

Karasek, R. A., Baker, D., Marxer, F., Ahlbom, A., & Theorell, T. (1981). Job decision latitude, job demands, and cardiovascular disease: A prospective study of Swedish men. *American Journal of Public Health, 71,* 694–705. doi:10.2105/AJPH.71.7.694

Karasek, R. A., & Theorell, T. (1990). *Healthy work: Stress, productivity and the reconstruction of work life.* New York, NY: Basic Books.

Kim, E. (2007). Occupational stress: A survey of psychotherapists in Korea and the United States. *International Journal of Stress Management, 14,* 111–120. doi:10.1037/1072-5245.14.1.111

Kraimer, M. L., & Wayne, S. J. (2004). An examination of POS as a multidimensional construct in the context of an expatriate assignment. *Journal of Management, 30,* 209–237. doi:10.1016/j.jm.2003.01.001

Lanza, M. (2006). Violence in nursing. In E. K. Kelloway, J. Barling, & J. J. Hurrell Jr. (Eds.), *Handbook of workplace violence* (pp. 147–167). Thousand Oaks, CA: Sage.

Lazarus, R. S. (1991). Psychological stress in the workplace. *Journal of Social Behavior and Personality, 6,* 1–13.

Lawoko, S., Soares, J. J. F., & Nolan, P. (2004). Violence towards psychiatric staff: A comparison of gender, job and environmental characteristics in England and Sweden. *Work and Stress, 18,* 39–55. doi:10.1080/02678370410001710337

Li, W.-C., Harris, D., & Chen, A. (2007). Eastern minds in Western cockpits: Meta-analysis of human factors in mishaps from three nations. *Aviation, Space, and Environmental Medicine, 78,* 420–425.

Liu, C., Spector, P. E., & Shi, L. (2007). Cross-national job stress: A quantitative and qualitative study. *Journal of Organizational Behavior, 28,* 209–239. doi:10.1002/job.435

Lu, C.-Q., Siu, O.-L., & Cooper, C. L. (2005). Managers' occupational stress in China: The role of self-efficacy. *Personality and Individual Differences, 38,* 569–578. doi:10.1016/j.paid.2004.05.012

Lu, C.-S., & Tsai, C.-L. (2008). The effects of safety climate on vessel accidents in the container shipping context. *Accident; Analysis and Prevention, 40,* 594–601. doi:10.1016/j.aap.2007.08.015

Lu, L., Gilmour, R., Kao, S. F., & Huang, M. T. (2006). A cross-cultural study of work/family demands, work/family conflict and wellbeing: The Taiwanese vs. British. *Career Development International, 11,* 9–27. doi:10.1108/13620430610642354

Matsui, T., Ohsawa, T., & Onglatco, M.-L. (1995). Work–family conflict and the stress-buffering effects of husband support and coping behavior among Japanese married working women. *Journal of Vocational Behavior, 47,* 178–192. doi:10.1006/jvbe.1995.1034

Matsumoto, D., Yoo, S. H., Hirayama, S., & Petrova, G. (2005). Development and validation of a measure of display rule knowledge: The Display Rule Assessment Inventory. *Emotion, 5,* 23–40. doi:10.1037/1528-3542.5.1.23

Matsumoto, D., Yoo, S. H., & Nakagawa, S. (2008). Culture, emotion regulation, and adjustment. *Journal of Personality and Social Psychology, 94,* 925–937. doi:10.1037/0022-3514.94.6.925

Maurer, T. J., Raju, N. S., & Collins, W. C. (1998). Peer and subordinate performance appraisal measurement equivalence. *Journal of Applied Psychology, 83,* 693–702. doi:10.1037/0021-9010.83.5.693

Mearns, K., Rundmo, T., Flin, R., Gordon, R., & Fleming, M. (2004). Evaluation of psychosocial and organizational factors in offshore safety: A comparative study. *Journal of Risk Research, 7,* 545–561. doi:10.1080/1366987042000146193

Merchant, J. A., & Lundell, J. (2001). Workplace violence intervention research workshop, April 5–7, 2000, Washington, DC: Background, rationale, and summary. *American Journal of Preventive Medicine, 20,* 135–140. doi:10.1016/S0749-3797(00)00289-0

Narayanan, L., Menon, S., & Spector, P. (1999). A cross-cultural comparison of job stressors and reactions among employees holding comparable jobs in two countries. *International Journal of Stress Management, 6,* 197–212. doi:10.1023/A:1021986709317

National Institute for Occupational Health and Safety. (1997). *Musculoskeletal disorders and workplace factors: A critical review of epidemiologic evidence for work-related musculoskeletal disorders of the neck, upper extremity, and low back.* Cincinnati, OH: NIOSH–Publications Dissemination.

Neal, A., & Griffin, M. A. (2006). A study of the lagged relationships among safety climate, safety motivation, safety behavior, and accidents at the individual and group levels. *Journal of Applied Psychology, 91,* 946–953. doi:10.1037/0021-9010.91.4.946

Newnam, S., Griffin, M. A., & Mason, C. (2008). Safety in work vehicles: A multilevel study linking safety values and individual predictors to work-related driving crashes. *Journal of Applied Psychology, 93,* 632–644. doi:10.1037/0021-9010.93.3.632

Pal, S., & Saksvik, P. O. (2008). Work–family conflict and psychosocial work environment stressors as predictors of job stress in a cross-cultural study. *International Journal of Stress Management, 15,* 22–42. doi:10.1037/1072-5245.15.1.22

Perrewé, P. L., & Zellars, K. L. (1999). An examination of attributions and emotions in the transactional approach to the organizational stress process. *Journal of Organizational Behavior, 20,* 739–752. doi:10.1002/(SICI)1099-1379(199909)20:5<739::AID-JOB1949>3.0.CO;2-C

Peterson, M. F., Smith, P. B., Akande, A., Ayestaran, S., Bochner, S., Callan, V., . . . Sinha, T. N. (1995). Role conflict, ambiguity, and overload: A 21-nation study. *Academy of Management Journal, 38,* 429–452. doi:10.2307/256687

Pugh, S. D. (2001). Service with a smile: Emotional contagion in the service encounter. *Academy of Management Journal, 44,* 1018–1027. doi:10.2307/3069445

Reise, S. P., Widaman, K. F., & Pugh, R. H. (1993). Confirmatory factor analysis and item response theory: Two approaches for exploring measurement invariance. *Psychological Bulletin, 114,* 552–566. doi:10.1037/0033-2909.114.3.552

Rohan, M. J. (2000). A rose by any name? The values construct. *Personality and Social Psychology Review, 4,* 255–277. doi:10.1207/S15327957PSPR0403_4

Sanchez, J. I., Spector, P. E., & Cooper, C. L. (2006). Frequently ignored methodological issues in cross-cultural stress research. In P. T. P. Wong & L. C. J. Wong (Eds.), *Handbook of multicultural perspectives on stress and coping* (pp. 187–201). Dallas, TX: Spring Publications.

Schaubroeck, J., Lam, S. S., & Xie, J. L. (2000). Collective efficacy versus self-efficacy in coping responses to stressors and control: A cross-cultural study. *Journal of Applied Psychology, 85,* 512–525. doi:10.1037/0021-9010.85.4.512

Schwartz, S. H. (1994). Are there universal aspects in the content and structure of values? *Journal of Social Issues, 50,* 19–45.

Selmer, J. (2007). Which is easier, adjusting to a similar or to a dissimilar culture? American business expatriates in Canada and Germany. *International Journal of Cross Cultural Management, 7,* 185–201. doi:10.1177/1470595807079385

Simon, M., Tackenberg, P., Nienhaus, A., Estryn-Behar, M., Conway, P. M., & Hasselhorn, H.-M. (2008). Back or neck-pain-related disability of nursing staff in hospitals, nursing homes, and home care in seven countries: Results from the European NEXT-study. *International Journal of Nursing Studies, 45,* 24–34. doi:10.1016/j.ijnurstu.2006.11.003

Siu, O.-L., Phillips, R., & Leung, T.-W. (2004). Safety climate and safety performance among construction workers in Hong Kong: The role of psychological strains as mediators. *Accident; Analysis and Prevention, 36,* 359–366. doi:10.1016/S0001-4575(03)00016-2

Smith, D. R. (2003). *Dermatological and musculoskeletal disorders of nursing home workers in Australia, Japan, Korea and Taiwan.* Unpublished doctoral dissertation, University of Southern Queensland, Toowoomba, Australia.

Smith, D. R., Mihashi, M., Adachi, Y., Koga, H., & Ishitake, T. (2006). A detailed analysis of musculoskeletal disorder risk factors among Japanese nurses. *Journal of Safety Research, 37,* 195–200. doi:10.1016/j.jsr.2006.01.004

Smith, D. R., Wei, N., Zhang, Y.-J., & Wang, R.-S. (2006). Musculoskeletal complaints and psychosocial risk factors among physicians in mainland China. *International Journal of Industrial Ergonomics, 36,* 599–603. doi:10.1016/j.ergon.2006.01.014

Sobeih, T. M., Salem, O., Daraiseh, N., Genaidy, A., & Shell, R. (2006). Psychosocial factors and musculoskeletal disorders in the construction industry: A systematic review. *Theoretical Issues in Ergonomics Science, 7,* 329–344. doi:10.1080/14639220500090760

Spangenberg, S., Baarts, C., Dyreborg, J., Jensen, L., Kines, P., & Mikkelsen, K. L. (2003). Factors contributing to the differences in work related injury rates between Danish and Swedish construction workers. *Safety Science, 41,* 517–530. doi:10.1016/S0925-7535(02)00007-3

Spector, P. E. (1988). Development of the Work Locus of Control Scale. *Journal of Occupational Psychology, 61,* 335–340.

Spector, P. E. (1992). A consideration of the validity and meaning of self-report measures of job conditions. In C. L. Cooper & I. T. Robertson (Eds.), *International review of industrial and organizational psychology: 1992* (pp. 123–151). West Sussex, England: Wiley.

Spector, P. E., Allen, T. D., Poelmans, S. A. Y., Lapierre, L. M., Cooper, C. L., O'Driscoll, M., . . . Widerszal-Bazyl, M. (2007). Cross-national differences in relationships of work demands, job satisfaction, and turnover intentions with work–family conflict. *Personnel Psychology, 60,* 805–835. doi:10.1111/j.1744-6570.2007.00092.x

Spector, P. E., Cooper, C. L., & Aguilar-Vafaie, M. E. (2002). A comparative study of perceived job stressor sources and job strain in American and Iranian managers. *Applied Psychology: An International Review, 51,* 446–457. doi:10.1111/1464-0597.00102

Spector, P. E., Cooper, C. L., Poelmans, S., Allen, T. D., O'Driscoll, M., Sanchez, J. I., . . . Lu, S. (2004). A cross-national comparative study of work–family stressors, working hours, and well-being: China and Latin America versus the Anglo world. *Personnel Psychology, 57,* 119–142. doi:10.1111/j.1744-6570.2004.tb02486.x

Spector, P. E., Cooper, C. L., Sanchez, J. I., O'Driscoll, M., Sparks, K., Bernin, P., . . . Yu, S. (2001). Do national levels of individualism and internal locus of control relate to well-being: An ecological level international study. *Journal of Organizational Behavior, 22,* 815–832. doi:10.1002/job.118

Spector, P. E., Cooper, C. L., Sanchez, J. I., O'Driscoll, M., Sparks, K., Bernin, P., . . . Yu, S. (2002). Locus of control and well-being at work: How generalizable are Western findings? *Academy of Management Journal, 45,* 453–466. doi:10.2307/3069359

Spector, P. E., Sanchez, J. I., Siu, O. L., Salgado, J., & Ma, J. (2004). Eastern versus Western control beliefs at work: An investigation of secondary control, socioinstrumental control, and work locus of control in China and the US. *Applied Psychology: An International Review, 53,* 38–60. doi:10.1111/j.1464-0597.2004.00160.x

Sutton, R. I. (1991). Maintaining norms about expressed emotions: The case of bill collectors. *Administrative Science Quarterly, 36,* 245–268. doi:10.2307/2393355

Triandis, H. C. (1995). *Individualism and collectivism.* Boulder, CO: Westview Press.

Triandis, H. C. (2001). Individualism–collectivism and personality. *Journal of Personality, 69,* 907–924. doi:10.1111/1467-6494.696169

U.S. Department of Labor. (2008). *Bureau of Labor Statistics: Injuries, illnesses and fatalities.* Retrieved from http://www.bls.gov/iif/home.htm#tables

van de Vijver, F. J. R., & Leung, K. (1997). *Methods and data analysis for cross-cultural research.* Thousand Oaks, CA: Sage.

Vandenberg, R. J. (2002). Toward a further understanding of an improvement in measurement invariance methods and procedures. *Organizational Research Methods, 5,* 139–158. doi:10.1177/1094428102005002001

Vandenberg, R. J., & Lance, C. E. (2000). A review and synthesis of the measurement invariance literature: Suggestions, practices, and recommendations for organizational research. *Organizational Research Methods, 3,* 4–69. doi:10.1177/109442810031002

Vassie, L., Tomàs, J. M., & Oliver, A. (2000). Health and safety management in UK and Spanish SMEs: A comparative study. *Journal of Safety Research, 31,* 35–43. doi:10.1016/S0022-4375(99)00028-6

Verhoeven, C., Maes, S., Kraaij, V., & Joekes, K. (2003). The job demand–control–social support model and wellness/health outcomes: A European study. *Psychology and Health, 18,* 421. doi:10.1080/0887044031000147175

Waluyo, L., Ekberg, K., & Eklund, J. (1996). Assembly work in Indonesia and in Sweden: Ergonomics, health, and satisfaction. *Ergonomics, 39,* 199–212. doi:10.1080/00140139608964451

Widerszal-Bazyl, M., Radkiewicz, P., Hasselhorn, H. M., Conway, P. M., & van der Heijden, B. (2008). The demand–control–support model and intent to leave across six European countries: The role of employment opportunities. *Work and Stress, 22,* 166–184. doi:10.1080/02678370801999750

Yang, N., Chen, C. C., Choi, J., & Zou, Y. (2000). Sources of work–family conflict: A Sino–U.S. comparison of the effects of work and family demands. *Academy of Management Journal, 43,* 113–123. doi:10.2307/1556390

Zacharatos, A., Barling, J., & Iverson, R. D. (2005). High-performance work systems and occupational safety. *Journal of Applied Psychology, 90,* 77–93. doi:10.1037/0021-9010.90.1.77

Zemba, Y., Young, M. J., & Morris, M. W. (2006). Blaming leaders for organizational accidents: Proxy logic in collective- versus individual-agency cultures. *Organizational Behavior and Human Decision Processes, 101,* 36–51. doi:10.1016/j.obhdp.2006.04.007

Zohar, D., & Luria, G. (2005). A multilevel model of safety climate: Cross-level relationships between organization and group-level climates. *Journal of Applied Psychology, 90,* 616–628. doi:10.1037/0021-9010.90.4.616

Part III

Causes and Risks

8

Safety Climate: Conceptual and Measurement Issues

Dov Zohar

Workplace injuries and illnesses result in 4% to 5% loss of gross domestic product (World Health Organization, 2008). Such a loss is expected to cost the American economy an estimated $550 billion a year (Bureau of Economic Analysis, 2008), in addition to human suffering and loss of life. A fatal work injury occurs every 2 hr in the United States, and a disabling injury every 8 s (National Safety Council, 1999). Large-scale accidents such as the Chernobyl or Bhopal disasters have provided dramatic evidence of the economic and human costs of industrial accidents. However, despite the economic and social significance of safety issues, they have received only cursory attention by management scholars (Fahlbruch & Wilpert, 1999; Glendon, Clarke, & McKenna, 2006; Shannon, Mayr, & Haines, 1997). An exception is the growing body of research on safety climate and culture, which has captured increasing attention since the inquiry into the Chernobyl disaster identified inadequate safety culture as a major underlying factor for the accident (International Atomic Energy Agency, 1986, 1991). A recent review indicated that the number of publications in this field has been increasing exponentially over the past decade (Glendon, 2008a). Furthermore, two recent meta-analyses, covering 202 studies (Nahrgang, Morgeson, & Hofmann, 2008) and 90 studies (Christian, Bradley, Wallace, & Burke, 2009), indicated that safety climate is a robust predictor of subjective and objective safety outcomes across industries and countries. However, this literature is characterized by conceptual ambiguity, evident in the fact that many authors fail to discriminate between safety climate and culture (Cox & Flin, 1998; Glendon, 2008b), in addition to including a host of variables that belong neither to climate nor to culture as defined in the organizational behavior literature.

This chapter is based on the premise that safety climate and culture must be clearly distinguished on grounds of discriminant validity. Using these constructs interchangeably, or operationalizing culture with climate scales, as is the common practice, results in conceptual slippage damaging to both. However, given the multitude of proposed solutions concerning ways of mapping safety climate onto safety culture, it hardly seems worthwhile suggesting yet another solution. A more beneficial strategy would be to increase conceptual clarity for each construct (considered in isolation) before attempting integration.

The purpose of this chapter, therefore, is to review the climate literature from an analytical perspective and to offer a model of safety climate that clarifies its nature. I first consider some basic attributes of organizational climate. Subsequently, I present a multilevel model specifying distinctions between organization- and group-level climate perceptions. Having defined the attributes of climate, I then focus on climate antecedents and its consequences, highlighting differences between these variable classes. Finally, I discuss measurement implications and highlight directions for future research.

Definitions of Organizational Climate

Organizational climate refers to shared perceptions among members of an organization with regard to its fundamental properties, in other words, policies, procedures, and practices (Ostroff, Kinicki, & Tamkins, 2003; Reichers & Schneider, 1990; Rentsch, 1990). A multilevel interpretation suggests that policies define strategic goals and means of goal attainment, whereas procedures provide tactical guidelines for action related to these goals and means. Practices, on the other hand, relate to the execution of policies and procedures by managers across the organizational hierarchy (Zohar, 2000; Zohar & Luria, 2005). Because organizations have multiple goals and means of attaining goals, senior managers must develop policies and procedures for each organizational facet (e.g., customer service, product quality, employee safety). To the extent that these policies are sufficiently clear and unequivocal, they allow a consensus among employees concerning their nature. This results in the formation of multiple climates in organizations, with employees focusing concurrently on different organizational facets such as the climates for innovation (Anderson & West, 1998), customer service (Schneider, Bowen, Ehrhart, & Holcombe, 2000), initiative (Baer & Frese, 2003), justice (Yang, Mossholder, & Peng, 2007), and safety (Dedobbeleer & Beland, 1991; Zohar, 1980, 2000).

Climate is an emergent property, characterizing groups of individuals. Operationally, it is assessed by aggregating individual perceptions to the required unit of analysis (organization, department, work group) and using the mean to represent the climate for that entity (Kozlowski & Klein, 2000; Reichers & Schneider, 1990). Research to date has identified three validation criteria for aggregated perceptions (Chan, 1998). The first is within-unit homogeneity, or consensus of perceptions. Without sufficient homogeneity, an aggregate score is not a valid indicator of climate (James, 1982). Because climate, like leadership and cohesion, is a group-level property, it follows that the individual level of analysis must be excluded from models of climate (Glick, 1988; Patterson, Payne, & West, 1996; Rousseau, 1988). Thus, variables such as personal beliefs concerning why accidents happen or job involvement should not be considered as climate variables. The second criterion is between-units variability, relating to units of analysis such as organizations or subunits within an organization. In other words, homogeneity of perceptions within the chosen unit of analysis must coincide with heterogeneity, or variance, between units (Glick, 1985; Patterson et al., 1996; Payne, 1990; Rousseau, 1988). The third validation criterion is that units of analysis should correspond to natural social units such as work groups, departments, or organizations. Although there has been some debate concerning this requirement (Joyce & Slocum, 1984), most authors consider it necessary

(Glick, 1988; Patterson et al., 1996; Payne, 1990). This contradicts the psychological climate perspective (James & Jones, 1974) whereby individuals sharing the same views of the organization are clustered by statistical means, although they may never have met or seen each other.

Previous research using indexes of agreement such as intraclass correlation (James, 1982), within-group correlation (R_{wg}; James, Demaree, & Wolf, 1984, 1993), or the average deviation index (Burke & Dunlap, 2002) have indicated that homogeneity of climate perceptions may vary. Because homogeneity statistics offer no test of statistical significance, Glick (1985) provided a heuristic for the R_{wg} coefficient whereby values of .70 and higher warrant aggregation of individual responses. Note, however, that this implies that climates may vary appreciably in terms of homogeneity (granted, of course, that a certain threshold value is surpassed). It follows, therefore, that climates can be described in terms of two independent parameters: (a) strength of climate (weak to strong), referring to the internal consistency with which climate perceptions are held; and (b) level of climate (low to high), referring to the relative position of the climate mean on the relevant continuum. Thus, for example, high safety climate relates to supportive policies concerning safety and health, though such a climate may be strong or weak, depending on the extent of agreement among employees in their respective organizations or subunits. This will have important implications for the effect of climate on safety behavior.

The Core Meaning of Safety Climate

As noted previously, organizations have multiple goals and means of attaining those goals, so that senior managers must develop facet-specific policies and procedures to which employees attend, resulting in multiple specific climates. Thus, safety climate relates to shared perceptions with regard to safety policies, procedures, and practices. However, assessment of such policies, procedures, and practices can be quite complex, requiring, among other things, establishment of differences between formally declared policies and procedures and their enforced counterparts (i.e., managerial practices). Formal policy is explicit, relating to overt statements and formal procedures, whereas enforced policy or enacted practices are tacit, derived from observing senior, middle, and lower management patterns of action concerning key policy issues. This distinction is akin to that made by Argyris and Schon (1996) between formally espoused theories of action, or policies, and theories-in-use. A similar distinction is associated with behavioral integrity (Simons, 2002), referring to the alignment between words and deeds on behalf of organizational managers. From a functional perspective, climate perceptions should refer only to policies-in-use, or enacted policies, rather than to their formal counterparts, because they inform employees of the probable consequences of safety behavior. Thus, a consensus should occur when management displays an internally consistent pattern of action concerning safety, even if it differs from formally declared policy. For example, site managers might expect workers to bend company safety rules, except in life-threatening situations or whenever production falls behind schedule, despite official claims to the contrary. If this is done consistently, it will promote a low safety climate, as described by Pate-Cornell (1990) and Wright (1986) with regard to managerial practices on offshore oil platforms.

Given that safety issues are inherent to every manufacturing process while competing with other issues such as speed or profitability, it follows that enforced safety policies and procedures can be construed in terms of the relative priorities of safety and production goals. Because relative priorities provide an economical means of interpreting the pragmatic meaning of enforced policies for company employees, it is proposed that safety climate perceptions refer to those policy attributes that indicate the true priority of safety. This agrees with the constructivist principle of least effort (Zipf, 1965), suggesting that employees will opt for the most economical means to assess enforced policies and procedures. The object of safety climate perceptions is, therefore, the (true) priority of safety, so that climate level reflects its consensual priority rather than numerous procedures considered individually. In other words, climate perceptions relate to "procedures-as-pattern" rather than to individual procedures. In this respect, safety climate is assumed to be a social construct (Rochlin, 1999), part of an active process of organizational sense-making (Drazin, Glynn, & Kazanjian, 1999; Weick, 1995), as opposed to passive observation of isolated safety procedures. Thus, for example, whenever safety issues are ignored or made contingent on production pressures, workers will infer low safety priority. All that is required for such a policy to become a source of (low) climate perceptions is that it remains unequivocal and stable.

Leadership as a Climate Antecedent

Among the various climate antecedents, leadership has attracted much of the attention. The quality of leader–member relationships has been assumed to play a key role in climate emergence due to the complexity of the organizational environment, presenting employees with competing demands that need to be managed simultaneously (Quinn & McGrath, 1985; Quinn & Rohrbaugh, 1983). For example, safe behavior tends to be differentially supported or rewarded under changing task conditions (e.g., falling behind schedule), and supervisors occasionally disregard procedural violations depending on production speed or efficiency demands (Zohar, 2003). High-quality relationships are characterized by mutual trust and openness (House & Shamir, 1993) and by the richness of verbal communication between leader and members (Klauss & Bass, 1982). Such leaders create more opportunities for sharing and clarifying perceptions (Kozlowski & Doherty, 1989) and offer better articulation of task cues (Kirkpatrick & Locke, 1996). These features should provide group members with better information for assessing what is prioritized, valued, and supported under a variety of conditions, promoting the development of shared climate perceptions.

In addition to facilitating shared climate perceptions, effective leaders have also been shown to promote higher or more positive safety climate in work groups performing risky tasks. This relationship has been shown for transformational (Bass, 1990, 1998) or high leader–member exchange (LMX) leaders (Graen & Uhl-Bien, 1995) across a variety of circumstances and industries (e.g., Barling,

Loughlin, & Kelloway, 2002; Gonzalez-Roma, Peiro, & Tordera, 2002; Hofmann & Morgeson, 1999; Hofmann, Morgeson, & Gerras, 2003; Zohar, 2002a; Zohar & Luria, 2004). Recent meta-analyses have reinforced the robustness of this relationship, resulting in strong corrected correlation estimates exceeding .5 or .6 (Christian et al., 2009; Nahrgang et al., 2008). These results support the idea that when work involves heightened physical risks, transformational or high-LMX leaders better inform members of the priority of safe behavior in the context of other competing demands, resulting in more positive safety climates. Furthermore, such leaders are more committed to employee safety as an extension of their global commitment to members' growth and development (Hofmann & Morgeson, 2003; Zohar, 2003), constituting the foundation of this leadership style (Bass, 1990).

Although the role of leadership as a climate antecedent has been well established, there is only limited research concerning underlying mechanisms. Such mechanisms should explain how leaders promote a more positive or stronger safety climate. Barling et al. (2002) suggested that transformational leaders employ their proactive orientation to work issues in the service of safety, promoting members' safety engagement and citizenship behaviors. Using social network analysis, Zohar and Tenne-Gazit (2008) indicated that transformational leaders promote higher density of group communication, resulting in a stronger group climate. Furthermore, such leaders also act as gatekeepers, maintaining higher priority for safety issues especially in organizations in which safety assumes a lower priority (Zohar & Luria, in press). Given the robustness of the leadership–climate relationship, further research into explanatory variables associated with this relationship is warranted.

Differentiation Between Climate and Leadership

Given the robustness and proximity of relationships between leadership and (safety) climate, a discussion of the discriminant validity of the two constructs is in order. *Leadership styles* refer to the nature and effectiveness of interpersonal relationships between leaders and members. The full-range leadership model, for example, construes leader–member relationships in terms of the continuum of passive to active/transactive to proactive/transformative (Bass, 1990). In contrast, the core meaning of *safety climate* refers to managerial or supervisor commitment to employees' safety (Flin, Mearns, O'Connor, & Bryden, 2000; Zohar, 2003) rather than to the nature or temporal orientation of interpersonal exchanges. Respective measurement scales operationalize these differences, using relationship-based referents for collecting leadership perceptions, and commitment-based referents for climate perceptions. Congruently, the factorial structure of leadership scales reflects different leadership styles, whereas that of climate scales reflects commitments and priorities associated with different performance facets.

Such distinctions have led climate scholars to postulate that leadership is a proximal antecedent rather than an embedded dimension of climate (e.g., Hofmann & Morgeson, 2003; Kozlowski & Doherty, 1989; Ostroff et al., 2003). The robustness of the relationship between the two constructs stems from the fact that leaders' interactions with group members constitute the primary source of information about the organizational environment, in addition to being the most salient attribute of this environment. Put differently, leader–member interactions provide the medium in which policies are implemented, yet the medium, although influencing the message (e.g., greater emphasis on safety under high-quality leader–member interactions) should not be confused with it.

This conceptual framework has received considerable support in safety research, indicating that although higher quality relationships between leaders and members predict a higher safety climate (e.g., Barling et al., 2002; Hofmann et al., 2003), this relationship is moderated by contextual factors. For example, Zohar (2002a) showed that relationships between different leadership styles and safety climate were moderated by the priority of safety, as communicated by the leader's immediate superior.

Leadership as a climate antecedent assumes also a key role in explaining the relationship between safety climate and motivation. As noted previously, safety behavior of employees poses a managerial challenge because of employees' bias against safe conduct under regular job conditions (Zohar & Erev, 2007). The negative value function for safe behavior can be modified by introducing short-term rewards that outweigh immediate costs, for which one readily available resource is leader–member exchange. An effective supervisor who is also committed to safety will observe whether work is performed properly, including the use of protective gear, and express approval or disapproval immediately afterward (Komaki, 1998). If this is done uniformly and consistently to all group members and in all situations, subordinates will infer a high safety priority, resulting in high (and strong) safety climate and, as a consequence, high safety motivation. Because supervisory contingencies are known to influence members' motivation and behavior (Komaki, 1998), this obviates the need to include external contingencies characteristic of most behavior-based safety interventions (see the meta-analysis by Stajkovic & Luthans, 1997). Hence, interventions that improve supervisory safety practices might offer a new strategy whose distinctive feature is that supervisory practice is modified to introduce change in safety climate and motivation on the shop floor.

The viability of this approach, identified as *supervision-based safety,* was tested by Zohar and colleagues (Zohar & Luria, 2003; Zohar & Polatchek, 2009), who provided evidence indicating that improved supervisory safety practices resulted in significant and stable changes in safety climate scores, safety behaviors, and minor injury rates. Future research should identify additional ways for inducing such change, taking advantage of the robust motivational and behavioral outcomes afforded by the law of effect. Given the human and economic cost of occupational accidents, this and other lines of research suggested previously should be considered not only as an intellectual challenge but also as a societal challenge.

A Multilevel Model of Safety Climate

Figure 8.1 presents a multilevel model of safety climate. The model shows the path from climate antecedents to outcomes, using a multilevel perspective. This path includes climate-mediated and -unmediated links between safety

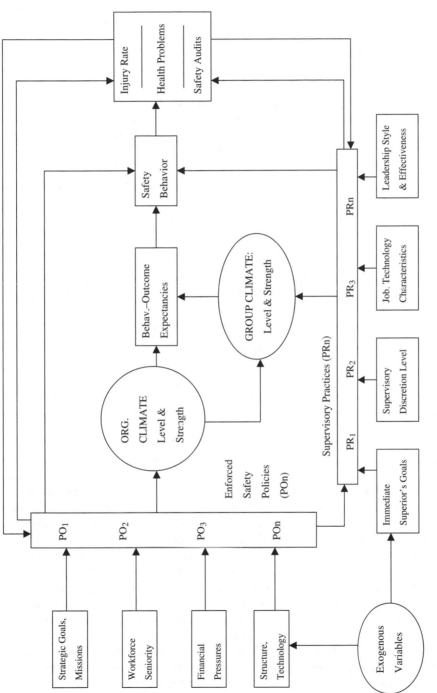

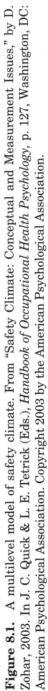

Figure 8.1. A multilevel model of safety climate. From "Safety Climate: Conceptual and Measurement Issues," by D. Zohar, 2003. In J. C. Quick & L. E. Tetrick (Eds.), *Handbook of Occupational Health Psychology*, p. 127, Washington, DC: American Psychological Association. Copyright 2003 by the American Psychological Association.

policies, supervisory leadership, employee safety behavior, and injury rate, as well as feedback loops suggesting that the incidence of unsafe behavior or injury could induce senior managers or supervisors to modify their emphasis on safety measures. It remains to be proven, though, that climate perceptions (partially) mediate the effect of policies and procedures, as well as supervisory practices, on role behavior and provide incremental prediction unaccounted for by direct effects.

The unmediated effect of managerial actions and practices can be accounted for by two factors. First, environmental constraints directly affect behavior. If safety devices are installed, employees must operate machines more safely, regardless of climate perceptions. Second, internal selection and attrition processes are important (Schneider, Goldstein, & Smith, 1995). Bringing safety violations to the attention of senior managers or making safety a performance criterion will probably result in discrimination against violators when personnel decisions are made. Over time, in companies with appropriate safety procedures, violators are likely to be transferred to less risky jobs or induced to leave the company. This too will affect the incidence of safe behavior, regardless of climate perceptions.

The following sections discuss specific aspects of the model in detail, including the three stages of climate–behavior relationship, safety compliance and safety engagement, organization and subunit levels, the role of supervisory discretion, and exogenous variables.

Three Stages of the Climate–Behavior Relationship

The model specifies the link between climate perceptions and organizational safety records. Recent meta-analyses of 122 safety climate studies indicated that safety climate had a negative relationship with injury rate, resulting in a corrected correlation estimate (r_c) of $-.23$ (Nahrgang et al., 2008; see also Christian et al., 2009). Although the empirical evidence concerning relationships between climate level and injury rate seems quite robust, the underlying variables remain less explored. I propose, therefore, that climate perceptions affect safety records in three stages: (a) Climate perceptions influence behavior–outcome expectancies, (b) expectancies influence prevalence of safety behavior, and (c) behavioral safety influences company safety records. The first stage—between climate perceptions and behavior–outcome expectancies—is implicit in the definition of climate presented previously. Given that climate perceptions are related to enacted policies that indicate the true priorities of key task facets, it follows that climate perceptions will influence outcome expectancies. In fact, employees pay attention to enacted policies rather than to their formalized counterparts because they indicate probable consequences—in other words, they inform behavior–outcome expectancies.

The second stage, relating to the effect of expectancies on behavior, is based on social learning and expected utility constructs (Bandura, 1986; Lawler, 1971; Vroom, 1964), although it can also be explained in terms of other theoretical constructs (James, James, & Ashe, 1990; Schneider & Reichers, 1983). Thus, the higher the perceived likelihood of obtaining a desired result by certain actions (e.g., stressing speed over safety) and the more valued the result, the greater the motivation to act in a specific manner. This presents the rationale for a positive relationship between safety climate level and behavioral safety in organizations. Climate strength should be the moderator variable for this relationship, because the less the homogeneity of climate perceptions, the weaker the climate–behavior relationship (Gonzalez-Roma et al., 2002; Zohar & Luria, 2005). Thus, climate strength should have a significant impact on the predictive power of climate level.

Finally, the third stage is based on much empirical evidence concerning the significance of human action in industrial accidents. Given that human error accounts for about 85% of accidents across industries (Heinrich, 1931; Reason, 1990, 1997), behavioral safety should be positively related with company safety records. Considered jointly, these stages result in a mediation model in which behavioral safety mediates the climate–outcome relationship. This mediation model was tested in meta-analytic studies, reporting a strong mediation effect for safety behaviors, linking safety climate with objective safety records (Christian et al., 2009; Nahrgang et al., 2008). In fact, safety climate had a strong relationship with employee safety behavior ($r_c = .62$), which was strongly related, in turn, with adverse safety events ($r_c = .36$).

Safety Compliance and Safety Engagement

The model can be expanded on the basis of a conceptual distinction between two dimensions of safety behavior, identified as safety compliance and safety engagement (Neal & Griffin, 2004). *Safety compliance* includes hazard or risk prevention activities such as compliance with safety rules and procedures, the use of personal protection equipment, safety-related training, and companywide implementation of safety rules and procedures (e.g., Goldenhar, Williams, & Swanson, 2003; Neal, Griffin, & Hart, 2000; Zacharatos, Barling, & Iverson, 2005). *Safety engagement* includes employee safety engagement, reflecting extra-role activities associated with a proactive approach to safety issues such as participation in safety improvement committees, communication with coworkers, preoccupation with possible hazards, and mindfulness about safety issues at large (e.g., Hofmann & Morgeson, 1999; Neal & Griffin, 2006; Parker, Axtell, & Turner, 2001). Recent meta-analyses (Christian et al., 2009; Nahrgang et al., 2008) indicated that both dimensions of safety behavior are equally and strongly related to safety climate ($r_c = .50$ and .62, respectively), with safety engagement resulting in a stronger negative relationship with injuries and adverse events than safety compliance ($r_c = -.30$ vs. $-.12$, respectively).

This theoretical model is congruent with the operant perspective for organizational climate or culture (Glenn, 1991; Thompson & Luthans, 1990), which also has been applied in the context of safety climate (Cooper, 2000; Hantula, 1999). An important concept is *meta-contingencies,* referring to stable, organizationwide contingencies for a whole class of role behaviors. When the various procedures are perceived by the workforce as converging on a particular priority for safety, this results in a specific meta-contingency for safety behavior. Based on the law of effect (Skinner, 1974), such meta-contingency should result in increased frequency of safety behavior and thus influence injury rates. Note, however, that this explanation does not preclude traditional, culture-based explanations of organizational practices and norms because any safety priority is related to certain values and basic assumptions (Schein, 2004). In other words, values and basic assumptions are antecedents of organizational policies and practices.

Organization and Subunit Levels

Another aspect of the climate model presented in Figure 8.1 is that climate can be investigated at two hierarchical levels: organizational and subunit or group level (Glick, 1988; Kozlowski & Klein, 2000; Patterson et al., 1996; Rousseau, 1988). To date, organization and subunit safety climates have largely been studied separately, dealing either with one unit of analysis or the other (Zohar, 2000). The same applies for other fields of organizational behavior research, in which researchers focus either on micro- or macrolevels of analysis (O'Reilly, 1991). Nonetheless, it has been repeatedly argued that organizational processes do take place simultaneously at several levels and that processes at different levels are linked in some way (Dansereau & Alutto, 1990; House, Rousseau, & Thomas-Hunt, 1995; Klein, Dansereau, & Hall, 1994; Kozlowski & Klein, 2000). In other words, processes that take place at one hierarchical level have an impact on other levels, mostly as a result of interdependence between individuals and of the need to balance hierarchical exchanges between organizational levels (Katz & Kahn, 1978; March & Simon, 1959). In the context of safety climate, this implies that climates have different meanings at different organizational levels, as well as cross-level relationships.

Several assumptions are required to make climate a multilevel construct. These relate to individuals as members both of an organization and of subunits in that organization. The first assumption postulates that policies and procedures that are established at the organization level must be implemented or executed by unit managers throughout the organizational hierarchy. That is, top managers are concerned with policymaking and the establishment of procedures to facilitate policy implementation. Supervisors at lower hierarchical levels execute these policies and associated procedures through interaction with subordinates. This creates a potential for discrepancy between formal and executed policy, including a reflexive discrepancy whereby top managers do not implement their own formal policies.

Second, policy execution is assumed to be affected by personal and technological group-level factors, including levels of work routinization. Low routinization requires greater discretion in policy implementation because procedures cannot cover all possible situations (Hage & Aiken, 1969; Perrow, 1967). Between-group differences relating to different ways of implementing company policies and procedures are, therefore, to be expected in a single organization. For example, unit supervisors may set lenient or severe safety standards within the boundaries set by top management.

Third, it is assumed that individual employees discriminate between procedures instituted by top management and those executed by unit managers, facilitated by two main sources of information. The first is the degree of difference between subunits, detected through social comparisons among employees in different subunits (Schneider & Reichers, 1983). For example, by social comparison, members of one subunit may conclude that their immediate superior is much more lenient regarding protective gear usage than other superiors. Thus, although "typical" or modal supervisory pressures would identify company-level policy regarding use of protective gear, the discrepancy between what most supervisors do and what a specific supervisor does would identify subunit practices. Another source of information concerns assessment of the degree to which supervisory behavior during interaction with group members is backed by company management. For example, if a supervisor initiates disciplinary action in response to a safety violation, this is indicative of supervisory emphasis on safety. The degree to which higher level managers are willing to back up this action is indicative of organizationwide emphasis. Together, this information can help employees to discriminate between company-level and group-level emphasis on safety.

Finally, level of analysis is assumed to simultaneously define the unit of aggregation and the target or referent of climate perceptions (Chan, 1998). At the organization level, climate perceptions are aggregated across the company, and company-level emphasis on safety is the referent object. At the group level, perceptions are aggregated within subunits, and supervisory emphasis is the primary referent object. By adjusting the referent of perceptions and assuming that individuals discriminate between procedural and supervisory emphasis on safety, a theoretical framework for a multilevel model is established.

Together, these assumptions explain the important cross-level phenomenon of group-level variation within a single organization-level climate. The key issue in group-level variation relates to the restraining effect of instituted procedures on supervisory practices. The first assumption listed previously indicates that unit managers must turn company-level procedures into situation-specific action directives. The second assumption indicates that this process requires discretionary decision making, because procedures cannot cover all possible contingencies (except in highly routinized work). Hence, unit managers must continually decide how to implement procedures, while taking into account situation-specific factors. It must be emphasized that supervisory roles entail considerable discretion because supervisors manage other people rather than deal directly with production technology. This creates interpersonal problems of sufficient complexity to allow supervision to be defined as inherently little routinized (Hage & Aiken, 1969; Perrow, 1967). For example, a supervisor must decide whether to put more or less emphasis on safety in a situation in which higher temperature may have made some workers fatigued or irritated (i.e., increased supervisory pressure could induce even greater fatigue or irritation). The discretionary power inherent in supervisory roles is a necessary and sufficient condition for creating group-level variation, resulting in corresponding climate variation.

The Role of Supervisory Discretion

The multilevel climate model was tested in a study covering 401 work groups nested in 36 manufacturing companies (Zohar & Luria, 2005). Results indicated that organization-level and group-level safety climates are globally aligned, and the effect of organization climate on safety behavior is fully mediated by group climate level. However, the data also revealed meaningful group-level variation in a single organization, attributable to supervisory discretion in implementing formal procedures associated with competing demands like safety versus productivity. Variables that limit supervisory discretion (i.e., organization climate strength and procedural formalization) reduced both between-groups climate variation and within-group variability (i.e., increased group-climate strength), although effect sizes were smaller than those associated with cross-level climate relationships.

These results support the idea that supervisory discretion is a necessary and sufficient condition for group-level climate variation in that the greater the supervisory discretion, the greater the expected variation of (group) climate levels in a single organization. This increases the likelihood of discrepancy between formal and executed policy at various levels in the organizational hierarchy. I thus propose a threshold framework in which, up to a certain point, group-level variation is assessed as remaining within the boundaries set by company policies, beyond which boundaries employees consider the variation as boundary crossing, resulting in misalignment or discrepancy. Such discrepancies can occur either within organizational levels ("Top management doesn't back up its own policy") or between levels ("Some unit managers exceed or fall short of company safety standards"). Organization-level factors influencing supervisory discretion include structure and culture. A relevant structural parameter is formalization (Hage & Aiken, 1969). Supervisors in a formalized organization, in which procedures are both highly specific (and thus numerous) and rigid, will enjoy little discretion, and policy boundaries will also be narrow and rigid (unless top management does not back them up). Because structure reflects culture, this is likely to be accompanied by considerable power distance between hierarchical levels (Hofstede, 1998). Other group-level factors can also influence supervisory discretion with regard to safety, for example, local hazards, supervisory expert power, and physical distance from headquarters. An experienced supervisor reporting to a passive superior will probably enjoy greater discretion, and, as a consequence, greater likelihood of discrepant group-level climate will result.

Assessing instituted procedures at company level and their execution at the group level as distinctively different assessment targets is similar to the distinction between procedural and interactional justice. In the organizational justice literature, *procedural justice* refers to employees' assessment of fairness in formal procedures, based on criteria such as consistency, bias suppression, and correctability (Skarlicki & Folger, 1997; Thibaut & Walker, 1975). *Interactional justice,* on the other hand, refers to employees' assessment of the quality of interpersonal treatment during enactment of formal procedures by their superiors. Supervisors' behavior is judged on such criteria as exhibiting respect, listening to concerns, providing explanations, and being truthful (Bies & Moag, 1986; Moorman, 1991). Studies of organizational justice have repeatedly indicated that both kinds of justice are assessed independently by employees, who are able to discriminate between them (Greenberg & Colquitt, 2005). Similarly, it is suggested that procedures as instituted by upper-level managers and their implementation by lower-level managers are distinctive attributes of the workplace to which workers attend when forming climate perceptions.

Exogenous Variables

Figure 8.1 also suggests that there may be two types of exogenous variables. One type includes variables likely to influence climate level or strength, although they are not part of this construct. For example, strategic goals and stakeholder pressures can induce higher safety climate, whereas financial pressure and a belief that safety is ultimately the responsibility of individual workers would result in lower climate. At the group level, individual supervisory leadership and the technology of particular subunits are also expected to influence climate level and strength. For example, increased technological hazards because of the use of inflammable raw materials might result in greater emphasis on safety in some work groups. The second type includes exogenous variables that have been shown to predict safety outcomes (e.g., workforce seniority, empowerment) though unrelated to safety climate, and these should be included as control variables in statistical models. They clarify the unique meaning of safety climate.

The mediation effect of climate perceptions is based on aspects of the definition of climate as outlined previously; that is, climate perceptions relate to the priority of safety as inferred from the global pattern of executed procedures. As related to this priority, climate perceptions influence action in many situations in which there are no specific procedures for appropriate role behavior. In other words, because procedures do not cover all work situations and contingencies (except in highly routinized work; see Hall, 1987; Perrow, 1979), there are many situations in which behavior must be guided by internal standards based on assessment of procedures-as-pattern. In such situations, climate perceptions will play an important mediating role, thereby exerting an incremental effect on behavior. In other words, the mediating effect of climate perceptions can be attributed to their potential influence on behavior–outcome expectancies in situations for which no specific procedures have been defined. Accident investigations and models of human error suggest that such situations are especially conducive to injury (I. D. Brown, 1991; Hopkins, 2006; Rasmussen, 1982, 1990; Reason, 1990, 1997).

In terms of safety behavior, climate perceptions play an additional mediation role because of employees' bias against safe conduct in regular job conditions (Zohar & Erev, 2007). Contrary to the assumption that self-preservation overrides other motives (Maslow, 1970), safety studies indicate that careless behavior prevails during regular job activities. For example, failure to use protective gear provided at the workplace accounts for about 40% of work accidents, a statistic that has not changed for more than 20 years (National Safety Council, 1999). The bias against safe behavior can be explained, in decision theory terms, as an outcome of assigning greater weight to short-term gains (i.e., melioration), coupled with underestimation of the likelihood of possible rare events (Herrnstein, Loewenstein, Prelec, & Vaughan, 1993). Safety precautions often entail a modest but immediate (hence certain) cost. For example, protective gear often causes personal discomfort such as sweating, blurred vision, or restricted manual dexterity. If the likelihood of injury during routine activity is underestimated and becomes infinitely small, the expected utility of unsafe behavior exceeds that of safe behavior. From the perspective of prospect theory (Kahneman & Tversky, 1979), the value function for loss associated with safe behavior is much steeper than that of gain. One factor that can modify the value function for safe behavior is contingent (and immediate, hence certain) social recognition or punishment from management (Stajkovic & Luthans, 1997). This has proved much more effective than pledge- or fear-based interventions, including supplying detailed risk information (Cooper, Phillips, Sutherland, & Makin, 1994), providing the basis for behavioral safety interventions (Glendon, Clarke, & McKenna, 2006; Krause, 2005; Krispin & Hantula, 1996; Saari & Nasanen, 1989). Thus, the incremental effect of safety climate perceptions in situations not covered by specific procedures is likely to be stronger than that of other climates because of the inherent bias toward unsafe behavior.

Implications for Safety Climate Measurement

Reviews of the literature indicate that authors of climate measures use management (upper or lower) commitment to the safety and health of employees as a primary target of climate perceptions (i.e., high commitment is functionally equivalent with a priority for safety over production). In a thematic analysis of available measurement scales, Flin et al. (2000) concluded that management commitment was the prime theme, appearing in 13 out of the 18 safety climate scales under review. Similar results were reported in another review of 15 partially overlapping measurement scales (Guldenmund, 2000). Examination of the measures covered in both reviews indicates that in addition to direct assessment of (perceived) management commitment, they include other subscales concerning procedural features of the safety system (e.g., training, audits, compliance, communication). This is often presented as an empirically derived list, based on findings suggesting that they predict important safety outcomes such as accident rate (e.g., Niskanen, 1994; Ostrom, Wilhelmsen, & Kaplan, 1993). To enhance discriminant validity, I propose that measures of safety climate should only include those procedural features indicative of managerial commitments to safety (in addition to direct, unmediated assessment of managerial commitments or priorities). This is akin to the use of artifacts, practices, and ceremonies as indicators of the tacit aspects of organizational culture (Schein, 2004), except that here I suggest retaining a single focus relating to the overriding priority of safety.

   Climate indicators can be subdivided into universal versus industry-specific items. Some indicators of safety priority refer to universal features in that they are applicable to all industries in which safety is a relevant issue. These include procedural features such as the (real) status of safety officer, effect of safe conduct on personnel decisions, investment in safety devices and safety training, and timely communication of safety information (e.g., Dedobbeleer & Beland, 1991; Glennon, 1982; Zohar, 1980, 2000). Other indicators relate to industry-specific features, for example, efficacy of the permit-to-work system in nuclear plants (Perrow, 1999), appropriateness of safety procedures under changing conditions aboard offshore oil installations (Mearns, Flin, Gordon, & Fleming, 1998), and insistence on universal precautions against blood-borne pathogens in health care clinics (DeJoy, Murphy, & Gershon, 1995). This means that safety climate measures may include three item classes: unmediated perceptions of (real) managerial commitment or direct assessment of relative priorities, mediated assessment through universal indicators, and assessment based on industry-specific indicators. The first two classes allow unlimited, between-units comparisons, but the third increases measurement sensitivity for within-unit and within-industry comparisons. A subset of items in each class should relate to situations in which safety and production come into overt conflict, identified here as "acid-test indicators." That is, it is assumed that employees will pay particular attention to managerial action in such situations, thus providing the clearest indication of true priorities. Management action when there is strong pressure to meet production deadlines, or when the required safety devices cost more than a few hundred dollars, will be assigned greater weight by employees in assessing true priorities.

Another classification of climate items concerns levels of analysis. A climate survey may include company-level and group-level items relating to commitments and resultant indicators of upper- and lower-level managerial practices. This agrees with the idea that referent objects of climate perceptions should be adjusted to the level of analysis. Thus, organization-level climate indicators should refer to issues such as financial expenditure on safety devices, reducing production speed in favor of safety, and personnel decisions based on safety criteria. Group-level indicators, however, should refer to issues such as supervisory monitoring and rewarding practices, individualized coaching of group members, and willingness to interrupt production to correct safety hazards. Therefore, although content of some items may vary considerably between different climate measures, depending on the work environment of the employees and level of analysis, subscales should retain the single underlying theme of true safety priority. By default, this means that other variables known to influence safety outcomes should be included as independent variables in theoretical and measurement models.

Boundary Stipulations for Safety Climate

This exposition of the safety climate construct can clarify relevant boundaries and explain consequences of inadvertently crossing them. When subscales refer to features of safety systems that are not related to safety priority or any other designated theme, conceptual ambiguity will arise. For example, when climate subscales relate to supervisory satisfaction, knowledge, and support (Safety Research Unit, 1993); workers' skills, abilities, and motivation (Niskanen, 1994); or optimism, self-esteem, and risk taking (Geller, Roberts, & Gilmore, 1996), conceptual ambiguity will result because they are not connected to any focal theme associated with the assessment of safety priority (apart from being individual-level variables). Such variables can be included in safety models in which climate is only one variable, among others that are equally independent. This distinction is especially relevant for risk perception items, often used in climate measures (Flin et al., 2000). Risk assessment should be included in measures of safety climate in which subscale items relate to risk resulting from management action or inaction, in other words, as an indicator of relative priorities rather than technological hazards (which vary between subunits regardless of climate levels).

Otherwise, it should be an independent variable in safety models. Similarly, items asking for assessment of the overall likelihood of being injured on the job over a period of 12 months (e.g., Dedobbeleer & Beland, 1991) should be avoided in samples in which likelihood of injury might be markedly influenced by factors over which management has little control.

In addition, if climate is an emergent property related to organization- or group-level properties, then individual-level variables whose aggregation is meaningless (e.g., individual beliefs or attitudes) should not be included in measurement instruments because this would create conceptual ambiguity. (For discussions of levels issues, see House et al., 1995; Kozlowsky & Klein, 2000; Rousseau, 1985.) For example, Williamson, Feyer, Cairns, and Biancotti (1997) devised a 62-item safety climate questionnaire designed to represent the different measures of safety climate published over the years. Although half of the items in this scale refer to senior management commitment and company-level procedures, the other half include individual-level items referring to personal beliefs (e.g., "Accidents will happen no matter what I do") and safety attributions (e.g., "When I have worked unsafely it has been because I was not trained properly"). Although the latter may have important safety implications, they ought to be independent (individual-level) variables rather than components of safety climate. This has important implications for statistical analysis, requiring hierarchical linear models instead of single-level regression models (Hofmann & Stetzer, 1996; Zohar, 2000).

Another boundary stipulation concerns the fact that meaningful aggregation requires homogeneity of perceptions within the chosen unit of analysis. Otherwise, the calculated mean scores might be thought to reflect climate level when, in fact, there is no climate at all (i.e., no consensus). This may be true of companies or installations in which management is inconsistent with regard to safety issues, resulting in little agreement among employees. For example, management might emphasize safety under normal operating conditions but deemphasize it when production of key products falls behind schedule. Such wavering will result in reduced agreement among employees. Disregarding this criterion, as in most published research, reinforces the use of variables for which there is little reason to expect consensus to begin with (e.g., perceived risk in a technologically diverse organization). (For exceptions, see Hofmann & Stetzer, 1996; Zohar, 2000.) If homogeneity statistics are included, it should be possible to assess which climate variables warrant aggregation and proceed accordingly. For example, in a study designed to improve supervisory safety practices, it turned out that, contrary to expectations, safety climate factors failed to meet criteria of homogeneity, hence the resulting perceptions were not considered as group-climate variables (Zohar, 2002b). This highlights the importance of considering both climate parameters—in other words, level and strength.

Conclusion

The ideas presented in this chapter have conceptual and methodological implications. Methodologically, climate measurement research should include the ongoing search for perceptual cues or indicators used by workers to assess the relative priority of safety. As noted, such indicators may be universal or industry specific, be explicit or implicit, and relate to different hierarchical levels. It is probable that some will provide more sensitive or reliable assessment of climate level and that certain combinations will result in better measurement instruments. Research designed to identify new, potentially better climate indicators might require several research strategies.

One strategy involves organization- and group-level comparisons between high- and low-accident companies. A review of the relevant literature identified a heterogeneous list of procedural variables associated with lower accident rates (Shannon, Mayr, & Haines, 1997), some of which have not been incorporated in the available scales. They include speed of hazard correction, completeness of accident investigation, monitoring unsafe behavior, composition and scope of duties of joint safety committees, and regularity of safety retraining. Other variables identified in this review should be excluded, however, despite their demonstrated discriminatory power (e.g., empowerment of workforce, good labor relations, and workforce seniority).

Another strategy involves qualitative data collection techniques such as focus group discussions. This was used, for example, in the development of an offshore oil-platform climate scale (Cox & Cheyne, 2000) in which employees were asked to discuss what they understood by the terms *safety* and *safety culture*. Subscales were based on issues identified in the focus groups, together with themes highlighted in other offshore and generic climate measures. This resulted in identification of various safety climate indicators such as "There is a good communication here about safety issues which affect me," "I do not receive praise for working safely," and "Sometimes I am not given enough time to get the job done safely." Note that these markers are universal, because they do not relate safety to unique attributes of offshore installations.

An additional strategy for uncovering relevant indicators is derived from the often-encountered discrepancy between formally espoused and enforced safety policies. Employees at various organizational levels are asked to recall incidents in which it became clear to them that management action diverged from formally espoused policies (Zohar & Luria, 2003). This strategy is based on the assumption that employees recall personally meaningful episodes and that their descriptions of these episodes reveal perceptual cues to which they attend in assessing true priorities. For example, a foreman in a metal processing plant reported that it took several days and repeated appeals to replace a worker's worn-out safety gloves because of management concern that gloves were being replaced too often. This contradicted management's formally declared drive to improve safety records. A worker in another work group in the same company reported that metal debris was left around an electric jigsaw (a safety hazard) until a safety audit by government inspectors was due, at which time it was removed. The contrast between ongoing tardiness and sudden activity revealed the managerial hypocrisy to this worker. These incidents suggest that ease of replacing protective equipment, or whether housekeeping is genuine or forced, could serve as safety climate indicators in some industries.

This methodology could also help identify acid-test indicators, because policy discrepancies often arise when safety and production are in direct conflict. For example, a foreman in a food processing plant reported that during the week before a major holiday, when demand was at its peak, he was pressured to clear clogged pipes in an oven in which temperature exceeded the safety level for such an operation by 30°C. This was contrary to the company's own rules. Bending safety rules because of work pressure might thus be an acid-test indicator.

This approach could be refined with situation-anchored rating scales of levels of work pressure to assess perceived relationships between work pressure and management willingness to bend safety rules (i.e., how much work pressure is encountered before management is willing to bend rules?). Assuming that safety rules can also be ordered along a continuum of risk, this should result in a refined assessment of real priorities (i.e., how much risk would management be willing to take at each level of work pressure?). The various strategies should make it possible to identify an increasing number of safety climate indicators, which could then be subjected to further psychometric testing.

Another direction for methodological development concerns psychometric comparisons of available scales. As noted, there are more than 20 climate measures that meet minimal criteria (Flin et al., 2000; Guldenmund, 2000), and new ones are continually being published (Cox & Flin, 1998; Glendon, 2008a). Because measurement scales provide operationalization of a construct, it is important to conduct evaluative research to converge on mutually agreed measures. Mueller, DaSilva, Townsend, and Tetrick (1999) conducted one such study, comparing four compatible safety climate measures to identify the best measurement model (R. L. Brown & Holmes, 1986; Coyle, Sleeman, & Adams, 1995; Dedobbeleer & Beland, 1991; Zohar, 1980). This was done by asking 500 working students to complete all four climate scales, followed by confirmatory factor analysis. The final model was a four-factor model that retained a high degree of overlap with Zohar's (1980) original eight-factor model. The four factors were management commitment to safety, rewards for working safely, effect of safe behavior on social standing, and effect of required work pace on safety. (Note that the first two factors are more in line with the suggested focus on safety priority.) There was also evidence for a single higher order factor of safety climate that could be useful in global comparisons of organizations. (This supports the use of universal climate indicators for global comparisons and specific ones for within-industry or within-company comparisons.) Studies of this sort should help to evaluate measurement models.

Theoretically, there is a need for research into the hypothesized path leading from climate antecedents to its behavioral and organizational outcomes (Figure 8.1). Although much research has focused on the climate–outcome relationship, there is a need for testing mediation processes associated with the entire path. Furthermore, much of the available evidence is tainted by single-source bias relating to self-report of behavior safety and injury data. The potential benefit of pursuing this line of work is evident from a study in which it was found that subscales (i.e., climate indicators) associated with open, rewarding supervisory safety practices were more predictive of subunit injuries than corrective, punitive practices (Zohar, 2002b).

Finally, if safety climate is to be used as a bridge to the larger organizational behavior literature, other important relationships, notably between leadership and climate, must be better investigated. As noted previously, research integrating leadership and safety climate suggests a mediation model whereby, in contexts in which job performance has direct safety implications, the quality of leader–member interaction influences leader commitment to members' welfare, in turn influencing safety climate perceptions in the group and, ultimately, safety behavior of group members. The robust leadership–climate relationship should encourage further research aimed at mediator and moderator variables likely to influence this relationship (e.g., consistency of managerial practice, which is likely to influence climate strength or leadership effects on group processes such as the adoption of a team-oriented approach to safety issues).

References

Anderson, N. R., & West, M. A. (1998). Measuring climate for work group innovation: Development and validation of the team climate inventory. *Journal of Organizational Behavior, 19,* 235–258. doi:10.1002/(SICI)1099-1379(199805)19:3<235::AID-JOB837>3.0.CO;2-C

Argyris, C., & Schon, D. A. (1996). *Organizational learning: Theory, method, and practice.* Reading, MA: Addison-Wesley.

Baer, M., & Frese, M. (2003). Innovation is not enough: Climates for initiative and psychological safety, process innovations, and firm performance. *Journal of Organizational Behavior, 24,* 45–68. doi:10.1002/job.179

Bandura, A. (1986). *Social foundations of thought and action.* Englewood Cliffs, NJ: Prentice Hall.

Barling, J., Loughlin, C., & Kelloway, K. E. (2002). Development and test of a model linking transformational leadership and occupational safety. *Journal of Applied Psychology, 87,* 488–496. doi:10.1037/0021-9010.87.3.488

Bass, B. M. (1990). *Bass and Stogdill's handbook of leadership* (3rd ed.). New York, NY: Free Press.

Bass, B. M. (1998). *Transformational leadership: Industry, military, and educational impact.* Mahwah, NJ: Erlbaum.

Bies, R. J., & Moag, J. S. (1986). Interactional justice: Communication criteria of fairness. In R. J. Lewicki, B. H. Sheppard, & M. H. Bazerman (Eds.), *Research on negotiations in organizations* (Vol. 1, pp. 43–55). Greenwich, CT: JAI Press.

Brown, I. D. (1991). Accident reporting and analysis. In J. R. Wilson & E. N. Corlett (Eds.), *Evaluation of human work* (pp. 755–778). New York, NY: Taylor & Francis.

Brown, R. L., & Holmes, H. (1986). The use of a factor-analytic procedure for assessing the validity of an employee safety climate model. *Accident Analysis and Prevention, 18,* 455–470. doi:10.1016/0001-4575(86)90019-9

Bureau of Economic Analysis. (2008). *National economic accounts.* Retrieved from http://www.bea.gov/national/index.htm#gdp

Chan, D. (1998). Functional relations among constructs in the same content domain at different levels of analysis: A typology of composition models. *Journal of Applied Psychology, 83,* 234–246. doi:10.1037/0021-9010.83.2.234

Christian, M. S., Bradley, J. C., Wallace, J. C., & Burke, M. J. (2009). Workplace safety: A meta-analysis of the roles of person and situation factors. *Journal of Applied Psychology, 94,* 1103–1127. doi:10.1037/a0016172

Cooper, M. D. (2000). Towards a model of safety culture. *Safety Science, 36,* 111–136. doi:10.1016/S0925-7535(00)00035-7

Cooper, M. D., Phillips, R. A., Sutherland, V. J., & Makin, P. J. (1994). Reducing accidents using goal setting and feedback: A field study. *Journal of Occupational and Organizational Psychology, 67,* 219–240.

Cox, S. J., & Cheyne, A. J. (2000). Assessing safety culture in offshore environments. *Safety Science, 34,* 111–129. doi:10.1016/S0925-7535(00)00009-6

Cox, S. J., & Flin, R. (1998). Safety culture: Philosopher's stone or man of straw? *Work and Stress, 12,* 189–201. doi:10.1080/02678379808256861

Coyle, I. R., Sleeman, S. D., & Adams, N. (1995). Safety climate. *Journal of Safety Research, 26,* 247–254. doi:10.1016/0022-4375(95)00020-Q

Dansereau, F., & Alutto, J. A. (1990). Level of analysis issues in climate and culture research. In B. Schneider (Ed.), *Organizational climate and culture* (pp. 193–236). San Francisco, CA: Jossey-Bass.

Dedobbeleer, N., & Beland, F. (1991). A safety climate measure for construction sites. *Journal of Safety Research, 22,* 97–103. doi:10.1016/0022-4375(91)90017-P

DeJoy, D. M., Murphy, L. R., & Gershon, R. M. (1995). Safety climate in health care settings. In A. C. Bittner & P. C. Champney (Eds.), *Advances in industrial ergonomics and safety* (Vol. 7, pp. 923–929). London, England: Taylor & Francis.

Drazin, R., Glynn, M. A., & Kazanjian, R. K. (1999). Multilevel theorizing about creativity in organizations: A sensemaking perspective. *Academy of Management Review, 24,* 286–307. doi:10.2307/259083

Fahlbruch, B., & Wilpert, B. (1999). System safety: An emerging field for I/O psychology. In C. L. Cooper & I. T. Robertson (Eds.), *International review of industrial and organizational psychology* (Vol. 14, pp. 55–93). New York, NY: Wiley.

Flin, R., Mearns, P., O'Connor, R., & Bryden, R. (2000). Measuring safety climate: Identifying the common features. *Safety Science, 34,* 177–192. doi:10.1016/S0925-7535(00)00012-6

Geller, E. S., Roberts, D. S., & Gilmore, M. R. (1996). Predicting propensity to actively care for occupational safety. *Journal of Safety Research, 27,* 1–8. doi:10.1016/0022-4375(95)00024-0

Glendon, I. (2008a). Safety culture: Snapshot of a developing concept. *Journal of Occupational Health and Safety, 24,* 179–189.

Glendon, I. (2008b). Safety culture and safety climate: How far have we come and where could we be heading? *Journal of Occupational Health and Safety, 24,* 249–271.

Glendon, I., Clarke, S. H., & McKenna, E. F. (2006). *Human safety and risk management* (2nd ed.). New York, NY: Taylor & Francis.

Glenn, S. S. (1991). Contingencies and meta-contingencies: Relations among behavioral, cultural, and biological evolution. In P. A. Lamal (Ed.), *Behavioral analysis of societies and cultural practices* (pp. 39–73). Washington, DC: Hemisphere.

Glennon, D. P. (1982). Safety climate in organizations. In *Proceedings of the 19th annual conference of the Ergonomics Society of Australia and New Zealand* (pp. 17–31). Parkville, Victoria, Australia: The Society.

Glick, W. H. (1985). Conceptualizing and measuring organizational and psychological climate: Pitfalls in multi-level research. *Academy of Management Review, 10,* 601–616. doi:10.2307/258140

Glick, W. H. (1988). Organizations are not central tendencies: Shadowboxing in the dark, Round 2. *Academy of Management Review, 13,* 133–137. doi:10.2307/258361

Goldenhar, L. M., Williams, L. J., & Swanson, N. G. (2003). Modeling relationships between job stressors and injury and near-miss outcomes for construction laborers. *Work and Stress, 17,* 218–240. doi:10.1080/02678370310001616144

Gonzalez-Roma, V., Peiro, J. M., & Tordera, N. (2002). An examination of the antecedents and moderator influences of climate strength. *Journal of Applied Psychology, 87,* 465–473. doi:10.1037/0021-9010.87.3.465

Graen, G. B., & Uhl-Bien, M. (1995). Relationship-based approach to leadership: Development of LMX theory of leadership over 25 years. *Leadership Quarterly, 6,* 219–247. doi:10.1016/1048-9843(95)90036-5

Greenberg, J., & Colquitt, J. A. (2005). *Handbook of organizational justice.* Mahwah, NJ: Erlbaum.

Guldenmund, F. W. (2000). The nature of safety culture: A review of theory and research. *Safety Science, 34,* 215–257. doi:10.1016/S0925-7535(00)00014-X

Hage, J., & Aiken, M. (1969). Routine technology, social structure, and organizational goals. *Administrative Science Quarterly, 14,* 366–378. doi:10.2307/2391132

Hall, R. H. (1987). *Organizations: Structures, processes, and outcomes* (4th ed.). Englewood Cliffs, NJ: Prentice Hall.

Hantula, D. (1999). Safety culture and behavioral safety: From contingencies to meta-contingencies. In *Proceedings of the ASSE symposium on best practices in safety management* (pp. 190–206). Philadelphia, PA: American Society of Safety Engineers.

Heinrich, H. W. (1931). *Industrial accident prevention: A scientific approach.* New York, NY: McGraw-Hill.

Herrnstein, R. J., Loewenstein, G. F., Prelec, D., & Vaughan, W. (1993). Utility maximization and melioration: Internalities in individual choice. *Journal of Behavioral Decision Making, 6,* 149–185. doi:10.1002/bdm.3960060302

Hofmann, D. A., & Morgeson, F. P. (1999). Safety-related behavior as a social exchange: The role of perceived organizational support and leader–member exchange. *Journal of Applied Psychology, 84,* 286–296. doi:10.1037/0021-9010.84.2.286

Hofmann, D. A., & Morgeson, F. P. (2003). The role of leadership in safety. In J. Barling & M. Frone (Eds.), *The psychology of workplace safety* (pp. 159–180). Washington, DC: American Psychological Association.

Hofmann, D. A., Morgeson, F. P., & Gerras, S. J. (2003). Climate as a moderator of the relationship between LMX and content-specific citizenship behavior: Safety climate as an exemplar. *Journal of Applied Psychology, 88,* 170–178. doi:10.1037/0021-9010.88.1.170

Hofmann, D. A., & Stetzer, A. (1996). A cross-level investigation of factors influencing unsafe behaviors and accidents. *Personnel Psychology, 49,* 307–339. doi:10.1111/j.1744-6570.1996.tb01802.x

Hofstede, G. (1998). Attitudes, values and organizational culture: Disentangling the concepts. *Organization Studies, 19,* 477–493. doi:10.1177/017084069801900305

Hopkins, A. (2006). Studying organizational cultures and their effects on safety. *Safety Science, 44,* 875–889. doi:10.1016/j.ssci.2006.05.005

House, R. J., Rousseau, D. M., & Thomas-Hunt, M. (1995). The meso paradigm: A framework for the integration of micro and macro organizational behavior. *Research in Organizational Behavior, 17,* 71–114.

House, R. J., & Shamir, B. (1993). Towards the integration of transformational, charismatic, and visionary theories. In M. M. Chemers & R. Ayman (Eds.), *Leadership theory and research: Perspectives and directions* (pp. 81–107). San Diego, CA: Academic Press.

International Atomic Energy Agency. (1986). *Summary report on the post-accident review meeting on the Chernobyl accident* (IAEA Safety Series 75-INSAG-1). Vienna, Austria: Author.

International Atomic Energy Agency. (1991). *Safety* culture (IAEA Safety Series 75-INSAG-4). Vienna, Austria: Author.

James, L. R. (1982). Aggregation bias in estimates of perceptual agreement. *Journal of Applied Psychology, 67,* 219–229. doi:10.1037/0021-9010.67.2.219

James, L. R., Demaree, R. G., & Wolf, G. (1984). Estimating within-group inter-rater reliability with and without response bias. *Journal of Applied Psychology, 69,* 85–98. doi:10.1037/0021-9010.69.1.85

James, L. R., Demaree, R. G., & Wolf, G. (1993). R_{wg}: An assessment of within-group interrater-agreement. *Journal of Applied Psychology, 78,* 306–309. doi:10.1037/0021-9010.78.2.306

James, L. R., James, L. A., & Ashe, D. K. (1990). The meaning of organizations: The role of cognition and values. In B. Schneider (Ed.), *Organizational climate and culture* (pp. 40–84). San Francisco, CA: Jossey-Bass.

James, L. R., & Jones, A. P. (1974). Organizational climate: A review of theory and research. *Psychological Bulletin, 81,* 1096–1112. doi:10.1037/h0037511

Joyce, W. G., & Slocum, J. W. (1984). Collective climate: Agreement as a basis for defining aggregate climates in organizations. *Academy of Management Journal, 27,* 721–742. doi:10.2307/255875

Kahneman, D., & Tversky, A. (1979). Prospect theory: An analysis of decision under risk. *Econometrica, 47,* 263–291. doi:10.2307/1914185

Katz, D., & Kahn, R. L. (1978). *The social psychology of organizations* (2nd ed.). New York, NY: Wiley.

Kirkpatrick, S. A., & Locke, E. A. (1996). Direct and indirect effects of three core charismatic leadership components on performance and attitudes. *Journal of Applied Psychology, 81,* 36–51. doi:10.1037/0021-9010.81.1.36

Klauss, R., & Bass, B. M. (1982). *Interpersonal communication in organizations.* New York, NY: Academic Press.

Klein, K. J., Dansereau, F., & Hall, R. J. (1994). Levels issues in theory development, data collection, and analysis. *Academy of Management Review, 19,* 195–229. doi:10.2307/258703

Komaki, J. L. (1998). *Leadership from an operant perspective.* New York, NY: Routledge.

Kozlowski, S. W., & Doherty, M. L. (1989). Integration of climate and leadership: Examination of a neglected issue. *Journal of Applied Psychology, 74,* 546–553. doi:10.1037/0021-9010.74.4.546

Kozlowski, S. W., & Klein, K. J. (2000). A multilevel approach to theory and research in organizations: Contextual, temporal, and emergent processes. In K. J. Kline & S. W. Kozlowski (Eds.), *Multilevel theory, research, and methods in organizations* (pp. 3–90). San Francisco, CA: Jossey-Bass.

Krause, T. R. (2005). *Leading with safety.* New York, NY: Wiley Interscience. doi:10.1002/047178527X

Krispin, J., & Hantula, D. (1996, October). *A meta-analysis of behavioral safety interventions in organizations.* Paper presented at the 1996 annual meeting of the Eastern Academy of Management, Philadelphia, PA.

Lawler, E. E. (1971). *Pay and organizational effectiveness: A psychological view.* New York, NY: McGraw Hill.

March, J. G., & Simon, H. A. (1959). *Organizations.* New York, NY: Wiley.

Maslow, A. (1970). *Motivation and personality* (2nd ed.). New York, NY: Harper & Row.

Mearns, K., Flin, R., Gordon, R., & Fleming, M. (1998). Measuring safety climate on offshore installations. *Work and Stress, 12,* 238–254. doi:10.1080/02678379808256864

Moorman, R. H. (1991). Relationship between organizational justice and organizational citizenship behaviors: Do fairness perceptions influence employee citizenship. *Journal of Applied Psychology, 76,* 845–855. doi:10.1037/0021-9010.76.6.845

Mueller, L., DaSilva, N., Townsend, J., & Tetrick, L. (1999, April). *An empirical evaluation of competing safety climate measurement models.* Paper presented at the annual meeting of the Society for Industrial and Organizational Psychology, Atlanta, GA.

Nahrgang, J. D., Morgeson, F. P., & Hofmann, D. A. (2008, April). *A meta-analytic investigation of individual and contextual influences on workplace safety, satisfaction, and well-being.* Paper presented at the annual meeting of the Society for Industrial and Organizational Psychology, San Francisco, CA.

National Safety Council. (1999). *Injury facts.* Itasca, IL: Author.

Neal, A., & Griffin, M. A. (2004). Safety climate and safety at work. In J. Barling & M. R. Frone (Eds.), *The psychology of workplace safety* (pp. 15–34). Washington, DC: American Psychological Association.

Neal, A., & Griffin, M. A. (2006). A study of the lagged relationships among safety climate, safety motivation, safety behavior, and accidents at the individual and group levels. *Journal of Applied Psychology, 91,* 946–953. doi:10.1037/0021-9010.91.4.946

Neal, A., Griffin, M. A., & Hart, P. M. (2000). The impact of organizational climate on safety climate and individual behavior. *Safety Science, 34,* 99–109. doi:10.1016/S0925-7535(00)00008-4

Niskanen, T. (1994). Safety climate in the road administration. *Safety Science, 17,* 237–255. doi:10.1016/0925-7535(94)90026-4

O'Reilly, C. A. (1991). Organizational behavior: Where we've been, where we're going. *Annual Review of Psychology, 42,* 427–458. doi:10.1146/annurev.ps.42.020191.002235

Ostroff, C., Kinicki, A. J., & Tamkins, M. M. (2003). Organizational culture and climate. In W. C. Borman, D. R. Ilgen, & R. J. Klimoski (Eds.), *Handbook of psychology* (Vol. 12, pp. 565–593). New York, NY: Wiley.

Ostrom, L., Wilhelmsen, C., & Kaplan, B. (1993). Assessing safety culture. *Nuclear Safety, 34,* 163–172.

Parker, S. K., Axtell, C., & Turner, N. (2001). Designing a safer workplace: Importance of job autonomy, communication quality, and supportive supervisors. *Journal of Occupational Health Psychology, 6,* 211–228. doi:10.1037/1076-8998.6.3.211

Pate-Cornell, M. E. (1990, November 30). Organizational aspects of engineering system safety: The case of offshore platforms. *Science, 250,* 1210–1217. doi:10.1126/science.250.4985.1210

Patterson, M., Payne, R., & West, M. (1996). Collective climates: A test of their sociopsychological significance. *Academy of Management Journal, 39,* 1675–1691. doi:10.2307/257074

Payne, R. (1990). Madness in our method: A comment on Jakofsky and Slocum's paper. *Journal of Organizational Behavior, 11,* 77–80. doi:10.1002/job.4030110110

Perrow, C. (1967). A framework for the comparative analysis of organizations. *American Sociological Review, 32,* 194–208. doi:10.2307/2091811

Perrow, C. (1979). *Complex organizations: A critical essay* (2nd ed.). Glenview, IL: Scott, Foresman.

Perrow, C. (1999). *Normal accidents: Living with high-risk technologies.* Princeton, NJ: Princeton University Press.

Quinn, R. E., & McGrath, M. R. (1985). The transformation of organizational culture: A competing values perspective. In P. J. Frost, L. F. Moore, M. R. Louis, C. C. Lundberg, & J. Martin (Eds.), *Organizational culture* (pp. 315–334). Beverly Hills, CA: Sage.

Quinn, R. E., & Rohrbaugh, J. (1983). A spatial model of effectiveness criteria: Towards a competing values approach to organizational analysis. *Management Science, 29,* 363–377. doi:10.1287/mnsc.29.3.363

Rasmussen, J. (1982). Human errors: A taxonomy for describing human malfunction in industrial installations. *Journal of Occupational Accidents, 4,* 311–333.

Rasmussen, J. (1990). The role of error in organizing behavior. *Ergonomics, 33,* 1185–1199. doi:10.1080/00140139008925325

Reason, J. T. (1990). *Human error.* Cambridge, England: Cambridge University Press.

Reason, J. T. (1997). *Managing the risks of organizational accidents.* Aldershot, England: Ashgate.

Reichers, A. E., & Schneider, B. (1990). Climate and culture: An evolution of constructs. In B. Schneider (Ed.), *Organizational climate and culture* (pp. 5–39). San Francisco, CA: Jossey-Bass.

Rentsch, J. R. (1990). Climate and culture: Interaction and qualitative differences in organizational meanings. *Journal of Applied Psychology, 75,* 668–681. doi:10.1037/0021-9010.75.6.668

Rochlin, G. I. (1999). Safe operations as a social construct. *Ergonomics, 42,* 1549–1560. doi:10.1080/001401399184884

Rousseau, D. M. (1985). Issues of level in organizational research: Multilevel and cross-level perspectives. In L. L. Cummings & B. M. Staw (Eds.), *Research in organizational behavior* (Vol. 7, pp. 1–37). Greenwich, CT: JAI Press.

Rousseau, D. M. (1988). The construction of climate in organizational research. In C. L. Cooper & I. T. Robertson (Eds.), *International review of industrial and organizational psychology* (Vol. 3, pp. 139–158). New York, NY: Wiley.

Saari, J., & Nasanen, M. (1989). The effect of positive feedback on industrial housekeeping and accidents. *International Journal of Industrial Ergonomics, 4,* 201–211. doi:10.1016/0169-8141(89)90003-6

Safety Research Unit. (1993). *The contribution of attitudinal and management factors to risk in the chemical industry* (Final report to the Health and Safety Executive). Guildford, England: University of Surrey.

Schein, E. H. (2004). *Organizational culture and leadership* (3rd ed.). San Francisco, CA: Jossey-Bass.

Schneider, B., Bowen, D. E., Ehrhart, M. G., & Holcombe, K. M. (2000). The climate for service: Evolution of a construct. In N. M. Ashkanasy, C. P. Wilderom, & M. F. Peterson (Eds.), *Handbook of organizational culture and climate* (pp. 21–36). Thousand Oaks, CA: Sage.

Schneider, B., Goldstein, H. W., & Smith, D. B. (1995). The ASA framework: An update. *Personnel Psychology, 48,* 747–773. doi:10.1111/j.1744-6570.1995.tb01780.x

Schneider, B., & Reichers, A. E. (1983). On the etiology of climates. *Personnel Psychology, 36,* 19–39. doi:10.1111/j.1744-6570.1983.tb00500.x

Shannon, H. S., Mayr, J., & Haines, T. (1997). Overview of the relationship between organizational and workplace factors and injury rates. *Safety Science, 26,* 201–217. doi:10.1016/S0925-7535(97)00043-X

Simons, T. (2002). Behavioral integrity: The perceived alignment between managers' words and deeds as a research focus. *Organization Science, 13,* 18–35.

Skarlicki, D. P., & Folger, R. (1997). Retaliation in the workplace: The roles of distributive, procedural, and interactional justice. *Journal of Applied Psychology, 82,* 434–443. doi:10.1037/0021-9010.82.3.434

Skinner, B. F. (1974). *About behaviorism.* New York, NY: Vintage.

Stajkovic, A. D., & Luthans, F. (1997). A meta-analysis of the effects of organizational behavior modification on task performance. *Academy of Management Journal, 40,* 1122–1149. doi:10.2307/256929

Thibaut, J., & Walker, L. (1975). *Procedural justice: A psychological analysis.* Hillsdale, NJ: Erlbaum.

Thompson, K. R., & Luthans, F. (1990). Organizational culture: A behavioral perspective. In B. Schneider (Ed.), *Organizational climate and culture* (pp. 319–344). San Francisco, CA: Jossey-Bass.

Vroom, V. H. (1964). *Work and motivation.* New York, NY: Wiley.

Weick, K. E. (1995). *Sense-making in organizations.* Thousand Oaks, CA: Sage.

Williamson, A. M., Feyer, A. M., Cairns, D., & Biancotti, D. (1997). The development of safety climate: The role of safety perceptions and attitudes. *Safety Science, 25,* 15–27. doi:10.1016/S0925-7535(97)00020-9

World Health Organization. (2008). *Occupational health.* Retrieved from http://www.who.int/occupational_health/en/

Wright, C. (1986). Routine deaths: Fatal accidents in the oil industry. *Sociological Review, 4,* 265–289.

Yang, J., Mossholder, K. W., & Peng, T. K. (2007). Procedural justice climate and group power distance: An examination of cross-level interaction effects. *Journal of Applied Psychology, 92,* 681–692. doi:10.1037/0021-9010.92.3.681

164   DOV ZOHAR

Zacharatos, A., Barling, J., & Iverson, R. D. (2005). High-performance work systems and occupational safety. *Journal of Applied Psychology, 90,* 77–93. doi:10.1037/0021-9010.90.1.77

Zipf, G. K. (1965). *Human behavior and the principle of least effort.* New York, NY: Hafner.

Zohar, D. (1980). Safety climate in industrial organizations: Theoretical and applied implications. *Journal of Applied Psychology, 65,* 96–102. doi:10.1037/0021-9010.65.1.96

Zohar, D. (2000). A group-level model of safety climate: Testing the effect of group climate on micro-accidents in manufacturing jobs. *Journal of Applied Psychology, 85,* 587–596. doi:10.1037/0021-9010.85.4.587

Zohar, D. (2002a). The effects of leadership dimensions, safety climate, and assigned priorities on minor injuries in work groups. *Journal of Organizational Behavior, 23,* 75–92. doi:10.1002/job.130

Zohar, D. (2002b). Modifying supervisory practices to improve sub-unit safety: A leadership-based intervention model. *Journal of Applied Psychology, 87,* 156–163. doi:10.1037/0021-9010.87.1.156

Zohar, D. (2003). The influence of leadership and climate on occupational health and safety. In D. A. Hofmann & L. E. Tetrick (Eds.), *Health and safety in organizations: A multilevel perspective* (pp. 201–230). San Francisco, CA: Jossey-Bass.

Zohar, D., & Erev, I. (2007). On the difficulty of promoting workers' safety behavior: Overcoming the underweighting of routine risks. *International Journal of Risk Assessment and Management, 7,* 122–136. doi:10.1504/IJRAM.2007.011726

Zohar, D., & Luria, G. (2003). The use of supervisory practices as leverage to improve safety behavior: A cross-level intervention model. *Journal of Safety Research, 34,* 567–577. doi:10.1016/j.jsr.2003.05.006

Zohar, D., & Luria, G. (2004). Climate as a social-cognitive construction of supervisory safety practices: Scripts as proxy of behavior patterns. *Journal of Applied Psychology, 89,* 322–333. doi:10.1037/0021-9010.89.2.322

Zohar, D., & Luria, G. (2005). A multilevel model of safety climate: Cross-level relationships between organization and group-level climates. *Journal of Applied Psychology, 90,* 616–628. doi:10.1037/0021-9010.90.4.616

Zohar, D., & Luria, G. (in press). Group leaders as gatekeepers: Testing safety climate variations across levels of analysis. *Applied Psychology.*

Zohar, D., & Polatchek, T. (2009). *The use of supervisory feedback as a means for safety climate and leadership improvement.* Manuscript in preparation.

Zohar, D., & Tenne-Gazit, O. (2008). Transformational leadership and group interaction as climate antecedents: A social network analysis. *Journal of Applied Psychology, 93,* 744–757. doi:10.1037/0021-9010.93.4.744

9

Work–Family Balance: A Review and Extension of the Literature

Jeffrey H. Greenhaus and Tammy D. Allen

Research on the work–family interface has grown substantially over the past several decades (Barnett, 1998; Eby, Casper, Lockwood, Bordeaux, & Brinley, 2005; Edwards & Rothbard, 2000; Greenhaus & Powell, 2006), due in large part to the increasing representation of dual-earner partners and single parents in the workforce. The past several years since the publication of the first edition of the *Handbook of Occupational Health Psychology* have been no exception as research and interest in the work–family interface continue to proliferate.

Most of the research has focused on understanding the interdependencies among work and family roles. Concepts such as work–family conflict and, more recently, work–family enrichment represent linking mechanisms (Edwards & Rothbard, 2000) that explain how experiences in one role affect experiences in the other role. This literature has provided considerable insight into the interconnections between employees' work and family lives. Another concept that is part of the discourse in the work–family literature with increasing frequency is work–family balance.

The goal of this chapter is twofold. Our first objective is to provide an updated review of the literature focusing on the negative and the positive aspects of combining work and family roles since the publication of the first edition of this *Handbook*. A considerable number of comprehensive qualitative and quantitative reviews of work–family research have been published in the last several years. Because our emphasis is on alerting readers to recent findings and trends in the literature, the current review is selective rather than exhaustive. Our second goal is to explicate the concept of work–family balance. Specifically, we review alternative meanings of work–family balance found in the literature. Next, we offer our definition of work–family balance and provide a tentative model. Then we present suggestions for future research designed to clarify the meaning, uniqueness, antecedents, and consequences of work–family balance.

The Negative Side of the Work–Family Interface

Work–family conflict (WFC), sometimes referred to as *work–family interference*, remains one of the most studied concepts in the work–family literature. WFC occurs when role pressures from work and family are mutually incompatible such that participation in one role is made more difficult by virtue of participation in the other role (Greenhaus & Beutell, 1985). Work interference with family (WIF) and family interference with work (FIW) are both possible (Mesmer-Magnus & Viswesvaran, 2005). WFC is of particular interest to occupational health psychologists because of its relationship with a variety of psychological and physical health outcomes (Greenhaus, Allen, & Spector, 2006).

Since the first edition of the *Handbook*, there have been multiple meta-analytic and qualitative reviews of the WFC literature. In addition, there have been several notable trends in the empirical work being conducted. In the following sections, we provide an update of knowledge concerning the predictors and outcomes associated with WFC. Next, we highlight research that has been based on longitudinal designs and international samples.

Predictors

As reviewed by Frone (2003), the predictors of WIF reside primarily in the work domain, whereas the predictors of FIW reside in the family domain. A meta-analysis of the predictors of WIF and FIW generally supports the notion that work-related factors such as job stressors tend to predict WIF, and family-related factors such as family stressors tend to predict FIW (Byron, 2005). However, the pattern of Byron's findings also revealed asymmetry in the domain effects. Specifically, whereas the work variables consistently demonstrated stronger relationships with WIF than with FIW, several of the nonwork variables demonstrated comparable relationships with WIF and FIW. Similar results were found in a meta-analysis conducted by Mesmer-Magnus and Viswesvaran (2005), who partialed out the effect of WIF when examining FIW and vice versa. As would be expected, job stressors had an appreciably higher effect size with WIF than with FIW (.29 vs. .09, respectively). However, the difference in effect sizes for nonwork stressors was considerably less, .14 for FIW and .08 for WIF. The implication is that researchers should not completely discount the association between family situational variables and WIF.

Meta-analytic research has also examined effect sizes associated with work–family policies. Byron (2005) reported a meta-analytic effect size of –.30 between flexibility and WIF and of –.17 with FIW. In contrast, Mesmer-Magnus and Viswesvaran (2006) reported an effect size of .00 with WIF and .06 with FIW. One of the main differences between the two studies was that Byron's analysis was limited to schedule flexibility. Subsequent research has suggested that flextime is more highly associated with WIF than is flexplace (Shockley & Allen, 2007). In another meta-analysis that focused specifically on telecommuting, Gajendran and Harrison (2007) reported a mean effect size of –.11 between telecommuting and WFC, suggesting a small but significant relationship.

To date, most of the research regarding individual differences has focused on demographic factors, but research on dispositional factors is growing. In her meta-analysis, Byron (2005) found that demographic factors such as gender and marital status were weak predictors of both WIF and FIW. However, these findings were moderated by parental and marital status. Specifically, when samples were comprised of a greater number of parents, women tended to report more

FIW and WIF than did men, and those who were single reported greater WIF and FIW than did those who were married. Although no meta-analyses have been conducted to date including dispositional variables, negative affect/neuroticism has been implicated in multiple WFC studies (e.g., Bruck & Allen, 2003; Wayne, Musisca, & Fleeson, 2004).

Several findings from Grzywacz, Arcury, et al. (2007) point to potentially fruitful areas of future inquiry of interest to occupational health psychology researchers. In a departure from most research that includes samples of professionals, Grzywacz and colleagues studied immigrants working in a poultry processing plant and found that stronger safety climate was associated with less WIF. In addition, physical workload was associated with WIF for women but not for men.

Outcomes

As noted previously, WFC has been of considerable interest to occupational health psychologists because of its link with both psychological and physical health-related outcomes (Greenhaus et al., 2006). Unlike predictors of WFC, domain-specific effects are not generally found with regard to outcomes. For example, after partialing out the effect of WIF when examining effect sizes associated with FIW, and vice versa, Mesmer-Magnus and Viswesvaran (2005) found that job satisfaction had a similar relationship with FIW (–.14) as with WIF (–.12).

One recent trend is the growing number of studies examining links between WFC and behaviors, including health-related behaviors associated with diet and exercise (e.g., Allen & Armstrong, 2006; Roos, Sarlio-Lahteenkorva, Lallukka, & Lahelma, 2007). Research suggests that food choices are used as a way to cope with conflicting demands between work and family (Devine et al., 2006). Recent research has also linked WFC with safety behaviors. Specifically, Cullen and Hammer (1997) reported that FIW, but not WIF, was associated with decreased compliance with safety rules and less willingness to participate in safety meetings. These findings suggest that work–family issues are important to address and integrate with other organizational programs that focus on employee health promotion and safety.

Longitudinal Studies

An often-cited criticism of the work–family literature has been the reliance on cross-sectional studies (e.g., Casper, Eby, Bordeaux, Lockwood, & Lambert, 2007). Researchers have taken heed of this criticism in that the number of longitudinal studies has grown during the past few years. One way to consider these findings is to ask if the results from longitudinal studies support conclusions based on the cross-sectional data. The answer is yes and no. The data are complicated by the use of different longitudinal time frames. However, even within the same time frames the results are mixed.

Several studies have been based on 6-month time lags. In one study, strain-based WIF was a result rather than a predictor of stress symptoms (Kelloway, Gottlieb, & Barham, 1999). In another study, a model in which strain-based WIF preceded health complaints provided a better fit to the data than did a model in which health complaints preceded strain-based WIF (Van Hooff et al., 2005). Time-based WIF was not associated with outcomes in Van Hooff et al.'s (2005) study, which did not include FIW. With regard to FIW, Kelloway et al. (1999) found that strain-based but not time-based FIW predicted stress symptoms and turnover intent. Grant-Vallone and Donaldson (2001) reported that a global bidirectional assessment of WFC was associated with lower well-being.

Several studies have used 1-year time lags. Hammer, Cullen, Neal, Sinclair, and Shafiro (2005) found bivariate relationships between both directions of interference at Time 1 and depression at Time 2, but results were nonsignificant when controls were included in regression analyses. These results held for both men and women. Kinnunen, Geurts, and Mauno (2004) found that WIF assessed at Time 1 was not related to outcomes assessed at Time 2 for men. For women, greater WIF was associated with job dissatisfaction, parental distress, and psychological symptoms. Kinnunen et al. also examined the data for reverse causal relationships and found that for men, low levels of satisfaction appeared to function as a precursor to WIF.

Frone, Russell, and Cooper (1997) used a 4-year time lag and found that FIW related to elevated levels of depression and poor physical health and that WIF predicted elevated levels of heavy alcohol consumption. Finally, Rantanen, Kinnunen, Feldt, and Pulkkinen (2008) found that time-based WIF was not an antecedent or an outcome of psychological well-being for men or for women across 1- and 6-year time lags.

Thus, the findings to date lead to the conclusion that the causal direction of work–family relationships and the temporal element of WFC need to be better understood. Moreover, temporal effects may differ for men and women, for time-based versus strain-based interference, and for WIF versus FIW. Long-term studies that include three or more measurement points are needed to more fully understand both the predictors and outcomes of WFC.

International Research

Another occurrence within the past few years has been an increase in research that takes an international or cross-cultural perspective. Not surprisingly, work and family issues have caught the attention of researchers across the globe. To date, comparative international studies have been limited in theoretical scope, primarily invoking individualism–collectivism to explain cross-national differences in the relationship between WFC and other variables (e.g., Lu, Gilmour, Kao, & Huang, 2006; Spector et al., 2007). These studies generally find weaker relationships involving WIF in countries assumed to be more collectivist than in countries thought to be more individualistic, presumably because in collectivist countries work and family are viewed as complementary. That is, work is thought to contribute to rather than detract from the family. By contrast, in individualist countries, work is more likely to be viewed as a selfish pursuit that can pose a threat to the family.

Another indication that work–family experiences may not be similar across all cultures comes from research conducted by Grzywacz, Arcury, et al. (2007), who found no association between WFC and health among a sample of immigrant Latino low-wage workers after controlling for job characteristics. However, these findings differed across gender. There was a relationship between WIF and greater anxiety and depressive symptoms for women but not for men. Moreover, Grzywacz et al. found that the degree of conflict reported was infrequent compared with research conducted on the typical American professional sample. Lyness and Kropf (2005) found evidence that gender makes a difference at a national level in a study of European managers. National gender equality was related to perceived work–family culture and the availability of flexible work arrangements, which in turn related to work–family balance. In sum, these findings suggest that understanding work and family experiences from a cross-national perspective is an important endeavor for future research. Such research should include an examination of values other than collectivism, such as gender role ideology, to further our understanding of how men and women may experience multiple role engagement differently across the globe.

The Positive Side of the Work–Family Interface

Although a conflict perspective continues to dominate the work–family literature, in recent years there has been a growing interest in examining the positive aspects of combining work and family roles. Out of this interest, several unique but highly related concepts have been developed. *Positive spillover* refers to the transfer of positively valenced affect, skills, behaviors, and values from the originating domain to the receiving domain, with beneficial effects on the receiving domain (Hanson, Hammer, & Colton, 2006). *Enrichment* is the extent to which experiences in one role improve the quality of life (performance and positive affect) in the other role through the transfer of resources or positive affect from one role to the other role (Greenhaus & Powell, 2006). *Facilitation* involves the extent to which involvement in one life domain provides gains (i.e., developmental, affective, capital, or efficiency) that contribute to enhanced functioning of another life domain (Wayne, Grzywacz, Carlson, & Kacmar, 2007), a broader concept than positive spillover or enrichment because it emphasizes system-level functioning (Grzywacz, Carlson, Kacmar, & Wayne, 2007). In this review, we use the term *enrichment* as a generic one intended to denote research on the positive effects of work and family on each other. Like conflict, enrichment is thought to be bidirectional, in which positive benefits can flow from the work domain to the family domain (work enrichment of family [WEF]) or from the family domain to the work domain (family enrichment of work [FEW]).

Predictors

The sets of variables that have been examined as predictors of work–family enrichment to date are limited. Greenhaus and Powell (2006) suggested that the antecedents of WEF/FEW would be resources acquired from the originating domain. Consistent with this line of thought, research to date suggests that family factors such as psychological involvement in the family and marital role commitment are predictors of FEW (e.g., Allis & O'Driscoll, 2008; Graves, Ohlott, & Ruderman, 2007). Similarly, work-related factors such as job involvement have been associated with WEF (Aryee, Srinivas, & Tan, 2005). Grzywacz and Butler (2005) found that characteristics of the job, such as greater decision latitude, variety, and complexity, were associated with greater WEF. Butler, Grzywacz, Bass, and Linney (2005) provided further support for this finding based on a within-person daily dairy design that linked skill level and control with WEF.

Research has also examined individual differences associated with enrichment. Higher levels of enrichment have been found for women than for men (Aryee et al., 2005; Rotondo & Kincaid, 2008; van Steenbergen, Ellemers, & Mooijarrt, 2007). Several studies have shown that personality is associated with enrichment (e.g., Grzywacz & Butler, 2005; Grzywacz & Marks, 2000; Wayne et al., 2004). Findings suggest that greater extraversion relates to greater WEF as well as to FEW. A secure attachment style has also been associated with greater enrichment in both directions (Sumer & Knight, 2001). Rotondo and Kincaid (2008) examined coping styles and found that direct-action coping was related to WEF but not FEW, whereas advice seeking was associated with FEW but not WEF.

Outcomes

Enrichment has been positively associated with job attitudes, such as job satisfaction and organizational commitment, in multiple studies (Aryee, Srinivas, & Tan, 2005; Boyar & Mosley, 2007; Carlson, Kacmar, Wayne, & Grzywacz, 2006; Geurts et al., 2005; Hanson et al., 2006). Positive work–family interactions have also been associated with positive family outcomes, such as marital satisfaction and family satisfaction (Hill, 2005; Voydanoff, 2005). In addition, van Steenbergen et al. (2007) reported that enrichment differentially predicted the work and nonwork outcomes of men and women. There is some indication that WEF more highly correlates with job satisfaction whereas FEW is more highly associated with family satisfaction (Carlson et al., 2006). Research also documents that positive work–family interactions are associated with general well-being (e.g., Allis & O'Driscoll, 2008). Williams et al. (2006) reported a positive relationship between FEW and sleep quality.

We are aware of only one study that has examined enrichment longitudinally. Hammer et al. (2005) found no significant bivariate relationship between direction of enrichment and depression measured 1 year later.

Summary

In his review, Frone (2003) drew several conclusions regarding the conflict and enrichment literature. These conclusions are consistent with those from the first edition of the *Handbook*. Research continues to support the importance of distinguishing between the different types of WFC. Research regarding the positive side of the work–family interface remains at a stage where firm conclusions regarding the predictors and outcomes of enrichment are premature. Conflict and enrichment appear for the most part to have unique predictors.

Predictors of WFC tend to be domain-specific stressors and negative affect, whereas the predictors of enrichment tend to be domain-specific resources and positive affect. However, there is also some evidence for shared predictors such as role involvement. There are a growing number of longitudinal studies informing our knowledge about WFC, but we know little about temporal issues associated with enrichment.

Several other conclusions from the first edition may need reevaluation. Recent meta-analytic work suggests that the domain-specificity argument may be overstated (e.g., Byron, 2005). Conclusions regarding gender differences may also warrant another look. Although meta-analytic research shows few mean differences between men and women, these findings appear to be moderated by parental and marital status. Moreover, interesting recent work suggests that men and women may differ in how they self-report WIF. Streich, Casper, and Salvaggio (2008) examined the extent that couples agree about the WIF of each partner. Husbands' average self-rating of WIF was significantly higher than their wives' ratings. There were no mean differences in self- and partner-rated WIF for wives. Although it is uncertain whether husbands overreport their own WIF or whether wives underreport their spouse's WIF, we believe that the relationship between gender and WFC (or enrichment for that matter) is not known conclusively.

Frone (2003) and other recent reviewers of the work–family literature have pointed to a number of limitations and criticisms (Casper et al., 2007; Eby et al., 2005) such as minimal consideration of individual differences, limited focus on family variables, and little understanding of patterns of change over time. As we mentioned earlier, some of these limitations are being addressed through the use of longitudinal research and studies that feature underrepresented samples. One limitation that remains unabated is the lack of experimentally controlled designs (for an exception, see van Steenbergen, Ellemers, Haslam, & Urlings, 2008). Such designs are sorely needed to provide sound evaluation of occupational health–oriented interventions and to help establish the causal direction of work–family relationships. Moreover, greater interdisciplinary collaboration among researchers may help ensure that both work and family domain variables receive adequate attention in the literature.

We now turn our attention to the concept of work–family balance. In the first edition of the *Handbook,* Frone (2003) presented a fourfold taxonomy of balance that conceived it as occurring when WFC is low and facilitation is high. Our view of balance is quite different and forms the subject of the rest of this chapter.

Work–Family Balance

The term *work–family balance* (or the more inclusive *work–life balance*) is used frequently in everyday life. Friends and self-help books encourage people to get more balance in their lives, and many employees lament the difficulties they have balancing work with other life commitments. In addition, balance is invoked in journalistic accounts of employees' work–family challenges as reflected by a *New York Times* article on the search for equilibrium in the "work–life balancing act" (Dwyer, 2005) and a *Business Week* article reminding the reader that it is never too late to gain greater work–life balance (McKee, 2008). The academic literature also contains references to balance in the title or the text (e.g., Duxbury & Higgins, 2001; Sumer & Knight, 2001).

Alternative Perspectives on Work–Family Balance

Despite the popularity of the term *work–family balance,* the meaning of balance remains elusive because many authors do not define balance and seem to view balance in a variety of different ways. Moreover, some scholars have expressed their displeasure with the balance concept. Halpern and Murphy (2005) rejected the work–family balance metaphor in favor of an alternative work–family interaction perspective, and Rapoport et al. (2002) encouraged organizations to go "beyond" work–family balance to advance gender equity and workplace performance. The balance notion seems to attract some scholars and repel others, and it is likely that the divergent attitudes toward balance reflect the ambiguity in the meaning of the concept.

BALANCE AS THE ABSENCE OF WORK–FAMILY CONFLICT. Work–family balance is often viewed as the absence of conflict between work and family roles. For example, Duxbury and Higgins (2001) equated the inability to balance work and family roles with high levels of work–family or work–life conflict, and they provided some evidence suggesting that "balance (*rather than conflict*)" (p. 6, italics added) may have increased during the 1990s. As noted earlier, Frone (2003) added work–family facilitation to the mix, proposing that balance represents minimal interference between roles and substantial positive effects of work and family roles on one another.

BALANCE AS HIGH INVOLVEMENT ACROSS MULTIPLE ROLES. Work–family balance is also viewed in terms of the degree of involvement, investment, or engagement in multiple roles. For example, Kirchmeyer (2000) suggested that individuals' personal resources of time, energy, and commitment must be well distributed across all life roles to achieve balance. Marks and MacDermid (1996) defined role balance as "the tendency to become fully engaged in the performance of every role in one's total role system, to approach every typical role and role partner with an attitude of attentiveness and care" (p. 421).

BALANCE AS HIGH EFFECTIVENESS AND SATISFACTION ACROSS MULTIPLE ROLES. A number of researchers view balance in terms of positive outcomes in multiple roles. For example, Kirchmeyer (2000) discussed the importance of "achieving satisfying experiences in all life domains" (p. 81), Kofodimos (1993) identified "a satisfying, healthy, and productive life that includes work, play, and love" (p. xiii) as characteristic of balance, and Caligiuri and Lazarova (2005) viewed balance in terms of "maintaining a happy and healthy personal life while being successful at work and . . . attaining a broadly defined sense of personal satisfaction" (p. 124). Grzywacz and Carlson (2007) emphasized role accomplishments but at a system (rather than individual) level. A common element in these definitions of balance is effectiveness (good functioning, successful, productive) and/or positive affect (satisfying, happy, healthy) in both work and family roles (or, in the case of life balance, in multiple roles).

An Assessment of Perspectives

Equating balance with the absence of WFC runs counter to everyday conceptions of balance. Some individuals may experience little interference of work with family life because their family commitments are so minimal that there is nothing to be interfered with, hardly the image of a balanced person. Conversely, individuals may experience moderate or high levels of WFC precisely because they are attempting to achieve more complete participation in both roles. More fundamentally, whereas WFC is a linking mechanism (Edwards & Rothbard, 2000) that specifies how one role affects another role, balance reflects an overall, holistic appraisal (Valcour, 2007) of one's experiences in work and family roles. Therefore, we do not think it is useful to equate balance with low conflict or, for that matter, with low conflict coupled with high facilitation.

A conceptualization of balance that emphasizes extensive involvement in work and family roles is compelling because individuals need to invest in work and family activities to reap the benefits of role participation. Viewing balance as high levels of effectiveness and satisfaction across work and family roles is also appealing because experiencing a wide range of accomplishments and fulfillments implies a sense of completeness or fullness to life. However, these approaches seem to ignore individual differences in values and interests. That is, the only way to achieve balance is through extensive involvement, effectiveness, or satisfaction in work and family roles even if individuals place a substantially greater value or importance on one role than the other role.

Moreover, these perspectives seem to implicitly invoke an image of a scale that must be equal—in involvement, effectiveness, or satisfaction—on both sides to achieve balance. In rejecting the balance metaphor, Halpern and Murphy (2005) likened the balance image to an individual at the fulcrum of a balance beam with work on one side and family on the other and suggested that "the message in this balance metaphor is clear—spend too much time at work and your family will suffer and vice versa" (p. 3). In a similar vein, Rapoport et al. (2002) believed that the notion of work–family balance implies that everybody's time should be split equally between the two roles or that choosing one role involves sacrificing the other. Although it is unlikely that scholars or lay people necessarily view balance as equal inputs or equal outcomes in the work and family domains, the perspectives discussed so far may unintentionally encourage an image of balance as a scale or beam that requires equal weights to achieve balance.

However, some researchers view work–family balance as a range of different distributions of attention, commitments, or outcomes that may differ from one person to another in accordance with individual preferences. For example, Kofodimos (1993) suggested that achieving balance involves "finding the allocation of time and energy that fits your values and needs" (p. 8), Bielby and Bielby (1989) viewed balance as a distribution of commitments to activities based on the activities' importance as a source of identity, and Lambert (1990) suggested that employees should determine the benefits and costs of maintaining a "particular balance" between work and home.

These views of balance are consistent with a person–environment fit perspective in the work–family literature in which fit is seen as a correspondence between individuals' work–family experiences (Barnett, 1998) or resources (Voydanoff, 2005) and their needs or aspirations. Viewing balance from a fit perspective implies that the distribution of involvement or outcomes in work and family roles has different consequences for feelings of work–family balance depending on individuals' priorities or values.

A New Definition of Work–Family Balance

Consistent with a fit perspective, we define *work–family balance* as an overall appraisal of the extent to which individuals' effectiveness and satisfaction in work and family roles are consistent with their life values at a given point in time. Individuals assess their effectiveness in each role against internal standards of performance, gauge the amount of satisfaction they derive from each role, and determine the degree to which their effectiveness and satisfaction are consistent with the value they attach to each role.

Although there are different classifications of life values, we use the notion of life role priority—the relative priority, focus, or emphasis placed on different life roles (Friedman & Greenhaus, 2000)—to illustrate the role of individual differences in producing work–family balance. Because we are concerned with the work–family interface, three life role priorities seem most relevant. Career-focused people and family-focused people place work and family, respectively, at the center of their lives and derive their strongest sense of identity from their higher priority role. Career-and-family focused people place approximately equal emphasis on both roles and derive their sense of self from their experiences and accomplishments in both domains.

According to our view of work–family balance, career-and-family focused individuals feel balanced only when they are highly effective and satisfied in both work and family roles because anything less would be inconsistent with the dual centrality of both roles. In contrast, career-focused individuals and family-focused individuals feel balanced when they are highly effective and satisfied in their higher priority role (work or family) regardless of whether they are as effective or as satisfied in the other role. In short, a balanced individual is highly effective and satisfied in a role or roles that are of highest priority.

Our perspective on balance has several elements worth noting. First, it is apparent that equally high effectiveness or satisfaction in work and family roles is not required to feel balanced unless both roles are of approximately equal priority or centrality. It is interesting to note that although dictionary definitions of balance are replete with references to equality (equally opposing forces, equality of mass, to be equal or equivalent), an additional definition of balance is the "harmonious or satisfying arrangement or proportion of parts or elements" (*American Heritage Dictionary,* 2000). Our view of balance is consistent with the latter meaning in that the parts or elements of life (work and family) are arranged harmoniously to the extent that effectiveness and satisfaction in these roles are consistent with life values.

Second, despite the importance of role involvement in the balance process, we view involvement as a contributor to work–family balance rather than as an indicator of balance per se. Although individuals may regret that they are not sufficiently involved in a role, we believe that their real concern is that they are not as effective or as satisfied in the role as they would like to be. Therefore, we believe that balance is best captured in terms of an appraisal of the outcomes achieved in the work and family domains.

Third, we suggest that experiencing a particular pattern of effectiveness and satisfaction as "harmonious" requires individuals to reflect deeply on their values and priorities rather than to conform to social pressures (e.g., gender role stereotypes) regarding what they should value. Outcomes should produce a more authentic feeling of balance when they are consistent with deeply held values (Friedman & Lobel, 2003) rather than values that are imposed by coercive social norms.

Fourth, because one may legitimately question whether individuals can feel balanced when they are substantially less effective or satisfied in a lower priority role than a higher priority role, we propose that an individual must experience at least a threshold, personally acceptable level of effectiveness and satisfaction in a lower priority role to experience balance. That is, a career-focused (or family-focused) individual who feels thoroughly ineffective and dissatisfied in the family (or work) domain is unlikely to experience harmony and balance.

Model of Work–Family Balance

As discussed in the previous section, we propose that feelings of balance are produced by an interaction of effectiveness and satisfaction in the work and family domains with life values (see Figure 9.1). WFC and enrichment play prominent roles in the work–family balance model because they can diminish (in the case of conflict) or enhance (in the case of enrichment) performance and satisfaction in a highly valued role, thereby having indirect effects on feelings of work–family balance.

Work and family role characteristics can have indirect effects on balance through WFC and enrichment. For example, work-related demands (e.g., job overload, inflexible work schedules) have been associated with WIF, and family-related demands (responsibility for dependents, interpersonal conflicts) have been associated with FIW (Frone, 2003). In a similar manner, work-related resources and family-related resources have been associated with WEF and FEW, respectively (Grzywacz & Marks, 2000; Hill, 2005; Voydanoff, 2004). Participation in roles that have reasonable demands and provide substantial resources can reduce WFC, increase enrichment, promote effectiveness and satisfaction, and ultimately produce feelings of balance. Figure 9.1 also indicates that dispositional characteristics are related to WFC and enrichment. Agreeable, conscientious, extraverted, and hardy individuals, as well as those with a secure relationship style, tend to experience low levels of conflict and high levels of enrichment (Bernas & Major, 2000; Bruck & Allen, 2003; Grzywacz & Marks, 2000; Sumer & Knight, 2001; Wayne et al., 2004).

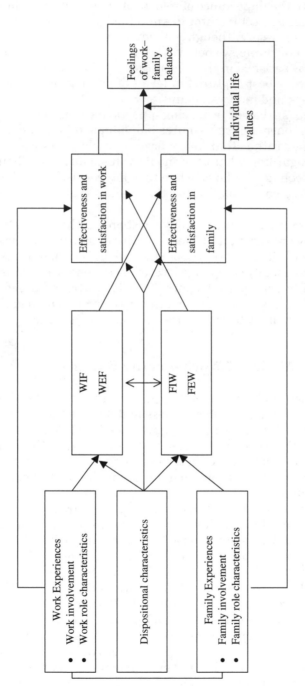

Figure 9.1. A model of work–family balance. WIF = work interference with family; WEF = work enrichment of family; FIW = family interference with work; FEW = family enrichment of work.

Note that role characteristics and dispositional factors also have direct effects on effectiveness and satisfaction that are independent of WFC and enrichment. For example, challenge, leadership, fairness, and support within the work domain and an extraverted, proactive personality may be more important contributors to job performance and satisfaction than are low FIW and high FEW. In other words, feelings of balance can be produced by any factor that promotes effectiveness and satisfaction in a highly valued role and are not solely a product of cross-role relationships.

We believe that our perspective overcomes the concerns raised by scholars who have rejected the notion of balance. Halpern and Murphy (2005) proposed replacing balance with a "work–family interaction" metaphor, a win-win situation in which "there are many benefits that accrue to people who both work and have families and other out-of-work life activities" (p. 3). However, what Halpern and Murphy called *work–family interaction* is similar to work–family enrichment, which contributes to work–family balance in our model. Moreover, Rapoport et al. (2002) indicated that they want individuals to experience work and family not as separate roles in need of balance but rather as "integrated," whereby they "should be able to function and find satisfaction in both work and personal life" (p. 17). Clearly, Rapoport et al.'s integration notion ("function and find satisfaction") is highly compatible with our view of work–family balance.

An Agenda for Future Research

Researchers should examine the factors that contribute to feelings of work–family balance as well as the effect of balance on important life outcomes, including psychological and physical health. Regarding the first issue, we encourage researchers to test the model we presented in this chapter. Because our model contains variables that represent the alternative perspectives on balance (low WFC, low WFC and high enrichment, high involvement across roles, high effectiveness and satisfaction across roles, and consistency of effectiveness and satisfaction with life values), it is possible to assess the relative power of each perspective to predict overall appraisals of balance (Valcour, 2007).

An examination of the proposed model should also provide insights into the particular cues that individuals use in evaluating their levels of balance. For example, is satisfaction in the work and family domains a stronger or weaker predictor of feelings of balance than effectiveness? In addition, although we have viewed balance in terms of role outcomes rather than role involvement, involvement in a role, especially time commitment, is such a concrete resource allocation decision (Edwards & Rothbard, 2000) that individuals may base their feeling of balance on how much they put into their work and family roles instead of (or in addition to) how much they get out of the roles.

Although our model may capture many of the important determinants of work–family balance, it does not directly address the strategies that individuals and their families should use to become more balanced and the actions that organizations should take to promote higher levels of work–family balance among their employees. Studies suggest that the application of time management activities (Adams & Jex, 1999), goal-oriented selection–optimization–compensation behaviors (Baltes & Heydens-Gahir, 2003), and informal accommodations of work to meet family needs (Behson, 2002) may either reduce WFC or attenuate the negative consequences of extensive conflict. It is important to determine whether these and other life management strategies have direct or indirect effects on feelings of work–family balance.

In addition to individual employees, couples also develop strategies to arrive at a pattern of work and family involvement for both partners that meets the needs of the family unit (Becker & Moen, 1999; Moen & Yu, 2000). Research should examine the effect of different family-adaptive strategies on the balance of each partner and the impact of an individual's balance on the family system as a whole (Grzywacz & Carlson, 2007).

The salience of personal and family strategies raises a broader issue regarding the role of decision making at the work–family interface. Greenhaus and Powell (2007) suggested that the decisions that individuals make regarding their participation in work and family roles can have implications for the level of balance they achieve in their lives. For example, the decision to work long hours can simultaneously produce high levels of job performance as well as substantial interference of work with family life with an unknown aggregate effect on work–family balance. A focus on decision making acknowledges the active role that individuals play in the unfolding of their lives and is consistent with a self-leadership perspective that recognizes the importance of proactive choices to enhance well-being (Neck & Manz, 2007). Because decisions made by individuals and families can affect a range of variables in our model (e.g., role involvement, work and family experiences, role performance, life values), it is important to understand the process by which these decisions are made and how they affect balance.

Our perspective on balance is based on life values at a given point in time. We recognize that career and family priorities can shift across the life course, often in response to major life transitions (Sweet & Moen, 2006). For example, an individual who is career focused at age 25 may become family focused following the birth of twins at age 35 and then return to a career focus again later in life after the children have left the home. Reflection on one's cumulative career and family experiences may result in different reports of work–family balance from reflection on one's current situation. An individual who felt balanced focusing on career earlier in life may come to regret that focus later in life and perceive that his or her sum total of life has been imbalanced. It is also possible that feelings of current balance are influenced by one's anticipation of future priority shifts. For example, an individual who is family focused while children are small may anticipate becoming career-and-family focused in the future and factor that into current perceptions of balance. In sum, the incorporation of temporal issues is a fertile area for future balance research.

In addition to individual and family strategies and decisions, the role of organizational initiatives in promoting balance requires further attention. Although supportive supervisors and organizational environments have been associated with low levels of WFC (Allen, 2001; Thompson, Beauvais, & Lyness, 1999), their effects on balance are less well known. A balance approach may also require organizations to think about family-supportive policies in new ways. Building on the life course perspective, one way that organizations can help promote work–family balance is to extend the concept of flexibility across the life span. Specifically, work arrangements that permit flexibility in career patterns are needed (Moen & Roehling, 2005). Giving individuals the opportunity to reduce hours or leave the workforce for a period of time, but also enabling them to return to full speed without penalty, can help individuals invest in their non-work roles in a way that permits a long-term approach to balance. Organizations may also link work–family programs with those focused on employee development. Employee development programs that provide opportunities for individuals to engage in introspection, reflection, and self-evaluation can help ensure that individuals make sound and thoughtful work–family decisions that are aligned with their core values.

Although we have been discussing the process by which individuals experience balance, it is also important to determine whether balance explains important life outcomes over and above the effects of related work–family concepts such as WFC and enrichment. Presumably, feelings of work–family balance enhance, and are an indicator of, psychological health and well-being. It may also be that poor health undermines the ability to effectively achieve balance. For example, individuals with health problems may involuntarily need to reduce their efforts in one or more domains of importance to them, resulting in a lack of balance.

It is also important to examine work–family balance for a wide array of populations. Because members of different racial, ethnic, or socioeconomic groups may have somewhat unique work and family experiences, it is not clear whether balance has the same meaning, antecedents, and consequences for members of different groups. For example, balance to a poverty-stricken individual may mean little more than being able to work enough hours to secure food and shelter for family members. Similarly, national culture, by virtue of its norms regarding work and family lives, may exert an influence on the meaning, antecedents, and outcomes of balance. Men and women may experience balance differently as a function of cultural values regarding gender role egalitarianism and extended family kinship systems (Aycan, 2008).

All of the issues we have discussed become magnified when we extend the concept of work–family balance to the broader notion of life balance, which might be described as an overall appraisal of the extent to which individuals' effectiveness and satisfaction in multiple life roles are consistent with their values regarding work, family, leisure, self-development, community, and spirituality. In fact, because life balance depends on such a wide array of activities, roles, and priorities, it may have a stronger effect on health and well-being than work–family balance. Although it is beyond the scope of this chapter to delve into the major issues surrounding the concept of life balance, extensive research is necessary to determine its meaning, antecedents, and consequences.

Conclusion

Our perspective on work–family balance addresses a largely implicit issue that seems to run through much of the popular and academic work–family literature, namely, how individuals can derive substantial accomplishment and fulfillment from those roles in life that are central to their self-identity. Our model identifies some of the factors that can contribute to feelings of balance. Nevertheless, considerable research is necessary to identify the mechanisms that produce balance and the actions that individuals, families, and organizations can take to enhance the harmony between work and family lives.

References

Adams, G. A., & Jex, S. M. (1999). Relationships between time management, control, work–family conflict, and strain. *Journal of Occupational Health Psychology, 4,* 72–77. doi:10.1037/1076-8998.4.1.72

Allen, T. D. (2001). Family-supportive work environments: The role of organizational perceptions. *Journal of Vocational Behavior, 58,* 414–435. doi:10.1006/jvbe.2000.1774

Allis, P., & O'Driscoll, M. (2008). Positive effects of nonwork-to-work facilitation on well-being in work, family and personal domains. *Journal of Managerial Psychology, 23,* 273–291. doi:10.1108/02683940810861383

Allen, T. D., & Armstrong, J. (2006). Further examination of the link between work–family conflict and physical health: The role of health-related behaviors. *American Behavioral Scientist, 49,* 1204–1221. doi:10.1177/0002764206286386

American Heritage Dictionary of the English Language, 4th ed. (2000). Retrieved from http://www.bartleby.com/61/56/B0035600.html

Aryee, S., Srinivas, E. S., & Tan, H. H. (2005). Rhythms of life: Antecedents and outcomes of work–family balance in employed parents. *Journal of Applied Psychology, 90,* 132–146. doi:10.1037/0021-9010.90.1.132

Aycan, Z. (2008). Cross-cultural approaches to work–family conflict. In K. Korabik, D. Lero, & D. Whitehead (Eds.), *Handbook of work–family integration* (pp. 353–370). San Diego, CA: Academic Press.

Baltes, B. B., & Heydens-Gahir, H. A. (2003). Reduction of work–family conflict through the use of selection, optimization, and compensation behaviors. *Journal of Applied Psychology, 88,* 1005–1018. doi:10.1037/0021-9010.88.6.1005

Barnett, R. C. (1998). Toward a review and reconceptualization of the work/family literature. *Genetic, Social, and General Psychology Monographs, 124,* 125–182.

Becker, P. E., & Moen, P. (1999). Scaling back: Dual-earner couples' work–family strategies. *Journal of Marriage and the Family, 61,* 995–1007. doi:10.2307/354019

Behson, S. J. (2002). Coping with family-to-work conflict: The role of informal work accommodations to family. *Journal of Occupational Health Psychology, 7,* 324–341. doi:10.1037/1076-8998.7.4.324

Bernas, K. H., & Major, D. A. (2000). Contributors to stress resistance: Testing a model of women's work–family conflict. *Psychology of Women Quarterly, 24,* 170–178. doi:10.1111/j.1471-6402.2000.tb00198.x

Bielby, W. T., & Bielby, D. D. (1989). Family ties: Balancing commitments to work and family in dual earner households. *American Sociological Review, 54,* 776–789. doi:10.2307/2117753

Boyar, S. L., & Mosley, D. C., Jr. (2007). The relationship between core self-evaluations and work and family satisfaction: The mediating role of work–family conflict and facilitation. *Journal of Vocational Behavior, 71,* 265–281. doi:10.1016/j.jvb.2007.06.001

Bruck, C. S., & Allen, T. D. (2003). The relationship between big five personality traits, negative affectivity, Type A behavior, and work–family conflict. *Journal of Vocational Behavior, 63,* 457–472. doi:10.1016/S0001-8791(02)00040-4

Butler, A. B., Grzywacz, J. G., Bass, B. L., & Linney, K. D. (2005). Extending the demands–control model: A daily diary study of job characteristics, work–family conflict and work–family facilitation. *Journal of Occupational and Organizational Psychology, 78,* 155–169. doi:10.1348/096317905X40097

Byron, K. (2005). A meta-analytic review of work–family conflict and its antecedents. *Journal of Vocational Behavior, 67,* 169–198. doi:10.1016/j.jvb.2004.08.009

Caligiuri, P., & Lazarova, M. (2005). Work–life balance and the effective management of global assignees. In S. A. Y. Poelmans (Ed.), *Work and family: An international research perspective* (pp. 121–145). Mahwah, NJ: Erlbaum.

Carlson, D. S., Kacmar, K. M., Wayne, J. H., & Grzywacz, J. G. (2006). Measuring the positive side of the work–family interface: Development and validation of a work–family enrichment scale. *Journal of Vocational Behavior, 68,* 131–164. doi:10.1016/j.jvb.2005.02.002

Casper, W. J., Eby, L. T., Bordeaux, C., Lockwood, A., & Lambert, D. (2007). A review of research methods in IO/OB work–family research. *Journal of Applied Psychology, 92,* 28–43. doi:10.1037/0021-9010.92.1.28

Cullen, J. C., & Hammer, L. B. (2007). Developing and testing a theoretical model linking work–family conflict to employee safety. *Journal of Occupational Health Psychology, 12,* 266–278. doi:10.1037/1076-8998.12.3.266

Devine, C. M., Jastran, M., Jabs, J., Wethington, E., Farell, T. J., & Bisogni, C. A. (2006). "A lot of sacrifices": Work–family spillover and the food choice coping strategies of low-wage employed parents. *Social Science and Medicine, 63,* 2591–2603. doi:10.1016/j.socscimed.2006.06.029

Duxbury, L., & Higgins, C. (2001). *Work–life balance in the new millennium: Where are we? Where do we need to go?* (CPRN Discussion Paper W/12). Ottawa, Ontario, Canada: Canadian Policy Research Networks.

Dwyer, K. P. (2005, December 4). Still searching for equilibrium in the work–life balancing act. *New York Times,* Section 10, pp. 1, 3.

Eby, L. T., Casper, W. J., Lockwood, A., Bordeaux, C., & Brinley, A. (2005). Work and family research in IO/OB: Content analysis and review of the literature (1980–2002). *Journal of Vocational Behavior, 66,* 124–197.

Edwards, J. R., & Rothbard, N. P. (2000). Mechanisms linking work and family: Clarifying the relationship between work and family constructs. *Academy of Management Review, 25,* 178–199. doi:10.2307/259269

Friedman, S. D., & Greenhaus, J. H. (2000). *Allies or enemies? What happens when business professionals confront life choices.* New York, NY: Oxford University Press.

Friedman, S. D., & Lobel, S. (2003). The happy workaholic: A role model for employees. *Academy of Management Executive, 17*(3), 87–98.

Frone, M. R. (2003). Work–family balance. In J. C. Quick & L. E. Tetrick (Eds.), *Handbook of occupational health psychology* (pp. 143–162). Washington, DC: American Psychological Association. doi:10.1037/10474-007

Frone, M. R., Russell, M., & Cooper, M. L. (1997). Relation of work–family conflict to health outcomes: A four-year longitudinal study of employed parents. *Journal of Occupational and Organizational Psychology, 70,* 325–335.

Gajendran, R. S., & Harrison, D. A. (2007). The good, the bad, and the unknown about telecommuting: Meta-analysis of psychological mediators and individual consequences. *Journal of Applied Psychology, 92,* 1524–1541. doi:10.1037/0021-9010.92.6.1524

Geurts, S. A. E., Taris, T. W., Kompier, M. A. J., Dikkers, J. S. E., van Hooff, M. L. M., & Kinnunen, U. M. (2005). Work–home interaction from a work psychological perspective: Development and validation of a new questionnaire, the SWING. *Work and Stress, 19,* 319–339. doi:10.1080/02678370500410208

Grant-Vallone, E. J., & Donaldson, S. I. (2001). Consequences of work–family conflict on employee well-being over time. *Work and Stress, 15,* 214–226. doi:10.1080/02678370110066544

Graves, L. M., Ohlott, P. J., & Ruderman, M. N. (2007). Commitment to family roles: Effects on managers' attitudes and performance. *Journal of Applied Psychology, 92,* 44–56. doi:10.1037/0021-9010.92.1.44

Greenhaus, J. H., Allen, T. D., & Spector, P. E. (2006). Health consequences of work–family conflict: The dark side of the work–family interface. In P. L Perrewé & D. C. Ganster (Eds.), *Research in occupational stress and well-being* (Vol. 5, pp. 61–98). Amsterdam, the Netherlands: JAI Press/Elsevier.

Greenhaus, J. H., & Beutell, N. J. (1985). Sources of conflict between work and family roles. *Academy of Management Review, 10,* 76–88. doi:10.2307/258214

Greenhaus, J. H., & Powell, G. N. (2006). When work and family are allies: A theory of work–family enrichment. *Academy of Management Review, 31,* 72–92.

Greenhaus, J. H., & Powell, G. N. (2007, July). *A conceptual analysis of decision making at the work-family interface.* Paper presented at the Second International Conference of Work and Family, IESE Business School, University of Navarra, Barcelona, Spain.

Grzywacz, J. G., Arcury, T. A., Marint, A., Carrillo, L., Burke, B., Coates, M. L., & Quandt, S. A. (2007). Work–family conflict: Experiences and health implications among immigrant Latinos. *Journal of Applied Psychology, 92,* 1119–1130. doi:10.1037/0021-9010.92.4.1119

Grzywacz, J. G., & Butler, A. B. (2005). The impact of job characteristics on work-to-family facilitation: Testing a theory and distinguishing a construct. *Journal of Occupational Health Psychology, 10,* 97–109. doi:10.1037/1076-8998.10.2.97

Grzywacz, J. G., & Carlson, D. S. (2007). Conceptualizing work–family balance: Implications for practice and research. *Advances in Developing Human Resources, 9,* 455–471. doi:10.1177/1523422307305487

Grzywacz, J. G., Carlson, D. S., Kacmar, K. M., & Wayne, J. H. (2007). A multi-level perspective on the synergies between work and family. *Journal of Occupational and Organizational Psychology, 80,* 559–574. doi:10.1348/096317906X163081

Grzywacz, J. G., & Marks, N. F. (2000). Reconceptualizing the work–family interface: An ecological perspective on the correlates of positive and negative spillover between work and family. *Journal of Occupational Health Psychology, 5,* 111–126. doi:10.1037/1076-8998.5.1.111

Halpern, D. F., & Murphy, S. E. (2005). From balance to interaction: Why the metaphor is important. In D. F. Halpern & S. E. Murphy (Eds.), *From work–family balance to work–family interaction: Changing the metaphor* (pp. 3–9). Mahwah, NJ: Erlbaum.

Hammer, L. B., Cullen, J. C., Neal, M. B., Sinclair, R. R., & Shafiro, M. V. (2005). The longitudinal effects of work–family conflict and positive spillover on depressive symptoms among dual-earner couples. *Journal of Occupational Health Psychology, 10,* 138–154. doi:10.1037/1076-8998.10.2.138

Hanson, G. C., Hammer, L. B., & Colton, C. L. (2006). Development and validation of a multidimensional scale of perceived work–family positive spillover. *Journal of Occupational Health Psychology, 11,* 249–265. doi:10.1037/1076-8998.11.3.249

Hill, E. J. (2005). Work–family facilitation and conflict, working fathers and mothers, work–family stressors and support. *Journal of Family Issues, 26,* 793–819. doi:10.1177/0192513X05277542

Kelloway, E. K., Gottlieb, B. H., & Barham, L. (1999). The source, nature, and direction of work and family conflict: A longitudinal investigation. *Journal of Occupational Health Psychology, 4,* 337–346. doi:10.1037/1076-8998.4.4.337

Kinnunen, U., Geurts, S., & Mauno, S. (2004). Work-to-family conflict and its relationship with satisfaction and well-being: A one-year longitudinal study on gender differences. *Work and Stress, 18,* 1–22. doi:10.1080/02678370410001682005

Kirchmeyer, C. (2000). Work–life initiatives: Greed or benevolence regarding workers' time? In C. L. Cooper & D. M. Rousseau (Eds.), *Trends in organizational behavior* (Vol. 7, pp. 79–93). West Sussex, England: Wiley.

Kofodimos, J. R. (1993). *Balancing act.* San Francisco, CA: Jossey-Bass.

Lambert, S. J. (1990). Processes linking work and family: A critical review and research agenda. *Human Relations, 43,* 239–257. doi:10.1177/001872679004300303

Lyness, K. S., & Kropf, M. B. (2005). The relationships of national gender equality and organizational support with work–family balance: A study of European managers. *Human Relations, 58,* 33–60. doi:10.1177/0018726705050934

Lu, L., Gilmour, R., Kao, S.-F., & Huang, M.-T. (2006). A cross-cultural study of work/family demands, work/family conflict and wellbeing: The Taiwanese vs. British. *Career Development International, 11,* 9–27. doi:10.1108/13620430610642354

Marks, S. R., & MacDermid, S. M. (1996). Multiple roles and the self: A theory of role balance. *Journal of Marriage and the Family, 58,* 417–432. doi:10.2307/353506

McKee, A. (2008, August 14). Work–life balance: It's never too late. *Business Week.* Retrieved from http://www.businessweek.com/magazine/content/ 08_34/b4097036735217.htm

Mesmer-Magnus, J. R., & Viswesvaran, C. (2005). Convergence between measures of work-to-family and family-to-work conflict: A meta-analytic examination. *Journal of Vocational Behavior, 67,* 215–232. doi:10.1016/j.jvb.2004.05.004

Mesmer-Magnus, J. R., & Viswesvaran, C. (2006). How family-friendly work environments affect work/family conflict: A meta-analytic examination. *Journal of Labor Research, 27,* 555–574. doi:10.1007/s12122-006-1020-1

Moen, P., & Roehling, P. (2005). *The career mystique: Cracks in the American dream.* Lanham, MD: Rowman & Littlefield.

Moen, P., & Yu, Y. (2000). Effective work/life strategies: Working couples, work conditions, gender, and life quality. *Social Problems, 47,* 291–326. doi:10.1525/sp.2000.47.3.03x0294h

Neck, C. P., & Manz, C. C. (2007). *Mastering self-leadership: Empowering yourself for personal excellence* (4th ed.). Upper Saddle River, NJ: Pearson Prentice Hall.

Rantanen, J., Kinnunen, U., Feldt, T., & Pulkkinen, L. (2008). Work–family conflict and psychological well-being: Stability and cross-lagged relations within one- and six-year follow-ups. *Journal of Vocational Behavior, 73,* 37–51. doi:10.1016/j.jvb.2008.01.001

Rapoport, R., Bailyn, L., Fletcher, J. K., & Pruitt, B. H. (2002). *Beyond work–family balance: Advancing gender equity and workplace performance.* San Francisco, CA: Jossey-Bass.

Roos, E., Sarlio-Lahteenkorva, S., Lallukka, T., & Lahelma, E. (2007). Associations of work–family conflicts with food habits and physical activity. *Public Health Nutrition, 10,* 222–229. doi:10.1017/S1368980007248487

Rotondo, D. M., & Kincaid, J. F. (2008). Conflict, facilitation, and individual coping styles across the work and family domains. *Journal of Managerial Psychology, 23,* 484–506. doi:10.1108/02683940810884504

Shockley, K. M., & Allen, T. D. (2007). When flexibility helps: Another look at the availability of flexible work arrangements and work–family conflict. *Journal of Vocational Behavior, 71,* 479–493. doi:10.1016/j.jvb.2007.08.006

Spector, P. E., Allen, T. D., Poelmans, S., Lapierre, L. M., Cooper, C. L., O'Driscoll, M., . . . Pagon, M. (2007). Cross-national differences in relationships of work demands, job satisfaction and turnover intentions with work–family conflict. *Personnel Psychology, 60,* 805–835. doi:10.1111/j.1744-6570.2007.00092.x

Streich, M., Casper, W. J., & Salvaggio, A. N. (2008). Examining couple agreement about work-family conflict. *Journal of Managerial Psychology, 23,* 252–272.

Sumer, H. C., & Knight, P. A. (2001). How do people with different attachment styles balance work and family? A personality perspective on work–family linkage. *Journal of Applied Psychology, 86,* 653–663. doi:10.1037/0021-9010.86.4.653

Sweet, S., & Moen, P. (2006). Advancing a career focus on work and family: Insights from the life course perspective. In M. Pitt-Catsouphes, E. E. Kossek, & S. Sweet (Eds.), *Work–family handbook: Multi-disciplinary perspectives and approaches* (pp. 189–208). Mahwah, NJ: Erlbaum.

Thompson, C. A., Beauvais, L. L., & Lyness, K. S. (1999). When work–family benefits are not enough: The influence of work–family culture on benefit utilization, organizational attachment, and work–family conflict. *Journal of Vocational Behavior, 54,* 392–415. doi:10.1006/jvbe.1998.1681

Valcour, M. (2007). Work-based resources as moderators of the relationship between work hours and satisfaction with work–family balance. *Journal of Applied Psychology, 92,* 1512–1523. doi:10.1037/0021-9010.92.6.1512

Van Hooff, M. L. M., Geurts, S. A. E., Taris, T. W., Kompier, M. A. J., Dikkers, J. S. E., Houtman, I. L. D., & Van Den Heufel, F. M. M. (2005). Disentangling the causal relationships between work–home interference and employee health. *Scandinavian Journal of Work, Environment and Health, 31,* 15–29.

van Steenbergen, E. F., Ellemers, N., & Mooijaart, A. B. (2007). How work and family can facilitate each other: Distinct types of work–family facilitation and outcomes for women and men. *Journal of Occupational Health Psychology, 12,* 279–300. doi:10.1037/1076-8998.12.3.279

van Steenbergen, E. F., Ellemers, N., Haslam, S. A., & Urlings, F. (2008). There is nothing either good or bad but thinking makes it so: Informational support and cognitive appraisal of the work–family interface. *Journal of Occupational and Organizational Psychology, 81,* 349–367. doi:10.1348/096317908X312669

Voydanoff, P. (2004). The effects of work demands and resources on work-to-family conflict and facilitation. *Journal of Marriage and the Family, 66,* 398–412. doi:10.1111/j.1741-3737.2004.00028.x

Voydanoff, P. (2005). Toward a conceptualization of perceived work–family fit and balance: A demands and resources approach. *Journal of Marriage and the Family, 67,* 822–836. doi:10.1111/j.1741-3737.2005.00178.x

Wayne, J. H., Musisca, N., & Fleeson, W. (2004). Considering the role of personality in the work–family experience: Relationships of the big five to work–family conflict and facilitation. *Journal of Vocational Behavior, 64,* 108–130. doi:10.1016/S0001-8791(03)00035-6

Wayne, J. H., Grzywacz, J. G., Carlson, D. S., & Kacmar, K. M. (2007). Work–family facilitation: A theoretical explanation and model of primary antecedents and consequences. *Human Resource Management Review, 17,* 63–76. doi:10.1016/j.hrmr.2007.01.002

Williams, A., Franche, R.-L., Ibrahim, S., Mustard, C. A., & Layton, F. R. (2006). Examining the relationship between work–family spillover and sleep quality. *Journal of Occupational Health Psychology, 11,* 27–37. doi:10.1037/1076-8998.11.1.27

10

Work Schedules, Health, and Safety

Carlla S. Smith, Simon Folkard, Philip Tucker, and Michael S. Evans

In recent years industrial and commercial activities that operate outside normal work hours have become increasingly common in many industrialized countries. Services such as banking, communications, transport, catering, and retailing are routinely available during evening hours and are often available 24 hr per day, 7 days per week. Consequently, the work schedules of a substantial proportion of the population now extend beyond regular daytime work hours, and both irregular schedules (often including evening or night work) and more regular shiftwork schedules have become widespread.

In the United States, 1997 survey data indicated that 27.6% of the workforce had irregular work schedules, and 16.8% of full-time employees had "alternative" schedules involving work outside normal daytime hours (6 a.m.–6 p.m.), 6.4% of whom worked night or rotating shifts (Beers, 2000). These proportions varied by occupation; rotating shifts were particularly common in security services (16.3%), mining (12.5%), and catering (8.7%) but infrequent among professionals and managers (1.7%). Night work was prevalent in health care, manufacturing, and manual occupations. Similarly, in a European survey, 28% of the workforce had variable work patterns, 10% had evening or night schedules, and 17% worked two-shift or three-shift rotating schedules (Boisard, Cartron, Gollac, & Valeyre, 2003). Further analyses showed that the proportion of shift workers remained relatively constant up to age 45 years but fell sharply at higher ages, particularly over 55 years (Boisard et al., 2003), reflecting older workers' difficulties in adjusting to shiftwork (Folkard, 2008b). Evidence from other national surveys suggests that shiftwork, including night work, is quite common across all regions of the world. In Asia, shift work is widely used in China (36.1% of employees), the Republic of Korea, and Malaysia. The same is true of the Americas (e.g., Chile, about 25% of employees) and the formal economies of the African countries that have been surveyed (i.e., Mauritius, Senegal, and Tunisia). However, shiftwork is rather less common in some transition economies outside the European Union, such as the Russian Federation (Lee, McCann, & Messenger, 2007).

The global trends toward a "24-hour society" suggest that these proportions are likely to rise; thus, the implications of shiftwork for physical and mental health are not only a matter of current concern but also likely to become increasingly important in the future (Costa, 2001; Rajaratnam & Arendt, 2001). The finding that older workers start leaving shiftwork from the age of 45 years onward is particularly worrying in view of the aging workforce in most industrialized countries.

Shiftwork has been variously defined, and in this chapter we use the term *shiftwork* to refer to any work schedule that differs from the standard daylight hours (e.g., 9 a.m. to 5 p.m. on weekdays). Organizations that adopt shiftwork systems can extend their hours of work past 8 hr by using successive teams of workers. The nature of shift systems varies widely along several dimensions, including whether they provide continuous or discontinuous cover, the number and length of shifts, the presence or absence of night work, the direction and speed of the shift rotation (or whether the shift rotates or not), the length of the shift cycles, the start and stop times of each shift, and the number and placement of days off.

The scientific community has long maintained that individuals who regularly work on abnormal work schedules (i.e., shiftwork of some type) are at greater risk of physical and psychological impairment or disease than typical day workers (e.g., Costa, 1996; Costa, Folkard, & Harrington, 2000). This risk is assumed to originate from the physical and psychological stress that develops from work schedule–related disruptions of their biological functions, sleep, and social and family life. The risk is further exacerbated by extended hours of work beyond the standard 40-hr week, a trend that has also been increasing over the past several years (Costa et al., 2000).

In this chapter, we explore the relationships between shiftwork and health. We do not aim at a comprehensive review of the vast and complex literature in this area but rather seek to illustrate the main problems by citing representative papers in the published research literature. We start by providing a general introduction to circadian rhythms to prepare the reader for the balance of the chapter. We then review the empirical evidence on shiftwork and various types of health-related strains or outcomes. We continue by examining some of the factors (e.g., age, personality) that have been investigated in the search for "shiftwork tolerant" individuals. We then explore the various types of interventions that have been attempted to enhance shiftwork effectiveness, and we end by summarizing the research findings and discussing implications for future research.

Theoretical Framework: Circadian Rhythms and Adjustment to Shiftwork

During the process of evolution, periodic changes in the environment, such as the light–dark cycle, have become internalized. It is now widely accepted that living organisms possess a body clock, such that they do not merely respond to environmental changes but actually anticipate them. This anticipation of environmental events is mediated by regular cyclic changes in body processes. In humans, the most pronounced of these are the approximately 24-hour circadian ("around a day") rhythms that occur in almost all physiological measures (Minors & Waterhouse, 1981).

Evidence that these circadian rhythms are at least partially controlled by an internal, or endogenous, body clock comes from studies in which people have been isolated from their normal environmental time cues, or *zeitgebers* (from the German for "time givers"). People continued to wake up and go to sleep on a regular basis, but instead of doing so every 24 hr, they did so about every 25 hr (e.g., Aschoff & Wever, 1962).

In most individuals, the circadian rhythms of other physiological measures, including body temperature and urinary electrolytes, typically show an identical period to that of their sleep–wake cycle. However, approximately a third of the people who have been studied in this way have spontaneously shown a rather different pattern of results, with their temperature rhythm continuing to run with a period of about 25 hr, but their sleep–wake cycle showing either a much shorter or a much longer period (Wever, 1979). It is interesting to note that this phenomenon of spontaneous internal desynchronization occurs more frequently in older people and in those with higher neuroticism scores (Lund, 1974), topics we discuss later in this chapter.

Circadian and Homeostatic Components

The fact that the temperature rhythm and sleep–wake cycle can run with distinctly different periods from one another suggests that the human circadian system comprises two, or perhaps more, underlying processes. The first of these is a relatively strong endogenous circadian process that is dominant in controlling the circadian rhythm in, for example, the secretion of melatonin by the pineal gland and is relatively unaffected by external factors. The second is a homeostatic process that is more prone to external influences and is dominant in controlling the sleep–wake cycle.

The endogenous circadian process exerts a considerably greater influence on the homeostatic process than vice versa. For example, internally desynchronized individuals show such a strong tendency to wake up at a particular point of the temperature rhythm, regardless of when they fell asleep, that their sleep periods can vary in duration from 4 hr to 16 hr (Czeisler, Weitzman, Moore-Ede, Zimmerman, & Kronauer, 1980). It follows that the sleep of shiftworkers is likely to be disrupted unless their temperature rhythms have adjusted to any changes in their sleep–wake cycle.

Adjustment to Shiftwork

Under normal circumstances, both the endogenous circadian process and the more exogenous homeostatic process are entrained to a 24-hr period by strong natural *zeitgebers,* and in particular the light–dark cycle. As a result, all circadian rhythms normally show a fixed-phase relationship to one another. The occasional late night may affect those rhythms controlled by the weaker homeostatic process but are less likely to upset the stronger circadian process and, hence, people's body temperature rhythm and the time at which they spontaneously wake up. This inherent stability in the human circadian system can, however, pose problems if a mismatch arises between the internal timing system and external time cues.

The simplest example of this occurs when people fly across time zones, because all the *zeitgebers* change. Body temperature rhythms usually take more than a week to delay their timing by the appropriate amount (Wegmann & Klein, 1985). For the first few nights, this often results in people waking up in the early hours of the morning and being unable to resume sleep. The rhythms in other processes adjust at different rates, depending on the degree to which they are controlled by the circadian and homeostatic process. As a result, the normal phase relationship between rhythms breaks down and is only slowly reestablished as the various rhythms adjust to the new time zone. This internal dissociation between rhythms is thought to be responsible for the disorientation and general malaise typical of jet lag.

These feelings of jet lag are normally worse following an eastward flight, which requires an advancing of the body's timing system, than following a westward one, which requires a delay. This directional asymmetry effect is related to the fact that the endogenous period of the circadian system is somewhat greater than 24 hr. Thus, in the absence of any *zeitgebers,* rhythms tend to delay rather than to advance, assisting adjustment to westward flights but inhibiting adjustment to eastward ones.

When shiftworkers go on the night shift, most environmental *zeitgebers* remain constant and discourage adjustment of the circadian system. The natural light–dark cycle, the clock time, and most social cues do not change while the timing of shiftworkers' work can be delayed by up to 16 hr and that of their sleep by up to 12 hr. From what we know so far, it is clear that the adjustment of a shiftworker's body clock to these changes is likely to be very slow, if indeed it occurs at all. A review by Folkard (2008a) concluded that only a small minority of permanent night workers showed sufficient adjustment of their melatonin rhythms for it to have been beneficial.

Review of Empirical Literature on Shiftwork and Health

In the previous section, we discussed how the experience of shiftwork, especially night work, provokes circadian disharmony, resulting in decreases in sleep quality and quantity. In the short term, the effects of these deficits are quite obvious (e.g., increased fatigue, sleepiness), and, if unabated, they can presumably lead to more serious medical conditions. In this section, we discuss these short-term and chronic health effects of working shifts.

Sleep and Fatigue

Sleep is the primary human function disrupted by shiftwork. Many bodily processes are at their lowest ebb at night, so it is not surprising that people who try to work at night and sleep during the day often report that they cannot do either very well. Shiftworkers who are forced to attempt to sleep during the day often have difficulty in falling asleep, and their sleep duration is usually substantially shorter than normal. This is because they are normally attempting to sleep at the wrong point within their circadian system. Indeed it has been estimated that about 10% of shiftworkers suffer from a condition termed *shift work sleep disorder* (Drake, Roehrs, Richardson, Walsh, & Roth, 2004).

The unfortunate outcome is that both the quality and quantity of shiftworkers' sleep suffer (Costa, 1996). One almost immediate result is fatigue (Luna, French, & Mitcha, 1997; Tepas & Carvalhais, 1990). Severe sleep disturbances may develop over time and result in the development of chronic fatigue, anxiety, nervousness, and depression, any or all of which frequently demand medical intervention (Costa et al., 2000). Such effects are aggravated by long working hours, which accompany extended (e.g., 12-hr) shifts or multiple jobs or roles (e.g., the working mother).

Accidents and Injuries

As we discussed in the previous section, shiftwork and the resulting biological dysfunction that often accompany it may culminate in serious errors and injury, especially on the night shift (Costa, 1996). The infamous industrial mishaps in the nuclear facilities at Three Mile Island and Chernobyl occurred during the night shift, and in both cases shift schedules and fatigue were cited as major contributing factors (Price & Holley, 1990). However, the task of demonstrating that risk is greater at night due to impaired alertness is fraught with difficulties. This is because in most industrial situations the a priori risk is not constant across the day and night. In many industries, longer, and hence safer, runs are kept for the night shift; the work pace may be slower, and there are often fewer workers present. This means that accident or injury rates often cannot be legitimately compared across the shifts because fewer "incidents" might be expected on the night shift. (Note that the term *incident* is used from here on to refer to both accidents and injuries.) Indeed, even in those few industrial situations in which the a priori risk of incidents would appear to be constant across the 24-hr day, there remains the problem that the probability of actually reporting an injury or accident that occurs may vary.

Reviews of the literature that have failed to take account of the a priori risk and the probability of reporting an incident have, perhaps not surprisingly, found rather mixed patterns of results. Thus, for example, Costa (1996) reviewed 19 studies and found that although eight studies showed the highest risk during the night shift, one study found the highest risk during the day shift, two during the morning shift, and two during the afternoon shift. This lack of consistency in studies that have failed to control for contaminating factors led Frank (2000) to comment that "there is little definitive information available of sufficient quality to make meaningful recommendations" (p. 34). However, when the contaminating factors are controlled for, there would appear to be several important and reasonably consistent trends in incidents associated with shiftwork.

First, having reviewed the available literature in this area, Folkard and Tucker (2003) concluded that, on average, risk increased in an approximately linear fashion over the three traditional types of shift (morning, afternoon, and night), with an increased risk of 18% for the afternoon shift and of 30% for the night shift, relative to that for the morning shift. Thus, in situations in which the a priori risk would appear to be constant across the three shifts, there is a consistent tendency for the relative risk of incidents to be higher on the afternoon than morning shift, and for it to be highest on the night shift.

Second, Folkard and Tucker (2003) found that the risk on the night shift increased over successive night shifts such that, on average, risk was about 6% higher on the second night, 17% higher on the third night, and 36% higher on the fourth night relative to the first night shift. They further showed that this increase in risk over successive night shifts was substantially greater than that found over successive day shifts where the average increases were only 2%, 7%, and 17%, respectively. A related finding is that, relative to day workers, night workers are more frequently involved in automotive accidents while driving home after work (Monk, Folkard, & Wedderburn, 1996).

The length of the shift would also appear to be important in determining the risk of incidents. Folkard and Lombardi (2006) reviewed the literature on trends relating the risk of incidents to hours on duty and estimated that, relative to an 8-hr shift, risk was on average increased by 13% on a 10-hr shift and by 27% on a 12-hr shift. These estimates were in close agreement with the values reported by Dembe, Erickson, Delbos, Banks, and Reville (2005). Nor are the risks associated with longer shifts confined to industrial incidents. Barger et al. (2005) conducted a case-control study of medical interns using a prospective nationwide, Internet-based survey. They reported that, compared with nonextended shifts, extended shifts (greater than 24 hr) were significantly associated with an increased risk of vehicle crashes (odds ratio of 2.3) and near-misses (odds ratio of 5.9) following their work shift. Finally, Tucker and colleagues (Tucker, Folkard, & Macdonald, 2003; Tucker, Lombardi, Smith, & Folkard, 2006) have shown that the risk of incidents is reduced in at least the first half hour following a rest break, suggesting that the provision of frequent short breaks might mitigate against some of the detrimental effects of night work and prolonged work shifts.

Psychological and Emotional Disorders

Psychological and emotional distress frequently accompanies shiftwork, not least because of the impact that shiftwork has on shiftworkers' personal lives (e.g., Bohle & Tilley, 1989). However, there is little conclusive evidence that shiftwork leads to increased risk of clinically diagnosable psychological health problems among shiftworkers (Cole, Loving, & Kripke, 1990). The extent to which shiftwork affects psychological well-being partly depends on the way in which the shift system is designed (e.g., the sequence of shifts or the presence of night work) and also the coping strategies that are adopted by the shiftworker (Tucker & Knowles, 2008).

Shiftwork may cause increased psychological strain through the effects of sleep loss (Barton et al., 1995), circadian disturbances (Cole et al., 1990), and psychosocial stress (e.g., time-based work–life conflict; Pisarski, Lawrence, Bohle, & Brook, 2008). Prolonged exposure to psychological strain may lead to the manifestation of physical health problems among shiftworkers (Barton et al., 1995). Moreover, the psychological distress that often accompanies shiftwork from its onset may be the primary factor that provokes many (approximately 20% to 50%, depending on the data source) to leave shiftwork (Costa, 1996).

Gastrointestinal and Metabolic Disorders

Gastrointestinal disorders are among the most common health complaints associated with shiftwork and night work (e.g., Angersbach et al., 1980; Vener, Szabo, & Moore, 1989). According to Costa et al. (2000), 20% to 75% of shift and night workers, compared with 10% to 25% of day workers, complain of irregular bowel movements and constipation, heartburn, gas, and appetite disturbances. Gastrointestinal complaints are commonly assessed in shiftwork studies, and most researchers report reliable effects, although the size of these effects is sometimes small. In many cases, these complaints eventually develop into chronic diseases, such as chronic gastritis and peptic ulcers (Costa, 1996).

Night work, not just shiftwork, appears to be the critical factor in the development of gastrointestinal disease (Angersbach et al., 1980). A review of 36 epidemiological studies, covering 50 years of data and 98,000 workers, indicated that disorders of the digestive tract were 2 to 5 times more common among shiftworkers who experienced night work than among day workers or shiftworkers who did not work at night (Costa, 1996). Tucker, Smith, Macdonald, and Folkard (2000) reported that the development of digestive problems was associated with working longer shifts (i.e., 12 hr vs. 8 hr) and relatively early shift changeovers (i.e., 6 a.m. vs. 7 a.m.).

Researchers have often speculated that gastrointestinal problems may be greater for shiftworkers because they have less access to healthy food compared with day workers, and their irregular hours encourage inconsistent dietary habits. Studies have found that night workers often tend to eat several snacks during the course of the shift rather eating a full meal (Kräuchi, Nussbaum, & Wirz-Justice, 1990; Lennernäs, Åkerstedt, & Hambraeus, 1995; Nikolova, Handjiev, & Angelova, 1990; Reinberg et al., 1979). However, even when hot meals are available, night workers are more likely to experience indigestion and report enjoying their meals less than their day-working counterparts (Waterhouse, Buckley, Edwards, & Reilly, 2003). Hence, it has been suggested that the higher prevalence of gastrointestinal problems among shiftworkers may be due to the disturbance of the biological rhythms involved in the ingestion, digestion, and absorption of food (Caruso, Lusk, & Gillespie, 2004).

Evidence suggests that shiftworkers' metabolic response to food is affected by the quality of food and the timing of their food intake. Consequently, shiftworkers are more likely to have high triglyceride levels, low levels of high-density lipoprotein cholesterol, and obesity (Karlsson, Knutsson, & Lindahl, 2001; Karlsson, Knutsson, Lindahl, & Alfredsson, 2003), with prevalence increasing in proportion to the duration of shiftworking (Ha & Park, 2005). Further evidence of links between shiftwork and metabolic disorders comes from a limited number of studies that have identified positive associations between shiftwork and incidence of diabetes (e.g., Karlsson, Alfredsson, Knutsson, Andersson, & Torén, 2005; Koller, Kundi, & Cervinka, 1978).

Cardiovascular Disorders

A comprehensive review concluded that "there is rather strong evidence in favour of an association between shiftwork and coronary heart disease"

(Knutsson, 2003, p. 105). In an impressive longitudinal study spanning 15 years, Knutsson, Akerstedt, Jonsson, and Orth-Gomer (1986) reported that the risk of cardiovascular disease increased as years in shiftwork increased. The association was independent of age and smoking history. Occupations with a high percentage of shiftworkers are also associated with a greater risk of heart disease (Costa et al., 2000). In a meta-analysis of the epidemiological literature on shiftwork and heart disease, Bøggild and Knutsson (1999) reported that shiftworkers have a 40% greater risk of cardiovascular mortality or morbidity than day workers.

The precise etiology of cardiovascular disorders among shiftworkers is unclear. It appears that cardiovascular disease may be more prevalent among rotating shiftworkers than among fixed-night workers (Fujino et al., 2006). This suggests that the repeated displacement of circadian rhythms may be responsible. One suggested mechanism links the disruption of circadian rhythms with metabolic disease (e.g., abnormal cholesterol levels and obesity; see above) and cardiovascular disease (Knutsson, 2003). Thus, it may be that at least some of the health problems prevalent among shiftworkers (i.e., gastrointestinal problems, metabolic disturbance, and cardiovascular disease) share common underlying causal elements, namely disturbance of eating habits and the processing of food.

It is also the case that shiftwork is associated with other risk factors for cardiovascular disease, such as sleeping dysfunction, smoking, and poor working conditions. Shiftwork can also function as a stressor, thus exacerbating the stress response over time and resulting in increased blood pressure, heart rate, cholesterol, and alterations in glucose and lipid metabolism (Costa, 1996). In a study of more than 2,000 Swedish men, Peter, Alfredsson, Knutsson, Siegrist, and Westerholm (1999) reported that, in addition to the direct effects of shiftwork on cardiovascular risk, psychosocial work factors in the form of effort–reward imbalance mediated the effects of shiftwork on cardiovascular risk. Therefore, the evidence to date strongly suggests that shiftwork is a contributing factor in the development of cardiovascular disease, but the specific etiology is complex and multifaceted.

Women's Reproductive Disorders

The influence of night and shiftwork on women's reproductive functions has been empirically investigated in several studies. Given that shiftwork disrupts periodic or cyclic functions, such as sleep and digestion, its negative effects on the female menstrual cycle are not surprising. In female shiftworkers, these effects include irregularities in cycle length or pattern (Hatch, Figa-Talamanca, & Salerno, 1999; Uehata & Sasakawa, 1982), spontaneous abortions, lower rates of pregnancies, premature delivery, and low birth weight (Nurminen, 1998).

A review by Figa-Talamanca (2006) observed that whereas irregular hours might be associated with slightly increased risk of spontaneous abortion and reduced fertility, regular night work does not seem to have the same effect. From this, it was concluded that schedule regularity may be the more important factor for reproductive outcome. It has been suggested that disruption of the circadian rhythm of melatonin and prolactin suppresses the ovarian function, affecting both the conception and normal development of the fetus (Figa-Talamanca, 2006; Nurminen, 1998).

In addition to coping with shiftwork, women frequently experience additional stress from domestic and child-care responsibilities. Female shiftworkers with children appear to be especially at risk, because research has shown that they have shorter and more frequently interrupted daytime sleep periods (Dekker & Tepas, 1990) and report greater tiredness than other groups of shiftworkers (Uehata & Sasakawa, 1982). However, some research has not found gender differences (Harma, 1993).

Cancer

An expert working group convened by the International Agency for Research on Cancer concluded that "shift-work that involves circadian disruption is probably carcinogenic to humans" (Straif et al., 2007, p. 1065). The strongest evidence points toward a significantly increased risk of breast cancer among women after 20 to 30 years of night-shift work. Research into links between shiftwork and other forms of cancer (i.e., prostate cancer, colon cancer, and overall cancer) has produced less clear evidence of causal associations (Kolstad, 2008). A meta-analysis of 13 studies identified a 51% increase in the risk of breast cancer among female night workers (Megdal, Kroenke, Laden, Pukkala, & Schernhammer, 2005). However, the interpretation of such data is often limited by potential confounding and inconsistent definitions of shiftwork, with several studies having focused on a single profession (Straif et al., 2007). Moreover, at least one study has identified a negative association between overnight shift work and breast cancer (O'Leary et al., 2006).

It has been suggested that exposure to light at night may increase the risk of breast cancer by suppressing the normal nocturnal production of melatonin (Davis, Mirick, & Stevens, 2001; Hansen, 2006). This is supported by epidemiological evidence, which suggests that women with visual impairment have 40% to 50% of the risk of breast cancer, as compared with controls (Hahn, 1991; Pukkala, Ojamo, Rudanko, Stevens, & Verkasalo, 2006). It has also been hypothesized that altered circadian rhythms may disrupt clock gene communication within cell cycle regulation in the mammary tissue (Stevens, 2006).

Review of Empirical Literature on Shiftwork Tolerance

A number of individual variables (e.g., age, gender, personality) may moderate the impact of shiftwork on health and safety. These variables are often treated analytically as predictors of *shiftwork tolerance,* which is defined as the absence of the most common complaints associated with shiftwork, such as sleep and gastrointestinal complaints (Harma, 1993).

Age

Over the age of 45 to 50 years, shiftworkers increasingly encounter difficulties in altering their sleep–wake cycles (Harma, 1993; Nachreiner, 1998). It has also been suggested that aging is associated with reduced amplitude circadian rhythms and a tendency toward internal desynchronization of circadian rhythms (Costa et al., 2000; Harma, 1993, 1996). However, in reviewing the literature on this, Monk (2005) concluded that although older people have more trouble coping with shiftwork, the evidence regarding circadian amplitude is, at best, mixed. The most consistent effect of aging would appear to be a change toward more morning orientation (Monk, 2005), such that the circadian activity peak occurs almost 2 hr earlier in older adults compared with younger people (Lieberman, Wurtman, & Teicher, 1989). These changes in circadian functioning imply that shift changes and night work are inadvisable for shiftworkers over age 50.

In addition, health problems increase with advancing age, and the effect of shiftwork generally is to increase that health risk or decrease shiftwork tolerance (Nachreiner, 1998; Tepas, Duchon, & Gersten, 1993) by further disrupting circadian functions and sleep. An interesting finding reported by Ogińska, Pokorski, and Oginski (1993) is that female shiftworkers' reports of subjective health improved after age 50, whereas the opposite was true for male shiftworkers. This gender difference may reflect the decreased child-care and domestic responsibilities of older women. Another study cited similar reasons for the increased alertness and decreased sleep difficulties reported by older female shiftworkers compared with their younger counterparts (Spelten, Totterdell, Barton, & Folkard, 1995).

There is currently considerable concern over the safety of aging shift workers because of the increasing age of the workforce and increases in the retirement age. However, there appears to be a complete lack of studies that have directly examined the combined effects of age and shiftwork on occupational injuries and accidents (Folkard, 2008b). In general, occupational injuries are less frequent in older workers, but those that do occur tend to be more serious (e.g., Rogers & Wiatrowski, 2005; Root, 1981). There is also suggestive evidence that older workers may be less able to both maintain their performance over the course of a night shift and cope with longer spans of successive night shifts (Folkard, 2008b).

Morningness and Circadian Type

Morningness (morning–evening orientation) is defined as the expressed preference for morning or evening activities; the guiding assumption is that people who express preferences for activities at the extremes of the 24-hr day (i.e., early morning or late evening) will, when feasible, behave in accord with those preferences (Horne & Ostberg, 1976; Smith, Reilly, & Midkiff, 1989).

Research has demonstrated that preference for early morning activity is related to an advanced phase (i.e., an earlier circadian peak), whereas preference for late evening activity is related to a delayed phase (i.e., a later circadian peak). Morning types are therefore thought to be especially suited to morning or early day shifts and evening types to evening or late-night shifts (see Tankova, Adan, & Buela-Casal, 1994). Morningness is also related to rigidity in sleep habits, or the inability to change sleep schedules, which is especially true for extreme morning types (Hildebrandt & Stratmann, 1979). However, empirical studies have indicated that morningness is only weakly to moderately related to health strains or shiftwork tolerance (e.g., Bohle & Tilley, 1989; Steele, Ma, Watson, & Thomas, 2000), and several conflicting studies exist (e.g., Costa, Lievore,

Casaletti, Gaffuri, & Folkard, 1989; Kaliterna, Vidacek, Prizmic, & Radosevic-Vidacek, 1995). It seems probable that, at least on rotating shift systems, any advantage of morningness for the morning or early day shift has to be weighed against a similar disadvantage on late evening and night shifts.

The notion of circadian type was created by Folkard, Monk, and Lobban (1979) to address other characteristics of circadian rhythms than phase (morningness). The construct rigidity–flexibility was developed to assess the stability of circadian rhythms, and the construct vigor–languidity to assess the amplitude of the rhythms. Folkard et al. (1979) hypothesized that flexibility–rigidity, or the flexibility of one's sleeping habits, and vigor–languidity, or one's ability to overcome drowsiness, are important contributors to adjustment to shiftwork; specifically, people with flexible and low-amplitude rhythms should better adjust to the demands of shiftwork. Both the flexibility and vigor dimensions have been reported to relate to long-term tolerance to shiftwork (Costa et al., 1989; Vidacek, Kaliterna, & Radosevic-Vidacek, 1987). In fact, in Vidacek et al.'s (1987) prospective study, vigor was the best predictor of shiftwork tolerance after 3 years. More recent studies have also supported the relationship between flexibility and vigor and shiftwork tolerance (e.g., Steele et al., 2000).

These individual differences in circadian rhythms have helped researchers to understand why some people prefer, and presumably adapt better to, different shift schedules. Although the use of these measures as selection or placement instruments for night workers and shiftworkers would be premature in view of the relative lack of validation data, they may be helpful in shiftwork counseling and education programs.

Personality

Researchers have also investigated other individual difference measures with respect to shiftwork tolerance. Introversion–extroversion is a well-known personality variable that, similar to morningness, has demonstrated relationships with circadian phase. Specifically, introverts have a somewhat earlier circadian phase (i.e., are more morning oriented) than extroverts (Blake, 1967; Vidacek et al., 1987), and circadian adjustment to shift schedules also seems to occur more slowly in introverts than in extroverts (Colquhoun & Condon, 1980). Researchers have also reported a relationship between neuroticism and shiftwork tolerance across several studies, such that shiftworkers who are more neurotic are less tolerant to shiftwork (e.g., Iskra-Golec, Marek, & Noworol, 1995). However, neuroticism does not appear to predict shiftwork tolerance (Kaliterna et al., 1995) but rather increases with exposure to shiftwork and thus behaves more like an outcome or strain measure than a moderator variable (Bohle & Tilley, 1989).

Interventions to Improve Shiftworkers' Health and Effectiveness

Attempts to improve shiftworkers' adaptation include the ingestion of pharmaceutical agents, exposure to bright lights, and education and counseling programs.

Pharmaceutical Agents

For decades, shiftworkers have used pharmacological aids to improve sleep, diminish fatigue, and enhance alertness, although long-term use of many of these drugs has not been advised because of potential side effects (Walsh, 1990). Melatonin seems to avoid the pitfalls of the earlier hypnotics and is a pineal hormone that promotes sleep and is present in humans and other species. Numerous controlled clinical studies have demonstrated the efficacy and safety of melatonin in enhancing sleep and adaptation to new shift schedules or time zones (Arendt & Deacon, 1997; Brzezinski et al., 2005; Herxheimer & Petrie, 2001). The long-term use of melatonin is, however, not without problems, and shiftworkers are advised to only take it under medical supervision (Arendt & Deacon, 1997).

In 2004 the psychostimulant modafinil was approved by the U.S. Food and Drug Administration for the treatment of shiftwork sleep disorder. Modafinil lacks the negative side effects of classic psychostimulants such as amphetamines (e.g., addiction, increased cardiovascular risk). As such, it is the only such approved prescription drug for the disorder (Boivin, Tremblay, & James, 2007). Trials indicated that modafinil taken by sufferers of shiftwork sleep disorder prior to the night shift reduced subjective and objective sleepiness, especially in the first half of the shift, and was also associated with a reduction in accident risk on the commute home in the morning. Although there was no polysomnographic change in daytime sleep between night shifts, workers on modafinil were more likely to report insomnia between night shifts (Czeisler et al., 2005).

Bright Light

Another recent intervention to aid adaptation to shift changes is the administration of bright light (see the review by Boivin & James, 2005). Research has indicated that exposure to very bright light (2,500 lux; indoor illumination is about 500 lux) can suppress the normal nocturnal secretion of melatonin and therefore delay sleep and entrain human circadian rhythms (for a review of the early research, see Eastman, 1990). These effects have also been demonstrated in field settings with shiftworkers (e.g., Stewart, Hayes, & Eastman, 1995). Some results, however, have been mixed and inconsistent (e.g., Budnick, Lerman, & Nicolich, 1995). To achieve the desired effects, shiftworkers must follow, and their employing organizations must support, a strict schedule of exposure to bright light over time, including rest days. The effort needed to achieve this outcome can be considerable, and therefore bright light exposure has not achieved the popularity of over-the-counter melatonin to enhance adaptation to shift changes and night work.

Education and Counseling Programs

Education and counseling programs have been used to impart information that may aid adaptation to shiftwork. Programs or workshops that deliver mostly general information about shiftwork and its effects on human functioning, as well as recommendations for coping with these issues, have been reported, for example, for emergency room physicians (Smith-Coggins, Rosekind, Buccino, Dinges, & Moser, 1997). Smith-Coggins and colleagues (1997) devised a well-controlled study using both objective and subjective criteria to assess the effectiveness of the workshop they presented to a group of physicians. However, their results indicated that although the physicians in the experimental group used the strategies they learned 85% of the time according to their log book entries, the intervention did not significantly improve the criteria (performance and mood).

The disappointing results in this well-controlled study support Tepas's (1993) argument that educational information alone is often not particularly helpful, and in some cases may actually be misleading or confusing. Tepas maintained that educational workshops are best used in the context of a larger effort to improve the existing shift schedule. Such a process was applied by Sakai, Watanabe, and Kogi (1993), who used an educational program to aid them in analyzing, planning, and implementing an improved shift rotation schedule in a disabled persons' facility.

In a similar vein, Wedderburn and Scholarios (1993) collected shiftworkers' opinions on guidelines for shiftworkers that were developed by a team of European shiftwork experts and published as the *Bulletin of Shiftwork Topics No. 3*. Of the 24 guidelines, six focused at the personal level were supported by a majority of the shiftworkers (e.g., on shiftwork, "I avoid taking sleeping pills" and "I avoid alcohol before sleeping"), and six were opposed by a majority (e.g., when working nights, "I use earplugs in bed" and "I avoid eating fatty foods"). These types of guidelines have often been, in some form, incorporated into shiftwork legislation.

Shiftwork Legislation

In an attempt to guard the health and safety of shiftworkers, shiftwork legislation has been developed by the European Community in the form of the European Directive 93/104, which deals with "certain aspects of the organisation of working time." This document discusses specific measures for night shiftworkers, such as health assessments before assignment to night work, reassessments at regular intervals, and reassessments in case of health complaints. Other issues include transferring workers out of night work and into day work for health reasons, limiting the average hours worked per week to 48, including overtime, and providing a minimum rest period of 11 hr per day and 24 hr per week. Most members of the European Union have now passed laws that conform to this directive (Costa et al., 2000).

International regulations have also dealt with equality of treatment for female shiftworkers, consideration of job design factors, expanded health and safety measures, and participatory practices for introducing change in the workplace (Kogi, 1998; Kogi & Thurman, 1993). When treated as law, these directives and regulations should have a profound influence on the health of night and shiftworkers by limiting some of the most dangerous practices. Unfortunately, beyond the Occupational Health and Safety Act of 1971, which requires employers to provide a workplace "free from recognized hazards likely to cause death or serious physical harm to [their] employees," we know of no legislation that has been specifically targeted toward night or shiftworkers in the United States.

Conclusion and Recommendations

Our goal in this chapter was to explore the relationships between shiftwork and health. The research evidence clearly indicates that shiftwork adversely affects sleep, promotes fatigue, and is associated with the occurrence of accidents and injuries. Shiftwork is also related to the development of psychological, gastro-intestinal, metabolic, cardiovascular, and women's reproductive disorders, as well as cancer. Although the data are insufficient to prove a causal relationship, the convergence of the evidence is strongly suggestive. The most destructive component is the amount of night work, not simply shiftwork, and the impact of night work increases with age. A number of interventions, with varying degrees of success, have also been developed to ease the plight of shiftworkers (e.g., melatonin ingestion, educational and counseling programs).

The main conclusion is distinctly negative, namely that shiftwork, and especially night work, which disrupts the human circadian system, is associated with increased health risk of minor and life-threatening disorders. Regardless of its impact on health, however, shiftwork will remain as a necessary way of structuring work because of the current and future demands of society. On a more positive note, we have considerable knowledge at our disposal to address these issues. The challenge for researchers and practitioners is to improve both the research and the tools (e.g., interventions) that we develop from that research. There are several ways in which this might be achieved.

To date, most shiftwork studies have been cross-sectional studies of workforces from which unknown numbers of shiftworkers may have already transferred out of shiftwork for health or personal reasons. As a consequence, only the "successful" shiftworkers remain in shiftwork. The result is that researchers may have greatly underestimated the negative impact of shiftwork. Conversely, studies of former shiftworkers may have overestimated the negative impact of shiftwork (Costa et al., 2000).

Another problem has been the relative lack of standardized measures used in shiftwork research, making comparisons across studies difficult. This issue was addressed by Barton et al. (1995), who proposed a battery of self-report instruments. The Standard Shiftwork Index (SSI) scales fall into three areas: (a) general, contextual variables (e.g., timing and duration of shifts, workload); (b) outcomes or criteria (e.g., digestive symptoms, job satisfaction); (c) and modifiers or moderators (e.g., morningness, coping strategies). Since 1995, various parts of the SSI have been used in a large number of studies by various shiftwork researchers (e.g., Tucker, Barton, & Folkard, 1996), and their results were reviewed by Tucker and Knowles (2008). We would urge researchers to consider using the SSI scales (which can be downloaded from the Working Time Society website: http://www.workingtime.org/index.php/Documents) in their future investigations to facilitate comparisons with other studies.

Personal control is yet another important issue in shiftwork research and practice. Psychologists have long known that personal control and choice are critical to maintain psychological and physical health and well-being (e.g., Folkman, 1984). It is not surprising that shiftwork researchers have discovered that the opportunity to exert individual control over the selection of the hours or shift one works is important in achieving shiftwork tolerance (e.g., Barton, 1994; Barton, Smith, Totterdell, Spelten, & Folkard, 1993). Therefore, individual choice or participation in the design of actual shift schedules should increase acceptance and positive attitudes toward the shift system (e.g., Sakai et al., 1993).

According to Knauth (1997), a tailor-made shift system should be a compromise between the employer's goals, the wishes of the employee, and ergonomic recommendations for the design of the shift systems. Knauth stated that only management's goals and ergonomic features have traditionally been considered when designing shift systems. However, if the new system is to achieve a high acceptance among shiftworkers, then a participatory process (i.e., their input) in the design and implementation of the new system is as necessary as the ergonomic features of the shift system. In fact, shiftwork experts consider worker participation in the design and implementation of shift systems to be so universally appropriate that it has been incorporated into international shiftwork regulations and directives (Kogi, 1998).

Until recently, one of the more neglected topics has been the effect of shiftwork on organizational variables such as employee retention and job performance. The negative effects on shiftworkers' well-being and work–life conflict can easily spill over into effects on job satisfaction and turnover intention. Such negative effects may be mitigated by supervisor and coworker support, as well as by appropriate shift system design (Pisarski et al., 2006).

In conclusion, decades of research indicate that shiftworkers are at greater health risk than comparable day workers. Using that knowledge, researchers have designed interventions to alleviate the risk. In the 21st century, our goals as applied researchers should be to improve and augment our research and the interventions developed from it.

References

Angersbach, D., Knauth, P., Loskant, H., Karvonen, M. J., Undeutsch, K., & Rutenfranz, J. (1980). A retrospective cohort study comparing complaints and diseases in day and shift workers. *International Archives of Occupational and Environmental Health, 45,* 127–140. doi:10.1007/BF01274132

Arendt, J., & Deacon, S. (1997). Treatment of circadian rhythm disorders: Melatonin. *Chronobiology International, 14,* 185–204. doi:10.3109/07420529709001155

Aschoff, J., & Wever, R. A. (1962). Spontanperiodik des Menschen bei Ausschluss aller Zeitgeber. *Naturwissenschaften, 49,* 337–342. doi:10.1007/BF01185109

Barger, L. K., Cade, B. E., Ayas, N. T., Cronin, J. W., Rosner, B., Seizer, F. E., & Czeisler, C. A. (2005). Extended work shifts and the risk of motor vehicle crashes among interns. *New England Journal of Medicine, 352,* 125–134. doi:10.1056/NEJMoa041401

Barton, J. (1994). Choosing to work at night: A moderating influence on individual tolerance to shift work. *Journal of Applied Psychology, 79,* 449–454. doi:10.1037/0021-9010.79.3.449

Barton, J., Smith, L., Totterdell, P., Spelten, E., & Folkard, S. (1993). Does individual choice determine shift system acceptability? *Ergonomics, 36,* 93–99. doi:10.1080/00140139308967859

Barton, J., Spelten, E., Totterdell, P., Smith, L., Folkard, S., & Costa, G. (1995). The Standard Shiftwork Index: A battery of questionnaires for assessing shiftwork-related problems. *Work and Stress, 9,* 4–30. doi:10.1080/02678379508251582

Beers, T. M. (2000, June). Flexible schedules and shift work: Replacing the "9–5" workday. *Monthly Labor Review,* 33–40.

Blake, M. J. (1967, August 19). Relationship between circadian rhythm of body temperature and introversion–extraversion. *Nature, 215,* 896–897. doi:10.1038/215896a0

Bøggild, H., & Knutsson, A. (1999). Shift work, risk factors and cardiovascular disease. *Scandinavian Journal of Work, Environment and Health, 25,* 85–99.

Bohle, P., & Tilley, A. J. (1989). The impact of night work on psychological well-being. *Ergonomics, 32,* 1089–1099. doi:10.1080/00140138908966876

Boisard, P., Cartron, D., Gollac, M., & Valeyre, A. (2003). *Time and work: Duration of work.* Dublin, Ireland: European Foundation for the Improvement of Living and Working Conditions.

Boivin, D. B., & James, F. O. (2005). Light treatment and circadian adaptation to shift work. *Industrial Health, 43,* 34–48. doi:10.2486/indhealth.43.34

Boivin, D. B., Tremblay, G. M., & James, F. O. (2007). Working on atypical schedules. *Sleep Medicine, 8,* 578–589. doi:10.1016/j.sleep.2007.03.015

Brzezinski, A., Vangel, M. G., Wurtman, R. J., Norrie, G., Zhdanova, I., Ben-Shishan, A., & Ford, I. (2005). Effects of exogenous melatonin on sleep: A meta-analysis. *Sleep Medicine Reviews, 9,* 41–50. doi:10.1016/j.smrv.2004.06.004

Budnick, L. D., Lerman, S. E., & Nicolich, M. J. (1995). An evaluation of scheduled bright light and darkness on rotating shiftworkers: Trial and limitations. *American Journal of Industrial Medicine, 27,* 71–82.

Caruso, C., Lusk, S., & Gillespie, B. (2004). Relationship of work schedules to gastrointestinal diagnoses, symptoms, and medication use in auto factory workers. *American Journal of Industrial Medicine, 46,* 586–598. doi:10.1002/ajim.20099

Cole, R. J., Loving, R. T., & Kripke, D. F. (1990). Psychiatric aspects of shiftwork. *Occupational Medicine, 5,* 301–314.

Colquhoun, W. P., & Condon, R. (1980). Introversion–extroversion and the adaptation of the body-temperature rhythm to night work. *Chronobiologia, 7,* 428.

Costa, G. (1996). The impact of shift and night work on health. *Applied Ergonomics, 27,* 9–16. doi:10.1016/0003-6870(95)00047-X

Costa, G. (2001). The 24-hour society: Between myth and reality. *Journal of Human Ergology, 30,* 15–20.

Costa, G., Folkard, S., & Harrington, J. M. (2000). Shift work and extended hours of work. In P. Baxter, P. H. Adams, T.-C. Aw, A. Cockcroft, & J. M. Harrington (Eds.), *Hunter's diseases of occupations* (9th ed., pp. 581–589). London, England: Arnold.

Costa, G., Lievore, F., Casaletti, G., Gaffuri, E., & Folkard, S. (1989). Circadian characteristics influencing interindividual differences in tolerance and adjustment to shiftwork. *Ergonomics, 32,* 373–385. doi:10.1080/00140138908966104

Czeisler, C. A., Walsh, J. K., Roth, T., Hughes, R. J., Wright, K., Kingsbury, L., . . . Dinges, D. F. (2005). Modafinil for excessive sleepiness associated with shift-work sleep disorder. *New England Journal of Medicine, 353,* 476–486. doi:10.1056/NEJMoa041292

Czeisler, C. A., Weitzman, E. D., Moore-Ede, M. C., Zimmerman, J. C., & Kronauer, R. S. (1980, December 12). Human sleep: Its duration and organization depend on its circadian phase. *Science, 210,* 1264–1267. doi:10.1126/science.7434029

Davis, S., Mirick, D. K., & Stevens, R. G. (2001). Night shift work, light at night, and risk of breast cancer. *Journal of the National Cancer Institute, 92,* 1557–1562.

Dekker, D. K., & Tepas, D. I. (1990). Gender differences in permanent shiftworker sleep behavior. In G. Costa, G. Cesana, K. Kogi, & A. Wedderburn (Eds.), *Shiftwork: Health, sleep, and performance* (pp. 77–82). Frankfurt, Germany: Peter Lang.

Dembe, A. E., Erickson, J. B., Delbos, R., Banks, S., & Reville, R. (2005). The impact of overtime and extended work hours on occupational injuries and illnesses: New evidence from the United States. *Occupational and Environmental Medicine, 62,* 588–597. doi:10.1136/oem.2004.016667

Drake, C. L., Roehrs, T., Richardson, G., Walsh, J. K., & Roth, T. (2004). Shift work sleep disorder: Prevalence and consequences beyond that of symptomatic day workers. *Sleep, 27,* 1453–1462.

Eastman, C. I. (1990). Circadian rhythms and bright light: Recommendations for shift work. *Work and Stress, 4,* 245–260. doi:10.1080/02678379008256987

Figà-Talamanca, I. (2006). Occupational risk factors and reproductive health of women. *Occupational Medicine, 56,* 521–531. doi:10.1093/occmed/kql114

Folkard, S. (2008a). Do permanent night workers show circadian adjustment? A review based on the endogenous melatonin rhythm. *Chronobiology International, 25,* 215–224. doi:10.1080/07420520 802106835

Folkard, S. (2008b). Shiftwork, safety and ageing. *Chronobiology International, 25,* 183–198. doi:10. 1080/07420520802106694

Folkard, S., & Lombardi, D. A. (2006). Modelling the impact of the components of long work hours on injuries and "accidents." *American Journal of Industrial Medicine, 49,* 953–963. doi:10.1002/ ajim.20307

Folkard, S., Monk, T. H., & Lobban, M. (1979). Towards a predictive test of adjustment to shiftwork. *Ergonomics, 22,* 79–91. doi:10.1080/00140137908924591

Folkard, S., & Tucker, P. (2003). Shiftwork, safety and productivity. *Occupational Medicine, 53,* 95–101. doi:10.1093/occmed/kqg047

Folkman, S. (1984). Personal control and stress and coping processes: A theoretical analysis. *Journal of Personality and Social Psychology, 46,* 839–852. doi:10.1037/0022-3514.46.4.839

Frank, A. L. (2000). Injuries related to shiftwork. *American Journal of Preventive Medicine, 18,* 33–36. doi:10.1016/S0749-3797(00)00139-2

Fujino, Y., Iso, H., Tamakoshi, A., Inaba, Y., Koizumi, A., Kubo, T., & Yoshimura, T. (2006). A prospective cohort study of shift work and risk of ischemic heart disease in Japanese male workers. *American Journal of Epidemiology, 164,* 128–135. doi:10.1093/aje/kwj185

Ha, M., & Park, J. (2005). Shiftwork and metabolic risk factors of cardiovascular disease. *Journal of Occupational Health, 47,* 89–95. doi:10.1539/joh.47.89

Hahn, R. A. (1991). Profound bilateral blindness and the incidence of breast cancer. *Epidemiology, 2,* 208–210. doi:10.1097/00001648-199105000-00008

Hansen, J. (2006). Risk of breast cancer after night- and shift work: Current evidence and ongoing studies in Denmark. *Cancer Causes and Control, 17,* 531–537. doi:10.1007/s10552-005-9006-5

Härmä, M. (1993). Individual differences in tolerance to shiftwork: A review. *Ergonomics, 36,* 101–109. doi:10.1080/00140139308967860

Härmä, M. (1996). Aging, physical fitness, and shiftwork tolerance. *Applied Ergonomics, 27,* 25–29. doi:10.1016/0003-6870(95)00046-1

Hatch, M. C., Figa-Talamanca, I., & Salerno, S. (1999). Work stress and menstrual patterns among American and Italian nurses. *Scandinavian Journal of Work, Environment and Health, 25,* 144–150.

Herxheimer, A., & Petrie, K. J. (2001). Melatonin for preventing and treating jet lag. *Cochrane Database of Systematic Reviews, 1,* Article No. CD001520.

Hildebrandt, G., & Stratmann, I. (1979). Circadian system response to night work in relation to the individual circadian phase position. *International Archives of Occupational and Environmental Health, 43,* 73–83. doi:10.1007/BF00378145

Horne, J. A., & Ostberg, O. (1976). A self-assessment questionnaire to determine morningness– eveningness in human circadian rhythms. *International Journal of Chronobiology, 4,* 97–110.

Iskra-Golec, I., Marek, T., & Noworol, C. (1995). Interactive effect of individual factors on nurses' health and sleep. *Work and Stress, 9,* 256–261. doi:10.1080/02678379508256561

Kaliterna, L., Vidacek, S., Prizmic, Z., & Radosevic-Vidacek, B. (1995). Is tolerance to shiftwork predictable from individual difference measures? *Work and Stress, 9,* 140–147.

Karlsson, B., Alfredsson, L., Knutsson, A., Andersson, E., & Torén, K. (2005). Total mortality and cause-specific mortality of Swedish shift- and dayworkers in the pulp and paper industry in 1952–2001. *Scandinavian Journal of Work, Environment and Health, 31,* 30–35.

Karlsson, B., Knutsson, A., & Lindahl, B. (2001). Is there an association between shift work and having a metabolic syndrome? Results from a population based study of 27,485 people. *Occupational and Environmental Medicine, 58,* 747–752. doi:10.1136/oem.58.11.747

Karlsson, B., Knutsson, A. K., Lindahl, B. O., & Alfredsson, L. S. (2003). Metabolic disturbances in male workers with rotating three-shift work: Results of the WOLF study. *International Archives of Occupational and Environmental Health, 76,* 424–430. doi:10.1007/s00420-003-0440-y

Knauth, P. (1997). Changing schedules: Shiftwork. *Chronobiology International, 14,* 159–171. doi:10. 3109/07420529709001153

Knutsson, A. (2003). Health disorders of shift workers. *Occupational Medicine, 53,* 103–108. doi:10. 1093/occmed/kqg048

Knutsson, A., Akerstedt, T., Jonsson, B. G., & Orth-Gomer, K. (1986). Increased risk of ischemic heart disease in shift workers. *Lancet, 2,* 89–92. doi:10.1016/S0140-6736(86)91619-3

Kogi, K. (1998). International regulations on the organization of shift work. *Scandinavian Journal of Work, Environment and Health, 24,* 7–12.

Kogi, K., & Thurman, J. E. (1993). Trends in approaches to night and shiftwork and new international standards. *Ergonomics, 36,* 3–13. doi:10.1080/00140139308967849

Koller, M., Kundi, M., & Cervinka, R. (1978). Field studies of shift work at an Austrian oil refinery: I. Health and psychosocial wellbeing of workers who drop out of shift work. *Ergonomics, 21,* 835–847. doi:10.1080/00140137808931787

Kolstad, H. A. (2008). Nightshift work and risk of breast cancer and other cancers: A critical review of the epiderniologic evidence. *Scandinavian Journal of Work, Environment and Health, 34,* 5–22.

Kräuchi, K., Nussbaum, P., & Wirz-Justice, A. (1990). Consumption of sweets and caffeine in the night shift: Relation to fatigue. In J. Horne (Ed.), *Sleep 90* (pp. 62–64). Bochum, Germany: Pontenagel Press.

Lee, S., McCann, D., & Messenger, J. C. (2007). *Working time around the world: Trends in working hours, laws and policies in a global comparative perspective.* New York, NY: Routledge.

Lennernäs, M., Åkerstedt, T., & Hambraeus, L. (1995). Shift related dietary intake in day- and shift workers. *Appetite, 25,* 253–265. doi:10.1006/appe.1995.0060

Lieberman, H. R., Wurtman, J. J., & Teicher, M. H. (1989). Aging, nutrient choice, activity, and behavioral responses to nutrients. *Annals of the New York Academy of Sciences, 561,* 196–208. doi:10.1111/j.1749-6632.1989.tb20982.x

Luna, T. D., French, J., & Mitcha, J. L. (1997). A study of USAF air traffic controller shiftwork sleep, fatigue, activity, and mood analyses. *Aviation, Space, and Environmental Medicine, 68,* 18–23.

Lund, R. (1974). Personality factors and desynchronization of circadian rhythms. *Psychosomatic Medicine, 36,* 224–228.

Megdal, S. P., Kroenke, C. H., Laden, F., Pukkala, E., & Schernhammer, E. S. (2005). Night work and breast cancer risk: A systematic review and meta-analysis. *European Journal of Cancer, 41,* 2023–2032. doi:10.1016/j.ejca.2005.05.010

Minors, D. S., & Waterhouse, J. M. (1981). *Circadian rhythms and the human.* Bristol, England: Wright PSG.

Monk, T. H. (2005). Aging human circadian rhythms: conventional wisdom may not always be right. *Journal of Biological Rhythms, 20,* 366–374. doi:10.1177/0748730405277378

Monk, T. H., Folkard, S., & Wedderburn, A. I. (1996). Maintaining safety and high performance on shiftwork. *Applied Ergonomics, 27,* 17–23. doi:10.1016/0003-6870(95)00048-8

Nachreiner, F. (1998). Individual and social determinants of shiftwork tolerance. *Scandinavian Journal of Work, Environment and Health, 24,* 35–42.

Nikolova, N., Handjiev, S., & Angelova, K. (1990). Nutrition of night and shiftworkers in transports. In G. Costa, G. Cesana, K. Kogi, & A. Wedderburn (Eds.), *Shiftwork: Health, sleep and performance* (pp. 538–547). Frankfurt, Germany: Peter Lang.

Nurminen, T. (1998). Shift work and reproductive health. *Scandinavian Journal of Work, Environment and Health, 24*(Suppl. 3), 28–34.

Ogińska, H., Pokorski, J., & Oginski, A. (1993). Gender, aging, and shiftwork intolerance. *Ergonomics, 36,* 161–168. doi:10.1080/00140139308967868

O'Leary, E. S., Schoenfeld, E. R., Stevens, R. G., Kabat, G. C., Henderson, K., Grimson, R., . . . Gammon, M. D. (2006). Shift work, light at night, and breast cancer on Long Island, New York. *American Journal of Epidemiology, 164,* 358–366. doi:10.1093/aje/kwj211

Peter, R., Alfredsson, L., Knutsson, A., Siegrist, J., & Westerholm, P. (1999). Does a stressful psychosocial work environment mediate the effects of shift work on cardiovascular risk factors? *Scandinavian Journal of Work, Environment and Health, 25,* 376–381.

Pisarski, A., Brook, C., Bohle, P., Gallois, C., Watson, B., & Vinch, S. (2006). *Extending a model of shift-work tolerance. Chronobiology International, 23,* 1363–1377.

Pisarski, A., Lawrence, S. A., Bohle, P., & Brook, C. (2008). Organizational influences on the work life conflict and health of shiftworkers. *Applied Ergonomics, 39,* 580–588. doi:10.1016/j.apergo.2008.01.005

Price, W. J., & Holley, D. C. (1990). Shiftwork and safety in aviation. *Occupational Medicine, 5,* 343–377.

Pukkala, E., Ojamo, M., Rudanko, S. L., Stevens, R. G., & Verkasalo, P. K. (2006). Does incidence of breast cancer and prostate cancer decrease with increasing degree of visual impairment. *Cancer Causes and Control, 17,* 573–576. doi:10.1007/s10552-005-9005-6

Rajaratnam, S. M., & Arendt, J. (2001). Health in a 24-h society. *Lancet, 358,* 999–1005. doi:10.1016/S0140-6736(01)06108-6

Reinberg, A., Migraine, C., Apfelbaum, M., Brigant, L., Ghata, J., Vieux, N., . . . Nicolai, A. (1979). Circadian and ultradian rhythms in the feeding behaviour and nutrient intakes of oil refinery operators with shift work every 3-4 days. *Diabete Metabolisme (Paris), 5,* 33–41.

Rogers, E., & Wiatrowski, W. J. (2005, October). Injuries, illnesses, and fatalities among older workers. *Monthly Labor Review,* 24–30.

Root, N. (1981, March). Injuries at work are fewer among older workers. *Monthly Labor Review,* 30–34.

Sakai, K., Watanabe, A., & Kogi, K. (1993). Educational and intervention strategies for improving a shift system: An experience in a disabled persons' facility. *Ergonomics, 36,* 219–225. doi:10.1080/00140139308967875

Smith, C. S., Reilly, C., & Midkiff, K. (1989). Evaluation of three circadian rhythm questionnaires with suggestions for an improved measure of morningness. *Journal of Applied Psychology, 74,* 728–738. doi:10.1037/0021-9010.74.5.728

Smith-Coggins, R., Rosekind, M. R., Buccino, K. R., Dinges, D. F., & Moser, R. P. (1997). Rotating shiftwork schedules: Can we enhance physician adaptation to night shifts? *Academic Emergency Medicine, 4,* 951–961. doi:10.1111/j.1553-2712.1997.tb03658.x

Spelten, E., Totterdell, P., Barton, J., & Folkard, S. (1995). Effects of age and domestic commitment on the sleep and alertness of female shiftworkers. *Work and Stress, 9,* 165–175. doi:10.1080/02678379508256551

Steele M. T., Ma, O. J., Watson, W. A., & Thomas, H. A. (2000). Emergency medicine residents' shift-work tolerance and preference. *Academic Emergency Medicine, 7,* 670–673. doi:10.1111/j.1553-2712.2000.tb02042.x

Stevens, R. G. (2006). Artificial lighting in the industrialized world: Circadian disruption and breast cancer. *Cancer Causes and Control, 17,* 501–507. doi:10.1007/s10552-005-9001-x

Stewart, K. T., Hayes, B. C., & Eastman, C. I. (1995). Light treatment for NASA shiftworkers. *Chronobiology International, 12,* 141–151. doi:10.3109/07420529509064509

Straif, K., Baan, R., Grosse, Y., Secretan, B., Ghissassi, F., Bouvard, V., . . . Cogliano, V. (2007). Carcinogenicity of shift-work, painting and fire-fighting. *The Lancet Oncology, 8,* 1065–1066. doi:10.1016/S1470-2045(07)70373-X

Tankova, I., Adan, A., & Buela-Casal, G. (1994). Circadian typology and individual differences: A review. *Personality and Individual Differences, 16,* 671–684. doi:10.1016/0191-8869(94)90209-7

Tepas, D. I. (1993). Educational programmes for shiftworkers, their families, and prospective shiftworkers. *Ergonomics, 36,* 199–209. doi:10.1080/00140139308967873

Tepas, D. I., & Carvalhais, A. B. (1990). Sleep patterns of shiftworkers. *Occupational Medicine: State of the Art Reviews, 5,* 199–208.

Tepas, D. I., Duchon, J. C., & Gersten, A. H. (1993). Shiftwork and the older worker. *Experimental Aging Research, 19,* 295–320. doi:10.1080/03610739308253940

Tucker, P., Barton, J., & Folkard, S. (1996). Comparison of eight and twelve hour shifts: Impacts on health, well-being, and alertness during the shift. *Occupational and Environmental Medicine, 53,* 767–772. doi:10.1136/oem.53.11.767

Tucker, P., Folkard, S., & Macdonald, I. (2003). Rest breaks and accident risk. *Lancet, 361,* 680. doi:10.1016/S0140-6736(03)12566-4

Tucker, P., & Knowles, S. R. (2008). Review of studies that have used the Standard Shiftwork Index: Evidence for the underlying model of shiftwork and health. *Applied Ergonomics, 39,* 550–564. doi:10.1016/j.apergo.2008.02.001

Tucker, P., Lombardi, D. A., Smith, L., & Folkard, S. (2006). The impact of rest breaks on temporal trends in injury risk. *Chronobiology International, 23,* 1423–1434. doi:10.1080/07420520601070315

Tucker, P., Smith, L., Macdonald, I., & Folkard, S. (2000). Effects of direction of rotation in continuous and discontinuous eight hour shift systems. *Occupational and Environmental Medicine, 57,* 678–684. doi:10.1136/oem.57.10.678

Uehata, T., & Sasakawa, N. (1982). The fatigue and maternity disturbances of night workwomen. *Journal of Human Ergology, 11,* 465–474.

Vener, K. J., Szabo, S., & Moore, J. G. (1989). The effect of shift work on gastrointestinal (GI) function: A review. *Chronobiologia, 16,* 421–439.

Vidacek, S., Kaliterna, L., & Radosevic-Vidacek, B. (1987). Predictive validity of individual differences measures for health problems in shiftworkers: Preliminary results. In A. Oginski, J. Pokorski, & J. Rutenfranz (Eds.), *Contemporary advances in shiftwork research* (pp. 99–106). Krakow, Poland: Medical Academy.

Walsh, J. K. (1990). Using pharmacological aids to improve waking function and sleep while working at night. *Work and Stress, 4,* 237–243. doi:10.1080/02678379008256986

Waterhouse, J., Buckley, P., Edwards, B., & Reilly, T. (2003). Measurement of, and some reasons for, differences in eating habits between night and day workers. *Chronobiology International, 20,* 1075–1092. doi:10.1081/CBI-120025536

Wedderburn, A. I., & Scholarios, D. (1993). Guidelines for shiftworkers: Trials and errors? *Ergonomics, 36,* 211–217. doi:10.1080/00140139308967874

Wegmann, H.-M., & Klein, K. E. (1985). Jet-lag and aircrew scheduling. In S. Folkard & T. H. Monk (Eds.), *Hours of work: Temporal factors in work scheduling* (pp. 263–276). Chichester, England: Wiley.

Wever, R. A. (1979). *The circadian system of man: Results of experiments under temporal isolation.* New York, NY: Springer.

11

The Impact of Organizational Justice on Occupational Health

Russell Cropanzano and Thomas A. Wright

A still growing body of research has established that organizational justice is an important predictor of workplace effectiveness (Cropanzano, Rupp, Mohler, & Schminke, 2001). This is the case whether *effectiveness* is defined from the perspective of the employee or from the perspective of the employer. From a worker's point of view, fair treatment encourages higher levels of satisfaction and commitment, as well as a greater desire to remain with the just organization. From a company's point of view, fair treatment encourages higher job performance and more helpful citizenship behaviors (for meta-analytic reviews of these effects, see Cohen-Charash & Spector, 2001; Colquitt, Conlon, Wesson, Porter, & Ng, 2001). Consequently, the case for organizational justice is based on fundamental human ethics and also on business needs (Cropanzano, Bowen, & Gilliland, 2007).

In this chapter, we review the empirical literature on justice and occupational health. We argue that in addition to the other problems it creates, injustice can cause symptoms of stress and damage workers' health. To make this case, we begin by defining some key terms pertaining to organizational justice. We then discuss three literatures. First we discuss the role of injustice in creating ill health and absenteeism, and then we turn our attention to research on injustice and burnout. Finally, we take up the growing and promising literature on justice and work–family conflict. In the interest of space constraints, we provide a thorough review of the empirical literature while deemphasizing abstract theoretical issues. For a more conceptually oriented analysis of this research, the reader is referred to Cropanzano, Goldman, and Benson (2005).

Three Forms of Justice

Scholars have identified at least three important forms of justice (Cropanzano, Byrne, Bobocel, & Rupp, 2001) each of which is based on employees' appraisals of important events in their work environments: the perceived fairness of outcomes obtained (*distributive justice*), the perceived fairness of processes (*procedural justice*), and the perceived fairness of the interpersonal treatment one receives (*interactional justice*). Justice scholars consider all three to be important (cf. Cohen-Charash & Spector, 2001). Stress researchers, however, have tended to devote more attention to distributive justice, less to procedural, and little to interactional.

Distributive justice pertains to the fairness of an allocation process. It is based on what one receives. Among burnout researchers in particular, the most common approach to distributive justice is equity. A distribution of benefits is *equitable* when individuals are compensated in accordance with their contributions. According to Adams's (1965; Adams & Freedman, 1976) equity theory, people calculate equity by using the ratio of their outcomes to their inputs (sometimes called *investments*). Their own outcome-to-input ratio is then compared with a target ratio, usually the outcomes-to-inputs of a similar other. A feeling of inequity is expected to result whenever these two ratios are unequal. This is the case when one is paid poorly relative to one's contributions (i.e., *under-reward*), but also when one is paid especially well relative to one's contributions (i.e., *over-reward*). Although the under-reward effect is certainly the more robust of the two, there is also evidence suggesting that individuals attempt to restore equity when they are paid somewhat too much (Walster, Walster, & Berscheid, 1973, 1978). As discussed later, burnout researchers have done much to advance our knowledge of workplace equity (e.g., Kop, Euwema, & Schaufeli, 1999; Schaufeli & Janczur, 1994; Schaufeli, van Dierendonck, & van Gorp, 1996), even obtaining evidence for the over-reward effect (van Dierendonck, Schaufeli, & Buunk, 1996, 2001).

Procedural justice, or process fairness, is the second form of justice that we consider. As Leventhal (1976, 1980) observed, fair procedures tend to be unbiased, consistent, accurate, correctable, and consistent with ethical standards and tend to take into account the concerns of all. As one might expect, it is an important predictor of occupational health (Schmitt & Dörfel, 1999). Procedural justice often interacts with distributive justice, such that the impact of an unfair allocation is weaker when the process is fair (Brockner, 2002; Brockner & Wiesenfeld, 1996). As discussed later, this moderator effect has been observed by some stress researchers (Janssen, 2004; Spell & Arnold, 2007; Tepper, 2001), though not all (Zohar, 1995).

The third form of justice, interactional justice, concerns the fairness of interpersonal treatment (Cropanzano et al., 2007). Interactional justice is sometimes divided into two parts: *informational justice* (i.e., the extent to which employees are kept informed) and *interpersonal justice* (i.e., the extent to which employees are treated with dignity and respect; Colquitt et al., 2001). Relatively little occupational health research has explored either interactional fairness or its two component parts, but there are a few promising exceptions (Elovainio, Kivimäki, & Helkama, 2001; Elovainio, Kivimäki, & Vahtera, 2002; Judge & Colquitt, 2004).

Injustice, Ill Health, and Absenteeism

In this section, we explore some initial evidence attesting to a relationship between justice and occupational health. As readers will see, unfair treatment appears to be associated with physical symptoms in employees. This poor health, in turn, may cause workers to subsequently be absent from their jobs.

From Injustice to Ill Health

A number of studies have obtained evidence that injustice is associated with symptoms of stress (cf. Cropanzano et al., 2005; Vermunt, 2002; Vermunt, Spaans, & Zorge, 1989; Vermunt, & Steensma, 2001). At times, the physical consequences can be quite severe. In a fascinating review, Siegrist (1996) discussed a number of studies indicting unfairness in the causal epidemiology of cardiovascular illness. Specifically, Siegrist compared three groups of working people: high effort accompanied by low reward (an inequity, of course), either high effort or else low reward (i.e., either hard work or low pay), and neither high effort nor low reward (i.e., no evidence of injustice, hard work, or low pay). Cardiovascular problems, as well as related risk factors, were most common among those who worked hard for low pay and less common among those in the other two groups. This suggests that distributive injustice is a problem, even beyond the independent effects of underpay and overwork (for additional evidence that justice impacts strain beyond the effect of workload, see Hendrix & Spencer, 1989; Maslach & Leiter, 2008; Schaufeli & Janczur, 1994).

From Injustice to Ill Health to Absenteeism: The Unfairness–Absenteeism Model

It is self-evident that poor health is not in the interest of workers, but it is useful to remind business leaders that it is not in the interest of their organizations either. In this regard, a number of studies have explored the link between justice and absenteeism. The general argument, of course, is that injustice damages workers' health. This poor health becomes one reason for individuals to miss work. De Boer, Bakker, Syroit, and Schaufeli (2002) termed this the *unfairness–absenteeism model* (p. 185). Although some studies have tested this entire theoretical framework (e.g., de Boer et al., 2002; Hendrix & Spencer, 1989), others have only investigated some of the links (e.g., Elovainio et al., 2001, 2002; Schmitt & Dörfel, 1999). Nevertheless, when this body of evidence is taken together, it appears that there is solid evidence supporting a causal sequence from injustice-to-health-to-absenteeism. Probably the earliest study to test this idea was conducted by Hendrix and Spencer (1989). Notably, pay inequity was associated with cold and flu episodes. These episodes, in turn, caused workers to be absent from their jobs. These effects manifested themselves even when other sources of strain were statistically taken into account. Of course, this study is limited in that it only measured distributive justice and did not also consider procedural and interactional fairness.

A decade later, Schmitt and Dörfel (1999) surveyed 295 workers in a German automotive factory. What they termed *psychosomatic well-being* (p. 447) was operationalized with two different variables: number of workdays missed due to illness and number of days that one was ill while at work. Results were reported for each separately, but also for a summed composite of the two. This composite variable was termed *sickness* (p. 450). Procedural justice predicted the number of days one worked while feeling sick. It also predicted the composite sickness measure. Furthermore, these two main effects were moderated by an interaction between justice and justice sensitivity. The effects of procedural justice were strongest among employees who were more sensitive to unfair treatment.

De Boer and his colleagues (2002) argued that both distributive and procedural injustice cause health complaints. Believing themselves to be in poor health, workers will then become more likely to miss work. The authors investigated the unfairness–absenteeism model with a group of 605 Belgian security guards. Health was measured with a checklist of physical symptoms. It is worth noting, however, that their measure of procedural justice contained items pertaining to not only process fairness but also to interactional fairness. In any case, this combined form of justice predicted health complaints and, operating through this variable, impacted absenteeism. Contrary to expectations, distributive justice did not show a direct or unmediated relationship to absenteeism.

One of the most comprehensive studies on the connection between justice, illness, and absenteeism was conducted by Elovainio et al. (2002). These researchers investigated the impact of two types of justice—procedural and interactional (Elovainio and his colleagues used the term *relational*)—among a sample of over 4,000 medical workers. Even when other workplace stressors were controlled, interactional justice was an important predictor of self-report health, psychological ailments, and even absenteeism. Procedural justice, which fared less well in this study, was associated with absenteeism.

To provide stronger causal inferences, Kivimäki, Elovainio, Vahtera, and Ferrie (2003) followed up their earlier investigation with a longitudinal field study. Even when baseline health and demographic factors were controlled, interactional justice again predicted reported health and absenteeism. Procedural justice showed somewhat more consistent effects than it did in the Elovainio et al. (2002) investigation. Kivimäki et al. found that process fairness was associated with health, psychological ailments, and absenteeism.

The unfairness–absenteeism model suggests two important conclusions. First, injustice can harm the health of its victims (e.g., Siegrist, 1996). Second, this harm may rebound back on the organization, as the resulting poor health can engender greater absenteeism and perhaps other problems as well (Cohen-Charash & Spector, 2001; Colquitt et al., 2001). There do not seem to be many strong beneficiaries of injustice.

Injustice and Burnout

According to Maslach, Schaufeli, and Leiter (2001), "burnout is a prolonged response to chronic emotional and interpersonal stressors on the job" (p. 397). Historically, burnout was understood to have three dimensions (Maslach & Jackson, 1981; 1986; Wright & Bonett, 1997; Wright & Cropanzano, 1998): emotional exhaustion, depersonalization or withdrawal, and diminished personal accomplishment. Over the years various other models have been proposed (cf. Halbesleben & Buckley, 2004), and the traditional three factors have been somewhat reconceptualized as emotional exhaustion, cynicism, and lack of efficacy (Maslach & Leiter, 2008). As readers will see, the literature integrating justice and burnout traces back some years. For this reason, most of the studies that we review used the original three dimensions. Nevertheless, there are exceptions to this generalization, and we note them as we discuss each study.

Inequity and Burnout

Research relating injustice to burnout has tended to emphasize the notion of distributive justice or, more generally, inequity, to the exclusion of procedural and interactional injustice. For example, in discussing the causes of burnout among nurses, Buunk and Schaufeli (1993) warned of the "imbalance between investments and outcomes in relationships with patients" (p. 56). Notice that this position shares much in common with the work of Siegrist (1996). Buunk and Schaufeli would no doubt agree that individuals can be overworked or underpaid, but the combination of the two—putting in too much while also getting back too little—creates a sense of unfairness that exacerbates health problems. As readers will see, evidence supports this contention.

THE PROVIDER–CLIENT RELATIONSHIP. Much of the seminal research exploring inequity and burnout focused on human service providers, such as nurses and physicians. These are rewarding but sometimes difficult jobs because they may necessitate intense interpersonal interactions between the health care professional and a patient. The sense that the provider is giving much but receiving little can be a source of imbalance or, in the terms used for this chapter, an inequity or distributive injustice (Buunk & Schaufeli, 1993). For this reason, early work connecting injustice to burnout tended to focus on the provider–client relationship.

To demonstrate this effect, van Dierendonck, Schaufeli, and Sixma (1994) surveyed 525 Dutch physicians. Van Dierendonck and his colleagues (1994) used a two-factor model of burnout. Emotional exhaustion was retained, but depersonalization and personal accomplishment were pooled into a global negative attitudes dimension. The researchers expected that inequity in the doctor–patient relationship would directly cause emotional exhaustion. Emotional exhaustion, in turn, would then cause negative attitudes (i.e., depersonalization combined with diminished personal accomplishment). Van Dierendonck et al. (1994) found support for these predictions, including the result that inequity predicted both burnout dimensions.

In a cross-national replication, Schaufeli and Janczur (1994) explored inequity and burnout among nurses in both Poland and the Netherlands. Among the Dutch nurses, an imbalanced relationship with patients predicted all three burnout dimensions: emotional exhaustion, depersonalization, and diminished personal accomplishment. Among the Polish nurses, it predicted exhaustion and depersonalization. Schaufeli and Janczur's findings were important because the effect of inequity manifested itself beyond a number of other predictors, such as hours employed and perceived control.

Bakker, Schaufeli, Demerouti, and colleagues (2000) sought to distinguish between two related ideas: burnout and depression. These constructs are similar, although Bakker, Schaufeli, Demerouti, et al. maintained that burnout is tied to the workplace whereas depression is more general and "context free." That is, depression can be experienced in a number of different life domains.

With this in mind, Bakker, Schaufeli, Demerouti and colleagues examined a sample of 154 Dutch high school teachers. They compared two types of unfairness. A lack of workplace reciprocity in relationships with students was expected to predict burnout, whereas a lack of reciprocity in private and intimate relationships was expected to predict depression. Burnout, in turn, was anticipated to further boost depression. Findings strongly supported this model.

Pulling together these findings into a comprehensive causal framework, Bakker, Schaufeli, Sixma, Bosveld, and van Dierendonck (2000) proposed that highly demanding patients create a lack of reciprocity among health care providers. This feeling of injustice, in turn, creates emotional exhaustion. Emotional exhaustion goes on to cause depersonalization and diminished personal accomplishment. When patients experience depersonalization or withdrawal from their providers, they respond by making even more demands. These additional demands further exacerbate the feelings of unfairness and, in turn, this creates additional burnout. Bakker, Schaufeli, Sixma, and colleagues tested this model in a longitudinal investigation of burnout among 207 physicians. Over the 5-year life of the study, the results were consistent with this causal framework, including the negative feedback loop.

THE EMPLOYEE–EMPLOYER RELATIONSHIP. Another potential source of inequity that we need to consider is an imbalanced relationship between workers and their employing organizations. Schaufeli et al. (1996) and van Horn, Schaufeli, and Enzmann (1999) maintained that this imbalance could create burnout. In support of this contention, Van Yperen (1998) found evidence that inequity in the relationship between nurses and their employing organizations exerted a main effect on burnout, especially with respect to emotional exhaustion and depersonalization. For completeness, it is worth revisiting the Hendrix and Spencer (1989) study we mentioned earlier. Although Hendrix and Spencer did find that pay equity was related to certain physical symptoms, it was not related to burnout in their full model. (There was a significant zero-order correlation between equity and burnout, however.) Pay equity is a somewhat narrow operationalization of distributive justice, and this may have been some of the problem.

The work of Van Yperen (1998) and Hendrix and Spencer (1989) is important, but it is limited in that it examined only one source of inequity: the organization. A complete test of these ideas needs to consider these two sources of inequity together. Schaufeli and his colleagues (1996) termed this the *dual-level social exchange model* (p. 225). In an initial exploration of these ideas, Schaufeli et al. surveyed two samples of student nurses. They found that both forms of inequity—that in the nurse–patient relationship and also that in the nurse–employer relationships—were associated with burnout. However, only inequity in the nurse–employer relationship was associated with organizational commitment. Kop et al. (1999) extended the dual-level social exchange model using a sample of police officers. In particular, they examined three relationships: those with civilians, those with coworkers, and those with their employer. Inequity in all three of these relationships contributed to symptoms of burnout. Kop and his colleagues further observed that police officers who had experienced burnout held less negative attitudes toward the use of violence than did their coworkers.

As a further test, van Horn et al. (1999) surveyed a large sample of secondary and elementary school teachers. Findings were only partially supportive with respect to the organizational relationship. Interpersonal inequity between teacher and student was less likely to engender burnout than did inequity between the teacher and the school. Although the null findings in the van Horn et al. study are disappointing, given the supportive findings obtained by Schaufeli et al. (1996) and Kop et al. (1999), the overall level of the support for the dual-level social exchange model seems solid.

Maslach and Leiter (2008) qualified much of the previous thinking on the burnout-justice association. These scholars updated the earlier three-part taxonomy of burnout, retaining the emotional exhaustion dimension but conceptualizing depersonalization more broadly as cynicism. They also treated diminished personal accomplishment as reduced efficacy. Focusing on emotional exhaustion and cynicism, Maslach and Leiter (p. 502) operationalized a congruent profile as one in which cynicism and exhaustion were aligned, such as when a person high on exhaustion is also high on cynicism. An incongruent profile occurs when these two dimensions are not aligned in the typical fashion, such as when one who is low on exhaustion is also high on cynicism. Over time, incongruent profiles tend to move into consistent alignment. This alignment can create engagement if the poorer score becomes consistent with the more favorable one, or else burnout if the favorable score becomes consistent with the poorer one.

If one accepts this theoretical posture, then a challenge for researchers is to predict these phase shifts. We would like to know what causes incongruent profiles to become congruent burnout. Maslach and Leiter (2008) identified six factors: workload, control, reward, community, values, and fairness. In a large-scale longitudinal study, Maslach and Leiter found that justice was an especially strong predictor of shifts. Specifically, when individuals showing an incongruent profile at Time 1 believed that they were rewarded appropriately with their contributions, they tended to become engaged with their work. However, when they viewed their rewards as inadequate relative to their contributions, they tended to shift to a consistent burnout profile. Maslach and Leiter's model is unique in that it focuses attention on the arrangement of the burnout dimensions rather than exclusively on their actual level.

TESTING A WORKPLACE INTERVENTION. Regardless of whether injustice comes from clients or from employers, there seems to be a consistent link between inequity and burnout. Given this, van Dierendonck, Schaufeli, and Buunk (1998) designed an intervention to reduce perceived injustice and, in turn, the resulting burnout. The program, which ran for five meetings, was targeted toward health care professionals, who joined groups of six to eight individuals led by trained psychologists. Design of the sessions was based on the aforementioned equity theory of distributive justice (e.g., Adams, 1965; Adams & Freedman, 1976; Walster et al., 1973, 1978). During the meetings, group leaders helped the participants to devise strategies for adjusting the size of their inputs and outcomes. Reducing inputs, increasing outcomes, or both tends to restore equity. Individuals were also encouraged to alter their expectations so as to conform more closely to their actual work situation.

The researchers evaluated their program with a quasi-experimental design that included a treatment condition and two control groups. In keeping with this, participants were evaluated three times: before the program began (baseline), 6 months later, and 1 year later. Overall, the sessions were very successful. Even a year later, participants in the treatment condition showed fewer feelings of inequity, lower levels of emotional exhaustion (though not of depersonalization or diminished accomplishment), and lower levels of absenteeism.

CURVILINEAR EFFECTS. As we have noted, Adams (1965; Adams & Freedman, 1976) asserted that both over-reward inequity and under-reward inequity produce aversive reactions in people who experience them. If this is so, then both should cause burnout. In particular, the relationship between equity and burnout should be curvilinear: Too little and too much should both be problematic. Confronting the issue directly, van Dierendonck and his colleagues (1996) explored this possibility in two samples, one of therapists and one of caretakers for the mentally disabled. In Study 1, therapists who felt that their clients gave them too little or too much were prone to emotional exhaustion. The other dimensions of burnout were not impacted, however. The findings in van Dierendonck et al.'s (1996) second study were even stronger. When considering the relationship between the caretaker and the client, equity showed a curvilinear relationship to emotional exhaustion, depersonalization, and diminished accomplishment. When considering the relationship with the organization, an additional curvilinear relationship was reported but only for emotional exhaustion. Using a longitudinal design, van Dierendonck et al. (2001) replicated these findings with a sample of 245 human service workers. As with the earlier study by van Dierendonck et al. (1996), equity was related in a curvilinear way to emotional exhaustion. This relationship held even when the measures were 1 year apart. Results were less supportive for depersonalization and diminished accomplishment.

COMMUNAL ORIENTATION AS A MODERATOR OF THE INEQUITY–BURNOUT RELATIONSHIP. In general, the relationship between inequity and burnout appears to be robust; those who feel that they are not receiving their fair share are prone to stress. However, this might not be the case for everyone. Van Yperen (1996) argued that certain individuals are high in communal orientation. These people tend to be altruistic—they take into account the needs and desires of others, sometimes at their own expense. Given this, it can be argued that human service workers, such as nurses, will be less likely to experience burnout symptoms when they are high in communal orientation. Those low in communal orientation, however, should show the traditional negative relationship between justice and burnout.

To test this possibility, Van Yperen, Buunk, and Schaufeli (1992) measured the three original Maslach and Jackson (1981, 1986) dimensions of burnout: emotional exhaustion, depersonalization, and diminished personal accomplishment. A sample of 194 nurses were also asked, "How often do you feel you invest more in the relationships with patients than you receive in return?" As anticipated, this one-item measure of imbalance or inequity tended to predict burnout. However, this effect was moderated by communal orientation. Highly communal individuals did not show a strong relationship between inequity and burnout. For those low in communal orientation, however, the relationship between inequity and burnout was strong and positive. This two-way interaction was observed among all three dimensions of burnout.

Van Yperen (1996) replicated these findings in a second sample of nurses. Nurses who felt that patients did not appreciate their contribution showed higher levels of burnout, unless they were also high in communal orientation. This was true for emotional exhaustion and depersonalization, whereas diminished personal accomplishment showed a strong trend in the expected direction. Building on these earlier findings regarding the relationship with patients, Van Yperen (1996) also explored inequity with respect to the nurses' employers. Observing that communal orientation refers "to concern for other people" (p. 340), he argued that this variable should not interact with inequity in nurses' relationships with their employers. Instead, Van Yperen (1996) hypothesized that an imbalanced relationship with one's organization would show only a main effect with burnout. This prediction was supported, especially for emotional exhaustion and depersonalization.

Procedural and Interactional Injustice and Their Relation to Burnout

As we have shown, burnout scholars have made considerable use of distributive justice, studied as a form of equity, whereby one's outcomes are evaluated with respect to one's investments. Although important, equity is not the only aspect of justice worthy of attention. As we discussed earlier, both procedural justice (the fairness of the process) and interactional justice (the fairness of interpersonal transactions) are important as well.

In a study of 317 workers in 59 different Spanish hotels, Moliner, Martínez-Tur, Peiró, Ramos, and Cropanzano (2008) studied the impact of all three forms of justice on burnout. They operationalized burnout as a single dimension, combining both depersonalization and emotional exhaustion but not including personal accomplishment. They separately assessed work engagement. Consistent with their predictions, Moliner et al. found that distributive justice increased procedural and interactional justice. Both procedural and interactional justice, in turn, decreased burnout and boosted engagement. Consequently, Moliner and her coauthors found that all three forms of justice affected burnout, but the effect of distributive was mediated by the effect of procedural and interactional justice. It is interesting to compare Moliner et al.'s findings with those of the earlier study by Elovainio, Kivimäki, and Helkama (2001). Unlike Moliner and her coauthors, Elovainio et al. (2001) did not assess burnout. Rather, they looked at indices of psychological strain, such as depression and nervousness. Nevertheless, and consistent with Moliner et al.'s findings, Elovainio and his colleagues (2001) found that both procedural and interactional justice were directly related to workplace stress.

There is also a sizable body of justice research indicating that outcomes and processes interact (Brockner, 2002). Specifically, if an outcome is either favorable or fair, then individuals should report less negative emotion and stress. On the other hand, if an outcome is either unfavorable or unfair, then people's responses will be negative unless the allocation process is seen as just (Brockner & Wiesenfeld, 1996). Stated more generally, individuals should respond without ill will if either the process or the outcome is fair. But if an unfair process is paired with an unfair outcome, or even with an unfavorable outcome, then people tend to react negatively.

Regarding work stress, Zohar (1995) reported what was probably the first attempt to test the process by outcome interaction. Zohar attempted to assess a new construct termed *role justice*. According to Zohar, role justice has to do with the fairness of the treatment that one receives from *role senders* (p. 489), people who help formulate one's workplace responsibilities and expectations. Unfortunately for our present purposes, Zohar did not measure burnout. Also unfortunately, role justice did not interact with other workplace stressors to predict stress. Zohar did observe main effects for role justice, however. The reason for these null findings might have been in the way role justice was operationalized. Zohar's measure was broad, and it did not separate justice into its procedural and distributive components. This could have masked the interaction between the two.

In two studies, Tepper (2001) tested the process by outcome interaction. In his Study 1, there were two outcome measures, depression and burnout symptoms. (Recall that burnout and depression are correlated, but distinct constructs; see Bakker, Schaufeli, Demerouti, et al., 2000.) Regardless, when predicting depression, Tepper's first study found the expected interaction between procedural and distributive justice. In Study 2, he assessed worker anxiety, depression, and emotional exhaustion (the latter, of course, is a dimension of burnout). As anticipated, procedures and outcomes interacted to predict all three of these criterion variables, providing solid support for Tepper's theoretical model. In a later study, Spell and Arnold (2007) replicated Tepper's findings for anxiety and depression, though these authors measured justice at the team level and not at the individual level of analysis.

Janssen (2004) tested a similar model among 118 public health workers. In particular, Janssen argued that large-scale workplace interventions create uncertainty, and this uncertainty can be a source of strain. In Brockner and Wiesenfeld's (1996) terms, innovation can be an unpleasant outcome for employees. Building on these ideas, Janssen suggested that both distributive and procedural justice would moderate the ill effects of innovation. That is, there should be a three-way interaction. Innovative behavior should be stressful, but only when both distributive justice and procedural justice are simultaneously low. To examine these ideas, Janssen measured two criterion variables: job-related anxiety and burnout. He also assessed all three dimensions of burnout but treated them as a single variable. Janssen obtained the predicted three-way interaction for both of these outcome variables.

Although research relating injustice to burnout is generally strong, we remind the reader that most studies have limited themselves to distributive justice. We recommend that future work follow the lead of Janssen (2004), Moliner et al. (2008), and Tepper (2001) in considering other forms of justice as well. As readers will see, the examination of procedural and interactional justice has improved our understanding of work–family conflict, a topic that we take up in our penultimate section.

Justice at the Interface of Work and Family

As Major (2007) insightfully observed, the domain of work and the domain of family are often viewed as the two most important in people's lives. It is no surprise, then, that organizational scientists have devoted a good deal of time to understanding the dynamics that occur at their boundary. Major observed that this literature has been known by a number of designations, including *work–family balance, work–family fit, work–family role integration, work–family enrichment,* and *work–family facilitation* (p. 891). The choice of monikers reflects an evolving emphasis in the field. Generally, the conceptualization of work–family transactions has moved from the negative (i.e., work–family conflict) to the more neutral (i.e., work–life balance), or even positive (i.e., work–family enrichment). As readers will see, justice scholars have tended to emphasize the negative consequences. This is reflected in the use of terms such as *work–family conflict* (e.g., Judge & Colquitt, 2004; Tepper, 2000) and *work–life conflict* (Siegel, Post, Brockner, Fishman, & Garden, 2005).

As one might expect, work can interfere with family life (i.e., work-to-family conflict), but it can also facilitate it. In a like fashion, one's family can interfere with work (i.e., family-to-work conflict) but can provide benefits as well (for good reviews, see Eby, Casper, Lockwood, Bordeaux, & Brinley, 2005; Kossek & Lambert, 2005; Parasuraman & Greenhaus, 2002; Chapter 9, this volume).

Using a community sample of 390 individuals, Tepper (2000) explored the impact of abusive supervision. Among other things, Tepper predicted that subordinates who were ill treated by their bosses would report less fairness and also more work–family conflict. He did not, however, treat fairness as an explicit cause. Regardless, his findings were intriguing. All three types of justice— distributive, procedural, and interactional—were significantly and negatively correlated with both work-to-family conflict and also with family-to-work conflict. The more justice, in other words, the less conflict was experienced by workers. Tepper went further, measuring three indicators of well-being: depression, anxiety, and emotional exhaustion. He found that each of these criterion variables was associated with all three types of fairness. These are important results and subsequent researchers were quick to build on them.

Judge and Colquitt (2004) made a number of changes from the original Tepper (2000) work. First, these authors measured only work-to-family conflict (and not family-to-work conflict), treating it as an indicator of stress. Prior research has shown that work-to-family conflict tends to be more serious than family-to-work conflict (Major, 2007). Second, the Judge and Colquitt model posited injustice as a cause, not simply as a correlate, of work-to-family conflict. Stated more generally, unfairness was anticipated to act as an environmental stressor (for a similar view, see Zohar, 1995). Work–family conflict, in turn, was a mediating variable between injustice and strain. Third, Judge and Colquitt used a somewhat different structure for justice perceptions. They divided interactional justice into its component parts: interpersonal justice (i.e., the extent to which one is treated with dignity and respect) and informational justice (i.e., the extent to which one is provided with social accounts and explanations for workplace events). Results were generally supportive. Judge and Colquitt found that procedural justice and interpersonal justice were significant predictors of work-to-family conflict. Distributive justice and informational justice, however, were not so associated. In its turn, work–family conflict then predicted self-reported stress.

Siegel and her colleagues (2005) took a somewhat different conceptual approach. They began with the tendency for work–life conflict to lower organizational commitment. They wished to discover a means of breaking this connection, whereby employees might be buffered from the ill effects of conflict. Siegel et al. posited that procedural justice (their model did not include distributive or interactional) might interact with work–life conflict. Specifically, they felt that work–life conflict would be strongly and negatively related to organizational commitment when workplace decisions were made in a procedurally unjust fashion. However, work–life conflict would be weakly related to organizational commitment when workplace decisions were made in a procedurally just fashion. The results of three separate studies, each using different methods and operationalizations, provided solid support for this prediction.

Work–life balance is already an important issue and may become even more so in the future (Major & Germano, 2006). General workplace unfairness might well contribute to work–family conflict (e.g., Judge & Colquitt, 2004). The research integrating these two literatures is small, but it holds considerable promise. As we have shown, there are areas of conceptual ambiguity, such as whether justice is better viewed as an antecedent or a moderator. Future research can help clarify such issues.

Conclusion

There is now a growing body of literature relating justice to workplace stress. This is important because it suggests that treating people fairly can reduce illnesses (Kivimäki et al., 2003; Siegrist, 1996). From a research perspective, however, the available work is somewhat scattered, prompting us to identify three traditions of study: research relating injustice to illness and absenteeism, research treating injustice as a predictor of workplace burnout, and research examining the relationship of injustice to work–life conflict. These distinct perspectives are not well integrated; often, scholars in each area do not even cite the work of scholars in another. This is unfortunate, as all pertain to occupational health and are likely to have much in common.

On the basis of our review, a number of directions for future research are worth considering. First, regarding the relationship between fairness and burnout, studies so far have emphasized distributive justice (i.e., equity). We encourage scholars to consider procedural and interactional fairness as well (cf. Moliner et al., 2008). Second, we found Maslach and Leiter's (2008) study to be of considerable interest. According to Maslach and Leiter, dimensions of burnout can become misaligned. At this juncture, one can reestablish consistency by improving on one dimension or by deteriorating on another. Injustice seems to be most important in an imbalanced situation, as it restores congruence by making the positive dimension more negative. Maslach and Leiter's model involves nothing less than a reinterpretation of the justice-burnout relationship. Clearly, their framework is in need of additional research. Finally, we also recommend additional research exploring the relationship between fairness and work–life balance because available work is promising but limited. The three studies we found (Tepper, 2000; Judge & Colquitt, 2004; Siegel et al., 2005) each use a different conceptual framework, making comparison and integration difficult.

From this short summary it is clear that there is much to be done. However, our review of the justice and occupational health literature is optimistic. It seems that fair treatment, managing subordinates in accordance with basic moral principles, may prove to be an invaluable means of promoting worker health while simultaneously advancing business goals.

References

Adams, J. S. (1965). Inequity in social exchange. In L. Berkowitz (Ed.), *Advances in experimental social psychology* (Vol. 2, pp. 267–299). New York, NY: Academic Press. doi:10.1016/S0065-2601(08)60108-2

Adams, J. S., & Freedman, S. (1976). Equity theory revisited: Comments and annotated bibliography. In L. Berkowitz (Ed.), *Advances in experimental social psychology* (Vol. 9, pp. 43–90). New York, NY: Academic Press.

Bakker, A. B., Schaufeli, W. B., Demerouti, E., Janssen, P. P. M., van Der Hulst, R., & Brouwer, J. (2000). Using equity theory to examine the difference between burnout and depression. *Anxiety, Stress, and Coping, 13,* 247–268.

Bakker, A. B., Schaufeli, W. B., Sixma, H. J., Bosveld, W., & van Dierendonck, D. (2000). Patient demands, lack of reciprocity, and burnout: A five-year longitudinal study among general practitioners. *Journal of Organizational Behavior, 21,* 425–441. doi:10.1002/(SICI)1099-1379(200006)21:4<425::AID-JOB21>3.0.CO;2-#

Brockner, J. (2002). Making sense of procedural fairness: How high procedural fairness can reduce or heighten the influence of outcome favorability. *Academy of Management Review, 27,* 58–76. doi:10.2307/4134369

Brockner, J., & Wiesenfeld, B. M. (1996). An integrative framework for explaining reactions to decisions: Interactive effects of outcomes and procedures. *Psychological Bulletin, 120,* 189–208. doi:10.1037/0033-2909.120.2.189

Buunk, B. P., & Schaufeli, W. B. (1993). Burnout: A perspective from social comparison theory. In W. B. Schaufeli, C. Maslach, & T. Marek (Eds.), *Professional burnout: Recent developments in theory and research* (pp. 53–69). New York, NY: Hemisphere.

Cohen-Charash, Y., & Spector, P. E. (2001). The role of justice in organizations: A meta-analysis. *Organizational Behavior and Human Decision Processes, 86,* 278–321. doi:10.1006/obhd.2001.2958

Colquitt, J. A., Conlon, D. E., Wesson, M. J., Porter, C. O. L. H., & Ng, K. Y. (2001). Justice at the millennium: A meta-analytic review of 25 years of organizational justice research. *Journal of Applied Psychology, 86,* 425–445. doi:10.1037/0021-9010.86.3.425

Cropanzano, R., Bowen, D. E., & Gilliland, S. W. (2007). The management of organizational justice. *The Academy of Management Perspectives, 21,* 34–48.

Cropanzano, R., Byrne, Z. S., Bobocel, D. R., & Rupp, D. R. (2001). Moral virtues, fairness heuristics, social entities, and other denizens of organizational justice. *Journal of Vocational Behavior, 58,* 164–209. doi:10.1006/jvbe.2001.1791

Cropanzano, R., Goldman, B., & Benson, L., III. (2005). Organizational justice. In J. Barling, K. Kelloway, & M. Frone (Eds.), *Handbook of work stress* (pp. 63–87). Beverly Hills, CA: Sage.

Cropanzano, R., Rupp, D. E., Mohler, C. J., & Schminke, M. (2001). Three roads to organizational justice. In J. Ferris (Ed.), *Research in personnel and human resources management* (Vol. 20, pp. 1–113). Greenwich, CT: JAI Press.

de Boer, E. M., Bakker, A. B., Syroit, J. E., & Schaufeli, W. B. (2002). Unfairness at work as a predictor of absenteeism. *Journal of Organizational Behavior, 23,* 181–197. doi:10.1002/job.135

Eby, L. T., Casper, W. J., Lockwood, A., Bordeaux, C., & Brinley, A. (2005). Work and family research in IO/OB: Content analysis and review of the literature (1980–2002) [Monograph]. *Journal of Vocational Behavior, 66,* 124–197.

Elovainio, M., Kivimäki, M., & Helkama, K. (2001). Organizational justice evaluations, job control, and occupational strain. *Journal of Applied Psychology, 86,* 418–424. doi:10.1037/0021-9010.86.3.418

Elovainio, M., Kivimäki, M., & Vahtera, J. (2002). Organizational justice: Evidence of a new psychosocial predictor of health. *American Journal of Public Health, 92,* 105–108. doi:10.2105/AJPH.92.1.105

Halbesleben, J. R. B., & Buckley, M. R. (2004). Burnout in organizational life. *Journal of Management, 30,* 859–879. doi:10.1016/j.jm.2004.06.004

Hendrix, W. H., & Spencer, B. A. (1989). Development and test of a multivariate model of absenteeism. *Psychological Reports, 64,* 923–938.

Janssen, O. (2004). How fairness perceptions make innovation behavior more or less stress. *Journal of Organizational Behavior, 25,* 201–215. doi:10.1002/job.238

Judge, T. A., & Colquitt, J. A. (2004). Organizational justice and stress: The mediating role of work–family conflict. *Journal of Applied Psychology, 89,* 395–404. doi:10.1037/0021-9010.89.3.395

Kivimäki, M., Elovainio, M., Vahtera, J., & Ferrie, J. E. (2003). Organisational justice and health of employees: Prospective cohort study. *Occupational and Environmental Medicine, 60,* 27–34. doi:10.1136/oem.60.1.27

Kop, N., Euwema, M., & Schaufeli, W. (1999). Burnout, job stress, and violent behavior among Dutch police officers. *Work & Stress, 13,* 326–340. doi:10.1080/02678379950019789

Kossek, E. E., & Lambert, S. J. (2005). *Work and life integrations: Organizational, cultural, and individual perspectives.* Mahwah, NJ: Erlbaum.

Leventhal, G. S. (1976). Fairness in social relationships. In J. W. Thibaut, J. T. Spence, & R. C. Carson (Eds.), *Contemporary topics in social psychology* (pp. 211–240). Morristown, NJ: General Learning Press.

Leventhal, G. S. (1980). What should be done with equity theory? In K. L. Gergen, M. S. Greenberg, & R. H. Willis (Eds.), *Social exchange: Advances in theory and research* (pp. 27–55). New York, NY: Plenum Press.

Major, D. A. (2007). Work–life balance. In S. G. Robelberg (Ed.), *Encyclopedia of industrial and organizational psychology* (Vol. 2, pp. 888–892). Thousand Oaks, CA: Sage.

Major, D. A., & Germano, L. M. (2006). The changing nature of work and its impact on the work–home interface. In F. Jones, R. Burke, & M. Westman (Eds.), *Work–life balance: A psychological perspective* (pp. 13–38). London, England: Psychology Press.

Maslach, C., & Jackson, S. E. (1981). The measurement and experience of burnout. *Journal of Organizational Behaviour, 2,* 99–113. doi:10.1002/job.4030020205

Maslach, C., & Jackson, S. E. (1986). *Maslach burnout inventory* (2nd ed.). Palo Alto, CA: Consulting Psychologists Press.

Maslach, C., & Leiter, M. P. (2008). Early predictors of job burnout and engagement. *Journal of Applied Psychology, 93,* 498–512. doi:10.1037/0021-9010.93.3.498

Maslach, C., Schaufeli, W. B., & Leiter, M. P. (2001). Job burnout. In S. T. Fiske, D. L. Schacter, & C. Zahn-Waxler (Eds.), *Annual review of psychology* (Vol. 53, pp. 397–422). Palo Alto, CA: Annual Reviews.

Moliner, C., Martínez-Tur, V., Peiró, J. M., Ramos, J., & Cropanzano, R. (2008). Organizational justice and extra-role customer service: The mediating role of well-being at work. *European Journal of Work and Organizational Psychology, 17,* 327–348. doi:10.1080/13594320701743616

Parasuraman, S., & Greenhaus, J. H. (2002). Toward reducing some critical gaps in work–family research. *Human Resource Management Review, 12,* 299–312. doi:10.1016/S1053-4822(02)00062-1

Schaufeli, W. B., & Janczur, B. (1994). Burnout among nurses: A Polish-Dutch comparison. *Journal of Cross-Cultural Psychology, 25,* 95–113. doi:10.1177/0022022194251006

Schaufeli, W. B., van Dierendonck, D., & van Gorp, K. (1996). Burnout and reciprocity: Towards a dual-level social exchange model. *Work & Stress, 10,* 225–237. doi:10.1080/02678379608256802

Schmitt, M., & Dörfel, M. (1999). Procedural injustice at work, justice sensitivity, job satisfaction, and psychosomatic well-being. *European Journal of Social Psychology, 29,* 443–453. doi:10.1002/(SICI)1099-0992(199906)29:4<443::AID-EJSP935>3.0.CO;2-C

Siegel, P. A., Post, C., Brockner, J., Fishman, A. Y., & Garden, C. (2005). The moderating influence of procedural fairness on the relationship between work–life conflict and organizational commitment. *Journal of Applied Psychology, 90,* 13–24. doi:10.1037/0021-9010.90.1.13

Siegrist, J. (1996). Adverse health effects of high-effort/low-reward conditions. *Journal of Occupational Health Psychology, 1,* 27–41. doi:10.1037/1076-8998.1.1.27

Spell, C. S., & Arnold, T. J. (2007). A multi-level analysis of organizational justice climate, structure, and employee mental health. *Journal of Management, 33,* 724–751. doi:10.1177/0149206307305560

Tepper, B. J. (2000). Consequences of abusive supervision. *Academy of Management Journal, 43,* 178–190. doi:10.2307/1556375

Tepper, B. J. (2001). Health consequences of organizational injustice: Test of main and interactive effects. *Organizational Behavior and Human Decision Processes, 86,* 197–215. doi:10.1006/obhd.2001.2951

van Dierendonck, D., Schaufeli, W. B., & Buunk, B. P. (1996). Inequity among human service professionals: Measurement and relation to burnout. *Basic and Applied Social Psychology, 18,* 429–451. doi:10.1207/s15324834basp1804_5

van Dierendonck, D., Schaufeli, W. B., & Buunk, B. P. (1998). The evaluation of an individual burnout intervention program: The role of inequity and social support. *Journal of Applied Psychology, 83,* 392–407. doi:10.1037/0021-9010.83.3.392

van Dierendonck, D., Schaufeli, W. B., & Buunk, B. P. (2001). Burnout and inequity among human service professionals: A longitudinal study. *Journal of Occupational Health Psychology, 6,* 43–52. doi:10.1037/1076-8998.6.1.43

van Dierendonck, D., Schaufeli, W. B., & Sixma, H. J. (1994). Burnout among general practitioners: A perspective from equity theory. *Journal of Social and Clinical Psychology, 13,* 86–100.

van Horn, J. E., Schaufeli, W. B., & Enzmann, D. (1999). Teacher burnout and lack of reciprocity. *Journal of Applied Social Psychology, 29,* 91–108. doi:10.1111/j.1559-1816.1999.tb01376.x

Van Yperen, N. W. (1996). Communal orientation and the burnout syndrome among nurses: A replication and extension. *Journal of Applied Social Psychology, 26,* 338–354. doi:10.1111/j.1559-1816.1996.tb01853.x

Van Yperen, N. W. (1998). Information support, equity and burnout: The moderating effect of self-efficacy. *Journal of Occupational and Organizational Psychology, 71,* 29–33.

Van Yperen, N. W., Buunk, B. P., & Schaufeli, W. B. (1992). Imbalance, communal orientation, and the burnout syndrome among nurses. *Journal of Applied Social Psychology, 22,* 173–189. doi:10.1111/j.1559-1816.1992.tb01534.x

Vermunt, R. (2002). Employee stress, injustice and the dual position of the boss. In S. W. Gilliland, D. D. Steiner, & D. P. Skarlicki (Eds.), *Emerging perspectives on managing organizational justice* (pp. 159–176). Greenwich, CT: Information Age.

Vermunt, R., Spaans, E., & Zorge, F. (1989). Satisfaction, happiness and well-being of Dutch students. *Social Indicators Research, 21,* 1–33. doi:10.1007/BF00302402

Vermunt, R., & Steensma, H. (2001). Stress and justice in organizations: An exploration into justice processes with the aim to find mechanisms to reduce stress. In R. Cropanzano (Ed.), *Justice in the workplace: From theory to practice* (Vol. 2, pp. 27–48). Mahwah, NJ: Erlbaum.

Walster, E., Walster, G. W., & Berscheid, E. (1973). New directions in equity research. *Journal of Personality and Social Psychology, 25,* 151–176. doi:10.1037/h0033967

Walster, E., Walster, G. W., & Berscheid, E. (1978). *Equity: Theory and research.* New York, NY: Allyn & Bacon.

Wright, T. A., & Bonett, D. G. (1997). The contribution of burnout to work performance. *Journal of Organizational Behavior, 18,* 491–499. doi:10.1002/(SICI)1099-1379(199709)18:5<491::AID-JOB804>3.0.CO;2-I

Wright, T. A., & Cropanzano, R. (1998). Emotional exhaustion as a predictor of job performance and voluntary turnover. *Journal of Applied Psychology, 83,* 486–493. doi:10.1037/0021-9010.83.3.486

Zohar, D. (1995). The justice perspective on job stress. *Journal of Organizational Behavior, 16,* 487–495. doi:10.1002/job.4030160508

Part IV

Symptoms and Disorders

12

Job-Related Burnout: A Review of Major Research Foci and Challenges

Arie Shirom

The purpose of the review in this chapter is to identify and describe the major issues in burnout research. I first discuss the controversy over the conceptual and operational definitions of *burnout,* including the possibility of overlap with depression and fatigue. I then synthesize past research on the associations of burnout with employee health and job performance. Finally, I provide recommendations for future research.

The literature on burnout is now vast: A bibliography covering the period 1990 to 2002 (Boudreau & Nakashima, 2002) identified 2,138 distinct items; a recent (September 2008) Google Scholar search of the key word *burnout* yielded more than 210,000 entries. A number of comprehensive reviews of various aspects of burnout at work have appeared in recent years (e.g., Halbesleben, 2006; Halbesleben & Buckley, 2004; Melamed, Shirom, Toker, Berliner, & Shapira, 2006). This chapter is not intended to duplicate either these recent reviews or their predecessors (e.g., Schaufeli & Enzmann, 1998). Instead, I focus on certain key issues in the research literature assessed as having considerable relevance to future research on burnout. Within this context, the chapter follows specific preferences. Most empirical studies on burnout are based on a cross-sectional study design and measure burnout by asking respondents to complete a self-report questionnaire. In this review, preference is given to longitudinal studies on burnout because they provide more credence to cause-and-effect statements. Preference is also given to recent quantitative reviews of the specific issues on which this chapter focuses.

Burnout is viewed as an affective reaction to ongoing stress whose core content is the gradual depletion over time of individuals' intrinsic energetic resources, including the components of emotional exhaustion, physical fatigue, and cognitive weariness (Shirom, 2003). This core content appears in most conceptual approaches to burnout. My review focuses on burnout of employees in work organizations, and it excludes research that deals exclusively with burnout in other life domains (e.g., athletes' burnout; Dale & Weinberg, 1990) and with crossover of burnout among marital partners (cf. Westman & Etzion, 1995).

In some countries, a syndrome of chronic fatigue highly similar to burnout is a legitimate basis for a compensation claim (Schaufeli, 2003) and represents a major reason for sickness absences and work disability (Ahola et al., 2008). In Sweden, the term *burnout* is used as a diagnosis on medical certificates

(Hallsten, 2005). In the Netherlands, about 30% of work disability recipients are classified as occupationally disabled on mental grounds, primarily reflecting cases of advanced burnout (Michielsen, Croon, Willemsen, De Vries, & Van Heck, 2007). In Sweden and the Netherlands, special rehabilitative facilities provide interdisciplinary health care to individuals diagnosed by occupational physicians as burnout cases (e.g., Michielsen et al., 2007). Schaufeli and Enzmann (1998) estimated that about 4% to 7% of the Dutch working population suffers from severe burnout, and Hallsten (2005) found that the estimated proportion of burnout among employees in a representative sample of the Swedish population was 7.4%, almost identical to the prevalence of serious burnout reported in similar studies carried out in Finland (Ahola et al., 2008). Burnout may transfer from one employee to another, either directly or indirectly (Bakker, Demerouti, & Schaufeli, 2003). Therefore, accumulated evidence supports the proposition that burnout at work can be regarded as a major public health problem and a cause for concern for health care policymakers.

When measured on several occasions in longitudinal studies, burnout was found to have moderate to high correlations over time. The cross-time correlations were found to range from .50 to .60, even with a time interval extending up to 8 years (Taris, Le Blanc, Schaufeli, & Schreurs, 2005). The relative stability of burnout over time is analogous to the stability found for other types of negative (e.g., depressive symptoms) and positive (e.g., life or job satisfaction) affective states (cf. Conley, 1984). One of the predictions of conservation of resources (COR; cf. Hobfoll, 1989) theory is that individuals who lack strong resources are more likely to experience cycles of resource losses. When not replenished, such cycles are likely to result in chronic depletion of energy, namely, progressive burnout, thus explaining the chronicity of burnout. A physiological explanation for this chronic nature has recently been provided by a study reporting that burnout and sleep disturbances or insomnia were reciprocally related over time (Armon, Shirom, Shapira, & Melamed, 2008).

Conceptual Basis of Burnout

The controversy over burnout's conceptual and operational definition (e.g., Kristensen, Borritz, Villadsen, & Christensen, 2005; Shirom, 2003) justifies the conceptual analysis presented in this section. The reason for the focus on the Maslach Burnout Inventory (MBI; Maslach & Jackson, 1981; Maslach, Jackson, & Leiter, 1996; Maslach, Schaufeli, & Leiter, 2001) is that it is the instrument most widely used in scholarly research on the subject (Shirom, 2003). I also discuss the alternative conceptualizations of burnout proposed by Pines and her colleagues (Pines & Aronson, 1988; Pines, Aronson, & Kafry, 1981) and by Shirom and Melamed (Melamed et al., 2006; Shirom & Melamed, 2006).

Maslach Burnout Inventory

The first version of the MBI reflected the field's preoccupation with professionals in people-oriented occupations. Subsequently, the construction of newer versions of the popular MBI, applicable to other occupational groups (Maslach et al., 1996), extended the study of burnout to other categories of employees. Maslach and her colleagues (Maslach, 1982; Maslach & Jackson, 1981) viewed burnout as a syndrome that consists of three components: emotional exhaustion, depersonalization, and reduced personal accomplishment. *Emotional exhaustion* refers to feelings of being depleted of one's emotional resources. This component was regarded as the basic individual stress component of the syndrome (Maslach et al., 2001) and, in a major review of available empirical evidence, was shown to precede the other two components (Taris et al., 2005). *Depersonalization,* referring to a negative, cynical, or excessively detached response to other people at work, represents the interpersonal component of burnout. *Reduced personal accomplishment,* referring to feelings of decline in one's competence and productivity and to one's lowered sense of self-efficacy, represents the self-evaluation component of burnout (Maslach, 1998, p. 69). These three dimensions were not deduced theoretically, but resulted from labeling exploratory factor-analyzed items initially collected to reflect the range of experiences associated with the phenomenon of burnout (Maslach, 1998, p. 68; Schaufeli & Enzmann, 1998, p. 51; Taris et al., 2005).

Maslach and her colleagues modified the original definition of the latter two components (cf. Maslach et al., 2001, p. 399). Depersonalization was replaced by *cynicism,* referring to the same cluster of symptoms. The new label for this component of the syndrome poses new problems. Cynicism is an emerging concept in psychology and organizational behavior, which is used to refer to negative attitudes involving frustration from and disillusionment with and distrust of organizations, persons, groups, or objects (Andersson & Bateman, 1997; Dean, Brandes, & Dharwadkar, 1998). Abraham (2000) suggested that work cynicism, one of the forms of cynicism that she identifies in her research, tends to be closely related to burnout and that it gauges several distinct attitudes, including distancing, hostility, rejection, and lack of concern. It follows that the discriminant validity of this component of burnout, relative to the current conceptualizations of employee or work cynicism, has yet to be established.

The third component was relabeled *reduced efficacy* or *ineffectiveness,* depicted to include the self-assessments of low self-efficacy, lack of accomplishment, lack of productivity, and incompetence (Leiter & Maslach, 2001). Each of these concepts—self-efficacy, self-rated performance, and personal competence—represents well-known and distinct fields of research in the behavioral sciences. The authors of the MBI have yet to clarify on what theoretical grounds these concepts should be grouped together in the same cluster of symptoms. Such a diverse cluster of symptoms related to effectiveness may obscure the meaning of the third component of the MBI. To illustrate, does reduced efficacy refer to one's personal judgment of how well one can execute courses of action required to deal with prospective situations, as self-efficacy is customarily defined (cf. Stajkovic & Luthans, 1998)? Alternatively, does this component of burnout reflect one's belief in one's knowledge and skills, as competence is often conceptualized (Foschi, 2000; Sandberg, 2000)? Or does it perhaps relate to self-rated job performance or performance expectations (e.g., Stajkovic & Luthans, 1998)? It appears that the second and third components of the MBI, as currently defined, probably represent several multifaceted constructs, each having different implications with regard to the emotional exhaustion component of burnout suggested by the authors of the MBI (cf. Moore, 2000, p. 341).

According to the MBI manual, the three dimensions should not be combined into a single total score (Maslach & Jackson, 1986, p. 2). This clear instruction to potential users of the MBI was supported in many studies that recommended not using the total score of the MBI on both theoretical and psychometric grounds (e.g., Kalliath, O'Driscoll, Gillespie, & Bluedorn, 2000; Koeske & Koeske, 1989; Moore, 2000). All meta-analytic studies found that the three MBI components are related to different sets of antecedents and consequences (Collins, 1999; Lee & Ashforth, 1996). It was argued (cf. Kristensen et al., 2005) that the MBI measures represent three independent constructs rather than a "syndrome."

The proponents of the MBI conceptualization burnout (Schaufeli & Taris, 2005) argue that they have developed clinically validated cutoff points for the three MBI scales, allowing them to be combined to define "cases" of burnout. However, they have yet to provide convincing theoretical arguments about why the three different clusters of symptoms that make up their conceptualization of burnout should "hang together" (Maslach et al., 2001). Moreover, Schaufeli and Taris (2005) argued that the MBI conceptualization of burnout allows researchers to use a specific coping behavior with burnout—distancing oneself or engaging in avoidance behavior—and a specific consequence of burnout—lack of personal accomplishment—because they are often found to be manifestations "of the same syndrome" (p. 259). In another context, Schaufeli (2003, p. 3) noted that the MBI is neither grounded in firm clinical observation nor based on sound theorizing and explained that it has been developed inductively by factor analyzing a rather arbitrary set of items. Therefore, one could conclude that there is no solid theoretical ground to support the argument that the three components of the MBI belong to the same underlying construct. In addition, accumulated evidence indicates that there are no specific antecedent variables or mechanisms leading to all three MBI components (Collins, 1999; Lee & Ashforth, 1996; Schaufeli & Enzmann, 1998).

Pines's Burnout Model and Measure

Pines and her colleagues defined burnout as the state of physical, emotional, and mental exhaustion caused by long-term involvement in emotionally demanding situations (Pines & Aronson, 1988, p. 9). This view does not restrict the application of the term *burnout* to the work context. Indeed, it was applied not only to employment relationships (Pines et al., 1981) and organizational careers (Pines & Aronson, 1988) but also to marital relationships (Pines, 1988, 1996) and to the aftermath of political conflicts (Pines, 1993).

Much like the MBI, the conceptualization of burnout emerged from clinical experiences and case studies. In the process of actually constructing a measure that purported to assess burnout—dubbed the *burnout measure* (BM)—Pines and her colleagues moved away from the conceptual definition that they originally proposed. In the BM, Pines and her colleagues viewed burnout as a syndrome of co-occurring symptoms that include helplessness, hopelessness, entrapment, decreased enthusiasm, irritability, and a sense of lowered self-esteem (cf. Pines, 1993). The BM is considered a one-dimensional measure yielding a single composite burnout score. Evidently, the overlap between the BM's conceptual definition and the BM's operational definition is minimal (cf. Schaufeli & Enzmann, 1998, p. 48). In addition, the discriminant validity of burnout, as assessed by the BM, relative to depression, anxiety, and self-esteem, is questionable (cf. Shirom & Ezrachi, 2001). Therefore, the BM probably represents a measure of psychological distress that encompasses physical fatigue, emotional exhaustion, depression, anxiety, and reduced self-esteem (e.g., Schaufeli & Van Dierendonck, 1993, p. 645).

Shirom–Melamed Burnout Model and Measure

The conceptualization of burnout underlying the Shirom–Melamed Burnout Measure (SMBM) was inspired by the work of Maslach and her colleagues and Pines and her colleagues, as described earlier. Burnout is viewed as an affective state characterized by one's feelings of being depleted of one's physical, emotional, and cognitive energies. Theoretically, the SMBM was based on Hobfoll's (1989, 1998) COR theory. The basic tenets of COR theory are that people are motivated to obtain, retain, and protect what they value. The things that people value are called *resources,* of which there are several types, including material, social, and energetic resources. The conceptualization of burnout formulated by Shirom (2003) on the basis of COR theory (Hobfoll & Shirom, 2000) relates to energetic resources only and covers physical, emotional, and cognitive energies. COR has often been used in past research to explain burnout (e.g., Halbesleben & Rathert, 2008; Neveu, 2007). Burnout is most likely to occur in situations where there is an actual resource loss, perceived threat of resource loss, or when one fails to obtain resources to offset those lost—situations defining stress in COR (Hobfoll, 1989, 1998).

Burnout, as based on COR and as operationally defined by the SMBM, was conceptualized as a multifaceted construct whose three facets were physical fatigue (i.e., feeling of tiredness and low energy), emotional exhaustion (i.e., lacking the energy to display empathy to others), and cognitive weariness (i.e., one's feelings of reduced mental agility). There were several theoretical reasons for focusing on these three facets. First, physical, emotional, and cognitive energy are individually possessed and are expected to be closely interrelated (Hobfoll & Shirom, 2000). COR theory postulates that personal resources affect one another and exist as a resource pool; lacking one is often associated with lacking another. Furthermore, COR theory argues that these resources represent a set of resources internal to the self that facilitates the development and use of other resources (Hobfoll, 2002). Third, the conceptualization of the SMBM clearly differentiates burnout from stress appraisals preceding burnout, from coping behaviors that individuals may engage in to ameliorate the negative aspects of burnout, such as distancing themselves from client recipients, and from probable consequences of burnout such as performance decrements. This stands in contrast to the two other conceptualizations of burnout outlined previously. Using confirmatory factor analysis, empirical research conducted with the SMBM confirmed the tricomponent view of the construct (cf. Melamed et al.,

2006; Shirom, Nirel, & Vinokur, 2006). A series of studies that confirmed expected relationships between the SMBM and physiological variables have lent support to its construct validity (for a review of these studies, see Melamed et al., 2006). A study comparing an aspect of the construct validity of the SMBM relative to the MBI (Shirom & Melamed, 2006) found that the two measures of burnout were comparable in terms of being predicted by the components of the job demand-control-support model (Karasek & Theorell, 1990).

Burnout and Depression

All approaches toward conceptualizing burnout include a component of felt fatigue or low levels of physical energy. These symptoms also appear as one of the nine criteria for diagnosis of a major depressive disorder and as one of the seven criteria leading to diagnosis of low-level depression, or dysthymia (Suls & Bunde, 2005). Although the *Diagnostic and Statistical Manual of Mental Disorders* (4th ed.; American Psychiatric Association, 1994) defines depressed mood most of the day, nearly every day, and loss of pleasure in almost all activities as core symptoms of the syndrome of depression, two of the other five symptoms used for the diagnosis of dysthymia include the symptoms of fatigue or low energy and diminished ability to think or concentrate. Conceptually, there is an overlap between the latter two symptoms and the MBI's scale of emotional exhaustion or the SMBM's scales of physical fatigue and cognitive weariness because similar symptoms appear in some depression symptoms scales, such as the Beck Depression Inventory (Beck, Ward, Mendelson, Mock, & Erbaugh, 1961). This overlap has led researchers to view depressive symptoms and burnout as essentially interchangeable (Hemingway & Marmot, 1999).

Theoretically, it could be suggested that burnout is a precursor of depressive symptoms. Individuals feel burned out when they perceive a continuous net loss, which cannot be replenished, of their physical, emotional, or cognitive energy. The net loss, due to experienced stresses, cannot be compensated for by expanding other resources or either borrowing or gaining additional resources by investing extant ones. Burned-out individuals may exacerbate their losses by entering an escalating spiral of losses (Hobfoll & Shirom, 2000). Thus, COR theory implies that during its early stages, burnout will be characterized by a process of the depletion of energy resources directed at coping with the threatening demands and by direct coping that usually entails a high level of arousal. When and if these coping behaviors prove ineffective, the individual may give up and engage in emotional detachment and defensive behaviors that may lead to depressive symptoms (cf. Shirom & Ezrachi, 2001). At this point, they may reach an advanced stage of burnout, wherein their symptoms of depression may become the predominant affect. Alternatively or concomitantly, they may reach advanced stages of burnout that manifest themselves in symptoms of psychological withdrawal, such as dehumanizing their customers or clients or displaying cynical behavior toward them. Conceptually, burnout is distinct in that it is dependent on the quality of the social environment at work (Schaufeli & Enzmann, 1998), whereas depression is a global state that pervades virtually every aspect of an individual's environment. Depressive symptomatology is affectively complex and includes lack of pleasurable experience, anger, guilt, apprehension, and physiological symptoms of distress. Moreover, cognitive views of depression regard it as being primarily related to pessimism about the self, capabilities, and the future (Fisher, 1984).

These theoretical possibilities have yet to be investigated. We still lack a basic understanding of the relationships between burnout and depression (see the discussion of the reciprocal relationships found in several studies between depression and prolonged or chronic fatigue in the next section). Melamed et al. (2006) proposed to view burnout as representing the accumulated effects of a variety of chronic stresses to which employees are exposed. However, as noted by Schaufeli and Enzmann (1998), longitudinal studies to date have not supported the notion that there is a time lag between the stress experience and feelings of burnout. It could be that stress and burnout change simultaneously; hence, the failure of the eight longitudinal studies examined by Schaufeli and Enzmann to reproduce over time the synchronous effects of stress on burnout found in most cross-sectional studies. Plausibly, the relationships between depression and burnout are also reciprocal, one influencing the other across time.

Empirical evidence has shown that burnout measures have positive moderate correlations with depression. Based on 12 studies, Schaufeli and Enzmann (1998) found that the emotional exhaustion component of burnout (gauged by the MBI) and depression share on average 26% of their variance. Schaufeli and Enzmann reported in their meta-analysis that the relationships between depression and the other MBI components—depersonalization and personal inefficacy—are much weaker, sharing 13% and 9% of their variance, respectively. Subsequent research has provided additional evidence that burnout and depression are positively and moderately correlated. For example, four recent studies—all based on large and representative samples and on different conceptualizations of burnout—concluded that although depression and burnout partially overlap, they are distinct constructs (Ahola & Hakanen, 2007; Lindeberg et al., 2008; Nyklicek & Pop, 2005).

Evidence supporting the discriminant validity of burnout and depression was synthesized in the recent review by Melamed et al. (2006). This review indicates that burnout and depression were found to be differentially related to certain physiological parameters and further that burnout (as gauged by the SMBM) predicted risk factors for cardiovascular disease after controlling for depression. A meta-analytic review of 18 studies (Glass & McKnight, 1996) suggested that depressive affect and burnout may share a common etiology and that their shared variance may be due to their concurrent development. Still, this meta-analytic study concluded that burnout and depressive symptomatology are not redundant concepts and that their shared variance does not indicate complete isomorphism.

Burnout and Chronic Fatigue

I use the term *fatigue* to refer to chronic or prolonged fatigue because these terms are used interchangeably in the relevant literature. Fatigue is not considered a specific disease (unless it extends over a period of 6 months, when, with additional important criteria, it could be diagnosed as chronic fatigue syndrome; cf. Shirom, 2003). Fatigue is a common patient complaint in a variety of medical settings, but when it appears without known comorbidity (e.g., anemia or any of the malignant diseases) it is difficult to identify an organic condition explaining it (Martin, Chalder, Rief, & Braehler, 2007). The prevalence rates of fatigue in the population depend on the way it is gauged; several studies based on representative samples of adult populations in different countries found prevalence rates that bear considerable similarity to those noted earlier for burnout. For example, the prevalence rate of fatigue in a representative sample of adults was found to be 6.1% in Germany (Martin et al., 2007), about 7% in the United States (Ricci, Chee, Lorandeau, & Berger, 2007), and from 16% to 21% in Sweden (Sullivan, Pedersen, Jacks, & Evengard, 2005).

Do burnout and fatigue represent different manifestations of the same underlying phenomenon? Conceptually, the overlap between fatigue and burnout has already been discussed in the section covering depression and burnout. However, there appears to be a disciplinary chasm between the two fields of research on burnout and fatigue. Although burnout has been studied primarily in the behavioral sciences, in disciplines that include psychology, sociology, and organizational behavior, fatigue has most often been studied in the medical sciences, in disciplines that include epidemiology and psychiatry. This is because fatigue is a major symptom accompanying diseases such as coronary heart disease, malignant diseases, renal failure, and many types of liver and blood diseases. Toxic treatment for malignancies is invariably accompanied by fatigue, and therefore there are many studies on fatigue in journals representing the medical specialization of oncology. Burnout has been investigated primarily in the work context: Fatigue has been investigated primarily in medical settings, as implied by the previously described characteristics of many types of diseases as well as by many types of treatment modules. There is also a considerable difference in the time dimension: Most measures of burnout—including those discussed earlier—gauge it over several weeks, whereas most studies of fatigue focus on how a patient feels at present. Although in burnout research there are only about half a dozen leading instruments to assess it, and the MBI is unquestionably the predominant measuring instrument, the situation is different in the area of fatigue research. Hundreds of different scales are used in fatigue research, most of them used only once or twice (Hjollund, Andersen, & Bech, 2007). Most of the heavily used fatigue scales conceptualize fatigue as a multidimensional construct, with some multi-item measures of fatigue using the two dimensions of physical and mental or cognitive fatigue (cf. Hjollund et al., 2007), in a manner similar to the previously described SMBM.

An additional important difference between burnout and fatigue research is that in fatigue research, the possible causal effects that characterize fatigue–depression linkages have been more systematically investigated in longitudinal studies whereas, as noted earlier, this is not the case in the burnout area of study. In the field of fatigue, as in burnout, several studies concluded that although there is some conceptual overlap, fatigue could be measured independently of conventional measuring instruments used to assess depression and anxiety (cf. Bultmann, Kant, Kasl, Beurskens, & van den Brandt, 2002). Most (but not all; for an exception see Harvey, Wadsworth,

Wessely, & Hotopf, 2008) recent longitudinal studies have found that fatigue and depression, although common in working populations and closely associated, act as independent risk factors for one another and are reciprocally related over time (Ahola & Hakanen, 2007; Huibers, Leone, van Amelsvoort, Kant, & Knottnerus, 2007).

What are some of the major similarities among the fields of study of burnout and of fatigue? Both represent exponential growth: The number of recent publications on burnout referred to earlier is close to the total number of papers covering different aspects of fatigue published during the past 15 years (Hjollund et al., 2007). An additional similarity lies in the fact that both are similarly stable across time (Leone, Huibers, Knottnerus, & Kant, 2008). Several empirical studies investigated both burnout and fatigue in the same study and systematically compared their respective antecedents or consequences. These studies differ in their design (e.g., cross-sectional vs. longitudinal), the measures of burnout and fatigue used, and in their respective analytic strategy. These differences make it difficult to identify an emerging pattern of burnout–fatigue relationships in the four studies that we identified (for references, see Leone et al., 2008). All four studies found that physical exhaustion, as a component of burnout, and general fatigue, as a component of fatigue, share a large proportion of their variance. All four studies found that, although burnout is more closely associated with work-related predictors (e.g., workload, overload), fatigue appears to be more closely related to dispositional variables, such as personality factors and styles.

Consequences of Burnout

As discussed next, researchers' interest in the consequences of burnout has focused on its effects on job performance and organizational effectiveness. But first I review an emerging field of study: the effects of employee burnout on employee health.

Employee Health

Accumulative evidence, recently summarized by Melamed et al. (2006), supports the view that, on the basis of longitudinal research conducted over the past 15 years, burnout, variously measured, might negatively impact workers' physical health. This is manifested by a two- to three-fold increased risk of CVD, even after adjusting for classical risk factors, such as blood lipid levels, obesity, smoking, age, and gender, in several longitudinal studies (cf. Melamed et al., 2006). More recent research has found that baseline levels of burnout predicted the incidence of Type 2 diabetes (Melamed, Shirom, Toker, & Shapira, 2006a), musculoskeletal disorders (Grossi, Thomten, Fandino-Losada, Soares, & Sundin, 2009; Melamed, 2009), and hospitalization (Toppinen-Tanner, Ahola, Koskinen, & Vaananen, 2009). A recent prospective study (Ahola, Vaananen, Koskinen, Kouvonen, & Shirom, in press) followed up 7,396 Finnish forest industry employees after assessing their baseline levels of burnout using the MBI (General Survey version). Ahola et al. (in press) used Cox proportional hazard regressions to predict mortality ($n = 199$) over a 10-year period, after controlling for baseline sociodemographic factors and health status and found that after these adjustments, and only for the younger participants, the emotional exhaustion component of the MBI predicted subsequent mortality. Several additional large-scale epidemiological studies have found evidence linking burnout to a variety of health outcomes. Honkonen et al. (2006) found that burnout was associated with musculoskeletal disease after controlling for several confounders, including depression. In another large-scale cross-sectional study (Purebl et al., 2006), burnout and CVD were found to be comorbid. These recent studies, some based on longitudinal design and some based on a cross-sectional design, generally support and buttress the conclusions reached by the Melamed et al. (2006) review.

Related research attempted to identify disease mediators, linking burnout and the aforementioned disease entities. One potential physiological mechanism relates to the finding of some studies that burned-out workers show low glucocorticoid (cortisol) levels and/or low cortisol responsivity compared with their nonburned-out counterparts (cf. Melamed et al., 2006). Glucocorticoids play a role in restraining activation of the immune system and other components of the stress response. Thus, a continuous absence of the protective effects of cortisol in burned-out individuals may promote a disinhibition of immune functions, resulting in turn in the hyperactivity of innate immune inflammatory responses. There is an increased recognition in the literature that inflammatory processes are central to the pathogenesis of chronic diseases, including CVD, diabetes, and cancer, and indeed there is some recent evidence supporting the possible linkage between burnout and inflammation biomarkers in the blood, such as C-reactive protein and fibrinogen (cf. Toker, Shirom, Shapira, Berliner, & Melamed, 2005; von Kanel, Bellingrath, & Kudielka, 2008).

Other potential mediators include the metabolic syndrome, sympathetic nervous system activation, and poor health behaviors. Obesity was recently reported in a longitudinal study to be negatively related to burnout (Armon, Shirom, Berliner, Shapira, & Melamed, 2008) and therefore probably does not represent a promising path linking burnout and CVD. Yet another recent longitudinal study provided strong support for the hypothesis that burnout and insomnia predict each other's incidence and intensification across time (Armon et al., 2008), thus suggesting that either might be a risk factor for the other across time. The relationships between burnout and health behaviors, including engaging in sport activities and maintaining a healthy diet, have yet to be investigated.

The study of physiological concomitants of burnout has already contributed to elucidating and supporting a theoretically based distinction between chronic stress and burnout and also between burnout and depression. Furthermore, it suggests that the stability of burnout over time may stem in part from the associated physiological derangements that feed back to the brain and help to maintain the chronicity of burnout (cf. Melamed et al., 2006). However, there are still several important challenges facing researchers investigating the burnout–CVD linkage. The first is that rather than being precursors of the disease state, symptoms included in most measures of burnout, primarily chronic fatigue, could be a manifestation of the atherosclerotic process leading to CVD. The atherosclerotic process starts early in life and takes years before it culminates in a disease state such as CVD. Inflammatory processes implicated in atherogensis could also be responsible for burnout and chronic fatigue. It is also possible that a third variable that precedes both burnout and the atherosclerotic process is causally responsible for both and that their relationship is spurious. Candidates for third variables are difficult life circumstances, disadvantaged social position, and objective and subjective low social status.

Performance in Organizations

Burnout, particularly when conceptualized to represent exhaustion, has been linked to several negative organizational outcomes. These adverse outcomes include increased incidence of medically certified sickness absences, which is independent of mental disorders and physical diseases (Ahola et al., 2008; Borritz, Rugulies, Christensen, Villadsen, & Kristensen, 2006), organizational deviance (Mulki, Jaramillo, & Locander, 2006), quality of care provided by physicians (Shirom et al., 2006), and the self-reported use of violence by police officers against civilians (Kop, Euwema, & Schaufeli, 1999). I focus on burnout job performance relationships.

Taris (2006) synthesized 16 studies that had investigated the associations between burnout and objective performance. Objective performance was chosen in this meta-analysis because of the well-known biases involved in using self-rated performance, including response biases, such as the wish to provide consistent responses on questionnaires. In 15 out of the 16 studies, the MBI was used to assess burnout; different measures of objective performance were employed in these studies, and most of them used a cross-sectional design. Taris found that the (corrected) meta-correlations between the emotional exhaustion subscale of the MBI in-role performance (based on three studies) and organizational citizenship behaviors (based on five studies) were −.22 and −.19, respectively. The findings of this meta-analytic study suggest that a reduction of the levels of exhaustion among employees may be advantageous to the organization and its clients alike. Because the relationships between the other two MBI subscales—depersonalization and lack of personal accomplishment—and the various measures of objective performance were found in this study to be ambiguous and inconclusive, it is recommended that future research concentrate on the relationship between exhaustion and performance.

Subsequently published studies largely confirmed the findings of Taris's (2006) meta-analysis. Thus, Halbesleben and Bowler (2007) found that the emotional exhaustion subscale of the MBI predicted supervisor-rated in-role and extra-role performance in two samples. Other recent studies (e.g., Bakker & Heuven, 2006), which used self-rated performance, obtained negative correlations with the same order of magnitude as those found by Taris. Therefore, it appears that burnout is not differentially related to self-assessed, supervisor-assessed, and objectively measured job performance. In general, burnout was found to be negatively related to subjectively assessed performance. Based on six studies, Schaufeli and Enzmann (1998) concluded that self-rated performance correlated weakly with the MBI emotional exhaustion scale, with only about 5% of the variance shared.

The evidence described previously lends credence to the major propositions of COR theory regarding the possible reasons for burnout's negative impact on job performance. The negative correlation between burnout and job performance is likely to be explained by burned-out individuals' impaired coping ability and their reduced level of motivation to perform, as confirmed in a recent study (Halbesleben & Bowler, 2007).

Future Research

More than 20 years ago, it was predicted that although more data on burnout would be gathered during the ensuing 20 years, researchers' understanding of this phenomena would not be augmented (Jackson, Schwab, & Schuler, 1986, p. 687). As demonstrated earlier, this pessimistic forecast for the field did not materialize because we increased our understanding of the chronicity of burnout, its antecedents, and its effects on employee health and job performance. However, vexing issues remain to be resolved by future research. In this concluding section, I describe some of the more important issues awaiting future research on the phenomenon of burnout. These issues supplement those already alluded to earlier.

Inconsistencies Among the Different Definitional Approaches

Earlier, I described the controversy over the construct validity of the MBI, the instrument that has been used by most researchers to operationally define burnout (Schaufeli & Enzmann, 1998). The questionable construct validity of the MBI led several groups of researchers to construct alternative instruments for the study of burnout. For example, Demerouti and her colleagues (Demerouti et al., 2003; Halbesleben & Demerouti, 2005) constructed the Oldenburg Burnout Inventory (OLBI). The OLBI expanded the original MBI scales of emotional exhaustion, which originally focused on physical exhaustion, to include both cognitive and emotional exhaustion, and also retained the depersonalization scale of the MBI relabeling it as *disengagement.* The OLBI posits that burnout is represented by two major dimensions, exhaustion and disengagement, but it does not provide a theoretical rationale for thus defining burnout (cf. Halbesleben & Demerouti, 2005). From a construct validity viewpoint, the job demands–resources model (Demerouti, Bakker, Nachreiner, & Schaufeli, 2001) posits that exhaustion stems from job demands, whereas disengagement is the result of a lack of job resources; this major prediction was supported in many studies (cf. Bakker & Demerouti, 2007). Therefore, the argument that the two dimensions of the OLBI represent the same underlying phenomenon does not accord with the earlier major prediction of the job demands–resources model because this model posits that different antecedents predict each dimension. In addition, the argument is inconsistent with the two studies reported by Halbesleben and Demerouti (2005), indicating that the two dimensions share only about 10% of their variance. From a psychometric viewpoint, yet another claimed advantage of the OLBI—that it uses two-directional wording for the items in each of its subscales—could actually represent a major disadvantage because it makes it difficult to determine whether the separate factors are substantively meaningful or represent method factors associated with item wording.

Another recently proposed measure of burnout is the Copenhagen Burnout Inventory (CBI; see Kristensen et al., 2005). The CBI conceives burnout as residing in three interconnected domains: life, work, and service to clients. Most of the items in the life domain repeat themselves in the work and service domains, with only a slight variation to represent context specificity. From our former discussion of the conceptual overlap between burnout and depression, arguably burnout in life, in general, is characterized by a closer conceptual affinity to depression in comparison with burnout at work. The three life domains underlying the CBI are conceptually embedded within each other; this raises the theoretical question of why they should be considered relatively independent of one another, thus providing a theoretical rationale to the argument that they should be measured as separate entities.

Burnout is a scientific construct in that it is used to describe a phenomenon of theoretical interest (Edwards & Bagozzi, 2000) and also, as demonstrated earlier, of considerable interest to practitioners. Based on the discussion of several new attempts to conceptualize burnout, two suggestions are recommended for future research. First, future research needs to provide a clear conceptual definition of burnout. Second, future research needs to analyze all items used to assess burnout within broader models that include causes, correlates, and effects of burnout. This suggestion for future research should generate evidence relevant to the nomological validity of burnout (Edwards & Bagozzi, 2000), evidence which is a necessary condition for claiming validity to any measure of burnout.

DISCRIMINATING BURNOUT FROM DEPRESSIVE SYMPTOMS. Regardless of the operational definition of burnout used in future research, an important area for future research is the discriminating validity of burnout and other types of emotional distress, particularly anxiety and depression. Earlier, I argued that burnout, anxiety, and depression are conceptually distinct emotional reactions to stress. Studies that support this contention were cited earlier (Schaufeli & Van Dierendonck, 1993). Still, the empirical overlap found in several meta-analytic studies (Glass & McKnight, 1996; Schaufeli & Enzmann, 1998) between depression and the emotional exhaustion scale of the MBI—the most robust and reliable out of the three scales that make up the MBI—is a cause for concern. The propositions that early stages of individuals' burnout are more likely to be accompanied by heightened anxiety, whereas more progressive stages of burnout may be linked to depressive symptoms need to be tested in longitudinal research.

RELATIONSHIP BETWEEN BURNOUT AND FATIGUE. Our concise review of past studies that investigated burnout–fatigue linkages allows the following recommendations to researchers in these fields. There is a lot to be gained by becoming acquainted with burnout–fatigue linkages, referring to one another's work, and comparing each field's major findings with those of the other field. This appears to be a feasible and easily implemented recommendation. On a higher level of cooperation, both fields have much to gain and little to lose by using each other's research instruments, thus allowing a convergence between them to be achieved in the future.

Individual Traits Predisposing Employees to Burnout

The effects of personality predispositions on the development of burnout appear to be an area of research waiting to be synthesized. In addition, it seems that the complex interactions between personality traits and burnout have yet to be described and understood. There is some evidence that personality factors explain additional variance in job burnout even after considering the effects of types of stress considered to be the most potent predictors of this phenomenon (e.g., Schaufeli & Enzmann, 1998). The lesson to burnout researchers is that it is plausible that individual traits predisposing employees to burnout interact with organizational features that are conductive to the development of burnout. As an example, when a major economic slump moves management to require that all employees increase their input of available personal energy and time to ensure the organization's survival, those employees who possess high self-esteem are less likely to experience burnout as a result (cf. Cordes & Dougherty, 1993).

Models of Stress That Most Powerfully Predict Burnout

Past reviews of the burnout literature (Halbesleben & Buckley, 2004; Moore, 2000; Shirom, 2003) viewed burnout as a consequence of one's exposure to chronic job stress. Most past longitudinal studies, however, have found that stresses and burnout tend to be reciprocally related, influencing each other across time (e.g., Shirom, Oliver, & Stein, 2009). A related open research question is which types of chronic stresses most likely to lead to burnout. In past research, the chronic stresses that were assessed include qualitative and quantitative overload, role conflict and ambiguity, lack of participation, and lack of social support. Among the major theoretical approaches to work-related stress and its outcomes (cf. Cooper, 1998), those that have been applied to investigate stress–burnout relationships are the demand–control–support model, the effort–reward imbalance perspective, and the person–environment fit model. In addition, the job demands–resources theoretical framework (Bakker & Demerouti, 2007) has been applied in many studies to predict burnout. It should be noted that these theoretical perspectives differ in their conceptualization of stress and place different emphases on individual personality differences and on situational variables that may moderate stress–burnout relations. In addition, the different models have not been systematically compared with regard to their predictive validity of burnout.

Burnout research still has to uncover the specific contexts in which stress exerts its effects on burnout. A meta-analysis of the literature (Collins, 1999) suggested that when the effects of different types of stress on burnout are compared across studies, larger effect sizes are obtained with job-specific stress measures relative to generic chronic stress measures, such as the role conflict and ambiguity referred to earlier. It is also possible that generic types of chronic stresses interact with job-specific types of stresses to influence burnout levels. Identifying the most potent stresses affecting burnout is a major challenge facing designers of intervention programs to ameliorate burnout.

Macrolevel Influences on Burnout and Organizational Burnout

There is a paucity of research on organizational-level burnout. In addition, for advancing our understanding of the role that burnout plays in determining organizational effectiveness, a profitable line of research could be relating unit-level burnout to unit-level and organizational-level outcomes.

Conclusion

Given the data provided on the prevalence of burnout in advanced market economies, improving understanding of the complex relationships between stress and burnout is critical for designing effective preventive interventions and for public policy efforts. Advances in knowledge are unlikely to result from research using fuzzy concepts and relying on instruments whose construct validity is dubious. For this reason, in this review I have selectively focused on theoretical and conceptual issues in burnout research.

Some of the major characteristics of burnout research highlighted earlier, including the stability of burnout over time, its negative impact on job performance, and the documented risk to physical health, all strongly point to the need to assess and treat burnout to prevent or at least reduce possible damage to health and to organizational effectiveness. On the basis of the available evidence on interventions applied to ameliorate burnout, it is strongly recommended that interventionists adopt a multidisciplinary approach composed of organizational, behavioral, psychological, and physiological and pharmacological approaches. This may prove to be more efficacious in bringing about long-term alleviation of burnout than do interventions with a unidisciplinary approach.

Burnout is likely to represent a pressing social problem in the years to come. Competitive pressures in the manufacturing industry that originate in the global market, the continuing process of consumer empowerment in service industries, and the rise and decline of the high-tech industry are among the factors likely to affect employees' levels of burnout in different industries. In addition, employees in many advanced market economies experience heightened job insecurity, demands for excessive work hours, the need for continuous retraining in the wake of the accelerating pace of change in informational technologies, and the blurring of the line separating work and home life. In many European countries, employers are enjoined by governmental regulations on occupational health to implement preventive interventions that concern job stress and burnout. This review is an attempt to steer future research on burnout to make future preventive interventions more effective.

References

Abraham, R. (2000). Organizational cynicism: Bases and consequences. *Genetic, Social, and General Psychology Monographs, 126,* 269–292.

Ahola, K., & Hakanen, J. (2007). Job strain, burnout, and depressive symptoms: A prospective study among dentists. *Journal of Affective Disorders, 104*(1–3), 103–110. doi:10.1016/j.jad.2007.03.004

Ahola, K., Kivimäki, M., Honkonen, T., Virtanen, M., Koskinen, S., Vahtera, J., & Lönnqvist, J. (2008). Occupational burnout and medically certified sickness absence: A population-based study of Finnish employees. *Journal of Psychosomatic Research, 64,* 185–193. doi:10.1016/j.jpsychores.2007.06.022

Ahola, K., Vaananen, A., Koskinen, A., Kouvonen, A., & Shirom, A. (in press). Burnout as a predictor of all-cause mortality among industrial employees: A 10-year prospective register-linkage study. *Journal of Psychosomatic Research.*

Andersson, L. M., & Bateman, T. S. (1997). Cynicism in the workplace: Some causes and effects. *Journal of Organizational Behavior, 18,* 449–469. doi:10.1002/(SICI)1099-1379(199709)18: 5{449::AID-JOB808}3.0.CO;2-O

Armon, G., Shirom, A., Berliner, S., Shapira, I., & Melamed, S. (2008). A prospective study of the association between obesity and burnout among apparently healthy men and women. *Journal of Occupational Health Psychology, 13,* 43–57. doi:10.1037/1076-8998.13.1.43

Armon, G., Shirom, A., Shapira, I., & Melamed, S. (2008). On the nature of burnout-insomnia relationships: A prospective study of employed adults. *Journal of Psychosomatic Research, 65,* 5–12. doi:10.1016/j.jpsychores.2008.01.012

Bakker, A. B., & Demerouti, E. (2007). The job demands–resources model: State of the art. *Journal of Managerial Psychology, 22,* 309–328. doi:10.1108/02683940710733115

Bakker, A. B., & Heuven, E. (2006). Emotional dissonance, burnout, and in-role performance among nurses and police officers. *International Journal of Stress Management, 13,* 423–440. doi:10.1037/1072-5245.13.4.423

Beck, A. T., Ward, C. H., Mendelson, M., Mock, J., & Erbaugh, J. (1961). An inventory for measuring depression. *Archives of General Psychiatry, 4,* 561–571.

Borritz, M., Rugulies, R., Christensen, K. B., Villadsen, E., & Kristensen, T. S. (2006). Burnout as a predictor of self-reported sickness absence among human service workers: Prospective findings from 3-year follow-up of the PUMA study. *Occupational and Environmental Medicine, 63,* 98–106. doi:10.1136/oem.2004.019364

Boudreau, R., & Nakashima, J. (2002). *A bibliography of burnout citations, 1990–2002.* Winnipeg, Canada: ASAC.

Bültmann, U., Kant, I., Kasl, S. V., Beurskens, A., & van den Brandt, P. A. (2002). Fatigue and psychological distress in the working population: Psychometrics, prevalence, and correlates. *Journal of Psychosomatic Research, 52,* 445–452. doi:10.1016/S0022-3999(01)00228-8

Collins, V. A. (1999). *A meta-analysis of burnout and occupational stress* (Unpublished doctoral dissertation). University of North Texas, Denton.

Conley, J. J. (1984). The hierarchy of consistency: A review and model of longitudinal findings on adult individual differences in intelligence, personality, and self-opinion. *Personality and Individual Differences, 5*(1), 11–25. doi:10.1016/0191-8869(84)90133-8

Cooper, C. L. (1998). *Theories of organizational stress.* New York, NY: Oxford University Press.

Cordes, C. L., & Dougherty, T. W. (1993). A review and an integration of research on job burnout. *Academy of Management Review, 18,* 621–656. doi:10.2307/258593

Dale, J., & Weinberg, R. (1990). Burnout in sport: A review and critique. *Journal of Applied Sport Psychology, 2,* 67–83. doi:10.1080/10413209008406421

Dean, J. W., Brandes, P., & Dharwadkar, R. (1998). Organizational cynicism. *Academy of Management Review, 23,* 341–352. doi:10.2307/259378

Demerouti, E., Bakker, A. B., Nachreiner, F., & Schaufeli, W. B. (2001). The job demands–resources model of burnout. *Journal of Applied Psychology, 86,* 499–512. doi:10.1037/0021-9010.86.3.499

Demerouti, E., Bakker, A. B., Vardakou, I., & Kantas, A. (2003). The convergent validity of two burnout instruments: A multitrait–multimethod analysis. *European Journal of Psychological Assessment, 19*(1), 12–23. doi:10.1027//1015-5759.19.1.12

Edwards, J. R., & Bagozzi, R. P. (2000). On the nature and direction of relationships between constructs and measures. *Psychological Methods, 5,* 155–174. doi:10.1037/1082-989X.5.2.155

Fisher, S. 1984. *Stress and the perception of control.* London, England: Erlbaum.

Foschi, M. (2000). Double standards for competence: Theory and research. *Annual Review of Sociology, 26,* 21–42. doi:10.1146/annurev.soc.26.1.21

Glass, D. C., & McKnight, J. D. (1996). Perceived control, depressive symptomatology, and professional burnout: A review of the evidence. *Psychology & Health, 11,* 23–48. doi:10.1080/08870449608401975

Grossi, G., Thomten, J., Fandino-Losada, A., Soares, J. J. F., & Sundin, O. (2009). Does burnout predict changes in pain experienced among women living in Sweden? A longitudinal study. *Stress and Health, 25,* 297–311.

Halbesleben, J. R. B. (2006). Sources of social support and burnout: A meta-analytic test of the conservation of resources model. *Journal of Applied Psychology, 91,* 1134–1145. doi:10.1037/0021-9010.91.5.1134

Halbesleben, J. R. B., & Bowler, W. M. (2007). Emotional exhaustion and job performance: The mediating role of motivation. *Journal of Applied Psychology, 92,* 93–106. doi:10.1037/0021-9010.92.1.93

Halbesleben, J. R. B., & Buckley, M. R. (2004). Burnout in organizational life. *Journal of Management, 30,* 859–879. doi:10.1016/j.jm.2004.06.004

Halbesleben, J. R. B., & Demerouti, E. (2005). The construct validity of an alternative measure of burnout investigating the English translation of the Oldenburg Burnout Inventory. *Work and Stress, 19,* 208–220. doi:10.1080/02678370500340728

Halbesleben, J. R. B., & Rathert, C. (2008). Linking physician burnout and patient outcomes: Exploring the dyadic relationship between physicians and patients. *Health Care Management Review, 33*(1), 29–39.

Hallsten, L. (2005). Burnout and wornout: Concepts and data from a national survey. In A. S. A. C. L. Cooper (Ed.), *Research companion to organizational health psychology* (pp. 516–536). Cheltenham, England: Edward Elgar.

Harvey, S. B., Wadsworth, M., Wessely, S., & Hotopf, M. (2008). The relationship between prior psychiatric disorder and chronic fatigue: Evidence from a national birth cohort study. *Psychological Medicine, 38,* 933–940. doi:10.1017/S0033291707001900

Hemingway, H., & Marmot, M. (1999). Evidence based cardiology—psychosocial factors in the aetiology and prognosis of coronary heart disease: Systematic review of prospective cohort studies. *British Medical Journal, 318,* 1460–1467.

Hjollund, N. H., Andersen, J., & Bech, P. (2007). Assessment of fatigue in chronic disease: A bibliographic study of fatigue measurement scales. *Health and Quality of Life Outcomes, 5*(1), 12. doi:10.1186/1477-7525-5-12

Hobfoll, S. E. (1989). Conservation of resources: A new attempt at conceptualizing stress. *American Psychologist, 44,* 513–524. doi:10.1037/0003-066X.44.3.513

Hobfoll, S. E. (1998). *The psychology and philosophy of stress, culture, and community.* New York, NY: Plenum Press.

Hobfoll, S. E. (2002). Social and psychological resources and adaptation. *Review of General Psychology, 6,* 307–324. doi:10.1037/1089-2680.6.4.307

Hobfoll, S. E., & Shirom, A. (2000). Conservation of resources theory: Applications to stress and management in the workplace. In R. T. Golembiewski (Ed.), *Handbook of organization behavior* (2nd rev. ed., pp. 57–81). New York, NY: Dekker.

Honkonen, T., Ahola, K., Pertovaara, M., Isometä, E., Kailmo, R., Nykyri, E., . . . Lönnqvist, J. (2006). The association between burnout and physical illness in the general population—Results from the Finnish Health 2000 Study. *Journal of Psychosomatic Research, 61,* 59–66. doi:10.1016/j.jpsychores.2005.10.002

Huibers, M. J. H., Leone, S. S., van Amelsvoort, L. G. P. M., Kant, I., & Knottnerus, J. A. (2007). Associations of fatigue and depression among fatigued employees over time: A 4-year follow-up study. *Journal of Psychosomatic Research, 63,* 137–142. doi:10.1016/j.jpsychores.2007.02.014

Jackson, S. E., Schwab, R. K., & Schuler, R. S. (1986). Toward an understanding of the burnout phenomenon. *Journal of Applied Psychology, 71,* 630–640. doi:10.1037/0021-9010.71.4.630

Kalliath, T. J., O'Driscoll, M. P., Gillespie, D. F., & Bluedorn, A. G. (2000). A test of the Maslach Burnout Inventory in three samples of healthcare professionals. *Work and Stress, 14,* 35–50. doi:10.1080/026783700417212

Karasek, R., & Theorell, T. (1990). *Healthy work: Stress, productivity, and the reconstruction of working life.* New York, NY: Basic Books.

Koeske, C. F., & Koeske, R. D. (1989). Construct validity of the Maslach Burnout Inventory: A critical review. *Journal of Applied Behavioral Science, 25,* 131–144. doi:10.1177/0021886389252004

Kop, N., Euwema, M., & Schaufeli, W. B. (1999). Burnout, job stress, and violent behaviour among Dutch police officers. *Work and Stress, 13,* 326–340. doi:10.1080/02678379950019789

Kristensen, T. S., Borritz, M., Villadsen, E., & Christensen, K. B. (2005). The Copenhagen Burnout Inventory: A new tool for burnout. *Work and Stress, 19,* 192–207. doi:10.1080/02678370500297720

Lee, R. T., & Ashforth, B. E. (1996). A meta-analytic examination of the correlates of the three dimensions of job burnout. *Journal of Applied Psychology, 81,* 123–133. doi:10.1037/0021-9010.81.2.123

Leiter, M. P., & Maslach, C. (2001). Burnout and health. In A. Baum, T. A. Revenson, & J. E. Singer (Eds.), *Handbook of health psychology* (pp. 415–422). Mahwah, NJ: Erlbaum.

Leone, S. S., Huibers, M. J. H., Knottnerus, J. A., & Kant, I. (2008). A comparison of the course of burnout and prolonged fatigue: A 4-year prospective cohort study. *Journal of Psychosomatic Research, 65,* 31–38. doi:10.1016/j.jpsychores.2008.03.018

Lindeberg, S. I., Eek, F., Lindbladh, E., Ostergren, P. O., Hansen, A. M., & Karlson, B. (2008). Exhaustion measured by the SF-36 vitality scale is associated with a flattened diurnal cortisol profile. *Psychoneuroendocrinology, 33,* 471–477. doi:10.1016/j.psyneuen.2008.01.005

Martin, A., Chalder, T., Rief, W., & Braehler, E. (2007). The relationship between chronic fatigue and somatization syndrome: A general population survey. *Journal of Psychosomatic Research, 63,* 147–156. doi:10.1016/j.jpsychores.2007.05.007

Maslach, C. (1982). *Burnout: The cost of caring.* Englewood Cliffs, NJ: Prentice Hall.

Maslach, C. (1998). A multidimensional theory of burnout. In C. L. Cooper (Ed.), *Theories of organizational stress* (pp. 68–85). Oxford, England: Oxford University Press.

Maslach, C., & Jackson, S. E. (1981). The measurement of experienced burnout. *Journal of Organizational Behavior, 2*(2), 99–113. doi:10.1002/job.4030020205

Maslach, C., & Jackson, S. E. (1986). *The Maslach Burnout Inventory.* Palo Alto, CA: Consulting Psychologist Press.

Maslach, C., Jackson, S. E., & Leiter, M. P. (1996). *Maslach Burnout Inventory Manual* (3rd ed.). Palo Alto, CA: Consulting Psychologists Press.

Maslach, C., Schaufeli, W. B., & Leiter, M. P. (2001). Job burnout. *Annual Review of Psychology, 52,* 397–422. doi:10.1146/annurev.psych.52.1.397

Melamed, S. (2009). Burnout and risk of regional musculoskeletal pain: A prospective study of apparently healthy employed adults. *Stress and Health, 25,* 313–321.

Melamed, S., Shirom, A., Toker, S., Berliner, S., & Shapira, I. (2006). Burnout and risk of cardiovascular disease: Evidence, possible causal paths, and promising research directions. *Psychological Bulletin, 132,* 327–353. doi:10.1037/0033-2909.132.3.327

Melamed, S., Shirom, A., Toker, S., & Shapira, I. (2006a). Burnout and risk of type 2 diabetes: A prospective study of apparently healthy employed persons. *Psychosomatic Medicine, 68,* 863–869. doi:10.1097/01.psy.0000242860.24009.f0

Michielsen, H. J., Croon, M. A., Willemsen, T. M., De Vries, J., & Van Heck, G. L. (2007). Which constructs can predict emotional exhaustion in a working population? A study into its determinants. *Stress and Health, 23,* 121–130. doi:10.1002/smi.1129

Moore, J. E. (2000). Why is this happening? A causal attribution approach to work exhaustion consequences. *Academy of Management Review, 25,* 335–349. doi:10.2307/259017

Mulki, J. P., Jaramillo, F., & Locander, W. B. (2006). Emotional exhaustion and organizational deviance: Can the right job and a leader's style make a difference? *Journal of Business Research, 59,* 1222–1230. doi:10.1016/j.jbusres.2006.09.001

Neveu, J.-P. (2007). Jailed resources: Conservation of resources theory as applied to burnout among prison guards. *Journal of Organizational Behavior, 28,* 21–42. doi:10.1002/job.393

Nyklícek, I., & Pop, V. J. (2005). Past and familial depression predict current symptoms of professional burnout. *Journal of Affective Disorders, 88,* 63–68. doi:10.1016/j.jad.2005.06.007

Pines, A. (1988). *Keeping the spark alive: Preventing burnout in love and marriage.* New York, NY: St. Martin's Press.

Pines, A. (1993). Burnout. In L. Goldberger & S. Breznitz (Eds.), *Handbook of stress* (2nd ed., pp. 386–402). New York, NY: Free Press.

Pines, A. (1996). *Couple burnout.* New York, NY: Routledge.

Pines, A., & Aronson, E. (1988). *Career burnout: Causes and cures.* New York, NY: Free Press.

Pines, A., Aronson, E., & Kafry, D. (1981). *Burnout: From tedium to personal growth.* New York, NY: Free Press.

Purebl, G., Birkas, E., Csoboth, C., Szumska, I., & Kopp, M. S. (2006). The relationship of biological and psychological risk factors of cardiovascular disorders in a large-scale national representative community survey. *Behavioral Medicine, 31,* 133–139. doi:10.3200/BMED.31.4.133-139

Ricci, J. A., Chee, E., Lorandeau, A. L., & Berger, J. (2007). Fatigue in the U.S. workforce: Prevalence and implications for lost productive work time. *Journal of Occupational and Environmental Medicine, 49,* 1–10. doi:10.1097/01.jom.0000249782.60321.2a

Sandberg, J. (2000). Understanding human competence at work: An integrative approach. *Academy of Management Journal, 43,* 9–25. doi:10.2307/1556383

Schaufeli, W. B. (2003). Past performance and future perspectives of burnout research. *South African Journal of Industrial Psychology, 29*(4), 1–15.

Schaufeli, W. B., & Enzmann, D. (1998). *The burnout companion to study and practice: A critical analysis.* Washington, DC: Taylor & Francis.

Schaufeli, W. B., & Taris, T. W. (2005). The conceptualization and measurement of burnout: Common grounds and worlds apart. *Work and Stress, 19,* 256–262. doi:10.1080/02678370500385913

Schaufeli, W. B., & Van Dierendonck, D. (1993). The construct validity of two burnout measures. *Journal of Organizational Behavior, 14,* 631–647. doi:10.1002/job.4030140703

Shirom, A. (2003). Job-related burnout. In J. C. Quick & L. E. Tetrick (Eds.), *Handbook of occupational health psychology* (pp. 245–265). Washington, DC: American Psychological Association. doi:10.1037/10474-012

Shirom, A., & Ezrachi, J. (2003). On the discriminant validity of burnout, depression, and anxiety: A reexamination of the burnout measure. *Anxiety, Stress, & Coping, 16,* 83–99.

Shirom, A., & Melamed, S. (2006). A comparison of the construct validity of two burnout measures in two groups of professionals. *International Journal of Stress Management, 13,* 176–200. doi:10.1037/1072-5245.13.2.176

Shirom, A., Nirel, N., & Vinokur, A. (2006). Overload, autonomy, and burnout as predictors of physicians' quality of care. *Journal of Occupational Health Psychology, 11,* 328–342. doi:10.1037/1076-8998.11.4.328

Shirom, A., Oliver, A., & Stein, E. (2009). Teachers' stressors and strains: A longitudinal study of their relationships. *International Journal of Stress Management, 16,* 312–332. doi:10.1037/a0016842

Stajkovic, A. D., & Luthans, F. (1998). Self-efficacy and work-related performance: A meta-analysis. *Psychological Bulletin, 124,* 240–261. doi:10.1037/0033-2909.124.2.240

Sullivan, P. F., Pedersen, N. L., Jacks, A., & Evengard, B. (2005). Chronic fatigue in a population sample. *Psychological Medicine, 35,* 1337–1348. doi:10.1017/S0033291705005210

Suls, J., & Bunde, J. (2005). Anger, anxiety, and depression as risk factors for cardiovascular disease: The problems and implications of overlapping affective dispositions. *Psychological Bulletin, 131,* 260–300. doi:10.1037/0033-2909.131.2.260

Taris, T. W. (2006). Is there a relationship between burnout and objective performance? A critical review of 16 studies. *Work and Stress, 20,* 316–334. doi:10.1080/02678370601065893

Taris, T. W., Le Blanc, P. M., Schaufeli, W. B., & Schreurs, P. J. G. (2005). Are there causal relationships between the dimensions of the Maslach Burnout Inventory? A review and two longitudinal tests. *Work and Stress, 19,* 238–255. doi:10.1080/02678370500270453

Toker, S., Shirom, A., Shapira, I., Berliner, S., & Melamed, S. (2005). The association between burnout, depression, anxiety, and inflammation biomarkers. *Journal of Occupational Health Psychology, 10,* 344–362. doi:10.1037/1076-8998.10.4.344

Toppinen-Tanner, S., Ahola, K., Koskinen, A., & Vaananen, A. (2009). Burnout predicts hospitalization for mental and cardiovascular disorders: 10-year prospective results from industrial sector. *Stress and Health, 25,* 287–296.

von Känel, R., Bellingrath, S., & Kudielka, B. M. (2008). Association between burnout and circulating levels of pro- and anti-inflammatory cytokines in schoolteachers. *Journal of Psychosomatic Research, 65,* 51–59. doi:10.1016/j.jpsychores.2008.02.007

Westman, M., & Etzion, D. (1995). Crossover of stress, strain and resources from one spouse to another. *Journal of Organizational Behavior, 16,* 169–181. doi:10.1002/job.4030160207

13

Workplace and Cardiovascular Disease: Relevance and Potential Role for Occupational Health Psychology

Paul A. Landsbergis, Peter L. Schnall,
Karen L. Belkic, Dean Baker,
Joseph E. Schwartz, and Thomas G. Pickering

The development of hypertension and cardiovascular disease (CVD) as global epidemics has occurred in parallel with urbanization, industrialization, and economic globalization (Gaziano, 2004). Workplace trends, resulting from economic globalization, appear to be increasing job stressors and may be having substantial effects on employee health. In developed countries, the prevalence of diabetes, obesity, hypertension, and sleeping problems is increasing. CVD incidence is barely declining and socioeconomic disparities in CVD mortality, incidence, and risk factors are increasing.

In this chapter, we first review the extensive body of research linking CVD, hypertension, and other CVD risk factors with work stressors. We then examine the physiological, behavioral, social, and psychological mechanisms by which work stressors can lead to cardiovascular outcomes. Finally, we describe strategies and programs for the prevention and management of work-related hypertension and CVD, including risk assessment, return-to-work programs, health promotion, job redesign, and legislation.

Social–Historical Context

CVD is the major cause of morbidity and mortality in the industrialized world and is projected to become the most common cause of death worldwide early in

This chapter is dedicated to the memory of our friend, colleague, and mentor, Thomas Pickering, MD, DPhil.

Some of the research findings in this chapter were supported in part by grants HL18232, HL30605, HL55165, and HL47540 from the National Heart, Lung, and Blood Institute, Bethesda, MD; grant OH OH07577 from the National Institute for Occupational Safety and Health, Cincinnati, OH; and the Signe and Olof Wallenius Foundation, Stockholm. Preparation of this manuscript was supported by a grant from the Center for Social Epidemiology, Venice Beach, CA.

the 21st century (Gaziano, 2004). However, nonindustrialized, nonurban populations (Cooper, Rotimi, & Ward, 1999) do not have high rates of CVD and hypertension. Coupled with the relatively recent emergence of standard CVD risk factors (e.g., cigarette smoking, sedentary labor, high cholesterol diets), this pattern suggests that CVD and hypertension are of relatively recent historical origin (Schnall & Kern, 1981). A major cross-cultural study found virtually no rise in blood pressure (BP) with age and no hypertension among hunter–gatherers, herders, or traditional family farmers (Waldron et al., 1982). In contrast, men and women in urban industrial societies have steady rises of BP with age, and hypertension is common (Schnall & Kern, 1981; Waldron et al., 1982).

The rising prevalence of hypertension in developed countries parallels the transformation of working life during the past century and a half, away from agricultural work and relatively autonomous craft-based work toward machine-based (including computer-based) labor, characteristic of mass production (Schnall, Belkic, Landsbergis, & Baker, 2000a). This transformation, often labeled *Taylorism,* is characterized by an assembly-line approach to job design in which high workload demands are often combined with low employee control or autonomy (i.e., "job strain"; Karasek & Theorell, 1990), and long work hours.

Over the past 30 years, an extensive body of evidence has documented that lower socioeconomic status (SES; Kaplan & Keil, 1993) and work stressors (Schnall, Belkic, Landsbergis, & Baker, 2000b) are risk factors for hypertension and CVD. Job control was "the biggest factor contributing to the socioeconomic gradient in CHD [coronary heart disease] risk across civil service employment grade" in the Whitehall study (Kawachi & Marmot, 1998, p. 162). For example, sedentary behavior and smoking "often arise in the context of individuals trapped in low-control work environments" (Kawachi & Marmot, 1998, p. 162). More advantaged communities and individuals have greater resources for promoting "hygienic" life-styles and reducing "alienating living and working conditions . . . conducive to initiating and maintaining unhealthful behaviors" (Wing, Casper, Riggan, Hayes, & Tyroler, 1988, p. 925).

Current Economic and Workplace Trends

Workplace trends, resulting from economic globalization, appear to be increasing job stressors and to be adversely impacting employee health. Governmental policies associated with economic globalization include deregulation, privatization of public services, and reduced social protections. Workplace trends include stagnant or falling real income, downsizing, "precarious" (i.e., temporary, part-time, contract) work, and new management systems such as "lean production" that intensify work (European Foundation, 2006; Landsbergis, 2003; National Institute for Occupational Safety and Health, 2002). Precarious work is associated with working at higher speeds, having less control over work pace, and receiving less training (Paoli & Merllié, 2001) and is more common among workers in lower status jobs (Robertson et al., 2006). In the United States, income for the bottom half of the income distribution has been largely stagnant for 30 years, so income inequality (i.e., the gap between richer and poorer) has increased dramatically since 1970 and is the highest in the developed world (Mishel & Bernstein, 2006). Studies have shown associations between CVD risk and privatization of public services (Ferrie, Shipley, Marmot, Stansfeld, & Smith, 1998), downsizing (Vahtera et al., 2004), and income inequality (Kaplan & Lynch, 1999).

Such trends have promoted substantial changes in job characteristics. In Europe, "time constraints" rose between 1977 and 1996 (European Foundation, 1997), and in the United States, increases between 1977 and 1997 were reported for "never enough time to get everything done on my job" (i.e., from 40% to 60%; Bond, Galinsky, & Swanberg, 1998). European surveys show a continuing rise in job demands between 1990 and 2005 but no change or slight declines in job control or autonomy since 1995 (European Foundation, 2006), suggesting an increase in the prevalence of job strain. Annual work hours for the U.S. paid labor force have not changed substantially in the past 30 years. However, because the proportion of women in the paid labor force has increased dramatically, the number of hours worked by middle-income husbands and wives with children, age 25 to 54, has risen from about 3,000 to 3,600 per year from 1982 to 2002 (Mishel & Bernstein, 2006). As a result of declines in work hours in other developed countries, annual U.S. work hours are now the longest in the developed world, about 8 to 10 more weeks per year than workers in Western Europe (Mishel & Bernstein, 2006).

Trends in CVD and CVD Risk Factors

In developing countries over the past 50 years, there has been a rapid increase in the prevalence of hypertension, smoking, obesity (Hajjar, Kotchen, & Kotchen, 2006), and CVD (Gaziano, 2004). In industrialized countries, although CVD mortality rates have fallen dramatically over the past 40 years (Gaziano, 2004), CVD incidence rates have shown little or no decline over the past 20 years (McGovern et al., 2001; Rosamond, Folsom, Chambless, & Wang, 2001). Although smoking prevalence and cholesterol levels have declined, there have been increases in diabetes and obesity (National Center for Health Statistics, 2006), and the previous trend of a decrease in hypertension prevalence is reversing (Hajjar et al., 2006).

The prevalence of inadequate sleep or insomnia is rising in the United States (National Sleep Foundation, 2005), Finland (European Foundation for the Improvement of Living and Working Conditions, 2005), and Sweden (Gustafsson & Lundberg, 2004). Sleeping problems are associated with elevated BP and heart rate (van der Hulst, 2003) and CVD risk (Ferrie et al., 2007). In addition, socioeconomic disparities in CVD mortality (Gonzalez, Artalejo, & Calero, 1998), CVD incidence (Tuchsen & Endahl, 1999), and in the United States, the prevalence of hypertension, diabetes, and smoking (Kanjilal et al., 2006) is rising. This temporal ecological pattern suggests that increases in work stressors produced by economic globalization may be playing an important role with respect to CVD risk factors, maintaining CVD incidence rates, and widening socioeconomic disparities in CVD and its risk factors.

Work Stressors Associated With CVD

Various work stressors have been investigated with respect to CVD and related outcomes.

- The most studied construct is *job strain,* work that combines high psychological work demands with low job-decision latitude or control (Karasek & Theorell, 1990). Eighteen of 34 studies of job strain and CVD published between 1981 and 2002 showed significant positive associations. An additional three studies had mixed positive and null results. The design of many of the studies tended to bias the results toward the null (i.e., produce weaker associations; Belkic, Landsbergis, Schnall, & Baker, 2004).
- *Effort–reward imbalance* defines deleterious job conditions as a mismatch between high workload and low control over long-term rewards (Siegrist et al., 2004). *Reward* includes concepts such as esteem reward (e.g., respect, support), income, and status control (e.g., promotion prospects, job security). Significant positive associations have been observed between exposure to effort–reward imbalance and CVD among men (Bosma, Peter, Siegrist, & Marmot, 1998; Kivimäki et al., 2002; Peter, Siegrist, Hallqvist, Reuterwall, & Theorell, 2002; Siegrist, 1996) and among men and women (Kuper, Singh-Manouz, Siegrist, & Marmot, 2002).
- *Threat-avoidant vigilant (TAV) work* (Belkic, Savic, Djordjevic, Ugljesic, & Mickovic, 1992) involves continuously maintaining a high level of vigilance to avoid disaster, such as loss of human life and is a feature of a number of occupations at high risk of CVD (e.g., urban mass transit operators, truck drivers, air traffic controllers, sea pilots). The strongest evidence for this risk factor comes from studies of single occupations, where professional drivers, particularly urban transport operators, emerge as the occupation with the most consistent evidence of elevated risk of CVD (Belkic, Emdad, & Theorell, 1998; Tuchsen, 2000) and hypertension (Greiner, Krause, Ragland, & Fisher, 2004).
- *Long work hours.* Epidemiological data concerning long work hours and CVD is sparse, though recent studies have suggested that working more than 60 hr per week may increase risk of heart disease (Liu & Tanaka, 2002; Sokejima & Kagamimori, 1998). Its importance has been emphasized in clinical observations (Shimomitsu & Odagiri, 2000; Steenland, 2000). *Karoshi,* CVD death due to long hours of demanding work, is a recognized entity in Japan (Shimomitsu & Odagiri, 2000) and is becoming acknowledged elsewhere (Michie & Cockcroft, 1996). Prolonged exposure to stressful working conditions appears to be particularly deleterious (Belkic, Schnall, Savic, & Landsbergis, 2000).
- *Shiftwork.* Night shift work has also been implicated in CVD risk; shift workers have an estimated 40% increased CVD risk compared with day workers (Boggild & Knutsson, 1999).
- *Downsizing.* Workforce reductions, or downsizing, were associated with a doubling of the risk of CVD mortality (Vahtera et al., 2004) among

Finnish public employees, mediated in part by increased levels of physical work demands and job insecurity and decreased level of skill discretion and participation (Kivimäki, Vahtera, Pentti, & Ferrie, 2000).

- *Organizational justice.* In the British Whitehall study, *relational justice* (i.e., primarily supervisor support) was associated with reduced risk of CVD (Kivimäki et al., 2005).

Synergism With Low Socioeconomic Status

For men, the impact of job strain on CVD is more consistent and stronger among blue-collar workers (Johnson & Hall, 1988; Theorell et al., 1998), with risk ratios as high as 10 (Hallqvist et al., 1998), compared with men in higher status jobs. A similar interaction with SES was observed for effort–reward imbalance (Kuper et al., 2002). Among women in the Framingham Heart Study, with baseline data collected in the 1960s, the association between job strain and CVD was higher in clerical workers than for all women (LaCroix, 1984). The combination of work and home stressors may help to explain increased CVD risk in women with lower SES (Haynes & Feinleib, 1980). However, among women in the Framingham Offspring Study, with baseline data that were collected between 1984 and 1987, women in high-status, putatively high-control jobs had the highest risk of developing CVD (Eaker, Sullivan, Kelly-Hayes, D'Agostino, & Benjamin, 2004). This finding may reflect a period of changing social roles—increasing labor force participation among women, including higher status jobs—with residual discrimination, including de facto limited authority as well as wage disparities.

Population Attributable Risk of CVD Due to Psychosocial Work Stressors

A population attributable risk (PAR%) of 7% to 16% was estimated for men in Sweden (Karasek & Theorell, 1990). In Denmark, the PAR% for monotonous high paced work (a conservative proxy measure for job strain) was estimated at 6% for men and 14% for women (Kristensen, Kronitzer, & Alfedsson, 1998). However, few studies have examined the combined or synergistic effect of workplace stressors, which would increase estimates of the proportion of CVD due to work. One Swedish study (Peter et al., 2002) did find that the combined effects of exposure to job strain and to effort–reward imbalance on CVD were stronger than the sum of the separate effects of each model.

Work Stressors and Hypertension

Few studies of work stressors and casual clinic BP have shown significant associations, with the exception of one large study (Guimont et al., 2006). However, strong evidence of an association is found in studies where BP is measured by an ambulatory (i.e., portable) monitor (Belkic et al., 2000). This difference may be explained in part by the imprecision and possible bias of taking casual clinic BP measurements. For example, relaxation can occur when people are away from work, resulting in lower BP. An alternative method is ambulatory blood pressure (ABP) monitoring in which a person wears an automatic BP monitor on his or her arm throughout the day (Pickering, Shimbo, & Haas, 2006). Compared with casual BP measurements, ambulatory monitoring provides a more reliable measure of BP because the number of readings is increased. It is also a more valid measure of mean BP because there is no observer bias and BP is measured during a person's normal daily activities and exposure to the stressors that influence persistent increases in BP. ABP is a better predictor than are casual clinic BP readings of target organ damage, such as increases in the size of the heart's left ventricle (Sega et al., 2001), and CVD (Pierdomenico et al., 2005).

Masked Hypertension

ABP monitoring allows for the identification of masked hypertension (MH), previously labeled *occult* hypertension (Belkic et al., 2001; Schnall, Belkic, Landsbergis, Schwartz, et al., 2000). MH is characterized by elevated ABP outside the clinician's office but normal BP when measured by the clinician in his or her office. The prevalence of MH among nonpatients with normal clinic BP ranges from 10% to 30% (Landsbergis et al., 2008). People with MH have a higher risk of target organ damage, such as increased left ventricular mass (Sega et al., 2001), increased carotid plaque burden (Hara et al., 2007), and increased CVD risk (Hansen et al., 2007) similar to patients with a diagnosis of hypertension and at significantly greater levels than truly normotensive people (i.e., normal clinic and ambulatory BP).

Epidemiologic Data

A variety of work stressors have been associated with BP levels or hypertension in epidemiologic studies. These include job strain, effort–reward imbalance, threat-avoidant vigilance, and long work hours.

JOB STRAIN. Of 11 cross-sectional studies of job strain (or its components) among men, the majority showed significant positive associations with work ABP (Belkic, Landsbergis, et al., 2000). In the five studies in which measurements were also made outside of work, job strain was associated with home or sleep systolic ABP. Both cohort studies of ABP performed among men found significant associations with job strain (Schnall, Landsbergis, Schwartz, Warren, & Pickering, 1998; Theorell et al., 1988). Of the six cross-sectional studies of job strain and ABP among women, four indicate a significant positive association with work systolic ABP (Brisson, 2000). Work systolic ABP among workers facing job strain is typically 4 mm Hg to 8 mm Hg higher than those without job strain.

The Work Site Blood Pressure Study, a longitudinal study of psychosocial factors and ABP, was begun in 1985 in New York City. At the first round of data collection (Time 1), men employed in "high strain" jobs were at increased risk of hypertension ($OR = 2.7$), had increased left ventricular mass index (Schnall et al., 1990), and had higher levels of work (6.7 mm Hg systolic, 2.7 mm Hg diastolic), home, and sleep ABP, controlling for potential confounders (Landsbergis, Schnall, Warren, Pickering, & Schwartz, 1994).

Examining data from Time 1 and a second round of data collection 3 years later (Time 2), a measure of repeated or cumulative exposure to job strain was constructed. The chronically exposed group exhibited an 11 mm Hg to 12 mm Hg higher systolic and 6 mm Hg to 9 mm Hg higher diastolic work ABP than the group unexposed at both times. These effect sizes are substantial, more than twice the difference between African Americans and Whites in this sample and more than the estimated effect of aging 25 years or gaining 50 lb in weight (Schnall et al., 1998). Those reporting job strain at Time 1 but no job strain at Time 2 exhibited a decrease in systolic ABP of 5.3 mm Hg at work and 4.7 mm Hg at home ($p < .05$; Schnall et al., 1998). The decrease in ABP associated with a decrease in job strain over time suggests that early detection and prevention strategies should be effective.

Men with job strain in the Work Site BP Study had a slightly higher risk of MH (defined as $\geq$ 85 mm Hg diastolic ABP and < 85 mm Hg casual BP); however, this association did not reach statistical significance (Belkic et al., 2001; Schnall, Belkic, Landsbergis, Schwartz, et al., 2000). Japanese male managerial employees had significantly higher awake ABP (and MH; K. Yamasue, personal communication, June 16, 2008) than did retirees of similar age (Yamasue, Hayashi, Ohshige, Tochikubo, & Souma, 2008). In unpublished results from a study of New York City health care workers, MH was significantly associated with shift work and with the combination of job strain and effort–reward imbalance.

EFFORT–REWARD IMBALANCE. Studies of high effort/low reward at work have shown significant positive associations with systolic ABP (Vrijkotte, van Doornen, & de Geus, 2000), hypertension in men (Peter & Siegrist, 1997), in men and women (Peter et al., 1998) and with a comanifestation of hypertension and high low-density lipoprotein cholesterol in men (Siegrist, Peter, Georg, Cremer, & Seidel, 1991).

TAV. Professional drivers, air traffic controllers, and sea pilots (jobs characterized by TAV) are reported to show increased risk of hypertension (Belkic et al., 2001). For urban mass transit operators this is related to number of years on the job (Ragland, Greiner, Holman, & Fisher, 1997). Elevated work ABP is also seen in this group compared with referents without exposure to TAV (Ugljesic, Belkic, Boskovic, Avramovic, & Mickovic, 1992).

LONG WORK HOURS. Only one study (from Japan) examined ABP and found evidence linking working more than 55 hr per week and ABP among men (Hayashi, Kobayashi, Yamaoka, & Yano, 1996). Self-report data from California indicated that employees working more than 50 hr per week had a 29% increased risk of self-reported hypertension compared with those working 11 to 39 hr per week (Yang, Schnall, Jauregui, Su, & Baker, 2006).

SYNERGISM WITH LOW SES. An interaction between job strain and low SES was also observed for BP among New York City men (Landsbergis, Schnall,

Pickering, Warren, & Schwartz, 2003) and Framingham men and women (Landsbergis, Schnall, Chace, Sullivan, & D'Agostino, 2005).

Mechanisms by Which Work Stressors Can Lead to CVD Outcomes

There are "intimate connections between the social environment and the central nervous system (CNS), and the CNS and the cardiovascular system via the autonomic and neuroendocrine systems" (Schnall et al., 2000a, p. 2). This interrelation has been labeled *econeurocardiology,* the biological paradigm by which social factors, such as work stressors, are perceived and processed by the CNS, resulting in pathophysiological changes that increase risk of CVD (Belkic, Schnall, Landsbergis, & Baker, 2000; Wolf, 2000). Athough the mechanisms remain to be fully elucidated, at least three possible pathways exist by which job stressors may influence CVD risk (Schnall, Landsbergis, & Baker, 1994): physiological mechanisms (including hypertension and atherosclerosis); increased risk of cardiac events in persons with manifest cardiac disease; and behavioral, social, and psychological pathways.

Physiological Mechanisms

A number of physiological mechanisms by which work stressors can lead to CVD have been identified. The most widely studied mechanism is hypertension.

HYPERTENSION. The strongest empirical evidence for a role for job stressors in the promotion of known CVD risk factors is for hypertension (Belkic et al., 2000a). Sympathetic nervous system overactivity (associated with job stressors) is also implicated in the clustering of hypertension and various atherogenic biochemical abnormalities, together known as the *cardiovascular metabolic syndrome* (CVM). CVM includes hypertension, increased total cholesterol, triglycerides, and insulin; decreased high-density lipoprotein cholesterol; central obesity; insulin resistance and glucose intolerance; and hypercoagulability and reduced fibrinolysis (Fossum, Hoieggen, Moan, Rostrup, & Kjeldsen, 2000).

Frankenhauser and Johansson (1986) confirmed the involvement of two neuroendocrine systems in the stress response: the *sympathoadrenal medullary system* (which secretes the catecholamines, epinephrine, and norepinephrine) and the *hypothalamic–pituitary–adrenal cortical system* (which secretes corticosteroids such as cortisol). Under demanding conditions where organisms can exert control, epinephrine levels increase and cortisol levels may decline (Frankenhaeuser & Johansson, 1986). However, in demanding but low control situations (analogous to job strain), both epinephrine and cortisol are elevated (Schwartz, Belkic, Schnall, & Pickering, 2000), which can have severe consequences for the cardiovascular system. Cortisol enhances and prolongs the effect of epinephrine (Theorell, 2000). The combination of these hormones appears to promote BP elevation (Schwartz et al., 2000a), dyslipidemia (Theorell, 2000b), and CVM (Fossum et al., 2000).

Short-term cortisol and adrenalin elevation has been associated with healthier coping in stressful situations (Karasek & Theorell, 1990). However, chronic elevation of cortisol appears in clinical depression, a risk factor for CVD (Rugulies, 2002) whereas low cortisol levels may also reflect exhausted function, which can be cardiodeleterious as well (Appels & Otten, 1992).

Personal control may reduce the duration of the stress response. Machine-paced and repetitive jobs and excessive overtime tend to prolong *unwinding,* that is, the return of neuroendocrine levels to baseline (Frankenhaeuser & Johansson, 1986). ABP studies indicate a carryover effect in which the work, home, and sleep BP in high strain workers is elevated above levels in other workers (Belkic, Landsbergis, et al., 2000). Another obstacle to unwinding may be the additional responsibility for household and children that many workers (particularly women) face when they return home. A Canadian study found evidence of synergism between family responsibilities and job strain in their effect on BP among college-educated women (Brisson et al., 1999).

ATHEROSCLEROSIS. Hypertension contributes to atherosclerosis (Steptoe & Marmot, 2000). In addition, low decision latitude is associated with high plasma fibrinogen, suggesting a link with coagulation and, thus, atherosclerosis (Brunner et al., 1996). Progression of atherosclerosis has been associated with low job decision latitude (Muntaner et al., 1998), high demands and low economic rewards at work (Lynch, Krause, Kaplan, Salonen, & Salonen, 1997), and job strain in men (Hintsanen et al., 2005). However, in another study, the association with job strain was seen in women but not men (Rosvall et al., 2002).

OTHER PHYSIOLOGICAL MECHANISMS. Although evidence is not always consistent, job stressors have been associated with Type 2 diabetes (Kawakami, Araki, Takatsuka, Shimizu, & Ishibashi, 1999; Kumari, Head, & Marmot, 2004), inadequate sleep (Dahlgren, Kecklund, & Akerstedt, 2006; Knudsen, Ducharme, & Roman, 2007; Nomura, Nakao, Takeuchi, & Yano, 2009), and lowered heart rate variability (Belkic, 2000a; Collins, Karasek, & Costas, 2005; Kageyama et al., 1998; van Amelsvoort, Schouten, Maan, Swene, & Kok, 2000; Vrijkotte et al., 2000). Low socioeconomic status has been associated with the acute phase inflammatory response (Pickering, 2007).

Occupational Risk Factors Associated With New Cardiac Events in Persons With Manifest CVD

The influence of sympathoadrenal activity on cardiovascular function includes increased myocardial oxygen demand and decreased supply that in vulnerable individuals (i.e., persons with manifest CVD) can lead to myocardial ischemia (Belkic, 2000b), destabilization of the cardiac electrical substrate (Belkic, 2000a), and increased risk of clot formation and disruption of unstable plaques (Steptoe & Marmot, 2000). Platelet activation and the concentration of fibrinogen also play a role in acute thrombosis (Steptoe & Marmot, 2000). Job strain may inhibit anabolic (i.e., regenerative) processes, which may contribute to an adverse, atherogenic metabolic profile (Theorell, 2000). Environmental stressors may act as potential triggers of life-threatening arrhythmias and sudden cardiac death in vulnerable persons (Belkic, 2000a). Young men who suffered a heart attack and return to high strain jobs may be particularly at risk of CVD-related mortality (Theorell, Perski, Orth-Gomer, Hamsten, & de Faire, 1991). Among 972 male and female patients followed after first heart attack, those facing chronic job strain had twice the risk of recurrent coronary disease events during 2.2 years of follow-up even after adjustment for 26 potentially confounding factors (Aboa-Éboulé et al., 2007).

Behavioral, Social, and Psychological Mechanisms

Although evidence is not always consistent, job stressors have been associated with cigarette smoking intensity and cessation (Belkic & Nedic, 2007; Kouvonen et al., 2006; Siegrist & Rodel, 2006), obesity (Belkic & Nedic, 2007; Caruso, Hitchcock, Dick, Russo, & Schmit, 2004; Kouvonen et al., 2006; Siegrist & Rodel, 2006), sedentary behavior (Johansson, Johnson, & Hall, 1991; Kouvonen et al., 2006), and alcohol use (Caruso et al., 2004; Kouvonen et al., 2006; Siegrist & Rodel, 2006).

JOB CHARACTERISTICS. Job stressors may increase the risk of hypertension and CVD in part by shaping behavior, personality, or increasing negative affect (e.g., anxiety, anger, depression), or by interacting with behavior, personality, or affect. Karasek's job demand–control model describes the adult socialization of personality traits and behavior patterns which occur at work. Chronic adaptation to low control–low demand situations (i.e., "passive" jobs) can result in reduced self-efficacy, greater external locus of control, reduced ability to solve problems or tackle challenges, and feelings of depression or learned helplessness (Karasek & Theorell, 1990). Conversely, when high (but not overwhelming) job demands are matched with greater authority and skill, more active learning and greater internal locus of control develop, enabling individuals to develop a broader range of coping strategies. For example, in Sweden, workers whose jobs became more passive over 6 years reported less participation in political and leisure activities. In contrast, workers in jobs that became more active participated more in these activities (Karasek & Theorell, 1990). In a U.S. study, evidence was seen for increased intellectual flexibility, nonauthoritarianism, capacity to take responsibility for one's actions, and intellectually demanding leisure time after 10 years among those with greater occupational self-direction, a concept similar to decision latitude (Kohn & Schooler, 1982). This research points to work organization not only as a source of stress and increased disease risk but also potentially as a key factor in the promotion of physical and mental health and the development of one's creative potential, effective coping, and social involvement outside work.

PERSONALITY AND NEGATIVE AFFECT. Empirical support for the concept of the "hypertensive personality" remains equivocal. Hypertension has been associated with internalized aggression (Perini et al., 1990) and with anxiety (Jonas, Franks, & Ingram, 1997; Markovitz, Matthews, Kannel, Cobb, & D'Agostino,

1993), although one study failed to find associations with anger or with anxiety among women (Markovitz et al., 1993). No psychological or personality variables were associated with ABP in the Work Site BP Study (Friedman et al., 2001). One limitation is the lack of a model that predicts specific interactions or mediation between work stressors and personality characteristics in the development of hypertension. For example, suppressed anger was associated with the prevalence of hypertension only among those reporting job stress in a study of male hourly workers (Cottington, Matthews, Talbott, & Kuller, 1986). Other studies have shown that asymptomatic participants with hypertension (Knox, Svensson, Waller, & Theorell, 1988) and those with normal BP with a family history of hypertension (Theorell, 1990) seemed to express fewer emotions and have a noncomplaining attitude (Karasek & Theorell, 1990). Theorell (1990) hypothesized that a stressful work environment "enforces a noncomplaining attitude and prevents development of active emotional coping" (p. 75). Thus, he observed an association between underreporting of stress and an increased physiologic response. Data among urban transport operators corroborate these premises: Operators with borderline or definite hypertension were distinguished from those with normal BP by having a low admitted fear during driving, although showing increased BP rise together with heightened selective attention during laboratory paradigms that mimicked stressful aspects of the traffic environment (Belkic et al., 1996; Emdad et al., 1997).

Job stressors may also increase the risk of CVD in part by influencing personality characteristics or negative affect. Many emotions "are responses to power and status differentials embedded within social situations" (Kubzansky, Kawachi, Weiss, & Sparrow, 1998, p. 55). Associations have been found between job stressors and anxiety (Bourbonnais, Comeau, & Vezina, 1999), burnout (Ahola et al., 2006), depression (Mausner-Dorsch & Eaton, 2000), and hostility (Bosma, Stansfeld, & Marmot, 1998). Depression has been associated prospectively with CVD (Rugulies, 2002).

Matthews and Haynes (1986) pointed out the following:

> [The Type A behavior pattern] is thought to be encouraged by Western society because it appears to offer special rewards and opportunities to those who can think, perform, and even play more rapidly and aggressively than their peers . . . the outcome of a set of predispositions interacting with specific types of eliciting situations, including those that are stressful or challenging. (p. 924)

Evidence exists that the hostility component of Type A is a risk factor for CVD (Smith, 1992), and some studies have found associations between hostility and job stressors (Bosma, Stansfeld, et al., 1998; Landsbergis, Schnall, Deitz, Friedman, & Pickering, 1992). Overcommitment in the effort–reward imbalance model is considered to be "a personal characteristic which is rather stable over time" (Siegrist, Peter, Junge, Cremer, & Seidel, 1990, p. 1128); however, it has been associated with job strain (Peter, 1997).

Finally, negative affectivity (NA) has been proposed as a confounder of the stress–illness association (McCrae, 1990). However, it has not been associated with BP (Landsbergis et al., 1992), and controlling for NA barely affected the association between low job control and CVD (Bosma, Stansfeld, et al., 1998). In short, contrary to widely held beliefs, there is currently little evidence supporting an etiologic role for psychological or personality factors in essential hypertension and limited evidence for CVD.

Prevention and Management of Work-Related Hypertension and CVD

The occupational health psychologist (OHP) can play a key role in the prevention, early detection, and management of work-related hypertension and CVD. As part of a public health strategy, we recommend a team approach in which OHPs work together with clinicians, health educators, ergonomists, epidemiologists, and other health professionals to identify high-risk workplaces and occupations, facilitate the provision of clinical care, and design and implement workplace interventions (Herbert et al., 1997).

Risk Assessment

The first step in this process is work-site surveillance. Experts in Japan, Europe, and the United States called for a program of surveillance at individual workplaces and monitoring at national and regional levels to identify the extent of work-stress related health problems and to provide baselines against which to evaluate efforts at amelioration (The Tokyo Declaration, 1998). First, the surveillance team needs to ascertain whether the current occupation(s) is high risk, whether workers are exposed to any physical, chemical, or psychosocial CVD risk factors at work (Belkic, Schnall, & Ugljesic, 2000). Questionnaires, such as the Job Content Questionnaire (Karasek et al., 1998), the Effort–Reward Imbalance Questionnaire (Siegrist et al., 2004), and the Occupational Stress Index (Belkic, Savic, Theorell, & Cizinsky, 1995) can help assess job characteristics and job stressors. Second, workplace screening, including ABP monitoring, should be conducted for biomedical CVD risk factors. This can help to identify clusters of work-related hypertension and help target work sites for primary and secondary prevention programs.

Another modality of risk assessment is an occupational history of individual workers. We have developed hands-on tools that trained graduate students to acquire this practical skill (available from http://www.workhealth.org/UCLA%20OHP%20class/UCLA%20OHP%20home%20page.html).

Preventing CVD and Improving Employee Cardiovascular Health

Both individual health promotion and workplace protection and prevention programs are needed to combat the epidemic of CVD. However, individual health promotion programs are often of limited efficacy without concomitant primary prevention strategies, including job redesign.

HEALTH PROMOTION. One role for the OHP is counseling patients to reduce their levels of unhealthy behaviors, such as smoking. However, cardiac risk factor counseling in isolation is often unsuccessful, particularly among occupational groups with a heavy burden of exposure to occupational stressors. For example, Fisher and Belkic (2000a) stated, "despite devotion of substantial time and the use of state-of-the-art methods . . . our efforts applied systematically among professional drivers were, at best, only minimally effective, unless there was a concomitant amelioration in stressful working conditions" (pp. 246–247). Although stress management interventions may have positive effects, if employees return to an unchanged work environment and high levels of job stressors, those beneficial effects are likely to be eroded (Nowack, 2000).

A number of researchers have recommended integrating workplace health promotion and occupational health to develop complementary behavioral and environmental interventions (Heaney & Goetzel, 1997). An example is the WellWorks Project conducted in 24 worksites in Massachusetts: "When workers were aware of change their employer had made to reduce exposures to occupational hazards, they were more likely to participate in both smoking control and nutrition activities" (Sorensen, Stoddard, Ockene, Hunt, & Youngstrom, 1996, p. 191). Employees in lower status jobs may be less likely to participate in health promotion programs (Lewis, Huebner, & Yarborough, 1996). Therefore, in the WellWorks Project, barriers to participation, such as blue-collar workers' time constraints and job responsibilities, were addressed through negotiation of time-off for participation in health promotion activities (Sorensen et al., 1995). A new form of cardiovascular health risk appraisal, being used by the New York State Department of Health, assesses employers' support for exercise programs, smoking cessation programs, or healthy food in their cafeterias, as well as organizational level interventions such as flexible work schedules, personal leave, child care programs, and collective bargaining (Golaszewski & Fisher, 2002).

TERTIARY PREVENTION AND RETURN TO WORK AFTER CARDIAC EVENTS. Cardiologists are called on to judge the cardiovascular work fitness of patients who have suffered cardiac events. Complicating the issue is that jobs in which public safety could be compromised with the occurrence of an acute cardiac event (deGaudemaris, 2000) are often those with high exposure to work stressors (e.g., urban transit operators, air traffic controllers; Fisher & Belkic, 2000). Advances in cardiovascular therapy permit the cardiovascular function of many patients to be restored so as to make returning to work potentially possible (deGaudemaris, 2000). The OHP could identify potentially modifiable stressors in the patient's work environment and together with the clinician formulate and implement a plan to provide a safer return to work after cardiac events. (For case examples, see Belkic, 2003.)

Job Redesign

The effectiveness of interventions to improve work organization and job design, reduce job stressors, and create a more healthy work organization have been documented (International Labor Office, 1992; Landsbergis, 2009). For example, an intervention among Swedish civil servants included worker committees which developed and carried out action plans to reduce work stressors. A significant decrease in apolipoprotein B/AI ratio (a risk factor for CVD) occurred in the intervention group but not in the control group, a change not explained by changes in exercise, diet, smoking, or weight (Orth-Gomer, Eriksson, Moser, Theorell, & Fredlund, 1994). An intervention on a bus line in Stockholm was designed to diminish time pressure and promote traffic flow. There was a significant decline in systolic BP (−10.7 mm Hg) in the intervention group that was greater than in the comparison group (−4.3 mm Hg; Rydstedt, Johansson, & Evans, 1998). A Swedish field study showed that systolic BP, heart rate, epinephrine and self-reported fatigue increased significantly from the start to the end of a day shift at a traditional auto assembly line but not at a more flexible work organization with small autonomous groups having greater opportunities to influence the pace and content of their work (Melin, Lundberg, Soderlund, & Granqvist, 1999). A recent review of 90 job stress intervention studies found that *systems approaches* (i.e., emphasizing primary prevention, integrating primary with secondary and tertiary prevention, and including meaningful participation of employees) appear to be the most effective in producing favorable organizational and individual outcomes (Lamontagne, Keegel, Louie, Ostry, & Landsbergis, 2007).

Efforts to regulate (Warren, 2000) or collectively bargain (Landsbergis, 2000) over work organization and work stressors have met with limited success in the United States. Promising recent developments are state legislation, which bans mandatory overtime and provides minimum staffing levels for health care workers, and the California paid family leave law (Milkman & Appelbaum, 2004). Valuable models include legislation in Scandinavia, the European Union (Levi, 2000), and Japan (Shimomitsu & Odagiri, 2000), which regulates work stressors as health hazards, and an agreement on work-related stress by major employer and union federations in Europe (European Trade Union Confederation, Union of Industrial and Employers Confederations of Europe, European Association of Craft Small and Medium-Sized Enterprises, & European Centre of Enterprises with Public Participation and of Enterprises of General Economic Interest, 2004).

OHPs can also work with labor–management committees and other health professionals to develop and evaluate the impact of job redesign programs, help convince employers of the long-term benefits of such programs, involve employees in such programs, and help develop appropriate legislation and regulations. In short, the OHP can potentially play a pivotal, multi-faceted role in helping to create and promote a "heart healthy" work environment.

References

Aboa-Éboulé, C., Brisson, C., Maunsell, E., Masse, B., Bourbonnais, R., Vezina, M., . . . Dagenais, G. R. (2007). Job strain and risk of acute recurrent coronary heart disease events. *JAMA, 298,* 1652–1660. doi:10.1001/jama.298.14.1652

Ahola, K., Honkonen, T., Kivimäki, M., Virtanen, M., Isometsä, E., Aromaa, A., Lönnqvist, J. (2006). Contribution of burnout to the association between job strain and depression: The Health 2000 Study. *Journal of Occupational and Environmental Medicine, 48,* 1023–1030. doi:10.1097/01.jom.0000237437.84513.92

Appels, A., & Otten, F. (1992). Exhaustion as precursor of cardiac death. *The British Journal of Clinical Psychology, 31,* 351–356.

Belkic, K. (2000a). Cardiac electrical stability and environmental stress. *Occupational Medicine: State of the Art Reviews, 15*(1), 117–120.

Belkic, K. (2000b). Myocardial oxygen supply and demand: Environmental triggers of imbalance. *Occupational Medicine: State of the Art Reviews, 15*(1), 132–136.

Belkic, K. (2003). *The Occupational Stress Index: An approach derived from cognitive ergonomics and brain research for clinical practice.* Cambridge, England: Cambridge International Science Publishing.

Belkic, K., Emdad, R., & Theorell, T. (1998). Occupational profile and cardiac risk: Possible mechanisms and implications for professional drivers. *International Journal of Occupational Medicine and Environmental Health, 11,* 37–57.

Belkic, K., Emdad, R., Theorell, T., Cizinsky, S., Wennberg, A., Hagman, M., . . . Olsson, K. (1996). *Neurocardiac mechanisms of heart disease risk among professional drivers. Final report.* Stockholm, Sweden: Swedish Fund for Working Life.

Belkic, K., Landsbergis, P., Schnall, P., & Baker, D. (2004). Is job strain a major source of cardiovascular disease risk? *Scandinavian Journal of Work, Environment & Health, 30,* 85–128.

Belkic, K., Landsbergis, P. A., Schnall, P., Baker, D., Theorell, T., Siegrist, J., . . . Karasek, R. (2000). Psychosocial factors: Review of the empirical data among men. *Occupational Medicine: State of the Art Reviews, 15*(1), 24–46.

Belkic, K., & Nedic, O. (2007). Workplace stressors and lifestyle-related cancer risk factors among female physicians: Assessment using the Occupational Stress Index. *Journal of Occupational Health, 49,* 61–71. doi:10.1539/joh.49.61

Belkic, K., Savic, C., Djordjevic, M., Ugljesic, M., & Mickovic, L. (1992). Event-related potentials in professional city drivers: Heightened sensitivity to cognitively relevant visual signals. *Physiology & Behavior, 52,* 423–427. doi:10.1016/0031-9384(92)90327-X

Belkic, K., Savic, C., Theorell, T., & Cizinsky, S. (1995). *Work stressors and cardiovascular risk: Assessment for clinical practice. Part I* (No. 256). Stockholm, Sweden: National Institute for Psychosocial Factors and Health, Karolinska Institute, WHO Psychosocial Center.

Belkic, K., Schnall, P., Landsbergis, P., & Baker, D. (2000). The workplace and CV health: Conclusions and thoughts for a future agenda. *Occupational Medicine: State of the Art Reviews, 15*(1), 307–322.

Belkic, K. L., Schnall, P. L., Landsbergis, P. A., Schwartz, J. E., Gerber, L., Baker, D., & Pickering, T. G. (2001). Hypertension at the workplace—An occult disease? The need for work site surveillance. *Advances in Psychosomatic Medicine, 22,* 116–138. doi:10.1159/000059280

Belkic, K., Schnall, P., Savic, C., & Landsbergis, P. A. (2000). Multiple exposures: Toward a model of total occupational burden. *Occupational Medicine: State-of-the-Art Reviews, 15*(1), 94–98.

Belkic, K., Schnall, P., & Ugljesic, M. (2000). Cardiovascular evaluation of the worker and workplace: A practical guide for clinicians. *Occupational Medicine: State of the Art Reviews, 15*(1), 213–222.

Boggild, H., & Knutsson, A. (1999). Shift work, risk factors, and cardiovascular disease. *Scandinavian Journal of Work, Environment & Health, 25,* 85–99.

Bond, J. T., Galinsky, E., & Swanberg, J. E. (1998). *The 1997 National Study of the Changing Workforce.* New York, NY: Families and Work Institute.

Bosma, H., Peter, R., Siegrist, J., & Marmot, M. (1998). Two alternative job stress models and the risk of coronary heart disease. *American Journal of Public Health, 88,* 68–74. doi:10.2105/AJPH. 88.1.68

Bosma, H., Stansfeld, S. A., & Marmot, M. G. (1998). Job control, personal characteristics, and heart disease. *Journal of Occupational Health Psychology, 3,* 402–409. doi:10.1037/1076-8998.3.4.402

Bourbonnais, R., Comeau, M., & Vezina, M. (1999). Job strain and evolution of mental health among nurses. *Journal of Occupational Health Psychology, 4,* 95–107. doi:10.1037/1076-8998.4.2.95

Brisson, C. (2000). Women, work, and cardiovascular disease. *Occupational Medicine: State of the Art Reviews, 15*(1), 49–57.

Brisson, C., Laflamme, N., Moisan, J., Milot, A., Masse, B., & Vezina, M. (1999). Effect of family responsibilities and job strain on ambulatory blood pressure among white-collar women. *Psychosomatic Medicine, 61,* 205–213.

Brunner, E., Smith, G. D., Marmot, M. G., Canner, R., Beksinska, M., & O'Brien, J. (1996). Childhood social circumstances and psychosocial and behavioral factors as determinants of plasma fibrinogen. *Lancet, 347,* 1008–1013. doi:10.1016/S0140-6736(96)90147-6

Caruso, C., Hitchcock, E., Dick, R., Russo, J., & Schmit, J. (2004). *Overtime and extended work shifts: Recent findings on illnesses, injuries, and health behaviors* (No. 2004–143). Cincinnati, OH: NIOSH.

Collins, S. M., Karasek, R. A., & Costas, K. (2005). Job strain and autonomic indices of cardiovascular disease risk. *American Journal of Industrial Medicine, 48,* 182–193. doi:10.1002/ajim.20204

Cooper, R. S., Rotimi, C. N., & Ward, R. (1999, February). The puzzle of hypertension in African-Americans. *Scientific American, 280,* 56–63.

Cottington, E. M., Matthews, K. A., Talbott, E., & Kuller, L. H. (1986). Occupational stress, suppressed anger, and hypertension. *Psychosomatic Medicine, 48,* 249–260.

Dahlgren, A., Kecklund, G., & Akerstedt, T. (2006). Overtime work and its effects on sleep, sleepiness, cortisol, and blood pressure in an experimental field study. *Scandinavian Journal of Work, Environment & Health, 32,* 318–327.

deGaudemaris, R. (2000). Clinical issues: Return to work and public safety. *Occupational Medicine: State of the Art Reviews, 15*(1), 223–230.

Eaker, E., Sullivan, L., Kelly-Hayes, M., D'Agostino, R., & Benjamin, E. (2004). Does job strain increase the risk for coronary heart disease or death in men and women? *American Journal of Epidemiology, 159,* 950–958. doi:10.1093/aje/kwh127

Emdad, R., Belkic, K., Theorell, T., Cizinsky, S., Savic, C., & Olsson, K. (1997). Work environment, neurophysiologic, and psychophysiologic models among professional drivers with and without cardiovascular disease: Seeking an integrative neurocariologic approach. *Stress Medicine, 13,* 7–21. doi:10.1002/(SICI)1099-1700(199701)13:1<7::AID-SMI709>3.0.CO;2-J

European Foundation for the Improvement of Living and Working Conditions. (1997). *Time constraints and autonomy at work in the European Union.* Dublin, Ireland: Author.

European Foundation for the Improvement of Living and Working Conditions. (2006). *Fifteen years of working conditions in the EU: Charting the trends.* Dublin, Ireland: Author.

European Foundation for the Improvement of Living and Working Conditions. (2005). *Finnish quality of work life surveys.* Dublin, Ireland: Author.

European Trade Union Confederation, Union of Industrial and Employers Confederations of Europe, European Association of Craft Small and Medium-Sized Enterprises, & European Centre of Enterprises with Public Participation and of Enterprises of General Economic Interest. (2004). *Framework agreement on work-related stress.* Retrieved from http://www.etuc.org/a/529

Ferrie, J. E., Shipley, M. J., Cappuccio, F. P., Brunner, E., Miller, M. A., Kumari, M., & Marmot, M. G. (2007). A prospective study of change in sleep duration: Associations with mortality in the Whitehall II cohort. *Sleep, 30,* 1659–1666.

Ferrie, J. E., Shipley, M. J., Marmot, M., Stansfeld, S., & Smith, G. D. (1998). The health effects of major organisational change and job insecurity. *Social Science & Medicine, 46,* 243–254. doi:10.1016/S0277-9536(97)00158-5

Fisher, J., & Belkic, K. (2000). A public health approach in clinical practice. *Occupational Medicine: State of the Art Reviews, 15*(1), 245–256.

Fossum, E., Hoieggen, A., Moan, A., Rostrup, M., & Kjeldsen, S. E. (2000). The cardiovascular metabolic syndrome. *Occupational Medicine: State of the Art Reviews, 15*(1), 146–150.

Frankenhaeuser, M., & Johansson, G. (1986). Stress at work: Psychobiological and psychosocial aspects. *International Review of Applied Psychology, 35,* 287–299. doi:10.1111/j.1464-0597.1986.tb00928.x

Friedman, R., Schwartz, J. E., Schnall, P. L., Landsbergis, P. A., Pieper, C., Gerin, W., Pickering, T. G. (2001). Psychological variables in hypertension: Relationship to casual or ambulatory blood pressure in men. *Psychosomatic Medicine, 63*(1), 19–31.

Gaziano, J. (2004). Global burden of cardiovascular disease. In D. Zipes, P. Libby, R. Bonow, & E. Braunwald (Eds.), *Heart disease* (pp. 1–19). London, England: Elsevier.

Golaszewski, T., & Fisher, B. (2002). Heart check: The development and evolution of an organizational heart health assessment. *American Journal of Health Promotion, 17,* 132–153.

González, M. A., Artalejo, F. R., & Calero, J. R. (1998). Relationship between socioeconomic status and ischaemic heart disease in cohort and case-control studies: 1960–1993. *International Journal of Epidemiology, 27,* 350–358. doi:10.1093/ije/27.3.350

Greiner, B., Krause, N., Ragland, D., & Fisher, J. (2004). Occupational stressors and hypertension: A multi-method study using observer-based job analysis and self-reports in urban transit operators. *Social Science & Medicine, 59,* 1081–1094. doi:10.1016/j.socscimed.2003.12.006

Guimont, C., Brisson, C., Dagenais, G., Milot, A., Vézina, M., Mâsse, B., . . . Blanchette, C. (2006). Effects of job strain on blood pressure: A prospective study of male and female white-collar workers. *American Journal of Public Health, 96,* 1436–1443. doi:10.2105/AJPH.2004.057679

Gustafsson, R., & Lundberg, I. (2004). *Arbetsliv och hälsa 2004.* Stockholm, Sweden: Arbetslivsinstitutet/Arbetsmiljöverket.

Hajjar, I., Kotchen, J., & Kotchen, T. (2006). Hypertension: Trends in prevalence, incidence, and control. *Annual Review of Public Health, 27,* 465–490. doi:10.1146/annurev.publhealth.27.021405. 102132

Hallqvist, J., Diderichsen, F., Theorell, T., Reuterwall, C., & Ahlbom, A. (1998). Is the effect of job strain on myocardial infarction due to interaction between high psychological demands and low decision latitude? Results from Stockholm Heart Epidemiology Program (SHEEP). *Social Science & Medicine, 46,* 1405–1415. doi:10.1016/S0277-9536(97)10084-3

Hansen, T. W., Kikuya, M., Thijs, L., Björklund-Bodegård, K., Kuznetsova, T., Ohkubo, T., . . . Staessen, J. A. (2007). Prognostic superiority of daytime ambulatory over conventional blood pressure in four populations: A meta-analysis of 7,030 individuals. *Journal of Hypertension, 25,* 1554–1564. doi:10.1097/HJH.0b013e3281c49da5

Hara, A., Ohkubo, T., Kikuya, M., Shintani, Y., Obara, T., Metoki, H., . . . Imai, Y. (2007). Detection of carotid atherosclerosis in subjects with masked hypertension and whitecoat hypertension by self-measured blood pressure at home: The Ohasama Study. *Journal of Hypertension, 25,* 321–327. doi:10.1097/HJH.0b013e3280115bbf

Hayashi, T., Kobayashi, Y., Yamaoka, K., & Yano, E. (1996). Effect of overtime work on 24-hour ambulatory blood pressure. *Journal of Occupational and Environmental Medicine, 38,* 1007–1011. doi:10.1097/00043764-199610000-00010

Haynes, S. G., & Feinleib, M. (1980). Women, work, and coronary heart disease: Prospective findings from the Framingham Heart Study. *American Journal of Public Health, 70,* 133–141. doi:10.2105/AJPH.70.2.133

Heaney, C. A., & Goetzel, R. Z. (1997). A review of health-related outcomes of multi-component worksite health promotion programs. *American Journal of Health Promotion, 11,* 290–307.

Herbert, R., Plattus, B., Kellogg, L., Luo, J., Marcus, M., Mascolo, A., & Landrigan, P. J. (1997). The union health center: A working model of clinical care linked to preventive occupational health services. *American Journal of Industrial Medicine, 31,* 263–273. doi:10.1002/(SICI)1097-0274(199703)31:3<263::AID-AJIM1>3.0.CO;2-Z

Hintsanen, M., Kivimaki, M., Elovainio, M., Pulkki-Raback, L., Keskivaara, P., Juonala, M., . . . Keltikangas-Järvinen, L. (2005). Job strain and early atherosclerosis: The Cardiovascular Risk in Young Finns study. *Psychosomatic Medicine, 67,* 740–747. doi:10.1097/01. psy.0000181271.04169.93

International Labor Office. (1992). *Conditions of Work Digest: Preventing stress at work.* Geneva, Switzerland: International Labor Office.

Johansson, G., Johnson, J. V., & Hall, E. M. (1991). Smoking and sedentary behavior as related to work organization. *Social Science & Medicine, 32,* 837–846. doi:10.1016/0277-9536(91)90310-9

Johnson, J. V., & Hall, E. M. (1988). Job strain, workplace social support, and cardiovascular disease: A cross-sectional study of a random sample of the Swedish working population. *American Journal of Public Health, 78,* 1336–1342. doi:10.2105/AJPH.78.10.1336

Jonas, B. S., Franks, P., & Ingram, D. D. (1997). Are symptoms of anxiety and depression risk factors for hypertension? Longitudinal evidence from the National Health and Nutrition Examination Survey I Epidemiologic Follow-Up Study. *Archives of Family Medicine, 6,* 43–49. doi:10.1001/archfami.6.1.43

Kageyama, T., Nishikido, N., Kobayashi, T., Kurokawa, Y., Kaneko, T., & Kabuto, M. (1998). Long commuting time, extensive overtime, and sympathodominant state assessed in terms of short-term heart rate variability among male white-collar workers in the Tokyo megalopolis. *Industrial Health, 36,* 209–217.

Kanjilal, S., Gregg, E. W., Cheng, Y. J., Zhang, P., Nelson, D. E., Mensah, G., & Beckles, G. L. A. (2006). Socioeconomic status and trends in disparities in 4 major risk factors for cardiovascular disease among US adults, 1971–2002. *Archives of Internal Medicine, 166,* 2348–2355. doi:10. 1001/archinte.166.21.2348

Kaplan, G. A., & Keil, J. E. (1993). Socioeconomic factors and cardiovascular disease: A review of the literature. *Circulation, 88,* 1973–1998.

Kaplan, G. A., & Lynch, J. (1999). Socioeconomic considerations in the primordial prevention of cardiovascular disease. *Preventive Medicine, 29,* S30–S35. doi:10.1006/pmed.1999.0540

Karasek, R., Brisson, C., Kawakami, N., Houtman, I., Bongers, P., & Amick, B. (1998). The job content questionnaire (JCQ): An instrument for internationally comparative assessments of psychosocial job characteristics. *Journal of Occupational Health Psychology, 3,* 322–355. doi:10.1037/1076-8998.3.4.322

Karasek, R., & Theorell, T. (1990). *Healthy work: Stress, productivity, and the reconstruction of working life.* New York, NY: Basic Books.

Kawachi, I., & Marmot, M. (1998). What can we learn from studies of occupational class and cardiovascular disease? *American Journal of Epidemiology, 148,* 160–163.

Kawakami, N., Araki, S., Takatsuka, N., Shimizu, H., & Ishibashi, H. (1999). Overtime, psychosocial working conditions, and occurrence of noninsulin dependent diabetes mellitus in Japanese men. *Journal of Epidemiology and Community Health, 53,* 359–363. doi:10.1136/jech.53.6.359

Kivimäki, M., Ferrie, J., Brunner, E., Head, J., Shipley, M., Vahtera, J., & Marmot, M. G. (2005). Justice at work and reduced risk of coronary heart disease among employees: The Whitehall II Study. *Archives of Internal Medicine, 165,* 2245–2251. doi:10.1001/archinte.165.19.2245

Kivimäki, M., Leino-Arjas, P., Luukkonen, R., Riihimaki, H., Vahtera, J., & Kirjonen, J. (2002). Work stress and risk of cardiovascular mortality: Prospective cohort study of industrial employees. *British Medical Journal, 325,* 857. doi:10.1136/bmj.325.7369.857

Kivimäki, M., Vahtera, J., Pentti, J., & Ferrie, J. E. (2000). Factors underlying the effect of organisational downsizing on health of employees: Longitudinal cohort study. *British Medical Journal, 320,* 971–975. doi:10.1136/bmj.320.7240.971

Knox, S., Svensson, J., Waller, D., & Theorell, T. (1988). Emotional coping and the psychophysiological substrates of elevated blood pressure. *Behavioral Medicine, 2,* 52–58.

Knudsen, H. K., Ducharme, L. J., & Roman, P. M. (2007). Job stress and poor sleep quality: Data from an American sample of full-time workers. *Social Science & Medicine, 64,* 1997–2007. doi:10.1016/j.socscimed.2007.02.020

Kohn, M. L., & Schooler, C. (1982). Job conditions and personality: A longitudinal assessment of their reciprocal effects. *American Journal of Sociology, 87,* 1257–1286. doi:10.1086/227593

Kouvonen, A., Kivimäki, M., Virtanen, M., Heponiemi, T., Elovainio, M., Pentti, J., . . . Vahtera, J. (2006). Effort–reward imbalance at work and the co-occurrence of lifestyle risk factors: Cross-sectional survey in a sample of 36,127 public sector employees. *BMC Public Health, 6,* 24. doi:10.1186/1471-2458-6-24

Kristensen, T. S., Kronitzer, M., & Alfedsson, L. (1998). *Social factors, work, stress, and cardiovascular disease prevention.* Brussels, Belgium: The European Heart Network.

Kubzansky, L. D., Kawachi, I., Weiss, S., & Sparrow, D. (1998). Anxiety and coronary heart disease: A synthesis of epidemiological, psychological, and experimental evidence. *Annals of Behavioral Medicine, 20*(2), 47–58. doi:10.1007/BF02884448

Kumari, M., Head, J., & Marmot, M. (2004). Prospective study of social and other risk factors for incidence of Type 2 diabetes in the Whitehall II Study. *Archives of Internal Medicine, 164,* 1873–1880. doi:10.1001/archinte.164.17.1873

Kuper, H., Singh-Manouz, A., Siegrist, J., & Marmot, M. (2002). When reciprocity fails: Effort–reward imbalance in relation to coronary heart disease and health functioning in the Whitehall II study. *Occupational and Environmental Medicine, 59,* 777–784. doi:10.1136/oem.59.11.777

LaCroix, A. Z. (1984). *High demands / low control work and the incidence of CHD in the Framingham cohort* (Unpublished doctoral dissertation). University of North Carolina, Chapel Hill.

Lamontagne, A., Keegel, T., Louie, A., Ostry, A., & Landsbergis, P. (2007). A systematic review of the job stress intervention evaluation literature: 1990–2005. *International Journal of Occupational and Environmental Health, 13,* 268–280.

Landsbergis, P. (2000). Collective bargaining to reduce CVD risk factors in the work environment. *Occupational Medicine: State-of-the-Art Reviews, 15*(1), 287–292.

Landsbergis, P. (2003). The changing organization of work and the health and safety of working people: A commentary. *Journal of Occupational and Environmental Medicine, 45,* 61–72. doi:10.1097/00043764-200301000-00014

Landsbergis, P. (2009). Interventions to reduce job stress and improve work organization and worker health. In P. Schnall, E. Rosskam, M. Dobson, D. Gordon, P. Landsbergis, & D. Baker (Eds.), *Unhealthy work: Causes, consequences, and cures* (pp. 193–209). Amityville, NY: Baywood Publishing.

Landsbergis, P., Schnall, P., Belkic, K., Schwartz, J., Baker, D., & Pickering, T. (2008). Work conditions and masked (hidden) hypertension—Insights into the global epidemic of hypertension. *Scandinavian Journal of Work, Environment, and Health, Suppl 2008, 6,* 41–51.

Landsbergis, P., Schnall, P., Chace, R., Sullivan, L., & D'Agostino, R. (2005). *Psychosocial job stressors and cardiovascular disease in the Framingham Offspring Study: A prospective analysis.* Poster session presented at the Fourth International Commission on Occupational Health Conference on Work Environment and Cardiovascular Disease, Newport Beach, CA.

Landsbergis, P. A., Schnall, P. L., Deitz, D., Friedman, R., & Pickering, T. (1992). The patterning of psychological attributes and distress by "job strain" and social support in a sample of working men. *Journal of Behavioral Medicine, 15,* 379–405. doi:10.1007/BF00844730

Landsbergis, P., Schnall, P., Pickering, T., Warren, K., & Schwartz, J. (2003). Lower socioeconomic status among men in relation to the association between job strain and blood pressure. *Scandinavian Journal of Work, Environment & Health, 29,* 206–215.

Landsbergis, P. A., Schnall, P. L., Warren, K., Pickering, T. G., & Schwartz, J. E. (1994). Association between ambulatory blood pressure and alternative formulations of job strain. *Scandinavian Journal of Work, Environment & Health, 20,* 349–363.

Levi, L. (2000). Legislation to protect worker CV health in Europe. *Occupational Medicine: State-of-the-Art Reviews, 15*(1), 269–273.

Lewis, R. J., Huebner, W. H., & Yarborough, C. M. (1996). Characteristics of participants and non-participants in worksite health promotion. *American Journal of Health Promotion, 11,* 99–106.

Liu, Y., & Tanaka, H. (2002). Overtime work, insufficient sleep, and risk of nonfatal acute myocardial infarction in Japanese men (The Fukuoka Heart Study Group). *Occupational and Environmental Medicine, 59,* 447–451. doi:10.1136/oem.59.7.447

Lynch, J., Krause, N., Kaplan, G. A., Salonen, R., & Salonen, J. T. (1997). Workplace demands, economic reward, and progression of carotid atherosclerosis. *Circulation, 96,* 302–307.

Markovitz, J., Matthews, K. A., Kannel, W. B., Cobb, J. L., & D'Agostino, J. B. (1993). Psychological predictors of hypertension in the Framingham Study: Is there tension in hypertension? *JAMA, 270,* 2439–2443. doi:10.1001/jama.270.20.2439

Matthews, K. A., & Haynes, S. G. (1986). Type A behavior pattern and coronary disease risk: Update and critical evaluation. *American Journal of Epidemiology, 123,* 923–960.

Mausner-Dorsch, H., & Eaton, W. (2000). Psychosocial work environment and depression: epidemiologic assessment of the demand–control model. *American Journal of Public Health, 90,* 1765–1770. doi:10.2105/AJPH.90.11.1765

McCrae, R. R. (1990). Controlling neuroticism in the measurement of stress. *Stress Medicine, 6,* 237–241. doi:10.1002/smi.2460060309

McGovern, P. G., Jacobs, D. R., Jr., Shahar, E., Arnett, D. K., Folsom, A. R., Blackburn, H., & Luepker, R. V. (2001). Trends in acute coronary heart disease mortality, morbidity, and medical care from 1985 through 1997: The Minnesota Heart Survey. *Circulation, 104,* 19–24.

Melin, B., Lundberg, U., Soderlund, J., & Granqvist, M. (1999). Psychophysiological stress reactions of male and female assembly workers: A comparison between two different forms of work organization. *Journal of Organizational Behavior, 20,* 47–61. doi:10.1002/(SICI)1099-1379(199901)20:1<47::AID-JOB871>3.0.CO;2-F

Michie, S., & Cockcroft, A. (1996). Overwork can kill: Especially if combined with high demand, low control, and poor social support. *British Medical Journal, 312,* 921–922.

Milkman, R., & Appelbaum, E. (2004). Paid family leave in California: New research findings. *The State of California Labor, 4,* 45–67.

Mishel, L., & Bernstein, J. (2006). *The state of working America.* Washington, DC: Economic Policy Institute.

Muntaner, C., Nieto, F. J., Cooper, L., Meyer, J., Szklo, M., & Tyroler, H. A. (1998). Work organization and artherosclerosis: Findings from the ARIC study. *American Journal of Preventive Medicine, 14,* 9–18. doi:10.1016/S0749-3797(97)00018-4

National Center for Health Statistics. (2006). *2006 Chartbook on trends in the health of Americans.* Hyattsville, MD: Author.

National Institute for Occupational Safety and Health. (2002). *The changing organization of work and the safety and health of working people* (No. 2002–116). Cincinnati, OH: Author.

National Sleep Foundation. (2005). *Sleep in America poll.* Washington, DC: Author.

Nomura, K., Nakao, M., Takeuchi, T., & Yano, E. (2009). Associations of insomnia with job strain, control, and support among male Japanese workers. *Sleep Medicine, 10,* 626–629.

Nowack, K. (2000). Screening and management of the workplace in relation to cardiovascular disease risk. *Occupational Medicine: State-of-the-Art Reviews, 15*(1), 231–233.

Orth-Gomer, K., Eriksson, I., Moser, V., Theorell, T., & Fredlund, P. (1994). Lipid lowering through work stress reduction. *International Journal of Behavioral Medicine, 1,* 204–214. doi:10.1207/s15327558ijbm0103_2

Paoli, P., & Merllié, D. (2001). *Third European Survey on Working Conditions.* Dublin: European Foundation for the Improvement of Living and Working Conditions.

Perini, C., Muller, F. B., Rauchfleisch, U., Battegay, R., Hobi, V., & Buhler, F. R. (1990). Psychosomatic factors in borderline hypertensive subjects and offspring of hypertensive parents. *Hypertension, 16,* 627–634.

Peter, R. (1997). Comparative analysis of the effort–reward imbalance model and the job strain model: Preliminary results from a Swedish case-control study. In The Heart at Work Network, *Socio-economic variations in cardiovascular disease in Europe: The impact of the work environment and lifestyle* (pp. 102–104). London, England: University College London, Department of Epidemiology and Public Health.

Peter, R., Alfredsson, L., Hammar, N., Siegrist, J., Theorell, T., & Westerholm, P. (1998). High effort, low reward, and cardiovascular risk factors in employed Swedish men and women: Baseline results from the WOLF Study. *Journal of Epidemiology and Community Health, 52,* 540–547. doi:10.1136/jech.52.9.540

Peter, R., & Siegrist, J. (1997). Chronic work stress, sickness absence, and hypertension in middle managers: General or specific sociological explanations? *Social Science & Medicine, 45,* 1111–1120. doi:10.1016/S0277-9536(97)00039-7

Peter, R., Siegrist, J., Hallqvist, J., Reuterwall, C., & Theorell, T. (2002). Psychosocial work environment and myocardial infarction: Improving risk estimation by combining two complementary job stress models in the SHEEP Study. *Journal of Epidemiology and Community Health, 56,* 294–300. doi:10.1136/jech.56.4.294

Pickering, T. G. (2007). Stress, inflammation, and hypertension. *Journal of Clinical Hypertension, 9,* 567–571. doi:10.1111/j.1524-6175.2007.06301.x

Pickering, T. G., Shimbo, D., & Haas, D. (2006). Ambulatory blood pressure monitoring. *The New England Journal of Medicine, 354,* 2368–2374. doi:10.1056/NEJMra060433

Pierdomenico, S. D., Lapenna, D., Bucci, A., Di Tommaso, R., Di Mascio, R., Manente, B., . . . Mezzetti, A. (2005). Cardiovascular outcome in treated hypertensive patients with responder, masked, false resistant, and true resistant hypertension. *American Journal of Hypertension, 18,* 1422–1428. doi:10.1016/j.amjhyper.2005.05.014

Ragland, D. R., Greiner, B. A., Holman, B. L., & Fisher, J. M. (1997). Hypertension and years of driving in transit vehicle operators. *Scandinavian Journal of Social Medicine, 25,* 271–279.

Robertson, R. E., Fallavollita, B. S., Siegel, L. L., Peterson, J. L., Campbell, J. R., Schwimer, D. A., . . . McMurray, J. S. (2006). *Employment Arrangements: Improved outreach could help ensure proper worker classification* (GAO-06-656). Washington, DC: U.S. Government Accountability Office.

Rosamond, W. D., Folsom, A. R., Chambless, L. E., & Wang, C.-H. (2001). Coronary heart disease trends in four United States communities. The Atherosclerosis Risk in Communities (ARIC) Study 1987–1996. *International Journal of Epidemiology, 30,* S17–S22.

Rosvall, M., Ostergren, P.-O., Hedblad, B., Isacsson, S.-O., Janzon, L., & Berglund, G. (2002). Work-related psychosocial factors and carotid atherosclerosis. *International Journal of Epidemiology, 31,* 1169–1178. doi:10.1093/ije/31.6.1169

Rugulies, R. (2002). Depression as a predictor for coronary heart disease: A review and meta-analysis. *American Journal of Preventive Medicine, 23,* 51–61. doi:10.1016/S0749-3797(02)00439-7

Rydstedt, L. W., Johansson, G., & Evans, G. W. (1998). The human side of the road: Improving the working conditions of urban bus drivers. *Journal of Occupational Health Psychology, 3,* 161–171. doi:10.1037/1076-8998.3.2.161

Schnall, P., Belkic, K., Landsbergis, P. A., & Baker, D. (2000a). Why the workplace and cardiovascular disease? *Occupational Medicine:State-of-the-Art Reviews, 15*(1), 1–5.

Schnall, P., Belkic, K., Landsbergis, P. A., & Baker, D. (2000b). The workplace and cardiovascular disease. *Occupational Medicine: State-of-the-Art Reviews, 15*(1).

Schnall, P., Belkic, K., Landsbergis, P., Schwartz, J., Gerber, L., Baker, D., & Pickering, T. G. (2000). Hypertension at the workplace—Often an occult disease: The relevance and potential in Japan for work site surveillance? *Japanese Journal of Stress Sciences, 15,* 152–174.

Schnall, P. L., & Kern, R. (1981). Hypertension in American society: An introduction to historical materialist epidemiology. In P. Conrad & R. Kern (Eds.), *The Sociology of Health and Illness: Critical Perspectives* (pp. 97–122). New York, NY: St. Martin's Press.

Schnall, P. L., Landsbergis, P. A., & Baker, D. (1994). Job strain and cardiovascular disease. *Annual Review of Public Health, 15,* 381–411. doi:10.1146/annurev.pu.15.050194.002121

Schnall, P. L., Landsbergis, P. A., Schwartz, J., Warren, K., & Pickering, T. G. (1998). A longitudinal study of job strain and ambulatory blood pressure: Results from a three-year follow-up. *Psychosomatic Medicine, 60,* 697–706.

Schnall, P. L., Pieper, C., Schwartz, J. E., Karasek, R. A., Schlussel, Y., Devereux, R. B., . . . Pickering, T. G. (1990). The relationship between "job strain," workplace diastolic blood pressure, and left ventricular mass index. Results of a case-control study [published erratum appears in *JAMA* 1992(9), 1209]. *JAMA, 263*(14), 1929–1935. doi:10.1001/jama.263.14.1929

Schwartz, J., Belkic, K., Schnall, P., & Pickering, T. (2000). Mechanisms leading to hypertension and CV morbidity. *Occupational Medicine: State of the Art Reviews, 15*(1), 121–132.

Sega, R., Trocino, G., Lanzarotti, A., Carugo, S., Cesana, G., Schiavina, R., . . . Mancia, G. (2001). Alterations of cardiac structure in patients with isolated office, ambulatory, or home hypertension: Data from the general population (Pressione Arteriose Monitorate E Loro Associazioni [PAMELA] Study). *Circulation, 104,* 1385–1392. doi:10.1161/hc3701.096100

Shimomitsu, T., & Odagiri, Y. (2000). Working life in Japan. *Occupational Medicine: State of the Art Reviews, 15*(1), 280–281.

Siegrist, J. (1996). Adverse health effects of high-effort/low-reward conditions. *Journal of Occupational Health Psychology, 1,* 27–41. doi:10.1037/1076-8998.1.1.27

Siegrist, J., Peter, R., Georg, W., Cremer, P., & Seidel, D. (1991). Psychosocial and biobehavioral characteristics of hypertensive men with elevated atherogenic lipids. *Atherosclerosis, 86,* 211–218. doi:10.1016/0021-9150(91)90217-Q

Siegrist, J., Peter, R., Junge, A., Cremer, P., & Seidel, D. (1990). Low status control, high effort at work and ischaemic heart disease: Prospective evidence from blue collar men. *Social Science & Medicine, 31,* 1127–1134. doi:10.1016/0277-9536(90)90234-J

Siegrist, J., & Rodel, A. (2006). Work stress and health risk behavior. *Scandinavian Journal of Work, Environment & Health, 32,* 473–481.

Siegrist, J., Starke, D., Chandola, T., Godin, I., Marmot, M., Niedhammer, I., & Peter, R. (2004). The measurement of effort–reward imbalance at work: European comparisons. *Social Science & Medicine, 58,* 1483–1499. doi:10.1016/S0277-9536(03)00351-4

Smith, T. W. (1992). Hostility and health: Current status of a psychosomatic hypothesis. *Health Psychology, 11,* 139–150. doi:10.1037/0278-6133.11.3.139

Sokejima, S., & Kagamimori, S. (1998). Working hours as a risk factor for acute myocardial infarction in Japan: Case-control study. *British Medical Journal, 317,* 775–780.

Sorensen, G., Himmelstein, J. S., Hunt, M. K., Youngstrom, R., Hebert, J. R., Hammond, S. K., . . . Ockene, J. K. (1995). A model for worksite cancer prevention: Integration of health protection and health promotion in the WellWorks Project. *American Journal of Health Promotion, 10*(1), 55–62.

Sorensen, G., Stoddard, A., Ockene, J. K., Hunt, M. K., & Youngstrom, R. (1996). Worker participation in an integrated health promotion/health protection program: Results from the WellWorks Project. *Health Education Quarterly, 23,* 191–203.

Steenland, K. (2000). Shift work, long hours, and CVD: A review. *Occupational Medicine: State-of-the-Art Reviews, 15*(1), 7–17.

Steptoe, A., & Marmot, M. (2000). Atherogenesis, coagulation, and stress mechanisms. *Occupational Medicine: State of the Art Reviews, 15*(1), 136–138.

Theorell, T. (1990). Family history of hypertension—An individual trait interacting with spontaneously occurring job stressors. *Scandinavian Journal of Work, Environment, & Health, 16*(suppl. 1), 74–79.

Theorell, T. (2000). Neuroendocrine mechanisms. *Occupational Medicine: State of the Art Reviews, 15*(1), 139–146.

Theorell, T., Perski, A., Akerstedt, T., Sigala, F., Ahlberg-Hulten, G., Svensson, J., & Eneroth, P. (1988). Changes in job strain in relation to changes in physiological states: A longitudinal study. *Scandinavian Journal of Work, Environment, & Health, 14,* 189–196.

Theorell, T., Perski, A., Orth-Gomer, K., Hamsten, A., & de Faire, U. (1991). The effects of the strain of returning to work on the risk of cardiac death after a first myocardial infarction before age 45. *International Journal of Cardiology, 30,* 61–67. doi:10.1016/0167-5273(91)90125-9

264   LANDSBERGIS ET AL.

Theorell, T., Tsutsumi, A., Hallqvist, J., Reuterwall, C., Hogstedt, C., Fredlund, P., . . . Johnson, J. V. (1998). Decision latitude, job strain, and myocardical infarction: A study of working men in Stockholm. *American Journal of Public Health, 88,* 382–388. doi:10.2105/AJPH.88.3.382

The Tokyo Declaration. (1998). The Tokyo Declaration. *Journal of the Tokyo Medical University, 56*(6), 760–767.

Tuchsen, F. (2000). High-risk occupations for cardiovascular disease. *Occupational Medicine. State-of-the-Art Reviews, 15*(1), 57–60.

Tuchsen, F., & Endahl, L. A. (1999). Increasing inequality in ischaemic heart disease morbidity among employed men in Denmark 1981–1993: The need for a new preventive policy. *International Journal of Epidemiology, 28,* 640–644. doi:10.1093/ije/28.4.640

Ugljesic, M., Belkic, K., Boskovic, S., Avramovic, D., & Mickovic, L. (1992). Porast arterijskog krvnog pritiska tokom rada i profil rizika kod stresogenih profesija: Novinari i vozaci gradskog saobracja [Increased arterial blood pressure during work and risk profile among high-stress occupations: Journalists and city mass transit drivers]. *Kardiologija, 13,* 150–154.

Vahtera, J., Kivimäki, M., Pentti, J., Linna, A., Virtanen, M., Virtanen, P., & Ferrie, J. E. (2004). Organisational downsizing, sickness absence, and mortality: 10-town prospective cohort study. *British Medical Journal, 328,* 555. doi:10.1136/bmj.37972.496262.0D

van Amelsvoort, L. G. P. M., Schouten, E. G., Maan, A. C., Swene, C. A., & Kok, F. J. (2000). Occupational determinants of heart rate variability. *International Archives of Occupational and Environmental Health, 73,* 255–262. doi:10.1007/s004200050425

van der Hulst, M. (2003). Long workhours and health. *Scandinavian Journal of Work, Environment, & Health, 29,* 171–188.

Vrijkotte, T. G., van Doornen, L. J., & de Geus, E. J. (2000). Effects of work stress on ambulatory blood pressure, heart rate, and heart rate variability. *Hypertension, 35,* 880–886.

Waldron, I., Nowatarski, M., Freimer, M., Henry, J. P., Post, N., & Witten, C. (1982). Cross-cultural variation in blood pressure: A qualitative analysis of the relationship of blood pressure to cultural characteristics, salt consumption, and body weight. *Social Science & Medicine, 16,* 419–430. doi:10.1016/0277-9536(82)90050-8

Warren, N. (2000). U.S. regulations for work organization. *Occupational Medicine: State-of-the-Art Reviews, 15*(1), 275–280.

Wing, S., Casper, M., Riggan, W., Hayes, C. G., & Tyroler, H. A. (1988). Socioenvironmental characteristics associated with the onset of decline of ischemic heart disease mortality in United States. *American Journal of Public Health, 78,* 923–926. doi:10.2105/AJPH.78.8.923

Wolf, S. (2000). The environment-brain-heart connection. *Occupational Medicine: State of the Art Reviews, 15*(1), 107–109.

Yamasue, K., Hayashi, T., Ohshige, K., Tochikubo, O., & Souma, T. (2008). Masked hypertension in elderly managerial employees and retirees. *Clinical and Experimental Hypertension, 30,* 203–211. doi:10.1080/10641960802068451

Yang, H., Schnall, P., Jauregui, M., Su, T., & Baker, D. (2006). Work hours and self-reported hypertension among working people in California. *Hypertension, 48,* 744–750. doi:10.1161/01.HYP.0000238327.41911.52

14

Pain, Musculoskeletal Injuries, and Return to Work

Robert J. Gatchel and Nancy Kishino

> In the United States alone the annual cost associated with the diagnosis and care of musculoskeletal trauma amounts to tens of billions of dollars. Moreover, these costs are continuing to increase at an alarming rate. Indeed, occupational musculoskeletal disorders are the leading causes of work disability in the United States today. (Mayer, Gatchel, & Polatin, 2000, p. xv)

It has been almost a decade since this statement was made. Since then, the near-epidemic dimensions of musculoskeletal disorders in the United States have remained unabated. Indeed, musculoskeletal pain is the most common cause of short-term and long-term workplace disability (Melhorn, Lazarovic, & Roehl, 2005). The costs and prevalence of work-related musculoskeletal pain disability in industrialized countries are extremely high. Epidemiological studies indicate that 85% of adults will miss work or seek professional care for musculoskeletal pain during their working career (Fordyce, 1995; Skovron, 1992; Waddell, 1996). Moreover, although few studies on *presenteeism* (i.e., the way productivity is negatively affected and reduced when an ill or injured employee continues to "punch the clock") have considered musculoskeletal and chronic pain conditions, it is well documented that health care costs and productivity losses associated with such chronic pain are estimated to be in the range of $70 billion to $100 billion each year (Gatchel, 2004). In fact, Loeppke and colleagues (2007) identified that approximately one half of the overall medical costs associated with back and neck pain are attributed to productivity losses involving "presentees." Fortunately, however, some major advances in clinical research, with the new emphasis on the biopsychosocial conceptualization of pain and disability, are beginning to provide solutions to this problem (Schultz & Gatchel, 2005).

The purpose of this chapter is to review the biopsychosocial model of musculoskeletal pain and its implications for treatment. We begin by describing the model, including the objective and subjective factors related to pain. We next discuss the primary, secondary, and tertiary levels of treatment for pain,

The writing of this chapter was supported in part by grants to the first author from the National Institutes of Health (3R01 MH 046452, 1K05 MH 071892, 1U01 DE 010713-12A2) and the Department of Defense (DAMD17-03-1-0055).

with the tertiary level requiring the most intense, interdisciplinary approach. Then, we discuss the effectiveness of interdisciplinary treatment and the roles of interdisciplinary treatment team members. *Functional restoration,* or the restoration of both physical functional capacity and psychosocial performance, should be the overarching aim of interdisciplinary treatment approaches. We conclude the chapter by discussing the effectiveness and major goals of functional restoration treatment programs.

Biopsychosocial Model of Musculoskeletal Pain

Pain is a complex experiential state consisting of a variety of variables. The complexity of pain increases when it persists over extended periods of time, during which a range of psychosocioeconomic factors can significantly interact with physical pathology to modulate a patient's self-report of pain and concomitant disability, and response to treatment (Gatchel, 2005). Chronic pain and disability are now appropriately viewed as complex and interactive biopsychosocial phenomena that cannot be broken down into distinct, independent psychosocial and physical components. This biopsychosocial model has replaced the outdated biomedical reductionist approach of medicine. As is reviewed later in this chapter, the critical elements of an interdisciplinary treatment approach (on the basis of this biopsychosocial model) have been demonstrated to be the most therapeutic and cost-effective approach to use when patients have progressed to the chronic pain stage (Gatchel & Okifuji, 2006). An important part of these successful results is improved socioeconomic outcomes, such as return to work.

The biopsychosocial model of pain, which is now accepted as the most heuristic approach to the understanding and treatment of pain disorders, views physical disorders associated with pain as a result of a complex and dynamic interaction among physiologic, psychologic, and social factors that perpetuate and may worsen the clinical presentation. Each person experiences pain uniquely. The range of psychological, social, and economic factors can interact with physical pathology to modulate patients' reports of symptoms and subsequent disability. The development of this biopsychosocial approach has proceeded rapidly during the past decade, and a great deal of scientific knowledge has been produced in this short period of time concerning the biobehavioral underpinnings of pain, the best care of individuals with complex pain problems, as well as pain prevention and coping techniques (Gatchel, Peng, Peters, Fuchs, & Turk, 2007).

In their comprehensive review of the biopsychosocial perspective of chronic pain, Turk and Monarch (2002) highlighted the fact that individuals differ significantly in how frequently they report physical symptoms, in their tendency to visit physicians when experiencing identical symptoms, and in their responses to the same treatments. Quite often, the nature of patients' responses to treatment has little to do with their objective physical conditions (Gatchel, 2005). Furthermore, from 30% to 50% of patients who seek treatment related to pain in primary care do not have specific diagnosable disorders (Dworkin & Massoth, 1994). Clearly, pain is a subjective experience.

Although pain itself is subjective, it is influenced by both subjective and objective factors. The most basic objective factor is *nociception,* that is, the stimulation of nerves that convey information about tissue damage to the brain. Pain results from the transduction, transmission, and modulation of sensory input, and this input may be filtered through individuals' genetic composition, prior learning histories, current physiological status, and sociocultural influences (Gatchel et al., 2007). Pain, therefore, cannot be comprehensively assessed without a full understanding of the person who is exposed to the nociception.

The distinction between nociception and pain is analogous to the distinction between disease and illness. The term *disease* is generally used to define an objective biological event that involves the disruption of specific body structures or organ systems caused by anatomical, pathological, or physiological changes, whereas *illness* is generally defined as a subjective experience or self-attribution that a disease is present (Turk & Monarch, 2002). An illness will yield physical discomfort, behavioral limitations, and psychosocial distress. Thus, the biopsychosocial model focuses on illness, which is the result of the complex interaction of biological, psychological, and social factors.

From the biopsychosocial perspective, diversity in pain or illness expression (including its severity, duration, and psychosocial consequences) can be expected. The interrelationships among biological changes, psychological status, and the sociocultural context all need to be taken into account in fully understanding pain, patients' perception, and their response to illness (Gatchel, 2005; Gatchel et al., 2007). This is especially true to achieve optimal rehabilitation in patients with occupational pain-related disorders (Sullivan, Feuerstein, Gatchel, Linton, & Pransky, 2005). A model or treatment approach that focuses on only one of these core sets of factors will be incomplete. Indeed, the treatment effectiveness of a biopsychosocial approach to pain has consistently demonstrated the heuristic value of this model (Gatchel & Okifuji, 2006; Turk & Monarch, 2002).

Primary, Secondary, and Tertiary Care

Time and intensity of care significantly differ depending on whether the care is primary, secondary, or tertiary. As Mayer et al. (2003) clearly delineated, the care of acute pain problems is considered *primary care,* usually consisting of control of the pain symptom. Primary care usually lasts between 0 to 12 weeks following the occurrence of a painful episode and includes, but is not restricted to, passive treatment modalities such as electrical stimulation, manipulation, temperature modulation methods, and analgesic medications. Moreover, as these authors noted, on the basis of the natural history of many pain disorders (especially musculoskeletal disorders), most patients recover spontaneously or with relatively limited primary care.

Secondary care refers to the first stage of reactivation during the transition from primary care to return to work or normal activities of daily living. This secondary care phase usually occurs 2 to 6 months after the initial pain occurrence and is designed for patients not responding to initial primary treatment, to facilitate a return to productivity before progressive physical deconditioning and psychosocioeconomic barriers become firmly entrenched. Secondary care is designed to avoid the occurrence of chronic disability by preventing physical deconditioning, potential negative psychosocial reactions, as well as social habituation to disability. As Mayer and colleagues (2003) highlighted, the rationale for secondary care rehabilitation is to recognize and manage early risk factors or signs for the development of disability, thus preventing chronic or permanent disability. Consequently, reactivation is often the most common need at this point in time.

Finally, *tertiary care* refers to rehabilitation directed at preventing or ameliorating permanent disability for the patient who already suffers the effects of disability and physical deconditioning. It is this tertiary care, or rehabilitation, that requires an interdisciplinary team approach to accurately assess the various interrelated factors of chronic disability and pain, which then must be linked to the careful administration of a multifaceted pain management program to effect recovery and reduce permanent disability. This is not to say that the interdisciplinary approach is not of significant value for secondary care (Gatchel et al., 2003). However, this form of tertiary care is quite different from secondary care because of the intensity of services required, duration of disability, treatment program protocol, greater specificity of physical and psychosocial assessment, and the greater level of coordination among health care professionals. A significant number of patients at the tertiary care stage may become financial burdens on their insurance carriers as well as on the health care system in general. They frequently fail to experience significant pain relief after repeated and extended contacts with several different physicians and other health care providers. And they do not receive long-term relief or a "cure" from traditional monotherapies, such as surgery, injections, or medications. This is not to say that patients are solely to blame; they are often exposed to ineffective treatment modalities.

Interdisciplinary Chronic Pain Management for Musculoskeletal Injuries and Disorders

Interdisciplinary treatment can be clearly distinguished from multidisciplinary treatment. The term *multidisciplinary* connotes the involvement of several health care providers. The integration of these services, as well as communication among providers, may be limited. The term *interdisciplinary,* in our use of the concept, involves greater coordination of services in a comprehensive program with all providers "under one roof," which maximizes frequent communication among the health care professionals providing care. A key ingredient of interdisciplinary care is a common philosophy of rehabilitation and active patient involvement (Gatchel & Okifuji, 2006; Turk & Stieg, 1987).

A myriad of studies and reviews have documented the clinical effectiveness of such interdisciplinary treatment of chronic pain patients (e.g., Deschner & Polatin, 2000; Gatchel, 2005; Gatchel & Okifuji, 2006; Okifuji, 2003; Turk & Swanson, 2007; Wright & Gatchel, 2002). Even systematic Cochrane Reviews have documented their effectiveness (Guzman et al., 2002; Schonstein, Kenny, Keating, & Koes, 2003). Turk and Swanson (2007) found that traditional monotherapies (e.g., surgery, injections, medications) were inferior to inter-disciplinary programs in terms of functional improvements, reduction of health care use, return-to-work rates, and closure of disability claims. These monother-apies were also found to be more expensive. Moreover, the long-term efficacy of these monotherapies has not been substantiated (Giordano & Schatman, 2008). Psychosocial distress, physical deconditioning, secondary gains and losses, and medication issues often result from monotherapies, thereby further complicating the presentation of pain.

The strengths of multiple disciplines working together to address complex issues confronting chronic musculoskeletal pain patients are greatly needed. The overall therapeutic focus should be toward independence and autonomy while acknowledging when certain physical limitations cannot be overcome. The Commission on Accreditation of Rehabilitation Facilities requires that a certified pain management team include at least a physician, specialized nurse, a physical therapist, and a clinical psychologist or psychiatrist. However, often, an occupational therapist is required because return to work and vocational retraining issues become important in managing chronic patient patients. The roles of each team member are as follows (adapted from Gatchel, Lou, & Kishino, 2006):

- *Medical director or physician.* A physician serves as the medical direc-tor of the treatment team, and he or she must have a firm background in providing medical rehabilitation for the types of musculoskeletal pain disorders frequently encountered. Formal training may vary from anesthesiology, orthopaedic surgery, psychiatry, or occupational medi-cine to internal medicine. The physician needs to assume a direct role in the medical management of the patients' musculoskeletal pain by providing the medical history to the treatment team and by taking direct responsibility for medication management for any other medical interventions. Often, other team members, as well as outside consul-tants, may be involved in the medical treatment of the patient, but it is the physician's responsibility to coordinate these medical contributions to the patients' care.
- *Nurse.* Although not all programs use nursing services, any pain man-agement program that provides anesthesiology services involving injections, nerve blocks, and other medical procedures will require a nurse. The nurse assists the physician, follows up the procedures, may interact with patients in the role of case manager, and provides patient education. The nurse may be viewed as a physician extender and edu-cator who has a strong impact on the patient.
- *Psychologist.* Although the physician and nurse play a major role in managing the physical status of patients, the psychologist plays the leading role in the day-to-day maintenance of the psychosocial aspects and status of the patient's care. Significant psychosocial barriers to positive outcomes of the treatment may develop as a patient progresses from acute through subacute to the chronic stage of a pain syndrome (such as fear avoidance, maladaptive coping, secondary gain issues; Gatchel, 2007). The psychologist is responsible for conducting a full

psychosocial evaluation, which includes identification of psychosocial barriers to recovery and the assessment of the patient's psychosocial strengths and weaknesses. A cognitive–behavioral treatment approach can then be used to address important psychosocial issues, such as pain-related depression, anxiety, fear, as well as psychopathology. A cognitive–behavioral treatment approach has been found to be the most appropriate modality to use with patients in a program such as this (Gatchel, 2005).

- *Physical therapist.* The physical therapist interacts daily with the patient regarding any issues related to physical progression toward recovery. Effective communication with other team members is crucial so that the patients' fear of exercise will not interfere with their reconditioning effort. The physical therapist also helps to educate the patient by addressing the physiological bases of pain and teaching ways of reducing the severity of pain episodes through the use of appropriate body mechanics and pacing.

- *Occupational therapist.* The occupational therapist is involved in both physical and vocational aspects of the patient's treatment. The great majority of patients participating in an interdisciplinary program are likely not to be working because of their pain. Often, they have become pessimistic about the prospect of returning to work. The occupational therapist addresses these vocational issues and the physical determinants of underlying disability. This therapist also plays an important educational role in teaching patients techniques for managing pain "on the job" in ways that do not jeopardize their employment status. Finally, the occupational therapist can play an important role as case manager in contacting employers to obtain job descriptions and other information, as well as vocational retraining if necessary.

Constant, effective communication among all treatment team members is required so that patient progress can be discussed and evaluated. It is important for patients to hear the same treatment philosophy and message from each of the treatment team members. Indeed, many times, patient wishes are in conflict with future treatment, and the patient may seek out any conflict between team members and use it to compromise treatment goals. A formal interdisciplinary treatment team meeting should occur at least once a week to review patient progress and to make any modifications in the treatment plan for each patient. Individually tailoring treatment for patients is essential. In addition, evaluating and monitoring treatment outcomes in a systematic fashion is essential for not only treatment outcomes evaluations but also for quality assurance purposes for the treatment team.

Functional Restoration

In recent years, there has been an emphasis on functional restoration as a driving force in the rehabilitation of musculoskeletal disorders (Gatchel, 2005; Schultz & Gatchel, 2005). The term *functional restoration,* originally developed by

Mayer and Gatchel (1988), refers to the restoration of both physical functional capacity and psychosocial performance. It requires a broad conceptualization of the entire problem, its diagnosis, and its management. When taking the patient's history, rather than collecting only the patient's self-report of pain and the diagnosis through imaging technology, functional restoration involves more information. Objective assessment of physical capacity and effort, compared with a normative database, adds a new dimension to diagnosis. This is consistent with a sports medicine approach in that it permits the development of individually tailored treatment programs of varied intensity and duration aimed primarily at restoring physical functional capacity and psychosocial performance. Objectives are more ambitious than merely attempting to alter pain complaints and to decrease medications. It is assumed that improvements in quality of life will be greatly enhanced by focusing on increasing physical capacity and decreasing social problems associated with pain. Attention is given to realistic goals, such as the following (adapted from Gatchel et al., 2006):

- returning the patient to productivity;
- maximizing function, thus minimizing pain;
- educating the patient to assume the responsibility for self-management and progress;
- reducing or eliminating future use of medical resources;
- avoiding recurrence of injury and maintaining therapeutic gains; and
- avoiding medication dependence and abuse.

These goals can all be objectively monitored and quantified. Indeed, numerous clinical investigators have discussed emphasizing such objective functional and psychosocial outcomes (Feuerstein & Zastowny, 1996; Hazard, 1995; Mayer & Gatchel; Mayer et al., 2000; Schultz & Gatchel).

The clinical effectiveness of functional restoration has been well documented. An early seminal study by Mayer and colleagues (1987) provides an example of the positive socioeconomic outcomes produced by a functional restoration program for the most costly type of musculoskeletal disorder: chronic low-back pain. In this study, patients who had undergone the functional restoration program were followed up 2 years after completion of the program. Results clearly demonstrated significant changes in a number of important socioeconomic outcome measures that were collected: Nearly 90% of the treatment group was actively working, as compared with only about 41% of a nontreatment comparison group; about twice as many comparison group patients required additional spine surgery and had unsettled Workers' Compensation litigation relative to the treatment group; the comparison group also had approximately 5 times more patient visits to health care professionals and had higher rates of recurrence of reinjury relative to the functional restoration group. There were also significant improvements in self-report measures and physical function measures, such as back strength and range of motion, in the functional restoration treatment group.

Since that time, the success of functional restoration has been independently replicated by Hazard et al. (1989) and Patrick et al. (2004) in this country; by Bendix and Bendix (1994) and Bendix et al. (1996) in Denmark;

Hildebrandt et al. (1997) in Germany; Corey, Koepfler, Etlin, and Day (1996) in Canada; Jousset et al. (2004) in France; and Shirado et al. (2005) in Japan. The fact that different clinical treatment teams functioning in different states (Texas and Vermont) and different countries, with markedly different socio-economic conditions and workers' compensation systems, produced comparable outcome results speaks highly for the robustness of the research findings and utility, as well as for the fidelity, of this functional restoration approach. In addition, Burke, Harms-Constas, and Aden (1994) demonstrated its efficacy in 11 different rehabilitation centers across seven states. Gatchel and Turk (1999) and Turk (2002) confirmed both the therapeutic- and cost-effectiveness of inter-disciplinary programs, such as functional restoration, for a wide range of chronic pain conditions. Hazard (1995) also reviewed the overall effectiveness of func-tional restoration. Thus, fortunately, we now have in our treatment armamen-tarium the ability to effectively manage what used to be recalcitrant chronic pain disorders.

It should also be pointed out that, besides functional restoration, other forms of interdisciplinary treatment programs for chronic pain have been shown to be efficacious with patients with chronic pain (Gatchel & Okifuji, 2006; Turk & Gatchel, 1999; Turk & Stacey, 1997). These other programs differ from func-tional restoration mainly in terms of their lesser emphasis on the direct quantifi-cation of function used to drive the sports medicine philosophy of that approach. Turk and Gatchel (1999) pointed out that the cost savings of all such comprehen-sive programs can be quite significant and that more research is needed to exam-ine what combinations of variables are most important in being able to prescribe the most efficient and effective therapeutic package, individually tailored to each patient, in an interdisciplinary treatment program.

Conclusion

There can now be no doubt that interdisciplinary functional restoration programs are both therapeutic and cost-effective for the treatment of chronic musculoskeletal disorders; they also produce positive socioeconomic outcomes, such as return to work. In early research, Flor, Fydrich, and Turk (1992) con-cluded that the overall therapeutic results emanating from interdisciplinary pain-management programs were quite promising, with significant changes demonstrated not only in self-reported pain and mood but also in important socioeconomic variables such as the return to work and the use of the health care system. At the time of that research, the cost of hospital and medical charges for chronic pain had been estimated to be in excess of $125 billion (Frymoyer & Durett, 1997). Even when the cost of the interdisciplinary core treatment of the interdisciplinary pain center was included, savings were realized (Flor et al., 1992). Research since then has confirmed the treatment and cost benefits of mul-tidisciplinary pain treatment centers (Gatchel & Okifuji, 2006; Turk & Swanson, 2007). One study even calculated a savings of more than $1 billion over a 19-year period (Turk & Gatchel, 1999).

More clinical research is still needed to examine what combinations of vari-ables are most important in being able to prescribe the most efficient and effective therapeutic package in an interdisciplinary treatment program for musculoskeletal injuries. As Turk and Gatchel (1999) concluded earlier, there are no data available to determine what set of patients with what characteristics are most likely to benefit from what set of treatment modalities, provided in what type of format. We are still in need of investigations to address this important issue of more precisely individually tailoring treatment programs to increase the time, cost, and outcome efficiency of the interdisciplinary functional restoration approach to musculoskeletal disorders as well as to other chronic pain syndromes.

References

Bendix, A. F., Bendix, T., Vaegter, K., Lund, C., Frolund, L., & Holm, L. (1996). Multidisciplinary intensive treatment for chronic low back pain: A randomized, prospective study. *Cleveland Clinic Journal of Medicine, 63*(1), 62–69.

Bendix, T., & Bendix, A. (1994). *Different training programs for chronic low back pain—A randomized, blinded one-year follow-up study.* Paper presented at the International Society for the Study of the Lumbar Spine, Seattle, WA.

Burke, S. A., Harms-Constas, C. K., & Aden, P. S. (1994). Return to work/work retention outcomes of a functional restoration program: A multi-center, prospective study with a comparison group. *Spine, 19,* 1880–1885.

Corey, D. T., Koepfler, L. E., Etlin, D., & Day, H. I. (1996). A limited functional restoration program for injured workers: A randomized trial. *Journal of Occupational Rehabilitation, 6,* 239–249. doi:10.1007/BF02110886

Deschner, M., & Polatin, P. B. (2000). Interdisciplinary programs: Chronic pain management. In T. G. Mayer, R. J. Gatchel, & P. B. Polatin (Eds.), *Occupational musculoskeletal disorders: Function, outcomes and evidence* (pp. 629–637). Philadelphia, PA: Lippincott Williams & Wilkins.

Dworkin, S. F., & Massoth, D. L. (1994). Temporomandibular disorders and chronic pain: Disease or illness? *The Journal of Prosthetic Dentistry, 72*(1), 29–38. doi:10.1016/0022-3913(94)90213-5

Feuerstein, M., & Zastowny, T. R. (1996). Occupational rehabilitation: Multidisciplinary management of work related musculoskeletal pain and disability. In R. J. Gatchel & D. C. Turk (Eds.), *Psychological approaches to pain management: A practitioner's handbook* (pp. 458–485). New York, NY: Guilford Press.

Flor, H., Fydrich, T., & Turk, D. C. (1992). Efficacy of multidisciplinary pain treatment centers: A meta-analytic flow. *Pain, 49,* 221–230. doi:10.1016/0304-3959(92)90145-2

Fordyce, W. E. (1995). *Back pain in the workplace: Management of disability in nonspecific conditions.* Seattle, WA: IASP Press.

Frymoyer, J. W., & Durett, C. L. (1997). The economics of spinal disorders. In J. W. Frymoyer, T. B. Ducker, J. P. Kostuik, J. N. Weinstein, & T. S. I. Whitecloud (Eds.), *The adult spine: Principles and practice* (2nd ed., Vol. 1, pp. 143–150). Philadelphia, PA: Lippincott-Raven.

Gatchel, R. J. (2004). Comorbidity of chronic mental and physical health disorders: The biopsychosocial perspective. *American Psychologist, 59,* 795–805. doi:10.1037/0003-066X.59.8.795

Gatchel, R. J. (2005). *Clinical essentials of pain management.* Washington, DC: American Psychological Association. doi:10.1037/10856-000

Gatchel, R. J., Lou, L., & Kishino, N. (2006). Concepts of multidisciplinary pain management. In M. V. Boswell & D. E. Cole (Eds.), *Weiner's pain management: A practical guide for clinicians* (7th ed., pp. 1501–1508). New York, NY: Taylor & Francis.

Gatchel, R. J., & Okifuji, A. (2006). Evidence-based scientific data documenting the treatment- and cost-effectiveness of comprehensive pain programs for chronic nonmalignant pain. *The Journal of Pain, 7,* 779–793. doi:10.1016/j.jpain.2006.08.005

Gatchel, R. J., Peng, Y., Peters, M. L., Fuchs, P. N., & Turk, D. C. (2007). The Biopsychosocial approach to chronic pain: Scientific advances and future directions. *Psychological Bulletin, 133,* 581–624. doi:10.1037/0033-2909.133.4.581

Gatchel, R. J., Polatin, P. B., Noe, C. E., Gardea, M. A., Pulliam, C., & Thompson, J. (2003). Treatment- and cost-effectiveness of early intervention for acute low back pain patients: A 1-year prospective study. *Journal of Occupational Rehabilitation, 13,* 1–9. doi:10.1023/A:1021823505774

Gatchel, R. J., & Turk, D. C. (1999). Interdisciplinary treatment of chronic pain patients. In R. J. Gatchel & D. C. Turk (Eds.), *Psychosocial factors in pain: Critical perspectives* (pp. 435–444). New York, NY: Guilford Press.

Giordano, J., & Schatman, M. E. (2008). An ethical analysis of crisis in chronic pain care: Facts, issues, and problems in pain medicine: Part I. Ethics. *Pain Physician, 11,* 483–490.

Guzman, J., Esmail, R., Karjalainen, K., Malmivaara, A., Irvin, E., & Bombardier, C. (2002). Multidisciplinary bio–psycho–social rehabilitation for chronic low-back pain. *Cochrane Database of Systematic Reviews, 1,* CD000963.

Hazard, R. G. (1995). Spine update: Functional restoration. *Spine, 20,* 2345–2348. doi:10.1097/00007632-199511000-00015

Hazard, R. G., Fenwick, J. W., Kalisch, S. M., Redmond, J., Reeves, V., Reid, S., & Frymoyer, J. W. (1989). Functional restoration with behavioral support. A one-year prospective study of patients with chronic low-back pain. *Spine, 14,* 157–161. doi:10.1097/00007632-198902000-00003

Hildebrandt, J., Pfingsten, M., Saur, P., & Jansen, J. (1997). Prediction of success from a multidisciplinary treatment program for chronic low-back pain. *Spine, 22,* 990–1001. doi:10.1097/00007632-199705010-00011

Jousset, N., Fanello, S., Bontoux, L., Dubus, V., Billabert, C., Vielle, B., . . . Richard, I. (2004). Effects of functional restoration versus 3 hours per week physical therapy: A randomized controlled study. *Spine, 29,* 487–493. doi:10.1097/01.BRS.0000102320.35490.43

Loeppke, R., Taitel, M., Richling, D., Parry, T., Kessler, R. C., Hymel, P., & Konicki, D. (2007). Health and productivity as a business strategy. *Journal of Occupational and Environmental Medicine, 49,* 712–721. doi:10.1097/JOM.0b013e318133a4be

Mayer, T. G., & Gatchel, R. J. (1988). *Functional restoration for spinal disorders: The sports medicine approach.* Philadelphia, PA: Lea & Febiger.

Mayer, T. G., Gatchel, R. J., Mayer, H., Kishino, N. D., Keeley, J., & Mooney, V. A. (1987). A prospective 2-year study of functional restoration in industrial low-back injury. An objective assessment procedure. *JAMA, 258,* 1763–1767. doi:10.1001/jama.258.13.1763

Mayer, T. G., Gatchel, R. J., & Polatin, P. B. (Eds.). (2000). *Occupational musculoskeletal disorders: Function, outcomes, and evidence.* Philadelphia, PA: Lippincott Williams & Wilkins.

Mayer, T. G., Polatin, P. B., Smith, B., Gatchel, R. J., Fardon, D., Herring, S. A., . . . Wong D. (2003). Spine rehabilitation: Secondary and tertiary nonoperative care. *The Spine Journal, 3,* 28–36. doi:10.1016/S1529-9430(02)00562-4

Melhorn, J. M., Lazarovic, J., & Roehl, W. K. (2005). Do we have a disability epidemic? In I. Z. Schultz & R. J. Gatchel (Eds.), *Handbook of complex occupational disability claims: Early risk identification, intervention and prevention* (pp. 7–24). New York, NY: Springer. doi:10.1007/0-387-28919-4_1

Okifuji, A. (2003). Interdisciplinary pain management with pain patients: Evidence for its effectiveness. *Seminars in Pain Medicine, 1,* 110–119. doi:10.1016/S1537-5897(03)00025-9

Patrick, L. E., Altmaier, E., & Found, E. (2004). Long-term outcomes in multidisciplinary treatment of chronic low-back pain: Results of a 13-year follow-up. *Spine, 29,* 850–855. doi:10.1097/00007632-200404150-00006

Schonstein, E., Kenny, D. T., Keating, J., & Koes, B. W. (2003). Work conditioning, work hardening and functional restoration for workers with back and neck pain. *Cochrane Database of Systematic Reviews, 1,* CD001822. doi: 10.1002/14651858.CD001822

Schultz, I., & Gatchel, R. (Eds.). (2005). *Handbook of complex occupational disability claims.* New York, NY: Springer. doi:10.1007/0-387-28919-4

Shirado, O., Ito, T., Kikumoto, T., Takeda, N., Minami, A., & Strax, T. E. (2005). A novel back school using a multidisciplinary team approach featuring quantitative functional evaluation and therapeutic exercises for patients with chronic low-back pain. *Spine, 30,* 1219–1225. doi:10.1097/01.brs.0000162279.94779.05

Skovron, M. L. (1992). Epidemiology of low back pain. *Bailliere's Clinical Rheumatology, 6,* 559–573. doi:10.1016/S0950-3579(05)80127-X

Sullivan, M. J. L., Feuerstein, M., Gatchel, R. J., Linton, S. J., & Pransky, G. (2005). Integrating psychosocial and behavioral interventions to achieve optimal rehabilitation outcomes. *Journal of Occupational Rehabilitation, 15,* 475–489. doi:10.1007/s10926-005-8029-9

Turk, D. C. (2002). Clinical effectiveness and cost effectiveness of treatment for patients with chronic pain. *The Clinical Journal of Pain, 18,* 355–365. doi:10.1097/00002508-200211000-00003

Turk, D. C., & Gatchel, R. J. (1999). Multidisciplinary programs for rehabilitation of chronic low back pain patients. In W. H. Kirkaldy-Willis & T. N. Bernard, Jr., (Eds.), *Managing low back pain* (4th ed., pp. 299–311). New York, NY: Churchill Livingstone.

Turk, D. C., & Monarch, E. S. (2002). Biopsychosocial perspective on chronic pain. In D. C. Turk & R. J. Gatchel (Eds.), *Psychological approaches to pain management: A practitioner's handbook* (2nd ed., pp. 3–29). New York, NY: Guilford Press.

Turk, D. C., & Stacey, B. R. (1997). Multidisciplinary pain centers in the treatment of chronic back pain. In J. W. Frymoyer (Ed.), *The Adult Spine* (2nd ed., pp. 253–274). New York, NY: Lippincott-Raven.

Turk, D. C., & Stieg, R. L. (1987). Chronic pain: The necessity of interdisciplinary communication. *The Clinical Journal of Pain, 3,* 163–167.

Turk, D. C., & Swanson, K. (2007). Efficacy and cost-effectiveness treatment of chronic pain: An analysis and evidence-based synthesis. In M. E. Schatman & A. Campbell (Eds.), *Chronic pain management: Guidelines for multidisciplinary program development* (pp. 15–38). New York, NY: Informa Healthcare.

Waddell, G. (1996). Low back pain: A 20th century health care enigma. *Spine, 21,* 2820–2825. doi:10.1097/00007632-199612150-00002

Wright, A. R., & Gatchel, R. J. (2002). Occupational musculoskeletal pain and disability. In D. C. Turk & R. J. Gatchel (Eds.), *Psychological Approaches to Pain Management: A Practitioner's Handbook* (2nd ed., pp. 349–364). New York, NY: Guilford Press.

15

Alcohol and Illicit Drug Use in the Workforce and Workplace

Michael R. Frone

Employee substance use is an issue of interest to managers, unions, and policy-makers because it may lead to costs being incurred by employers due to potential negative effects involving employee health, attendance, productivity, and safety. Moreover, workplace substance use by some employees may negatively affect the larger group of employees who do not use alcohol or illicit drugs at work. Occupational health psychologists, however, have devoted little attention to the issue of employee substance use. The bulk of research that does exist has been conducted by substance use researchers and is located in substance use and public health journals. One outcome of this lack of involvement by occupational health psychologists is that employee substance use research does not take full advantage of theoretical perspectives and measures developed in occupational health psychology, industrial and organizational psychology, and organizational behavior. The goal of this chapter, therefore, is to summarize briefly for occupational health psychologists the literature on employee substance use. The first section of this chapter defines some key terms. The second section explores the prevalence of alcohol and illicit drug use among employees. The third section summarizes key causes of employee substance use. The fourth section looks at organizational consequences of employee substance use. The final section provides concluding thoughts.

Definition of Terms

Before exploring the prevalence, causes, and consequences of employee substance use, several issues need to be clarified. This section begins by presenting a general definition of psychoactive drugs and a summary of the major classes of psychoactive drugs. Next, the distinction between illicit and licit use of drugs is explored. This is followed by consideration of terms that characterize levels of substance use and types of substance impairment. Finally, the temporal context of substance use and impairment is examined, which highlights the distinction between substance use and impairment in the workforce and in the workplace.

What Is a Psychoactive Drug?

A *psychoactive drug* is a chemical substance that acts primarily on the central nervous system, resulting in changes in consciousness, perception, emotion, cognition, or behavior. Psychoactive substances are commonly classified according to their primary pharmacological effects, though there is one exception. The exception is inhalants, which represent a broad class of substances. Although inhalants have effects similar to depressants, they are grouped by their route of administration.

Narcotic analgesics are substances whose primary effect is to reduce pain, though they also reduce tension and increase euphoria. They include (a) opium; (b) natural derivatives of opium, also called opiates (e.g., morphine, codeine); (c) semisynthetic opioids derived from opiates (e.g., heroin, oxycodone, hydrocodone); and (d) synthetic opioids (e.g., methadone). *Depressants* act to slow down the central nervous system and produce a drowsy or calm feeling, and include barbiturates, sedatives, benzodiazapines or minor tranquilizers, antipsychotics or major tranquilizers, and alcohol. *Stimulants* act to increase central nervous system activity and produce a sense of euphoria. They include amphetamines, ephedrine, cocaine, caffeine, and nicotine. *Hallucinogens* alter consciousness in unpredictable ways. In contrast to other psychoactive drugs, hallucinogens do not merely amplify familiar states of mind but rather induce experiences that are qualitatively different from those of ordinary consciousness. There are four categories of hallucinogens: serotonergic hallucinogens (e.g., LSD, mescaline, psilocybin), methylated amphetamines (e.g., MDMA or ecstasy, MDA), anticolinergic hallucinogens (e.g., atropine, scolopine), and dissociative anesthetics (e.g., PCP or angel dust, ketamine). *Cannabis* includes marijuana and hashish and has many of the same effects reported for hallucinogens, analgesics, and sedatives. *Inhalants* produce psychoactive effects similar to depressants and include a variety of volatile solvents (e.g., gasoline, lighter fluids, paint thinners, toluene) and anesthetics (nitrous oxide, ether, chloroform).

Illicit Versus Licit Drug Use

In addition to their pharmacological effects, psychoactive drugs can be classified according to their legal availability and extent of governmental regulation. This classification scheme is called *drug scheduling* and is used in a number of countries, though the exact scheduling scheme may differ across countries. In the United States, five schedules were created in the U.S. Controlled Substances Act of 1970. All other substances not falling into one of the five schedules produce a residual category of unscheduled substances. As used in most population studies of substance use, *illicit drug use* refers to (a) the use of psychoactive substances that are illegal to possess and unavailable by medical prescription (i.e., Schedule I drugs) or (b) the illicit use of any psychoactive drug that requires a medical prescription (i.e., Schedule II, III, and IV drugs), which occurs when the drug is used without a prescription or used with a prescription but taken more frequently or in higher dosage than prescribed. In contrast, with a few exceptions, *licit drug use* refers to (a) the use of prescribable drugs (i.e., Schedule II, III, and IV drugs) with a prescription and as prescribed, (b) the use of scheduled substances that can be obtained over the counter without a medical prescription (i.e., Schedule V drugs), and (c) the use of unscheduled substances (e.g., alcohol, nicotine, caffeine). Thus, for the purpose of this chapter, alcohol is a licit psychoactive substance for employed adults with the exception of a narrow age range of individuals 18 to 20 years old. Also, substances used as inhalants are unscheduled and are therefore legal to possess. Nonetheless, past discussion of illicit drugs and assessments of the prevalence of illicit drug use often include inhalants.

Substance Use and Impairment

Substance use has several dimensions. *Prevalence of use* refers to the percentage of individuals in some population who have used a substance at least once over some fixed period of time (e.g., during the preceding 12 months or past month or past week). *Frequency of use* refers to the number of days that a substance is used over some fixed period of time. *Quantity used* refers to the amount or number of units (e.g., drinks) used or consumed on a typical occasion of use. Quantity used is typically assessed for alcohol but not for other substances. In contrast to alcohol, where standard drinks can be defined for respondents that contain approximately the same level of absolute alcohol, it is difficult to get standard dosages or quantity consumed for illicit drug use because of differing chemical properties, routes of administration, and levels of purity. Measures of alcohol use sometime combine the frequency of use and quantity used. For example, heavy drinking is often defined as consuming five or more drinks in a day. So it is common to see assessments of the frequency of consuming five or more drinks in a day (i.e., frequency of heavy drinking).

Substance impairment has two dimensions: intoxication and withdrawal. *Substance intoxication* refers to acute and reversible central nervous system impairment due to the direct pharmacological action of a substance resulting in various behavioral, cognitive, and affective changes (e.g., American Psychiatric Association, 2000; Maisto, Galizio, & Connors, 2008). *Substance withdrawal* refers to central nervous system impairment due to cessation of or reduction in substance use that has been heavy and prolonged resulting in various behavioral, cognitive, and affective changes (e.g., American Psychiatric Association, 2000; Saitz, 1998). Also included in the definition of withdrawal is the hangover syndrome usually linked to alcohol use. An alcohol hangover is believed to represent, at least partly, a mild form of acute alcohol withdrawal (e.g., Moore, 1998; Swift & Davidson, 1998; Wiese, Shlipak, & Browner, 2000).

Temporal Context of Use and Impairment

Past research has typically only assessed employees' overall use of or impairment from psychoactive substances. Overall substance use or impairment represents use or impairment across all contexts. Thus, past research has primarily explored substance use and impairment in the workforce, which largely reflects use and impairment away from work and outside an employed individual's normal work hours. In contrast, relatively little research has focused on substance use in the workplace even though such information is important to employers and policymakers. Substance use in the workplace represents the consumption of a substance at times occurring just before or during formal work hours (Ames, Grube, & Moore, 1997; Frone, 2004, 2006a, 2006b). Specifically, *workplace substance use* refers to the consumption of alcohol or illicit drugs (a) within 2 hours of starting one's work shift, (b) during a lunch break, (c) during other work breaks, and (d) while performing one's job. Workplace substance impairment represents impairment (i.e., intoxication or withdrawal) due to alcohol or illicit drugs experienced during work hours. This distinction between use and impairment in the workforce and use and impairment in the workplace may be important for research looking at the workplace causes of employee substance use and the productivity outcomes associated with employee substance use.

Prevalence of Substance Use and Impairment

This section begins by presenting data from the United States and available international data on the prevalence of workforce alcohol and illicit drug use and impairment. It then presents data from the United States and available international data on the prevalence of workplace alcohol and illicit drug use and impairment.

Workforce Prevalence

ALCOHOL USE AND IMPAIRMENT. Recent U.S. national prevalence data on overall alcohol use (Frone, 2008b) reveal that during a 12-month period, 73.6% of the workforce (92.5 million workers) used alcohol, 30.6% (38.4 million workers) drank enough to become intoxicated, and 22.6% (28.4 million workers) experienced a hangover. Looking at the frequency of alcohol use, weekly alcohol use was reported by 32.7% of workers, monthly use was reported by 19.5% of workers, and less than monthly use was reported by 21.4% of workers. Drinking to intoxication on a weekly basis was reported by 3.4% of the workforce, monthly intoxication was reported by 6.4% of the workforce, and less than monthly intoxication was reported by 20.9% of the workforce. Experiencing a hangover on a weekly basis was reported by 1.4% of the workforce, monthly hangover was reported by 3.6% of the workforce, and less than monthly hangover was reported by 17.6% of the workforce.

In regard to prevalence data on workforce alcohol use outside the United States, Pidd and colleagues (2006) surveyed a national sample of Australian workers and reported that 89.4% of the workforce used alcohol in the past 12 months and 43.9% drank at levels defined as risky. Finally, using a representative sample of the workforce in Alberta, Canada, the Alberta Alcohol and Drug Abuse Commission (2003) reported that 81% of workers reported using alcohol during the preceding 12 months.

ILLICIT DRUG USE AND IMPAIRMENT. Prevalence rates for overall illicit drug use in the U.S. workforce (Frone, 2006b) reveal that 14.1% (17.7 million workers) used at least one illicit drug during the preceding 12 months. When the type of illicit drug is considered, 11.3% of the workforce (14.2 million workers) used marijuana, 1.0% (1.3 million workers) used cocaine, and 4.9% (6.2 million workers) illicitly used a prescription drug (i.e., stimulants, sedatives, tranquilizers, analgesics). The prevalence rates for being impaired by drugs (i.e., using enough to get high or stoned) showed that 11.2% (14.1 million workers) were impaired by an illicit drug, 10.6% (13.3 million workers) were impaired by marijuana, 0.9% (1.2 million workers) were impaired by cocaine, and 2.2% (2.8 million workers) were impaired by the illicit use of a prescription drug.

As to the frequency of illicit drug use, weekly use of any illicit drug was reported by 4.5% of the workforce, monthly use was reported by 2.5% of the workforce, and less than monthly use was reported by 7.1% of the workforce. Impairment from any illicit drug on a weekly basis was reported by 3.6% of the workforce, monthly drug impairment was reported by 1.9% of the workforce, and less than monthly drug impairment was reported by 5.7% of the workforce.

Finally, three groups of vulnerable workers were identified by cross-classifying gender (male vs. female), age (18–30 vs. 31–65), and occupation (low vs. high risk; for a detailed discussion, see Frone, 2006b). Among young women in the high-risk occupations, 43.2% reported using an illicit drug in the past 12 months and 42.6% reported being impaired by an illicit drug. Among young men in the high-risk occupations, 55.8% reported using an illicit drug and 37.8% reported being impaired by an illicit drug. Also, young men in the low-risk occupations showed elevated prevalence rates, with 24.7% reporting illicit drug use and 20.9% reporting substance use impairment. Despite these high prevalence rates, it is important to point out that the estimated population of individuals in these three subgroups reporting overall illicit drug use represented 5.5% of the overall U.S. workforce. This means that these high rates of illicit substance use represent a potential problem for a narrow range of employers whose workforce is largely young men and women in specific occupations.

Regarding prevalence data on workforce illicit drug use outside the United States, Bywood, Pidd, and Roche (2006) found that 17.3 % of the Australian workforce used an illicit drug during the prior 12 months. Smith, Wadsworth, Moss, and Simpson (2004), using a large regional probability sample from the United Kingdom, reported that 13% of the workforce used an illicit drug during the preceding 12 months and 7% reported use during the preceding month. Finally, 10% of the workforce in Alberta, Canada, reported using an illicit drug (Alberta Alcohol and Drug Abuse Commission, 2003).

Workplace Prevalence

ALCOHOL USE AND IMPAIRMENT. Recent U.S. national data (Frone, 2006a) show that workplace alcohol use and impairment was reported by an estimated 15.3% of the U.S. workforce (19.2 million workers) during the preceding 12 months. Specifically, an estimated 1.8% (2.3 million workers) drank before work, 7.1% (8.9 million workers) drank during the workday (i.e., during lunch breaks, during other breaks, or while working), 1.7% (2.1 million workers) worked under the influence of alcohol, and 9.2% (11.6 million workers) worked with a hangover.

Data on the frequency of drinking before work show that weekly use was reported by 0.1% of the workforce, monthly use was reported by 0.5% of the workforce, and less than monthly use was reported by 1.3% of the workforce. Drinking during the workday was reported to occur weekly by 1.0% of the workforce, monthly by 1.7% of the workforce, and less than monthly by 4.4% of the workforce. Working while under the influence of alcohol was reported to occur weekly by 0.3% of the workforce, monthly by 0.4% of the workforce, and less than monthly by 1.0% of the workforce. Finally, working with a hangover was reported to occur weekly by 0.5% of the workforce, monthly by 1.4% of the workforce, and less than monthly by 7.3% of the workforce.

Regarding workplace prevalence data outside the United States, Pidd et al. (2006) summarized several published and unpublished findings on Australian workers. Among 337 Australian urban train drivers, 3.1% drank within 3 hr of coming to work and 2% drank during actual work hours. Among 4,193 Australian police officers, 26% reported occasionally drinking at work. Among 319 Australian construction apprentices, 29.3% (2.6% at least weekly and 26.7% less than weekly) drank during work hours. Also, a regional sample of 1,200 Australian workers found that 4% reported drinking at work. A study of the workforce in Alberta, Canada, found that 4% of workers reported drinking alcohol within 4 hours of coming to work (Alberta Alcohol and Drug Abuse Commission, 2003). With regard to frequency, drinking before work was reported to occur weekly by 0.4% of the workforce, monthly by 0.6% of the workforce, and less than monthly by 3% of the workforce. Drinking while at work among Alberta workers was reported to occur weekly by 2% of the workforce. With regard to frequency, drinking at work was reported to occur weekly by 2% of the workforce, monthly by 1.0% of the workforce, and less than monthly by 8% of the workforce.

ILLICIT DRUG USE AND IMPAIRMENT. Past year prevalence rates for workplace illicit drug use in the United States (Frone, 2006b) reveal that 3.1% of the workforce (3.9 million workers) used at least one illicit drug—1.6% (2 million workers) used marijuana, 0.1% (169,000 workers) used cocaine, and 1.8% (2.3 million workers) illicitly used a prescribable drug. Regarding working under the influence of an illicit drug, 2.9% (3.6 million workers) were impaired by an illicit drug—1.7% (2.2 million workers) were impaired by marijuana, 0.2% (233,000 workers) were impaired by cocaine, and 1.4% (1.8 million workers) were impaired by a prescribable drug.

Weekly use at the workplace was reported by 1.8% of the workforce, monthly use was reported by 0.5% of the workforce, and less than monthly use was reported by 0.9% of the workforce. Workplace illicit drug impairment was reported to occur weekly by 1.2% of the workforce, monthly by 0.6% of the workforce, and less than monthly by 1.0% of the workforce. In terms of temporal context, 2.7% of the workforce (3.4 million workers) used illicit drugs within 2 hr of reporting to work, 1.8% (2.3 million workers) used during lunch breaks, 1.2% (1.5 million workers) used during other work breaks, and 1.7% (2.2 million workers) used while working.

Finally, as noted earlier, three groups of vulnerable workers were identified by cross-classifying gender, age, and occupation. Among young women in high-risk occupations, 10.6% reported workplace illicit drug use in the past 12 months and 11.4% reported workplace drug impairment. Among young men in the high-risk occupations, 28.0% reported workplace illicit drug use and 26.3% reported workplace drug impairment. Also, young men in the low-risk occupations showed somewhat elevated prevalence rates, with 7.7% reporting workplace illicit drug use and 6.8% reporting workplace drug impairment. Despite the high prevalence rates in these three subgroups, it is again important to point out that that the estimated population of individuals in these three subgroups reporting workplace illicit drug use represented 1.9% of the overall U.S. workforce.

Data from outside the United States show that 2.5% of the Australian workforce reported going to work under the influence of illicit drugs (Bywood et al., 2006). In Alberta, Canada, 2% of workers reported using an illicit drug within 4 hr of coming to work and 1% reported using an illicit drug while at work. Illicit drug use before work was reported to occur weekly by 0.7% of the workforce, monthly by 0.2% of the workforce, and less than monthly by 1.1% of the workforce. Illicit drug use while at work was reported to occur weekly by 0.4% of the workforce, monthly by 0.3% of the workforce, and less than monthly 0.3% of the workforce (Alberta Alcohol and Drug Abuse Commission, 2003).

Causes of Employee Substance Use

The potential causes of employee substance use can be classified along two primary dimensions (Frone, 2003, 2008b): causes that are external to the workplace (i.e., genetics, demographics, personality characteristics, socialization, and environmental factors) and causes internal to the workplace (i.e., socialization, experiences, and exposures at work). Although many factors external to the workplace may influence employee substance use, three categories of external predictors may be particularly salient to employee substance use: employee demographics, personality, and substance use outcome expectancies. In addition, three categories of predictors internal to the workplace are also relevant to employee substance use: workplace substance use climate, workplace social control, and work stressors.

Causes External to the Workplace

DEMOGRAPHICS. Prior research demonstrates that gender and age are related to substance use among workers. Employed adolescent boys and adult men report higher levels of overall alcohol and illicit drug use than employed adolescent girls and adult women, respectively (e.g., Bacharach, Bamberger, & Sonnenstuhl, 2002; Frone, 2003, 2006b; Frone, Russell, & Barnes, 1996; Frone, Russell, & Cooper, 1995; Hoffmann, Larison, & Sanderson, 1997). Moreover, past research among employed adolescents and adults revealed that males are more likely than females to engage in workplace substance use (e.g., Frone, 2003, 2006a, 2006b). Regarding age, the general substance use research literature shows that the prevalence of alcohol and illicit drug use increases from early adolescence until it peaks and begins to drop during the latter part of early adulthood (e.g., Anthony & Arria, 1999; O'Malley, Johnston, & Bachman, 1999). Consistent with this curvilinear relation, research on employed adolescents shows that age is positively related to overall and workplace substance use (e.g., Frone, 2003), whereas age is negatively related to overall and workplace substance use among employed adults (e.g., Bacharach et al., 2002; Frone, 2006a, 2006b; Hoffmann et al., 1997).

PERSONALITY. Prior research suggests that two domains of personality are related to substance use: behavioral undercontrol and negative affectivity. *Behavioral undercontrol* represents a tendency to focus on short-term incentives and to inhibit behavioral responses to cues of impending or possible punishment. Impulsivity, rebelliousness or intolerance of rules, and risk taking propensity are distinct dimensions of behavioral undercontrol that are positively associated with overall substance use among adolescents and adults (e.g., Colder & Chassin, 1997; Elkins, King, McGue, & Iacono, 2006; Jackson & Sher, 2003; King & Chassin, 2004). *Negative affectivity,* or the propensity to experience negative mood states and psychological distress, also has been identified as a vulnerability factor for substance use among adolescents and adults (e.g., Colder & Chassin, 1997; Cooper, Frone, Russell, & Mudar, 1995; Elkins et al., 2006). However, few studies have explored the relation of negative affectivity and behavioral undercontrol to workforce or workplace substance use. Grant and Langan-Fox (2007) explored the relation of the Big Five personality traits (i.e., openness to experience, conscientiousness, extraversion, agreeableness, and neuroticism) to overall employee substance use. They found that only negative affectivity predicted overall substance use. Although Frone (2003) failed to find a relation of negative affectivity to overall and workplace substance use among young workers, several dimensions of behavioral undercontrol were related to employee substance use. Impulsivity and risk taking were positively related to overall alcohol and marijuana use, and rebelliousness (i.e., intolerance of rules) was positively related to workplace alcohol use.

SUBSTANCE USE OUTCOME EXPECTANCIES. *Outcome expectancies* are "anticipations of one's own automatic reactions to various situations and behaviors" (Kirsch, 1999, p. 4) and therefore act as determinants of behavior. For example, individuals may consume alcohol after experiencing a stressful event if they expect to be more relaxed after consuming alcohol. In fact, individuals hold a number of different expectancies regarding the outcomes of using psychoactive substances (e.g., George et al., 1995; Goldman, Brown, & Christiansen, 1987; Schafer & Brown, 1991). Two anticipated effects of psychoactive substances are especially relevant to organizational research: affect regulation and performance regulation. *Affect regulation expectancies* refer to the expectation that a psychoactive substance will reduce negative emotions and increase positive emotions (e.g., Cooper et al., 1995; Goldman et al., 1987; Schafer & Brown, 1991). Many studies have documented a positive relation between affect regulation expectancies and overall levels of alcohol use in samples of adolescents and adults (e.g., Cooper et al., 1995). Although few expectancy studies have focused on the substance use of employed individuals, research shows that affect regulation expectancies are positively related to overall alcohol and marijuana use among adolescent and adult employees (Frone, 2003; Frone, Russell, & Cooper, 1993).

However, the only study exploring the relation of affect regulation expectancies to workplace alcohol and marijuana use failed to find significant relations in a sample of adolescent workers (Frone, 2003).

Performance regulation expectancies refer to the expectation that a psychoactive substance will impair or improve cognitive and motor performance (e.g., Goldman et al., 1987; Schafer & Brown, 1991). For example, individuals who believe that alcohol will improve their ability to think and function are more likely to report heavy drinking (e.g., Christiansen & Goldman, 1983). The only study to explore this issue among employed individuals found that performance regulation expectancies were positively related to overall alcohol and marijuana use and to workplace alcohol and marijuana use in a sample of adolescent workers (Frone, 2003).

Causes Internal to the Workplace

WORKPLACE SUBSTANCE USE CLIMATE. *Workplace substance use climate* has been defined broadly as employees' perceptions of the extent to which their work environment is supportive of alcohol and drug use at work (Frone, 2009). Ames and colleagues have suggested that workplace substance use climate comprises three dimensions (e.g., Ames & Grube, 1999; Ames & Janes, 1992). The first dimension is the perceived physical availability of alcohol and drugs at work. This dimension represents the ease of obtaining alcohol or other drugs at work and the ease of using them during work hours and during breaks. The second dimension represents descriptive norms or the extent to which members of an individual's workplace social network use or work while impaired by alcohol or drugs at work. The third dimension represents injunctive norms or the extent to which members of an individual's workplace social network approve of using or working under the influence of alcohol or drugs at work.

Findings from the few studies that have assessed the relation of workplace substance use climate to employees' use of alcohol or illicit drugs are mixed. Macdonald, Wells, and Wild (1999) found that reports of drugs being easily available from coworkers were positively related to having an alcohol use problem. However, Ames and Grube (1999) failed to find a relation between physical availability of alcohol at work and an individual's drinking at work. Similarly, Frone (2003) found that physical availability of alcohol and marijuana at work was unrelated to both overall and workplace alcohol and marijuana use, respectively. Although few studies have explored the relation of workplace descriptive or injunctive norms to employees' use of alcohol or illicit drugs, their results generally support a positive relation to overall and workplace substance use (e.g., Ames & Grube, 1999; Bacharach et al., 2002; Frone, 2003; Kjærheim, Mykletun, Aasland, Haldorsen, & Andersen, 1995; Macdonald et al., 1999).

A U.S. national study by Frone (2009) explored the relation of workplace substance use climate to the work outcomes of the majority of employees who do not use alcohol and drugs at work. The results of this study revealed that all three dimensions of workplace substance use climate (i.e., availability, descriptive norms, and injunctive norms) were negatively related to workplace safety, positively related to work strain, and negatively related to employee morale.

These results suggest that exposure to a permissive substance use climate at work may have broader relevance to the majority of employees who do not use alcohol and drugs at work.

WORKPLACE SOCIAL CONTROL. Substance use may be higher among employees who are not integrated into or regulated by the work organization (Ames, Grube, & Moore, 2000; Trice & Sonnenstuhl, 1990). Therefore, *workplace social control* refers to a broad set of work conditions that put employees at lower or higher risk of alcohol and illicit drug use, such as levels of commitment or attachment to an organization, level of mobility during work hours, visibility of work behaviors, level of supervision, and formal and informal polices and disciplinary actions regarding substance use. A few studies have assessed workplace social control, focusing primarily on supervisor monitoring and job visibility. Some research supports a relation between a lack of workplace social control and overall and workplace substance use (Frone, 2003; Trice & Sonnenstuhl, 1990), whereas other research fails to support this relation (Macdonald et al., 1999).

WORKPLACE STRESS. The dimension of the work environment that has received the most empirical attention in relation to employee substance use is work stress (for a broader review, see Frone, 1999, 2008b). It is widely believed that employee alcohol and illicit drug use represents a strategy to cope with negative emotions resulting from exposure to aversive physical and psychosocial qualities of the work environment (Ames & Janes, 1992; Frone, 1999; Trice & Sonnenstuhl, 1990). This expectation derives from the notion of tension reduction developed in the literature on alcohol use (Conger, 1956). Stated generally, the tension-reduction hypothesis has two propositions. The *stress-response dampening proposition* states that substance use before exposure to a stressor will reduce the experience of tension or strain normally resulting from the exposure (e.g., Sayette, 1999). The *stress-induced substance use proposition* states that exposure to stressors will lead to substance use as a means of mitigating the experienced tension and strain (e.g., Frone, 1999; Sayette, 1999). Most work-stress research has tested the stress-induced substance use proposition that more frequent exposure to work stressors is expected to cause more frequent or heavier use of alcohol and drugs after exposure to the stressors. In contrast, little research has tested the stress-response damping proposition that employees may use substances before exposure to work stressors to reduce anticipated negative affect. The general expectation that workplace stress is a cause of employee substance use also is consistent with a broader literature that supports the use of substances for affect regulation (e.g., Cooper et al., 1995; Peirce, Frone, Russell, Cooper, & Mudar, 2000).

Research on work stress and substance use has focused primarily on alcohol use, with relatively little attention devoted to illicit drug use. Most research testing the direct relation between within-role work stressors and alcohol use has failed to support such a relation (see Frone, 1999, 2008b). One exception is research on work–family conflict, which has been consistently related to overall measures of employee alcohol use and abuse in cross-sectional and longitudinal studies (e.g., Bromet, Dew, & Parkinson, 1990; Frone, 2000; Frone et al., 1996, 1997; Roos, Lahelma, & Rahkonen, 2006).

One reason for the lack of a direct relation between within-role work stressors and alcohol use may be that past research focused exclusively on measures of overall use that primarily assess consumption that occurs at times and in settings far removed from the workday. Measures of substance use that consider the temporal context of use may provide a more consistent link to work stressors (Frone, 1999). To explore this possibility, Frone (2008a) examined the relation of work overload and job insecurity to overall and temporally specific measures of alcohol and illicit drug use. The temporally specific measures assessed alcohol and drug use within 2 hr of starting work, during the workday, and within 2 hr of leaving work. Consistent with past research, the results failed to support a link between the within-role work stressors and measures of overall alcohol and illicit drug use. However, the results provided support for the relations of work stressors to alcohol and illicit drug use before work, during the workday, and after work. In addition, the temporal assessment of substance use allowed tests of and provided support for both the stress-response dampening (i.e., substance use before work) and stress-induced substance use (i.e., substance use during and after work) propositions of the tension reduction hypothesis.

Other studies have begun to explore variables that may mediate or moderate the relation between work stressors and substance use. Although some studies of within-role work stressors failed to support the mediating role of negative affect (e.g., Cooper, Russell, & Frone, 1990; Richman, Shinsako, Rospenda, Flaherty, & Freels, 2002), other studies support this indirect effect (e.g., Greenberg & Grunberg, 1995; Martin, Blum, & Roman, 1992). In addition to negative affect, Delaney, Grube, Greiner, Fisher, and Ragland (2002) found that inability to unwind after work mediated the relation between job problems and alcohol use.

Two studies supported the mediating role of negative affect in work–family conflict and alcohol use (Frone, Barnes, & Farrell, 1994; Vasse, Nijhuis, & Kok, 1998). Three studies tested and provided support for moderating effects on the relation of work stressors and work–family conflict to alcohol use (Bacharach et al., 2002; Frone et al., 1993, 1995; Grunberg, Moore, Anderson-Connolly, & Greenberg, 1999). For example, building from identity theory, Frone et al. (1995) found that both job demands and role ambiguity were positively related to heavy drinking only among employees who reported that their work role was psychologically important for self-definition. Finally, two studies tested and provided support for a moderated mediation model of work stress and alcohol use using within-role work stressors (Cooper et al., 1990; Grunberg, Moore, & Greenberg, 1998). For example, Grunberg and colleagues (1998) found that that work demands, interpersonal criticism from supervisors and coworkers, and feeling stuck in one's job were positively related to job dissatisfaction. Furthermore, they found that job dissatisfaction was related to problem drinking only among those who reported that they drank to reduce negative emotions.

Organizational Consequences of Employee Substance Use

The organizational consequences of employee substance use have received much attention and speculation. Although it is widely believed that the use of alcohol and other psychoactive drugs among employees has a strong and consistent negative relation to employee productivity, past research suggests that these relations are neither consistent nor robust (Frone, 2004, 2008b; Normand et al., 1994). This section first summarizes research exploring the relation of employee alcohol and illicit drug use in three categories of organizational consequences: (a) attendance outcomes, (b) task performance and other on-the-job behaviors, and (c) job accidents and injury outcomes (for additional information, see Frone, 2004, 2008b; Normand et al., 1994). It then describes a general model of substance use and employee productivity that highlights the potential complexity of these relations (Frone, 2004).

Attendance Outcomes

On the basis of a small set of studies, several older reviews suggest that absenteeism is the most consistently documented organizational outcome related to employee substance use (e.g., Martin, Kraft, & Roman, 1994; Normand et al., 1994; Zwerling, 1993). More recent research suggests that the relation between employee substance use and poor attendance is mixed, with some studies supporting a positive relation (e.g., Cunradi, Greiner, Ragland, & Fisher, 2005; McFarlin & Fals-Stewart, 2002) and others failing to support this relation (e.g., Boles, Pelletier, & Lynch, 2004; Moore, Grunberg, & Greenberg, 2000; Vasse et al., 1998). Given these inconsistent findings, an interesting study was conducted by McFarlin and Fals-Stewart (2002). In a timeline follow-back assessment of alcohol use over the preceding 4 weeks and an examination of company records for days absent during this period, these researchers found that workers were approximately 2 times more likely to be absent from work the day after alcohol was consumed. In contrast, alcohol use was not related to same day absenteeism or to being absent 2 or more days after drinking. Notwithstanding this study's strengths, the quantity of alcohol consumed was not assessed. As discussed later, being absent is likely the outcome of impairment (i.e., intoxication or hangover) due to heavy alcohol use and not the mere use of alcohol on a given day. The fact that the sample consisted primarily of young men, who generally drink more heavily than other groups of workers, might explain the relation they found between the dichotomous alcohol measure (i.e., drank vs. did not drink) and absenteeism. However, to understand the underlying process that links alcohol use to absenteeism, failing to assess quantity consumed may (a) lead to the misleading conclusion that any alcohol use is related to absenteeism and (b) underestimate the size of the relation between alcohol impairment and absenteeism.

Task Performance and Other On-the-Job Behaviors

Basic laboratory research on the acute effects of substance use generally shows that alcohol, marijuana, opioid analgesics, tranquilizers, and sedatives either have no effect or impair performance on a variety of tasks, such as time estimation, divided attention, tracking, vigilance, postural stability, and complex reaction time. In contrast, stimulants (which include cocaine) either have no effect or improve performance in laboratory settings. Several laboratory studies have explored the acute effect of alcohol use on performance using work-related simulations. Even at low levels (e.g., blood-alcohol concentrations of .04% to .09%), acute exposure to alcohol can impair various dimensions of cognitive and psychomotor performance used for many jobs, such as drill press operation, punch press operation, assembly tasks, welding, maintaining a power plant on a merchant ship, piloting a merchant ship, and managerial performance. In contrast, work-related simulations have failed to find an effect of alcohol hangover on managerial performance and ship power plant operation. Work simulation studies have not explored the acute effect of illicit psychoactive drugs on cognitive and psychomotor performance (for more detail, see Frone 2008b).

Despite the fact that laboratory studies have strong internal validity, the statistically significant cognitive and psychomotor deficits may be weak in practical terms. Moreover, because laboratory studies and work simulations may have limited external validity, it is not yet clear whether and how strongly their findings translate into actual changes in on-the-job behavior and performance (e.g., Heishman, 1998; Macdonald et al., 2003). Compared with laboratory research, field research has stronger external validity (though weaker internal validity) and has explored a broader set of performance and on-the-job behavioral outcomes. Several field studies have reported that employee alcohol or illicit drug use is related to poorer job performance (e.g., Ames et al., 1997; Blum, Roman, & Martin, 1993; Burton et al., 2005), whereas other research has failed to support such a relation (e.g., Boles et al., 2004; Burton et al., 2005; Moore et al., 2000). Research also has found that alcohol and illicit drug use is related to lower levels of positive contextual performance, such as working overtime, volunteering for additional work, or trying to improve the job (Lehman & Simpson, 1992), and to higher levels of counterproductive behavior, such as psychological and physical withdrawal at work and the perpetration of aggression and antagonistic behaviors at work (e.g., Ames et al., 1997; Lehman & Simpson, 1992; McFarlin, Fals-Stewart, Major, & Justice, 2001; Moore et al., 2000).

Accident and Injury Outcomes

Data on employee substance use and work injuries come from two sources. The first source is data from coroner and medical examiner records, drug testing programs, and emergency room visits. Zwerling (1993) estimated that acute alcohol impairment is present in approximately 10% of fatal work injuries and 5% of nonfatal work injuries. Based on the average positivity rates for over 35 million employee drug tests over a 5-year period (2002–2006) conducted by Quest Diagnostics Incorporated (2007), 3.0% of postaccident drug tests were positive for at least one illicit drug in the federally mandated safety-sensitive workforce, and 5.8% of postaccident drug tests were positive in the general workforce. Although interesting, these findings are insufficient evidence that substance use played a causal role in accidents or injuries. The primary problems with studies that report the proportion of substance-related injuries are the lack of a control condition and, in the case of illicit drug use, the inability of urine tests to discern the timing of use relative to the injury or accident and the level of impairment. But the causal role of overall illicit drug use can be addressed by comparing the positivity rate from postaccident drug tests with the positivity rate from random drug tests. If employee drug use plays a major role in workplace accidents and injuries, the positivity rate for postaccident drug tests (3.0% in the safety-sensitive workforce, 5.8% in the general workforce) should be substantially higher than the positivity rate for random drug tests (1.8% in the safety-sensitive workforce, 6.3% in the general workforce). Thus, these comparisons do not support a causal role for overall employee drug use in workplace accidents and injuries.

The second source of data comes from epidemiologic field studies that attempt to estimate the relation between employee substance use and work accidents or injuries. Several reviews conducted during the 1990s concluded that there was no consistent and robust relation between employee substance use and workplace accidents or injuries. Nonetheless, because of various methodological weaknesses in the empirical studies, earlier reviews also suggested that it was premature to conclude that employee substance use plays no causal role in the etiology of workplace injuries and accidents. More recent field studies show that with few exceptions (e.g., Frone, 1998), employee alcohol and illicit drug use are not significantly related to workplace injuries (for reviews, see Frone, 2004, 2008b).

A General Model of Employee Substance Use and Productivity

Inconsistency exists in research findings relating employee substance use to various dimensions of organizational outcomes. Some of the inconsistency is found across field studies exploring different outcomes (e.g., attendance, task performance, injuries), and some is found comparing laboratory studies of acute impairment with field studies of chronic patterns of use. These inconsistencies may not be surprising because many researchers seem to assume that the mere consumption of a psychoactive substance, regardless of its temporal context or the amount consumed, will have the same effect across all productivity outcomes for all employees. The general alcohol and drug literature, however, suggests that the underlying process linking employee substance use to workplace productivity may be much more complicated. Failing to account for this complexity may explain much of the inconsistency in past research findings.

To account for these inconsistencies and to highlight the potential complexity in the relations between employee substance use and productivity outcomes, Frone (2004) developed the conceptual model depicted in Figure 15.1. This section summarizes the major features of this model, though the reader is referred to the original source for a detailed discussion of its development, relevant constructs, implications, and supporting evidence.

The first general feature of the model is that the temporal context of substance use is matched to specific organizational outcomes. In past research, researchers typically assessed employees' overall alcohol and drug use (i.e., workforce substance use), which largely reflected substance use off the job (i.e., use away from work and outside an individual's normal work hours) rather than workplace substance use that reflected use and impairment on the job. Thus, the model explicitly distinguishes between off-the-job and on-the-job substance

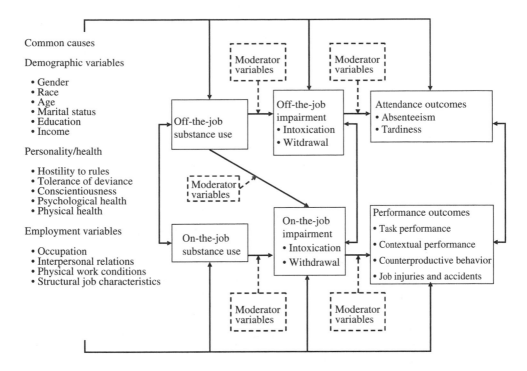

Figure 15.1. Model of employee substance use and productivity. From "Alcohol, Drugs, and Workplace Safety Outcomes: A View From a General Model of Employee Substance Use and Productivity," by M. R. Frone. In J. Barling & M. R. Frone (Eds.), *The Psychology of Workplace Safety* (p. 135), 2004, Washington, DC: American Psychological Association. Copyright 2004 by the American Psychological Association.

use and impairment. It is also important to distinguish between attendance and performance outcomes. Attendance outcomes represent the failure to come to work on time (i.e., tardiness) or the failure to come to work at all (i.e., absenteeism). Performance outcomes represent behaviors and outcomes that occur on the job, such as accidents and injuries, task performance, contextual performance, and counterproductive behaviors. As shown in Figure 15.1, the model proposes that there is a correspondence between the temporal context of employee substance use and impairment and the type of productivity outcomes affected. In other words, off-the-job substance use and impairment primarily predict attendance outcomes and on-the-job substance use and impairment predict performance outcomes.

The second general feature of the model is that it distinguishes between substance use and substance impairment (see the definitions provided earlier). The model proposes that substance impairment is the proximal cause of poor productivity outcomes and mediates the more distal effect of substance use. Specifically, increasing levels of off-the-job substance use are expected to cause higher levels of intoxication and more severe withdrawal (when substance use is decreased) off the job, which then causes poor attendance. Likewise, higher levels of off-the-job substance use may be related to intoxication at work because individuals may still have a nonzero blood level when they arrive at work, and withdrawal symptoms at work may be more severe among chronic heavy off-the-job substance users if they do not consume the substance during their work shift. Also, higher levels of on-the-job substance use are expected to cause higher levels of on-the-job intoxication. In turn, on-the-job intoxication and withdrawal are expected to negatively affect performance outcomes.

The third general feature of the model is that it calls attention to the need to control for common causes of employee substance use and the various productivity outcomes. Care must be taken in the interpretation of some prior studies that have supported relations between employee substance use and the various organizational outcomes. Much of this research has lacked adequate controls for common causes of substance use, substance impairment, and productivity. Differences across studies in the potential confounding variables that were modeled may partly explain inconsistencies across studies in the extent to which employee substance use was related to specific outcomes.

The final general feature of the model is that it highlights the need to consider variables that may moderate the various relations involving substance use, substance impairment, and the organizational outcomes. The various moderating processes discussed by Frone (2004) include pharmacological, dispositional, motivational, and situational influences. As shown in Figure 15.1, different variables may moderate the relation between substance use and substance impairment and between substance impairment and the productivity outcomes.

Conclusions

The goal of this chapter was to review briefly the literature on substance use in the workforce and in the workplace for occupational health psychologists. The literature on the scope of employee alcohol and illicit drug use support several general conclusions. First, detailed prevalence data on alcohol and illicit drug use in the workforce and in the workplace are beginning to be published in the United States. However, published prevalence data from other countries are scarce. Second, despite the attention devoted to illicit drug use by employers, policymakers, and companies conducting drug tests, the use of alcohol by employees is likely to be more problematic for employers than employee use of illicit drugs. Alcohol use and impairment are more prevalent than illicit drug use and impairment in the workforce and workplace. Third, illicit drug use primarily reflects the use of marijuana. Fourth, comparing the prevalence of workforce substance use with the prevalence of workplace substance use shows that most substance use and impairment occurs outside the workplace. In other words, 79% of U.S. employees who use alcohol do not report any workplace alcohol use, and 78% of those who report illicit drug use do not report any workplace illicit drug use. Finally, alcohol and illicit drug use in the workforce and in the workplace are not distributed uniformly in the working population. The primary factors related to the distribution of substance use are gender, age, and occupation. This means that not all employers are affected equally and that substance use, especially illicit drug use, may not be a major issue for most employers. Nonetheless, those employers who draw from the three high-risk segments of the workforce identified earlier may be more likely to deal with problems related to overall and workplace substance use.

Research looking at the causes and outcomes of employee substance use is inconsistent and inconclusive. This is partly due to a lack of research in some areas and partly due to conceptual and measurement shortcomings. Future research needs to be much more sophisticated and integrated if we are to (a) better understand the role of causes that are external (e.g., demographics, personality, substance use outcome expectancies) and internal (e.g., workplace substance use climate, workplace social control, work stressors) to the workplace and (b) better understand the complex relation of employee substance use to organizational outcomes. Regarding organizational outcomes, not only do we need to study the outcomes of employees who use alcohol and illicit drugs, we also need to study the impact of exposure to a permissive workplace substance use climate on the majority of employees who do not use substances and are not impaired during the workday. A broad discussion of future research directions would be too long for this review. Therefore, the interested reader is referred to Frone (1999, 2004, 2006a, 2006b, 2008b) and Normand et al. (1994).

To develop defensible and effective evidence-based policies and interventions regarding employee substance use, relevant stakeholders will require more integrative and higher quality research. It is hoped that this review will motivate occupational health psychologists to begin reading the literature on employee substance use and to begin designing new research on the scope of substance use in the workforce and in the workplace and a new generation of integrative theoretical research on the causes and organizational outcomes of employee substance use.

References

Alberta Alcohol and Drug Abuse Commission. (2003). *Substance use and gambling in the Alberta workplace, 2002: A replication study.* Edmonton, Canada: Author.

American Psychiatric Association. (2000). *Diagnostic and statistical manual of mental disorders* (4th ed., text rev.). Washington, DC: Author.

Ames, G. M., & Grube, J. W. (1999). Alcohol availability and workplace drinking: Mixed method analyses. *Journal of Studies on Alcohol, 60,* 383–393.

Ames, G. M., Grube, J. W., & Moore, R. S. (2000). Social control and workplace drinking norms: A comparison of two organizational cultures. *Journal of Studies on Alcohol, 61,* 203–219.

Ames, G. M., Grube, J. W., & Moore, R. S. (1997). The relationship of drinking and hangovers to workplace problems: An empirical study. *Journal of Studies on Alcohol, 58,* 37–47.

Ames, G. M., & Janes, C. J. (1992). A cultural approach to conceptualizing alcohol and the workplace. *Alcohol Health and Research World, 16,* 112–119.

Anthony, J. C., & Arria, A. M. (1999). Epidemiology of substance abuse in adulthood. In P. J. Ott, R. E. Tarter, & R. T. Ammerman (Eds.), *Sourcebook on substance abuse: Etiology, epidemiology, assessment, and treatment* (pp. 32–49). Boston, MA: Allyn & Bacon.

Bacharach, S. B., Bamberger, P. A., & Sonnenstuhl, W. J. (2002). Driven to drink: Managerial control, work-related risk factors, and employee problem drinking. *Academy of Management Journal, 45,* 637–658. doi:10.2307/3069302

Blum, T. C., Roman, P. M., & Martin, J. K. (1993). Alcohol consumption and work performance. *Journal of Studies on Alcohol, 54,* 61–70.

Boles, M., Pelletier, B., & Lynch, W. (2004). The relationship between health risks and work productivity. *Journal of Occupational and Environmental Medicine, 46,* 737–745. doi:10.1097/01.jom.0000131830.45744.97

Bromet, E. J., Dew, M. A., & Parkinson, D. K. (1990). Spillover between work and family: A study of blue-collar working women. In J. Eckenrode & S. Gore (Eds.), *Stress between work and family* (pp. 133–151). New York, NY: Plenum Press.

Burton, W. N., Chen, C.-Y., Conti, D. J., Schultz, A. B., Pransky, G., & Edington, D. W. (2005). The association of health risks with on-the-job productivity. *Journal of Occupational and Environmental Medicine, 47,* 769–777.

Bywood, P., Pidd, K., & Roche, A. (2006). *Illicit drugs in the Australian workforce: Prevalence and patterns of use.* Canberra, Australia: National Centre for Education and Training on Addiction.

Christiansen, B. A., & Goldman, M. S. (1983). Alcohol related expectancies versus demographic/background variables in the prediction of adolescent drinking. *Journal of Consulting and Clinical Psychology, 51,* 249–257. doi:10.1037/0022-006X.51.2.249

Colder, C. R., & Chassin, L. (1997). Affectivity and impulsivity: Temperament risk for adolescent alcohol involvement. *Psychology of Addictive Behaviors, 11,* 83–97. doi:10.1037/0893-164X.11.2.83

Conger, J. (1956). Reinforcement theory and the dynamics of alcoholism. *Quarterly Journal of Studies on Alcohol, 17,* 296–305.

Controlled Substances Act, 21 U.S.C. § 812 (1970).

Cooper, M. L., Frone, M. R., Russell, M., & Mudar, P. (1995). Drinking to regulate positive and negative emotions: A motivational model of alcohol use. *Journal of Personality and Social Psychology, 69,* 990–1005. doi:10.1037/0022-3514.69.5.990

Cooper, M. L., Russell, M., & Frone, M. R. (1990). Work stress and alcohol effects: A test of stress-induced drinking. *Journal of Health and Social Behavior, 31,* 260–276. doi:10.2307/2136891

Cunradi, C. B., Greiner, B. A., Ragland, D. R., & Fisher, J. (2005). Alcohol, stress-related factors, and short-term absenteeism among urban transit operators. *Journal of Urban Health, 82,* 43–57. doi:10.1093/jurban/jti007

Delaney, W. P., Grube, J. W., Greiner, B., Fisher, J. M., & Ragland, D. R. (2002). Job stress, unwinding, and drinking in transit operators. *Journal of Studies on Alcohol, 63,* 420–429.

Elkins, I. J., King, S. M., McGue, M., & Iacono, W. G. (2006). Personality traits and the development of nicotine, alcohol, and illicit drug disorders: Prospective links from adolescence to young adulthood. *Journal of Abnormal Psychology, 115,* 26–39. doi:10.1037/0021-843X.115.1.26

Frone, M. R. (1998). Predictors of work injuries among employed adolescents. *Journal of Applied Psychology, 83,* 565–576. doi:10.1037/0021-9010.83.4.565

Frone, M. R. (1999). Work stress and alcohol use. *Alcohol Research & Health, 23,* 284–291.

Frone, M. R. (2000). Work–family conflict and employee psychiatric disorders: The national comorbidity survey. *Journal of Applied Psychology, 85,* 888–895. doi:10.1037/0021-9010.85.6.888

Frone, M. R. (2003). Predictors of overall and on-the-job substance use among young workers. *Journal of Occupational Health Psychology, 8,* 39–54. doi:10.1037/1076-8998.8.1.39

Frone, M. R. (2004). Alcohol, drugs, and workplace safety outcomes: A view from a general model of employee substance use and productivity. In J. Barling & M. R. Frone (Eds.), *The Psychology of workplace safety* (pp. 127–156). Washington, DC: American Psychological Association.

Frone, M. R. (2006a). Prevalence and distribution of alcohol use and impairment in the workplace: A U.S. national survey. *Journal of Studies on Alcohol, 67,* 147–156.

Frone, M. R. (2006b). Prevalence and distribution of illicit drug use in the workforce and in the workplace: Findings and implications from a U.S. national survey. *Journal of Applied Psychology, 91,* 856–869. doi:10.1037/0021-9010.91.4.856

Frone, M. R. (2008a). Are work stressors related to employee substance use? The importance of temporal context in assessments of alcohol and illicit drug use. *Journal of Applied Psychology, 93,* 199–206. doi:10.1037/0021-9010.93.1.199

Frone, M. R. (2008b). Employee alcohol and illicit drug use: Scope, causes, and organizational consequences. In J. Barling & C. L. Cooper (Eds.), *The Sage handbook of organizational behavior: Vol. 1. Micro approaches* (pp. 519–540). Thousand Oaks, CA: Sage.

Frone, M. R. (2009). Does a permissive workplace substance use climate affect employees who do not use alcohol and drugs at work? A U.S. national study. *Psychology of Addictive Behaviors, 23,* 386–390. doi:10.1037/a0015965

Frone, M. R., Barnes, G. M., & Farrell, M. P. (1994). Relationship of work–family conflict to substance use among employed mothers: The role of negative affect. *Journal of Marriage and the Family, 56,* 1019–1030. doi:10.2307/353610

Frone, M. R., Russell, M., & Barnes, G. M. (1996). Work–family conflict, gender, and health-related outcomes: A study of employed parents in two community samples. *Journal of Occupational Health Psychology, 1,* 57–69. doi:10.1037/1076-8998.1.1.57

Frone, M. R., Russell, M., & Cooper, M. L. (1993). Relationship of work–family conflict, gender, and alcohol expectancies to alcohol use/abuse. *Journal of Organizational Behavior, 14,* 545–558. doi:10.1002/job.4030140604

Frone, M. R., Russell, M., & Cooper, M. L. (1995). Job stressors, job involvement, and employee health: A test of identity theory. *Journal of Occupational and Organizational Psychology, 68,* 1–11.

Frone, M. R., Russell, M., & Cooper, M. L. (1997). Relation of work–family conflict to health outcomes: A four-year longitudinal study of employed parents. *Journal of Occupational and Organizational Psychology, 70,* 325–335.

George, W. H., Frone, M. R., Cooper, M. L., Russell, M., Skinner, J. B., & Windle, M. (1995). A revised alcohol expectancy questionnaire: Factor structure confirmation and invariance in a general population sample. *Journal of Studies on Alcohol, 56,* 177–185.

Goldman, M. S., Brown, S. A., & Christiansen, B. A. (1987). Expectancy theory: Thinking about drinking. In H. T. Blane & K. E. Leonard (Eds.), *Psychological theories of drinking and alcoholism* (pp. 181–226). New York, NY: Guilford Press.

Grant, S., & Langan-Fox, J. (2007). Personality and the occupational stressor–strain relationship: The role of the big five. *Journal of Occupational Health Psychology, 12,* 20–33. doi:10.1037/1076-8998.12.1.20

Greenberg, E. S., & Grunberg, L. (1995). Work alienation and problem alcohol behavior. *Journal of Health and Social Behavior, 36,* 83–102. doi:10.2307/2137289

Grunberg, L., Moore, S., Anderson-Connolly, R., & Greenberg, E. S. (1999). Work stress and self-reported alcohol use: The moderating role of escapist reasons for drinking. *Journal of Occupational Health Psychology, 4,* 29–36. doi:10.1037/1076-8998.4.1.29

Grunberg, L., Moore, S., & Greenberg, E. S. (1998). Work stress and problem alcohol behavior: A test of the spill-over model. *Journal of Organizational Behavior, 19,* 487–502. doi:10.1002/(SICI)1099-1379(199809)19:5<487::AID-JOB852>3.0.CO;2-Z

Heishman, S. J. (1998). Effects of abused drugs on human performance: Laboratory assessment. In S. B. Karach (Ed.), *Drug abuse handbook* (pp. 206–235). New York, NY: CRC Press.

Hoffmann, J. P., Larison, C., & Sanderson, A. (1997). *An analysis of worker drug use and workplace policies and programs (DHHS Pub. No. SMA 97–3142).* Washington, DC: U.S. Government Printing Office.

Jackson, K. M., & Sher, K. J. (2003). Alcohol use disorders and psychological distress: A prospective state–trait analysis. *Journal of Abnormal Psychology, 112,* 599–613. doi:10.1037/0021-843X.112.4.599

King, K. M., & Chassin, L. (2004). Mediating and moderating effects of adolescent behavioral undercontrol and parenting in the prediction of drug use disorders in emerging adulthood. *Psychology of Addictive Behaviors, 18,* 239–249. doi:10.1037/0893-164X.18.3.239

Kirsch, I. (1999). Response expectancy: An introduction. In I. Kirsch (Ed.), *How expectancies shape experience* (pp. 3–13). Washington, DC: American Psychological Association.

Kjærheim, K., Mykletun, R., Aasland, O. G., Haldorsen, T., & Andersen, A. (1995). Heavy drinking in the restaurant business: The role of social modeling and structural factors of the work-place. *Addiction, 90,* 1487–1495. doi:10.1111/j.1360-0443.1995.tb02811.x

Lehman, W. E. K., & Simpson, D. D. (1992). Employee substance use and on-the-job behaviors. *Journal of Applied Psychology, 77,* 309–321. doi:10.1037/0021-9010.77.3.309

Macdonald, S., Anglin-Bodrug, K., Mann, R. E., Erickson, P., Hathaway, A., Chipman, M., & Rylett, M. (2003). Injury risk associated with cannabis and cocaine use. *Drug and Alcohol Dependence, 72,* 99–115. doi:10.1016/S0376-8716(03)00202-3

Macdonald, S., Wells, S., & Wild, T. C. (1999). Occupational risk factors associated with alcohol and drug problems. *The American Journal of Drug and Alcohol Abuse, 25,* 351–369. doi:10.1081/ADA-100101865

Maisto, S. A., Galizio, M., & Connors, G. J. (2008). *Drug use and abuse* (5th ed.). Belmont, CA: Wadsworth.

Martin, J. K., Blum, T. C., & Roman, P. M. (1992). Drinking to cope and self-medication: Characteristics of jobs in relation to workers' drinking behavior. *Journal of Organizational Behavior, 13,* 55–71. doi:10.1002/job.4030130106

Martin, J. K., Kraft, J. M., & Roman, P. M. (1994). Extent and impact of alcohol and drug use problems in the workplace: A review of empirical evidence. In S. Macdonald & P. M. Roman (Eds.), *Research advances in alcohol and drug problems: Vol. 2. Drug testing in the workplace.* New York, NY: Plenum Press.

McFarlin, S. K., & Fals-Stewart, W. (2002). Workplace absenteeism and alcohol use: A sequential analysis. *Psychology of Addictive Behaviors, 16,* 17–21. doi:10.1037/0893-164X.16.1.17

McFarlin, S. K., Fals-Stewart, W., Major, D. A., & Justice, E. M. (2001). Alcohol use and workplace aggression: An examination of perpetration and victimization. *Journal of Substance Abuse, 13,* 303–321. doi:10.1016/S0899-3289(01)00080-3

Moore, R. S. (1998). The hangover: An ambiguous concept in workplace alcohol policy. *Contemporary Drug Problems, 25,* 49–63.

Moore, S., Grunberg, L., & Greenberg, E. (2000). The relationships between alcohol problems and well-being, work attitudes, and performance: Are they monotonic? *Journal of Substance Abuse, 11,* 183–204. doi:10.1016/S0899-3289(00)00020-1

Normand, J., Lempert, R. O., & O'Brien, C. P. (1994). *Under the influence? Drugs and the American work force.* Washington, DC: National Academy Press.

O'Malley, P. M., Johnston, L. D., & Bachman, J. G. (1999). Epidemiology of substance abuse in adolescence. In P. J. Ott, R. E. Tarter, & R. T. Ammerman (Eds.), *Sourcebook on substance abuse: Etiology, epidemiology, assessment, and treatment* (pp. 14–31). Boston, MA: Allyn & Bacon.

Peirce, R. S., Frone, M. R., Russell, M., Cooper, M. L., & Mudar, P. (2000). A longitudinal model of social contact, social support, depression, and alcohol use. *Health Psychology, 19,* 28–38. doi:10.1037/0278-6133.19.1.28

Pidd, K., Berry, J. G., Harrison, J. E., Roche, A. M., Driscoll, T. R., & Newson, R. S. (2006). *Alcohol and work: Patterns of use, workplace culture and safety. Injury research and Statistics Series Number 28* (AIHW cat no. INJCAT 82). Adelaide, Australia: Australian Institute of Health and Welfare.

Quest Diagnostics Incorporated. (2007). *The drug testing index.* Lyndhurst, NJ: Author.

Richman, J. A., Shinsako, S. A., Rospenda, K. M., Flaherty, J. A., & Freels, S. (2002). Workplace harassment/abuse and alcohol-related outcomes: The mediating role of psychological distress. *Journal of Studies on Alcohol, 63,* 412–419.

Roos, E., Lahelma, E., & Rahkonen, O. (2006). Work–family conflicts and drinking behaviours among employed men and women. *Drug and Alcohol Dependence, 83,* 49–56. doi:10.1016/j.drugalcdep.2005.10.009

Saitz, R. (1998). Introduction to alcohol withdrawal. *Alcohol Health and Research World, 22,* 5–12.

Sayette, M. A. (1999). Does drinking reduce stress? *Alcohol Research & Health, 23,* 250–255.

Schafer, J., & Brown, S. A. (1991). Marijuana and cocaine effect expectancies and drug use patterns. *Journal of Consulting and Clinical Psychology, 59,* 558–565. doi:10.1037/0022-006X.59.4.558

Smith, A., Wadsworth, E., Moss, S., & Simpson, S. (2004). *The scale and impact of illegal drug use by workers* (Research Report 193). London, England: Health and Safety Executive.

Swift, R., & Davidson, D. (1998). Alcohol hangover: Mechanisms and mediators. *Alcohol Health and Research World, 22,* 54–60.

Trice, H. M., & Sonnenstuhl, W. J. (1990). On the construction of drinking norms in work organizations. *Journal of Studies on Alcohol, 51,* 201–220.

Vasse, R. M., Nijhuis, F. J. N., & Kok, G. (1998). Associations between work stress, alcohol consumption, and sickness absence. *Addiction, 93,* 231–241. doi:10.1046/j.1360-0443.1998.9322317.x

Wiese, J. G., Shlipak, M. G., & Browner, W. S. (2000). The alcohol hangover. *Annals of Internal Medicine, 132,* 897–902.

Zwerling, C. (1993). Current practice and experience in drug and alcohol testing. *Bulletin on Narcotics, 45,* 155–196.

Part V ———————————————

Interventions
and Treatment

16

Job Stress Interventions and Organization of Work

Norbert K. Semmer

Although many attempts to prevent stress at work have been directed toward the individual (Ganster, 1995; Murphy & Sauter, 2004), there are compelling reasons to focus on changing the workplace itself (Semmer, 2006). The latter is difficult, though, because changing organizations implies changing a complex social system, which often meets much resistance and can have unintended side effects. The former emphasis on people's behavior reflects the domain of psychology. Often, people's stress symptoms are prematurely attributed to their alleged inability to cope rather than to characteristics of the work environment. The emphasis on individuals and their behavior is one-sided and calls for a balancing emphasis on the work environment as a target for change (Semmer & Zapf, 2004). I emphasize "in addition to" rather than "instead of." One sometimes hears the claim that all one needs to do is "remove the causes" of stress. This greatly underestimates the complex interplay between the environment, with its options and restrictions on the one hand, and people, with their ways of coping, on the other. It also underestimates the extent to which many stressful work environments have positive stressful aspects as well, for instance in terms of stimulation and challenge. Not surprisingly, therefore, interventions that change the work environment yield mixed results (Semmer, 2006), and this picture has not fundamentally changed since the first edition of this handbook.

Changes related to the work itself may imply either primary prevention (i.e., creating working conditions that are not conducive to the development of stress symptoms for the healthy) or secondary prevention (i.e., preventing existing, but minor, stress symptoms from becoming chronic by altering aspects of the work environment that are responsible for them; see Quick, Quick, Nelson, & Hurrell, 1997). Interventions can simultaneously be primary and secondary in nature, being directed at a large number of people, some with problems and some not.

Influence of Work on Health

Stress at work can have an impact on people's health and well-being (e.g., Beehr, 1995; Murphy & Sauter, 2004; Kahn & Byosiere, 1992; Karasek & Theorell, 1990; Quick et al., 1997; Sonnentag & Frese, 2003). The health risks apply to depression, psychosomatic complaints, back pain, cardiovascular disease, and other disorders (Belkic, Landsbergis, Schnall, & Baker, 2004; Siegrist, 2002; Sonnentag & Frese, 2003). Theory and research on stress imply that work should be challenging but not overly so, provide variability but control too, afford reasonably clear role expectations but not conflicting ones, provide stimulation but not be overly demanding, be embedded in supportive social relationships as well as demanding yet supportive leadership, and offer a reasonable psychological contract with rewards and security (Warr, 2007).

There are several domains of work stressors, including (a) features of tasks, such as complexity and variety; (b) work conditions, such as ergonomic conditions and speed; (c) role requirements, especially ambiguity or conflict; (d) social conditions, such as conflicts, appreciation and fairness; and (e) wider organizational conditions, such as job security and organizational culture (Quick et al., 1997). Of these, control and influence play a major role (Karasek & Theorell, 1990; Spector, 1998), as do conditions that create impediments to successful task performance (Sonnentag & Frese, 2003) and the rewards offered by organizations to people who have to deal with stressful situations (Siegrist, 2002).

Domains of Intervention

Interventions for healthy work may focus on ergonomic changes, job content, and work organization. Quick et al. (1997) referred to these as *task and physical demands* (p. 157). Many calls for changing the work environment imply this focus. Less attention is given to the social environment, or what Quick et al. (1997) referred to as *role and interpersonal demands* (p. 157). Unclear and conflicting expectations have long been recognized as central aspects of stress (Kahn & Byosiere, 1992). Such features as conflicting relationships with others have been shown to constitute important social stressors, whereas social support has been established as a possible source of relief (Beehr, 1995; Kahn & Byosiere, 1992).

The following sections concentrate, first, on attempted changes in technical and task demands and then on changes in the social environment. This discussion is followed by an account of comprehensive interventions that cannot be assigned to any one approach. Of course, there is hardly any intervention that does not target multiple aspects. Here, I have tried to categorize interventions according to their dominant focus. Only a small number of studies can be cited; they are selected mainly for illustration purposes.

Interventions Concerning Tasks and Work Environment

Task interventions refer to the job design in terms of tasks (e.g., variability) and the organization of work (e.g., control), which are important for health and well-being (Kompier, 2003). Many concepts for "good" or "human" job design were developed with motivation in mind rather than health and well-being (cf. Hackman & Oldham, 1980), but they often show effects on the latter as well (cf. Parker & Wall, 1998).

As an example, one of the best-known studies in this area concerns an intervention in a department of a confectionery company (Wall & Clegg, 1981), prompted by problems such as low morale, poor relations between management and the shop floor, and concomitant problems such as high turnover. Changes concentrated on two aspects of Hackman and Oldham's (1980) job characteristics model. Task identity was increased by removing barriers in the production hall to make the whole process visible, and autonomy was given to the group, which now could decide on the allocation of tasks, rest breaks, production speed, and the like. Measures were taken 5 months after the project started, but before changes took effect, and then again 18 and 28 months later. Changes were observed in the aspects of the model that were targeted (i.e., perceived identity, autonomy) but not in skill variety and significance, making a Hawthorne effect unlikely. There were improvements in intrinsic motivation, job satisfaction, performance, and mental health. These effects were observed for all three intervals, but the long-term effects were strongest. Despite the lack of a control group, the study convincingly demonstrated that the effects were specific to the changes of increases in autonomy and identity, because "nonequivalent dependent variables" (Shadish, Cook, & Campbell, 2002, p. 158) did not change. However, a later study that had a similar approach although showing some positive findings (e.g., for job satisfaction) failed to replicate the findings with regard to mental health (Wall, Kemp, Jackson, & Clegg, 1986).

From these and other studies, it is possible to reach two key conclusions. First, it is possible to achieve positive health-related outcomes by changing the nature of tasks. Second, the results of different studies are not necessarily consistent. Of the measures that refer to health and well-being, job satisfaction improved in both studies mentioned, but mental health improved in only one of them. This is an example. The literature shows that inconsistencies are more the rule than the exception and therefore deserve to be discussed further. This point is taken up later.

Smith and Zehel (1992) illustrated another point about task interventions. Their study concerned wrappers, meat processors, and cutters in a meat processing company. Its original focus on upper-extremity cumulative trauma disorders was broadened to more general aspects of stressful work conditions, such as machine pacing, short cycles, harsh physical environment, and the potential for job loss. Focus groups recommended job rotation, which was introduced.

After 1 year, the wrappers showed reduced musculoskeletal problems and psychosomatic complaints and improved appraisal of work conditions (e.g., concerning pressure to work fast). Meat processors showed a mixed picture. The cutters benefited somewhat in terms of musculoskeletal complaints, psychosomatic symptoms, and pressure to work hard, but they reported less job control and lower job satisfaction. It is of interest that the wrappers, who had the worst conditions at the outset, benefited the most clearly. The cutters, however, who originally had the most skilled and prestigious jobs, evidently resented the skill devaluation resulting from rotating to the other tasks and therefore deteriorated in job satisfaction, although they improved with respect to strain.

This study illustrates two points. First, results may differ for different groups. Second, some symptoms (i.e., classic stress symptoms—see the section on outcome variables) may improve, whereas other indicators of well-being (i.e., attitudinal variables such as job satisfaction) deteriorate. In addition, this study presents an example of an investigation that does not fully make use of its potential: Quantitative data were gathered but not properly analyzed, and the report confines itself to a narrative description. Note that this criticism does not simply say that they do not have the optimal design. Rather, the emphasis is on the fact that the authors were not fully exploiting their data, even within the limits of their design.

Other studies show that improvements depend on additional variables, as when enhancement of control, and concomitant job satisfaction, depended on perceived supervisor support (Logan & Ganster, 2005). Bond, Flaxman, and Bunce (2008) showed that enhanced control affected mental health and absenteeism in the intervention group but not in the control group, and the effects were stronger for people high in flexibility. This study also demonstrated that the effects of control-enhancing measures were, indeed, mediated by enhanced perception of control. These two studies also illustrate increasing methodological sophistication since the last edition of this handbook.

Work Conditions

The second category of intervention refers to work conditions, such as workload and work time. Two studies of driving examiners reported interventions concerning workload. Meijman, Mulder, van Dormolen, and Cremer (1992) investigated schedules of nine, 10, or 11 driving examinations per day, with each condition lasting a week. In the 11-exams condition, tension at the end of the working day was higher, as were adrenalin levels. A mental task revealed reduced efficiency. Observers riding along in the cars noted that the examiners issued more warnings and rebukes concerning violation of rules. In addition, the failure rate for the two last exams of the day was higher in this condition.

Parkes and Sparkes (1998, Case 3.8) also compared different numbers of exams per day. Perceived demands and anxiety were reduced, and cognitive performance and job satisfaction increased with reduced load. Exams were reduced from nine to eight per day as a result of the study, and perceived demands were still lower 5 years after the first assessment. Anxiety levels were lower than could have been expected without the intervention (according to an analysis of covariance). So both of these studies document positive short-term effects, and Parkes and Sparkes's study yields indications of a positive long-term effect.

Kompier, Cooper, and Geurts (2000, Case 1) reported a study in which work time for bus drivers was reduced. The intervention led to a reduction in back pain (significant in comparison with that of the control group) and several other changes, not all of which were, however, significantly different from those of the control group. (Significance was, however, not easy to achieve, as the control group contained only 26 persons.) This was a study with a rather strong design, having a control group. In addition, a variety of measures was used. However, there was a possible confound with a person-focused intervention (a workshop on health promotion). But altogether this study constitutes a rather good example, with encouraging results.

Role Clarity and Social Relationships

As argued earlier, interventions that reduce interpersonal conflict, strengthen social ties, and clarify goals and expectations might decrease unnecessary stress and increase health. However, one finds only a few studies concerned with stress that focus on this type of intervention (see Quick et al., 1997; Quick, Bhagat, Dalton, & Quick, 1987).

In a study by Quick (1979), goal setting by supervisor–employee interaction significantly reduced role conflict and role ambiguity. Reduced absenteeism was demonstrated after 5 months but not maintained after 8 months. Quick, Kulisch, Jones, O'Connor, and Peters (as cited in Quick et al., 1997) could not replicate the positive effects on role problems, and absenteeism actually increased. It seems likely that positive effects of this kind of intervention depend strongly on a participatory approach, which was more characteristic of the first than of the second study (see Quick et al., 1997). In a similar vein, Schaubroeck, Ganster, Sime, and Ditman (1993) found weak effects of role clarification overall but a dose-response relationship between the amount of role clarification actually achieved and psychological health. Both latter studies underscore the role of implementation quality.

Heaney, Price, and Rafferty (1995) presented an experimental intervention aimed at increasing participants' competence and propensity to recognize and mobilize social support and to use problem-solving techniques in groups. Participants, who were providing care for mentally ill or disabled people, were expected to train their peers. After 3 months, significant improvements were found for the participants concerning supervisor support and feedback, self-appraisal of coping, team functioning, and depressive and psychosomatic symptoms. Effects were weaker when peers were included. Additional analyses identified characteristics of people who were at risk of deterioration in important variables, such as well-being. This high-risk subgroup did show a decline in well-being in the control group but not in the intervention group.

Schweiger and DeNisi (1991) reported on the effects of communication about an imminent merger in two companies. One company made efforts to disseminate honest information, for example, by a telephone hot line and regular meetings. Uncertainty, stress, job satisfaction, and the perception of the company as trustworthy and caring all initially got worse in both plants. These developments continued, however, in the control plant but stabilized in the experimental plant. There is no information on the effects of the merger itself, but the study does indicate that honest information can buffer the negative effects of anticipated threatening developments. In a similar vein, Greenberg (2006) showed that training supervisors in interactional justice attenuated the effects of a pay cut on sleep problems.

Summarizing these studies, it appears that interventions aiming at role clarification and feedback have a good chance of affecting role ambiguity and role conflict. There are some effects on absenteeism, though they are inconsistent. Implementation quality seems to be important. Interventions that focus on social support were effective in only one of three cases (Heaney et al., 1995). Training supervisors with regard to improving organizational justice seems promising. Overall, results imply that social interventions do have the potential for positive effects.

Multiple Changes

Many of the studies discussed so far had several targets. Nevertheless, it seemed easier to identify a major focus in them than in the five studies that follow.

Theorell and Wahlstedt (1999) and Wahlstedt and Edling (1997) reported changes in a postal sorting terminal, including (a) the forming of new production areas, each with its own budget and with a smaller number of supervisors, so that staff influence on the work situation was increased; (b) granting a new status for "senior postmen"; (c) hiring new people; (d) introducing work groups; (e) introducing the possibility of obtaining hot meals; and (f) changing the shift system. After 1 year, perceived skill discretion and authority in decision making had increased. Sick leave was reduced, but sleep problems increased. Gastrointestinal complaints did not change on average. Perceived amount of change in working conditions did, however, correlate with reduced sleep problems and gastrointestinal complaints, suggesting a dose–response relationship, as in the study by Schaubroeck et al. (1993).

An intervention in a mail delivery office (Theorell & Wahlstedt, 1999) included (a) more control and social support, (b) clarification of management roles, (c) better information, (d) more staff, and (e) a new sorter table (to reduce musculoskeletal problems). Changes were implemented in two stations, more so in one of them, and employees could choose at which station they wanted to work. After a year, perceived ergonomic conditions (e.g., repetitive arm movements) had not changed, social support had improved in the more modern station, and decision authority had improved in the more traditional site. Psychological demands had decreased in both stations. Musculoskeletal problems decreased, although significantly only at the more modern site. These changes were related to improvements in social support by superiors and were largely confined to those under the age of 35.

Kawakami, Araki, Kawashima, Masumoto, and Hayashi (1997) reported an attempt to reduce stressors by (a) improving machine speed and performance, (b) reducing the number of checks required, (c) increasing training, (d) standardizing procedures, and (e) enhancing social support by supervisors. After 1 year, perception of working conditions had not changed. There were no effects for blood pressure. Depressive symptoms decreased significantly in the intervention group but not in the control group. The group–time interaction was significant. A similar effect was found for sick leave.

One case that was reported by Kompier, Aust, van den Berg, and Siegrist (2000, Case 8) included (a) reorganization of work, (b) establishment of group work (including own coordination of shift schedules), (c) more free weekends, (d) regular meetings, (e) ergonomic improvements, and (f) health education. Both absenteeism and turnover decreased, and job satisfaction increased.

Case 3 in Kompier et al. (1998) demonstrated an improvement in social climate and work atmosphere following the introduction of semiautonomous groups, along with ergonomic improvements and better management of absenteeism. This study also reports a significant decrease in absenteeism.[1]

A project in the Finnish forest industry (Kalimo & Toppinen, 1999) included (a) work reorganization (e.g., by integrating production, maintenance, and support), (b) training (e.g., concerning leadership), and (c) improved cooperation and communication. After 2 years, and then again after 10 years, more respondents reported improvements than deteriorations, most notably for communication with superiors, challenging work, and autonomy. However, perceived time pressure had increased. Health indicators did not change.

A Dutch hospital introduced (a) job enrichment and improved work organization; (b) ergonomic and technical changes; (c) improved work-rest schedules; (d) supervisor training; and (e) health promotion activities, such as stress management (Lourijsen, Houtman, Kompier, & Gründemann, 1999). After 3 years, perceived job content, emotional stress, and appreciation had improved, but work pace was perceived to have increased. Emotional exhaustion and health complaints were unchanged. Moreover, at postmeasurement, a control hospital, which also was active, had improved organization of work and work pace and had fewer complaints about work characteristics than did the intervention hospital. However, the significant drop in absenteeism at the intervention hospital is impressive, starting out higher than both the comparison hospital and the national average but ending lowest.

In Europe, particularly in Germany, "health circles" have become popular (Aust & Ducki, 2004; Beermann, Kuhn, & Kompier, 1999). They are similar to quality circles, and topics often overlap because the problems that cause stress often are the same as those that impair quality (Schurman & Israel, 1995). Typically, groups meet for a number of sessions, usually with an external moderator. Risks and complaints are assessed (i.e., by interview, questionnaire, or analysis of company data) and discussed in the circle, and suggestions are handed over to management. Topics concern, for example, ergonomic changes, improvement of communication and training, and work reorganization (Beermann et al., 1999; Ducki, Jenewein, & Knoblich, 1998; Slesina, Beuels, & Sochert, 1998).[2] Evaluations generally are rather positive, but they typically relate to satisfaction with the circle, sometimes to the number of suggestions implemented (estimated to be about one third by Slesina et al., 1998) but hardly ever to perceived improvements in working conditions or to health parameters. Friczewski (1994) reported significant improvement in social relations and in physical and psychological well-being. Ducki et al. (1998) reported that

---

[1] These authors reported a number of other cases in which some kind of management of absenteeism was employed. Even though employees may positively evaluate absenteeism consultancy, it is not clear whether the management of absenteeism can be regarded as stress prevention. Rather, the reduction in absenteeism might reflect normative changes ("absence culture") rather than changes in the stressfulness of work (see Spector, 1997). Reduced absenteeism can therefore be attributed to changes in working conditions only in the study reported here.

[2] Health circles might seem similar to health committees in U.S. health promotion projects, such as employee assistance programs. These latter programs, however, typically focus on behavior change, and the environmental component (e.g., fitness facilities, smoking bans, healthy food, support groups) typically refers to environments that support specific health behaviors, not job design, or work organization (Gebhardt & Crump, 1990; O'Donnell, 2002).

absenteeism decreased in that part of a company where a health circle was implemented but increased in the others. Pfaff and Bentz (2000) reported a perceived increase in the quality of supervision and social relationships following a 1-day health workshop. A health circle in a transport company resulted in changes in ergonomics, shift systems, teamwork structure, more open communication, and the institution of behavior change programs. Absenteeism dropped from 13.5% to less than 10% (Marstedt & Mergner, 1995). Kornadt, Schmook, Wilm, and Hertel (2000) found significant improvements regarding ergonomics, time management, and communication among teleworkers. Altogether, there are promising signs but few hard data to support clear conclusions.

The health circle concept has much in common with the participatory action research (PAR) concept (Israel, Baker, Goldenhar, Heaney, & Schurman, 1996; Parkes & Sparkes, 1998; Schurman & Israel, 1995). Both advocate active participation and the development of proposals based on the assessment of local circumstances rather than on premanufactured packages. Reports about the PAR approach are often informative, especially with regard to process evaluation and identification of crucial principles and pitfalls but often not stringent with regard to outcome evaluation.

The studies discussed in this section are quite diverse. What seems striking is the drop in absenteeism in many cases, sometimes occurring in conjunction with improved perceptions of working conditions but in other cases accompanied by both positive and negative changes. Those negative changes often involved increases in time pressure. Changes in health are mixed, with many null findings and findings that differ for various indicators. For health circles, there are a few promising signs but too little research to allow clear conclusions.

Issues to Consider

To be able to draw conclusions in a diverse and complex field, and to advance research on organizational stress interventions, I believe a number of issues need to be considered. They refer to criteria for effectiveness and to methodological considerations.

Are Organization-Based Interventions Effective?

Altogether, the studies reported convey the impression that work-related interventions do have potential for positive effects (cf. Taris et al., 2003). It is, however, hard to predict specifically which changes are likely to occur, and this prediction becomes more difficult the more distant the variables in question are from the immediate intervention. Thus, many studies report changes in the perception of the work variables they targeted (e.g., autonomy and variety, role ambiguity, supervisor support). Sometimes, these changes affect stress, well-being, and health variables, sometimes they do not, and sometimes they affect some but not others (cf. Elo, Ervasti, Kuosma, & Mattila, 2008). The outcomes that seem to have the greatest chance of improvement are job satisfaction and absenteeism. However, absenteeism sometimes is reduced without concomitant changes in perceived working characteristics. Finally, workload and, to some degree, turnover, seem to be especially prone to deteriorate, even when other features improve.

Some authors have drawn much more pessimistic conclusions from this state of affairs (e.g., Briner & Reynolds, 1999). A meta-analysis by van der Klink, Blonk, Schene, and van Dijk (2001) concluded that effects of organizational interventions are negligible. However, these results are based on five studies only. Furthermore, effect sizes are averaged per study. Thus, the effect size (d) for the study by Heaney et al. (1995), mentioned earlier, was estimated at .005. Richardson and Rothstein (2008) examined true experiments only, which excludes many important studies; furthermore, they also averaged outcome variables.

Should we, however, expect an unequivocal "yes" to a question as general as "Does organizational stress intervention attain its objectives?" The answer to that broad question must inevitably be, "Sometimes, for some people, and on some measures," and the main issue then becomes determining what can be expected when. We are far from answering that question; but some answers, and some refinements of the question, can be suggested. I first discuss whether uniform outcomes across outcome measures ought to be expected. This is followed by suggestions concerning process variables and by more general methodological remarks. The chapter closes with a short discussion of prerequisites and pitfalls for interventions.

Outcome Variables

The interventions discussed aim at changing working conditions (in a broad sense) as their immediate targets. Measures such as perceived autonomy in the case of job enrichment, impediments in ergonomic interventions, or role ambiguity in role clarification studies therefore seem especially important. They are, in a sense, a "manipulation check." If these variables do not change, the intervention did not reach its proximal goal. It therefore cannot be expected to attain more distal goals (although this is not impossible, as other variables, such as felt appreciation and respect, may improve well-being).

The next target concerns measures of health and well-being. Here we find measures of depression, anxiety, and psychosomatic complaints, back and neck pain, medically diagnosed illness, or physiological risk factors. Unfortunately, formulations on stress at work yield rather few indications of specific relationships between stress factors and indicators of well-being that could guide us in choosing among the many measures possible. The meaning of different indicators of well-being is not widely discussed in that literature, and the choice of measures often does not seem to be based on such considerations.

Warr (2007) suggested three dimensions of well-being, based on the circumplex model of emotion: displeasure versus pleasure (usually equated with satisfaction), anxiety versus comfort, and enthusiasm versus depression. This model could be used to choose measures and to make sure that each dimension is represented. The dimensions are correlated, and they can be combined into a metaconstruct of subjective well-being (Diener, 1994). They are, however, not identical, and it is perfectly possible to find effects on one dimension but not another. The same applies to physiological measures. Arousal is not a unitary phenomenon (Meijman & Mulder, 1998), and its various indicators (which are likely to have different temporal characteristics) cannot be expected to all go up or down at the same time.

There are indications that various dimensions of work have specific relations to aspects of well-being. Thus, content variables (e.g., autonomy) seem to have stronger relations to satisfaction, whereas demand variables (e.g., workload) correlate more with high-arousal negative affect, such as anxiety, or psychosomatic symptoms (see Demerouti, Bakker, Nachreiner, & Schaufeli, 2001; Houkes, Janssen, de Jonge, & Nijhuis, 2001; Warr, 2007). Divergent effects are possible, as when people in high-level jobs are more satisfied but at the same time report more anxiety, or when the cutters who rotated between tasks of different status in the study by Smith and Zehel (1992) showed an improvement in health parameters but deterioration in job satisfaction, which seems to be more sensitive to the status component.

All this implies that it is not reasonable to expect all indicators of well-being and health to show changes in means following intervention. There may be differential impact, and there are different time frames (Dormann & Zapf, 2002). Improvement on some measures might be a perfectly reasonable result. And even if some other measures deteriorate, one might consider looking at a balance of positive and negative effects because in many cases, tradeoffs will be involved.

Two outcome measures deserve a special comment. Job satisfaction is sometimes regarded with skepticism (Sonnentag, 1996), mainly because it might be the consequence of lowered standards (resulting in what Bruggemann, 1974, called "resigned job satisfaction"; see also Bussing, Bissels, Fuchs, & Perrar, 1999). Nevertheless, global job satisfaction seems to be quite a sensitive indicator of a general evaluation of the work situation, which is related to variables such as life satisfaction and general well-being (Diener, 1994; Faragher, Cass, & Cooper, 2005), health (Faragher et al., 2005), turnover (Baillod & Semmer, 1994), a number of job-related behaviors (Roznowski & Hulin, 1992), and—contrary to common belief—performance (Judge, Thoresen, Bono, & Patton, 2001).

Absenteeism, if assessed by company records, has the advantage of being independent of self-report and of being especially convincing to employers. It is, however, affected by many factors, such as normative considerations (Spector, 1997). In light of this, the impressive reductions in absenteeism sometimes found are rather surprising. They are likely to be connected to the fact that an intervention is taking place and that the organization is therefore perceived as showing concern for its employees. This is akin to a Hawthorne effect.

Creating "Good" Working Conditions Versus Trade-Offs

I argued earlier that a uniform effect on outcome measures might not be a reasonable expectation. A similar argument can be made about working conditions. Most good things come with a price, and that applies to improvements in working conditions as well (cf. Semmer, 2006).

An illustrative example is a study concerning police officers (Orth-Gomer, 1983). Changing a shift system from counterclockwise to clockwise rotation had led to improvements on a number of health-related parameters. Nevertheless, the officers went back to their old schedule because it gave them larger blocks of free time. Thus, the new system was "healthier" but at the same time interfered with private life. (It is interesting to note that after the study was finished, the police officers reversed their decision and opted for the "healthy" variant, but the point is that there are trade-offs involved.)

Morgeson and Campion (2003) argued that changes corresponding to the motivational model (i.e., work content variables, as in job enrichment) increase satisfaction but often also increase work stress (i.e., workload), because mental demands increase. And indeed, higher workload does seem to be a common side effect of job enrichment and teamwork interventions. Some of this may be inherent in enrichment concepts, because these imply more parameters to be accounted for, more coordination and planning efforts, and so forth. Some of it may be a result of implementation problems, such as increased task assignments going along with enriched jobs. In any case, however, there are trade-offs to consider, and it may often be naive to expect only positive effects. Other aspects to be considered are loss of status (e.g., for superiors or specialists) and increased group conflicts as a result of group autonomy (because groups cannot "delegate" conflict-prone decisions to their superiors any more; Wall et al., 1986).

The potential "status" aspect of stress factors also deserves more attention. Sometimes people take pride in dealing with harsh conditions (Meara, 1974). Older train drivers sometimes opt for straining night rides on intercity long-distance trains because these also carry the most prestige. Workers may resist removing some stressful aspects of their work, arguing that their job entails some harsh conditions ("This is a steel plant and not a girls' boarding school"; Slesina et al., 1998, p. 201). A good implementation policy might avoid, or attenuate, some of these effects, but probably not all of them. The question, then, may be whether a change has more advantages than disadvantages rather than whether it is "good" or not. Incidentally, from this perspective job satisfaction seems a particularly good measure because it also implies weighting positive and negative aspects of one's work (cf. Semmer, 2006).

Process Considerations

Although quantitative analyses tell us about success or failure, process accounts may lead to more insight about the mechanisms involved (Griffiths, 1999; Kristensen, 2000; Nytro, Saksvik, Mikkelsen, Bohle, & Quinlan, 2000). Carefully documented qualitative accounts can be extremely informative about the dangers and pitfalls of worksite interventions (e.g., Schurman & Israel, 1995). Short but repeated measures of process variables, such as quality of meetings (e.g., attendance, atmosphere, satisfaction), behavior of facilitators, presence of superiors, and so forth, and careful documentation of external events may be included in quantitative analyses (Semmer, 2006).

Often, however, authors do not report much at all about the quality of the implementation. For example, how were facilitators trained, what mistakes did they make (e.g., in terms of "taking over," in terms of forming coalitions within an organization)? This makes it hard to know whether failures were a result of poor concepts, poor implementation, obstruction by people inside the organization, or other factors (see Kristensen's, 2005, distinction between theory failures and program failures). Also, we often learn little about the stress introduced by the change process itself. After all, most projects are run while everything else is going on, implying lack of time and resources for the project (Kompier, Cooper, et al., 2000) and many temptations to go back to old routines when faced with difficulties (Frei, Hugentobler, Schurman, & Alioth, 1993). Kompier and coworkers (Kompier, Aust, et al., 2000; Kompier & Cooper, 1999; Kompier, Cooper, et al., 2000; Kompier et al., 1998) provided good examples by including a section on "obstructing" and "stimulating" factors. Some more recent studies provide good examples for systematic process evaluation (Aust, Rugulies, Finken, & Jensen, 2010; Busch, Clasen, Duresso, Ducki, & Bamberg, 2009; Nielsen, Fredslund, Christensen, & Albertsen, 2006).

It is deplorable that the link between this area and other attempts to alter organizations is so weak. Thus, the literature on Productivity Measurement and Enhancement System (Pro-MES; e.g., Pritchard, 1995) or on quality circles (e.g., Cordery, 1996) conveys many messages similar to those found in accounts of organizational stress interventions. The training literature suggests that the posttraining environment (e.g., support from supervisors in trying out new skills) is no less important than the training itself (Ford, Kozlowski, Kraiger, Salas, & Teachout, 1997). By contrast, much of the stress intervention literature seems to assume that a "good" intervention "maintains itself," so to speak.

An important element in many interventions is a participatory approach, which implies control and empowerment for those involved (Aust & Ducki, 2004). Participatory approaches may combine both the work situation and the person as targets in a "personalized" way. For example, Arnetz, Sjögren, Rydéhn, and Meisel (2003) did a study in which each individual workplace of people who had musculoskeletal problems was analyzed from an ergonomic point of view, and both physical and psychological stressors were assessed as well. This resulted in interventions, including ergonomic improvements, that were tailored to the individual's work situation.

Methodological Considerations

The poor methodological quality of many studies is often deplored (e.g., Briner & Reynolds, 1999; Burke & Richardsen, 2000). I do not discuss such issues in general (see Shadish et al., 2002) nor the arguments regarding the difficulties of doing rigorous research in organizations (Cox, Karanika, Griffiths, & Houdmont, 2007) because most readers undoubtedly are familiar with both. Rather, I discuss a few more specific points.

One point concerns samples containing people with different characteristics and different status with regard to the target of the intervention. There often are differences between improvement for those who already have developed symptoms of stress and prevention for those who have not (see Bunce & Stephenson, 2000; Kompier & Kristensen, 2000). Many studies will contain participants from both populations. There is no reason to assume, however, that the effects will be equal for the two groups. Some symptoms may prevail even when the stress factors that caused them have been removed (Frese & Zapf,

1988), as when former shift workers are found to have more health problems than current shift workers (Frese & Semmer, 1986). For those without symptoms, however, there will not be much room for improvement (i.e., a floor effect).

Another topic concerns attrition. The analyses reported by Heaney et al. (1995) are good examples for modeling the characteristics of those who have a high probability of not participating or of leaving their job. Analyses such as these should be conducted more often. Similarly, considering actual exposure can yield important insights (Busch et al., 2009; Randall, Griffiths, & Cox, 2005).

With regard to long-term effects, it often is argued that evaluation lags are too short. Given the little known about onset and disappearance of stress symptoms (Dormann & Zapf, 2002), this is plausible. What is less plausible, however, is the underlying assumption that an intervention that has been well-implemented will be effective forever. Work environments are continuously changing: A new supervisor may change the whole working climate or may restrict or enhance people's autonomy; new colleagues have not gone through the original change process; new technology may be introduced, and so on. In my view, there is no way out of this dilemma. The longer the time frame, the less likely effects can be attributed to the original intervention. The only thing one could try to do is assess working conditions and possible health outcomes continuously. This might profitably be combined with a periodic review of the status of the project (for a similar approach, see Pritchard, 1990). Such reviews might uncover erosions of changes that were implemented, negative side effects, discontinuities because of new demands, new technology, new people, and so forth, and suggest efforts to revive the project.

The question of trade-offs, already mentioned, applies also to design. Indeed, some aspects of good designs are threats to others. Thus, many measurement points over extended periods of time will improve the design in theory but may also increase reactivity of measures and the risk of attrition and thus lead to biased samples and measures (Kompier & Kristensen, 2000). Shorter measures may be a way out, but this will decrease their reliability. Again, a trade-off is necessary rather than seeking solutions without flaws.

There is reason to believe that statistical significance is being overemphasized (as in psychology in general; Smith, 1996). In most studies, samples will not be very large, which increases the danger of statistical Type II errors. Small samples also increase the chances that results across studies will be inconsistent because, in each study, only a small proportion of the effects will be detected (Maxwell, 2004). It seems advisable to publish exact data on all effects, regardless of their statistical significance, so that they can be used in meta-analyses. Practical, rather than statistical, significance should receive more attention, and methods for this have been developed (e.g., Jacobson & Revenstorf, 1988; cf., Bunce & Stephenson, 2000).

We should be more concerned with changing standards during interventions. A project may raise expectations that go well beyond what is finally implemented, and this might make changes that did occur look much smaller. Sometimes the meaning of a concept (e.g., autonomy) may change during a project, as participants talk and think about possibilities they might never have considered as being realistic for them before. Thus, beta and gamma changes may occur, which, if undetected, lead to erroneous conclusions (see Logan & Ganster, 2005).

Finally, as many authors have stated, the value of case studies should be recognized more, and their role as a complement to (quasi-) experimental studies should be acknowledged (Griffiths, 1999; Kompier & Kristensen, 2000). This should not be taken to mean that no methodological rigor is required or that subjective impressions of change agents can be substituted for well-documented accounts of events. Rather than deploring poor designs on the one side, and bemoaning the difficulties of implementing rigorous designs on the other, researchers should present the maximum information possible. As Kazdin (1981) pointed out, the real issue is whether we have good reasons to render alternative interpretations implausible. Case studies sometimes have unique possibilities for doing this—for instance, by temporally aligning (objectively recorded) effects with (objectively recorded) events (e.g., Busch et al., 2009). What types of data are recorded, therefore, may be of equal or greater importance than the overall design, and case studies with well-documented data can be extremely valuable.

Conclusions

In light of the problems just discussed, and in light of the many problems involved in changing organizations, the state of affairs seems less pessimistic than it appears at first—at least if one accepts that the issue is not one of attaining uniformly positive effects but rather one of a balance of effects. There are many positive findings and many null effects but not many negative ones, although intervening in a complex system will always run the risk of negative effects (Aust et al., in press). Moreover, the quality of studies seems to be improving, and we can expect to have a much better database in the years to come.

It also is important not to pit person-oriented and work-oriented approaches against each other. If anything, the evidence is stronger for person-oriented than for work-oriented interventions (Richardson & Rothstein, 2008; van der Klink et al., 2001), although the time effects are not so clear. Also, an increasing number of studies suggest that personal resources (e.g., self-efficacy) may be necessary for taking advantage of opportunities such as increased autonomy (de Rijk, Le Blanc, & Schaufeli, 1998; Jimmieson, 2000; Meier, Semmer, Elfering, & Jacobshagen, 2008; Schaubroeck & Merritt, 1997). One effect of stress may be that it undermines the very resources needed to deal with it effectively (Semmer, McGrath, & Beehr, 2005). Unless personal resources are strengthened by person-oriented approaches, changes in working conditions may not live up to their potential or may even be resisted by those who need them most but who also have the greatest anxieties with regard to anticipated changes. The strong emphasis on active participation in practically all approaches (Aust, Peter, & Siegrist, 1997; Karasek & Theorell, 1990; Quick et al., 1997; Schurman & Israel, 1995; Slesina et al., 1998) reflects this concern. All this argues for a collaboration of person-oriented and work-oriented strategies (see Munz, Kohler, & Greenberg, 2001).

Two additional remarks concern the role of experts and of management. Experts have a delicate role to play. They must provide information, advice, and facilitation but avoid becoming responsible for producing the changes. And they must avoid putting their own theories above the client's concerns (Aust et al., in press). Unless proposals are rooted in a diagnosis of problems in the specific context, they might reflect the experts' approach more than the problems of the organization. Especially, many problems do not involve the "big" issues suggested by theory, but rather seemingly trivial problems such as eliminating sources of draft, improving lighting, or having access to spare parts (Ducki et al., 1998; Slesina et al., 1998).

It is often noted that management support is crucial and difficult to achieve, but there is little information on how it can be achieved and maintained. Sometimes, it is suggested that the cost-saving potential of interventions might convince management (see Cascio, 2000). However, the fact that many organizations are reluctant to conduct a careful evaluation suggests that cost savings may not be that important—or if they are, it is the conviction about cost savings that counts and not hard data. Furthermore, managers themselves often indicate that other considerations are more important to them, and many rank health-related outcomes higher than cost saving (U.S. Department of Health and Human Services, 1993). For example, Mintzberg (1975) found that managers have a general tendency to base decisions about projects on how much they trust the judgment of those who present the project to them. It is my hunch that it is important not to "sell" projects to managers too hard. Rather, consultants should refrain from getting involved in projects in which management commitment is not assured, and they should make this clear from the outset. If commitment can be gained, it needs to entail time and effort allocated to the project, not just lip service.

My final remark concerns the Hawthorne effect. It is often labeled "unspecific"; that is, not directly related to the specifics of the intervention, sometimes with the connotation of being somehow artificial. If it is true, however, that stress at work has much to do with "daily humiliations" (Cooper, Schabracq, & Winnubst, 1996), and that many problems result from lack of respect, fairness, and appreciation (Rutte & Messick, 1995; Semmer, Jacobshagen, Meier, & Elfering, 2007), then sensing these elements both in one's interpersonal encounters and in one's tasks and working conditions may be at the heart of the problem rather than being unspecific. If this is true, we should not avoid Hawthorne effects. Rather, we should try to achieve them.

References

Aust, B., & Ducki, A. (2004). Comprehensive health promotion interventions at the workplace: Experiences with health circles in Germany. *Journal of Occupational Health Psychology, 9,* 258–270. doi:10.1037/1076-8998.9.3.258

Aust, B., Peter, R., & Siegrist, J. (1997). Stress management in bus drivers: A pilot study based on the model of effort–reward imbalance. *International Journal of Stress Management, 4,* 297–305. doi:10.1023/B:IJSM.0000008709.11196.19

Aust, B., Rugulies, R., Finken, A., & Jensen, C. (2010). When workplace interventions lead to negative effects: Learning from failures. *Scandinavian Journal of Public Health, 38*(Suppl. 3), 106–119.

Arnetz, B. B., Sjögren, B., Rydéhn, B., & Meisel, R. (2003). Early workplace intervention for employees with musculoskeletal-related absenteeism: A prospective controlled intervention study. *Journal of Occupational and Environmental Medicine, 45,* 499–506. doi:10.1097/01.jom. 0000063628.37065.45

Baillod, J., & Semmer, N. (1994). Fluktuation und Berufsverläufe bei Computerfachleuten [Turnover and career paths of computer specialists]. *Zeitschrift für Arbeits- und Organisationspsychologie, 38,* 152–163.

Beehr, T. A. (1995). *Psychological stress in the workplace.* London, England: Routledge.

Beermann, B., Kuhn, K., & Kompier, M. (1999). Germany: Reduction of stress by health circles. In M. Kompier & C. Cooper (Eds.), *Preventing stress, improving productivity. European case studies in the workplace* (pp. 222–241). London, England: Routledge.

Belkic, K. L., Landsbergis, P. A., Schnall, P. L., & Baker, D. (2004). Is job strain a major source of cardiovascular disease risk? A critical review of the empirical evidence, with a clinical perspective. *Scandinavian Journal of Work, Environment & Health, 30,* 85–128.

Bond, F. W., Flaxman, P. E., & Bunce, D. (2008). The influence of psychological flexibility on work redesign: Mediated moderation of a work reorganization intervention. *Journal of Applied Psychology, 93,* 645–654. doi:10.1037/0021-9010.93.3.645

Briner, T. B., & Reynolds, S. (1999). The costs, benefits, and limitations of organizational level stress interventions. *Journal of Organizational Behavior, 20,* 647–664. doi:10.1002/(SICI)1099-1379(199909)20:5<647::AID-JOB919>3.0.CO;2-1

Bruggemann, A. (1974). Zur Unterscheidung verschiedener Formen von "arbeitszufriedenheit" [On different forms of "job satisfaction"]. *Arbeit und Leistung, 28,* 281–284.

Bunce, D., & Stephenson, K. (2000). Statistical considerations in the interpretation of research on occupational stress management interventions. *Work & Stress, 14,* 197–212.

Burke, R. J., & Richardsen, A. M. (2000). Organizational-level interventions designed to reduce occupational stressors. In P. Dewe, M. Leiter, & T. Cox (Eds.), *Coping, health, and organizations* (pp. 191–209). London, England: Taylor & Francis.

Busch, C., Clasen, J., Duresso, R., Ducki, A., & Bamberg, E. (2009). *Evaluation of a team-based stress management intervention for low-qualified workers.* Unpublished manuscript, University of Hamburg, Germany.

Bussing, A., Bissels, T., Fuchs, V., & Perrar, K.-M. (1999). A dynamic model of work satisfaction: Qualitative approaches. *Human Relations, 52,* 999–1028. doi:10.1177/001872679905200802

Cascio, W. F. (2000). *Costing human resources* (4th ed.). Cincinnati, OH: Southwestern College.

Cooper, C. L., Schabracq, M. J., & Winnubst, J. A. M. (1996). Preface. In M. J. Schabracq, J. A. Winnubst, & C. L. Cooper (Eds.), *Handbook of work and health psychology* (pp. xv–xvi). Chichester, England: Wiley.

Cordery, J. L. (1996). Autonomous work groups and quality circles. In M. A. West (Ed.), *Handbook of work group psychology* (pp. 225–246). Chichester, England: Wiley.

Cox, T., Karanika, M., Griffiths, A., & Houdmont, J. (2007). Evaluating organizational-level work stress interventions: Beyond traditional methods. *Work and Stress, 21,* 348–362. doi:10.1080/02678370701760757

Demerouti, E., Bakker, A. B., Nachreiner, F., & Schaufeli, W. B. (2001). The job demands–resources model of burnout. *Journal of Applied Psychology, 86,* 499–512. doi:10.1037/0021-9010.86.3.499

de Rijk, A. E., Le Blanc, P. M., & Schaufeli, W. B. (1998). Active coping and need for control as moderators of the job demand-control model: Effects on burnout. *Journal of Occupational and Organizational Psychology, 71,* 1–18.

Diener, E. (1994). Assessing subjective well-being: Progress and opportunities. *Social Indicators Research, 31,* 103–157. doi:10.1007/BF01207052

Dormann, C., & Zapf, D. (2002). Social stressors at work, irritation, and depressive symptoms: Accounting for unmeasured third variables in a multi-wave study. *Journal of Occupational and Organizational Psychology, 75,* 33–58. doi:10.1348/096317902167630

Ducki, A., Jenewein, R., & Knoblich, H.-J. (1998). Gesundheitszirkel: Ein instrument der organisationsentwicklung [Health circles: An instrument for organizational development]. In E. Bamberg, A. Ducki, & A. Metz (Eds.), *Handbuch betriebliche gesundheitsförderung* [Handbook of worksite health promotion] (pp. 267–281). Göttingen, Germany: Hogrefe.

Elo, A.-L., Ervasti, J., Kuosma, E., & Mattila, P. (2008). Evaluation of an organizational stress management program in a municipal public works organization. *Journal of Occupational Health Psychology, 13,* 10–23. doi:10.1037/1076-8998.13.1.10

Faragher, E. B., Cass, M., & Cooper, C. L. (2005). The relationship between job satisfaction and health: A meta-analysis. *Occupational and Environmental Medicine, 62,* 105–112. doi:10.1136/oem.2002.006734

Ford, J. E. L., Kozlowski, S. W. J., Kraiger, K., Salas, E., & Teachout, M. (Eds.). (1997). *Improving training effectiveness in work organizations.* Mahwah, NJ: Erlbaum.

Frei, F., Hugentobler, M., Schurman, S., & Alioth, A. (1993). *Work design for the competent organization.* New York, NY: Quorum Books.

Frese, M., & Semmer, N. (1986). Shiftwork, stress, and psychosomatic complaints: A comparison between workers in different shift work schedules. *Ergonomics, 29,* 99–114.

Frese, M., & Zapf, D. (1988). Methodological issues in the study of work stress: Objective versus subjective measurement and the question of longitudinal studies. In C. L. Cooper & R. Payne (Eds.), *Causes, coping, and consequences of stress at work* (pp. 375–411). Chichester, England: Wiley.

Friczewski, F. (1994). Das Volkswagen-gesundheitszirkelprojekt [The Volkswagen health circle project]. In G. Westermayer & B. Bahr (Eds.), *Betriebliche gesundheitszirkel* [Workplace health circles] (pp. 123–127). Göttingen, Germany: Verlag für Angewandte Psychologie.

Ganster, D. C. (1995). Interventions for building healthy organizations: Suggestions from the stress research literature. In L. R. Murphy, J. J. Hurrell, S. L. Sauter, & G. P. Keita (Eds.), *Job stress interventions* (pp. 323–336). Washington, DC: American Psychological Association. doi:10.1037/10183-021

Gebhardt, D. L., & Crump, C. E. (1990). Employee fitness and wellness programs in the workplace. *American Psychologist, 45,* 262–272.

Greenberg, J. (2006). Losing sleep over organizational injustice: Attenuating insomnia reactions to underpayment inequity with supervisory training in interactional justice. *Journal of Applied Psychology, 91,* 58–69. doi:10.1037/0021-9010.91.1.58

Griffiths, A. (1999). Organizational interventions: Facing the limits of the natural science paradigm. *Scandinavian Journal of Work, Environment, and Health, 25,* 589–596.

Hackman, J. R., & Oldham, G. R. (1980). *Work redesign.* Reading, MA: Addison-Wesley.

Heaney, C. A., Price, F. H., & Rafferty, J. (1995). Increasing coping resources at work: A field experiment to increase social support, improve work team functioning, and enhance employee mental health. *Journal of Organizational Behavior, 16,* 335–352. doi:10.1002/job.4030160405

Houkes, I., Janssen, P. P. M., de Jonge, J., & Nijhuis, F. J. N. (2001). Specific relationships between work characteristics and intrinsic work motivation, burnout and turnover intention: A multi-sample analysis. *European Journal of Work and Organizational Psychology, 10,* 1–23. doi:10.1080/13594320042000007

Israel, B. A., Baker, E. A., Goldenhar, L. M., Heaney, C. A., & Schurman, S. J. (1996). Occupational stress, safety, and health: Conceptual framework and principles for effective prevention interventions. *Journal of Occupational Health Psychology, 1,* 261–286. doi:10.1037/1076-8998.1.3.261

Jacobson, N. S., & Revenstorf, D. (1988). Statistics for assessing the clinical significance of psychotherapy techniques: Issues, problems, and new developments. *Behavioral Assessment, 10,* 133–145.

Jimmieson, N. L. (2000). Employee reactions to behavioural control under conditions of stress: The moderating role of self-efficacy. *Work & Stress, 14,* 262–280.

Judge, T. A., Thoresen, C. J., Bono, J. E., & Patton, G. K. (2001). The job satisfaction–job performance relationship: A qualitative and quantitative review. *Psychological Bulletin, 127,* 376–407. doi:10.1037/0033-2909.127.3.376

Kahn, R. L., & Byosiere, P. (1992). Stress in organizations. In M. D. Dunnette & L. M. Hough (Eds.), *Handbook of industrial and organizational psychology* (Vol. 3, pp. 571–650). Palo Alto, CA: Consulting Psychologists Press.

Kalimo, R., & Toppinen, S. (1999). Finland: Organizational well-being. Ten years of research and development in a forest industry corporation. In M. Kompier & C. Cooper (Eds.), *Preventing stress, improving productivity. European case studies in the workplace* (pp. 52–85). London, England: Routledge.

Karasek, R., & Theorell, T. (1990). *Healthy work.* New York, NY: Basic Books.

Kawakami, N., Araki, S., Kawashima, M., Masumoto, T., & Hayashi, T. (1997). Effects of work-related stress reduction on depressive symptoms among Japanese blue-collar workers. *Scandinavian Journal of Work, Environment & Health, 23,* 54–59.

Kazdin, A. E. (1981). Drawing valid inference from case studies. *Journal of Consulting and Clinical Psychology, 49,* 183–192.

Kompier, M. (2003). Job design and well-being. In M. Schabracq, J. Winnubst, & C. Cooper (Eds.), *The handbook of work & health psychology* (2nd ed., pp. 429–454). Chichester, England: Wiley.

Kompier, M. A. J., Aust, B., van den Berg, A. M., & Siegrist, J. (2000). Stress prevention in bus drivers: Evaluation of 13 national experiments. *Journal of Occupational Health Psychology, 5,* 11–31. doi:10.1037/1076-8998.5.1.11

Kompier, M., & Cooper, C. (Eds.). (1999). *Preventing stress, improving productivity. European case studies in the workplace.* London, England: Routledge.

Kompier, M. A. J., Cooper, C. L., & Geurts, S. A. E. (2000). A multiple case study approach to work stress prevention in Europe. *European Journal of Work and Organizational Psychology, 9,* 371–400. doi:10.1080/135943200417975

Kompier, M. A. J., Geurts, S. A. E., Gründemann, R. W. M., Vink, P., & Smulders, P. G. W. (1998). Cases in stress prevention: The success of a participative and stepwise approach. *Stress Medicine, 14,* 144–168.

Kompier, M. A. J., & Kristensen, T. S. (2000). Organizational work stress interventions in a theoretical, methodological and practical context. In J. Dunham (Ed.), *Stress in the workplace: Past, present, and future* (pp. 164–190). London, England: Whurr.

Kornadt, U., Schmook, R. Wilm, A., & Hertel, G. (2000). Health circles for teleworkers: Selective results on stress, strain and coping styles. *Health Education Research, 15,* 327–338.

Kristensen, T. S. (2000). Workplace intervention studies. *Occupational Medicine, 15,* 293–305.

Kristensen, T. S. (2005). Intervention studies in occupational epidemiology. *Occupational and Environmental Medicine, 62,* 205–210. doi:10.1136/oem.2004.016097

Logan, M. S., & Ganster, D. C. (2005). An experimental evaluation of a control intervention to alleviate job-related stress. *Journal of Management, 31,* 90–107. doi:10.1177/0149206304271383

Lourijsen, E., Houtman, I., Kompier, M., & Gründemann, R. (1999). The Netherlands: A hospital, "healthy working for health." In M. Kompier & C. Cooper (Eds.), *Preventing stress, improving productivity. European case studies in the workplace* (pp. 86–120). London, England: Routledge.

Marstedt, G., & Mergner, U. (1995). *Gesundheit als produktives Potential* [Health as productive potential]. Berlin, Germany: Sigma.

Maxwell, S. E. (2004). The persistence of underpowered studies in psychological research: Causes, consequences, and remedies. *Psychological Methods, 9,* 147–163. doi:10.1037/1082-989X.9.2.147

Meara, H. (1974). Honor in dirty work: The case of American meat cutters and Turkish butchers. *Sociology of Work and Occupations, 1,* 259–283.

Meier, L. L., Semmer, N. K., Elfering, A., & Jacobshagen, N. (2008). The double meaning of control: Three-way interactions between internal resources, job control, and stressors at work. *Journal of Occupational Health Psychology, 13,* 244–258. doi:10.1037/1076-8998.13.3.244

Meijman, T. F., & Mulder, G. (1998). Psychological aspects of workload. In P. J. D. Drenth, H. Thierry, & C. J. de Wolff (Eds.), *Handbook of work and organizational psychology* (2nd ed., pp. 5–33). Hove, England: Psychology Press.

Meijman, T. F., Mulder, G., van Dormolen, M., & Cremer, R. (1992). Workload of driving examiners: A psychophysiological field study. In H. Kragt (Ed.), *Enhancing industrial performance* (pp. 245–258). London, England: Taylor & Francis.

Mintzberg, H. (1975, July-August). The manager's job: Folklore and fact. *Harvard Business Review, 53,* 49–61.

Morgeson, F. P., & Campion, M. A. (2003). Work design. In W. C. Borman, D. R. Ilgen, & R. J. Klimoski (Eds.), *Handbook of psychology: Vol. 12. Industrial and organizational psychology* (pp. 423–452). Hoboken, NJ: Wiley.

Munz, D. C., Kohler, J. M., & Greenberg, C. I. (2001). Effectiveness of a comprehensive worksite stress management program: Combining organizational and individual interventions. *International Journal of Stress Management, 8,* 49–62. doi:10.1023/A:1009553413537

Murphy, L. R., & Sauter, S. L. (2004). Work organization interventions: State of knowledge and future directions. *Social and Preventive Medicine, 49,* 79–86.

Nielsen, K., Fredslund, H., Christensen, K. B., & Albertsen, K. (2006). Success or failure? Interpreting and understanding the impact of interventions in four similar worksites. *Work and Stress, 20,* 272–287. doi:10.1080/02678370601022688

Nytro, K. Saksvik, P. O.,Mikkelsen, A., Bohle, P., & Quinlan, M. (2000). An appraisal of key factors in the implementation of occupational stress intervention. *Work & Stress, 14,* 213–225. doi:10.1080/02678370010024749

O'Donnell, M. P. (Ed.). (2002). *Health promotion in the workplace* (3rd ed.). Albany, NY: Delmar.

Orth-Gomer, K. (1983). Intervention on coronary risk factors by adapting a shift work schedule to biological rhythmicity. *Psychosomatic Medicine, 34,* 407–415.

Parker, S., & Wall, T. (1998). *Job and work design*. Thousand Oaks, CA: Sage.

Parkes, K. R., & Sparkes, T. I. (1998). *Organizational interventions to reduce work stress: Are they effective? (HSE Contract Research Report 193 / 1998)*. Colegate, England: Her Majesty's Stationery Office.

Pfaff, H., & Bentz, J. (2000). Intervention und evaluation im DaimlerChrysler werk Berlin [Intervention and evaluation at DaimlerChrysler Berlin]. In B. Badura, M. Litsch, & C. Vetter (Eds.), *Fehlzeiten-Report* 2000 [Absenteeism report] (pp. 176–190). Berlin, Germany: Springer.

Pritchard, R. D. (1990). *Measuring and improving organizational productivity*. New York, NY: Praeger.

Pritchard, R. D. (Ed.). (1995). *Productivity measurement and improvement: Organizational case studies*. Westport, CT: Praeger.

Quick, J. C. (1979). Dyadic goal setting and role stress: A field study. *Academy of Management Journal, 22*, 241–252. doi:10.2307/255587

Quick, J. C., Bhagat, R. S., Dalton, J. E., & Quick, J. D. (Eds.). (1987). *Work stress: Health care systems in the workplace*. New York, NY: Praeger.

Quick, J. C., Quick, J. D., Nelson, D. L., & Hurrell, J. (1997). *Preventive stress management in organizations*. Washington, DC: American Psychological Association. doi:10.1037/10238-000

Randall, R., Griffiths, A., & Cox, T. (2005). Evaluating organizational stress-management interventions using adapted study designs. *European Journal of Work and Organizational Psychology, 14*, 23–41. doi:10.1080/13594320444000209

Richardson, K. M., & Rothstein, H, R. (2008). Effects of occupational stress management intervention programs: A meta-analysis. *Journal of Occupational Health Psychology, 13*, 69–93. doi:10.1037/1076-8998.13.1.69

Roznowski, M., & Hulin, C. (1992). The scientific merit of valid measures of general constructs with special reference to job satisfaction and job withdrawal. In C. J. Cranny, S. C. Smith, & E. F. Stone (Eds.), *Job satisfaction: How people feel about their jobs and how it affects their performance* (pp. 123–163). New York, NY: Lexington.

Rutte, C. G., & Messick, D. M. (1995). An integrated model of perceived unfairness in organizations. *Social Justice Research, 8*, 239–261. doi:10.1007/BF02334810

Schaubroeck, J., Ganster, D. C., Sime, W. E., & Ditman, D. (1993). A field experiment testing supervisory role clarification. *Personnel Psychology, 46*, 1–25. Schaubroeck, J., & Merritt, D. E. (1997). Divergent effects of job control on coping with work stressors: The key role of self-efficacy. *Academy of Management Journal, 40*, 738–754.

Schurman, S. J., & Israel, B. A. (1995). Redesigning work systems to reduce stress: A participatory action research approach to creating change. In L. R. Murphy, J. J. Hurrell, S. L. Sauter, & G. P. Keita (Eds.), *Job stress interventions* (pp. 235–263). Washington, DC: American Psychological Association. doi:10.1037/10183-016

Schweiger, D. M., & DeNisi, A. S. (1991). Communication with employees following a merger: A longitudinal field experiment. *Academy of Management Journal, 34*, 110–135. doi:10.2307/256304

Semmer, N. K. (2006). Job stress interventions and the organization of work. *Scandinavian Journal of Work, Environment & Health, 32*, 515–527.

Semmer, N. K., Jacobshagen, N., Meier, L. L., & Elfering, A. (2007). Occupational stress research: The "stress-as-offense-to-self" perspective. In J. Houdmont & S. McIntyre (Eds.), *Occupational health psychology: European perspectives on research, education and practice* (Vol. 2, pp. 43–60). Castelo da Maia, Portugal: ISMAI.

Semmer, N. K., McGrath, J. E., & Beehr, T. A. (2005). Conceptual issues in research on stress and health. In C. L. Cooper (Ed.), *Handbook of stress medicine and health* (2nd ed., pp. 1–43). New York, NY: CRC Press.

Semmer, N. K., & Zapf, D. (2004). Gesundheits- und verhaltensbezogene interventionen in organisationen [Health- and behavior-related interventions at the worksite]. In H. Schuler (Ed.), *Organisationspsychologie—Gruppe und organisation* [Organizational psychology—Groups and organizations] (pp. 773–843). Göttingen, Germany: Hogrefe.

Shadish, W. R., Cook, T. D., & Campbell, D. T. (2002). *Experimental and quasi-experimental designs for generalized causal inference*. Boston, MA: Houghton Mifflin.

Siegrist, J. (2002). Effort–reward imbalance at work and health. In P. L. Perrewé & D. C. Ganster (Eds.), *Research in occupational stress and well being* (Vol. 2, pp. 261–291). Amsterdam, Netherlands: Elsevier.

Slesina, W., Beuels, F.-R., & Sochert, R. (1998). *Betriebliche gesundheitsforderung: Entwicklung und evaluation von gesundheitszirkeln zur pravention arbeitsbedingter erkrankungen* [Health promotion at the worksite: Development and evaluation of health circles to prevent work related illness]. Weinheim, Germany: Juventa.

Smith, F. L. (1996). Statistical significance testing and cumulative knowledge in psychology: Implications for training of researchers. *Psychological Methods, 1,* 115–129.

Smith, M. J., & Zehel, D. (1992). A stress reduction intervention programme for meat processors emphasizing job design and work organization (United States). In V. Di Martino (Ed.), *Preventing stress at work* (pp. 204–213). Geneva, Switzerland: International Labour Office.

Sonnentag, S. (1996). Work group factors and individual well-being. In M. A. West (Ed.), *Handbook of work group psychology* (pp. 345–367). Chichester, England: Wiley.

Sonnentag, S., & Frese, M. (2003). Stress in organizations. In W. C. Bormann, D. R. Ilgen, & R. J. Klimoski (Eds.), *Comprehensive handbook of psychology: Vol. 1. Industrial and Organizational Psychology* (pp. 453–491). New York, NY: Wiley. doi:10.1002/0471264385.wei1218

Spector, P. E. (1997). *Job satisfaction: Application, assessment, causes, and consequences.* Thousand Oaks, CA: Sage.

Spector, P. E. (1998). A control theory of the job stress process. In C. L. Cooper (Ed.), *Theories of organizational stress* (pp. 153–169). Oxford, England: Oxford University Press.

Taris, T. W., Kompier, M. A. J., Geurts, S. A. E., Schreurs, P. J. G., Schaufeli, W. B., de Boer, E., . . . Wattez, C. (2003). Stress management interventions in the Dutch domiciliary care sector: Findings from 81 organizations. *International Journal of Stress Management, 10,* 297–325. doi:10.1037/1072-5245.10.4.297

Theorell, T., & Wahlstedt, K. (1999). Sweden: Mail processing. In M. Kompier & C. Cooper (Eds.), *Preventing stress, improving productivity. European case studies in the workplace* (pp. 195–221). London, England: Routledge.

U.S. Department of Health and Human Services. (1993). 1992 National survey of worksite health promotion activities: Summary. *American Journal of Health Promotion, 7,* 452–464.

van der Klink, J. J. L., Blonk, R. W. B., Schene, A. H., & van Dijk, F. J. H. (2001). The benefits of interventions for work-related stress. *American Journal of Public Health, 91,* 270–276. doi:10.2105/AJPH.91.2.270

Wahlstedt, K. G. I., & Edling, C. (1997). Organizational changes at a postal sorting terminal—Their effects upon work satisfaction, psychosomatic complaints, and sick leave. *Work & Stress, 11,* 279–291.

Wall, T. D., & Clegg, C. W. (1981). A longitudinal field study of group work redesign. *Journal of Organizational Behaviour, 2,* 31–49. doi:10.1002/job.4030020104

Wall, T. D., Kemp, N. J., Jackson, P. R., & Clegg, C. W. (1986). An outcome evaluation of autonomous work groups: A long-term field experiment. *Academy of Management Journal, 29,* 280–304.

Warr, P. (2007). *Work, happiness, and unhappiness.* Mahwah, NJ: Erlbaum.

17

Worksite Health Interventions: Targets for Change and Strategies for Attaining Them

Catherine A. Heaney

During the past decade, much attention has been given to enhancing our understanding of how best to initiate, implement, and evaluate worksite interventions to protect and promote health. Historically, our knowledge about worksite hazards and individual risk factors for ill health has significantly surpassed our ability to develop and implement effective worksite-based interventions to address these hazards and risk factors (National Institute for Occupational Safety and Health [NIOSH], 2002; Parkes & Sparkes, 1998; Schult, McGovern, Dowd, & Pronk, 2006). However, intervention effectiveness research was recognized as a priority of the National Occupational Research Agenda in the United States (NIOSH, 1996), with significantly increased resources invested in occupational intervention research (NIOSH, 2006).

Perhaps in response to this investment and the increase in intervention activity, several systematic reviews of worksite health intervention research have recently been conducted (Bambra, Egan, Thomas, Petticrew, & Whitehead, 2007; Egan et al., 2007; Lamontagne, Keegel, Louie, Ostry, & Landsbergis, 2007; Parks & Steelman, 2008; Rivilis et al., 2008). A major conclusion from these reviews is that, although some of the worksite interventions have brought about improvements in employee health, the results are inconsistent and represent only modest effects. This chapter identifies current challenges to mounting effective worksite health interventions and suggests strategies for overcoming these challenges. More specifically, the various targets for change and the processes or strategies for change that are incorporated into worksite-based interventions are addressed. Lastly, given the central role of participatory strategies in worksite interventions, these strategies are described and critiqued.

Conceptual Model

An integrative conceptual framework for examining the relationship between work and health is based on a comprehensive model of stress and health initially developed by researchers at the University of Michigan (French & Kahn, 1962; Katz & Kahn, 1978) and more recently updated for broad applications in occupational safety and health (Israel, Baker, Goldenhar, Heaney, & Schurman, 1996).

This conceptual framework (depicted in Figure 17.1) presents the interplay of environmental, social, organizational, and individual factors as they influence employee health. Individuals experience conditions in the physical, social, and organizational environments. These conditions are referred to as *stressors* if they are likely to be perceived as harmful or threatening (Lazarus & Folkman, 1984) or if they place a demand on employees that results in a physiological adaptational response (Selye, 1993). Exposure to stressors may have a direct effect on health (e.g., when an equipment breakdown directly causes injury), or effects on health may be mediated through individual employees' perceptions and responses (e.g., when an equipment breakdown causes an employee to worry). The intensity and duration of the stressor, in combination with an employee's response to the stressor, influence the likelihood that exposure to the stressor will result in adverse physiological, psychological, or behavioral consequences. Each step of the process outlined in Figure 17.1 is influenced by employees' individual resources and the social resources provided within the organizational context. Thus, this model reflects a complex and dynamic process.

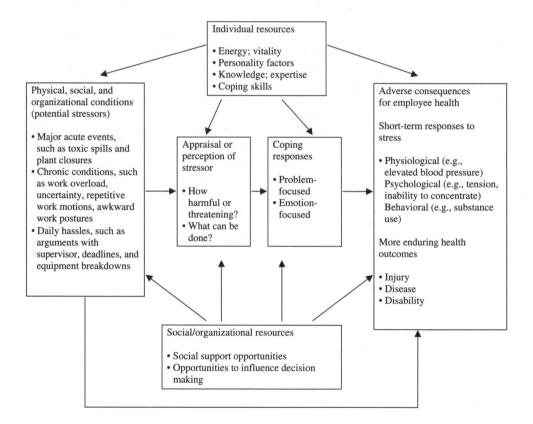

Figure 17.1. Conceptual framework for work, stress, and health. From "Worksite Health Interventions: Targets for Change and Strategies for Attaining Them," by C. A. Heaney. In J. C. Quick and L. E. Tetrick (Eds.), *Handbook of Occupational Health Psychology* (p. 307), 2003, Washington, DC: American Psychological Association. Copyright 2003 by the American Psychological Association.

Targets for Change

Although the major constructs of this conceptual model implicitly suggest the importance of multiple points of intervention for promoting and protecting worker health, Figure 17.2 explicitly presents the potential targets of intervention for influencing the process described in Figure 17.1. For example, Figure 17.2 shows that public policy, organizational policy and procedures, job tasks,

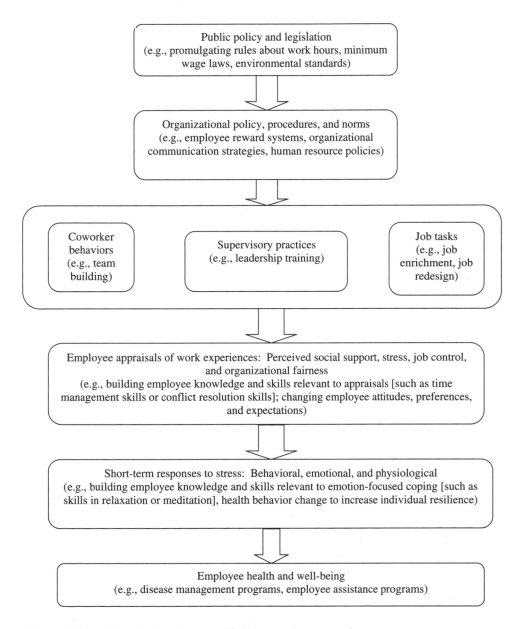

Figure 17.2.   Targets for change with intervention examples.

and the behaviors of supervisors and coworkers all contribute to employees' experience of work. Thus, interventions at any of these levels may influence employee appraisals of stress, social support, job control, and other work characteristics. The descending flow (indicated by the arrows in Figure 17.2) suggests that higher level targets for change may constrain or otherwise influence lower level targets. For example, minimum wage laws constrain organizational employee compensation policies. These policies, in turn, influence how supervisors conduct performance reviews of employees. All of these factors may influence the extent to which employees perceive that they are fairly compensated for their work. Of course, employee expectations and attitudes also influence employee appraisals of fairness.

Although much research has investigated the link between employee appraisals of their work experiences and health, little research has addressed the linkages among specific organizational factors, supervisory behaviors, and employee appraisals. For example, only a small number of studies have attempted to identify the organizational structures and policies or the supervisory behaviors that lead to employee perceptions of job control and social support (Gilbreath & Benson, 2004; Harenstam, 2008). At this point, the extent to which the organizational factors and supervisory behaviors that contribute to employee appraisals of job control and social support are specific to local context versus widely applicable across worksites is not known.

Several planning frameworks in public health intervention development suggest that targets of intervention be chosen on the basis of the following criteria: (a) importance and prevalence of the health problem; (b) prevalence of the risk factor; (c) strength of association between the risk factor and the health problem; and (d) modifiability of the risk factor (Bartholomew, Parcel, & Kok, 1998; Green & Kreuter, 1999; Jeffery, 1989). When these public health criteria are applied to the conceptual model presented in Figure 17.1, they translate into the following questions (Heaney & van Ryn, 1990):

1. What adverse health conditions are being experienced by employees?
2. What are the various physical, social, and organizational conditions that are potential stressors in this workplace?
3. Who is experiencing these stressors and perceiving them as stressful (e.g., a few idiosyncratic individuals or an identifiable subgroup)? How widespread is the perception of stress?
4. To what extent are these perceptions of stress linked to short-term and long-term adverse outcomes?
5. How modifiable is the stressor? Can exposure to the stressor be reduced?
6. If exposure to the stressor cannot be reduced, what individual and social resources are effective buffers against the adverse effects of the stressor?

However, these criteria are rarely applied systematically during the planning of worksite health interventions. Instead, the choice of change target has been determined more by philosophy, disciplinary assumptions, and perceived feasibility rather than critical assessment of empirical criteria. Occupational health and safety practitioners who are trained as engineers or safety science specialists tend to give priority to reducing exposure to worksite hazards or stressors by engineering them out of the work process (Goldenhar & Schulte, 1994). However, interventions addressing stress-related health problems have tended to emphasize individual level targets for change (Murphy & Sauter, 2004). Research indicates that both managers and employees are most likely to view psychosocial stress as strongly influenced by individual factors (Singer, Neale, & Schwartz, 1989). Indeed, when asked about their preferences or expectations for intervention, employees seem to prefer interventions that target employee knowledge and skills about stress management or that target employee health behaviors more generally (Elo, Ervasti, Kuosma, & Mattila, 2008; Saksvik, Nytro, Dahl-Jorgensen, & Mikkelsen, 2002). These beliefs are aligned with the fundamental attribution error in social psychology (Ross & Nisbett, 1991) and the context minimization error in community psychology (Shinn & Toohey, 2003), which describe the tendency of observers to overestimate the importance of individual characteristics and underestimate the importance of situational or contextual factors when describing the causes of phenomena. Such information processing biases may contribute to the continuing overemphasis on individual level targets for change in worksite interventions to reduce stress.

However, a social ecological perspective emphasizes the dynamic interplay among the parts of a system and suggests that sole reliance on any one target or level of intervention is unlikely to yield optimal results (Sallis, Owen, & Fisher, 2008). This perspective reminds us that the effectiveness of change at one level is likely to be dependent on the extent to which factors at the other levels are aligned with or facilitative of that change. For example, the quality of a supervisor's relationship with his or her boss has been shown to influence the extent to which the supervisor is able to have a positive impact on his or her employees' attitudes toward work (Tangirala, Green, & Ramanujam, 2007). Indeed, managers have expressed reservations about engaging in worksite health interventions if they perceive that upper management is not willing to support or reward the effort (Saksvik et al., 2002). Thus, an intervention that plans for integrated change across multiple targets at multiple levels (e.g., employee, supervisor, work team, organization) will be most likely to effectively reduce health problems.

In addition, a social ecological perspective suggests that effective change at one level is likely to bring about changes at other levels. Sometimes, such changes are unintended, unexpected, and in a worse case scenario, unwanted. For example, it has been suggested that the implementation of autonomous work groups may result in changes in coworker relationships that undermine the availability of coworker support (Semmer, 2006).

A social ecological perspective also suggests the importance of identifying *high impact leverage points* (Stokols, 1996, p. 290) as targets for change. These leverage points are people, behaviors, roles, and environmental conditions that exert a disproportionately large influence on employee health and well-being. For example, Rasmussen et al. (2006) found that the elected safety representatives in a Danish manufacturing facility were tremendously central to the success of an intervention intended to reduce the incidence of eczema and traumatic injuries. By involving these safety representatives in the planning of any production system changes and encouraging them to seek input from a broader base of employees, the intervention was successful at improving the safety climate in the facility and reducing the incidence of injuries and illness. House (1981) suggested that the front-line supervisor can be an important leverage point. If front-line supervisors increase their supportive exchanges with coworkers and subordinates, many employees stand to benefit in terms of enhanced social support. Finally, opinion leaders may serve as high-impact leverage points because of their ability to bring about changes in others' attitudes and behaviors (Lam & Schaubroeck, 2000).

Strategies for Change

Although the model in Figure 17.2 shows a variety of potential targets for change, it provides little guidance in terms of identifying strategies for change. *Strategies for change* are the activities that change agents engage in or implement to bring about the desired intervention outcomes. Once a target for change has been identified, how does one go about effecting that change in as timely, appropriate, and cost-effective a manner as possible? What tactics should be used to reduce the likelihood of undesirable outcomes while optimizing desired change?

Most planning frameworks suggest that social science theories, intervention effectiveness research, program evaluation results, and knowledge gained from local needs and resource assessments should inform choices of tactics and strategies (Bartholomew et al., 1998; Green & Kreuter, 1999). In the following discussion, strategies for change are categorized as (a) individual-level change strategies that focus on changing employees' beliefs, attitudes, and behaviors and (b) organizational-level change strategies that focus on changing organizational structures, policies, priorities, and procedures.

Individual-Level Change Theories

When attempting to change employee beliefs, attitudes, and behaviors, theories of social influence and social learning have been used to guide intervention development. The most commonly used theories include social–cognitive theory (Bandura, 1986), the transtheoretical model of change (Prochaska, Redding, & Evers, 2008), fear arousal theories (Witte, Meyer, & Martell, 2001), and the theory of reasoned action (Ajzen, Albarracin, & Hornik, 2007). Although these various theories place differing amounts of emphasis on cognitive, affective, and behavioral processes, they all aid in identifying the major explanatory factors that influence the target of change, and in some cases, they also identify strategies for modifying the explanatory factors. For example, social–cognitive theory (Bandura, 1986) places great emphasis on efficacy expectations (i.e., beliefs regarding one's ability to successfully carry out a course of action or perform a behavior) and outcome expectations (i.e., beliefs that the performance of a behavior will have desired effects or consequences) as explanatory factors for behavior. The theory further posits that both types of expectations can be influenced through observational and experiential learning (Bandura, 1986). Thus, to increase health care employees' compliance with universal precautions, an intervention might incorporate learning activities that allow employees to hear about or observe others' successful use of the desired procedures and to practice the procedures themselves to develop confidence in their ability to carry them out. Theories that have undergone rigorous testing and have been applied in many different settings and with various target populations are the most useful for developing intervention strategies (Glanz, Rimer, & Viswanath, 2008).

Although psychological theories of learning and social influence have been well integrated into health promotion interventions in other settings (Glanz et al., 2008), worksite health interventions (and particularly occupational safety and health programs) have not been adequately informed by social science theory (Goldenhar, Lamontagne, Katz, Heaney, & Landsbergis, 2001). However, a few studies serve as useful examples of how worksite intervention strategies that are attempting individual level change can be well guided by theory. For example, Sinclair, Gershon, Murphy, and Goldenhar (1996) used protection motivation theory to guide their development of an intervention to change employee behavior to reduce needlestick injuries among workers in the health care industry. As another example, Green, DeJoy, and Olejnik (2005) used concepts from social–cognitive theory to guide the development and evaluation of an ergonomics-training program for computer users. In the worksite health promotion arena, Glasgow, Terborg, Hollis, Severson, and Boles (1995) based their heart disease prevention program on the transtheoretical model of change, providing intervention activities matched to employees' levels of motivational readiness.

Organizational-Level Change Theories

Worksite health researchers and practitioners have made less use of organizational change theory and its associated body of research than they have of theories describing individual-level change. Several factors may inhibit application of organizational change theory and research to worksite health programs. One such factor is that the outcomes of interest for most published organizational change interventions revolve around the health of the organization (i.e., productivity, efficiency, profits) rather than the health of the employee. And although several conceptualizations of healthy organizations include the well-being of employees (Lawler, Mohrman, & Ledford, 1995; Pfeffer, 1998), much of the research does not examine health outcomes. Thus, the process of translating results from the organizational change literature to the field of worksite health is not straightforward. A second factor that may inhibit the application of organizational change theories is that they tend to emphasize the influence of the organizational context on the change process (Molinsky, 1999). Such contextualizing limits the ability of the program developer to apply the findings from one organization to another and strongly suggests that "off the shelf" programs are not likely to be effective if adopted without modification (Argyris, 1993; Colarelli, 1998). Perhaps because of the contextual nature of the conceptual frameworks, organizational change research tends to be more idiographic than nomothetic (Quick, 1997). In other words, much of the research is oriented toward understanding change processes within a particular organization rather than examining change processes across organizations. Methodologies focus on case studies and include more ethnographic approaches rather than experimental or epidemiological methods. Thus, the application of the findings in the literature tends to be in terms of lessons learned from diverse cases rather than empirically derived generalizations about effective change processes. Although these lessons learned can be instructive, they may be less compelling to intervention developers who have been steeped in positivist, experimental research traditions.

In spite of these complexities and inconsistencies, various organizational change scholars have suggested strategies for maximizing the success of planned change efforts (Boonstra, 2004; Kanter, Stein, & Jick, 1992; Kotter, 1996; Schein, 1987). There are striking similarities among the guidelines put forth by different authors. Their intellectual roots are firmly entrenched in Lewin's (1951) influential model for conceptualizing change. Lewin posited three stages to the change process: unfreezing the old behavior, moving to a new behavior, and then refreezing or stabilizing the new behavior. Building on this framework, organizational change theorists linked the stages to action steps that change agents should take to facilitate progress through the stages.

The *unfreezing* stage involves creating a readiness for change among members of the organization. This stage needs to address employee beliefs about the need for change, perhaps by disconfirming current conceptions of and stimulating dissatisfaction with the status quo (Cummings & Worley, 2001). Employee beliefs about the likelihood that change can be successfully accomplished should also be addressed to build a shared sense of collective capacity (Weiner, Amick, & Lee, 2008). According to Lewin's (1951) original theory, this stage involves conducting a *force field analysis* that identifies the major forces that both facilitate and hinder change. This process encourages organization members to think about why change has not already occurred and how the change process should be crafted to be optimally successful. Cummings and Worley (2001) suggested that this involves creating a vision for the planned change.

The *moving* stage centers on the development and implementation of an action plan to bring about the desired change. Such a plan should include developing political support for the change among the relevant stakeholders, identifying and accessing the needed resources, providing leadership and assigning responsibility for the change, modifying organizational structures and policies to support the change effort, and providing training and problem-solving assistance (Cummings, 2004; Kanter et al., 1992; Kotter, 1996; Schein, 1987).

The *refreezing* stage involves sustaining the momentum of the change effort and institutionalizing the change. This is a particularly important stage if the change effort has been initiated or managed by researchers or experts from outside the organization who will leave once the change effort has been implemented. Strategies associated with this stage include reinforcing changes by making rewards contingent on compliance with them, socializing newcomers into the organizational culture that informed the change effort, and disseminating the change more broadly throughout the organization to normalize it (Cummings, 2004).

Participatory Strategies in Worksite Health Interventions

Employee participation has been an important component of long-standing traditions in organizational change theory and research. For example, it is a central component of organizational development (Cummings, 2004; Levin, 2004), action research (Argyris, 1993), and popular quality-improvement programs such as Total Quality Management (Hackman & Wagerman, 1995; Klein, Ralls, Smith-Major, & Douglas, 2000). Levin (2004) suggested that the two cornerstones of a successful organizational change process are participation and collective reflection. *Participation* refers to the creation of opportunities for employees to take an active role in shaping their working situation, by generating knowledge about the change process that incorporates employees' views of the status quo and their preferred responses to current challenges or problems. *Collective reflection* describes a type of learning process in which everyone involved in the change process has the opportunity to be informed about the unfolding change effort, share feedback with each other, and contribute to problem solving and ongoing improvement in the change effort.

Organizational scholars and practitioners support employee participation in change efforts for a number of reasons (Cummings, 2004; Klein et al., 2000; Levin, 2004). Participatory strategies are viewed as consistent with democratic values and with employee preferences for having control over their work lives. In addition, both theory and change agents' practice-based experiences suggest that employee participation, by incorporating worker expertise and a broad array of relevant information and skills into decision making, produces qualitatively better decisions and action plans for change (Vink, Imada, & Zink, 2008). Participation in the development and implementation of new initiatives also reduces employee resistance to change programs and enhances employees' willingness to persevere in the face of setbacks during the change process (Nielsen, Randall, & Albertsen, 2007). Lastly, participation is positively associated with organizational commitment, perceptions of organizational fairness, and employee morale (Cummings, 2004; Klein et al., 2000).

Worksite health practitioners and researchers have embraced employee participation in the planning, development, implementation, and evaluation of worksite health programs (Goldenhar et al., 2001; Semmer, 2006). Sometimes, employee participation is used as a strategy for bringing about a desired targeted change and sometimes employee participation is a desired target of change in itself. Worksite health promotion programs have incorporated employee participation to maximize the effectiveness of efforts to reduce employee risk behaviors. Strategies have included seeking employee input into the assessment of employee health needs (e.g., through employee surveys or focus groups), having employee advisory boards guide the planning process, and having employee groups take full responsibility for the implementation of health promotion efforts (Linnan et al., 1999). In occupational safety and health, *participatory ergonomics,* defined as "the involvement of people in planning and controlling a significant amount of their own work activities, with sufficient knowledge and power to influence both processes and outcomes in order to achieve desirable goals" (Wilson & Haines, 1997, pp. 492–493), best exemplifies programs that emphasize employee participation both as a means to effecting ergonomic innovation and as an important outcome in itself. Participatory strategies have also been a central component of some worksite-stressor reduction interventions (see, e.g., Bourbonnais, Brisson, Vinet, Vezina, & Lower, 2006; Elo et al., 2008; Israel, Schurman, & House, 1989; Landsbergis & Vivona-Vaughan, 1995; Mikkelsen & Gundersen, 2003). Belief in the benefits of employee participation in health and safety efforts is so strong that it has been identified as a required component of a psychologically healthy workplace by the American Psychological Association (2009) and codified into law in the European Union and other parts of the world (Council of the European Union, 1994; Harris, 2004).

Although participatory strategies have gained in popularity, the nature of those strategies has varied greatly. The word *participation* has been used to indicate strategies ranging from the provision of information to employees by management (e.g., company newsletters, "state-of-the-company" presentations), to opportunities for employees to voice concerns or suggestions (e.g., suggestion boxes, open forums), to joint labor–management problem-solving groups with unequal influence in decision making, and finally to initiatives with joint control of resources and influence (Cotton, Vollrath, Froggatt, Lengnick-Hall, & Jennings, 1988; Robertson & Minkler, 1994). Several authors have provided classification schemes for participatory strategies, identifying the important decision points in designing these types of strategies (Cotton et al., 1988; Eklund, 2000; Klein et al., 2000). These classification schemes are synthesized in Table 17.1.

A few worksite health programs that have used participatory strategies illustrate some of the different choices that have been made. Most programs use representative participation, with representatives chosen in a number of ways. Representatives have been elected by their peers (Landsbergis & Vivona-Vaughan, 1995), chosen by their managers (Bourbonnais, Brisson, Vinet, Vezina, & Lower, 2006), recruited by labor and management leaders (Israel et al., 1989), and self-selected through expressions of employee interest (Bohr, Evanoff, & Wolf, 1997; Bond & Bunce, 2001). The scope of the issues addressed has ranged from one health behavior issue (Eriksen & Gottlieb, 1998), to a set of employee health risk behaviors (Glasgow, Terborg, Hollis, Severson, & Boles, 1995), to ergonomic issues relevant to a work unit (Bohr et al., 1997; Granzow & Theberge, 2008), to a broader charge of reducing adverse psychosocial work factors (Bourbonnais, Brisson, Vinet, Vezina, & Lower, 2006; Elo et al., 2008; Mikkelsen & Gundersen, 2003). The duration and intensity of the participatory processes also varied tremendously. In a recent review of participatory ergonomics programs, the duration of the programs ranged from a few weeks to more than 7 years (Rivilis et al., 2008). Several of the recently conducted participatory worksite health interventions involved weekly or bimonthly meetings held over the course of 3 to 6 months (Bond & Bunce, 2001; Bourbonnais, Brisson, Vinet, Vezina, & Lower, 2006; Mikkelsen & Gundersen, 2003).

Much of the earlier research examining employee participation strategies focused on the outcomes of employee satisfaction and performance (for reviews, see Cotton et al., 1988; Klein et al., 2000; Lawler, 1992). These reviews concluded that the use of participatory strategies has had mixed results. Cotton et al. (1988) suggested that these mixed results may be a result of the great variety of ways in which participation has been operationalized and that the most effective participatory strategies are those that are ongoing, direct, and that

Table 17.1.   Strategy Choice Points for Employee Participation Initiatives

Category	Choice point
Scope of initiative	• What range of issues will be addressed? • To what extent will decisions be made relevant to personal job performance, work teams, and/or larger organizational units? • Is the participatory process anticipated to continue indefinitely or for a discrete time period? • Will the program be initiated in a small number of organizational units or instituted organization-wide?
Group composition and process	• Will participation be mandatory or voluntary? • To what extent will all employees be provided opportunities for participation versus participation of employee representatives? If the latter, how will representatives be chosen? • To what extent will others in the organization review (and potentially modify) decisions made by the group? • Will participation occur through formal and/or informal processes?
Organizational support for initiative	• How much and what types of training will be provided to employees so that they can participate effectively? • To what extent will employees be allowed to participate on work time (e.g., be released from other job duties, be allocated time outside of meetings to perform follow up)? • To what extent will organizational structures and processes be modified to reinforce participation (e.g., reward system, hiring practices)?

Note. From "Worksite Health Interventions: Targets for Change and Strategies for Attaining Them," by C. A. Heaney. In J. C. Quick and L. E. Tetrick (Eds.), *Handbook of Occupational Health Psychology* (p. 315), 2003, Washington, DC: American Psychological Association. Copyright 2003 by the American Psychological Association. Ideas adapted from Cotton, Vollrath, Froggatt, Lengnick-Hall, and Jennings (1988); Eklund (2000); Klein, Ralls, Smith-Major, and Douglas (2000); and Wilson and Haines (1997).

provide employees with significant influence in decision making relevant to how they perform their jobs. Subsequent reviews questioned the methodology used by Cotton et al. (1988) and did not successfully replicate their results (Leana, Locke, & Schweiger, 1990; Wagner, 1994).

However, it should be noted that participatory worksite health interventions have generally chosen strategies that are contrary to the suggestions of Cotton et al. (1988). Rather than using direct, ongoing participatory strategies offering significant influence over decision making, programs have tended to use representative processes (often with a small number of representatives for a large number of employees) of limited duration and scope. Recent systematic reviews of participatory worksite health interventions also concluded that the programs have had mixed results, but offer little guidance about how best to optimize effectiveness through the choice points listed in Table 17.1 (Egan et al., 2007; Rivilis et al., 2008). This remains a critical priority for future worksite health intervention research.

Although a comprehensive review of the relevant literature on participatory strategies is beyond the scope of this chapter, a number of themes emerge from published accounts of participatory worksite health programs and from reviews of employee-participation strategies more broadly. First, little attention has been paid to Lewin's (1951) unfreezing stage of change. Researchers or change agents from outside the organization initiated many of the worksite health interventions. Thus, it may be particularly important to engage in activities that encourage employees to perceive the need for change. Rasmussen et al. (2006) attributed some of the success of their program in a Danish manufacturing facility to the fact that it addressed specific health problems (i.e., incidence of traumatic injuries and eczema) that were widely recognized by employees.

Even when employee "felt need" for change was established in some of the participatory interventions, other important components of Lewin's (1951) force field analysis often remained unaddressed. Granzow and Theberge (2008) pointed out that many organizations have had a history of conflict-ridden and confrontational labor management relations, as well as previous failed planned change efforts. This history provides a context for worksite health interventions that may hinder workers' faith in the participatory process, with workers perceiving the purpose of the participatory strategies to be more manipulative (e.g., to enhance employee morale) than productive (e.g., to improve quality of work life). In addition, front-line supervisors may resist participatory strategies if they fear an erosion of their power and influence (Klein et al., 2000). They may resent a perceived increase in workload as they are assigned to guide the participatory efforts and instructed to release other employees from their usual duties, and they may infer a lack of top management support for the effort if organizational structures and processes are not modified to complement the participatory initiative (Saksvik et al., 2002). None of the published accounts of participatory interventions reviewed for this chapter described strategies for identifying and addressing these sources of resistance to change.

Second, most of the participatory interventions concentrated on problem identification and solution generation but gave short shrift to the implementation process. In some cases, the implementation of the action plans developed through participatory processes was viewed as the responsibility of management (Bourbonnais, Brisson, Vinet, Vezina, Abdous, et al., 2006; Kobayashi, Kaneyoshi, Yokota, & Kawakami, 2008). In other cases, the steering committee or intervention team was expected to implement changes, but members did not have access to the necessary resources nor authority to implement changes at an organizational level beyond the local work unit (e.g., Saksvik et al., 2002).

No matter how changes were expected to be implemented, there was little recognition of the need for employees to be able to collectively reflect on the changes once implemented and to make adjustments to the action plans depending on how employees were responding to them. This ongoing transactional process between reflection and action is central to certain models of organizational development (Levin, 2004) and action research (Argyris, 1993) but is not emphasized in many participatory strategies for worksite health interventions. If such a process is included in a worksite health intervention, it is typically available only to the small number of employees who constitute the steering or advisory committees for the programs (Bourbonnais, Brisson, Vinet, Vezina, & Lower, 2006; Granzow & Theberge, 2008). Without broader participation in this collective reflection process, employees are unlikely to optimally learn about effective change processes nor to perceive the extent to which the intervention is having an effect.

Third, the scope of participatory worksite health interventions is often limited to the work unit or department. For example, in the Kobayashi et al. (2008) study, employees were instructed to focus on "low cost improvements for immediate change in their work" (p. 458). In participatory ergonomic programs, employees are often directed to focus on specific aspects of their work practices or local work environments (Rivilis et al., 2008). Indeed, across most of the participatory worksite interventions, action plans that addressed work unit level processes were more likely to be implemented than broader organizational level change (Bond & Bunce, 2001; Bourbonnais, Brisson, Vinet, Vezina, & Lower, 2006; Mikkelsen & Gundersen, 2003). However, to "refreeze" or institutionalize these work unit changes, it is likely that broader organizational processes, such as reward systems, communication practices, and training policies, will also need to change. Without this alignment across multiple levels of the organization, momentum is unlikely to be sustained, particularly once the external change agents withdraw.

Perhaps the limited scope of the participatory strategies, the lack of support for the implementation of change from multiple levels of the organization, and the lack of opportunities to collectively reflect on implemented changes have contributed to both the inconsistent results of the participatory interventions and the lack of increased job control experienced by employees in organizations that have mounted such interventions. It is striking to note that in 10 out of 18 studies of participatory interventions reviewed by Egan et al. (2007), employees did not report an increase in job control after the intervention.

Conclusion

The social ecological perspective (Sallis et al., 2008) and the systems science approach (Green, 2006) strongly suggest that worksite interventions incorporate multiple targets of change at multiple levels of influence. However, an overwhelming preponderance of the studies describing the relationship between work organization and employee health focus on the relationship between employee appraisals of their work conditions and their health, rather than on the organizational practices and the behaviors of supervisors and coworkers that contribute to those appraisals (Harenstam, 2008). This tends to perpetuate the overemphasis of worksite health interventions on individual level change. Multilevel studies across multiple organizations will help to identify organizational structures and practices that consistently influence employee perceptions of stress, social support, control, organizational justice, and organizational commitment to employees' health and well-being. In addition, we need well-documented local efforts to ascertain these linkages within specific organizations. Such activity will support the inclusion of a broader array of targets for change for worksite health programs.

At the same time, it is important to move past the either/or framing of the choice of targets for change. Worksite health interventions that incorporate change at multiple levels provide the opportunity for organizational structures and processes to reinforce adaptive employee norms and facilitate healthy behaviors (Sorensen, Quintiliani, Pereira, Yang, & Stoddard, 2009) and for individual behaviors to support and augment the effects of the implementation and institutionalization of organizational processes that reduce exposure to hazards and enhance healthy decision making (Semmer, 2006).

With a few notable exceptions, the worksite health intervention literature continues to provide little attention to issues of strategy. Published accounts of interventions rarely provide detailed descriptions of the program activities and change processes, nor do they explicate the basis for decisions about strategies for change. It is even rarer for intervention research to formally compare the effectiveness of various strategies for bringing about targeted changes. For example, no published studies have compared the implementation and effectiveness of worksite health interventions that incorporate employee participation in the change process with interventions that are guided solely by outside experts.

More specifically, the use of theory to inform the development of change strategies, whether at the individual level or organizational level, remains scarce. The example of participatory strategies described earlier is instructive. Such strategies are popular and the empirical evidence suggests that, in general, they contribute to health-enhancing outcomes. However, the results across studies differ markedly, and it is likely that these inconsistent results are related to variations in how the participatory strategies were designed and implemented. Clearly, the basic tenets of organizational stage theory (Levin, 2004; Lewin, 1951) have not been widely used to inform the development of these strategies. A more in-depth application of theory to practice may increase the likelihood that participatory strategies will successfully bring about health promoting outcomes.

Only with more systematic attention to the development and implementation phases of intervention research (Goldenhar et al., 2001) will we be able to maximize the effectiveness of worksite health interventions and accomplish the vision set forth by the NIOSH Worklife Initiative: "Workplaces that are free of recognized hazards, with health-promoting and sustaining policies, programs, and practices; and employees with ready access to effective programs and services that protect their health, safety, and well-being" (NIOSH, 2009).

References

Ajzen, I., Albarracin, D., & Hornik, R. (Eds.). (2007). *Prediction and change of health behavior: Applying the reasoned action approach.* Hillsdale, NJ: Erlbaum.

American Psychological Association. (2009). The psychologically healthy workplace program. Retrieved from http://www.phwa.org/

Argyris, C. (1993). *Knowledge for action: A guide to overcoming barriers to organizational change.* San Francisco, CA: Jossey-Bass.

Bambra, C., Egan, M., Thomas, S., Petticrew, M., & Whitehead, M. (2007). The psychosocial and health effects of workplace reorganisation. 2. A systematic review of task restructuring interventions. *Journal of Epidemiology and Community Health, 61,* 1028–1037. doi:10.1136/jech. 2006.054999

Bandura, A. (1986). *Social foundations of thought and action*. Englewood Cliffs, NJ: Prentice Hall.

Bartholomew, L. K., Parcel, G. S., & Kok, G. (1998). Intervention mapping: A process for developing theory- and evidence-based health education programs. *Health Education & Behavior, 25*, 545–563. doi:10.1177/109019819802500502

Bohr, P. C., Evanoff, B. A., & Wolf, L. D. (1997). Implementing participatory ergonomics teams among health care workers. *American Journal of Industrial Medicine, 32*, 190–196. doi:10.1002/(SICI)1097-0274(199709)32:3<190::AID-AJIM2>3.0.CO;2-1

Bond, F. W., & Bunce, D. (2001). Job control mediates change in a work reorganization intervention for stress reduction. *Journal of Occupational Health Psychology, 6*, 290–302. doi:10.1037/1076-8998.6.4.290

Boonstra, J. J. (Ed.). (2004). *Dynamics of organizational change and learning*. Amsterdam, Netherlands: Wiley. doi:10.1002/9780470753408

Bourbonnais, R., Brisson, C., Vinet, A., Vezina, M., Abdous, B., & Gaudet, M. (2006). Effectiveness of a participative intervention on psychosocial work factors to prevent mental health problems in a hospital setting. *Occupational and Environmental Medicine, 63*, 335–342. doi:10.1136/oem.2004.018077

Bourbonnais, R., Brisson, C., Vinet, A., Vezina, M., & Lower, A. (2006). Development and implementation of a participative intervention to improve the psychosocial work environment and mental health in an acute care hospital. *Occupational and Environmental Medicine, 63*, 326–334. doi:10.1136/oem.2004.018069

Colarelli, S. M. (1998). Psychological interventions in organizations: An evolutionary perpsective. *American Psychologist, 53*, 1044–1056. doi:10.1037/0003-066X.53.9.1044

Cotton, J. L., Vollrath, D. A., Froggatt, K. L., Lengnick-Hall, M. L., & Jennings, K. R. (1988). Employee participation: Diverse forms and different outcomes. *Academy of Management Review, 13*, 8–22. doi:10.2307/258351

Council of the European Union (1994, September 22). *Council Directive 94/45/EC of 22 September 1994 on the establishment of a European Works Council or a procedure in Community-scale undertakings and Community-scale groups of undertakings for the purposes of informing and consulting employees.* Retrieved from http://eur-lex.europa.eu/LexUriServ/LexUriServ.do?uri=CELEX:31994L0045:EN:HTML

Cummings, T. (2004). Organizational development and change: Foundations and applications. In J. J. Boonstra (Ed.), *Dynamics of organizational change and learning* (pp. 25–42). Hoboken, NJ: Wiley. doi:10.1002/9780470753408.ch2

Cummings, T., & Worley, C. (2001). *Organizational development and change* (7th ed.). Cincinnati, OH: Southwestern College Publishing.

Egan, M., Bambra, C., Thomas, S., Petticrew, M., Whitehead, M., & Thomson, H. (2007). The psychosocial and health effects of workplace reorganisation. 1. A systematic review of organisation-level interventions that aim to increase employee control. *Journal of Epidemiology and Community Health, 61*, 945–954. doi:10.1136/jech.2006.054965

Eklund, J. (2000). Development work for quality and ergonomics. *Applied Ergonomics, 31*, 641–648. doi:10.1016/S0003-6870(00)00039-9

Elo, A.-L., Ervasti, J., Kuosma, E., & Mattila, P. (2008). Evaluation of an organizational stress management program in a municipal public works organization. *Journal of Occupational Health Psychology, 13*, 10–23. doi:10.1037/1076-8998.13.1.10

Eriksen, M. P., & Gottlieb, N. H. (1998). A review of the health impact of smoking control at the workplace. *American Journal of Health Promotion, 13*(2), 83–104.

French, J. R. P., & Kahn, R. (1962). A programmatic approach to studying the industrial environment and mental health. *Journal of Social Issues, 18*, 1–47.

Gilbreath, B., & Benson, P. G. (2004). The contribution of supervisor behavior to employee psychological well-being. *Work & Stress, 18*, 255–266. doi:10.1080/02678370412331317499

Glanz, K., Rimer, B. K., & Viswanath, K. (Eds.). (2008). *Health behavior and health education: Theory, research, and practice* (4th ed.). San Francisco, CA: Jossey-Bass.

Glasgow, R. E., Terborg, J. R., Hollis, J. F., Severson, H. H., & Boles, S. M. (1995). Take heart: Results from the initial phase of a work-site wellness program. *American Journal of Public Health, 85*, 209–216. doi:10.2105/AJPH.85.2.209

Goldenhar, L. M., Lamontagne, A. D., Katz, T., Heaney, C. A., & Landsbergis, P. (2001). The intervention research process in occupational safety and health: An overview from the NORA intervention effectiveness research team. *Journal of Occupational and Environmental Medicine, 43*, 616–622. doi:10.1097/00043764-200107000-00008

Goldenhar, L. M., & Schulte, P. A. (1994). Intervention research in occupational health and safety. *Journal of Occupational Medicine, 36,* 763–775.

Granzow, K., & Theberge, N. (2009). On the line: Worker democracy and the struggle over occupational health and safety. *Qualitative Health Research, 19*(1), 82–93. doi:10.1177/1049732308327349

Green, L. W. (2006). Public health asks of systems science: To advance our evidence-based practice, can you help us get more practice-based evidence? *American Journal of Public Health, 96,* 406–409. doi:10.2105/AJPH.2005.066035

Green, L. W., & Kreuter, M. W. (1999). *Health promotion planning: An educational and ecological approach* (3rd ed.). Mountain View, CA: Mayfield.

Greene, B., DeJoy, D., & Olejnik, S. (2005). Effects of an active ergonomics-training program on risk exposure, worker beliefs, and symptoms in computer users. *Work, 24,* 41–52.

Hackman, J. R., & Wagerman, R. (1995). Total quality management: Empirical, conceptual, and practical issues. *Administrative Science Quarterly, 40,* 309–342. doi:10.2307/2393640

Harenstam, A. (2008). Organizational approach to studies of job demands, control, and health. *Scandinavian Journal of Work, Environment and Health, Supplement, 6,* 144–149.

Harris, P. (2004). From health and safety to employee participation? The impact of the New Zealand health and safety in employment amendment act (2002) [online]. *International Employment Relations Review, 10,* 1–12.

Heaney, C. A. (2003). Worksite health interventions: Targets for change and strategies for attaining them. In J. C. Quick & L. E. Tetrick (Eds.), *Handbook of occupational health psychology* (pp. 305–324). Washington, DC: American Psychological Association.

Heaney, C. A., & van Ryn, M. (1990). Broadening the scope of worksite stress programs: A guiding framework. *American Journal of Health Promotion, 4,* 413–420.

House, J. S. (1981). *Work stress and social support.* Reading, MA: Addison-Wesley.

Israel, B. A., Baker, E. A., Goldenhar, L. M., Heaney, C. A., & Schurman, S. J. (1996). Occupational stress, safety, and health: Conceptual framework and principles for effective prevention interventions. *Journal of Occupational Health Psychology, 1,* 261–286. doi:10.1037/1076-8998.1.3.261

Israel, B. A., Schurman, S. J., & House, J. S. (1989). Action research on occupational stress: Involving workers as researchers. *International Journal of Health Sciences, 19*(1), 135–155.

Jeffery, R. W. (1989). Risk behaviors and health: Contrasting individual and population perspectives. *American Psychologist, 44,* 1194–1202. doi:10.1037/0003-066X.44.9.1194

Kanter, R. M., Stein, B. A., & Jick, T. D. (Eds.). (1992). *The challenge of organizational change: How companies experience it and leaders guide it.* New York, NY: Free Press.

Katz, D., & Kahn, R. (1978). *The social psychology of organizations.* New York, NY: Wiley.

Klein, K. J., Ralls, R. S., Smith-Major, V., & Douglas, C. (2000). Power and participation in the workplace: Implications for empowerment theory, research, and practice. In J. Rappaport & E. Seidman (Eds.), *Handbook of community psychology* (pp. 273–295). New York, NY: Kluwer Academic/Plenum.

Kobayashi, Y., Kaneyoshi, A., Yokota, A., & Kawakami, N. (2008). Effects of a worker participatory program for improving work environments on job stressors and mental health among workers: A controlled trial. *Journal of Occupational Health, 50,* 455–470. doi:10.1539/joh.L7166

Kotter, J. P. (1996). *Leading change.* Boston, MA: Harvard Business School Press.

Lam, S. S. K., & Schaubroeck, J. (2000). A field experiment testing frontline opinion leaders as change agents. *Journal of Applied Psychology, 85,* 987–995. doi:10.1037/0021-9010.85.6.987

Lamontagne, A. D., Keegel, T., Louie, A. M., Ostry, A., & Landsbergis, P. (2007). A systematic review of the job stress intervention evaluation literature, 1990–2005. *International Journal of Occupational and Environmental Health, 13,* 268–280.

Landsbergis, P. A., & Vivona-Vaughan, E. (1995). Evaluation of an occupational stress intervention in a public agency. *Journal of Organizational Behavior, 16,* 29–48. doi:10.1002/job.4030160106

Lawler, E. E. (1992). *The ultimate advantage: Creating the high-involvement organization.* San Francisco, CA: Jossey-Bass.

Lawler, E. E., Mohrman, S. A., & Ledford, G. E., Jr. (1995). *Creating high performance organizations.* San Francisco, CA: Jossey-Bass.

Lazarus, R., & Folkman, S. (1984). *Stress, appraisal, and coping.* New York, NY: Springer.

Leana, C., Locke, E. A., & Schweiger, D. M. (1990). Fact and fiction in analyzing research on participative decision making: A critique of Cotton, Volrath, Froggatt, Lengnick-Hall, and Jenkins. *Academy of Management Review, 15,* 137–146.

Levin, M. (2004). Organizing change processes: Cornerstones, methods, and strategies. In J. J. Boonstra (Ed.), *Dynamics of organizational change and learning* (pp. 71–84). Hoboken, NJ: Wiley. doi:10.1002/9780470753408.ch4

Lewin, K. (1951). Field theory and learning. In D. Cartwright (Ed.), *Field theory in social science: Select theoretical papers* (pp. 60–86). New York, NY: HarperCollins.

Linnan, L. A., Fava, J. L., Thompson, B., Emmons, K., Basen-Engquist, K., Probart, C., . . . Heimendinger, J. (1999). Measuring participatory strategies: Instrument development for worksite populations. *Health Education Research, 14,* 371–386. doi:10.1093/her/14.3.371

Mikkelsen, A., & Gundersen, M. (2003). The effect of a participatory organizational intervention on work environment, job stress, and subjective health complaints. *International Journal of Stress Management, 10,* 91–110. doi:10.1037/1072-5245.10.2.91

Molinsky, A. L. (1999). Sanding down the edges: Paradoxical impediments to organizational change. *Journal of Applied Behavioral Science, 35*(1), 8–24. doi:10.1177/0021886399351002

Murphy, L. R., & Sauter, S. (2004). Work organization interventions: State of knowledge and future directions. *Social and Preventive Medicine, 49,* 79–86.

National Institute for Occupational Safety and Health. (1996). *National Occupational Research Agenda.* (DHHS Publication No. 96-115). Washington, DC: Author.

National Institute for Occupational Safety and Health. (2002). *The changing organization of work and the safety and health of working people.* (DHHS Publication No. 2002-116). Washington, DC: Author.

National Institute for Occupational Safety and Health. (2006). *The team document: Ten years of leadership advancing the National Occupational Research Agenda.* (DHHS Publication No. 2006-121). Washington, DC: Author.

National Institute for Occupational Safety and Health. (2009). *NIOSH worklife initiative.* Retrieved from http://www.cdc.gov/niosh/worklife/

Nielsen, K., Randall, R., & Albertsen, K. (2007). Participants' appraisals of stress management interventions. *Journal of Organizational Behavior, 28,* 793–810. doi:10.1002/job.450

Parkes, K. R., & Sparkes, T. J. (1998). *Organizational interventions to reduce work stress: Are they effective? A review of the literature* (Contract Research Report No. 193/1998). Oxford, England: University of Oxford.

Parks, K. M., & Steelman, L. (2008). Organizational wellness programs: A meta-analysis. *Journal of Occupational Health Psychology, 13*(1), 58–68. doi:10.1037/1076-8998.13.1.58

Pfeffer, J. (1998). *The human equation: Building profits by putting people first.* Boston, MA: Harvard Business School Press.

Prochaska, J. O., Redding, C. A., & Evers, K. E. (2008). The transtheoretical model and stages of change. In K. Glanz, B. K. Rimer, & K. Viswanath (Eds.), *Health behavior and health education: Theory, research, and practice* (pp. 97–121). San Francisco, CA: Jossey-Bass.

Quick, J. C. (1997). Idiographic research in organizational behavior. In C. L. Cooper (Ed.), *Creating tomorrow's organizations: A handbook for future research in organizational behavior* (pp. 475–492). Chichester, England: Wiley.

Rasmussen, K., Glasscock, D. J., Hansen, O. N., Carstensen, O., Jepsen, J. F., & Nielsen, K. J. (2006). Worker participation in change processes in a Danish industrial setting. *American Journal of Industrial Medicine, 49,* 767–779. doi:10.1002/ajim.20350

Rivilis, I., Van Eerd, D., Cullen, K., Cole, D., Irvin, E., Tyson, J., & Mahood, Q. (2008). Effectiveness of participatory ergonomic interventions on health outcomes: A systematic review. *Applied Ergonomics, 39,* 342–358. doi:10.1016/j.apergo.2007.08.006

Robertson, A., & Minkler, M. (1994). New health promotion movement: A critical examination. *Health Education Quarterly, 21,* 295–312.

Ross, L., & Nisbett, R. (1991). *The person and the situation: Perspectives in social psychology.* New York, NY: McGraw-Hill.

Saksvik, P. O., Nytro, K., Dahl-Jorgensen, C., & Mikkelsen, A. (2002). A process evaluation of individual and organizational occupational stress and health interventions. *Work & Stress, 16,* 37–57. doi:10.1080/02678370110118744

Sallis, J. F., Owen, N., & Fisher, E. B. (2008). Ecological models of health behavior. In K. Glanz, B. K. Rimer, & K. Viswanath (Eds.), *Health behavior and health education: Theory, research, and practice* (pp. 465–485). San Francisco, CA: Jossey-Bass.

Schein, E. H. (1987). *Process consulting.* Reading, MA: Addison-Wesley.

Schult, T. M. K., McGovern, P. M., Dowd, B., & Pronk, N. (2006). The future of health promotion/disease prevention programs: The incentives and barriers faced by stakeholders.

Journal of Occupational and Environmental Medicine, 48, 541–548. doi:10.1097/01.jom.0000222565.68934.0b

Selye, H. (1993). History of the stress concept. In L. Goldberger & S. Breznitz (Eds.), *Handbook of stress: Theoretical and clinical aspects* (2nd ed., pp. 7–17). New York, NY: Free Press.

Semmer, N. K. (2006). Job stress interventions and the organization of work. *Scandinavian Journal of Work, Environment, & Health, 32,* 515–527.

Shinn, M., & Toohey, S. (2003). Community contexts of human welfare. *Annual Review of Psychology, 54,* 427–459. doi:10.1146/annurev.psych.54.101601.145052

Sinclair, R. C., Gershon, R. M., Murphy, L. R., & Goldenhar, L. M. (1996). Operationalizing theoretical constructs in bloodborne pathogens training curriculum. *Health Education Quarterly, 23,* 238–255.

Singer, J., Neale, M., & Schwartz, G. (1989). The nuts and bolts of assessing occupational stress: A collaborative effort with labor. In L. R. Murphy & T. F. Schoenborn (Eds.), *Stress management in work settings* (pp. 3–30). New York, NY: Praeger.

Sorensen, G., Quintiliani, L., Pereira, L., Yang, M., & Stoddard, A. (2009). Work experiences and tobacco use: Findings from the Gear Up for Health study. *Journal of Occupational and Environmental Medicine, 51*(1), 87–94. doi:10.1097/JOM.0b013e31818f69f8

Stokols, D. (1996). Translating social ecological theory into guidelines for community health promotion. *American Journal of Health Promotion, 10,* 282–298.

Tangirala, S., Green, S. G., & Ramanujam, R. (2007). In the shadow of the boss's boss: Effects of supervisors' upward exchange relationships on employees. *Journal of Applied Psychology, 92,* 309–320. doi:10.1037/0021-9010.92.2.309

Vink, P., Imada, A., & Zink, K. (2008). Defining stakeholder involvement in participatory design processes. *Applied Ergonomics, 39,* 519–526. doi:10.1016/j.apergo.2008.02.009

Wagner, J. A. (1994). Participation's effect on performance and satisfaction: A reconsideration of the research evidence. *Academy of Management Review, 19,* 312–330.

Weiner, B. J., Amick, H., & Lee, S. Y. (2008). Conceptualization and measurement of organizational readiness for change: A review of the literature in health services research and other fields. *Medical Care Research and Review, 65,* 379–436. doi:10.1177/1077558708317802

Wilson, J. R., & Haines, H. M. (1997). Participatory ergonomics. In G. Salvendy (Ed.), *Handbook of human factors and ergonomics* (2nd ed., pp. 490–513). New York, NY: Wiley.

Witte, K., Meyer, G., & Martell, D. P. (2001). *Effective health risk messages: A step-by-step guide.* Thousand Oaks, CA: Sage.

18

Employee Assistance Programs: Strengths, Challenges, and Future Roles

Cary L. Cooper, Philip J. Dewe, and Michael P. O'Driscoll

The Economist recently featured an article on the potential backlash in the United States against the impact of globalization in terms of a shift in employment practices. It argued that globalization is leading to higher mobility between employers, to more job insecurity, to a short-term contract culture of employment, and ultimately to substantial employee stress. From our perspective, the U.S. workplace has always had substantial elements of all of these characteristics, with the process of globalization only marginally moving it faster and further along the continuum toward a completely "contingent" workforce. The issue for the business community in the rest of the world is whether they should be travelling in this same direction. The developed world has moved toward the Americanization of work as more and more companies are outsourcing, delayering, and using terms such as *interim management* and the like, with many more employees, in effect, selling their services to organizations on a freelance or short-term basis.

This has led to what employers now refer to euphemistically as the *flexible workforce,* although in family-friendly terms it is anything but flexible. The psychological contract between employer and employee in terms of "reasonably permanent employment for work well done" is truly being undermined as more and more employees no longer regard their employment as secure and many more are engaged in short-term contract or part-time work. Indeed, in an International Survey Research survey of 400 companies in 17 countries employing over 8 million workers throughout Europe, the "employment security" of workers significantly declined between the mid to late 1980s and the late 1990s: in the United Kingdom from 70% to 48%, in Germany from 83% to 55%, in France from 64% to 50%, in the Netherlands from 73% to 61%, in Belgium from 60 to 54%, and in Italy from 62% to 57%. In addition, in the United Kingdom, for example, from the early 1980s to the end of the 1990s, the number of men working part-time doubled, with the number of people employed in firms of more than 500 employees having slumped to about a third of the employed population and nearly one in 10 workers being self-employed. The future of work seems to be in small- to medium-sized businesses or in self-employed portfolio careers or as outsourced workers in virtual organizations. Cooper and Jackson (1997) predicted the following:

> Most organizations will have only a small core of full-time permanent employees, working from a conventional office. They will buy most of the skills they need on a contract basis, either from individuals working at home and linked to the company by computers and modems, or by hiring people on short-term contracts to do specific jobs or carry out specific projects. In this way, companies will be able to maintain the flexibility they need to cope with a rapidly changing world. (p. 2)

These changes and those that are anticipated in the future are leading to increases in workplace stress (Cartwright & Cooper, 2009). The big picture issue is how stress at work can be effectively managed. There are several options to consider in looking at the management and prevention of stress, which can be termed as primary, secondary, and tertiary levels of intervention. In this chapter, we focus on the tertiary level of intervention, reflected in employee assistance programs (EAPs), which have become fairly widely adopted by many organizations (especially in Western countries) as a mechanism for attending to workplace stress and other performance-related problems. We begin with an overview of the different levels of intervention.

Levels of Intervention

Primary prevention is concerned with taking action to reduce or eliminate stressors (i.e., sources of stress) and to promote a supportive and healthy work environment. *Secondary prevention* is concerned with the prompt detection and management of mental concerns such as depression and anxiety by increasing individual and collective awareness of stress and improving stress-management skills. *Tertiary prevention* is concerned with the rehabilitation and recovery process of those individuals who have suffered, or are suffering from, mental or physical ill health as a result of stress (Cooper & Cartwright, 1994).

Primary Prevention

The most effective way of tackling stress is to eliminate it at its source. This may involve changes in personnel policies, such as improving communications systems, redesigning jobs, or allowing more decision making and autonomy at lower levels. Obviously, as the type of action required by an organization will vary according to the kinds of stressors operating, any intervention needs to be guided by a prior diagnosis or stress audit to identify what these stressors are and whom they are affecting.

Stress audits typically take the form of a self-report questionnaire administered to employees on an organization-wide, site, or departmental basis. A widely validated example of such a diagnostic instrument is A Shortened

Stress Evaluation Tool, known as ASSET, an organizational stress-screening tool (Faragher, Cooper, & Cartwright, 2004; Johnson & Cooper, 2003). In addition to identifying the sources of stress at work and those individuals who are most vulnerable to stress, the questionnaire will usually measure levels of employee job satisfaction and coping behavior, as well as physical and psychological health on a comparative basis with similar occupational groups and industries. Stress audits are an effective way of identifying problematic areas and directing organizational resources to areas where they are most needed. Audits also provide a means of regularly monitoring stress levels and employee health over time and provide a baseline whereby subsequent interventions can be evaluated.

Secondary Prevention

Initiatives that fall into this category generally focus on training and education and involve awareness-raising activities and skills training programs (Biron, Cooper, & Bond, 2009). Stress education and stress-management courses serve a useful function in helping individuals to recognize the symptoms of stress in themselves and others and to extend or develop their coping skills and stress resilience. The form and content of this kind of training can vary immensely but often include simple relaxation techniques, lifestyle advice and planning, and basic training in time management, assertiveness, and problem-solving skills. This aim of these programs is to help employees to review the psychological effects of stress and to develop a personal stress-control plan.

Tertiary Prevention

One of the main aspects of tertiary prevention that organizations can consider to assist in the recovery and rehabilitation of stressed employees is workplace counseling. In this approach, organizations provide access to confidential professional counseling services for employees who are experiencing problems in the workplace or personal setting. Such services are typically provided by outside agencies that operate entirely independently of the organization and to whom the employee is referred or is advised to consult. In some instances, such counseling can be provided in-house, financed by the employer, although the independence of such a service is hard to ensure. A relatively recent development of workplace-based professional counseling is the EAP, which can be in-house or (more usually) delivered through an expert external agency or contractor. Normally, it is fully funded by the employer as an employee benefit. As such, it is distinguished from other forms of workplace counseling and is relatively integrated into other organizational systems of human resources and line management. An EAP provides counseling, information, and/or referral to appropriate internal or external counseling treatment and support services for troubled employees. Workplace counseling and EAPs are the most common forms of stress management, because they can be introduced quickly and provide a resource for dealing immediately with employee distress.

Defining and Describing an Employee Assistance Program

Berridge, Cooper, and Highley (1997) defined an EAP as a systematic, organized, and ongoing provision of counseling, advice, and assistance, provided or funded by the employer, designed to help employees and (in most cases) their families with problems arising from work-related and external sources. The authors stated that there are many definitions of EAPs, reflecting the wide range of participants in such programs, the varying interest groups as providers or purchasers, and the differing views of professional commentators. The U.K. Employee Assistance Professionals Association (EAPA; 2009) defined an EAP as

> a worksite-based program designed to assist (1) work organizations in addressing productivity issues and (2) "employee clients" in identifying and resolving personal concerns including but not limited to, health, marital, family, financial, alcohol, drug, legal, emotional, or other personal issues that may affect job performance. (p. 6)

This definition highlights certain requisite characteristics of any EAP, that is, its clear extent of coverage of all or selected employees and their dependants, its systematic provision of counseling by right rather than by privilege or patronage, and its adherence to levels of service quality on an independent, verified basis. It also emphasizes the drive for professionalism, which is necessary to confer occupational status and social recognition of an expert personal service in a confidential and fiduciary relationship. The focus here is on the EAP's compatibility and integration with corporate goals and culture and with managerial practices in the motivation and development of staff members. The provider contractor accepts working within the framework of the organizations structures and processes while retaining professional standards of service. This definition tends to mirror American practice, which is succinctly described as "a programme that provides direct service to an organization's workers who are experiencing many different types of problems in their personal or work lives" (Cunningham, 1994, p. 5).

A comprehensive definition was developed by Berridge and Cooper (1993):

> A programmatic intervention associated with the work context, usually at the level of the individual employee, using behavioural science knowledge and methods for the control of certain work-related problems (notably alcoholism, drug abuse, and mental health) that adversely affect job performance, with the objective of enabling the individual to return to making her or his full job contribution and reattaining fully functioning in personal life. (p. 89)

This definition attempts to reconcile the two potentially conflicting foci of attention of an EAP: the client and the employing organization.

In Britain and Europe more widely, EAPs tend to have two primary objectives:

● to help the employees distracted by a range of personal concerns, including (but not limited to) emotional, stress, relationship, family,

alcohol, drug, financial, legal, and other problems to cope with such concerns and learn to themselves control the stresses produced; and
- to assist the organization in the identification and amelioration of productivity issues in employees whose job performance is adversely affected by such personal concerns (EAPA, 1994).

Therefore, the intended beneficiaries of the EAP are both the individual (the primary focus in European practice) and her or his employing organization (less directly in Europe but more emphasized in U.S. practice). At the personal level, the objective of employee counseling is not personal restructuring (i.e., psychotherapy) but the effect on individual coping and adjustment to work- and nonwork life can be considerable. An EAP can also generate benefits at the organizational level because "being more or less deeply embedded into the organizational processes of the firm, it becomes part of organizational discourse, it reflects and nourishes the organizational culture, and it becomes part of the organizational learning, problem-solving and adaptation mechanisms" (Berridge & Cooper, 1994, p. 5).

The variability of objectives for EAPs can result in many differing modes of program delivery. The modus operandi of external providers is often the main factor because standardization of the mode of delivery key to their provision of a high-quality service with economical use of internal production factors. The choice of provider may be central in determining whether the employer or organization adopts an EAP with a suitable delivery method. The main dimensions of delivery methods are shown in Table 18.1.

In the United States, in-house, on-site (i.e., cell 1 in Table 18.1) provision is still widely found, especially among large employers and in government service. In Britain and Europe, the later developments of EAPs in a different and more stringent economic climate have predisposed delivery methods to be by external providers who use a network of counselors (i.e., cell 4) to provide services for a variety of large and smaller employer clients.

The essential components of an EAP should reflect the provider's and the employer's preferred method of implementing an EAP, the resources available to the organization, the needs of its employees, as well as the size and the configuration of the organization (Davis & Gibson, 1994; Lee & Gray, 1994). Berridge et al. (1997) provided the following list that covers many of the essential elements that distinguish the EAP by its integrated approach and its systematic design, meshing with the administrative and social systems of the organization and its environment:

- a systematic survey of the organization to determine the nature, causes, and extent of problems perceived by individuals, also taking into account the viewpoints of all the stakeholders and functional specialists in the organization;
- a continuing commitment on the part of the employing organization at the top level to provide counseling, advisory, and assistance services to "troubled" employees on a no-blame and no-cost, totally confidential basis;
- an effective program of promotion and publicity of the EAP to all employees as potential clients, emphasizing in particular its confidentiality, access, and scope in issues covered;

Table 18.1 Delivery Methods for Employee Assistance Programs (EAPs) and Counseling Services

	In-house provision of EAP and counseling services	External contractor provision of EAP and counseling services
On-site EAP and counseling services	1. Often relatively direct control by occupational health or human resources management departments	2. Unusual, but may be found where many functions/services are subcontracted, or have been "floated off" from former in-house services
Externally located EAP and counseling services	3. Unusual but may occur for reasons of confidentiality, using an adjacent location, or as part of a "mixed model" provision, such as a partnership with a contractor	4. Customary delivery model in Britain, using provider company's offices, or affiliate counselors' consulting rooms or home premises

Note.   From *Employee Assistance Programmes and Workplace Counselling* (p. 18) by J. Berridge, C. Cooper, and C. Highley, 1997, Chichester, England: Wiley. Copyright 1997 by Wiley. Reprinted with permission.

- a linked program of education and training on the goals and methods of the EAP for all staff members in terms of the definition of troubled employees; the individual's responsibility for well-being; the roles of managers, supervisors, and shop stewards within the design and implementation of the EAP; and the duties and capabilities of counselors, including any limitations on their activities;
- a procedure for contact with the EAP and referral to counseling, details of procedures for self-referral, and (if appropriate) managerial referral;
- a definition of problem-assessment procedures, including diagnosis routes, confidentiality guarantees, timeliness, scope of counselors' training, as well as their accreditation, competencies, and organizational knowledge;
- a protocol outlining the extent of short-term counseling and longer-term treatment and assistance;
- a statement of the macro- and micro-linkages with other services in the community, or with specialist resources or support mechanisms;
- a procedure for the follow up and monitoring of employees subsequent to their use of the EAP service, with the necessary provisions for their appropriate use and deployment;
- an administrative channel for the feedback of aggregated statistics on the age and short- and longer-term outcomes of the EAP, provided by the contractor; and
- an evaluation procedure of individual and corporate benefits of the EAP on the most impartial basis that is practical (i.e., that draws on EAPA, 1994, 1997).

These are the key activities that make EAPs an entity distinct from other forms of workplace counseling services, whether internal or external. However, although desirable, these elements are not all found in most EAPs (Berridge et al., 1997).

Assessment of the Effectiveness of Employee Assistance Programs

Although EAPs have been in existence, in different forms, for about 40 years and have been implemented in a wide variety of organizations (Arthur, 2000; Highley & Cooper, 1994), often less attention has been given to evaluating their impact than to developing and conducting EAPs. Given the amount of time, energy, and funding invested in mounting and implementing EAPs, the relative inattention to assessing their effectiveness is somewhat surprising. Reasons for this state of affairs vary but include a lack of clearly defined success criteria (Arthur, 2000; Berridge & Cooper, 1994), resistance on the part of EAP providers toward having their efforts evaluated (Davis & Gibson, 1994), concerns over confidentiality of information on clients (Highley & Cooper, 1994), unavailability of information in a usable form for evaluation research (Davis & Gibson, 1994), and methodological difficulties associated with conducting valid assessments of EAP effectiveness (Arthur, 2000).

Highley and Cooper (1994) elaborated on some of the more critical issues in EAP evaluations. One problem that confronts research in this area, as well as in assessments of all organizational interventions, is the definition of what the program is intended to achieve. As noted earlier in this chapter, EAPs frequently have multiple goals, including enhancing employee morale and motivation, promoting an image of the organization as caring for the welfare of its employees, improving productivity (e.g., by reducing absenteeism and tardiness, as well as through more direct effects on job performance), and reducing disciplinary problems. In addition, EAPs may be adopted by an organization to reduce the financial costs of medical and disability claims (Every & Leong, 1995). Given the range of intended benefits and that achieving significant improvements in all of these areas is unlikely, the assessment of whether a particular intervention has been effective poses considerable challenges for the evaluator (Noblet & Lamontagne, 2009).

Several different assessment criteria have been applied in evaluations of EAP effectiveness. French, Zarkin, and Bray (1995) summarized four major components that should be incorporated into research on EAPs:

- Process evaluation, which documents the nature of the EAP, the manner in which it is delivered, and the intensity of service delivery. Such evaluation assesses whether implementation of the EAP has been optimal, hence maximizing the likelihood of positive benefits.
- Cost analysis, which focuses on collecting data concerning the financial and perhaps other (e.g. time, human resources) costs associated with the intervention.
- Outcome analysis, which examines the consequences of the EAP intervention, such as those itemized previously.

- Cost-effectiveness, which is predominantly an assessment of the outcomes of the program in relation to the financial costs of implementing it.

Although French and his colleagues concentrated primarily on the financial aspects of EAPs, other commentators have reviewed different evaluation criteria. For instance, Becker, Hall, Fisher, and Miller (2000) noted that it is important to assess both quantitative (e.g., financial) and qualitative effectiveness criteria. The latter include possible improvements in employees' work-related motivation, better management-employee relations, enhanced organizational climate, and reduced psychological strain among employees. These criteria are as important as the more strictly quantitative benefits that organizations hope to achieve by adopting EAPs.

It is also important to consider the criteria required for evaluation research to generate valid conclusions about the relative benefits of an EAP. Arthur (2000) noted the following about evaluation research:

> [It] should include the collection of uniform and standardised data that would allow comparison with other studies, a true experimental research design, the inclusion of employees who use other kinds of mental health services, linking the mental health status of individuals with their counseling utilisation rates, the use of adequate control groups, collection of data at least 3 years prior to and 3 years following the EAP intervention, random assignment of employees to different treatment and non-treatment conditions, the employment of work-performance indicators, and a cost-benefit or economic analysis. (p. 553)

Few if any EAP effectiveness studies incorporate all of these criteria, and Arthur (2000) commented that more has been written about how to do such research than actual reports of EAP evaluations. In addition, because of several factors, which we outline later, evidence for the effectiveness of EAPs is inconsistent at best.

Despite the difficulties of conducting evaluation research in this field, recent investigations have demonstrated both the benefits and the limitations of EAPs. A full review of this literature is not intended here; rather, we summarize findings from a sample of studies that illustrate some general themes emerging from this line of research. For example, Westhuis, Hayashi, Hart, Cousert, and Spinks (1998) evaluated a drug and alcohol treatment program among over 12,000 military personnel in the United States. Their research incorporated several of the features outlined by Arthur (2000) as necessary for a valid evaluation of effectiveness, including a quasi-experimental design that collected measures pre- and postintervention and two data sources (i.e., the participants' commanding officer and the drug and alcohol counselor responsible for the EAP intervention). Comparison of treatment combinations suggested that a combined treatment approach, which entailed individual counseling and group therapy along with increasing educational awareness led to the most successful rehabilitation outcomes. Success in this context was defined broadly in terms of return to service.

In their assessment of EAP effectiveness relating to substance abuse and work performance problems, Hiatt, Hargrave, and Palmertree (1999) also collected data from employees' supervisors and EAP counselors. This research was conducted on what the authors referred to as a "broad brush" EAP, but they did not provide a detailed explanation of the specific elements of the intervention. Nevertheless, improvements in performance-related criteria were observed, especially in job attendance.

Effectiveness studies frequently include satisfaction as a criterion variable (Arthur, 2000). Typically, employee satisfaction with EAP interventions has been found to be quite high, and counselor satisfaction is (perhaps not surprisingly) also high (Harlow, 1998). For example, Macdonald and his colleagues reported that over 90% of employees in a Canadian transportation company indicated high levels of satisfaction with the EAP services provided, and 69% said that these services had a positive effect on their overall quality of life. With respect to job performance, 46% of employees reported some or great improvement in their own job performance. Reports from counselors in the program also suggested a favorable reaction to the outcomes of the program (Macdonald, Lothian, & Wells, 1997; Macdonald, Wells, Lothian, & Shain, 2000).

Winwood and Beer (2008) also outlined what makes a good EAP. Identifying what they believe to be the "core technology" of EAPs, Winwood and Beer described the critical features as including collaboration on the training and development of those managing troubled employees, timely and confidential provision of problem identification and assessment opportunities, the use of constructive techniques that address in the immediate short term job performance problems, the referral of employees for treatment and assistance, the establishment and maintenance of service provision and consultation in relation to other services that may be required, and program evaluation at both the organizational and individual level and in terms of identifiable performance outcome measures (2008). In the view of these authors, if consistency of service is going to be maintained, EAPs need to be protocol-focused, agreed on, easily accessible, and with clear accountabilities that are capable of being audited.

In contrast to these positive evaluations of EAPs, some studies have reported little or no systematic advantages over other forms of treatment or counseling. For instance, in a well-controlled investigation of the effects of an EAP on Australian government employees, Blaze-Temple and Howat (1997) found that, although EAP counseling was effective, there was no substantial advantage in terms of cost-effectiveness of EAP-based counseling over self-arranged counseling. Similarly, in a comprehensive study of the effects of various stress management training interventions on both employee mental health and organizational variables (e.g., absenteeism), Whatmore, Cartwright, and Cooper (1999) found that most of the gains that had been observed at 3 months postintervention had virtually dissipated by 6 months following completion of the intervention, suggesting that positive benefits may not be sustained, particularly if there is no systematic follow-up.

Kirk and Brown (2003) noted that the organizational rationale for using EAPs is a belief that managing workplace stress (and related issues) will lead to improvements in productivity and therefore profitability via reduced absenteeism and turnover and improved job satisfaction or morale. They suggested that the widespread growth of EAPs globally might be attributed (at least partially) to the recognition of workplace stress as a significant and important problem that organizations need to deal with along with increases in litigation over stress-related problems (Highley & Cooper, 1996). Unfortunately, however, there has not been a corresponding level of interest in evaluating the effectiveness of EAPs as a tool for managing stress. Kirk and Brown provided an overview of the history of EAP usage in Australia and its role in the management of stress and well-being.

One problem identified by Kirk and Brown (2003), which also has been reflected by other reviewers of EAPs, is that a clear and agreed-on definition of EAPs is nonexistent; rather, a plethora of intervention types has been subsumed under this label. This makes it extremely difficult, if not impossible, to rigorously evaluate the effectiveness of EAPs because the form and content of interventions can vary dramatically. Kirk and Brown observed that it is common for evaluations to report high levels of employee satisfaction with EAP services. Although this is important information, it is of limited value in terms of any objective assessment of their value. Overall, it would appear (from the limited evidence available) that EAPs can and often do yield positive benefits for individual employees (e.g., in terms of stress reduction), but their impact on productivity and other organizationally relevant outcomes is far from clear. Along with other commentators, Kirk and Brown made a plea for more methodologically sound approaches to the systematic evaluation of EAP effectiveness.

In summary, this brief overview of EAP evaluations illustrates that findings on the outcomes of EAPs are mixed (see Arthur, 2000) and that it is simply not possible to draw general conclusions about the effectiveness of these interventions. As noted earlier, one reason for this lack of conclusiveness lies in the design of EAP evaluations, which are often suboptimal and do not include longitudinal pre- and postintervention assessments, data comparative with other forms of intervention, multiple sources of information (e.g., managers and organizational clients, as well as counselors and employees), and the variety of types of information needed to ensure that benefits are not limited to self-reports of satisfaction levels or financial outcomes.

There is no doubt that program evaluations in the field of EAPs, as in other areas of evaluation, are challenging and fraught with potential pitfalls. Some of these were noted earlier. An additional problem is that the term *EAP* encompasses a wide range of different types and foci of intervention, ranging from substance abuse programs through to stress-management training and even more global wellness programs. The multidimensionality of EAPs means that it may not be possible to derive general conclusions that reflect all intervention types and formats. Rather, it may be more appropriate to examine the specific goals of a particular program and the extent to which those goals have been achieved. Nevertheless, it is evident that evaluations of EAPs need to be more systematic and rigorous than has often been the case until now, and they must examine a range of outcomes that demonstrate benefits to a variety of stakeholders.

Employee Assistance Programs and Coping With Stress

It is clear from the earlier sections of this chapter that there is a "considerable amount of activity" (Kompier & Cooper, 1999, p. 1) in the field of stress management through the use of EAPs, although this activity may be confined to large organizations (Whatmore et al., 1999). There is, however, a belief that organizations may not benefit from the marketing claims made about EAPs in terms of improved productivity, morale, and performance (Arthur, 2000). Evidence that the effectiveness of such programs is mixed can be partly explained in terms of the difficulties associated with evaluation, the fact that symptom relief is at times separated out from performance measures, because little work has been carried out on the long-term effects of such programs, and because the primary responsibility for stress management is more often than not left to the individual (see Arthur, 2000; Cooper & Cartwright, 1994; Reynolds & Briner, 1994). Even so, those making use of EAPs generally appear satisfied with the interventions they receive (Arthur, 2000; Kirk & Brown, 2003) and difficulties associated with gauging EAP effectiveness may be more the result of the ad hoc way in which they are implemented (Bull, 1997) and the fact that their purpose and objectives are not always clearly expressed (Health and Safety Commission, 1999).

Although there is no standardized model of EAP practice (Arthur, 2000), this in itself cannot be responsible for the debate surrounding the use and effectiveness of EAPs. When considering the application of such programs, it may first be necessary to take a step back and reflect on the importance of theory, the issue of ethics, the question of organizational context, and the concerns of managers. Several authors (e.g., Arthur, 2000; Briner & Reynolds, 1999; Dewe, 1994; Murphy, 1995) have pointed to the need to make more explicit use of theory when considering the relevance and utility of EAPs and the issues they are expected to resolve. The view expressed is that traditional cause and effect assertions linking stress to performance are "no longer good enough" (Briner & Reynolds 1999, p. 658) and that such approaches may no longer be "serviceable" (Lazarus, 1991, p. 1) or even be able to support a workable theory when dealing with those suffering from stress at work. This is not to challenge the historical importance of interactional (i.e., cause and effect) models of stress nor the information they have provided. It is simply to draw attention to the fact that "treating everyone as though they were alike, and work environments as though they have common effects on everyone" (Lazarus 1991, p. 10) may now be too superficial an approach to EAP intervention (Arthur, 2000).

Moving forward requires that stress be thought of in transactional terms (Lazarus, 1999). That is, stress does not reside solely in the individual or solely in the environment but in the transaction between the two. Even more important is that thinking of stress in transactional terms points to the processes of appraisal as the link between the individual and the environment. This shifts attention to the process of stress and away from seeing individuals and environments as "separate causal antecedents of stress" (Lazarus, 1991, p. 11). This transactional view offers a different perspective on work stress and therefore a more cognitive-individual-process oriented approach to stress management and EAPs. In summary, the emphasis from a transactional perspective when considering stress interventions is on recognizing the individual and the environment as a "single analytic unit, rather than as separate sets of variables to be manipulated independently" (Lazarus, 1991, p. 10).

There is considerable debate about the application of the transactional model to a work setting (Brief & George, 1991; Dewe, 1991, 1992; Frese & Zapf, 1999; Harris, 1991; Perrewé & Zellars, 1999; Schaubroeck, 1999). The issue that is relevant here concerns its individual-level focus. Although there is agreement that stress is essentially an individual-level phenomenon, the significance of work in people's lives leads some to suggest that it is more important to identify those work conditions that "adversely affect most worker exposed to them" (Brief & George, 1991, p. 16) rather than to focus on interindividual processes. The argument that the transactional model's interindividual level of analysis limits the directions that can be given to those involved in stress management and "does not necessarily provide . . . insight into ways of correcting the stressful circumstances" (Harris, 1991, p. 27) still needs to be tested empirically, because whether it is possible to produce favorable environmental changes for all is in itself a moot point (Briner & Reynolds, 1999; Lazarus, 1991).

Other issues are also debated when the transactional approach to stress is the focus of attention. These include, for example, whether objective rather than subjective measurement of stress holds more promise for stress intervention strategies (Frese & Zapf, 1999), the utility of problem-focused versus emotion-focused coping (Cooper, Dewe, & O'Driscoll, 2001) in managing stressful encounters, and the importance of *primary appraisal*—that is, the meanings individuals give to events—and how such meanings should be treated when considering different stress interventions. Accepting that it is the transactional encounter itself that should now become the unit of analysis (Lazarus, 1991) offers those responsible for EAPs a theoretical framework and a set of conceptual pathways that emphasize that such interventions "must be part of holistic strategies" (Arthur, 2000, p. 557) and reinforces that programs targeting only one level of intervention are not as successful as those that combine multiple levels of intervention (Cooper & Sadri, 1991). Even more important is that unless EAPs, and for that matter other stress management programs, are set within some theoretical framework, then attempts to help those whose working lives we study may "be simple and clear—but also hopelessly wrong" (Briner & Reynolds, 1999, p. 661).

The transactional approach to stress also draws attention to issues of power and control. From this perspective the issue becomes one of the resources available to individuals to cope with the demands of work. It draws attention to the influence that organizational structures and culture can have in constraining and directing individuals to think and act in particular ways (Dewe, 1994; Handy, 1988), raising questions about how far individuals can actually act on their own behalf (Thoits, 1995). The transactional approach offers as a framework a more "sophisticated matching of the person and the environment" (Lazarus, 1991, p. 10). Each is bound to the other through the adaptational encounter and "forces a more comprehensive strategy to evolve" (Dewe 1994, p. 30) when considering the role of EAPs.

Three other issues are important when considering the use of EAPs or any stress-management program. The first draws attention to the fact that although many organizations are concerned enough about the demands of work to put in place EAPs, little attempt has been made to find out what managers understand by stress—their implicit theory of stress (Westman & Eden, 1991), the extent to which they think their organization has a responsibility to address such problems, what motives lie behind the introduction of such programs (Reynolds & Briner, 1994), and whether they actually regard stress as a problem and how they perceive the risk (Daniels, 1996).

The second issue concerns the ethical considerations surrounding the use of EAPs. At the heart of the matter is the concept of informed consent. A number of issues must be confronted, including information on what the program involves and its duration; the nature of individuals' involvement; why they are being asked to participate and on what basis they are being invited; a clear description of potential risks and/or benefits to individuals; how issues such as privacy, confidentiality, and anonymity are to be respected; how the information gathered is going to be used; who has access to that information and how it is to be stored; and the rights of participants to decline to take part, to withdraw from the program, to refuse to answer any particular question, and to continue to ask questions so that informed consent is maintained. When considered in these terms, the manager's right to manage may need to be reviewed in light of the individual's right to make an informed judgment.

A third important issue concerns cultural factors relevant to EAP use and effectiveness. As we noted earlier, EAPs are becoming a global phenomenon and are being used in various countries as a method for reducing stress and enhancing employee well-being. However, there is no doubt that they are more prevalent in Western countries (e.g., the United States, United Kingdom, Europe) and less common in other parts of the world. Bhagat, Steverson, and Segovis (2007) provided a valuable review of the cross-national use of EAPs and some of the key issues surrounding their implementation. In particular, they discussed the need to redesign EAPs to meet the cultural needs and expectations inherent in different countries. A program or service developed and found to be relatively effective in one country will not necessarily exhibit the same benefits when implemented in a culturally and economically different context.

Bhagat and his colleagues (2007) commented that there are several reasons for this differential uptake of EAPs. For example, different rates of unemployment across countries may influence the perceived necessity to manage stress-related issues. Where unemployment is low, and hence workers can be replaced with relative ease, employers may not see the value of expending time, energy, and money on dealing with employee stress. Second, cultures that are more individualistic in orientation may place more emphasis on the psychological health and well-being of individual workers, whereas collectivistic societies give more consideration to the group or collective; therefore, it is likely that EAPs will be more prevalent in individualistic than in collectivistic cultures. Finally, in some countries there may be a greater social stigma associated with seeking help for personal problems from a professional counselor or psychologist. Bhagat et al. observed that "some societies emphasize the belief that problems that adversely affect a person's psychological well-being should only be shared with members of the immediate family, close friends, or the in-group" (p. 225). Under these circumstances, it is less likely that individuals would avail themselves of help from an unknown professional.

Of particular interest in Bhagat et al.'s (2007) article is their discussion of the dimensions of individualism/collectivism (I/C) that may be pertinent to the use and effectiveness of EAPs. Following the work of Triandis (1998), Bhagat et al. discussed how different patterns of I/C may influence whether EAPs are viewed as an acceptable and desirable mechanism for addressing stress and other performance-related problems. As noted earlier, generally collectivistic cultures do not engage with EAPs to the same level as individualistic cultures, and there are also marked differences in the forms of EAP provision within those culture types. Bhagat et al. developed a "cultural matrix" of coping with stress and how this might relate to the use of EAPs as an avenue for stress-reduction. From this matrix they derived four propositions concerning the prevalence of EAPs in different cultural contexts. In brief, they argued that EAPs are more likely to be used in cultures that are individualistic, rational, and rule-based; in contrast, cultures that are collectivistic, affective, and relationship-based are likely to emphasize support from social groups rather than institutionalized systems such as EAPs.

We believe that the matrix constructed by Bhagat and his colleagues (2007) offers a valuable framework for examining international patterns of EAP use, as well as some important suggestions on the relative effectiveness of EAP systems in different cultural contexts. Exploration of cultural factors would be a major step toward increasing understanding of relevant psychosocial contributors to EAP use and effectiveness.

Future Role of Employee Assistance Plans

Three areas appear to be consistently referred to when considering the future development of EAPs: (a) agreeing on a clear understanding of the role of EAPs and whether contemporary theory supports them in such a role, (b) establishing methods for evaluating their role, and (c) considering the nature of the problems EAPs will be required to address in the future. In most reviews of EAPs, as for stress management generally (Geurts & Grundemann, 1999), there is agreement that one of the challenges facing organizations is to increase awareness of work stress generally and stress prevention in particular. But this challenge is not simply to get people to agree that stress prevention (or in this case EAPs) is mutually beneficial but to seriously consider questions such as "Why do organizations introduce stress management intervention?" (Briner, 1997, p. 65) and "For whom and to what ends?" (Reynolds & Briner, 1994, p. 73), and what role in this process of increasing awareness and establishing programs is played by management (Daniels, 1996), primary care groups (Arthur, 2000), outside experts, and employees (Murphy, 1993).

The other theme allied to this issue of awareness is that of theory-based program development. It is clear from this chapter that theory has been noticeably absent in the rush to establish stress management interventions. This has led to definitional and conceptual confusion and "too many baseless assumptions" (Briner, 2000, p. 6) about the relationship between work and stress and therefore the extent to which, based on such assumptions, stress interventions can reasonably be expected to be successful (Briner & Reynolds, 1999). It is now time to redirect attention toward "the goal of answering some basic theoretical and empirical questions concerning organizational stress" (Briner & Reynolds,

1999, p. 661) that take us way from separating out the work environment and individual to applying the principles of transaction, "requiring a very different perspective on work stress" (Lazarus, 1991, p. 6).

The significance of the transactional process for EAPs lies in the fact that it forces a more comprehensive strategy to evolve (Dewe, 1994), one that recognizes that EAPs in themselves are not sufficient to counteract the effects of stress (Arthur, 2000). It is more closely related to the way in which individuals see their job and requires as much attention to be given to process as has been given to structure (Lazarus, 1999), and it establishes a link between theory and practice, emphasizing as a result a subject-centered or collaborative approach rather than an expert-centered approach that "remains at some distance from the problems and individuals" (Shipley & Orlans, 1988, p. 111).

A second challenge facing the development of EAPs is their evaluation. Evaluation is of course inextricably linked with theory. If little attention is paid to the nature of stress then "at best measurement of effectiveness is partial" (Liukkonen, Cartwright, & Cooper, 1999, p. 49). Although it may be possible, by analyzing examples of best practice, to establish those factors that may contribute to a successful approach (Geurts & Grundemann, 1999), the "success of stress prevention depends on a subtle combination of two approaches, that is, 'bottom-up' (participation) and 'top-down' (top management support)" (Kompier & Cooper, 1999, p. 335). More attention must now be given to evidence-based approaches (Briner, 2000). The difficulties of establishing a link between outcomes and intervention need more focused attention (Kompler & Cooper, 1999), accepting that the identification of costs and benefits associated with programs such as EAPs may only be achieved by adopting "a wider and more holistic approach" (Liukkonen et al., 1999, p. 49), requiring both quantitative and qualitative measurement and a more systematic approach to EAP design and implementation.

Before turning to the role of EAPs in the future it is important to provide a context for considering the future direction of EAPs as an intervention. It is clear that the costs of work stress, particularly in terms of health absence, turnover, and presenteeism run into billions for organizations, economies, and individuals (Cooper & Dewe, 2008). It is also clear that government departments and agencies are being charged with improving the quality of the work experience. The recent U.K. report (Black, 2008) on "Working for a Healthier Tomorrow" pointed out that "health and well-being extend far beyond avoiding or reducing the costs of absence or poor performance; [it] requires a changed perception of health and well-being and a willingness from both employers and employees to invest resources and change behaviours" (p. 51).

Evidence-based reviews support the belief that there is "a clear business case" (Rolfe, Foreman, & Tylee, 2006, p. 49) that comprehensive intervention practices work and that good health is good work (Waddell & Burton, 2006). Most interventions are, of course, aimed at supporting those where work stress is identified as the problem. However, focusing solely on stress at work may overshadow the broader issue of overall mental health and well-being, which encompasses but is not constrained to work stress.

Although progress is being made, particularly in terms of work stress, and although some managers feel comfortable in dealing with issues of stress and well-being, that feeling does not extend to mental health disorders, even though mental health problems "are almost as common in the workplace as they are anywhere else" (Sainsbury Centre for Mental Health, 2007, p. 6). The level of mental health disorders at work is greater than generally acknowledged, cannot be understood by focusing solely on work-related causes, and is not receiving the attention it should. Working from official data sources, the Sainsbury Centre for Mental Health (2007) report on mental health at work stated that in the United Kingdom, employers can expect to find that around "1 in 6 of their workforce is affected by depression, anxiety, or other mental health conditions" (p. 6). Work by the Shaw Trust and Future Foundation (2006) suggests that employers significantly underestimate the extent to which employees "are experiencing, stress, anxiety, depression, and other forms of mental ill-health" (p. 10).

It is clear that employers need support to deal with mental health problems in the workplace. This support, suggested the Shaw Trust and Future Foundation (2006), should aim to raise awareness of such problems, initiate programs that help to educate managers and employees about mental health issues at work, and help governments and organizations to work together to put policies and processes in place that help to support current practices and develop new ones. In initiating such support, the training of line managers becomes crucial, but this should be done in a way that reflects more of a partnership approach with organizations looking both inside and outside when developing best practices and building expertise to help manage mental health problems. Outside expertise and the notion of partnership not only includes engaging with mental health professionals who can advise and provide services but also extending this expertise to include working with medical practitioners and other occupational health specialists to provide supportive rehabilitation and inventive programs to help manage workplace mental health problems.

Two other issues are important when thinking about EAPs. The first is the impact of the positive psychology movement, with its emphasis on positive organization behaviors (Roberts, 2006), and the second concerns the importance of identifying those factors that facilitate or inhibit rehabilitation and return to work (Thomson & Rick, 2008). The first issue has at its center the development of positive workplaces where employees can maximize their potential, develop their abilities, and flourish. Employers are encouraged to recognize the powerful impact of positive emotions harnessed through the recognition of good performance, the provision of resources that harness motivated performance, the fact that good health is good business, and that well-being builds on being valued, feeling in control, competent, and contributing in a meaningful way (Nelson, Little, & Frazier, 2008). The second issue is one that resonates with all those interested in well-being: early and supportive rehabilitation. As Thomson and Rick (2008) pointed out, rehabilitation requires written policies appropriately managed and practiced that include, for example, the development of a rehabilitation plan with clear milestones and targets for a full return to work, opportunities for agreed therapeutic interventions, flexible return to work options, and workplace evaluations and adjustments that empower employees.

What is the role of EAPs in the future? If, for example, legislation and litigation begin to establish a picture of what the courts think the organization's responsibility for the general health and well-being of their employees should be, will this change the role of how EAPs are used from reactive to proactive procedures? Will they be required to adopt some sort of audit function? Will EAPs have to juggle, for example, the need to comply with health and safety legislation on the one hand, with individual rights as to privacy, confidentiality, informed consent on the other, not to mention human resources issues such as selection, assessment, promotion, and training and employment issues such as employment agreements and grievances and issues of equity, fairness, and trust in terms of the psychological contract? This will require an even greater emphasis on evaluation: evaluative techniques, processes, and procedures including an audit trail of what a systematic intervention strategy involves including specific audit points and reporting requirements.

Will EAPs in the future also be responsible or required to deal with issues of work–life balance and the conflicts that may emerge from negative home–work interactions? Will EAPs become part of a wider social responsibility of organizations that involves issues of family-friendly policies, issues of diversity including gender, ethnicity, ageism, and discrimination? Will such programs also be part of a move toward human resource accounting where organizations attempt to report on their investment in people and the value they place on a healthy workforce? Finally, the changes mentioned at the beginning of this chapter, coupled with the demands on organizations to meet social and legislative goals, also require those who study work stress to become far more rigorous in the way EAPs are researched and evaluated so that we can contribute meaningfully to those whose working lives we study.

References

Arthur, A. R. (2000). Employee assistance programmes: The emperor's new clothes of stress management? *British Journal of Guidance & Counselling, 28,* 549–559. doi:10.1080/03069880020004749

Becker, L. R., Hall, M., Fisher, D., & Miller, T. (2000). Methods for evaluating a mature substance abuse prevention/early intervention program. *The Journal of Behavioral Health Services & Research, 27,* 166–177. doi:10.1007/BF02287311

Berridge, J., & Cooper, C. L. (1993). Stress and coping in U.S. organizations: The role of the employee assistance programme. *Work & Stress, 7,* 89–102.

Berridge, J., & Cooper, C. L. (1994). The employee assistance programme: Its role in organizational coping and excellence. *Personnel Review, 23,* 4–20. doi:10.1108/00483489410072190

Berridge, J., Cooper, C., & Highley, C. (1997). *Employee assistance programmes and workplace counselling.* Chichester, England: Wiley.

Bhagat, R. S., Steverson, P. K., & Segovis, J. C. (2007). International and cultural variations in Employee Assistance Programmes: Implications for managerial health and effectiveness. *Journal of Management Studies, 44,* 222–242. doi:10.1111/j.1467-6486.2007.00686.x

Biron, C., Cooper, C. L, & Bond, F. (2009). Mediators and moderators of organizational stress interventions to prevent occupational stress. In S. Cartwright & C. L. Cooper (Eds.), *The Oxford handbook of organizational well-being* (pp. 441–465). Oxford, England: Oxford University Press.

Black, C. (2008, March 17). *Working for a healthier tomorrow: Review of the health of Britain's working age population.* Presentation to the Secretary of State for Health and the Secretary of State for Works and Pensions. London, England: The Stationery Office.

Blaze-Temple, D., & Howat, P. (1997). Cost benefit of an Australian EAP. *Employee Assistance Quarterly, 12,* 1–24. doi:10.1300/J022v12n03_01

Brief, A. P., & George, J. M. (1991). Psychological stress and the workplace: A brief comment on Lazarus's outlook. *Journal of Social Behavior and Personality, 6,* 15–20.

Briner, R. B. (1997). Improving stress assessment: Toward an evidence-based approach to organizational stress interventions. *Journal of Psychosomatic Research, 43,* 61–71. doi:10.1016/S0022-3999(97)00010-X

Briner, R. B. (2000). Stress management 2: Effectiveness of interventions. *Employee Health Bulletin, 18,* 2–7.

Briner, R. B., & Reynolds, S. (1999). The costs and limitations of organizational level stress interventions. *Journal of Organizational Behavior, 20,* 647–664. doi:10.1002/(SICI)1099-1379(199909)20:5<647::AID-JOB919>3.0.CO;2-1

Bull, A. (1997). Organizational stress: Sources and responses. In C. Feltham (Ed.), *The gains of listening: Perspectives on counselling at work* (pp. 28–46). Buckingham, England: Open University Press.

Cartwright, S., & Cooper, C. L. (2009). *The Oxford handbook of organizational well-being.* Oxford, England: Oxford University Press.

Cooper, C. L., & Cartwright, S. (1994). Healthy mind; healthy organization–A proactive approach to occupational stress. *Human Relations, 47,* 455–471. doi:10.1177/001872679404700405

Cooper, C., & Dewe, P. (2008). Well-being—absenteeism, presenteeism, costs, and challenges. *Occupational Medicine, 58,* 522–524. doi:10.1093/occmed/kqn124

Cooper, C. L., Dewe, P. J., & O'Driscoll, M. P. (2001). *Organizational stress: A review and critique of theory, research, and applications.* London, England: Sage.

Cooper, C. L., & Jackson, S. E. (1997). *Creating tomorrow's organizations: A handbook for future research in organizational behaviour.* Chichester, England: Wiley.

Cooper, C. L., & Sadri, G. (1991). The impact of stress counselling at work. *Journal of Social Behavior and Personality, 6,* 411–424.

Cunningham, G. (1994). *Effective employee assistance programs: A guide for EAP counsellors.* London, England: NFER-Nelson.

Daniels, K. (1996). Why aren't managers concerned about occupational stress? *Work & Stress, 10,* 352–366. doi:10.1080/02678379608256813

Davis, A., & Gibson, L. (1994). Designing employee welfare provisions. *Personnel Review, 23,* 33–45. doi:10.1108/00483489410072208

Dewe, P. J. (1991). Primary appraisal, secondary appraisal, and coping: Their role in stressful work encounters. *Journal of Occupational Psychology, 64,* 331–351.

Dewe, P. J. (1992). Applying the concept of appraisal to work stressors: Some exploratory analysis. *Human Relations, 45,* 143–164. doi:10.1177/001872679204500203

Dewe, P. J. (1994). EAPs and stress management: From theory to practice to comprehensiveness. *Personnel Review, 23,* 21–32. doi:10.1108/00483489410072217

Employee Assistance Professionals Association. (2009). *Standards of practice and professional guidelines for employee assistance programs.* London, England: Author.

Employee Assistance Professionals Association. (1997). *U.K. EAPA guidelines for the audit and evaluation of workplace counselling programmes.* London, England: Author.

Every, D., & Leong, D. (1995). Exploring EAP cost-effectiveness: Profile of a nuclear power plant internal EAP. *Employee Assistance Quarterly, 10,* 1–12. doi:10.1300/J022v10n01_01

Faragher, E. B., Cooper, C. L., & Cartwright, S. (2004). A Shortened Stress Evaluation Tool (ASSET). *Stress & Health, 20,* 189–201. doi:10.1002/smi.1010

French, M., Zarkin, G., & Bray, J. (1995). A methodology for evaluating the costs and benefits of employee assistance programs. *Journal of Drug Issues, 25,* 451–470.

Frese, M., & Zapf, D. (1999). On the importance of the objective environment in stress and attribution theory. Counterpoint to Perrewe and Zellars. *Journal of Organizational Behavior, 20,* 761–765. doi:10.1002/(SICI)1099-1379(199909)20:5<761::AID-JOB951>3.0.CO;2-Y

Geurts, S., & Grundemann, R. (1999). Workplace stress and stress prevention in Europe. In M. Kompier & C. Cooper (Eds.), *Preventing stress, improving productivity: European case studies in the workplace* (pp. 9–32). London, England: Routledge.

Handy, J. A. (1988). Theoretical and methodological problems within occupational stress and burnout research. *Human Relations, 41,* 351–369. doi:10.1177/001872678804100501

Harlow, K. (1998). Employee attitudes toward an internal employee assistance program. *Journal of Employment Counseling, 35,* 141–150.

Harris, J. R. (1991). The utility of the transactional approach for occupational stress research. *Journal of Social Behavior and Personality, 6,* 21–29.

Health and Safety Commission. (1999). *Managing stress at work: A discussion document.* London, England: Health and Safety Executive.

Hiatt, D., Hargrave, G., & Palmertree, M. (1999). Effectiveness of job performance referrals. *Employee Assistance Quarterly, 14,* 33–43. doi:10.1300/J022v14n04_03

Highley, J., & Cooper, C. L. (1994). Evaluating EAPs. *Personnel Review, 23,* 46–59. doi:10.1108/00483489410072226

Johnson, S., & Cooper, C. L. (2003). The construct validity of the ASSET stress measure. *Stress & Health, 19,* 181–185. doi:10.1002/smi.971

Kirk, A. K., & Brown, D. F. (2003). Employee assistance programs: A review of the management of stress and well-being through workplace counselling and consulting. *Australian Psychologist, 38,* 138–143. doi:10.1080/00050060310001707137

Kompier, M., & Cooper, C. L. (1999). Improving work, health, and productivity through stress prevention. In M. Kompier & C. Cooper (Eds.), *Preventing stress, improving productivity: European case studies in the workplace* (pp. 1–8). London, England: Routledge.

Lazarus, R. S. (1991). Psychological stress in the workplace. *Journal of Social Behavior and Personality, 6,* 1–13.

Lazarus, R. S. (1999). *Stress and emotion: A new synthesis.* London, England: Free Association Books.

Lee, C., & Gray, J. A. (1994). The role of employee assistance programmes. In C. L. Cooper & S. Williams (Eds.), *Creating healthy work organizations* (pp. 215–242). Chichester, London: Wiley.

Liukkonen, P., Cartwright, S., & Cooper, C. (1999). Costs and benefits of stress prevention in organizations: Review and new methodology. In M. Kompier & C. Cooper (Eds.), *Preventing stress, improving productivity: European case studies in the workplace* (pp. 33–51). London, England: Routledge.

Macdonald, S., Lothian, S., & Wells, S. (1997). Evaluation of an employee assistance program at a transportation company. *Evaluation and Program Planning, 20,* 495–505. doi:10.1016/S0149-7189(97)00028-1

Macdonald, S., Wells, S., Lothian, S., & Shain, M. (2000). Absenteeism and other workplace indicators of employee assistance program clients and matched controls. *Employee Assistance Quarterly, 15,* 41–57. doi:10.1300/J022v15n03_04

Murphy, L. R. (1995). Occupational stress management: Current status and future directions. In C. Cooper & D. M. Rousseau (Eds.), *Trends in organizational behavior* (pp. 1–14). Chichester, England: Wiley.

Nelson, D. L., Little, L. M., & Frazier, M. L. (2008). Employee well-being: The heart of positive organizational behavior. In A. Kinder, R. Hughes, & C. Cooper (Eds.), *Employee well-being support: A workplace resource* (pp. 51–60). Chichester, England: Wiley. doi:10.1002/9780470773246.ch4

Noblet, A. J., & Lamontagne, A. D. (2009). The challenges of developing, implementing, and evaluating interventions. In S. Cartwright & C. L. Cooper (Eds.), *The Oxford handbook of organizational well-being* (pp. 466–496). Oxford, England: Oxford University Press.

Perrewé, P. L., & Zellars, K. L. (1999). An examination of attributions and emotions in the transactional approach to the organizational stress process. *Journal of Organizational Behavior, 20,* 739–752. doi:10.1002/(SICI)1099-1379(199909)20:5<739::AID-JOB1949>3.0.CO;2-C

Reynolds, S., & Briner, R. (1994). Stress management at work: With whom, for whom, and to what ends? *British Journal of Guidance & Counselling, 22,* 75–89.

Roberts, L. M. (2006). Shifting the lens on organizational life: The added value of positive scholarship. *Academy of Management Review, 31,* 292–305.

Rolfe, H., Foreman, J., & Tylee, A. (2006). *Welfare or farewell? Mental health and stress in the workplace* (Discussion Paper 28). London, England: National Institute of Economic and Social Research.

Sainsbury Centre for Mental Health. (2007, December). Mental health at work: Developing the business case (Policy Paper 8). London, England: Author.

Schaubroeck, J. (1999). Should the subjective be the objective? On studying mental processes, coping behavior, and actual exposures in organizational stress research. *Journal of Organizational Behavior, 20,* 753–760. doi:10.1002/(SICI)1099-1379(199909)20:5<753::AID-JOB950>3.0.CO;2-W

Shaw Trust and Future Foundation. (2006, June). *Mental health: The last workplace taboo. Independent research into what British business thinks.* London, England: Shaw Trust.

Shipley, P., & Orlans, V. (1988). Stress research: An interventionist perspective. In J. J. Hurrell, L. R. Murphy, & S. L. Sauter (Eds.), *Occupational stress: Issues and developments in research* (pp. 110–122). New York, NY: Taylor & Francis.

Thoits, P. A. (1995). Stress, coping, and social support processes: Where are we? What next? *Journal of Health and Social Behavior, Special Number,* 53–79. doi:10.2307/2626957

Thomson, L., & Rick, J. (2008). An organizational approach to the rehabilitation of employees following stress-related illness. In A. Kinder, R. Hughes, & C. Cooper (Eds.), *Employee well-being support: A workplace resource* (pp. 223–238). Chichester, England: Wiley. doi:10.1002/9780470773246.ch19

Triandis, H. C. (1998). Vertical and horizontal individualism and collectivism: Theory and research implications for international comparative management. In Cheng, J. L., & Peterson, R. B. (Eds.). *Advances in international comparative management* (pp. 7–35). Greenwich, CT: JAI Press.

Waddell, G., & Burton, A. K. (2006). *Is work good for your health and well-being?* London, England: The Stationery Office.

Westhuis, D., Hayashi, R., Hart, L., Cousert, D., & Spinks, M. (1998). Evaluating treatment issues in a military drug and alcohol treatment program. *Research on Social Work Practice, 8,* 501–519. doi:10.1177/104973159800800501

Westman, M., & Eden, D. (1991). Implicit stress theory: The spurious effects of stress on performance ratings. *Journal of Social Behavior and Personality, 6,* 127–140.

Whatmore, L., Cartwright, S., & Cooper, C. (1999). United Kingdom: Evaluation of a stress management programme in the public sector. In M. Kompier & C. Cooper (Eds.), *Preventing stress, improving productivity: European case studies in the workplace* (pp. 149–174). London, England: Routledge.

Winwood, M. A., & Beer, S. (2008). What makes a good employee assistance programme? In A. Kinder, R. Hughes, & C. Cooper (Eds.), *Employee well-being support: A workplace resource.* Chichester, England: Wiley. doi:10.1002/9780470773246.ch16

19

Occupational Health and Safety Leadership

Jane Mullen and E. Kevin Kelloway

Research documenting the effects of leadership on employee well-being has been available for over 40 years (Day & Hamblin, 1964), and the conclusions of this research would not surprise any adult who has held a job for any length of time (Gilbreath, 2004). Poor leadership is associated with increased levels of employee stress (Offermann & Hellman, 1996) and a variety of other negative consequences (Kelloway, Sivanathan, Francis, & Barling, 2005). What may be surprising is just how extensive the effects of leadership are on individuals' well-being. In addition to the well-documented effects of leadership on employee stress (for reviews, see Kelloway et al., 2005; Arnold, Turner, Barling, Kelloway, & McKee, 2007), leadership has emerged as a predictor of cardiovascular outcomes (e.g., Kivimäki, Ferrie, Brunner, Head, Shipley, Vahtera, & Marmot, 2005; Wager, Feldman, & Hussey, 2003), a salient predictor of safety outcomes (e.g., Barling, Loughlin, & Kelloway, 2002; Kelloway, Mullen, & Francis, 2006) in organizations, and is plausibly related to employees' engagement in healthy lifestyle practices (Bamberger & Bacharach, 2006; Kelloway, Teed, & Prosser, 2008).

In this chapter, we review this literature. We begin with a consideration of leadership style as a foundation for understanding how leaders affect individual well-being in organizations. Following this, we consider the effects of leadership on safety, psychological well-being, healthy lifestyle practices, and physiological well-being. We highlight the potential effect of leaders' behaviors for young workers, suggesting that this population is particularly vulnerable to any effects of poor leadership. We conclude with a consideration of issues for future research.

Leadership Styles

Style of leadership influences the well-being of individuals in organizations in several important ways. In this section, we consider transformational leadership, passive leadership, and abusive supervision.

Transformational Leadership

The theory of transformational leadership (Bass, 1985) is one of the most influential leadership theories in recent management literature and has generated significant empirical interest among researchers. *Transformational leadership* is defined as influencing subordinates by "broadening and elevating followers' goals and providing them with confidence to perform beyond the expectations specified in the implicit or explicit exchange agreement" (Dvir, Eden, Avolio, & Shamir, 2002, p. 735). Empirical evidence suggests that transformational leadership and its individual dimensions predicts subordinates' performance in field experiments (Barling, Weber, & Kelloway, 1996; Dvir et al., 2002), field studies (Bass, Avolio, Jung, & Berson, 2003; Kelloway, Barling, Kelley, Comtois, & Gatien, 2003), laboratory studies (Kirkpatrick & Locke, 1996), and meta-analytic studies (DeGroot, Kiker, & Cross, 2000).

Researchers are becoming increasingly interested in the effects of transformational leadership behavior on health and safety related outcomes (e.g., Hepworth & Towler, 2004; Zohar & Tenne-Gazit, 2008). For example, Kuoppala, Lamminpaa, Liira, and Vainio (2008) reviewed 27 empirical studies that examined the effects of leadership on measures of employee health and well-being (e.g., job well-being, sick leave, disability pension, job satisfaction, job performance). The results of the meta-analysis indicated a moderately strong relationship between the dimensions of leadership and enhanced job well-being (e.g., lower anxiety, job stress, depression), reduced sick leave, and reduced disability pensions. Transformational leaders can positively and indirectly influence employee psychological well-being by evoking positive emotions through their interactions with subordinates (Bono, Foldes, Vinson, & Muros, 2007). Transformational leaders also enhance employee well-being through their effects on the perceived meaning and purpose employees gain from their work (Arnold et al., 2007; Sparks & Schenk, 2001). The findings are consistent with research from the field of positive psychology, which demonstrates that one's sense of meaning and the intrinsic rewards (e.g., enjoyment) that are derived from their work play an important role in the development of psychological well-being (Westaby, Versenyi, & Hausmann, 2005).

In light of the empirical evidence and the overall trend supporting the positive effects of leadership on employee well-being and occupational safety (e.g., Barling et al., 2002; Mullen & Kelloway, 2009; Zohar & Tenne-Gazit, 2008), transformational leaders play an important role in the development of healthy workplaces. In their healthy workplace framework of psychosocial and physical factors, Kelloway and Day (2005) suggested that leadership is one of the key determinants of employee well-being. Employee well-being and organizational effectiveness are also found to be enhanced through various healthy workplace practices, including employee involvement, employee growth and development, work–life balance, health and safety, and employee recognition (Grawitch, Gottschalk, & Munz, 2006), all of which are influenced by leader behavior (for a review, see Kelloway et al., 2005).

Passive Leadership

Constructive forms of leadership (e.g., transformational leadership, transactional leadership) have been contrasted with poor styles of managing known as *passive leadership* (Kelloway et al., 2005). Passive leadership encompasses management-by-exception (passive) behavior (Bass & Avolio, 1990), which is characterized by leaders waiting until performance issues become serious before they take corrective action. In addition to management-by-exception (passive) behaviors, researchers have differentiated an additional form of passive leadership known as *laissez-faire leadership* (Bass, 1985; Kelloway et al., 2006). Laissez-faire leadership is characterized by inaction, being unavailable when needed by subordinates, failing to clarify performance expectations, and avoiding both decision-making and leadership responsibilities (Judge & Piccolo, 2004). Because of the similarities found between management-by-exception (passive) leadership and laissez-faire leadership, researchers have combined the dimensions into a single higher-order passive leadership dimension (Kelloway et al., 2006; Teed, Kelloway, & Mullen, 2008). The higher-order passive leadership dimension is empirically distinct from and negatively correlated with transformational leadership.

Although passive forms of leadership are generally considered to be ineffective styles of leadership, few researchers have empirically examined the impact of passive leadership on employee health and safety (e.g., Skogstad, Einarsen, Torsheim, Aasland, & Hetland, 2007). Kelloway et al. (2006) provided empirical support for the importance of examining the effects of both positive and negative leadership styles on health and safety related outcomes. Their study showed that the absence of leadership is equally important to the presence of other forms of active leadership (e.g., transformational leadership) for the development of employee health and well-being.

Abusive Supervision

Leader behaviors that are characterized as abusive (Tepper, 2000), undermining (Duffy, Gangster, & Pagon, 2002), aggressive (Schat, Desmarais, & Kelloway, 2006), tyrannical (Ashforth, 1994), and emotionally abusive (Keashly, 1997) are beginning to receive increasing attention in the management literature. *Abusive supervision* (Tepper, 2007) is the most commonly used term to describe the various forms of poor leadership and is defined as "subordinates' perceptions of the extent to which their supervisors engage in the sustained display of hostile verbal and nonverbal behaviors, excluding physical contact" (Tepper, 2000, p. 178). Examples of abusive supervision include publicly ridiculing subordinates, blaming subordinates for mistakes they did not make (Tepper, Duffy, & Shaw, 2001), and using derogatory names and intimidation (Keashly, 1998).

The fragmented, yet rapidly expanding, body of empirical research that directly tests the relationships between abusive supervision and employee outcomes supports the plethora of anecdotal evidence suggesting that abusive behavior by supervisors has deleterious effects on employee health and well-being, work-related attitudes, and job performance (for a review, see Tepper, 2007). Moreover, as highlighted by Kelloway et al. (2005) in their review of poor leadership, support for the negative consequences of abusive supervision may also be drawn from the workplace violence literature (e.g., Barling, Rogers, & Kelloway, 2001). Studies that have examined physical violence at work suggest that abusive leader behavior may have more harmful consequences than abusive behaviors that are enacted by customers. For example, LeBlanc and Kelloway (2002) examined the effects of public and coworker aggression and violence on personal and organizational outcomes. The results showed direct effects of coworker aggression on emotional well-being, psychosomatic well-being, and affective commitment. In contrast, public aggression indirectly affected the study outcomes through employee fear of future violence. The data supporting the indirect effects of public aggression on individual and organizational outcomes reported in the workplace violence literature (see also Rogers & Kelloway, 1997; Schat & Kelloway, 2003) suggest that abuse from a supervisor may be a stronger predictor of employee health and well-being than the abusive behaviors of nonorganizational members.

Leadership and Safety

The occupational health and safety literature is rapidly expanding with respect to empirical studies that demonstrate the link between various styles of leadership (e.g., transformational, passive, abusive) and safety-related outcomes. A majority of the studies have examined the effects of active styles of leadership (e.g., transformational) on employee safety-related attitudes and behaviors. A transformational leadership-based approach represents a proactive approach to safety leadership in which the leader develops and communicates a vision for creating a healthy workplace and inspires all employees to actively participate in healthy workplace practices. Employees are highly motivated to create and sustain a safe work environment because they value health and well-being and believe in the importance of working safely, as opposed to complying with safety policies as a means to avoid punishment or to gain rewards.

Empirical studies consistently support the relationship between transformational leadership behaviors and perceived safety climate within organizations (Barling et al., 2002; Hofmann & Morgeson, 1999; Zohar, 2002a, 1980; Zohar & Tenne-Gazit, 2008), defined as the "shared perceptions of managerial policies, procedures and practices" (Zohar, 2002a, p. 75; Zohar, 1980) relating to safety. The studies contribute to our understanding of how leaders create and maintain a positive safety climate within organizations (e.g., promoting social networks and friendship).

Leadership behaviors similar to those described by transformational leadership theory are associated with positive employee safety behaviors. Researchers have demonstrated the positive effects of supportive leadership on task (e.g., safety compliance) and contextual (e.g., safety participation) performance (e.g., Hofmann & Morgeson, 1999). For example, Mullen (2005) found that employees reported a greater willingness to voluntarily raise safety concerns (e.g., safety participation) when supervisors were perceived as supportive and likely to listen to their concerns. Hofmann, Morgeson, and Gerras (2003) found that high-quality social exchanges between leaders and employees resulted in expanded role definitions (e.g., employees perceived safety as part of their job responsibilities), which in turn predicted employee safety citizenship behavior. The link between high-quality leader social exchange and employee safety role definitions was moderated by employee perceptions of safety climate.

Alternatively, managers who exhibit passive forms of safety leadership (e.g., management-by-exception [passive], laissez-faire) communicate the message that safety is not important. Employees, in turn, perceive that safety is not valued in their organization, resulting in negative safety behavior and increased injury rates (e.g., see Zohar, 2002a, 2002b). Kelloway et al. (2006) conducted a study to examine the effects of both transformational leadership and passive leadership on employee safety outcomes. Passive leadership accounted for significant incremental variance in safety consciousness, safety climate, safety-related events, and injuries, beyond that explained by transformational leadership. Teed et al. (2008) examined the effects of inconsistent leadership on employee safety outcomes (e.g., displaying both transformational and passive leadership behaviors). Inconsistent leadership weakened the positive relationship between transformational leadership, employee safety citizenship behavior, and employee safety attitudes. Thus, better safety outcomes are achieved when leaders are consistently champions of safety.

The studies provide empirical support for the notion that a passive, uninvolved approach to safety leadership results in negative safety outcomes. Passive leaders intensify negative safety outcomes, and the results indicate that the beneficial effects of transformational leadership may not be maximized if leaders' behaviors are inconsistent.

The effects of abusive supervision on safety-related outcomes have received considerably less attention from researchers. In a qualitative investigation aimed at understanding why employees engage in unsafe behavior at work, participants from various occupations identified abusive leadership as a key factor that explains unsafe employee behavior (Mullen, 2004). For example, participants did not use appropriate safety equipment to avoid teasing from managers and coworkers. Managers also intimidated and coerced participants to perform unsafe job tasks to meet performance demands.

Mullen and Fiset (2008) examined the effects of abusive supervision on employee safety behavior within the health care setting. They developed and empirically validated a model proposing that abusive supervision negatively impacts employee safety participation and psychological health. The link between abusive supervision and safety participation was fully mediated by employee perceptions of safety climate. The results provided further support for the salient influence of leader behavior on perceived safety climate within organizations. Furthermore, consistent with reactance theory (e.g., Brehm & Brehm, 1981), the results suggest that employees who experience abusive treatment from their manager may seek to restore a sense of justice by purposely withholding voluntary extra-role safety behaviors. For example, when managers bully or intimidate employees into meeting high production demands at the cost of performing safe work practices, employees perceive managers as being unsupportive of safety policies (e.g., negative safety climate perceptions), and may retaliate in an indirect manner by withholding safety citizenship behaviors (e.g., voluntarily identifying potential hazards, participating in safety programs or suggesting innovative ways to improve job safety).

The studies highlight the importance of early organizational socialization experiences of employees when they join an organization. *Organizational socialization* is defined as ongoing processes through which employees learn the values, beliefs, behaviors, social knowledge, and skills that are necessary to effectively fulfill their role within an organization (Van Maanen & Schein, 1979). Socialization facilitates new employees' adjustment to the organization and clearly communicates the behaviors that are expected of them. In terms of safety, we draw on the definition of socialization to define *safety socialization* as the ongoing processes, policies, and practices through which employees learn the safety values and beliefs, safety-related behaviors, and work-related practices that are necessary to create and maintain a safe work environment. Drawing on previous safety leadership literature, there is strong empirical evidence supporting the link between leadership (effective and poor) and various aspects of socialization, including the stages of socialization (e.g., Wanous, 1992), employee information seeking and learning about their work environment (e.g., Morrison, 1993), content of the socialization process (e.g., Ashforth & Saks, 1996), and the activities designed by an organization to help individuals through the socialization.

Leadership and Psychological Well-Being

Much of the research on occupational health and well-being focuses on the impact of perceived job stress on *employee strain,* which is defined as the potential psychological, physical, and behavioral outcomes of negative perceived stress (Barling, 1990). *Employee psychological strain,* which includes anxiety, depression, difficulty making decisions, and forgetfulness (Broadbent, Cooper, FitzGerald, & Parkes, 1982; Tepper, 2001), is influenced by a variety of stressors, including perceptions of job insecurity, work schedules, role conflict, job content, and job control (for a review, see Kelloway & Day, 2005; Sparks, Faragher, & Cooper, 2001). There is growing recognition that the social context within organizations, particularly supervisor–subordinate interpersonal relations, affects employee psychological well-being. Poor leadership is among the commonly cited sources of perceived employee stress and psychological strain (e.g., Kelloway et al., 2005; Tepper, 2000). For example, Skogstad et al. (2007) reported that increased levels of perceived role stress, interpersonal conflict, and workplace bullying mediated the effects of laissez-faire leadership on employee psychological distress.

Abusive supervision has been linked with decreased psychological well-being, including diminished self efficacy (Duffy et al., 2002), increased burnout (Grandey, Kern, & Frone, 2007), frustration, and feelings of helplessness (Ashforth, 1997). Schat and Kelloway (2003) found that organizational support buffered the negative effects of psychological aggression (e.g., from managers and coworkers) on employee health-related outcomes (e.g., emotional well-being, somatic health, job-related affect). Burton and Hoobler (2006) reported that abusive supervision was associated with decreased levels of individual self-esteem. Furthermore, the link between abusive supervision and self-esteem was moderated by gender, such that the effects of abusive supervision were stronger for women than they were for men. Harvey, Stoner, Hochwarter, and Kacmar (2007) examined the effects of abusive supervision on employee job strain (e.g., tension, emotional exhaustion). The results indicated that individuals who were high in positive affect and who used ingratiation tactics experienced lower levels of job strain than individuals who were low in positive affect and refrained from using ingratiation tactics. Thus, the negative effects of abusive supervision on job strain may be neutralized by individual dispositional tendencies and behaviors that are used to influence the attitudes of others.

Despite the dominant focus on poor leadership and its negative health-related consequences, an emerging body of research suggests that effective leaders have the potential to positively influence employee psychological well-being. For example, support from managers has been linked with lower levels of perceived stress, job strain, burnout, and depression (e.g., Lee & Ashforth, 1996; Moyle, 1998; Rooney & Gottlieb, 2007; van Dierendonck, Haynes, Borrill, & Stride, 2004). Transformational leaders provide social support for their employees, and studies provide evidence for the efficacy of transformational leadership behavior in reducing employee stress. Sosik and Godshalk (2000) found that transformational leadership behavior (e.g., social support provided through mentoring) was associated with increased mentoring functions received by protégés, which in turn predicted reduced job-related stress. Furthermore, mentoring functions received by protégés moderated the link between transformational leadership and stress, such that the relationship was stronger for the sample that received high mentoring functions than for the sample that received the low mentoring functions.

Arnold et al. (2007) demonstrated a positive link between transformational leadership and employee psychological well-being, and the mediating role of meaningful work. Data from two studies provided support for both fully mediated and partially mediated models, suggesting that transformational leaders positively influence employee well-being through behaviors and verbal interactions that convey the importance, meaning, and purpose of one's work. The authors noted that the relationship between leadership and well-being was stronger (e.g., fully mediated by meaningful work) in the study that examined stigmatized work roles as opposed to valued work roles (e.g., health care providers).

Using an experience sampling methodology and within-person analyses, Bono et al. (2007) examined the moderating effects of transformational leadership behavior on the link between employees' emotional regulation and both stress and satisfaction at work. Participants experienced greater optimism, happiness, and enthusiasm when their supervisor engaged in transformational leadership behaviors, compared with employees who did not. The results also demonstrated long-lasting effects (i.e., 2 hr) of emotional regulation on employee self-reported stress levels but short-lived effects on job satisfaction. It is of interest to note that transformational leadership buffered the negative effects of emotional regulation on job satisfaction but not on stress, which suggests the possibility of different underlying processes that explain the effects. The results of Bono et al.'s (2007) study have important implications for stress-management interventions. Researchers must consider the role leaders play in tertiary interventions that are focused on providing employee support to cope with stress, in addition to preventative interventions focused on changing the job stressors (e.g., leaders supporting authenticity in the workplace).

Overall, the data suggest that the supportive behavior of transformational leaders may help employees cope with psychological strain resulting from some perceived job stressors (e.g., role ambiguity, meaning derived from work) but not others (e.g., psychological strain resulting from emotional regulation at work).

Leadership and Health Behaviors

Researchers are increasingly interested in examining how leadership affects various behavioral indicators of employee well-being. For example, abusive supervision was found to be positively associated with subordinate problem drinking, including the increased occurrence of feelings of guilt associated with drinking, feelings that drinking behavior should be reduced, having the first drink in the morning (e.g., an "eye opener"), and feeling annoyed when criticized about drinking behavior (Bamberger & Bacharach, 2006). Kelloway et al. (2005) argued that poor quality leadership within organizations strongly influences employees' perceptions of the demands they experience in their job and, thus, the mechanisms they use to cope with job stressors. Job demands have been linked to smoking, greater smoking intensity, and high fat food intake (Hellerstedt & Jeffery, 1997). Results of a study that examined the success of a smoking cessation program showed that participants were more likely to experience a smoking relapse when their manager did not create a social climate that was supportive of the program (Eriksen, 2006). In contrast, a health promotion program aimed at reducing rates of smoking, alcohol abuse, poor fitness, and obesity was more successful when leaders were highly involved and supportive of the program (Whiteman, Snyder, & Ragland, 2001).

Kelloway et al. (2008) examined the effects of organizational response on employee health behaviors following a virus outbreak. Individual perceptions of organizational response reflected how well the leaders within the organization kept individuals informed, provided support to those who became ill, showed concern for individuals' well-being, and took steps to protect individuals and to ensure that the outbreak would not occur in the future. The results of the study showed that organizational response was a strong predictor of stress (e.g., fear) and, in turn, psychological strain. Furthermore, poor organizational response also indirectly predicted increased self-protective behavior (e.g., hygiene practices such as hand washing). The authors of the study note that although increased hygiene practices were beneficial in this case, the findings do suggest the possibility that excessive levels of fear during times of crisis may result in maladaptive coping (e.g., obsessive self-protective behaviors).

Overall, the accumulating data in the literature contribute to the growing recognition that poor leadership behavior can have negative health consequences for individuals, including increased stress, psychological strain, and unhealthy coping behavior. The results of the studies are consistent with findings of previous research on employee well-being and further support the notion that poor leadership has a negative impact on employee health-related behaviors, as opposed to having no effect.

Leadership and Physiological Outcomes

Recent epidemiological studies of work stress provide longitudinal evidence that explains how leadership is linked to physiological health outcomes and the biological onset of disease. Work stress, including the perceived lack of support from supervisors and job control, has been linked to coronary heart disease both directly (e.g., through the activation of neuroendocrine stress pathways) and indirectly (e.g., through unhealthy lifestyle behavior such as poor diet, smoking, low physical activity; Chandola et al., 2008). Researchers have also examined the effects of leadership on various health risks that are associated with cardiovascular disease. Karlin, Brondolo, and Schwartz (2003) examined the effects of supervisory support on systolic blood pressure (SBP), diastolic blood pressure (DBP), and heart rate. The results showed that immediate supervisor support was negatively related to SBP, especially during high-stress conditions. The findings are consistent with a growing number of studies that have demonstrated the beneficial impact of positive social interactions (e.g., supportive, fair) on the cardiovascular system (for a review, see Heaphy & Dutton, 2008), including lower SBP and DBP (Brondolo et al., 2003; Wager et al., 2003) and strengthened immune systems (Kiecolt-Glaser, McGuire, Robles, & Glaser, 2002).

Leadership and Young Workers

Researchers are becoming increasingly concerned with the impact of early work experiences on young workers' health and safety (e.g., Loughlin & Lang, 2005). Young workers are believed to be at an increased risk of being injured on the job due to the nature of the work they perform, limited job knowledge, skills and training, and developmental factors (National Institute for Occupational Safety and Health, 2003).

Researchers have also identified poor leadership behavior as a contributing factor that inadvertently increases the risk of workplace injuries and strain among young workers (e.g., Kelloway et al., 2005). Poor organizational leadership is a root cause of many job stressors outlined in models of job stress (e.g., Karasek & Theorell, 1990; Sauter, Murphy, & Hurrell, 1990). Leaders are responsible for specifying workloads and hours of work for young workers. Increased or unrealistic work demands can become a source of workplace stress and are linked with decreased well-being. For example, Mortimer, Harley, and Staff (2002) suggested that compatibility between work and school is an important predictor of psychological health among young workers. Work hours (i.e., 20 or more hr per week) have been negatively linked with academic performance in high school (e.g., Carr, Wright, & Brody, 1996) and positively associated with school absences (Schoenhals, Tienda, & Schneider, 1998).

Young workers' health has also been found to be negatively affected by interpersonal stressors at work (Frone, 2000). Lubbers, Loughlin, and Zweig (2005) found that interpersonal conflict with supervisors was negatively associated with job self-efficacy, which in turn predicted decreased psychological and physical health indicators 10 weeks later. The results of the study also suggested that interpersonal conflict with supervisors during early work experiences of young workers played a greater role than intrinsic job characteristics in the prediction of job self-efficacy and strain outcomes.

Using a grounded theory approach, Starratt and Grandy (2008) explored young workers' experiences of abusive supervision and proposed a theoretical model of abusive leadership. Participants reported various psychological outcomes that resulted from interactions with abusive supervisors, including feelings of helplessness (i.e., being unable to change the undesirable situation), humiliation, and stress. The results of this study extended previous definitions and studies of abusive supervision (e.g., Tepper, 2007) by providing a comprehensive account of the abusive behaviors that young workers experience in the workplace and the psychological strain resulting from such experiences.

In contrast, empirical evidence also highlights the positive role that leaders play in the development and socialization of young workers' health- and safety-related attitudes and behavior. Safety socialization facilitates a young worker's adjustment to the organization and clearly communicates the behaviors that are expected of them. Transformational leaders are an integral component of the safety socialization process; studies consistently demonstrate the positive safety outcomes that can be achieved when leaders communicate their beliefs of the importance and value of safety, communicate safety expectations by modeling healthy and safe work practices, and show concern for young workers' well-being (e.g., Barling et al., 2002; Kelloway et al., 2006; Teed et al., 2008).

The emerging data for young workers appear to be consistent with findings from studies that focus primarily on adult health and well-being. However, much work remains as researchers have yet to fully explore how theoretical models of work stress and leadership generalize to young workers (Loughlin & Lang, 2005).

Implications for Research and Practice

Although leadership research tends to focus on indices of performance, there are now sufficient data to support the unambiguous conclusion that leadership also affects individual well-being in organizations. Given the potential direct and indirect costs of poor health and impaired well-being for both individuals and organizations, the need for more research explicating these relationships is apparent. We suggest that such research would be most productive if several observations were taken into account.

First, future research efforts should include self-report, behavioral, and physiological indices of strain (Semmer, Grebner, & Elfering, 2004). Organizational stress researchers are becoming increasingly concerned with the widespread reliance on self-report measures (e.g., Francis & Barling, 2005) and have encouraged the increased use of physiological indices of strain, including SBP, DBP, heart rate, and neuroendocrine response (i.e., hormones including oxytocin and cortisol; Heaphy, 2007; Sonnentag & Frese, 2003). A combination of multiple indices of strain will greatly contribute to the study of work stress (Yarnell, 2008).

Including such measures in organizational research has both considerable benefit and some cost. As outcome variables, many physiological measures have the desirable property of responding immediately to social interactions (see Heaphy & Dutton, 2008). However, measuring physiological responses poses a challenge for organizational researchers because such measures (e.g., blood samples) can be intrusive, expensive, and often limited to lab studies as opposed to natural workplace settings. Expanding the domain of well-being may suggest the need for interdisciplinary collaboration. Organizational researchers are not typically conversant with physiological indices and may need to acquire specific expertise to interpret these data appropriately.

Second, although it has become commonplace to call for a greater focus on temporal relations in stress research, we believe that the increasing popularity of experience sampling methodologies offers considerable benefit for examining the effects of leadership on well-being (e.g., Scollon, Kim-Prieto, & Diener, 2003). In particular, the use of experience sampling allows for the understanding of individual leadership "events" rather than global assessment of leadership style. We suggest that a focus on events may be a more productive route to understanding the implications of social interactions such as those between a leader and a subordinate (see, e.g., Glomb, 2002). Recent evidence suggesting that leaders can evince both a transformational and a passive "style" (Kelloway et al., 2006) suggests the importance of focusing on leadership in the short term (e.g., daily, weekly).

Third, we believe that researchers need to examine the potential moderating and mediating mechanisms relating leadership to health outcomes. For example, Kelloway et al. (2005) suggested that leadership may be a "root cause" of organizational stressors, indicating that leadership may predict work stressors, which in turn may predict well-being. There is now some empirical support for this suggestion (e.g., Nielsen, Randal, Yarker, & Brenner, 2008). Future research could profitably examine other mechanisms (e.g., moderation) as well as other leadership styles as predictors of individual well-being and perceptions of work stressors.

Finally, and consistent with our foregoing review, we suggest that there is a particular need to examine the effect of organizational leaders on the health and safety of young workers. It is not clear whether models of leadership derived from the adult workforce apply equally well to young workers; indeed, we note that there is considerable variation within the category of "young worker" (Barling & Kelloway, 1999). Given the importance of early employment experiences as a formative influence (Kelloway & Barling, 1999; Kelloway & Harvey, 1999), future research is well-advised to consider this population in more detail.

Conclusion

A great deal of anecdotal and research evidence supports the proposition that organizational leadership has an effect on virtually every aspect of individual health and safety in organizations. Although this conclusion may seem self-evident, there is also an ongoing need to explicate the mechanisms through which these effects occur. The availability of effective techniques of leadership development (i.e., the observation that good leadership can be learned) suggests the possibility of effective interventions that will positively affect individual well-being in organizations.

References

Arnold, K. A., Turner, N., Barling, J., Kelloway, E. K., & McKee, M. C. (2007). Transformational leadership and psychological well-being: The mediating role of meaningful work. *Journal of Occupational Health Psychology, 12,* 193–203. doi:10.1037/1076-8998.12.3.193

Ashforth, B. E. (1994). Petty tyranny in organizations. *Human Relations, 47,* 755–778. doi:10.1177/001872679404700701

Ashforth, B. E. (1997). Petty tyranny in organizations. A preliminary examination of antecedents and consequences. *Canadian Journal of Administrative Sciences, 14,* 126–140.

Ashforth, B. E., & Saks, A. M. (1996). Socialization tactics: Longitudinal effects on newcomer adjustment. *Academy of Management Journal, 39*(1), 149–178. doi:10.2307/256634

Bamberger, P. A., & Bacharach, S. B. (2006). Abusive supervision and subordinate problem drinking: Taking resistance, stress, and subordinate personality into account. *Human Relations, 59,* 723–752. doi:10.1177/0018726706066852

Barling, J. (1990). *Employment stress and family functioning.* New York, NY: Wiley.

Barling, J., & Kelloway, E. K. (1999). Introduction. In J. Barling & E. K. Kelloway (Eds.), *Young workers: Varieties of experience* (pp. 3–15). Washington, DC: American Psychological Association. doi:10.1037/10309-009

Barling, J., Loughlin, C., & Kelloway, E. (2002). Development and test of a model linking safety-specific transformational leadership and occupational safety. *Journal of Applied Psychology, 87,* 488–496. doi:10.1037/0021-9010.87.3.488

Barling, J., Rogers, A. G., & Kelloway, E. K. (2001). Behind closed doors: In-home workers' experience of sexual harassment and workplace violence. *Journal of Occupational Health Psychology, 6,* 255–269. doi:10.1037/1076-8998.6.3.255

Barling, A. J., Weber, T., & Kelloway, E. K. (1996). Effects of transformational leadership training on attitudinal and financial outcomes: A field experiment. *Journal of Applied Psychology, 81,* 827–832. doi:10.1037/0021-9010.81.6.827

Bass, B. M. (1985). *Leadership and Performance beyond expectations.* New York, NY: Free Press.

Bass, B. M., & Avolio, B. J. (1990). *Transformational leadership development: Manual for the Multifactor Leadership Questionnaire.* Palo Alto, CA: Consulting Psychologist Press.

Bass, B. M., Avolio, B. J., Jung, D., & Berson, Y. (2003). Predicting unit performance by assessing transformational and transactional leadership. *Journal of Applied Psychology, 88,* 207–218. doi:10.1037/0021-9010.88.2.207

Bono, J. E., Foldes, H., Vinson, G., & Muros, J. P. (2007). Workplace emotions: The role of supervision and leadership. *Journal of Applied Psychology, 92,* 1357–1367. doi:10.1037/0021-9010.92.5.1357

Brehm, J., & Brehm, S. (1981). *Psychological reactance: A theory of freedom and control.* New York, NY: Academic Press.

Broadbent, D. E., Cooper, P. F., FitzGerald, P., & Parkes, K. R. (1982). The Cognitive Failures Questionnaire (CFQ) and its correlates. *The British Journal of Clinical Psychology, 21*(1), 1–16.

Brondolo, E., Rieppi, R., Erickson, S. A., Bagiella, E., Shapiro, P. A., McKinley, R. P., & Sloan, R. P. (2003). Hostility, interpersonal interactions, and ambulatory blood pressure. *Psychosomatic Medicine, 65,* 1003–1011. doi:10.1097/01.PSY.0000097329.53585.A1

Burton, J., & Hoobler, J. (2006). Subordinate self-esteem and abusive supervision. *Journal of Managerial Issues, 18,* 340–355.

Carr, R., Wright, J., & Brody, C. (1996). Effects of high school work experience a decade later: Evidence from the National Longitudinal Study. *Sociology of Education, 69,* 66–81. doi:10.2307/2112724

Chandola, T., Britton, A., Brunner, E., Hemingway, H., Malik, M., Kumari, M., . . . Marmot, M. (2008). Work stress and coronary heart disease: What are the mechanisms. *European Heart Journal, 29,* 640–648. doi:10.1093/eurheartj/ehm584

Day, R. C., & Hamblin, R. L. (1964). Some effects of close and punitive styles of supervision. *American Journal of Sociology, 69,* 499–510. doi:10.1086/223653

DeGroot, T., Kiker, D. S., & Cross, T. C. (2000). A meta-analysis to review organizational outcomes related to charismatic leadership. *Canadian Journal of Administrative Sciences, 17,* 356–371.

Duffy, M. K., Gangster, D., & Pagon, M. (2002). Social undermining in the workplace. *Academy of Management Journal, 45,* 331–351. doi:10.2307/3069350

Dvir, T., Eden, D., Avolio, B. J., & Shamir, B. (2002). Impact of transformational leadership on follower development and performance: A field experiment. *Academy of Management Journal, 45,* 735–744. doi:10.2307/3069307

Eriksen, W. (2006). Work factors as predictors of smoking relapse in nurses' aides. *International Archives of Occupational and Environmental Health, 79,* 244–250. doi:10.1007/s00420-005-0048-5

Francis, L., & Barling, J. (2005). Organizational injustice and psychological strain. *Canadian Journal of Behavioural Science, 37,* 250–261. doi:10.1037/h0087260

Frone, M. R. (2000). Interpersonal conflict at work and psychological outcomes: Testing a model among young workers. *Journal of Occupational Health Psychology, 5,* 246–255. doi:10.1037/1076-8998.5.2.246

Gilbreath, B. (2004). Creating healthy workplaces: The supervisor's role. In C. Cooper & I. Robertson (Eds.), *International review of industrial and organizational psychology* (Vol. 19, pp. 93–118). Chichester, England: Wiley.

Glomb, T. M. (2002). Workplace frustration and aggression: Informing conceptual models with data from specific encounters. *Journal of Occupational Health Psychology, 7,* 20–36. doi:10.1037/1076-8998.7.1.20

Grandey, A. A., Kern, J., & Frone, M. (2007). Verbal abuse from outsiders versus insiders: Comparing frequency, impact on emotional exhaustion, and the role of emotional labour. *Journal of Occupational Health Psychology, 12,* 63–79. doi:10.1037/1076-8998.12.1.63

Grawitch, M. J., Gottschalk, M., & Munz, D. C. (2006). The path to a healthy workplace: A critical review linking healthy workplace practices, employee well-being, and organizational improvements. *Consulting Psychology Journal: Practice and Research, 58,* 129–147. doi:10.1037/1065-9293.58.3.129

Harvey, P., Stoner, J., Hochwarter, W., & Kacmar, C. (2007). Coping with abusive bosses: The neutralizing effects of ingratiation and positive affect on negative employee outcomes. *The Leadership Quarterly, 18,* 264–280. doi:10.1016/j.leaqua.2007.03.008

Heaphy, E. (2007). Bodily insights: Three lenses for positive organizational relationships. In J. Dutton & B. Ragins (Eds.), *Exploring positive relationships at work: Building a theoretical and research foundation* (pp. 47–71). Mahwah, NJ: Erlbaum.

Heaphy, E. D., & Dutton, J. (2008). Positive social interactions and the human body at work: Linking organizations and physiology. *Academy of Management Review, 33*(1), 137–163.

Hellerstedt, W. L., & Jeffery, R. W. (1997). The association of job strain and health behaviors in men and women. *International Journal of Epidemiology, 26,* 575–583. doi:10.1093/ije/26.3.575

Hepworth, W., & Towler, A. (2004). The effects of individual differences and charismatic leadership on workplace aggression. *Journal of Occupational Health Psychology, 9,* 176–185. doi:10.1037/1076-8998.9.2.176

Hofmann, D. A., & Morgeson, F. P. (1999). Safety-related behavior as a social exchange: The role of perceived organizational support and leader–member exchange. *Journal of Applied Psychology, 84,* 286–296. doi:10.1037/0021-9010.84.2.286

Hofmann, D. A., Morgeson, F. P., & Gerras, S. (2003). Climate as a moderator of the relationship between leader–member exchange and content specific citizenship. *Journal of Applied Psychology, 88,* 170–178. doi:10.1037/0021-9010.88.1.170

Judge, T. A., & Piccolo, R. F. (2004). Transformational and transactional leadership: A meta-analytic test of their relative validity. *Journal of Applied Psychology, 89,* 755–768. doi:10.1037/0021-9010.89.5.755

Karasek, R., & Theorell, T. (1990). *Healthy work: Stress, productivity, and the reconstruction of working life.* New York, NY: Basic Books.

Karlin, W., Brondolo, E., & Schwartz, J. (2003). Workplace social support and ambulatory cardiovascular activity in New York city traffic agents. *Psychosomatic Medicine, 65,* 167–176. doi:10.1097/01.PSY.0000033122.09203.A3

Keashly, L. (1997). Emotional abuse in the workplace: Conceptual and empirical issues. *Journal of Emotional Abuse, 1,* 85–117. doi:10.1300/J135v01n01_05

Kelloway, E. K., & Barling, J. (1999). When children work: Implications for individuals, organizations, and society. *International Journal of Management Reviews, 1,* 159–170. doi:10.1111/1468-2370.00010

Kelloway, E. K., Barling, J., Kelley, E., Comtois, J., & Gatien, B. (2003). Remote transformational leadership. *Leadership and Organization Development Journal, 24,* 163–171. doi:10.1108/01437730310469589

Kelloway, E. K., & Day, A. (2005). Building healthy workplaces. What we know so far. *Canadian Journal of Behavioural Science, 37,* 223–235. doi:10.1037/h0087259

Kelloway, E. K., & Harvey, S. (1999). Learning to work: The development of work beliefs. In J. Barling & E. K. Kelloway (Eds.). *Young workers: Varieties of experience* (pp. 37–58). Washington, DC: American Psychological Association. doi:10.1037/10309-002

Kelloway, E. K., Mullen, J. E., & Francis, L. (2006). Divergent effects of passive and transformational leadership on safety outcomes. *Journal of Occupational Health Psychology, 11,* 76–86. doi:10.1037/1076-8998.11.1.76

Kelloway, E. K., Mullen, J. E., & Francis, L. (2008, March). *The stress of an epidemic.* Paper presented at the meeting of the Work, Stress, and Health Conference, Washington, DC.

Kelloway, E. K., Sivanathan, N., Francis, L., & Barling, J. (2005). Poor leadership. In J. Barling, E. K. Kelloway, & M. Frone (Eds.), *Handbook of workplace stress* (pp. 89–112). Thousand Oaks, CA: Sage.

Kelloway, E. K., Teed, M., & Prosser, M. (2008). Leading to a healthy workplace. In A. Kinder, R. Hughes, & C. L. Cooper (Eds). *Employee well-being support: A workplace resource* (pp. 25–38). Chichester, England: Wiley.

Kiecolt-Glaser, J. K., McGuire, L., Robles, T. F., & Glaser, R. (2002). Psychoneuroimmunology: Psychological influences on immune function and health. *Journal of Consulting and Clinical Psychology, 70,* 537–547. doi:10.1037/0022-006X.70.3.537

Kirkpatrick, S. A., & Locke, E. A. (1996). Direct and indirect effects of three core charismatic leadership components on performance and attitudes. *Journal of Applied Psychology, 81,* 36–51. doi:10.1037/0021-9010.81.1.36

Kivimäki, M., Ferrie, J. E., Brunner, E., Head, J., Shipley, M. J., Vahtera, K., & Marmot, M. (2005). Justice at work and reduced risk of coronary heart disease among employees: The Whitehall II study. *Archives of Internal Medicine, 165,* 2245–2251. doi:10.1001/archinte.165.19.2245

Kuoppala, J., Lamminpaa, A., Liira, J., & Vainio, H. (2008). Leadership, job well-being, and health effects: A systematic review and meta-analysis. *Journal of Occupational and Environmental Medicine, 50,* 904–915. doi:10.1097/JOM.0b013e31817e918d

LeBlanc, M. M., & Kelloway, E. K. (2002). Predictors and outcomes of workplace violence and aggression. *Journal of Applied Psychology, 87,* 444–453. doi:10.1037/0021-9010.87.3.444

Lee, R. T., & Ashforth, B. E. (1996). A meta-analytic examination of the correlates of the three dimensions of job burnout. *Journal of Applied Psychology, 81,* 123–133. doi:10.1037/0021-9010.81.2.123

Loughlin, C., & Lang, K. (2005). Young workers. In J. Barling, E. K. Kelloway, & M. Frone (Eds.), *Handbook of workplace stress* (pp. 405–430). Thousand Oaks, CA: Sage.

Lubbers, R., Loughlin, C., & Zweig, D. (2005). Common pathways to health and performance: Job self-efficacy and affect among young workers. *Journal of Vocational Behavior, 67,* 199–214. doi:10.1016/j.jvb.2004.03.002

Morrison, E. (1993). Longitudinal study of the effects of information seeking on newcomer socialization. *Journal of Applied Psychology, 78,* 173–183. doi:10.1037/0021-9010.78.2.173

Mortimer, J., Harley, C., & Staff, J. (2002). The quality of work and youth mental health. *Work and Occupations, 29,* 166–197. doi:10.1177/0730888402029002003

Moyle, P. (1998). Longitudinal influences of managerial support on employee well-being. *Work & Stress, 12*(1), 29–49. doi:10.1080/02678379808256847

Mullen, J. (2004). Investigating factors that influence safety behavior at work. *Journal of Safety Research, 35,* 275–285. doi:10.1016/j.jsr.2004.03.011

Mullen, J. E. (2005). Testing a model of employee willingness to raise safety issues. *Canadian Journal of Behavioural Science, 37,* 273–282. doi:10.1037/h0087262

Mullen, J. E., & Fiset, J. (2008, March). *The effects of abusive supervision on employee occupational health and safety outcomes.* Paper presented at the 9th meeting of the World Conference on Injury Prevention and Safety Promotion, Merida, Mexico.

Mullen, J. E., & Kelloway, E. K. (2009). Safety leadership: A longitudinal study of the effects of transformational leadership on safety outcomes. *Journal of Occupational and Organizational Psychology, 82,* 253.

National Institute for Occupational Safety and Health. (2003). *Preventing deaths, injuries, and illnesses of young workers* (DHHS Publication No. 2003-128). Cincinnati, OH: Author.

Nielsen, K., Randal, R., Yarker, S., & Brenner, S. (2008). The effects of transformational leadership on followers' perceived work characteristics and psychological well-being: A longitudinal study. *Work & Stress, 22,* 16–32. doi:10.1080/02678370801979430

Offermann, L. R., & Hellmann, P. S. (1996). Leadership behavior and subordinate stress: A 360° view. *Journal of Occupational Health Psychology, 1,* 382–390. doi:10.1037/1076-8998.1.4.382

Rogers, K., & Kelloway, E. K. (1997). Violence at work: Personal and organizational outcomes. *Journal of Occupational Health Psychology, 2,* 63–71. doi:10.1037/1076-8998.2.1.63

Rooney, J., & Gottlieb, B. (2007). Development and initial validation of a measure of supportive and unsupportive managerial behaviors. *Journal of Vocational Behavior, 71,* 186–203. doi:10.1016/j.jvb.2007.03.006

Sauter, S., Murphy, L., & Hurrell, J. (1990). Prevention of work-related psychological disorders: A national strategy proposed by the National Institute for Occupational Safety and Health (NIOSH). *American Psychologist, 45,* 1146–1158. doi:10.1037/0003-066X.45.10.1146

Schat, A., Desmarais, S., & Kelloway, E. K. (2006). *Exposure to workplace aggression from multiple sources: Validation of a measure and test of a model.* Unpublished manuscript, McMaster University, Hamilton, Ontario, Canada.

Schat, A., & Kelloway, E. K. (2003). Reducing the adverse consequences of workplace aggression and violence: The buffering effects of organizational support. *Journal of Occupational Health Psychology, 8,* 110–122. doi:10.1037/1076-8998.8.2.110

Schoenhals, M., Tienda, M., & Schneider, B. (1998). The educational and personal consequences of adolescent employment. *Social Forces, 77,* 723–762. doi:10.2307/3005545

Scollon, C. N., Kim-Prieto, C., & Diener, E. (2003). Experience sampling: Promises and pitfalls, strengths, and weaknesses. *Journal of Happiness Studies, 4,* 5–34. doi:10.1023/A:1023605205115

Semmer, N. K., Grebner, S., & Elfering, A. 2004. Beyond self-report: Using observational, physiological, and situation-based measures in research on occupational stress. In P. L. Perrewé & D. C. Ganster (Eds.), *Emotional and physiological processes and positive intervention strategies: Research in occupational stress and well-being* (pp. 205–263). Boston, MA: JAI Press.

Skogstad, A., Einarsen, S., Torsheim, T., Aasland, M., & Hetland, H. (2007). The destructiveness of laissez-faire leadership behavior. *Journal of Occupational Health Psychology, 12*(1), 80–92. doi:10.1037/1076-8998.12.1.80

Sonnentag, S., & Frese, M. (2003). Stress in organizations. In W. C. Borman, D. R. Ilgen, & R. J. Klimoski (Eds.), *Comprehensive handbook of psychology: Vol. 12. Industrial and organizational psychology* (pp. 453–491). New York, NY: Wiley.

Sosik, J., & Godshalk, V. (2000). Leadership styles, mentoring functions received, and job-related stress: A conceptual model and preliminary study. *Journal of Organizational Behavior, 21,* 365–390. doi:10.1002/(SICI)1099-1379(200006)21:4<365::AID-JOB14>3.0.CO;2-H

Sparks, K., Faragher, B., & Cooper, C. L. (2001). Well-being and occupational health in the 21st century workplace. *Journal of Occupational and Organizational Psychology, 74,* 489–509. doi:10.1348/096317901167497

Sparks, J. R., & Schenk, J. A. (2001). Explaining the effects of transformational leadership: An investigation of the effects of higher-order motives in multilevel marketing organizations. *Journal of Organizational Behavior, 22,* 849–869. doi:10.1002/job.116

Starratt, A., & Grandy, G. (2008, September). *Young workers' experiences of abusive leadership: A grounded theory approach.* Paper presented at the meeting of the British Academy of Management Conference, Harrogate, England.

Teed, M., Kelloway, E. K., & Mullen, J. E. (2008, March). *Young workers' safety: The impact of inconsistent leadership.* Paper presented at the meeting of the Work, Stress, and Health Conference, Washington, DC.

Tepper, B. J. (2000). The consequences of abusive supervision. *Academy of Management Journal, 43,* 178–190. doi:10.2307/1556375

Tepper, B. J. (2001). Health consequences of organizational injustice: Tests of main effects and interactive effects. *Organizational Behavior and Human Decision Processes, 86,* 197–215. doi:10.1006/obhd.2001.2951

Tepper, B. J. (2007). Abusive supervision in work organizations: Review, synthesis, and research agenda. *Journal of Management, 33,* 261–289. doi:10.1177/0149206307300812

Tepper, B. J., Duffy, M. K., & Shaw, J. D. (2001). Personality moderators of the relationship between abusive supervision and subordinates' resistance. *Journal of Applied Psychology, 86,* 974–983. doi:10.1037/0021-9010.86.5.974

van Dierendonck, D., Haynes, C., Borrill, C., & Stride, C. (2004). Leadership behavior and subordinate well-being. *Journal of Occupational Health Psychology, 9,* 165–175. doi:10.1037/1076-8998.9.2.165

Van Maanen, J. V., & Schein, E. H. (1979). Toward a theory of organizational socialization. In B. M. Staw (Ed.), *Research in organizational behavior* (Vol. 1, pp. 209–264). Greenwich, CT: JAI Press.

Wager, N., Feldman, G., & Hussey, T. (2003). The effect on ambulatory blood pressure of working under favourably and unfavourably perceived supervisors. *Occupational and Environmental Medicine, 60,* 468–474. doi:10.1136/oem.60.7.468

Wanous, J. P. (1992). *Organizational entry: Recruitment, selection, and socialization of newcomers* (2nd ed.). Reading, MA: Addison Wesley.

Westaby, J. D., Versenyi, A., & Hausmann, R. C. (2005). Intentions to work during mental illness: An exploratory study of antecedent conditions. *Journal of Applied Psychology, 90,* 1297–1305. doi:10.1037/0021-9010.90.6.1297

Whiteman, J., Snyder, D., & Ragland, J. (2001). The value of leadership in implementing and maintaining a successful health promotion program in the Naval Surface Force, U.S. pacific Fleet. *American Journal of Health Promotion, 15,* 437–440.

Yarnell, J. (2008). Stress at work: An independent risk factor for coronary heart disease. *European Heart Journal, 29,* 579–580. doi:10.1093/eurheartj/ehm641

Zohar, D. (1980). Safety climate in industrial organizations: Theoretical and applied implications. *Journal of Applied Psychology, 65,* 96–102. doi:10.1037/0021-9010.65.1.96

Zohar, D. (2002a). The effects of leadership dimensions, safety climate, and assigned priorities on minor injuries in work groups. *Journal of Organizational Behavior, 23,* 75–92. doi:10.1002/job.130

Zohar, D. (2002b). Modifying supervisory practices to improve submit safety: A leadership-based intervention model. *Journal of Applied Psychology, 87,* 156–163. doi:10.1037/0021-9010.87.1.156

Zohar, D., & Tenne-Gazit, O. (2008, July). Transformational leadership and group interaction as climate antecedents: A social network analysis. *Journal of Applied Psychology, 93,* 744–757. doi:10.1037/0021-9010.93.4.744

Part VI _____

Methodology
and Evaluation

20

An Epidemiological Perspective on Research Design, Measurement, and Surveillance Strategies

Stanislav V. Kasl and Beth A. Jones

In this chapter, we address a number of methodological issues that we view as important to studies of the impact of the work environment on health and well-being. The framework and the perspective we use are those of occupational and psychosocial epidemiology. This epidemiologic perspective borrows equally from classical epidemiology and the social–behavioral sciences. In a handbook of occupational health psychology, this perspective dovetails well with the approaches to studying the impact of the work environment that come to us from more traditional health psychology. On occasion, our procedure will be to describe the strategy used in classical occupational epidemiology (e.g., the study of physical and chemical exposures at work) and then to discuss modifications and elaborations of strategies needed to make the methods more suitable for the study of psychosocial work exposures. Epidemiology does not present us with unique or superior methodological solutions to problems that frequently challenge social and behavioral scientists working in occupational health psychology; rather, it offers additional or alternative approaches that can broaden our range of useful strategies in the study of the work environment. Excellent studies of physical and chemical exposures in the workplace, affecting biomedical outcomes, are exemplars that can give new insights for designing studies of psychosocial work exposures affecting psychological or behavioral outcomes, but they are generally insufficiently complex to be widely applicable models for studying psychosocial work exposures. Finally, epidemiologic approaches, with their tradition of studying environmental exposures, remind us that examining the impact of the work environment on health and well-being demands a broadly interdisciplinary approach rather than a single disciplinary approach, such as health psychology with its lesser emphasis on environmental exposures.

The primary methodological topics to be covered in this chapter include study designs, measurement of exposures, and surveillance strategies. A few comments about issues that cut across these topics will serve as an entrée to their presentation. And the use of the occupational and psychosocial epidemiology perspective is intended to help those inadequately familiar with epidemiologic methods to become better acquainted with their usefulness.

Issues Linking Study Design and Measurement of Exposures

Even though study designs and measurement of exposure are topics discussed later separately, it is useful to recognize that methodological strengths or potential weaknesses in one domain may be linked to, or are contingent on, strengths and weaknesses in another domain. For example, the impact of limitations in measurement of psychosocial work exposures may vary depending on the method used, such as laboratory-based biological data compared with self-reports of symptoms of distress; when outcomes are measured by self-reports as well, our concern about limitations of measurement of exposure increases. Similarly, cross-sectional designs may increase our concern about measurement shortcomings, whereas prospective designs may lessen some concerns, especially the influence of the outcome on measurement of exposure. Inappropriate analysis of data may undermine specific study strengths such as the use of a prospective design. And, of course, availability of additional variables that can be included in analyses as controls for potential confounders can dramatically alter uncertainties about the proper interpretation of findings that would normally result from design or measurement limitations.

It is not clear to what extent methodological concerns are also contingent on the kind of theory (if any) that has guided a study. Obviously, the use of a particular theoretical approach in designing a study, such as the demand–control–support model or the effort–reward imbalance model (Bosma, Peter, Siegrist, & Marmot, 1998; Kivimäki et ak., 2006; Kuper & Marmot, 2003; Siegrist et al., 2004), can be undermined by the omission of a crucial variable or the inadequate operationalization of an important construct. Problems also arise when a theory is marginally appropriate to a particular occupational setting, such as the use of the demand–control model when studying physicians; in this case, high levels of decision authority in fact represent high levels of demand and responsibility (Calnan, Wainwright, Forsythe, Wall, & Almond, 2001). This may lead to inadequate analyses and to inappropriate interpretations of findings. But beyond such examples, it would seem that guidelines about good research designs and strong measurement are not particularly altered by the kind of theory that underpins a study.

Study Design Considerations

The broad objectives of studies in occupational epidemiology can be characterized as follows: (a) to demonstrate the etiological role of an exposure variable, (b) to show that this role remains after adjustments for necessary confounders and control variables, and (c) to learn as much as possible about the underlying mechanisms and the moderating influences involved in the etiological relationship.

The classical design in occupational epidemiology, frequently used and still useful, is relatively straightforward: establish differences in disease-specific morbidity or mortality by occupation and place of work, and then search for environmental agents in the workplace, the exposure to which might explain these differences. This strategy works well enough when certain conditions are near optimal: (a) when self-selection into occupations (e.g., because of health status or personal characteristics) and company selection policies are minimal, and any selection that exists either does not produce confounding or can be controlled statistically; (b) when the specific nature and extent of exposure can be pinpointed and quantified; (c) when identification of cases and non-cases is complete and without bias, that is, not contingent on seeking or receiving treatment and not influenced by knowledge of exposure status; (d) when latency between exposure and detection is relatively short, an ideal that is more likely to be met for injuries and musculoskeletal disorders than for many cancers or cardiovascular disease; (e) when the disease is rare and the relative risk of disease, given exposure, is high; and (f) when the disease has a simple etiology in that work setting and moderators of the exposure–disease relationship are weak or nonexistent. The original story of angiosarcoma of the liver and exposure to polyvinylchloride (e.g., Creech & Johnson, 1974) illustrates these optimal conditions admirably.

This classical design in occupational epidemiology is only a useful reference point for studies conducted within the domain of occupational health psychology; it is not an adequate study design model because many of the conditions are not satisfied. In other words, studies of physical and chemical exposures in relation to occupational cancers or workplace injuries are not enough of a model for the study of the impact of the psychosocial work environment on health and well-being. (A similar point will be made later when we consider the applicability of classical surveillance strategies to occupational health psychology.) However, the identification of the particular conditions that make the study of some exposure–disease link relatively uncomplicated is still quite valuable when we face a research problem that is more complex, if not intractable. Most often, the problems we encounter in occupational health psychology have to do with: (a) identifying the correct or relevant exposure variables and measuring them appropriately; (b) taking sufficient account of the influence of mediators and moderators, which may include a whole host of personal and trait characteristics, as well as behavioral and psychological processes taking place over time; (c) studying outcomes that have a complex etiology, that develop gradually, and where the relative risk of disease, given exposure, is rather weak. Other issues, such as self-selection concerns or biases in the detection of an outcome, would not seem to be a priori more troublesome in occupational health psychology than in classical occupational epidemiology.

Because the vast majority of studies of the health impact of work exposures use observational (i.e., nonexperimental) designs, it is useful to identify and discuss elements of observational designs that represent strengths. In our opinion, these elements are suitable targets for implementation at the point of designing a study of psychosocial work characteristics and health.

The Environmental Condition (Exposure) Is Objectively Defined and Measured

Admittedly, this is a position that, although quite noncontroversial in occupational epidemiology, is a subject of considerable debate in occupational health psychology, particularly in the context of studying work stress and, more broadly, psychosocial work conditions. This debate, often using the uncomfortable and inadequate terminology of "subjective versus objective" measurement, is not uncommon in other areas of psychology, such as the work that has dealt with the residential environment (e.g., Archea, 1977; Taylor, 1980; Wohlwill, 1973). We have previously elaborated on the reasons for anchoring the study to the objective assessment of the exposure conditions (Kasl, 1998; Kasl & Jones, 2001), and we deal with it separately in the section on measurement.

Mediating Processes Are Studied, and Vulnerability or Protective Factors That Interact With Exposure Are Included

The goal is to include all the relevant psychological and behavioral variables that are emphasized by those who use primarily psychological formulations of the process (e.g., Perrewé & Zellars, 1999) or who have come out on the "subjective" side of the measurement debate (e.g., Vagg & Spielberger, 1998; Williams & Cooper, 1998). However, unlike the purely psychological formulations in which the first step in the theorized causal process is the subjectively defined work exposure and there is no assessment of the objective features of the work environment, in the occupational epidemiology perspective that we are recommending, the first step is the objectively defined exposure and the mediating psychological and behavioral processes are anchored to it. Of course, this point is part of the overall debate about exposure measurement, and we return to it later.

The Cohort Is Identified Before Any Exposure, Self-Selection Into Exposure Conditions Is Minimized, and the Cohort Can Be Followed Through the Transition Into Exposure and for Short-Term and Long-Term Effects of Exposure

This is perhaps the most idealized, that is, difficult to achieve, design strength in our listing, but it is one that is especially pertinent to occupational health psychology. In studies of the health impact of physical and chemical exposures, the start of exposure may be relatively easily established, such as by date of the person's entry into the particular work setting or by the date of introduction of a new industrial process. The quantification of exposure may also be reasonably straightforward, such as the cumulative duration of radiation exposure by level of radiation. In addition, using medical records to establish that individuals in the cohort are initially free of a disease, such as cancer, is often relatively easy. Similarly, innovations in the field of molecular biomarkers (McMichael, 1994) can facilitate the measurement of internal exposures and of early biological response, such as precursors to cancer or early pathologic changes.

The situation in occupational health psychology is frequently more difficult and more complex. First, the field seldom uses the strategy of studying newcomers into a job (e.g., Saks & Ashforth, 2000), a design that would seem to hold considerable promise, particularly for the study of early adaptation and coping. Second, opportunities for using natural experiments, with changes in the work setting that generate comparable groups of exposed and unexposed workers and that allow for baseline (i.e., prechange) data collection, are relatively rare. Some exceptions include (a) studies of effects of job loss based on finding unexpected factory closures where all the workers lose their jobs (Morris & Cook, 1991), (b) studies of effects of job insecurity based in companies involved in downsizing and planned mergers (Ferrie, Shipley, Marmot, Stansfeld, & Smith, 1995; Ferrie, Shipley, Stansfeld, Smith, & Marmot, 2003), and (c) studies of unexpected changes in job demands and work environment (Kittel, Kornitzer, & Dramaix, 1980). These natural experiments provide baseline data and establish a temporal sequence of changes, thus improving our ability to argue for a cause-and-effect relationship.

These comments are meant to sensitize the investigator to the limited value of setting up an apparently strong design, a longitudinal follow-up of a cohort of workers; often the best one can do is observe small changes in a cohort that is in a steady state, that is, undergoing no changes in work conditions and having already accommodated to the work setting. The beginning and the end of follow-up are relatively arbitrary points in the lives of the workers. The measurement of exposure (and quantifying the dose) is a particularly troublesome issue, given the presumed importance of the mediating psychological processes; length of tenure in a particular job is a poor substitute for measuring the previous history of these psychological processes at various points in the past. The assumption that the respondent's position on these dimensions (e.g., psychological demands) at the arbitrary start of the follow-up is representative of the whole tenure in that job would seem somewhat dubious. This suggests that the steady-state cohort that is being studied during an arbitrary temporal window on their working lives will consist of three (hypothetical) types of individuals: those who are studied "too early" to observe any effects, those who are studied "too late" because the effects have already taken place, and those for whom the temporal window is "just right" to reveal effects. Unfortunately, we rarely have external criteria for identifying these three hypothetical subgroups so that we could select only the third one for study. In contrast, in prospective studies of incidence of physical disease outcomes, such as myocardial infarction, we delete those with history of the disease at baseline from the cohort. And we try to choose the age range for the study cohort to maximally reflect the period of risk for first events. However, when studying psychological and behavioral processes, and assessing exposures and outcomes with continuous measures, we do not set up a truly prospective design (before disease occurrence) but merely a longitudinal one where we study changes measured from one time point to another. (For a discussion of the overly optimistic evaluations of the benefits of longitudinal follow-up studies, see Taris & Kompier, 2003.)

The comments in the previous paragraph are linked to the assumption that there is a standard and preferred way of analyzing such longitudinal data. The statistical model that is normally set up examines the outcome at Time 2 in relation to exposure at Time 1, controlling for the value of the outcome at Time 1 (in addition to other control variables). It is inappropriate to fail to control for the value of the outcome at Time 1 (e.g., Niedhammer, Goldberg, Leclerc, Bugel, & David, 1998) or to predict the outcome at Time 2 from the average of values of exposure at both Time 1 and Time 2 (e.g., Cheng, Kawachi, Coakley, Schwartz, & Colditz, 2000). Because the standard way of analyzing the longitudinal data means predicting changes net of the existing baseline (cross-sectional) association of exposure and outcome, the cohort should include enough individuals for whom the effects of exposure have not yet played themselves out so that it may be an informative design.

Special Study Designs in Occupational and Psychosocial Epidemiology

Elsewhere (Kasl & Jones, 2001), we listed a number of traditional designs in psychosocial epidemiology and discussed associated strengths and weaknesses. These designs were (a) random assignment to exposure or beneficial intervention, (b) prospective designs in which some cohort members change exposure status, (c) traditional prospective cohort designs, (d) cross-sectional population surveys, and (e) case-control retrospective designs. This is a textbook classification and is not as useful as grouping studies in an ad hoc fashion according to types of approaches actually used in occupational epidemiology (e.g., Kasl & Amick, 1995). We comment on three interesting varieties of design approaches.

Studies With Limited Information Using Occupational Titles

Typically, these are studies of total mortality (e.g., Fletcher, 1991), cause-specific mortality, such as suicide (Boxer, Burnett, & Swanson, 1995), or selected morbidities, such as myocardial infarction (e.g., Bolm-Audorff & Siegrist, 1983) or major depressive disorders (e.g., Eaton, Anthony, Mandel, & Garrison, 1990). The studies do not tell us more than they seem to, namely, what occupations have high and low rates. We cannot identify the specific aspects of these jobs that contribute to the differential rates; also, confounders remain uncontrolled, and what segments of the total etiological process (i.e., risk factor differences, differential incidence given risk factors, case fatality) are reflected by these rates remains unclear.

Some studies have adopted the supplementary strategy of imputing values for the demand–control model dimensions, based on data from separate surveys of individuals (e.g., Hammar, Alfredsson, & Johnson, 1998; Schwartz, 2000; Steenland, Johnson, & Nowlin, 1997). Although this is an inventive bootstrap strategy, the concern is that the imputation is too narrowly based in a single theoretical model and alternative models have not been usually explored. Furthermore, because occupational titles explain a fair amount of variance in some dimensions such as physical demands and decision latitude, and relatively little in other dimensions, such as psychological demands and supervisor support (Bültmann, Kant, van Amelsvoort, van den Brandt, & Kasl, 2001; Karasek & Theorell, 19901), this imputation strategy seems more appropriate for some dimensions and less so for others.

Intensive Studies of Single Occupations

The occupational health literature contains many studies of single occupations. Earlier work tended to focus on such occupations as air traffic controllers, bus drivers, police officers, and health care personnel (Kasl & Amick, 1995). The more recent work has continued the interest in drivers and transportation workers (e.g., Gustavsson et al., 1996; Peter, Geibler, & Siegrist, 1998; Piros, Karlehagen, Lappas, & Wilhelmsen, 2000) and health care workers (e.g., Bourbonnais, Comeau, & Vezina, 1999; Kirkcaldy & Martin, 2000; Williams, Dale, Glucksman, & Wellesley, 1997). The study of a single occupation would seem inappropriate when we are still at the point of trying to show that it is associated with high rates of some adverse outcome, or if we are worried that any association between exposure and outcome may not be generalizable to other work settings. Aside from these considerations, the primary questions about this approach are: What is the payoff from this research strategy, other than learning more about a particular occupation? If earlier work on many occupations points to these as high-stress occupations, or if they have high rates of a particular health problem, will this strategy advance our understanding of the health impact of the work environment? The answer is that it depends. If the difference in the level of exposure to some hazard that describes the original difference across many occupations can be made even bigger and clearer or more precise by studying only individuals within a single occupation, then we learn more. If, for example, the presumed hazard among bus drivers is a result of bad traffic conditions on the bus route (Netterstrom & Juel, 1988; Winklebly, Ragland, Fisher, & Syme, 1988), then finding bus drivers on rural routes with little traffic would be a good contrast that may control for many exogenous variables. If, however, the presumed hazard is uniformly high for most of the job occupants, then the risk factors for an adverse health outcome will be primarily related to individual differences in perceptions, responding, coping, and personal characteristics because their high level of exposure is held constant. Moreover, these predictors may be unique for that setting and will not account for the high rates of some health problems in this occupation, compared with other occupations, which was the original observation in search of explanations. Thus, the work setting for air traffic controllers in high density air traffic areas seems fairly homogeneous, and some of the risk factors that have emerged reflected individual characteristics, such as Type A personality, amicability, and conscientiousness (Lee, Niemcryk, Jenkins, & Rose, 1989). We might also note a dilemma faced by investigators who study single occupations: whether to use a generic instrument for measuring psychosocial workplace exposures useful in any occupation (Landsbergis & Theorell, 2000), which may not be sufficiently appropriate for that particular work setting, or to develop a tailor-made instrument, which will make it difficult to compare findings from other occupations.

Designs That Describe Acute Changes in Biological Variables

The monitoring of acute effects of work stressors on biological variables is a research strategy that has become quite popular. The designs include 24-hour monitoring, changes during the working day, and comparisons of working and nonworking occasions, such as before the workday begins, after the workday ends, during sleep, and during vacation. The biological indicators most often used are blood pressure, cortisol, and catecholamines. It is unlikely that self-report measures of stress, distress, and symptoms would be suitable in these designs because the frequent data collection over a short period of time could have strong reactive effects, with repeated self-observations possibly leading to drift in the meaning (i.e., validity) of the measure.

One simple approach has been to measure the increase in some biological indicator from the start of the workday to the end, and to relate the magnitude of the increase to type of job and to work conditions. The presumption is that larger increases will be observed in more demanding or hazardous work settings. For example, in a study of blood pressure in a prison setting, work-related increases among guards were greater in maximum-security than in minimum-security prisons (Ostfeld, Kasl, D'Atri, & Fitzgerald, 1987). Among other correctional personnel, those involved in treatment had higher increases than service and clerical workers; this was particularly so for women. In interpreting these findings, one assumes that a change during the day, such as a small decline, is a function of a relatively nonstressful work setting, rather than reflecting strong anticipation effects of coming to a difficult work setting, in which case the values at the start of the day are already elevated.

Studies of changes in biological indicators during the workday have been significantly enriched by also examining changes that cross the work and nonwork boundary, also known as studies of "spillover" or "unwinding" (e.g., James & Bovbjerg, 2001; Luecken et al., 1997; Sluiter, Frings-Dresen, Meijman, & van der Beek, 2000; Steptoe, Lundwall, & Cropley, 2000). The detection of failure to recover from putative work-linked high levels of catecholamines and cortisol comes close to the ideal of studying acute biological changes that have great promise as risk factors for adverse health events: Repeated occasions of such patterns of acute reactivity appear likely to translate into irreversible changes with clinical significance. However, one must not forget that the link to specific disease outcomes is yet to be securely established (Sluiter et al., 2000). It should also be noted that the spillover studies must be able to account for the possible contributing influences of nonwork demands and stressors. Failure to recover from high levels at work is presumably indicative of a stressful job only if the nonwork situation is relatively low on stress. Otherwise, such failure to recover is ambiguous, perhaps reflecting the simultaneous impact of several role domains.

Some Issues in the Measurement of Psychosocial Workplace Exposures

One of the most persistent issues in this area of measurement is the debate concerning the proper place for objective versus subjective measurement strategies. The illuminating and helpful exchange between Perrewé and Zellars (1999) and Frese and Zapf (1999) is a testimony to the undying nature of this controversy. As we indicated earlier, the perspective that we use for this chapter, that of occupational and psychosocial epidemiology, puts us solidly aligned with the position enunciated by Frese and Zapf: The objective measurement of the environmental condition (i.e., exposure) is a crucial component of an occupational health study and its omission is likely to limit the interpretability of its findings. Over the years, we have maintained this position (Kasl, 1978, 1987, 1991, 1998); the opposing viewpoints from the two sides of the debate continue to be formulated in similar ways. Hurrell, Nelson, and Simmons (1998) have provided an excellent and balanced overview of this continuing debate.

We find it illuminating that although the argument of Frese and Zapf (1999) is essentially quite pragmatic, based on accumulated research experience, the position of Perrewé and Zellars (1999) is more closely derived from theory, the transactional model of the stress process (Lazarus, 1966). It is from this model that they derive "a research agenda for the study of the organizational stress process that focuses on the appraisal of objective stressors, attributions regarding the felt stress, and the subsequent affective emotions" (Perrewé and Zellars, 1999, p. 740). We disagree with this statement because it truncates the phenomenon that needs to be studied and weakens the research strategy that needs to be applied to it, in two crucial ways. It leaves out the objective stressors and it omits a variety of outcomes, both proximal and distal, to the "affective emotions." The latter concern is important, because the transactional process may differ substantially, depending on the outcomes being studied. For example, outcomes such as sickness absence, heavy alcohol consumption, and lower back disorders may involve additional appraisal and attribution processes that should also be studied. Other outcomes, such as biological risk factors and clinical outcomes, may necessitate the inclusion of other transactional steps, such as health care seeking and adherence to medications.

Arguments in Favor of Objective Measurement Strategies

The various considerations in favor of objective versus subjective measurement strategies may be summarized as follows:

- We will have a clearer linkage to the "actual" environmental conditions and will know much better what aspects of the environment needs changing, should that be the contemplated next step.
- We will have a clearer picture of the etiological process, because the complete set of important antecedent influences on the subjective measures will be otherwise unclear.
- There will be less potential measurement confounding when the outcomes linked to the exposure are psychological and behavioral.
- There will be a clearer separation of where the independent variable ends and the mediator or dependent variables begin. With subjective measures describing the transactional process, the components (e.g., appraisals and attributions) in actuality may not be separate steps and may not take place in the theoretically predicted order (Kasl, 1998).

Arguments in Favor of a Subjective Measurement Strategy

The following are arguments in favor of using a subjective measurement strategy:

- The psychological meaning of exposure, and the experience of it, varies substantially across individuals within the same work setting.

- Cognitive and emotional processing strongly moderates the overall etiological process, and the subjective exposure clarifies the etiological mechanism.
- Environmental manipulation is not possible, and only differential reactivity of individuals can be addressed, thus making the appraisals the better target of any contemplated interventions.
- Objective measures are irrelevant because they describe conditions that are outside of any possible causal chain (Kasl, 1998).

There would seem to be several possibilities for fine-tuning the debate so that it is less polarized. For example, there are some outcomes, such as musculoskeletal disorders, where there appears to be an exquisitely complex interplay of biomechanical and ergonomic factors with psychosocial variables (e.g., Devereux, Buckle, & Vlachonikolis, 1999; Macfarlane, Hunt, & Silman, 2000; Smedley, Egger, Cooper, & Coggon, 1997), so that the need for objective measurement of work dimensions seems essential. However, the accumulated evidence linking psychosocial exposures in the workplace to cardiovascular disease is rather impressive (e.g., Schnall, Belkic, Landsbergis, & Baker, 2000), and yet this research domain has not generally used objective measures. It should also be noted that the strategy of using both self-report measures of work dimensions and independent assessments of these dimensions by expert raters (e.g, Bosma et al., 1997) is a useful strategy, because the latter type of measurement removes concerns over individual biases affecting the self-report measures, such as negative affectivity. However, little work has been done toward understanding better where precisely these measures may differ and in what ways. The primary question so far has been: Do they predict health outcomes, such as coronary heart disease, in a similar way or do the associations differ?

Pragmatic considerations should also be part of this debate. Fundamentally, self-report measures tend to be more easily developed, cheaper, and more convenient. Moreover, it is not difficult to develop generic instruments that can be used across many occupations. However, objective measures for assessing dimensions of the work environment are seen as expensive, clumsy, hard to develop, and with their own set of limitations. In addition, they tend to be specific to a few jobs, thus limiting their usefulness. However, these are somewhat polarizing perceptions. Although the proposed methodology by Hacker (1993) does indeed seem complicated and labor-intensive, there are settings in which objective measurement appears less challenging. For example, Greiner, Ragland, Krause, Syme, and Fisher (1997) have been able to develop a useful objective measure of occupational stress for urban transit operators. In certain settings, such as in jobs involving human–computer interactions (e.g., Smith, Conway, & Karsh, 1999), many features of the job setting are relatively easy to assess objectively and may even be part of ongoing recordkeeping: technology breakdowns, technology slowdowns, and electronic performance monitoring. And objective measures that are based on data provided by informed personnel managers seem quite feasible even in large epidemiological surveys such as the Whitehall II study (Bosma et al., 1997). In general, considerable methodological work continues to be carried out that explores the validity, reliability, and usefulness of self-reports versus alternative data collection strategies for measuring work exposures. Studies have targeted chemical exposures, biomechanic and ergonomic task demands, and psychosocial work dimensions (e.g., Benke et al., 2001; Fritschi, Siemiatycki, & Richardson, 1996; Hansson et al., 2001; Ostry et al., 2001a, 2001b; Stewart & Stenzel, 2000; Waldenström, Josephson, Persson, & Theorell, 1998). Investigators who keep up with this literature may find there useful new measurement strategies.

The strategy of examining data by job titles or job classifications represents a minimal concession to the argument for objective measurement. It was noted earlier that occupational titles explain a fair amount of variance in some dimensions, such as physical demands and decision latitude, and relatively little in other dimensions, such as psychological demands and supervisor support (Bültmann et al., 2001; Karasek & Theorell, 1990). Such variation in strength of associations is surely informative and represents an opportunity to learn more about the meaning of our measures. It is interesting to note, for example, that a similar variation was observed in a methodological study using experienced job evaluators in a sawmill industry setting (Ostry et al., 2001b). The evaluators were able to reliably estimate the job control dimension, but for job demands the reliability was poorest of all the dimensions assessed.

The situation in which job titles explain a very small amount of variance in a particular dimension, such as job demands, raises a number of challenges: Are the job titles too crude a classification schema to pick up variations in job demands, and do we therefore need smaller units of analysis, which will more accurately reflect the actual tasks for that particular respondent? Or is it that more refined classifications will not explain more variance in job demands because these are highly subjective assessments not linked to the objective work situation? Does the meaning of high job demands differ by occupations so that analyses of it as a risk factor, such as for coronary heart disease, need to account for this in statistical model building instead of ignoring job titles altogether? Does the weak association between job titles and job demands pose problems for developing work-based interventions? Does such a weak association mean that job demands simply reflect preexisting traits such as neuroticism or affective negativity, or are they truly perceptions of the work situation, however idiosyncratic?

The last sentence is an obvious segue into the controversy over negative affectivity and what role it plays—and should play—in occupational health psychology studies. The original concern raised in the context of work stress studies (Kasl, 1978) dealt with the potential triviality of reporting cross-sectional stress–strain relationships, given the conceptual and operational overlap of measures of these "independent" and "dependent" variables. This issue eventually refocused on the role of negative affectivity (NA; Watson, Pennebaker, & Folger, 1987), a presumed individual difference variable that reflects a general tendency to experience and report negative emotions and evaluations, and distressing symptoms. The primary questions are: Does NA influence the measurement of subjective exposures and indicators of strain and distress in a way that creates a biased inflation of the observed association (whether cross-sectional or longitudinal), which then needs to be removed statistically? Or does NA have "a substantive role" as a vulnerability factor (Payne, 2000; Spector, Zapf, Chen,

& Frese, 2000), and controlling for it distorts or obscures the true etiological relationships?

A number of observations can be made regarding this debate:

- The vast majority of studies measures NA with symptom scales reflecting anxiety or neuroticism. We do not have any direct measures of NA as a dispositional tendency; we only have measures based on actual reporting of symptoms.
- The issues raised are not relevant when a study uses objective measures of exposure and biomedical outcomes. For associations between subjective work exposures and biomedical outcomes, the issue of biased inflation of associations still does not apply, but the issue of a proper interpretation of the exposure variable can be raised.
- We do have empirical evidence regarding the issue of how much difference it makes if we statistically partial out the influence of NA: (a) relatively little (Spector, Chen, & O'Connell, 2000), particularly if biomedical outcomes are involved (Bosma et al., 1997); (b) quite a bit (Burke, Brief, & George, 1993); (c) depends on what pairs of variables are involved in the adjustment (Brennan & Barnett, 1998; Chen & Spector, 1991); (d) Payne's (2000) suggestion that there is no harm in comparing results without and with statistical control for NA effects is eminently sensible, because knowing more is better than knowing less, and such additional information is fully in the spirit of carrying out sensitivity analyses. Doing it does not oblige us to choose a particular interpretation; (e) The Spector, Zapf, et al. (2000) article flows entirely from the initial hypothetical premise "if indeed NA has a substantive role," (p. 79), but empirical support for the premise is not easy to obtain. It is important to realize that the discussion of how one could investigate this premise empirically drifts inexorably toward the suggestion that one would have to do this in the context of also having objective data on work exposures. This whole topic remains an active research area (e.g., Mora, Halm, Leventhal, & Ceric, 2007), and there continue to be new theoretical developments, such as combining NA and social inhibition in a construct called "Personality D" (Denollet, 2005).

We end this section with a few comments on the need to go beyond existing, established instruments (e.g., Landsbergis & Theorell, 2000) and the need to develop additional measures as new work issues emerge. Some of the new issues that are gaining in importance are precarious employment (Benavides, Benach, Diez-Roux, & Roman, 2000), downsizing (Kivimäki, Vahtera, Pentti, & Ferrie, 2000), job insecurity (Domenighetti, D'Avanzo, & Bisig, 2000; Strazdins, D'Souza, Lim, Broom, & Rodgers, 2004), underemployment and temporary employment (Friedland & Price, 2003; Kivimäki et al., 2003), and lean production teams (Jackson & Mullarkey, 2000), and they call for additional instruments. New developments in the workplace, such as computerization, seem to demand not just assessment of new dimensions of work but may also require paying attention to the associated changes in the whole organizational structure (Burris,

1998). The accelerating change from a manufacturing economy to a service economy may put strain on our theoretical models that are more tied to the former than the latter (Marshall, Barnett, & Sayer, 1997).

Surveillance Strategies for Psychosocial Work Hazards

Medical surveillance in the workplace has been described as "the systematic collection and evaluation of employee health data to identify specific instances of illness or health trends suggesting an adverse effect of work exposures, coupled with actions to reduce hazardous workplace exposures" (Rempel, 1990, p. 435). The primary prevention strategy is based on industrial hygiene exposure assessment, and secondary prevention is based on early and rapid detection of adverse health outcomes associated with particular work settings (Rempel, 1990). The primary prevention approach presumes that one has good documentation of the health risks associated with an exposure. Secondary prevention is often linked to the strategy of sentinel health events (Rutstein et al., 1983). Such events represent a disease, or disability, or untimely death that is related to occupation, and the occurrence of which signals the need for epidemiological or hygiene studies and prevention intervention. The July–September 1990 issue of *Occupational Medicine* and the supplement to the December 1989 issue of the *American Journal of Public Health* provide useful overviews of the many issues and strategies.

Some of the literature on occupational surveillance is concerned with chemical and biological exposures (Koh & Aw, 2003), where clear-cut exposure–health outcome relations are possible and where hazard surveillance is most effective. It is also here that one can use molecular biomarkers as indicators of susceptibility. Otherwise, most surveillance strategies are based on monitoring selected adverse health outcomes that are based on research findings in traditional occupational medicine, not occupational health psychology. For example, a recent Pan American Health Organization expert panel (Choi, Eijkemans, & Tennassee, 2001) selected three sentinel events for surveillance: occupational fatal injuries, pesticide poisoning, and low back pain. In general, the successful state programs for occupational disease surveillance concentrate on conditions that have a short latency period, are easily diagnosed, and are easily linked to a workplace hazards (Henderson, Payne, Ossiander, Evans, & Kaufman, 1998). Surveillance is often based on specific existing databases, such as insurance claims for disability in a specific industry (Park, Krebs, & Miner, 1996) or hospital emergency department records for work-related inhalations (Henneberger, Metayer, Layne, & Althouse, 2000). Broader and more systematic surveillance may need outreach efforts, often under state sponsorship and funding (Davis, Wellman, & Punnett, 2001; Forst, Hryhorczuk, & Jaros, 1999; Rosenman, Reilly, & Kalinowski, 1997). Nationwide data are often based on analyses of cause-specific mortality rates by occupations (e.g., Aronson, Howe, Carpenter, & Fair, 1999) or on linkages of two or more national data sets (e.g., Leigh & Miller, 1998).

Surveillance efforts that emphasize workplace exposures are considerably less frequent, often limited to a specific industry, such as construction (Becker,

2000) and nuclear weapons facilities (Ruttenber et al., 2001). At the national level, the National Institute of Occupational Safety and Health has been the source of several hazard surveillance surveys dealing with chemical, physical, and biological agents (Boiano & Hull, 2001). Monitoring of psychosocial work exposures is quite rare (e.g., Houtman et al., 1998); however, such "monitoring" is no different from surveying workers in many occupations and industries and administering one or more of the established instruments. These data may then be used to impute exposure to other workers in those occupations who were not surveyed (Schwartz, 2000).

Although epidemiology does not usually include the putative etiological factor with the diagnostic criteria, the diagnosis of "occupational disease" in occupational medicine comes from a more clinical tradition. Such a diagnosis can be quite a complicated exercise (Cherry, 1999; Palmer & Coggon, 1996), and its use in surveillance may involve additional pragmatic but nonmedical considerations: union–company contracts, workers' compensation guidelines, insurance reimbursement, judgments of referring clinicians, and so on. The monitoring strategies noted tend to both oversimplify the diagnostic issues as well as focus on conditions (i.e., short latency, simple etiology, easy link to workplace hazard) where the diagnosis is reasonably justifiable. This is done in the service of detecting hazards that can be eliminated, not for the purposes of conducting an accurate epidemiological study of prevalence.

In trying to develop surveillance strategies for psychosocial work exposures leading to a variety of biomedical and psychological outcomes, we may not be able to borrow much from traditional occupational medicine (Kasl, 1992). It is difficult to translate surveillance strategies, developed for chemical–physical–biological exposures and for health outcomes that are relatively easily linked to work hazards, into ways of monitoring psychosocial work exposures and health outcomes with complex etiologies. Consider the strategy of sentinel health events. We might choose a rare but notable outcome such as suicide (Sauter, Murphy, & Hurrell, 1990). Presumably, we would pay attention to suicides that occur in the workplace, but this does not make it an "occupational suicide" the way an injury at work does. Suicides occurring elsewhere could still be related to work but these would be missed, and suicides at work could be due to nonwork related reasons. Because there is little evidence that suicides are sufficiently often work-related, one might end up doing a large number of psychological autopsies to detect the one that seems to have a primarily work-related etiology. Of course, nothing prevents us from linking cause-specific mortality data (i.e., suicide) to occupational titles to identify jobs with high rates, but this is no longer the sentinel health events strategy. We can also note that surveillance in occupational medicine uses a variety of sources of data to provide health outcome data: occupational health clinics, law-mandated physician reporting, registries, Occupational Safety and Health Administration 200 logs, workers' compensation data, and so on. However, none of these would be suitable for dealing with psychological outcomes or common diseases such as coronary heart disease.

Surveillance based on identifying workplace hazards runs into a different set of problems. Because some of the psychosocial work exposures, such as job demands, are poorly linked to occupations, we cannot use job titles or expert raters to identify this hazard. We are primarily looking for individuals who report high demands; this is not surveillance, this is conducting epidemiological surveys. Even for work exposures that are more closely linked to occupational titles, such as decision latitude, identifying jobs alone is a relatively poor strategy given the additional importance of psychosocial characteristics of individuals that moderate the etiological picture. Thus, the task is really to identify combinations of psychosocial work exposures and personal vulnerabilities of job occupants, rather than only exposures, which again moves us beyond the simple notion of surveillance. For many chemical, physical, and biological hazards, however, psychosocial moderators tend to be unimportant, with the possible exception of psychosocial influences on use of protective equipment and safety behaviors.

If surveillance is seen as a shortcut to identifying hazard-disease linkages that bypasses the traditional epidemiological cohort surveys that are more expensive and labor-intensive, then it would seem that occupational health psychology offers few worthwhile possibilities for such shortcuts. Mostly, we need to fall back on traditional research strategies to provide us with additional information on the impact of the psychosocial work environment on health and well-being. Fortunately, as this handbook demonstrates, the accumulated evidence is considerable and provides a sound scientific basis for identifying work dimensions that are likely to represent health hazards.

Conclusion

In this chapter, we chose the perspectives of occupational and psychosocial epidemiology to discuss and elaborate on three broad methodological topics: study designs, measurement of exposures, and surveillance strategies. The procedure we adopted was to describe the specific strategies and practices used in classical occupational (i.e., medical) epidemiology and to note what lessons we could learn from these as we try to apply them to occupational health psychology. Then, we noted limitations of applicability, discussed the reasons for these limitations, and suggested modifications and elaborations of such strategies to make them more useful for the study of psychosocial work exposures and psychological outcomes typical of occupational health psychology. In this strategy of organizing the presentation of the material, we sought to emphasize the broadly interdisciplinary approach epidemiology can provide. Our goal in this chapter was not to offer a different model of research but to enrich our thinking about how occupational health psychology can best approach the study of the health impact of the work setting.

References

Archea, J. (1977). The place of architectural factors in behavioral theories of privacy. *Journal of Social Issues, 33,* 116–137.

Aronson, K. J., Howe, G. R., Carpenter, M., & Fair, M. E. (1999). Surveillance of potential associations between occupations and causes of death in Canada, 1965–1991. *Occupational and Environmental Medicine, 56,* 265–269. doi:10.1136/oem.56.4.265

Benavides, F. G., Benach, J., Diez-Roux, A. V., & Roman, C. (2000). How do types of employment relate to health indicators? Findings from the Second European Survey of Working Conditions. *Journal of Epidemiology and Community Health, 54*, 494–501. doi:10.1136/jech.54.7.494

Benke, G., Sim, M., Fritschi, L., Aldred, G., Forbes, A., & Kaupinnen, T. (2001). Comparison of occupational exposure using three different methods: Hygiene panel, job exposure matrix (JEM), and self-reports. *Applied Occupational and Environmental Hygiene, 16*(1), 84–91. doi:10.1080/104732201456168

Boiano, J. M., & Hull, R. D. (2001). Development of a national survey and database associated with NIOSH hazard surveillance initiatives. *Applied Occupational and Environmental Hygiene, 16*, 128–134. doi:10.1080/104732201460217

Bolm-Audorff, U., & Siegrist, J. (1983). Occupational morbidity data in myocardial infarction. *Journal of Occupational Medicine, 25*, 367–371.

Bosma, H., Marmot, M. G., Hemingway, H., Nicholson, A. C., Brunner, E., & Stansfeld, S. A. (1997). Low job control and risk of coronary heart disease in Whitehall II (prospective cohort) study. *British Medical Journal, 314*, 558–565.

Bosma, H., Peter, R., Siegrist, J., & Marmot, M. (1998). Two alternative job stress models and the risk of coronary heart disease. *American Journal of Public Health, 88*, 68–74. doi:10.2105/AJPH.88.1.68

Bourbonnais, R., Comeau, M., & Vezina, M. (1999). Job strain and evolution of mental health among nurses. *Journal of Occupational Health Psychology, 4*, 95–107. doi:10.1037/1076-8998.4.2.95

Boxer, P. A., Burnett, C., & Swanson, N. (1995). Suicide and occupation: A review of the literature. *Journal of Occupational and Environmental Medicine, 37*, 442–452.

Brennan, R. T., & Barnett, R. C. (1998). Negative affectivity: How serious a threat to self-report studies of psychological distress? *Women's Health, 4*, 369–383.

Bültmann, U., Kant, I., van Amelsvoort, L. G. P. M., van den Brandt, P. A., & Kasl, S. V. (2001). Differences in fatigue and psychological distress across occupations: Results from the Maastricht Cohort Study of Fatigue at Work. *Journal of Occupational and Environmental Medicine, 43*, 976–983. doi:10.1097/00043764-200111000-00008

Burke, M. J., Brief, A. P., & George, J. M. (1993). The role of negative affectivity in understanding relations between self-reports of stressors and strains: A comment on the applied psychology literature. *Journal of Applied Psychology, 78*, 402–412. doi:10.1037/0021-9010.78.3.402

Burris, B. H. (1998). Computerization of the workplace. *Annual Review of Sociology, 24*, 141–157. doi:10.1146/annurev.soc.24.1.141

Calnan, M., Wainwright, D., Forsythe, M., Wall, B., & Almond, S. (2001). Mental health and stress in the workplace: The case of general practice in the U.K. *Social Science & Medicine, 52*, 499–507. doi:10.1016/S0277-9536(00)00155-6

Chen, P. Y., & Spector, P. E. (1991). Negative affectivity as the underlying cause of correlations between stressors and strains. *Journal of Applied Psychology, 76*, 398–407. doi:10.1037/0021-9010.76.3.398

Cheng, Y., Kawachi, I., Coakley, E. H., Schwartz, J., & Colditz, G. (2000). Association between psychosocial work characteristics and health functioning in American women: Prospective study. *British Medical Journal, 320*, 1432–1436. doi:10.1136/bmj.320.7247.1432

Cherry, N. (1999). Occupational disease. *British Medical Journal, 318*, 1397–1399.

Choi, B. C. K., Eijkemans, G. J. M., & Tennassee, L. M. (2001). Prioritization of occupational sentinel health and hazard surveillance: The Pan American Health Organization experience. *Journal of Occupational and Environmental Medicine, 43*, 147–157. doi:10.1097/00043764-200102000-00014

Creech, J. L., & Johnson, M. N. (1974). Angiosarcoma of liver in the manufacturing of polyvinylchloride. *Journal of Occupational Medicine, 16*, 150–151.

Davis, L., Wellman, H., & Punnett, L. (2001). Surveillance of work-related carpal tunnel syndrome in Massachusetts, 1992–1997. A report from the Massachusetts Sentinel Event Notification System for Occupational Risk (SENSOR). *American Journal of Industrial Medicine, 39*, 58–71. doi:10.1002/1097-0274(200101)39:1<58::AID-AJIM6>3.0.CO;2-3

Denollet, J. (2005). DS14: Standard assessment of negative affectivity, social inhibition, and Type D personality. *Psychosomatic Medicine, 67*, 89–97. doi:10.1097/01.psy.0000149256.81953.49

Devereux, J. J., Buckle, P. W., & Vlachonikolis, I. G. (1999). Interactions between physical and psychosocial risk factors at work increase the risk of back disorders: An epidemiological approach. *Occupational and Environmental Medicine, 56*, 343–353. doi:10.1136/oem.56.5.343

Domenighetti, G., D'Avanzo, B., & Bisig, B. (2000). Health effects of job insecurity among employees in the Swiss general population. *International Journal of Health Services, 30,* 477–490. doi:10.2190/B1KM-VGN7-50GF-8XJ4

Eaton, W. W., Anthony, J. C., Mandel, W., & Garrison, R. (1990). Occupations and the prevalence of major depression disorder. *Journal of Occupational Medicine, 32,* 1079–1087. doi:10.1097/00043764-199011000-00006

Ferrie, J. E., Shipley, M. J., Marmot, M. G., Stansfeld, S., & Smith, G. D. (1995). Health effects of anticipation of job change and nonemployment: Longitudinal data from Whitehall II study. *British Medical Journal, 311,* 1264–1269.

Ferrie, J. E., Shipley, M. J., Stansfeld, S. A., Smith, G. D., & Marmot, M. (2003). Future uncertainty and socioeconomic inequalities in health: The Whitehall II Study. *Social Science & Medicine, 57,* 637–646. doi:10.1016/S0277-9536(02)00406-9

Fletcher, B. (1991). *Work, stress, disease, and life expectancy.* Chichester, England: Wiley.

Forst, L. S., Hryhorczuk, D., & Jaros, M. (1999). A state trauma registry as a tool for occupational injury surveillance. *Journal of Occupational and Environmental Medicine, 41,* 514–520. doi:10.1097/00043764-199906000-00019

Frese, M., & Zapf, D. (1999). On the importance of the objective environment in stress and attribution theory. Counterpoint to Perrewé and Zellars. *Journal of Organizational Behavior, 20,* 761–765. doi:10.1002/(SICI)1099-1379(199909)20:5<761::AID-JOB951>3.0.CO;2-Y

Friedland, D. S., & Price, R. H. (2003). Underemployment: Consequences for the health and well-being of workers. *American Journal of Community Psychology, 32,* 33–45. doi:10.1023/A:1025638705649

Fritschi, L., Siemiatycki, J., & Richardson, L. (1996). Self-assessed versus expert-assessed occupational exposures. *American Journal of Epidemiology, 144,* 521–527.

Greiner, B. A., Ragland, D. R., Krause, N., Syme, S. L., & Fisher, J. M. (1997). Objective measurement of occupational stress factors—An example with San Francisco urban transit operators. *Journal of Occupational Health Psychology, 2,* 325–342. doi:10.1037/1076-8998.2.4.325

Gustavsson, P., Alfredsson, L., Brunnberg, H., Hammar, N., Jakobsson, R., Reutenvall, C., & Ostlin, P. (1996). Myocardial infarction among male bus, taxi, and lorry drivers in middle Sweden. *Occupational and Environmental Medicine, 53,* 235–240. doi:10.1136/oem.53.4.235

Hacker, W. (1993). Objective work environment: Analysis and evaluation of objective work characteristics. In L. Levi & F. LaFerla, *A healthier work environment: Basic concepts and methods of measurement* (pp. 42–57). Copenhagen, Denmark: World Health Organization Regional Office for Europe.

Hammar, N., Alfredsson, L., & Johnson, J. V. (1998). Job strain, social support at work, and incidence of myocardial infarction. *Occupational and Environmental Medicine, 55,* 548–553. doi:10.1136/oem.55.8.548

Hansson, G. A., Balogh, I., Bystrom, J. U., Ohlsson, K., Nordander, C., Asterland, P., . . . Skerfving, S. (2001). Questionnaire versus direct technical measurements in assessing postures and movements of the head, upper back, arms, and hands. *Scandinavian Journal of Work, Environment, & Health, 27,* 30–40.

Henderson, A. K., Payne, M. M., Ossiander, E., Evans, C. G., & Kaufman, J. D. (1998). Surveillance of occupational diseases in the United States. *Journal of Occupational and Environmental Medicine, 40,* 714–719. doi:10.1097/00043764-199808000-00009

Henneberger, P. K., Metayer, C., Layne, L. A., & Althouse, R. (2000). Nonfatal work-related inhalations: Surveillance data from hospital emergency departments, 1995–1996. *American Journal of Industrial Medicine, 38,* 140–148. doi:10.1002/1097-0274(200008)38:2<140::AID-AJIM4>3.0.CO;2-L

Houtman, I. L. D., Goudswaard, A., Dhondt, S., van den Grinten, M. P., Hildebrandt, V. H., & van der Poel, E. G. T. (1998). Dutch monitor on stress and physical load risk factors, consequences, and preventive action. *Occupational and Environmental Medicine, 55,* 73–83. doi:10.1136/oem.55.2.73

Hurrell, J. J., Jr., Nelson, D. L., & Simmons, B. L. (1998). Measuring job stressors and strains: Where we have been, where we are, and where we need to go. *Journal of Occupational Health Psychology, 3,* 368–389. doi:10.1037/1076-8998.3.4.368

Jackson, P. R., & Mullarkey, S. (2000). Lean production teams and health in garment manufacture. *Journal of Occupational Health Psychology, 5,* 231–245.

James, G. D., & Bovbjerg, D. H. (2001). Age and perceived stress independently influence daily blood pressure levels and variation among women employed in wage jobs. *American Journal of Human Biology, 13,* 268–274. doi:10.1002/1520-6300(200102/03)13:2<268::AID-AJHB1038>3.0.CO;2-Z

Karasek, R., & Theorell, T. (1990). *Healthy work.* New York, NY: Basic Books.

Kasl, S. V. (1978). Epidemiological contributions to the study of work stress. In C. L. Cooper & R. L. Payne (Eds.), *Stress at work* (pp. 3–38). Chichester, England: Wiley.

Kasl, S. V. (1987). Methodologies in stress and health: Past difficulties, present dilemmas, future directions. In S. V. Kasl & C. L. Cooper (Eds.), *Stress and health: Issues in research methodology* (pp. 307–318). Chichester, England: Wiley.

Kasl, S. V. (1991). Assessing health risks in the work setting. In H. E. Schroeder (Ed.), *New directions in health psychology assessment* (pp. 95–125). New York, NY: Hemisphere.

Kasl, S. V. (1992). Surveillance of psychological disorders in the workplace. In G. P. Keita & S. L. Sauter (Eds.), *Work and well-being: An agenda for the 1990s* (pp. 73–95). Washington, DC: American Psychological Association. doi:10.1037/10108-004

Kasl, S. V. (1998). Measuring job stressors and studying the health impact of the work environment: An epidemiologic commentary. *Journal of Occupational Health Psychology, 3,* 390–401. doi:10.1037/1076-8998.3.4.390

Kasl, S. V., & Amick, B. C. (1995). The impact of work stress on health and well-being. In J. C. McDonald (Ed.), *The epidemiology of work related diseases* (pp. 239–266). London, England: BMJ Press.

Kasl, S. V., & Jones, B. A. (2001). Some methodological considerations in the study of psychosocial influences on health. In A. Vingerhoets (Ed.), *Advances in behavioral medicine* (pp. 25–48). London, England: Harwood Academic.

Kirkcaldy, B. D., & Martin, T. (2000). Job stress and satisfaction among nurses. *Stress Medicine, 16,* 77–89. doi:10.1002/(SICI)1099-1700(200003)16:2<77::AID-SMI835>3.0.CO;2-Z

Kittel, F., Kornitzer, M., & Dramaix, M. (1980). Coronary heart disease and job stress in two cohorts of bank clerks. *Psychotherapy and Psychosomatics, 34,* 110–123.

Kivimäki, M., Vahtera, J., Pentti, J., & Ferrie, J. E. (2000). Factors underlying the effect of organizational downsizing on health of employees: Longitudinal cohort study. *British Medical Journal, 320,* 971–975. doi:10.1136/bmj.320.7240.971

Kivimäki, M., Vahtera, J., Virtanen, M., Elovainio, M., Pentti, J., & Ferrie, J. (2003). Temporary employment and risk of overall and cause-specific mortality. *American Journal of Epidemiology, 158,* 663–668. doi:10.1093/aje/kwg185

Kivimäki, M., Virtanen, M., Elovainio, M., Kouvonen, A., Vaananen, A., & Vahtera, J. (2006). Work stress in the etiology of coronary heart disease–A meta-analysis. *Scandinavian Journal of Work Environment and Health, 32*(6), 431–442.

Koh, D., & Aw, T.-C. (2003). Surveillance in occupational health. *Occupational and Environmental Medicine, 60,* 705–710. doi:10.1136/oem.60.9.705

Kuper, H., & Marmot, M. (2003). Job strain, job demands, decision latitude, and risk of coronary heart disease within the Whitehall II study. *Journal of Epidemiology and Community Health, 57,* 147–153. doi:10.1136/jech.57.2.147

Landsbergis, P., & Theorell, T. (2000). Measurement of psychosocial workplace exposure variables. *Occupational Medicine, 15*(1), 163–188.

Lazarus, R. S. (1966). *Psychological stress and the coping process.* New York, NY: McGraw-Hill.

Lee, D. J., Niemcryk, S. J., Jenkins, C. D., & Rose, R. M. (1989). Type A, amicability, and injury: A prospective study of air controllers. *Journal of Psychosomatic Research, 33,* 177–186. doi:10.1016/0022-3999(89)90045-7

Leigh, J. P., & Miller, T. R. (1998). Occupational illnesses within two national data sets. *International Journal of Occupational & Environmental Health, 4,* 99–113.

Luecken, L. J., Suarez, E. C., Kuhn, C., Barefoot, J. C., Blumenthal, J. A., Siegler, J. C., & Williams, R. B. (1997). Stress in employed women: Impact of marital status and children at home on neurohormone output and home strain. *Psychosomatic Medicine, 59,* 352–359.

Macfarlane, G. J., Hunt, I. M., & Silman, A. J. (2000). Role of mechanical and psychosocial factors in the onset of forearm pain: Prospective population based study. *British Medical Journal, 321,* 676–679. doi:10.1136/bmj.321.7262.676

Marshall, N. L., Barnett, R. C., & Sayer, A. (1997). The changing workforce, job stress, and psychological distress. *Journal of Occupational Health Psychology, 2,* 99–107. doi:10.1037/1076-8998.2.2.99

McKernan, J. (2000). Development of a hazard surveillance methodology for residential construction. *Applied Occupational and Environmental Hygiene, 15,* 890–895. doi:10.1080/104732200750051094

McMichael, A. J. (1994). Invited commentary—"Molecular epidemiology": New pathway or new traveling companion. *American Journal of Epidemiology, 140,* 1–11.

Mora, P. A., Halm, E., Leventhal, H., & Ceric, F. (2007). Elucidating the relationship between negative affectivity and symptoms. *Annals of Behavioral Medicine, 34,* 77–86. doi:10.1007/BF02879923

Morris, J. R., & Cook, C. G. (1991). A critical review of the effect of factory closures on health. *British Journal of Industrial Medicine, 56,* 557–563.

Netterstrom, B., & Juel, K. (1988). Impact of work-related and psychosocial factors on the development of ischemic heart disease among urban bus drivers in Denmark. *Scandinavian Journal of Work, Environment, & Health, 14,* 231–238.

Niedhammer, I., Goldberg, M., Leclerc, A., Bugel, I., & David, S. (1998). Psychosocial factors at work and subsequent depressive symptoms in the Gazel cohort. *Scandinavian Journal of Work, Environment, & Health, 24,* 197–205.

Ostfeld, A. M., Kasl, S. V., D'Atri, D. A., & Fitzgerald, E. F. (1987). *Stress, crowding, and blood pressure in prison.* Hillsdale, NJ: Erlbaum.

Ostry, A. S., Marion, S. A., Demers, P. A., Hershler, R., Kelly, S., Teschke, K., . . . Hertzman, C. (2001a). Comparison of expert-rater methods for assessing psychosocial job strain. *Scandinavian Journal of Work, Environment, & Health, 27,* 70–75.

Ostry, A. S., Marion, S. A., Demers, P. A., Hershler, R., Kelly, S., Teschke, K., & Hertzman, C. (2001b). Measuring psychosocial job strain with the Job Content Questionnaire using experienced job evaluators. *American Journal of Industrial Medicine, 39,* 397–401. doi:10.1002/ajim.1030

Palmer, K., & Coggon, D. (1996). ABC of work related disorders: Investigating suspected occupational illness and evaluating the workplace. *British Medical Journal, 313,* 809–811.

Park, R. M., Krebs, J. M., & Miner, F. E. (1996). Occupational disease surveillance using disability insurance at an automotive stamping and assembly complex. *Journal of Occupational and Environmental Medicine, 38,* 1111–1123. doi:10.1097/00043764-199611000-00011

Payne, R. L. (2000). Comments on "Why negative affectivity should not be controlled in job stress research: Don't throw out the baby with the bath water." *Journal of Organizational Behavior, 21,* 97–99. doi:10.1002/(SICI)1099-1379(200002)21:1<97::AID-JOB965>3.0.CO;2-H

Perrewé, P. L., & Zellars, K. L. (1999). An examination of attributions and emotions in the transactional approach t o the organizational stress process. *Journal of Organizational Behavior, 20,* 739–752. doi:10.1002/(SICI)1099-1379(199909)20:5<739::AID-JOB1949>3.0.CO;2-C

Peter, R., Geibler, H., & Siegrist, J. (1998). Associations of effort–reward imbalance at work and reported symptoms in different groups of male and female public transport workers. *Stress Medicine, 14,* 175–182. doi:10.1002/(SICI)1099-1700(199807)14:3<175::AID-SMI775>3.0.CO;2-4

Piros, S., Karlehagen, S., Lappas, G., & Wilhelmsen, L. (2000). Psychosocial risk factors for myocardial infarction among Swedish railway engine drivers during 10 years follow-up. *Journal of Cardiovascular Risk, 7,* 389–394.

Rempel, D. (1990). Medical surveillance in the workplace: Overview. *Occupational Medicine, 5*(3), 435–438.

Rosenman, K. D., Reilly, M. J., & Kalinowski, D. J. (1997). A state-based surveillance system for work-related asthma. *Journal of Occupational and Environmental Medicine, 39,* 415–425. doi:10.1097/00043764-199705000-00007

Rutstein, D. D., Mullan, R. J., Frazier, T. M., Halperin, W. E., Melius, J. M., & Sestito, J. P. (1983). Sentinel health events (occupational): A basis for physician recognition and public health surveillance. *American Journal of Public Health, 73,* 1054–1062. doi:10.2105/AJPH.73.9.1054

Ruttenber, A. J., McCrea, J. S., Wade, T. D., Schonbeck, M. F., Lamontagne, A. D., VanDyke, M. V., & Martyny, J. W. (2001). Integrating workplace exposure database for occupational medicine services and epidemiologic studies at a former nuclear weapons facility. *Applied Occupational and Environmental Hygiene, 16,* 192–200. doi:10.1080/104732201460334

Saks, A. M., & Ashforth, B. E. (2000). The role of dispositions, entry stressors, and behavioral plasticity in predicting newcomers' adjustment to work. *Journal of Organizational Behavior, 21,* 43–62. doi:10.1002/(SICI)1099-1379(200002)21:1<43::AID-JOB985>3.0.CO;2-W

Sauter, S. L., Murphy, L. R., & Hurrell, J. J., Jr. (1990). Prevention of work-related psychological disorders. *American Psychologist, 45,* 1146–1158.

Schnall, P. L., Belkic, K., Landsbergis, P., & Baker, D. (Eds.). (2000). The workplace and cardio-vascular disease. *Occupational Medicine, 15*(1).

Schwartz, J. (2000). Imputation of job characteristics scores. *Occupational Medicine, 15*(1), 172–175.

Siegrist, J., Starke, D., Chandola, T., Godin, I., Marmot, M., Niedhammer, I., & Peter, R. (2004). The measurement of effort–reward imbalance at work: European comparisons. *Social Science & Medicine, 58,* 1483–1499. doi:10.1016/S0277-9536(03)00351-4

Sluiter, J. K., Frings-Dresen, M. H. W., Meijman, T. F., & van der Beek, A. J. (2000). Reactivity and recovery from different types of work measured by catecholamines and cortisol: A systematic literature overview. *Occupational, & Environmental Medicine, 57,* 298–315. doi:10.1136/oem.57.5.298

Smedley, J., Egger, P., Cooper, C., & Coggon, D. (1997). Prospective cohort study of predictors of incident low back pain in nurses. *British Medical Journal, 314,* 1225–1228.

Smith, M. J., Conway, F. T., & Karsh, B.-T. (1999). Occupational stress in human computer inter-action. *Industrial Health, 37,* 157–173. doi:10.2486/indhealth.37.157

Spector, P. E., Chen, P. Y., & O'Connell, B. J. (2000). A longitudinal study of relations between job stressors and job strains while controlling for prior negative affectivity and strains. *Journal of Applied Psychology, 85,* 211–218. doi:10.1037/0021-9010.85.2.211

Spector, P. E., Zapf, D., Chen, P. Y., & Frese, M. (2000). Why negative affectivity should not be con-trolled in job stress research: Don't throw out the baby with the bath water. *Journal of Organizational Behavior, 21,* 79–95. doi:10.1002/(SICI)1099-1379(200002)21:1<79::AID-JOB964>3.0.CO;2-G

Steenland, K., Johnson, J., & Nowlin, S. (1997). A follow-up study of job strain and heart disease among males in the NHANESl population. *American Journal of Industrial Medicine, 31,* 256–259. doi:10.1002/(SICI)1097-0274(199702)31:2<256::AID-AJIM16>3.0.CO;2-0

Steptoe, A., Lundwall, K., & Cropley, M. (2000). Gender, family structure, and cardiovascular activity during working day and evening. *Social Science & Medicine, 50,* 531–539.

Stewart, P., & Stenzel, M. (2000). Exposure assessment in the occupational setting. *Applied Occupational and Environmental Hygiene, 15,* 435–444. doi:10.1080/104732200301395

Strazdins, L., D'Souza, R. M., Lim, L. L.-Y., Broom, D. H., & Rodgers, B. (2004). Job strain, job inse-curity, and health: Rethinking the relationship. *Journal of Occupational Health Psychology, 9,* 296–305. doi:10.1037/1076-8998.9.4.296

Taris, T. W., & Kompier, M. (2003). Challenges in longitudinal designs in occupational health psy-chology. *Scandinavian Journal of Work, Environment, & Health, 29,* 1–4.

Taylor, R. B. (1980). Conceptual dimensions of crowding reconsidered. *Population and Environment, 3,* 298–308. doi:10.1007/BF01255344

Vagg, P. R., & Spielberger, C. D. (1998). Occupational stress: Measuring job pressure and organi-zational support in the workplace. *Journal of Occupational Health Psychology, 3,* 294–305. doi:10.1037/1076-8998.3.4.294

Waldenström, M., Josephson, M., Persson, C., & Theorell, T. (1998). Interview reliability for assessing mental work demands. *Journal of Occupational Health Psychology, 3,* 209–216. doi:10.1037/1076-8998.3.3.209

Watson, D., Pennebaker, J. W., & Folger, R. (1987). Beyond negative activity: Measuring stress and satisfaction in the workplace. In J. M. Ivancevich & D. C. Ganster (Eds.), *Job stress: From theory to suggestion* (pp. 141–157). New York, NY: Haworth Press.

Williams, S., & Cooper, C. L. (1998). Measuring occupational stress. The development of the Pressure Management Indicator. *Journal of Occupational Health Psychology, 3,* 306–321. doi:10.1037/1076-8998.3.4.306

Williams, S., Dale, J., Glucksman, E., & Wellesley, A. (1997). Senior house officers work related stressors, psychological distress, and confidence in performing clinical tasks in accident and emergency: A questionnaire study. *British Medical Journal, 314,* 713–718.

Winkleby, M. A., Ragland, O. R., Fisher, J. M., & Syme, S. L. (1988). Excess risk of sickness and disease in bus drivers: A review and synthesis of epidemiologic studies. *International Journal of Epidemiology, 17,* 255–262. doi:10.1093/ije/17.2.255

Wohlwill, J. F. (1973). The environment is not in the head. In W. F. E. Preiser (Ed.), *Environmental design research: Vol. 2. Symposia and workshops* (pp. 166–181). Stroudsburg, PA: Dowden, Hutchinson & Ross.

21

Program Evaluation: The Bottom Line in Organizational Health

Joyce A. Adkins, Susan Douglas Kelley,
Leonard Bickman, and Howard M. Weiss

The practice of occupational health psychology (OHP) is flourishing. The acceptance and growth of OHP has been founded on documented need and value. In a highly competitive global market, organizations have become increasingly attuned to the need for evidence-based decision making. Resources are targeted to strategies and actions that contribute to business plans for cost containment, improved productivity, and risk abatement and control. As a result, OHP practitioners must ensure that their practices prove their value in addressing the needs and context of their organizational clients while also maintaining solid roots in a scientific and ethical foundation. Challenges in program evaluation and in evaluation research arise out of the inherently applied nature of the activity. The dynamic context and numerous uncontrolled variables in an occupational environment create challenges to effective measurement of organizational health interventions, whether those interventions come as policies, practices, or programs.

Often, little time and few dedicated resources are available to conduct thorough literature reviews, carefully time and control program implementation, obtain a valid and reliable control group or randomize participants to selected exposures, and confront ethical concerns of withholding program availability from any individual or group of employees. Even if the work environment could be carefully controlled, the influence of individual differences and nonwork-life spillover into the worklife domain makes it difficult to draw firm conclusions about ultimate program outcomes (Mauno, Kinnunen, & Ruokolainen, 2006). When confronted with these complex issues, practitioners may be tempted to avoid the situation by neglecting to design or implement an evaluation plan. Others may choose to restrict the value of evaluations by focusing on more easily obtained data such as program activity levels, utilization rates, or customer satisfaction ratings compared with implementation costs. In using any of these strategies, they sacrifice the opportunity to actively demonstrate the effectiveness of their work and to make a valuable contribution to science. Despite the obstacles, thorough and effective program evaluation strategies are vital to the sustained acceptance of OHP in the workplace and to its growth as a professional discipline.

This chapter addresses the design and implementation of program evaluation strategies in an occupational health environment. Basic strategies and techniques of evaluation design and implementation will be discussed first, followed by a consideration of value, utility, and ethics associated with the use of program evaluation products.

Program Evaluation Facts and Myths

This section focuses on distinguishing facts from myths about program evaluation. Decisions related to the cost, rigor, and feasibility of an evaluation should be influenced by clear understanding of the scope and purpose of the evaluation, involvement of key stakeholders, and acknowledgement of contextual considerations. Careful consideration of these issues is necessary prior to determining the type of evaluation design and the development of a clearly defined program theory.

Facts

Program evaluation involves the use of scientific methods to collect and analyze information about a policy or program with the intent of coming to a determination about its relevance, progress, efficiency, effectiveness, and outcomes or impact. The strategies and procedures used in program evaluation are generally borrowed from the social, behavioral, and managerial sciences, and the utility of evaluation is central to the managerial process (Veney & Kaluzny, 1998), making evaluation a natural fit for OHP.

The form and scope of an evaluation depend on its purpose or the questions being asked about a program or policy, the interests of the relevant stakeholders, and the context in which the evaluation is being conducted (Rossi, Lipsey, & Freeman, 2007). An evaluation's purpose may be internally derived to provide valuable information for a program and an organization, externally derived from the upper layer of management within the same organization or from external funding sources, or some combination. The group of stakeholders, including individual consumers or decision makers and groups with collective interests, may have both shared and competing interests that must be negotiated to determine the questions to be asked and the methods to answer them. The organizational and political context in which the evaluation occurs must be explicitly acknowledged to enhance the actual use of evaluation findings.

Myths

Three myths or beliefs about evaluation should be critically examined before proceeding further. The first deals with the cost of an evaluation. In practice, some organizations have budgeted evaluation costs by assessing a fixed percentage of the total cost of the program. However, following this approach, the most expensive programs would get the most evaluation resources when in fact it may be more important to invest more resources in programs that are the least expensive and therefore more likely to be adopted. Cost of the evaluation should be associated with the type of questions being addressed, the certainty associated with the results, and the degree and experience required of the evaluation team. Thus, complex questions, better evaluation designs (e.g., inclusion of a control group or multiple measures), and more experienced evaluators are usually more costly.

Second, there is often resistance to using the most rigorous evaluation design, which is the true experiment or randomized clinical trial. Although this design is discussed later in this chapter, it is important to note that there have been thousands of successful randomized experimental design evaluations (Bickman & Reich, 2009). It is good to start planning using the strongest and most rigorous design feasible because designs tend to degrade when put in place in the real work environment.

A third mistaken belief is that one can simply accept what people in the organization or program tell one about the feasibility of conducting the evaluation. Good planning includes checking out the facts oneself and not depending on estimates of others. One of the biggest problems evaluations typically encounter is a shortfall in the number of participants who are projected to participate in the evaluation. Having a sufficient number of participants in the evaluation is a critical component to statistical power, giving the evaluation team the ability to detect an effect if one is really present. Overestimates of participants may occur because program personnel overestimate for many reasons the number of clients they will serve; these reasons include to obtain funding, to show the potential need for the program, or because of optimism about the program's popularity. In addition, the evaluator may overestimate the number of participants who will volunteer, or he or she may not include exclusionary rules (e.g., only one member of a family can participate) in estimating the number of persons or organizational units that will participate in the evaluation.

Types of Program Evaluation

Program evaluation is a multidimensional process that can legitimately focus on different facets of program design and implementation. Prior to beginning an evaluation, an *evaluability assessment* can help determine whether a meaningful evaluation is possible. This is done by assessing the clarity and plausibility of program goals, the agreement on criteria or standards to judge performance, the availability of relevant data that can be feasibly collected, and the agreement among stakeholders about how evaluation results will be used (Thurston, Graham, & Hatfield, 2003; Trevisan & Yi, 2003; Wholey, 2004). An outcome of an evaluability assessment could be the identification before the evaluation begins of needed program modifications due to an ill defined target population, poor program delivery, or other potential flaws in the program's design.

A *needs assessment,* also referred to as *design evaluation,* asks questions related to the relevance of the program as determined by the nature and extent of the problem to be addressed. As such, this program evaluation function focuses on defining the problem, the target population, and how the program fits into the overall organizational strategy. Other relevant needs assessment issues include an examination of alternative approaches to solving the problem and in fact whether the problem should be solved at all and if so how much attention and how many resources should be allocated to solving it (Veney & Kaluzny, 1998).

There are two main types of traditional program evaluation: formative, or process, and summative, or outcome, evaluations. *Formative evaluations* examine the program implementation process. Such evaluations serve to monitor and correct problems and are conducted during ongoing program operations. Collection of these data can assist in fine-tuning program operations and ensuring that processes continue on target. *Summative evaluations* determine whether the program or policy had the desired impact or outcomes. A good evaluation will look at outcomes that were planned as well as those that were unintended. Planned outcomes are typically the objectives of the program. Outcomes are usually differentiated from impact. Outcome factors include those variables that are proximal to the program, whereas impacts usually mean more distant outcomes. For example, an outcome of a drug treatment program may be the reduction of drug use for those who complete the program, whereas a reduction in burglaries may be considered an impact. Costs and cost–benefits are also important targets of program evaluations.

Needs assessments generally accompany program planning; formative or process-oriented evaluations provide feedback for management of program implementation; and summative, or impact-oriented, evaluations examine the final outcomes of the program or policy. Although many program evaluators attempt to categorize techniques and strategies into one part of the evaluation or program life cycle, in practice the boundaries tend to blur. Each provides important information and warrants consideration in an overall evaluation strategy. Program evaluation strategies provide valuable decision-making data to answer the when, who, what, how, and—importantly—why questions of program success or failure. Indeed, prioritizing program evaluation and measurement of relevant health and work outcomes has been associated with promising health and productivity management efforts (Goetzel et al., 2007).

Role of Program Theory

The need for a clearly defined program theory is well established in evaluation and provides the foundation necessary to formulate the questions, design the evaluation, and interpret the results (Bickman, 1987; Chen & Rossi, 1983; Wholey, 1979). *Program theory* refers to a plausible, sensible, or logical conceptualization of how a program is expected or presumed to work (Bickman, 1987). It is different from, but clearly relies on, the scientific theory, orientation, or perspective of the practitioner. When fully developed and articulated, the program theory allows for increased certainty that the results of the evaluation accurately represent the program. A clearly specified theory or model also allows for either program replication or adjustment of the conditions to achieve a different result. This is opposed to black box evaluations that examine only the inputs and outputs of a program, without a clear understanding of how the program works. Identifying or constructing program linkages moves the evaluation "inside the box" and generally falls within the scope of program theory.

Unfortunately, many evaluations lack a clear theoretical and conceptual underpinning (Aust & Ducki, 2004; Donaldson, 1997). The assumptions underlying the work often remain implicit and unspecified, providing little in the way of explanation and rendering data amassed less meaningful. Limitations arising from evaluation methodology are often cited as critical factors associated with the lack of demonstrated long-term effectiveness of OHP interventions, although it is certainly acknowledged that field-based research is challenging (Heaney, 2003). For example, although organizational context is an essential component of organizational health, it is not adequately addressed in most health promotion program evaluations (Poland, Frohlich, & Cargo, 2009). Yet program planners and evaluators who clearly identify, fully develop, and explicitly describe their guiding theory produce evaluation strategies that yield more satisfying and useful results.

An established strategy to graphically represent an underlying program theory is the logic model. *Logic models* vary but generally include standard elements such as program inputs (e.g., financial costs and personnel time incurred in program implementation), specific program activities, mediating variables or processes that may influence how the program works, and program outputs ranging from proximate to distal outcomes. As depicted in Figure 21.1, inputs and outputs constitute only the beginning of the process in evaluating OHP programs. These variables are then linked to expected program outcomes and ultimately to desired or targeted organizational goals or outcomes.

To effectively develop a logic model, the links associated with inputs, outputs, outcomes, and the expected role of extraneous or contextual variables are determined by the assumptions associated with the theoretical model of the practitioner or evaluator (Bickman, 1987). Involvement of the program stakeholders is key to developing a high quality logic model to uncover unstated assumptions, clarify potential relationships among variables, and importantly, build consensus and collaboration in the overall evaluation process (Adler, 2002; Kaplan & Garrett, 2005). Both qualitative (e.g., case studies, observations, semistructured interviews) and quantitative (e.g., surveys) methods are recommended as systematic approaches to elucidating stakeholder views, with the actual development of the logic model as an iterative process of correction and enhancement (den Heyer, 2002; Frechtling, 2007; Goldman & Schmalz, 2006; Gugiu & Rodriguez-Campos, 2007; Kellogg Foundation, 2004; Porteous, Sheldrick, & Stewart, 2002; Unrau, 2001).

Because programs and practices are not implemented in a vacuum, mediating, moderating, or competing variables can exert a substantial influence. Organizational intervention programs that are multifaceted rather than focused on a single, isolated process have been found to be more effective in meeting organizational objectives (Florin et al., 2006; Schurman & Israel, 1995). Florin and colleagues (2006) provided a comprehensive logic model of multiple community-based interventions for tobacco cessation, with each program intended to meet specific objectives as well as to work together to increase systemic change. Evaluation strategies, therefore, often look at the combined effect of multiple programs and tease out individual program effects whenever practical through clear designs, specific measures, and strategic data analysis.

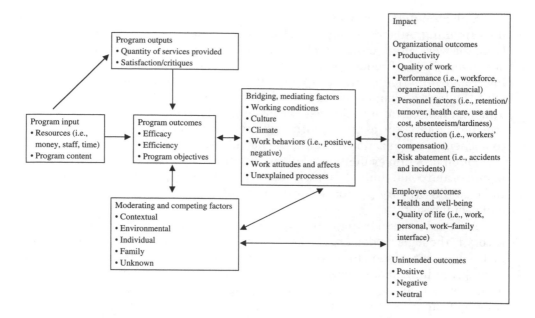

Figure 21.1.   Program evaluation process elements. Arrows represent processes, links, or assumptions, either implicit or explicit, known or hypothesized, consistent with a program theory or logic model. From "Program Evaluation: The Bottom Line in Organizational Health," by J. A. Adkins and H. M. Weiss, 2003. In J. C. Quick and L. E. Tetrick (Eds.), *Handbook of Occupational Health Psychology* (p. 402), Washington, DC; American Psychological Association. Copyright 2003 by the American Psychological Association.

Steps in Implementing an Organizational Health Evaluation Strategy

Evaluation measures provide a means of documenting the initial need, ongoing implementation, and subsequent impact of implementation of new programs as well as changes in existing practices, policies, or procedures. As so aptly stated by Light and colleagues (Light, Singer, & Willet, 1990, p. viii), analysis cannot fix what design bungles. Planning for the evaluation and the program should occur simultaneously. Evaluation plans are rarely taken directly from a standard manual or blueprint and must be individualized for the program and the stakeholders' needs. Although reviews of previous evaluations on similar programs can be of assistance, the specific programs, stakeholders, and the overall environment or context often have unique features that must be reflected in the evaluation plan. As noted earlier, correctly estimating the number of participants in the evaluation is critical to the successful implementation of an evaluation. Without verifiable numbers, estimates may be significantly discrepant, endangering the success of the study. Furthermore, inclusion of program evaluation at the outset of a program or policy can contribute to organizational learning. Therefore, evaluation strategies are most effective when designed in advance as an integral part of the initial program design and through a continuous quality improvement cycle informing development, implementation, and effectiveness (Goldenhar, Lamontagne, Katz, Heaney, & Landsbergis, 2001).

Clarify the Question, Problem, or Issue

To begin any data collection, a clear purpose, target, or question is fundamental. Increased ambiguity in the beginning will only lead to vague results. An initial design or needs assessment can provide relevant information that would lead to the development of an evaluation plan during program development. In an ideal world, an evaluation component would be a natural part of all programs, and we advocate an increase in program-generated evaluations. However, the world is not always ideal and externally conducted, after-the-fact evaluations are frequently encountered. In such cases, the evaluator will likely need to assist in clarifying the evaluation question and operationalizing constructs to develop meaningful measures and evaluation strategies.

Consultation with program staff and other stakeholders can assist in developing a shared understanding of the essential elements of the program, generally improving the evaluation results (Bickman, 1987). By allowing input from and educating stakeholders about potential uses of the information, the evaluator is afforded the opportunity to identify obstacles, build consensus, and engender ownership of the evaluation and subsequent results (Patton, 2008; Rossi et al., 2007). In utilization-focused evaluation, Patton (2008) described a process for collaborating with key stakeholders to determine the evaluation focus, strategies and methods, program theory, and intended use of findings. He promoted the role of evaluator as a facilitator of the process who looks to actively involve stakeholders in all aspects of evaluation, balancing the credibility and potential use of evaluation results with adherence to professional standards and principles (e.g., Farrington, 2003). Although developing a cooperative working relationship with relevant stakeholders assists in understanding the program objectives and implementation process, external evaluators are best served by going beyond the objectives of the program staff to look for both positive and negative effects that might not be expected by either the designers or implementers, so that an effective and comprehensive program theory can be identified and developed (Bickman, 1987).

Conceptualize the Program Theory

Each discipline approaches a situation differently and will likely explain the outcomes and assumptions based on their own worldview. OHP, as an interdisciplinary field, draws measures and methods from multiple fields. Each component discipline, whether psychology, public health, organizational behavior, or preventive health holds a different piece of the strategic puzzle. Efforts have emerged to integrate the pieces into a single picture (Macik-Frey, Quick, & Nelson, 2007; Murphy & Cooper, 2000). However, many of the underlying foundations still lie with each puzzle piece. It is up to the practitioner to collect the puzzle pieces and fit them together in a way that makes sense to the organization or evaluation and is in line with the program logic model. Use of multidisciplinary teams or committees can assist in reducing potential for disciplinary partisanship in both program development and evaluation (Quick, Quick, Nelson, & Hurrell, 1997). Many valid approaches and models can be used as the basis for an evaluation. The key is clarifying and documenting the theory and its assumptions so the results of the evaluation can be clearly understood. Only those assumptions that can be subjected to assessment will assist in program replication or correction.

In addition to attending to program theory in evaluation, monitoring of program implementation is essential. Nielsen, Fredslund, Christensen, and Albertsen (2006) provided an excellent example of where the inclusion of both process and outcomes evaluation allowed the interpretation of unexpected results of an organizational-level health promotion intervention as likely due to implementation failure rather than theory failure. Although the program, in theory, may work well, if it is not implemented with fidelity, the expected results may not be forthcoming. It would be hard to say in that case whether the program would work as designed if implemented as designed. Yet not all programs succeed even when implemented precisely as planned. Lack of success may also occur when the underlying assumptions of the program model, even those supported by scientific theory and empirical evidence, fail to hold true.

Pretesting or piloting is often helpful to illuminate black box or implicit assumptions in the program design and can serve the same purpose in the evaluation design. If the assumptions of the program theory associated with the evaluation design are faulty, the evaluation results can be questionable. If the evaluation fails to find successful outcomes, it may be a result of the program or it may be a result of a flawed theory or flawed assumptions. In a classic example, Rog and Bickman (1984) reported an evaluation of a stress management program that assumed employees experienced stress primarily associated with home and family. They designed their program around that assumption and implemented the program with fidelity. Unfortunately, the evaluation data found that employees experienced stress on the job, not at home. Regardless of implementation, established programs are not likely to achieve their objectives if the underlying conditions or assumptions are flawed. If the program does succeed, it may not be possible to replicate those results if the program logic was faulty.

The program theory also drives the selection of measures and the strategy used in measurement. Individually oriented models hold that improving organizational health is achieved through assisting employees to expand personal resources through training or to manage strain through increased support. Criteria for success would likewise rely on individual changes that presumably result in overall organizational benefits. More organizationally based models rely on making changes in organizational structure or processes and focus on organizationally based measures. Some models take a systems view and seek to examine an integrated measure of both individual and organizational predictors and outcomes. In fact, the concept of organizational health hinges on the intersection of organizational effectiveness and personal well-being, with research aims focused on identifying factors that predict both individual and organizational health outcomes (Adkins, 1999; Adkins, Quick, & Moe, 2000; Quick, Macik-Frey, & Cooper, 2007). Indeed, it has been suggested that occupational health programs and policies may be more effective when interventions target both individuals and organizations (Heaney, 2003; National Institute for Occupational Safety and Health [NIOSH], 2002). Multiple theories can be used to guide data collection, which is particularly useful in cases where there are multiple and/or competing assumptions about how a program works (Weiss, 2000).

Determine Measurement Strategies

The act of measurement itself may in some cases serve to create the beginning ripples of change. Therefore, taking preintervention measures whenever possible provides a foundation from which the direction and magnitude of change or program impact can be assessed.

ORGANIZATIONAL HEALTH RISK APPRAISALS. The concept of an *organizational health risk appraisal* (OHRA) is extracted from individual health management (Adkins et al., 2000). *Individual health risk appraisals* (HRAs) provide an overview of individual health risk and protective factors and generally tend to be behaviorally oriented. Following that reasoning, OHRAs provide a basic evaluation of psychosocial or behavioral risk factors and protective factors found within the organization. Depending on the question that requires attention, the OHRA can be either general and broad-based or more focused and targeted on discrete behaviors or conditions. This information is collected primarily through self-report measures such as surveys, questionnaires, or other methods designed to query attitudes and opinions from the workforce. Self-report data can provide a baseline snapshot of the preintervention organization and can also assist in looking at changes that take place over time and across employment groups.

Evaluations have typically relied on questionnaire data to provide information for planning, targeting, and evaluating stress reduction and management programs, under several labels (e.g., Akerboom & Maes, 2006; Griffin, Hart, & Wilson-Evered, 2000). A foundation of information linking work conditions and processes with health outcomes and organizational effectiveness has been generated through cross-sectional survey or questionnaire methods (Burton et al., 2005; Evans, 2004; Kessler et al., 2003; Kessler et al., 2004; NIOSH, 2002; Quick et al., 1997). In their agenda for research and development, NIOSH (2002) recommended national surveys of work organization risk factors to track changes in working conditions associated with employee health. Epidemiologic methodology can provide a wealth of survey data, but it can also entail a tendency to minimize the importance of theory. In addition, although useful in capturing a significant amount of data from a large group in a short time, questionnaires provide only a snapshot in time of the organization; the results can be misleading if used as the sole piece of information because of the reliance on self-report and the need for further validation of relevant measures (Evans, 2004).

ORGANIZATIONAL HEALTH AND SAFETY ASSESSMENTS. Just as a complete physical or psychological evaluation of an individual provides a more complete and in-depth picture than can be seen with an HRA, a comprehensive organizational health assessment (OHA) provides a more complete view of the organization. The underlying concept associated with OHAs can be seen in a variety of workplace stress and organizational diagnosis processes. Given that an OHA must address a complex system of interlinking individual, job, process, and organizational factors (Shoaf, Genaidy, Karwowski, & Huang, 2004), a mixed methods approach including quantitative and qualitative strategies is recommended.

The diagnostic process begins with a question, issue, or target area. The question is best posed through consultation with organizational and program leaders to facilitate a partnership approach, thus increasing the usefulness and acceptance of the results. A strategy is then formulated to develop measures that will illuminate the issue in question. In general, the strategy includes use of a standardized questionnaire in conjunction with supplemental questions targeted at the particular population(s) and target issue. The use of a standardized questionnaire provides an opportunity to benchmark or compare with established norms (e.g., Vahtera, Kivimäki, Pentti, & Theorell, 2000). Targeted questions fill in specific information that may be unique to the population or issue under study. Once the written data are obtained, more in-depth information is gathered through semistructured interviews with individuals and groups. Those data are then qualitatively analyzed to add depth and detail to written information. Additional details are gleaned from behavioral observations and relevant organizational records. Information about resources available for support and intervention along with current and past programs used to address relevant issues is also obtained. To minimize the potentially myopic view of a single practitioner, a multidisciplinary team is used to collect and analyze the data and develop recommendations. The information is then integrated into a composite report that is presented to the relevant decision makers.

Organizational assessments can provide a foundation for an overall organizational intervention and evaluation strategy. The process can provide a comprehensive needs assessment and paint a detailed picture of the organization preintervention. In doing so, it pinpoints targets of high leverage opportunity, populations at risk, and level of risk. As a general evaluation strategy, the use of a combination of quantitative, qualitative, self-report, historical, and current documented factual information provides a rich data set. In addition, using multiple measures from several sources provides a means of building convergent validity. Results can provide insight into both the design and the ongoing implementation of change programs and policies. Repeated measures across time can be used to assess the direction and magnitude of the change in indicators used. As a systemic assessment, the OHA promotes systemic interventions and thus calls for systemic, interdependent strategies.

Craft an Evaluation Design

Technical issues are as fundamental to program evaluation as to any other field of scientific inquiry. Certainly, programs can fail because of a faulty theory or poor implementation. However, a poor evaluation design can also produce findings that mask the success or failure of a program. Despite the complex, applied nature of the evaluation process, scientific rigor is critical to drawing valid conclusions. Programs that can affect individual and organizational health and well-being should be evaluated using the highest standards possible. Therefore, technical issues associated with design and analysis requires concentrated attention in program evaluation efforts.

The evaluation problem is generally straightforward: How can decision makers determine whether an intervention, such as an OHP program, policy, or practice, is needed, functioning as intended, and producing the intended outcomes? At its core, the problem is no different than any research question. In more basic research paradigms, comparison conditions are created to test implications of theory. In the applied research paradigm of program evaluation, comparison conditions are created to test the efficacy of interventions. In both cases, the critical concern is the level of confidence in judgments about the differences between conditions associated with program exposure or participation and nonexposure or nonparticipation. Issues of internal validity and statistical conclusion validity (Cook & Campbell, 1979) apply in both circumstances because both involve judgments about confidence in inferences that group membership (i.e., program participant versus nonparticipant) makes a difference in the dependent variable of interest, whether that variable is individual, organizational, or systemic health and well-being.

Although the core problem is equivalent, the contextual differences between the two problems are substantial and important. In program evaluation, operations are never arbitrary. They are the essential reason for study. The independent variable is the program. The dependent variable is the individual or organizational issue of concern. Unfortunately, the ability to implement designs that provide maximal confidence in inferences about the causes of group differences can be severely constrained by practical considerations. All these problems enter into the program evaluation context.

Despite contextual issues, the true experiment (Cook & Campbell, 1979) remains the design of choice in all feasible situations. In a randomized experiment, participants (whether individuals, departments, or some other group entity) are randomly assigned to one or more intervention and/or control groups. Effective experimental design provides a high level of confidence that group differences are a result of the program being evaluated. Such confidence is maximized when alternative reasons for group differences can be logically eliminated. Two sources of alternative explanations for group differences are generally identified: differences in the nature of the members in the participant and nonparticipant groups and differences in experiences between participants and nonparticipants other than the program of interest. A detailed discussion of randomized experiments in applied research is beyond the scope of this chapter (see Bickman & Reich, 2009; Boruch, Weisburd, Turner, Karpyn, & Littell, 2009; Rossi et al., 2007; Stufflebeam & Shinkfield, 2007); however, several issues warrant mention here as they relate to threats to internal validity (i.e., the cause–effect relationship).

First, random assignment does not necessarily produce group equivalence in the sense that individual members of groups are equivalent on all key variables. It can only produce average equivalence across conditions. Even here, randomization is not foolproof. Its logic will produce expected average equivalence, not necessarily actual equivalence in any particular case. Mean levels of measured and unmeasured variables will be equal, on average, for participant and nonparticipant groups (Boruch et al., 2009). However, given small samples and single studies, it is likely that participant and nonparticipant groups in any particular program will still have initial differences that may be important for causal inference. This point is important but is not intended to justify the use of weaker designs by arguing the flaws of random assignment. Rather, it emphasizes that the characteristics of research design enhance or reduce confidence levels in inferences about the final program outcomes and highlights the importance of ensuring adequate statistical power when planning the evaluation. Such confidence may be maximized with random assignment, but causality is in no way assured, even with textbook design precision.

Random assignment also fails to account for group differences that can occur once the program is implemented. Differential dropout rates for participant and nonparticipant groups are common occurrences in the field. This attrition has the effect of biasing causal inferences unless it can be assumed that factors associated with attrition are equivalent across groups. Examining condition-specific dropout rates and characteristics of stayers and leavers in both conditions can aid in judgments about the severity of the problem, but neither is foolproof.

Random assignment also does not ensure control over whether the participant does or does not experience the program intervention and at what level. When programs are implemented across groups in the same organization, members of one group can become aware of the experiences of another group and their behavior may be affected. Program effects can leak to nonparticipant groups and that diffusion of the program intervention masks inferences about effects made from the examination of group differences. In addition, members of participant groups often differ in the extent to which they actually experience or are actively involved with relevant program elements, with some members themselves not complying with procedures and others receiving weaker exposure through procedural flaws of implementation. These programs are even more problematic when broad changes are made at the organizational level with the intention of affecting a large group of people but exist clearly even in individually focused programs such as stress-management training programs. Methods exist for estimating causal effects in the face of noncompliance (Little & Yau, 1998), but such methods are limited in scope and have methodological assumptions that may not always be defensible. These problems exist in spite of an evaluator's ability to assign participants to conditions at random. Of course, doing that simple task is sometimes difficult in program evaluation where participants are often assigned based on need, desire, or other considerations.

A vital distinction when considering the use of randomized experiments in program evaluation is between internal and external validity. Internal validity affects the ability to draw causal inferences, whereas external validity relates to the generalizability of findings. Program evaluation by nature is conducted in context; yet the more tightly controlled the design, the less likely the findings will be generalizable. When considering the potential number of threats to internal and external validity, the randomized experiment is clearly the most credible design (Bickman & Reich, 2009) whenever feasible. Nevertheless, a number of other valid and practical designs for applied research can prove useful and should be considered in addition to the randomized experiment, including quasi-experiments, qualitative studies, mixed methods approaches, and research synthesis such as meta-analysis (for a more thorough discussion, see Bickman & Rog, 2009).

Analyze Program Usefulness

Although basic and evaluation research share the same design objective of maximizing confidence in causal inferences, that similarity should not hide the important differences in the broader objectives. Basic research serves the master of theory. Its structure is deduction and its aim is examining the credibility of theoretical propositions. Program evaluation serves the decision maker, who is interested in the usefulness of a specific program or intervention, particularly as compared with alternative courses of action. Therefore, the criteria used to evaluate the reasonableness of an underlying theoretical proposition are not the same criteria used to evaluate the effectiveness of an intervention. Yet the basic research criterion of statistical significance remains the most used criterion of program effectiveness (Lipsey & Cordray, 2000).

Statistical significance testing has come under attack (Schmidt, 1996), but its logic rests on a deductive model that is defensible for judging the results of basic research studies. As such, it is a useful tool to help gauge whether a theoretically driven expectation is supportable. It is also an important tool for gauging program effectiveness and outcomes, but it is not enough. Decision makers need information about usefulness and efficacy. They must judge gains against costs and be able to compare programs in cost–benefit terms. To do so, they must be able to simultaneously look at multiple outcomes that programs will affect. The criterion of statistical significance examines the effects of program outcome against the alternative explanation of chance, which is necessary but not sufficient for program evaluation.

It is recommended that evaluators go beyond reporting simple statistical significance tests and report effect sizes, which provide information on the strength of the effects of the independent variables (Lipsey & Cordray, 2000). Different methods exist for assessing effect sizes, but generally they attempt to express the size of an intervention effect in terms of standardized mean differences, or standard deviation units, between participant and nonparticipant groups. Essentially, the question is how much of an increase (or decrease) in standard scores on the selected outcome measures can be expected from the program or intervention? Effect sizes are useful because they allow comparison of results across multiple studies, as well as a criterion for determining the usefulness of a single study. For example, using established benchmarks to evaluate effect sizes (Cohen, 1988), a decision maker can determine where significant differences may be practically meaningful. In addition, the meaningfulness of the effect size may vary with the situation. Although a small effect size may be significant, it may be less practically meaningful as it may correspond to a small mean difference. However, in some applied contexts, even quite small effects can be practically significant.

Use of effect sizes allows different interventions to be compared in the same units, allows for multiple studies to be cumulated, and allows for moderators of program effectiveness to be identified through these cumulations. Because effect sizes are influenced by such things as the strength of an intervention and the variance in the participant population, they are of less use in examining results for basic research. However, in the context of evaluation, these factors are part of the core of the program itself. Will this intervention work, and for whom? As a consequence, effect sizes have more meaning for program evaluation.

Although the examination of effect sizes is an advance over relying entirely on statistical significance tests, it still does not get to the issue of usefulness directly. In addition, program objectives are seldom well captured by single outcomes. In such cases, multiple effect sizes will exist, and some reasonable method for summarizing effects across outcomes within single studies is needed. In response to these and other issues, recent attempts have been made to examine the usefulness of programs using multiattribute utility analysis.

Although not yet used widely, multiattribute utility analysis essentially requires that the multiple outcomes of interest be scaled, usually by expert judges, on equivalent metrics of utility (Cascio & Boudreau, 2008). For many organizational programs, that metric is dollar values, but dollar value need not be the only way to judge utility. In gauging program effectiveness and outcomes, utility estimates for standard deviation changes in the various criteria of interest are generated, and the utility of a program can be assessed by combining such estimates with effect sizes and summing across outcomes. An added advantage is that these utility estimates can be compared with costs for implementing the program. Finally, multiattribute utility analysis requires evaluators, program managers, and decision makers to carefully think through the nature of the desired outcomes and their importance, which also speaks to the importance of the collaborative design of a comprehensive program logic model for the evaluation.

Focusing on the importance of technical issues is not intended to discourage program evaluation efforts. Just as OHP integrates knowledge from multiple disciplines such as psychology, public health, and organizational science, program evaluation integrates the research and practice skills associated with the scientist–practitioner model. The OHP practitioner must balance perspectives of multiple disciplines, and the program evaluator must realistically balance the practical constraints of the program with the technical requirements of scientific inquiry. Just as a multidisciplinary team is an effective strategy for developing and implementing OHP programs, a consultative relationship or evaluation team that blends strengths of practice and science can serve to build a technically sound and practically useful evaluation strategy.

Value Added Using Evaluation Results

Information obtained from program evaluation studies, regardless of validity and reliability, must be applied for the usefulness to be realized. The value of an evaluation lies mainly in the utility of the results in informing policy or improving programs (Leviton & Hughes, 1981; Weiss, 1993). Use can take many forms.

In general, the stated purpose is to provide information for decision making or problem solving to validate or change the program under study. Although it certainly makes sense that program evaluation results would be an ideal tool to use to inform policy and program decision making, evaluations rarely result in dramatic changes (Weiss, Murphy-Graham, Petrosino, & Gandhi, 2008).

Weiss, Murphy-Graham, and Birkeland (2005) described four types of use from a broad review of the evaluation literature: instrumental, political, conceptual, and imposed. Pure instrumental use, or direct influence on policy and practice, although desirable, is rare. Political use is largely symbolic and provides legitimation, where evaluation results either justify or refute a preexisting course of action. The third type of use, conceptual, reflects situations in which the evaluation process and results may be used indirectly to influence thinking about an issue without actually resulting in an immediate concrete change. Instead, results may become part of an integrated body of information that is accumulated and used over time in the evolution of programs in general. This accumulated information eventually influences changes in attitudes and ultimately affects policy, programs, or practices on a larger scale than in a single organization or industry, as has been the case in the development and growth of OHP. Finally, imposed use occurs as a result of external pressure. The growing emphasis on evidence-based interventions is an example of imposed use that has spawned greater scientific interest in the translation of research into practice through directly attending to issues of efficacy, effectiveness, dissemination, and implementation (Glasgow & Marcus, 2003; Goldenhar et al., 2001; Mendel, Meredith, Schoenbaum, Sherbourne, & Wells, 2008; Rabin, Brownson, Haire-Joshu, Kreuter, & Weaver, 2008).

Evaluation information is often used less for concrete decision making than for its capacity to empower users of the information (Patton, 2008). Insights from the evaluation feed the program evolution. Resultant information can reduce uncertainty, confirm results from other sources, control implementation schedules, or trigger modifications in implementation or direction of an existing program or policy. In a classic meta-analysis of evaluation research, Leviton and Hughes (1981) identified a number of factors still applicable today that increase the probability of use of evaluation results. The following sections describe these factors in detail.

Relevance

Information that is perceived as relevant to policy or program concerns and that addresses decision-maker needs is more likely to be used. Developing relevant information requires a partnership of the OHP evaluator with the program being evaluated. The OHP practitioner is grounded in both organizational operations and behavioral science, creating an important role as a knowledge broker and translator of psychosocial or behavioral science information to organization and program managers. To be effective in that role, the practitioner may be required to formulate the findings from the evaluation in language that is practical and actionable and to integrate seemingly contradictory pieces of information that may arise from the process. Development of an effective program logic model will aid in this process. When a needs assessment is conducted, practitioners are afforded the opportunity to become familiar with the business objectives, culture, and language of the organization. Both the goals of the program and the objectives of the evaluation can then be tied to the overall organizational short-term and long-term goals and objectives, increasing the likelihood that all products will be perceived as a part of and therefore relevant to the business plan. The questions formulated from that assessment set the stage for the development of answers that are relevant and applicable to the situation. In addition, relevance is affected by the timing of results. Windows of opportunity in decision-making processes occur in every organization and in every program. Data that are realized in the window become imminently more useful. Increasing knowledge of organizational processes will likewise increase awareness of windows of opportunity.

Communication and Involvement

A flow of undistorted and unbiased communication between the potential user or consumer of evaluation information and the producer of that information results in both a better understanding of initial needs and a more effective method of dissemination of accurate information. In addition, as the level of user involvement increases, ownership of the process and the resultant information also increases. Information flow in organizations tends to be impeded by those who may feel threatened by potentially negative findings. Identifying and involving those individuals with a stake in the outcome of the evaluation can help to minimize resistance and facilitate the crafting of results in a format that is palatable.

Presentation of the information is also critical. Clearly established goals, explicit recommendations, and easy to understand written and verbal communication will obviously enhance the probability that the information will be used (Skinner, 2004). Clarity and specificity can also assist in reducing potential misuse. Qualitative information, such as that obtained in an organizational assessment, can provide relevant examples to help users understand quantitative findings. Sensitive communication of negative or unanticipated findings combined with direct communication with organizational leaders and managers can reduce the amount of organizational censorship or distortion that can take place when program personnel or other affected groups feel threatened by the evaluation process, as may be the case in any evaluation but perhaps most significantly in evaluations that are either externally required or imposed from higher levels within the organization.

Credibility and Quality

An evaluation is not the only source of information available to decision makers. It is therefore generally taken in context with preconceptions, day-to-day experiences, and other sources of information, often serving as a source of corroboration. Issues of power and resources within organizations will influence the entire evaluation process, from whether one occurs at all to whether and how findings are used (Skinner, 2004). Knowledge of the context will assist in developing information that fills informational gaps. Obviously, the results of the evaluation cannot be predicted in advance. However, information that is completely out of line with expectations or with other sources of information is likely to meet with skepticism. Such information would require extensive explanation and justification of the quality of the work. However, even high quality evaluations may not be used in decision making (Weiss et al. 2005, 2008) if not perceived as credible.

Credibility, although highly subjective, takes into account the place of evaluation as a source of knowledge among other types of information and also takes into account issues of organizational power and resources as well as aspects of quality. The quality of evaluation findings is determined by several factors, including the evaluator's role related to the program, evaluation questions, evidence gathered to answer those questions, depth and breadth of the evaluation, design and methods, analytic plan, and context (Bickman & Reich, 2009). The importance of quality increases when findings must be persuasive or in situations posing a high potential for information misuse. Credibility of information increases when the source is seen as fair and impartial with no specific stake in the outcome. Therefore, for practitioners who develop evaluation components for their own programs, high methodological quality and well-developed perceptions of credibility in the organization will become increasingly important.

Commitment, Advocacy, and Politics

Evaluations are conducted in the political context of an organization. Advocates of multiple positions battle for and against issues that correspond with their own interests. Understanding that context is critical. In the end, results generally are used by specific individuals rather than a group or an organization as a whole. The presence of a champion for the evaluation will increase the likelihood of the results being heard and used. The emotional investment of that champion and their position in the organization can have a substantial impact on the advocacy of both OHP programs and evaluations. To ensure effectiveness, advance marketing and building solid relationships in the planning and implementation phase will set the stage for a receptive attitude once the results of the evaluation are completed. Building relationships within the organization is a critical but often neglected activity of both program managers and evaluators. Targeting information to key users and marketing the importance of that information to decision makers promotes meaningful use of evaluation results.

Ethical Considerations

Evaluators have obligations to diverse groups, including the client organization, stakeholders in the program, program managers and staff, program beneficiaries, and other professionals in their discipline. These obligations include conducting evaluations with fairness, objectivity, and professionalism (Farrington, 2003). Evaluations must begin with realistic objectives and questions that the evaluator or evaluation team is capable of answering. Valid constructs and measures followed by skilled and unbiased data collection and thoughtful analysis lead to results that can be relied on to guide policy or program decisions. In the process, it is important that individuals and the organization are protected from harm. Protection involves a respect for confidentiality and may require informed consent from those who participate. Ethical challenges arise when it appears that the project cannot be accomplished as defined. There may be questions about how much information is enough to answer the question, how much analysis is required as opposed to straight presentation of the information, or when causal inferences are appropriate to the data and methodology of the evaluation. Requests may be made from a variety of factions to present the findings in the best possible light. Information can be misused by clients or by individuals within the organization to support their own ideas or interests. Finally, findings can result in harmful action taken against participants in the evaluation, participants in the program, or employees in the organization if the findings fail to support health-engendering practices. Because of the potential for harm, it is incumbent on practitioners to consider the potential consequences of the evaluation process and to ensure that a process is established that will protect the participants, the organizational client, and the professional integrity of the evaluation itself.

Conclusion

The landscape of OHP practice continues to evolve and expand. To continue to grow and adapt to a dynamic workplace, it is important to know what works and to be able to understand as fully as possible why it works, creating an effective core technology and procedures. It is critical for practitioners to envision the future and to find, develop, and acquire skills to implement alternative strategies to meet the needs of their client organizations. Effectively designed, conducted, and well-documented program evaluations provide the cornerstone for continued success.

References

Adkins, J. A. (1999). Promoting organizational health: The evolving practice of occupational health psychology. *Professional Psychology, Research, and Practice, 30,* 129–137. doi:10.1037/0735-7028.30.2.129

Adkins, J. A., Quick, J. C., & Moe, K. O. (2000). Building world class performance in changing times. In L. R. Murphy & C. L. Cooper (Eds.), *Healthy and productive work: An international perspective* (pp. 107–132). Philadelphia, PA: Taylor & Francis.

Adler, M. A. (2002). The utility of modeling in evaluation planning: The case of the coordination of domestic violence services in Maryland. *Evaluation and Program Planning, 25,* 203–213. doi:10.1016/S0149-7189(02)00016-2

Akerboom, S., & Maes, S. (2006). Beyond demand and control: The contribution of organizational risk factors in assessing the psychological well-being of health care employees. *Work & Stress, 20,* 21–36. doi:10.1080/02678370600690915

Aust, B., & Ducki, A. (2004). Comprehensive health promotion interventions at the workplace: Experiences with health circles in Germany. *Journal of Occupational Health Psychology, 9,* 258–270. doi:10.1037/1076-8998.9.3.258

Bickman, L. (1987). Using program theory in evaluation. In L. Bickman, *New directions for program evaluation* (pp. 5–18). San Francisco, CA: Jossey-Bass.

Bickman, L., & Reich, S. M. (2009). Randomized controlled trials: A gold standard with feet of clay? In S. I. Donaldson, C. A. Christie, & M. M. Marks (Eds.), *What counts as credible evidence in applied research and evaluation practice?* (pp. 51–77). Thousand Oaks, CA: Sage.

Bickman, L., & Rog, D. (Eds.). (2008). The Sage handbook of applied social research methods. Thousand Oaks, CA: Sage.

Boruch, R. F., Weisburd, D., Turner, H. M., Karpyn, A., & Littell, J. (2008). Randomized controlled trials for evaluation and planning. In L. Bickman & D. Rog (Eds.), *The Sage handbook of applied social research methods* (pp. 147–181). Thousand Oaks, CA: Sage.

Burton, W. N., Chen, C. Y., Conti, D. J., Schultz, A. B., Pransky, G., & Edington, D. W. (2005). The association of health risks with on-the-job productivity. *Journal of Occupational and Environmental Medicine, 47,* 769–777.

Cascio, W. F., & Boudreau, J. W. (2008). *Investing in people: Financial impact of human resource initiatives.* Upper Saddle River, NJ: FT Press.

Chen, H., & Rossi, P. (1983). Evaluating with sense: The theory-driven approach. *Evaluation Review, 7,* 283–302. doi:10.1177/0193841X8300700301

Cohen, J. (1988). *Statistical power analysis for the behavioral sciences* (2nd ed.). Hillsdale, NJ: Erlbaum.

Cook, T. D., & Campbell, D. T. (1979). *Quasi-experimentation: Design and analysis for field settings.* Boston, MA: Houghton-Mifflin.

den Heyer, M. (2002). The temporal logic model concept. *The Canadian Journal of Program Evaluation, 17,* 27–47.

Donaldson, S. I. (1997). Worksite health promotion: A theory-driven, empirically based perspective. In L. R. Murphy, J. J. Hurrell, S. L. Sauter, & G. P. Keita (Eds.), *Job stress interventions* (pp. 73–90). Washington, DC: American Psychological Association.

Evans, C. J. (2004). Health and work productivity assessment: State of the art or state of flux? *Journal of Occupational and Environmental Medicine, 46,* S3–S11. doi:10.1097/01.jom.0000126682.37083.fa

Farrington, D. P. (2003). Methodological quality standards for evaluation research. *The Annals of the American Academy of Political and Social Science, 587*(1), 49–68. doi:10.1177/0002716202250789

Florin, P., Celebucki, C., Stevenson, J., Mena, J., Salago, D., White, A., . . . Dougal, M. (2006). Cultivating systemic capacity: The Rhode Island tobacco control enhancement project. *American Journal of Community Psychology, 38*(3–4), 213–220.

Frechtling, J. A. (2007). *Logic modeling methods in program evaluation.* San Francisco, CA: Jossey-Bass.

Glasgow, R. E., & Marcus, A. C. (2003). Why don't we see more translation of health promotion research to practice? Rethinking the efficacy-to-effectiveness transition. *American Journal of Public Health, 93,* 1261–1267. doi:10.2105/AJPH.93.8.1261

Goetzel, R. Z., Shechter, D., Ozminkowski, R. J., Marmet, P. F., Tabrizi, M. J., & Roemer, E. C. (2007). Promising practices in employer health and productivity management efforts: Findings from a benchmarking study. *Journal of Occupational and Environmental Medicine, 49,* 111–130. doi:10.1097/JOM.0b013e31802ec6a3

Goldenhar, L. M., Lamontagne, A. D., Katz, T., Heaney, C., & Landsbergis, P. (2001). The intervention research process in occupational safety and health: An overview from the National Occupational Research Agenda Intervention Effectiveness Research Team. *Journal of Occupational and Environmental Medicine, 43,* 616–622. doi:10.1097/00043764-200107000-00008

Goldman, K. D., & Schmalz, K. J. (2006). Logic models: The picture worth ten thousand words. *Health Promotion Practice, 7*(1), 8–12. doi:10.1177/1524839905283230

Griffin, M. A., Hart, P. M., & Wilson-Evered, E. (2000). Using employee opinion surveys to improve organizational health. In L. R. Murphy & C. L. Cooper (Eds.), *Healthy and productive work: An international perspective* (pp. 15–36). New York, NY: Taylor & Francis.

Gugiu, P. C., & Rodriguez-Campos, L. (2007). Semistructured interview protocol for constructing logic models. *Evaluation and Program Planning, 30,* 339–350. doi:10.1016/j.evalprogplan.2007.08.004

Heaney, C. A. (2003). Worksite health interventions: Targets for change and strategies for attaining them. In J. C. Quick & L. E. Tetrick (Eds.), *Handbook of occupational health psychology* (pp. 305–323). Washington, DC: American Psychological Association. doi:10.1037/10474-015

Kaplan, S. A., & Garrett, K. E. (2005). The use of logic models by community-based initiatives. *Evaluation and Program Planning, 28,* 167–172. doi:10.1016/j.evalprogplan.2004.09.002

Kellogg Foundation. (2004). *Using logic models to bring together planning, evaluation, and action: Logic model development guide.* Retrieved from http://www.wkkf.org/knowledge-center/Resources-Page.aspx?q=logic+model

Kessler, R. C., Ames, M., Hymel, P. A., Loeppke, R., McKenas, D. K., Richling, D. E., . . . Ustun, T. B. (2004). Using the World Health Organizational Health and Work Performance Questionnaire (HPQ) to evaluate the indirect workplace costs of illness. *Journal of Occupational and Environmental Medicine, 46*(6), S23–S37. doi:10.1097/01.jom.0000126683.75201.c5

Kessler, R. C., Barber, C., Beck, A., Berglund, P., Cleary, P. D., McKenas, D., . . . Wang, P. (2003). The World Health Organizational Health and Work Performance Questionnaire (HPQ). *Journal of Occupational and Environmental Medicine, 45,* 156–174. doi:10.1097/01.jom.0000052967.43131.51

Leviton, L. C., & Hughes, E. (1981). Research on the utilization of evaluations: A review and synthesis. *Evaluation Review, 5,* 525–548. doi:10.1177/0193841X8100500405

Light, R. J., Singer, J. D., & Willet, J. B. (1990). *By design: Planning research on higher education.* Cambridge, MA: Harvard University Press.

Lipsey, M. W., & Cordray, D. S. (2000). Evaluation methods for social research. *Annual Review of Psychology, 51,* 345–375. doi:10.1146/annurev.psych.51.1.345

Little, R. J., & Yau, L. H. (1998). Statistical techniques for analyzing data from prevention trials: Treatment of no-shows using Rubin's causal model. *Psychological Methods, 3,* 147–159. doi:10.1037/1082-989X.3.2.147

Macik-Frey, M., Quick, J. C., & Nelson, D. L. (2007). Advances in occupational health: From a stressful beginning to a positive future. *Journal of Management, 33,* 809–840. doi:10.1177/0149206307307634

Mauno, S., Kinnunen, U., & Ruokolainen, M. (2006). Exploring work- and organization-based resources as moderators between work–family conflict, well-being, and job attitudes. *Work & Stress, 20,* 210–233. doi:10.1080/02678370600999969

Mendel, P., Meredith, L. S., Schoenbaum, M., Sherbourne, C. D., & Wells, K. B. (2008). Interventions in organizational and community context: A framework for building evidence on dissemination and implementation in health services research. *Administration and Policy in Mental Health, 35,* 21–37. doi:10.1007/s10488-007-0144-9

Murphy, L. R., & Cooper, C. L. (2000). *Healthy and productive work.* New York, NY: Taylor & Francis.

National Institute for Occupational Safety and Health (NIOSH). (2002). *The changing organization of work and the safety and health of working people.* Cincinnati, OH: Author.

Nielsen, K., Fredslund, H., Christensen, K. B., & Albertsen, K. (2006). Success or failure? Interpreting and understanding the impact of interventions in four smaller worksites. *Work & Stress, 20,* 272–287. doi:10.1080/02678370601022688

Patton, M. Q. (2008). *Utilization-focused evaluation* (4th ed.). New York, NY: Sage.

Poland, B., Frohlich, K. L., & Cargo, M. (2009). Context as a fundamental dimension of health promotion program evaluation. In L. Potvin & D. McQueen (Eds.), *Health promotion evaluation practices in the Americas* (pp. 299–317). New York, NY: Springer. doi:10.1007/978-0-387-79733-5_17

Porteous, N. L., Sheldrick, B. J., & Stewart, P. J. (2002). Introducing program teams to logic models: Facilitating the learning process. *The Canadian Journal of Program Evaluation, 17,* 113–141.

Quick, J. C., Macik-Frey, M., & Cooper, C. L. (2007). Managerial dimensions of organizational health. *Journal of Management Studies, 44,* 189–205. doi:10.1111/j.1467-6486.2007.00684.x

Quick, J. C., Quick, J. D., Nelson, D. L., & Hurrell, J. J. (1997). *Preventive stress management in organizations.* Washington, DC: American Psychological Association. doi:10.1037/10238-000

Rabin, B. A., Brownson, R. C., Haire-Joshu, D., Kreuter, M. W., & Weaver, N. L. (2008). A glossary for dissemination and implementation research in health. *Journal of Public Health Management and Practice, 14,* 117–123.

Rog, D., & Bickman, L. (1984). The feedback research approach to evaluation: A method to increase evaluation utility. *Evaluation and Program Planning, 7,* 169–175. doi:10.1016/0149-7189(84)90042-9

Rossi, P. H., Lipsey, M. W., & Freeman, H. E. (2007). *Evaluation: A systematic approach* (7th ed.). Thousand Oaks, CA: Sage.

Schurman, S. J., & Israel, B. A. (1995). Redesigning work systems to reduce stress: A participatory action research approach to creating change. In L. R. Murphy, J. J. Hurrell, S. L. Sauter, & G. P. Keita (Eds.), *Job stress interventions* (pp. 235–263). Washington, DC: American Psychological Association. doi:10.1037/10183-016

Schmidt, F. L. (1996). Statistical significance testing and cumulative knowledge in psychology: Implications for training of researchers. *Psychological Methods, 1,* 115–129. doi:10.1037/1082-989X.1.2.115

Shoaf, C., Genaidy, A., Karwowski, W., & Huang, S. H. (2004). Improving performance and quality of working life: A model for organizational health assessment in emerging enterprises. *Human Factors and Ergonomics in Manufacturing, 14,* 81–95. doi:10.1002/hfm.10053

Skinner, D. (2004). Primary and secondary barriers to the evaluation of change. *Evaluation, 10,* 135–154. doi:10.1177/1356389004045078

Stufflebeam, D. L., & Shinkfield, A. J. (2007). *Evaluation theory, models, and applications.* New York, NY: Jossey-Bass.

Thurston, W. E., Graham, J., & Hatfield, J. (2003). Evaluability assessment: A catalyst for program change and improvement. *Evaluation & the Health Professions, 26,* 206–221. doi:10.1177/0163278703026002005

Trevisan, M. S., & Yi, M. H. (2003). Evaluability assessment: A primer. *Practical Assessment, Research, & Evaluation, 8*(20). Retrieved from http://PAREonline.net/getvn.asp?v=8&n=20

Unrau, Y. A. (2001). Using client exit interviews to illuminate outcomes in program logic models: A case example. *Evaluation and Program Planning, 24,* 353–361. doi:10.1016/S0149-7189(01)00029-5

Vahtera, J., Kivimäki, M., Pentti, J., & Theorell, T. (2000). Effect of change in the psychosocial work environment on sickness absence: A seven-year follow up of initially healthy employees. *Journal of Epidemiology and Community Health, 54,* 484–493. doi:10.1136/jech.54.7.484

Veney, J. E., & Kaluzny, A. D. (1998). *Evaluation and decision making for health services* (3rd ed.). Ann Arbor, MI: Health Administration Press.

Weiss, C. H. (1993). Where politics and evaluation research meet. *American Journal of Evaluation, 14,* 93–106. doi:10.1177/109821409301400119

Weiss, C. H. (2000). Which links in which theories shall we evaluate? *New Directions for Evaluation, 87,* 35–45. doi:10.1002/ev.1180

Weiss, C. H., Murphy-Graham, E., & Birkeland, S. (2005). An alternate route to policy influence: How evaluations affect D.A.R.E. *American Journal of Evaluation, 26,* 12–30. doi:10.1177/1098214004273337

Weiss, C. H., Murphy-Graham, E., Petrosino, A., & Gandhi, A. G. (2008). The fairy godmother— and her warts: Making the dream of evidence-based policy come true. *American Journal of Evaluation, 29,* 29–47. doi:10.1177/1098214007313742

Wholey, J. (1979). *Evaluation: Promise and performance.* Washington, DC: Urban Institute Press.

Wholey, J. S. (2004). Evaluability assessment. In J. S. Wholey, H. P. Hatry, & K. E. Newcomer (Eds.), *Handbook of practical program evaluation* (pp. 33–62). San Francisco, CA: Jossey-Bass.

Index

About the Editors

James Campbell Quick, PhD, is John and Judy Goolsby Distinguished Professor, Goolsby Leadership Academy at the University of Texas at Arlington, and visiting professor, Lancaster University Management School, United Kingdom. He is a fellow of the Society for Industrial and Organizational Psychology, American Psychological Association (APA), and of the American Institute of Stress. He was awarded an APA presidential citation in 2001 and the 2002 Harry and Miriam Levinson Award by the American Psychological Foundation. He and his brother Jonathan originated preventive stress management, a term included in the 2007 *APA Dictionary of Psychology.* He has more than 100 publications in 10 languages and holds a 2009 University Award for Distinguished Record of Research. Colonel (Ret.) Quick was awarded the Legion of Merit by the United States Air Force and the Maroon Citation by Colgate University. He is married to the former Sheri Grimes Schember; both are members of the Chancellor's Council of the University of Texas System and the Silver Society, American Psychological Foundation.

Lois E. Tetrick, PhD, received her doctorate in industrial and organizational psychology from the Georgia Institute of Technology in 1983. Upon completion of her doctoral studies, she joined the faculty of the Department of Psychology at Wayne State University and remained there until 1995, when she moved to the Department of Psychology at the University of Houston. She joined the faculty at George Mason University as the director of the Industrial and Organizational Psychology Program in 2003. Dr. Tetrick is editor of the *Journal of Occupational Health Psychology.* She coedited the first edition of the *Handbook of Occupational Health Psychology* with James Campbell Quick and *Health and Safety in Organizations* with David Hofmann. She also coedited *The Employment Relationship: Examining Psychological and Contextual Perspectives* with Jacqueline Coyle-Shapiro, Lynn Shore, and Susan Taylor. Dr. Tetrick is a fellow of the European Academy of Occupational Health Psychology, the American Psychological Association (APA), the Society for Industrial and Organizational Psychology (SIOP), and the Association for Psychological Science. She served as president of SIOP (2007–2008), chair of the Human Resources Division of the Academy of Management (2001–2002), SIOP representative on the APA Council of Representatives (2003–2005), and member of the APA Board of Scientific Affairs (2006–2009). Her research interests are occupational health and safety, occupational stress, the work–family interface, and the psychological contracts and exchange relationships between employees and their organizations.